England in the Later Middle Ages

First published to wide critical acclaim in 1973, England in the Later Middle Ages has become a seminal text for students studying this significant period in English history. This spirited work surveys the period from Edward I to the death of Richard III at the Battle of Bosworth, which heralded in the Tudor Age. The study discusses the important aspects of the age such as

- The reign of Edward I and Edward II
- Edward III and the Hundred Years War
- Plague and the changing economy
- Church and state in the Later Middle Ages
- The rise and fall of the Lancastrian empire
- The Wars of the Roses

The second edition of this book, while maintaining the structure of the original, brings the study up to date. There has been much new research since its first publication and the author has made substantial revisions to take account of fresh interpretations. The introductory chapter and the section dealing with plague and the economy have been re-written; and each chapter includes a discussion of historiographical developments since the original publication.

Maurice Keen is a distinguished historian of the Middle Ages and Fellow of Balliol College, Oxford. His many publications include *The Outlaws of Medieval Legend* (re-issued 2000), *Chivalry* (Yale, 1984) and *Nobles, Knights and Men at Arms in the Middle Ages* (Hambledon Press, 1996).

England in the Later Middle Ages

A political history

Second edition

M. H. Keen

Fellow of Balliol College, Oxford

Routledge
Taylor & Francis Group

LONDON AND NEW YORK

In memoriam
ERNEST JACOB

First published 1973 by Methuen & Co. Ltd

First published as a University Paperback 1975

Reprinted three times

Reprinted 1986

Reprinted 1988, 1990, 1993, 1995, 1997, 2000
by Routledge

Second edition published in 2003
by Routledge

11 New Fetter Lane, London EC4P 4EE
29 West 35th Street, New York, NY 10001

Routledge is an imprint of the Taylor & Francis Group

© 1973, 2003 Maurice Keen

Typeset in Galliard by BC Typesetting Ltd, Bristol
Printed and bound in Great Britain by
MPG Books Ltd, Bodmin, Cornwall

British Library Cataloguing in Publication Data
A catalogue record for this book is available from the British Library

Library of Congress Cataloging-in-Publication Data
Keen, Maurice Hugh.
England in the later Middle Ages: a political history/Maurice Keen. –
2nd ed.
p. cm.
Includes bibliographical references and index.
ISBN 0–415–27293–9 (paperback) – ISBN 0–415–27292–0 (hardcover)
1. Great Britain–Politics and government – 1066–1485.
2. Constitutional history, Medieval. I. Title.
DA225.K4 2003
942.03–dc21   2003011016

ISBN 0–415–27292–0 (cased)
     0–415–27293–9 (limp)

Contents

Preface

This book is concerned with the period of English medieval history that has always been for me the most interesting. I am attracted by it for a reason that may perhaps seem old-fashioned: because its story is full of martial events, of the adventures in wars in England and beyond the sea of men of fame and ancestry, like the Black Prince and that Earl of Shrewsbury whom the French in fear and respect christened *le roi Talbot*. I have no doubt that my predilections colour my view of the period. Perhaps this book would have been better written by someone with a deep knowledge of the legal and administrative records of late Plantagenet England (a knowledge to which I can lay no claim), for these are the sources that are currently shedding most new light on the history of the age. But I believe that there may still be this to be said for looking at it in a rather traditional way; that if they could be consulted, the men of the period would probably have hoped that their times would be remembered most for their great victories, Falkirk and Crecy and Poitiers and Agincourt.

Writing a textbook is not altogether an agreeable task; it teaches one too much about one's own ignorance. Faced with topics with which one's own acquaintance is entirely superficial – in my own case, notably, the problems of late medieval economic history and ecclesiastical history – what can one do but reproduce, as best one may, the views of others who are better informed? I am conscious of a very great debt to the books of those scholars who have made this period of English history their special field. I am also conscious that the period is one in which the results of extensive and important research, undertaken over the last twenty years, are beginning to multiply in print, and that at the present moment it is one where almost all views are interim views. Statements made now are likely to date quickly. I have tried nevertheless to be definite in presenting my points of view; a textbook can, in my experience, be occasionally useful simply because the student can find in it unsound opinions to attack.

I have received much generous help in writing this book. My principal debts are to Mr G. L. Harriss of Magdalen College, Oxford, who read through the whole text in typescript and made many valuable suggestions and criticisms, and to Mr C. R. J. Currie, a research student of my own college, who went through substantial parts of it in an effort to root out as many as he could of the errors of fact – of proper names, precise dates and relationships – that he knew had always marred my work. Where he read he found much to correct, but I am afraid there will be many more mistakes of mine that will appear uncorrected. I must also thank a number of scholars and friends who have looked at parts of the book and have assisted me with criticism and advice: Miss Barbara Harvey, Dr Michael Prestwich, Dr Christopher Allmand, and Dr Seymour Philips. Dr Prestwich and Dr J. R. Maddicott both most kindly allowed me to read their doctoral theses, both of which were at the time unpublished; without their help I am not sure what I could have made of the early part of the period, the years with which I am least familiar. Mr K. J. Leyser very kindly allowed me to look at a copy of the late Mr K. B. McFarlane's Ford Lectures on the English nobility in the later Middle Ages, perhaps the most influential and seminal set of lectures ever given on this period of English history. I must finally thank Mrs Glynis Donovan, Mrs Mary Clapinson and Mr David Vaisey for their help with the proofs; and Miss Pat Lloyd, Mrs Mary Budge and, above all, my wife, for assistance at various stages of writing and typing, and with the index.

There is a special debt that I have tried to record in the dedication of this book, to the late Dr E. F. Jacob. I at least have never met a scholar who has been more generous in sharing with others his insights, based on a profound knowledge and understanding. How much he showed me, or suggested, I shall never be able to record, because so much was given, so unobtrusively, in the course, almost entirely, of casual conversations. The most pleasurable of all to remember were talks near the banks of rivers, where he was full of wisdom on the ways of fish as on the ways of the past, and always had much to say about both.

Maurice Keen
Balliol College
Oxford
1973

Preface to the revised edition

This book was originally written more than thirty years ago. I was then a young man, and had clear and, I hoped, coherent ideas about what I wanted to say and the themes I wished to stress. When the publisher suggested to me the preparation of a revised edition, I realised that the task would not be an easy one. Teaching the period that the book covers and reading around it has naturally, over thirty years, led me to modify my views on many matters and on some has altered them. There has been, moreover, over those thirty years, an exponential expansion of new, scholarly, research based writing on England in the later Middles Ages, of which a revised edition needs to take account. But it was clear to me that if I tried to alter too much, the coherence that I hoped and hope was there in my original presentation would be lost. An untidy mish mash of old and new would not improve on the book as first written. Making judgements about what to change and what to leave as it first stood looked likely to be a tricky and testing assignment, and so it has proved to be.

Fortunately for me, my mind has not changed on one central issue, that the great wars of the English with the French and the Scots in the later Middle Ages, and the tides of fortune and misfortune in those wars, were a formative and dominant influence on English political history through the period that my book covers. That has meant that I have been able to allow the greater part of my original text to stand, and to retain the original chapter divisions. In every chapter I have found passages and paragraphs which I have needed to alter or re-write. Where new material or fresh interpretations have demanded notice, my rewriting has often been quite extensive. Chapter 8, always the least satisfactory in my own eyes, has been completely rewritten. The general shape of the old book and its thrust remain not much changed, however, and the authorial stamp remains that of the person that I was, all of thirty years ago.

What to do about the footnotes of the original edition presented a particularly thorny problem when I agreed to attempt a revision. In my original version I tried to make these as ample, historiographically, as I might: but time has rendered the apparatus of 1973 in this respect completely outdated. It was clearly not feasible simply to substitute new references for old in existing footnotes, since new work with new pre-occupations will not fit the old slots. The policy I have in the end adopted is a radical one. The footnotes have been drastically reduced: with very few exceptions I have preserved in this revised edition only those that support a quotation from an original source or the comment of an authority directly invoked. To compensate for the elimination of historiographical footnotes, I have appended at the end of each chapter a 'note on secondary reading', concentrating in these notes on what seems to me to have been the most significant work to appear since I first wrote. Since this is primarily a textbook, and some readers' interests will therefore be focused selectively on matters discussed in one chapter or a group of chapters, I have repeated full details of publications (date, place of publication, etc.) in each of these notes, chapter by chapter.

My book is about the history of England, as its title states. The original edition included as an Appendix a 'Note on the political history of Scotland and Ireland'. So much has been written since then of the later medieval history of these two lands, and it has been of such high quality, as to render this attempt at genuflexion towards the 'British dimension' of the history of these islands totally inadequate, as well as obsolete – and even, perhaps, discourteously formal. I have therefore excluded it. To compensate, I have added substantially to the final sections of the main bibliography at the end of the book, devoted to the histories of Scotland, Ireland, and Wales.

I recorded in my original preface my indebtedness to those scholars who have made late medieval English history their special field: that debt has been greatly enlarged since then. Three new and particular debts of gratitude, arising out of this revision, I must acknowledge. The first is to Professor Michael Prestwich, for his advice about how I should approach the task, about what most called for modification or rewriting, and for supplying me with the invaluable guidance of bibliographies that he had himself compiled. The second is to Carole Clement, for the patient typing up of revisions, and her assistance in moulding new matter into the old. The third is to Dr Christopher Fletcher for his invaluable assistance with intractable proofs. The publishers have at every point been most courteous and helpful.

I was courting my wife when I first started to write this book. But for her support through the tribulations incidental both to writing and then to revision, there would be no first edition and no revised edition either.

Maurice Keen
Oxford, 2003

Abbreviations

A.H.R.	*American Historical Review*
A.P.S.	*Acts of the Parliament of Scotland*
B.E.C.	*Bibliothèque de l'École des Chartes*
B.I.H.R.	*Bulletin of the Institute of Historical Research*
B.J.R.L.	*Bulletin of the John Rylands Library*
C.C.R.	*Calendar of the Close Rolls*
C.H.J.	*Cambridge Historical Journal*
C.P.R.	*Calendar of the Patent Rolls*
C.S.P.	*Calendar of State Papers*
Econ.H.R.	*Economic History Review*
E.E.T.S.	Early English Text Society
E.H.R.	*English Historical Review*
Foed.	*Foedera Conventiones Literae et cujuscunque generis Acta Publica*, ed. T. Rymer (London, 1704–32)
H.J.	*Historical Journal*
K. de L.	*Oeuvres de Froissart*, ed. Kervyn de Lettenhove (Brussels, 1870–7)
L. and P.	*Letters and Papers Illustrative of the Wars of the English in France*, ed. J. Stevenson (Rolls Series, 1861–4)
L.Q.R.	*Law Quarterly Review*
P.B.A.	*Proceedings of the British Academy*
P.L.	*The Paston Letters*, ed. J. Gairdner (London, 1872–5: the references throughout are to the numbers of the letters in this edition)
P.P.C.	*Proceeding and Ordinances of the Privy Council*, ed. H. Nicholas (London, 1834–7)
P.W.	*Parliamentary Writs*, ed. F. Palgrave (London, 1827–34)
R.P.	*Rotuli Parliamentorum*
R.S.	Rolls Series
S.H.R.	*Scottish Historical Review*
Storey, *H. of L.*	R. L. Storey, *The End of the House of Lancaster* (London, 1966)

Tout, *Chapters*   T. F. Tout, *Chapters in the Administrative History of Medieval England* (Manchester, 1920–33)

T.R.H.S.   *Transactions of the Royal Historical Society*

V.C.H.   *Victoria History of the Counties of England*

1 Introduction

The structure of government and politics

The year 1290 may seem a strange date at which to commence a political history of the late Middle Ages in England. It marks neither the beginning nor the end of a reign: in fact it was the eighteenth year of King Edward I, who had another seventeen years of authority ahead of him. All the same, it is an important date. It was in that year that the death of the Maid of Norway, titular queen of Scotland, started a chain of events which were to lead in 1296 to the outbreak of a great war of the English against the Scots. Two years before that, in 1294, another major war had commenced, with France; this is why the 'auld alliance', of France and Scotland against England, came into being at this point in the 1290s. From then onwards, with only short intervals, England was to remain at war with Scotland, or France, or both, until the end of the medieval period. These prolonged hostilities exposed her government and its resources to unprecedented strains. The consequences, both of the wars directly and of the strains and pressures that they engendered, were only beginning to work themselves out when the first Tudor, Henry VII, came to the throne in 1485.

The course of the great wars of the late Middle Ages shaped England's gradual achievement of self-conscious, insular identity as a nation-state. The period from 1290 to 1485 is therefore a very important one in her political history. It is also a confused and troubled period (though not more troubled, probably, than that which preceded it). As Shakespeare's plays remind us, this was a violent age, in the course of which no less than five kings lost their thrones and in whose civil wars a long and sorry list of noblemen lost their lives in the field or on the block. This aspect of the late Middle Ages in England is what made their history unpalatable to the scholars of the nineteenth century, with their confidence in constitutional principles and progress. The trouble was not, however, as Stubbs and his generation believed, that the great men of the late Middle Ages were the moral and intellectual inferiors of their ancestors and their descendants. The difficulties of the period arose rather because its recurrent warfare exposed the system of government which had been developed earlier, and the balance of political forces in the kingdom, to new stresses. These stresses generated for the kingdom's rulers a greater need for cooperation, on the one hand from those who controlled the purse strings for the financing of large scale campaigns, and on the other from their greater subjects, who had their own views on policies and governance and who were too powerful to manage on the basis of authority alone. That cooperation was not always forthcoming, and when it broke down problems easily became acute.

Since so much of the history with which this book will be concerned revolves about these two matters, taxation and magnate power, and about the wars which made them crucial factors in political and social development, it will be prudent to take a closer look at both at the outset. But before we do that we must first say something very briefly about the structure of royal government at the beginning of the period – about the system on which the wars imposed new strains.

According to the legal theory of the late thirteenth century, all secular authority in the kingdom stemmed ultimately from the crown. In reality, however, royal government was neither all powerful, nor legally omnicompetent. Its scope was limited by its objectives: it was not designed to foster the public welfare by providing direction and essential services, as in a modern state, but to uphold the dignity of the king as a great hereditary lord, and to protect his legal rights and those of his subjects. The law which the king's courts enforced was not based in royal command; it was the common inheritance of the people, founded in the custom of time past. The king might, with the assent and advice of his council, amend the law in detail, as Edward I did in the early part of his reign through a series of famous statues, but it was not, strictly speaking, his law. Moreover, the common law of the king's courts was not the only law that ran in England, nor his the only authority that enforced it. The church, an international community, had its own law, and its own courts enforced its rules on all men in spiritual matters (which included all matrimonial and testamentary causes). There were great franchises, such as that of the Bishop of Durham, within whose limits their lords exercised the rights that pertained to the king elsewhere. A host of lords of lesser franchises and the citizens of chartered boroughs enjoyed privileges which entitled them to enforce law and local custom with varying degrees of independence, and which gave them, as it were, a private share in the business of governing. At the fringes of the realm, in Wales and its marches and on the northern border with Scotland, the king's government shaded off into remote control. The king's duchy of Aquitaine and his lordship of Ireland were administered separately from England, and his authority there was exercised over societies whose customs and outlook were foreign, pure southern French in the one case, and in the other deeply affected by the clan life of the native Irish.

For all these limitations on its range, competence and initiative, the English royal administrative system was, at the end of the thirteenth century, precociously developed by contemporary European standards, especially in its central bureaucracy. This bureaucracy was organized around a series of departments, each equipped with one of the royal seals which, as formal authenticating instruments, made it possible to coordinate the private decisions of the king and his trusted advisers into public action, executive, legal, or administrative. The king's household, which travelled about with him, was his personal business head-quarters, and included a staff of trained clerks. These clerks were able and experienced men, well capable in emergencies of turning the expertise that they had acquired in supervising the king's everyday expenses in the chamber and wardrobe to tackle such formidable tasks as the victualling and payment of an armed host, and of managing, at a pinch, the whole of his correspondence, official and private. In his household the king kept his privy seal, to authenticate the letters that he sent out from his itinerant court – diplomatic correspondence, summonses to appear before him, instructions to the chancellor to draw up official documents in accordance with his and his counsellors' decisions. Quite early in the fourteenth century the business passing under this privy seal – especially diplomatic and conciliar business – became so considerable that it developed into a separate office, and its keeper became the third officer of state, after the chancellor and the treasurer. When this happened, the signet seal kept by the king's secretary became the seal used to authenticate his private letters, and warrants under the signet were from time to time accepted as authority by the chancery for the issue of letters under the great seal of England.

The great seal, kept by the chancellor, was the most important of the king's seals. The use of the great seal for all purposes except routine business required to be warranted (usually by a letter under the privy seal). It was used to give authority to all important acts of state, to public treaties, statutes, and letters patent appointing men to official posts or commissioning them to discharge essential administrative and judicial duties. There were also many regular writs instituting proceedings in the courts, which had to be sued from the chancery and sealed there. In short, the chancery was the lynchpin of general administration, and the chancellor, who was usually a bishop, was in consequence always a man of influence. He was automatically a member of the royal council, and came to be often the chief spokesman who explained the king's need for fiscal aid to parliaments. He had a substantial staff of clerks to help him in his business, clerics who could expect a benefice (indeed probably more than one benefice) to provide them with a stipend, and for whom, if they made their mark, there were rosy prospects of ecclesiastical promotion.

The third office of state, beside the privy seal office and the chancery, was also the oldest and the most professional, the exchequer. It had acquired early a seal of its own, the seal of the exchequer. Responsible for supervising and accounting for the collection, audit and expenditure of the king's revenue in accordance with its own strict rules of procedure, it was also a court dealing with cases in which the king's fiscal rights were involved. The treasurer (like the chancellor, often a bishop) presided over it, aided by the barons of the exchequer, men learned in the law and in the exchequer's own complicated processes. Every item of the king's revenue, and every payment made at his order, was entered on its massive rolls. The accounts, both of local officials (as the sheriff) and of the royal household, were audited by it. Its task was more formidable than that of either of the other departments, and in many ways even more vital. The exchequer alone, through the treasurer, could give the king and his councillors any idea of how far his resources really would stretch. Needless to say, it did not manage to keep the kings of England's royal accounts in balance; it would have needed much more than clerical efficiency to achieve that.

The normal home of the exchequer and the chancery was at Westminster: it was there too that the king's central courts held their sessions. The King's Bench was the highest court in the land, aside from the king's own council and parliament, and was so called because of its concern with all matters that affected the crown. The Court of Common Pleas (often called the 'bench' simply) dealt with cases between parties and corrected the errors of lower courts. The judges of these courts, appointed by the crown, were men of great influence, often called to council, who gave important assistance in the drafting of royal statutes. After 1290, few of these judges were clerks, as so many of their predecessors had been, and few had had a clerical education. They were recruited now usually from among the serjeants (senior barristers, who had a monopoly of pleading in the central courts). The law was becoming a professional lay occupation, and these men had trained in their business of pleading by attending the courts and watching their procedures as 'apprentices' in the law. On account of the multiplication of the statutes (a notable feature of the late thirteenth century), and of the number and variety of writs instituting proceedings, mastery of the common law and its intricacies had become a branch of learning in its own right. In spite of its long delays and the expense incidental to litigation, the common law was highly prized by the king's subjects, and the law courts were always busy.

The great offices of state and the central courts were the essential links between the king's council, the heart and the centre of government where executive decisions were taken and legal remedies framed, and the local administration. The most important figure in local government at the end of the thirteenth century was still, as it had long been, the king's sheriff. It was he who, in the county court that met once a month, published royal statutes; he who supervised (in this same county court) the election of representatives when these were summoned to parliaments. He was responsible for the pursuit and custody of criminals, for empanelling juries to try cases, and in general for having all things ready when the king's justices visited his shire. Most judicial work was carried out by justices appointed from time to time to take the assizes, deliver the gaols, or to hear and determine cases between parties: more rarely the counties were visited by justices in eyre, appointed in the exchequer, with power to hear all pleas and to undertake a general review of the administration of the king's rights (these eyres were unpopular, and lapsed in the course of the fourteenth century). It was the sheriff's task to see that the decisions of these judges were implemented, and to levy the fines that they imposed. In his fiscal capacity the sheriff was responsible to the exchequer. Twice a year he had to appear there and account for all the moneys that he had received, the farm of his county, fines imposed by the courts, and any other dues to the crown that he had collected – less what he had spent in the county at the king's orders, in wages, for victualling the king's castles and repairing his buildings, and so on.

The sheriff was the maid of all work in the county, but by the 1290s he was no longer by any means the omnicompetent royal servant that he had once been, and the late Middle Ages were to witness the further decline of his office. A series of other officials, most of them like the sheriff recruited from among the substantial county gentry, discharged specialized duties in the localities. There was the coroner, who kept the record of the pleas of the crown, and held inquests into matters in which the king had a customary legal interest, such as murders and wrecks. There were the escheators who looked after the king's rights as a feudal landlord, to wardships, marriages, and reliefs. There were the keepers appointed to look after estates which for one reason or another were in the king's hand, as for instance those of a bishopric during a vacancy, the collectors of customs at the ports, the keepers of the royal forests. In all financial matters the exchequer supervised the activities of this host of officials. The outbreak of wars, in the 1290s and after, multiplied the tasks and enhanced further the importance of the crown's local servants. Taxes had to be collected, and men arrayed for military service, and the assistance of men of local substance was called for in the discharge of such offices as collectors of subsidies and commissioners of array. At the same time, concern over the maintenance of public order (whose deterioration was seen by many as a by-product of the strains of war) contributed to an increasing reliance on the same sort of people in the pursuit of crime and law enforcement, first as keepers of the peace in the counties, and later as justices of the peace. The overall effect of this proliferation of local offices was to give the sector of society that historians broadly call 'the gentry' a newly significant part to play in the governance of the kingdom regionally and in the service of the crown.

The system of administration that was in operation before the wars began to generate new stresses was sufficient to its foremost intended task, the enforcement of the king's hereditary rights. Those rights were however not wide enough, and above all were not productive enough financially to enable him to cope with such an emergency as a major war without further assistance. From his private and prerogative resources the king drew an income in the region of £20,000. Besides this he had the regular revenue brought in by the customs, the levy on wool (6s. 8d. a sack) and certain other exports, payable at the ports, and originally granted to Edward I in the parliament of 1275. In his day this brought in something like £12,000 a year. The income from these combined sources was just about enough to meet the king's regular expenditure on his household, his works, his administration, and the keeping of his castles. There was nothing left over for emergencies, let alone for such a costly emergency as a campaign.

We shall have to look in later chapters at the detailed problems of raising hosts for campaigning and paying for them. It was a very expensive business. There was no standing army. Though there was a general obligation on all men between the ages of sixteen and sixty to serve in defence of the realm, troops who served in a host expected to be paid wages. The cavalry of armoured knights carried expensive equipment, a costly coat of mail with plate at the joints, and they were mounted on great warhorses which could be worth as much as £40 or even £80 (the cavalry soldier supplied his own equipment, but the king paid for horses lost in his service). A man had to be wealthy to support the estate of knighthood, and the knights were a military aristocracy; in 1301 Edward I was able to summon about 900 from all over his kingdom to serve in the Caerlaverock campaign. To every mounted cavalryman in the host there might be ten or even twenty footmen, mostly archers, an increasing proportion of them usually being mounted for purposes of mobility. In the fourteenth century archers became more important than before with the development of the longbow, the great English six-foot bow of oak or yew which could penetrate armour up to a range of nearly 400 yards and had a rapid rate of fire. The service of archers was cheap compared with that of cavalrymen (in Edward III's time a knight bachelor was paid two shillings a day, a foot archer two pence), but they had to be paid, fed, and increasingly often mounted as well. Over and above these forces, the king needed for a major campaign to recruit expert miners and engineers, to build siege engines, and, if he intended to cross the sea, to hire and impound ships. Here already is an onerous tale of the outlay necessary for a single expedition. As long as hostilities were active a king needed three or four times his ordinary annual revenue if he was to pay his way.

The expense of campaigning meant that, if war broke out, the king had inevitably to look to his subjects for grants of taxation. There was no real question of their refusing to aid him: it was an acknowledged principle that subjects were bound to aid their ruler when necessity and the common interest demanded. But because the king had no automatic right to a stipulated contribution by way of tax, some form of communal assent was required to legitimize the collection of any levy that would be classed as 'extra-ordinary', that is to say, not due to the crown by established customary right. That spelt a need for the king to negotiate with some body or assembly that could be held to represent the 'community of the realm' and therefore empowered to assent to taxation on his behalf. Within the course of the half century following 1290, the assembly called parliament came to be identified as the proper forum in which such assent should be given, and a parliament, moreover, that included the 'commons', the representatives of the shires and boroughs of the kingdom. Before the outbreak of the great wars, the role of parliaments had been perceived as principally advisory and judicial (and as by no means necessarily involving the presence of representatives of the local communities). 'The king has his court in his council in his parliaments, where judicial doubts are determined and new remedies are approved for new wrongs', wrote the author of the law book *Fleta*.[1] The recurrent need for financial aid to meet military expenditure was the key factor, over the years from 1290 to 1340, in parliament's development into an institution, the primary significance of whose meetings was fiscal and political, rather than judicial. The regular attendance, at parliaments, of the representatives of the shires and of the boroughs, in the same time, brought the crown into direct, negotiatory contact with leading men in local society. As with the contemporaneous proliferation of local offices, the effect was to involve more closely with the counsels of the realm and in its political life the sector of society from among whom representatives (especially those of the shire) were chosen.

The grants that the king's subjects made to him were normally of two kinds. One was an extra levy on exports, in particular on wool (such were the *maltoltes* that Edward I and Edward III negotiated with assemblies of merchants, and the subsidies on wool which later monarchs were granted by parliaments). The other was a 'lay subsidy', the payment by the king's secular subjects of a given fraction of their movable property and their income, by way of a tax. Early in Edward III's reign the fraction became stereotyped at a fifteenth in the shires and a tenth in the boroughs; and in 1334 the assessments for such subsidies were standardized for future purposes in all localities – so that henceforward a lay subsidy could normally be reckoned to bring in about £36,000. The clergy, who in the late thirteenth century were occasionally assessed for parliamentary taxes, in the fourteenth established their right to make their own grants of tenths in their convocations (of York and Canterbury; their standard assessment was that reached for the tax of a tenth imposed by Pope Nicholas IV in 1291). The yield of subsidies, both lay and clerical, could be cut or increased after the assessments had become standardized, by the grant of fractions or multiples of a subsidy (a double subsidy, a subsidy and a half or a third).

For the purpose of financing the king's wars grants of assented taxation had serious shortcomings. They were occasional, granted for a specific campaign or in a specific military emergency; the idea that a king needed regular grants of taxation was never accepted in medieval England. The conditions on which they were granted were often unwelcome to the king. Besides, they always took a long time to collect (whereas his needs were usually immediate), and they were often insufficient – indeed, if hostilities lasted beyond a year or so they almost always were. These shortcomings regularly drove the kings of England to seek to raise funds by other means besides assented taxation. The two most obvious methods of doing so were by borrowing, and by the more rigorous exploitation of the king's customary and prerogative rights.

Tyranny – which is what the effort to make the king's rights yield more than they ordinarily did looked like in the eyes of his subjects – was in the long run self-defeating. The king had many rights that he could exploit; to tallage (tax) his demesne boroughs and manors at his will; to take scutage (the ancient tax in lieu of feudal military service) from his tenants in chief; to purchase compulsorily and at his own price ('purvey') goods for his household. He could send out justices in eyre to delve into the bottomless history of his subjects' petty crimes and misdemeanours, and make them pay for them, and he could seek to enforce the forest laws protecting his woods and venison more effectively. The return on measures such as these was, however, unrewarding in proportion to the effort involved, nothing like enough to relieve the king of the need for further, assented taxation. Then, when the king did assemble men to ask them to grant him subsidies, he would inevitably find himself faced with demands for the relaxation or abandonment of the rights that he had been seeking to enforce, and in his need he seldom had much option but to make concessions. It was in just this way that, in the course of the fourteenth century, popular pressure succeeded in putting an end to the general eyres, which had once been simultaneously a way of swelling the king's coffers and the central government's most effective means of maintaining a tight control over local administration.

The dangers of borrowing were less straightforward. Loans to the crown were inseparable from war taxation in the late Middle Ages. Subsidies took time to collect, and it became normal to ask for loans in anticipation of their payment, through commissioners appointed to negotiate personally with potential lenders in the counties. It was to the wealthy, bishops, abbots and knights, and to communities such as boroughs that the commissioners naturally addressed their requests. The subject had not much real option of refusing them; it was much less inconvenient, probably, to lend than to serve the king in person, which at a pinch he might be obliged to do, and anyway he was being offered good security for his loan – repayment out of the subsidy when it came in. If he did try to refuse, he ran a serious risk of being summoned to explain why he had done so, a most uncomfortable prospect. English society in the late Middle Ages, and especially its prosperous sector, was small enough for the ill will of the king and his officers to matter a great deal to quite ordinary people.

Small sums, contributed by individuals and communities who lent voluntarily because they knew that they could be compelled to do so, only dented the king's necessities in wartime. He needed to raise much larger loans as well. In the late thirteenth and early fourteenth century he usually applied to Italian bankers, later more often to the native merchant community. On such loans the crown might have to pay interest, perhaps at a high rate (interest was not paid on its semi-compulsory loans from subjects). The normal method of repayment of both kinds of loan was by 'assignment'; the exchequer gave the lender tallies, notched sticks recording the sum lent, which were assigned for repayment at a future date from a particular revenue – say the subsidy for Oxfordshire, or the customs of Southampton. The creditor then collected the cash from the king's officials himself. All too often it happened, however, that when he came to cash his tally he found that there was no money available – some other creditor had been before him, maybe. In this case he might with luck get his tally renewed, and payment deferred to a later date; but the same thing might happen again. As time went on, if hostilities endured, the exchequer's revenues became weighed down with assignments, and a backlog of bad debt began to accumulate. The customs might have to be pledged to major creditors; and fresh loans might have to be raised, not now in anticipation of subsidies but to repay old debts. Confusion then began to mar the system of accounting. The longer a war continued, the more difficult the exchequer's losing battle against mounting insolvency was likely to become.

Impoverishment and indebtedness were directly damaging to the royal reputation, and so to kingly authority. They exposed the king's exercise of his patronage (one of the key tools of his political management) to hostile attention; why was he giving away so much when he ought to be harbouring his resources? They promoted competition and appeals to private influence for priority in the repayment of royal debts. In these circumstances, the harmony between the king and his leading subjects that was vital to effective government came easily under strain, with potentially dire consequences. For, as Sir John Fortescue pointedly remarked, 'his subjects will rather go with a lord that is rich, and may pay their wages and expenses, than with a king that hath nought in his purse'. Fortescue was here thinking about the problems facing Henry VI's government, impoverished by the long struggle to maintain his father's French conquests, as it listed toward insolvency on the eve of the Wars of the Roses. He had another pertinent remark to make about the dangers of royal poverty, with different circumstances in mind. Necessity, he noted, might drive the king

> to find exquisite means of getting goods, as to put in default some of his subjects that be innocent, and upon the rich men more than the poor, because they may the better pay; and to show rigour there as favour ought to be showed, and favour there as rigour should be showed; to the perversion of justice and perturbation of the peace and quiet of the realm.[2]

This was an even more certain way of sowing divisions between the king and his magnates. (Fortescue was probably thinking here of Richard II, who found out the hard way how right he was.) In either of the situations that Fortescue envisaged, problems arising from the difficulty referred to earlier, that the king's greater subjects were too powerful to manage on the basis of authority alone, were likely to become acute.

Amongst the king's greater subjects, with whose affairs the rest of this chapter will be principally concerned, we must distinguish at the start two groups: the great lay barons and their ecclesiastical colleagues. The bishops and the greater abbots whom the king summoned to parliaments by individual writs were great landowners, feudal tenants in chief of the king: that was why they were so summoned. They were no less determined than were the lay magnates to maintain the integrity of their wide estates, of which they considered themselves custodians for the saints to whom their churches were dedicated. But their wealth was not hereditary, and their office and experience set them apart; they were not involved in the competition for dynastic advantage that pre-occupied the lay baronage, and the background of their education was religious, not martial. Royal influence had helped most of them to their dignities; and many among the bishops had risen directly through the administrative service of the crown. This did not always make them committed royalists in politics, but they usually looked on political issues with a bias that favoured the monarchy. Late in the fourteenth century and in the fifteenth, when cadets of noble houses were more numerous among the episcopate than they had been, leading churchmen tended, it is true, to become more easily entangled in the feuds of their fellow peers. Even then, however, theirs was a moderating influence in politics, in favour of stable government and marked by a less martial concept of the common interest than that of the lay lords.

It was the lay lords who presented the real problem of management for the crown. There is a story that, when Edward I instituted the *Quo Warranto* inquiries and summoned all those lords who held franchises to prove their title to them in his courts, the Earl of Warenne appeared before the royal judges brandishing an 'ancient and rusty sword'. 'Behold, my lords', he cried, 'this is my warrant. My ancestors came with William the Bastard and conquered their lands by the sword; and by the sword I will defend them against any who may wish to take them. For the king did not by himself conquer and subject the land, but our ancestors were his partners and companions in the business.'[3] These words are full of significance. The great lay lords did regard themselves as a class apart, companions of the king with special privileges and responsibilities. In war they did act as his partners: contingents recruited and captained by them always, in the fourteenth and fifteenth centuries, formed a substantial proportion of the royal hosts, and often the major one. In Wales and Scotland, in Edward I's day, they often served without pay, and later, for service in France, they showed themselves willing to wait, sometimes for years, for wages of war for themselves and their men. On account of their great wealth, the public good order of the king's realm was quite as vital to their interests as his, and they looked on themselves as his companions in maintaining domestic governance as well as in war. They expected to give the king counsel about the government of his realm, and that he should heed it. If he and his officials threatened them in their rights, or played fast and loose with the laws that were the common inheritance of the people, they regarded it as their right, indeed their duty as his 'born counsellors',[4] to restrain him, and by force if no other way could be found. Men who had such an exalted view of their station as this, and who were respected by others as the king's 'partners' or 'companions', needed to be handled very delicately by their monarch. In peace and war alike, their co-operation was vital to him. The nicely balanced combination of firmness and favour that was needed to secure it was not always easy to achieve.

The lay magnates could not have claimed the status and privileges that they did, but for their immense wealth, which, as Fortescue saw clearly, was what could make them difficult to manage. The foundation of this wealth was the individual magnate's inheritance, the network of estates and jurisdictional rights that descended to him by hereditary right (primogeniture was the rule among males; equal division between co-heiresses). From this inheritance, the territorial accumulation that was the fruit of the careful dynastic forethought of his ancestors, the magnate drew his income, partly from rents, partly from farming, partly from the profits of justice – from fines and dues levied in the courts that his reeves and bailiffs presided over on his manors.

The inheritance of a great lay magnate was likely to be scattered through many shires (with local concentrations), and its administration demanded the services of an extensive staff of officials. It was usually divided into a series of receiverships – one for each area in which there was a concentration of estates. In each receivership the lord would appoint a steward to supervise the running of his estates, and a receiver to collect his rents and dues; these would be paid into a central treasury, probably called the 'wardrobe', at one of his castles. The work of these officials was controlled and coordinated by the magnate's council, which would naturally include experts in estate management and men learned in the law. On a miniature scale the administration of the inheritance was thus a replica of the royal administration, and a magnate's councillors were quite as conscious of their duty to enforce all his rights and as ingenious in their pursuit of this object as the king's judges and the officials of the exchequer were on the crown's behalf.

All the great magnates held at least a part of their inheritances in chief from the crown by feudal tenure, and many of them the major part. As a system of reciprocal services (usually military) connecting lord and tenant, feudalism was already, before the late thirteenth century, obsolete, but it remained the basis of English common law concerning land tenure. This meant that the king retained his right to his feudal 'incidents': to the wardship of the heir of a dead tenant in chief if he was under age, and to dispose in marriage of his heiresses; and that tenants in chief might not alienate lands held of the king without a royal license. Still more important, the estates of a tenant in chief who died without heirs reverted ('escheated') to the crown. It was therefore only with the crown's connivance that a magnate could hope to augment his territories by marriage or by collateral inheritance. Direct royal patronage could, of course, enrich him even more splendidly. There were always inheritances which looked like falling in for lack of heirs, the reversion of which was in the king's gift, and rich wardships, not to mention grants that were to be had from time to time from lands forfeited to the crown by the treason of those who had previously held them. Besides this there were many offices of dignity and profit at the crown's disposal, Lord Chamberlain, Warden of the Cinque Ports, Keeper of the King's Forest, chief justice of north or south Wales – to mention a few among the most dignified and profitable.

Though there were considerable disparities of wealth between individual magnate families, the lay magnates constituted a relatively homogeneous political elite. They were bound to one another by ties of intermarriage, by their common interest as great landowners, by broadly shared perceptions of their standing and social role, and by shared pride in their ancestral tradition of service to the king and his realm. At the same time, however, they were also in a degree natural competitors. It was the policy of every magnate to seek to augment his inheritance; ambition aside, it was his duty to his kindred to do so. Because magnates were so heavily dependent on royal favour for the furtherance of their territorial and dynastic ambitions, the king needed to use the arts of management very carefully in his dealings with them, and in his exercise of patronage towards them (and their clients and associates). Of course everyone expected to see loyal service rewarded, and no one grumbled much at the advancement of, say, William Montagu in Edward III's reign to be Earl of Salisbury, or of Henry de Grosmont to be the first Duke of Lancaster. Both men had earned their recompense by service in war, diplomacy and domestic politics. It was quite another thing to witness the rise of one such as Piers Gaveston, Edward II's favourite whom he made Earl of Cornwall, which was the result of favour alone. It was not difficult for jealous rivals to denounce a *parvenu* to the peerage like Gaveston as an evil counsellor who was using his influence to plunder his king's resources and make himself rich. Such an evil counsellor exercised the sort of influence that magnates might see it as their duty in the common interest to restrain – by force if there were no other way of doing so. It was the easier to convince others besides magnates that this course might be necessary and justified if, as was the case at the time when Edward II was showering title and riches upon Gaveston, the king's wars were going badly. The charge that the king's patrimony had been depleted by overlavish patronage of the undeserving was one often on the lips of the discontented, coupled usually with the demand that unjustified grants be resumed, so as to lighten the burden of his overtaxed subjects.

When the lords denounced evil counsellors, or demanded that this or that be changed or amended for the common profit, it was very dangerous for the king to ignore them. Their voice was not theirs only, but that also of their followers, the retainers and dependants who had taken fees from them and were pledged to their service. The framework of relations which bound together these followers, and others more loosely connected, in the 'affinity' that focused round a magnate's 'lordship', is what historians have christened 'bastard feudalism'. The name is a little misleading: it denotes not a late and degenerate form of feudalism, only a system that in certain superficial respects resembled tenurial feudalism. A great many of the political ills of late medieval England have been attributed to it, often with rather less than justice. We need therefore to consider what the sort of associations were that the label 'bastard feudal' seeks to identify. This is not altogether simple, since it is an historian's term of art, not contemporary usage, differently nuanced in the interpretation of different commentators.[5]

   A great magnate family, with its wide hereditary estates, stood at the centre of a multi-class social group that drew its cohesion from attachment to a particular lord. For this society, the focal centres were the private castles and manors of the lord in question. Wherever he went, he would be accompanied by his permanent household staff: a list of the household people of John de Bek, Lord d'Eresby in the late thirteenth century, includes his steward (a knight), the wardrober (the clerk who supervised his accounts), a chaplain, two friars and a boy clerk, the marshal, and a substantial group of lesser men, ushers, butlers, porters, farriers. This was John de Bek's permanent staff only; there would always be more people with a lord's household – sons of important tenants, knights and esquires who had taken the lord's fees, messengers, and at each of his residences he would find a great staff of grooms, huntsmen, and menial servants waiting for him. John Smyth's description of the household of Thomas Lord Berkeley, famous as the gaoler of Edward II, gives a fine picture of the kind of society thus gathered together:

> The knights that had wages by the day and their double liveries of gowns furred were usually twelve, each of them with two servants and a *garçon* or page, and allowance for the like number of horses; the esquires that also

had wages by the day, each of them [with] one man and a page and allowance for their horses, were twenty four . . . from whence it may be conjectured what the number of inferior degrees might in probability be. I am confident that the number of his standing house, each day fed, were three hundred at the least.[6]

Communal living and the lord's liberality gave this society a coherence that was prized by men at large, for all ate together in the lord's great hall (and in the early days a good many slept together there too). 'Command the officers to admit your acknowledged men, familiar friends, and strangers too, with merry cheer', so runs the advice to a lord in a late medieval tract on the management of a household, 'and always, as much as you may, eat in the hall before your household, for that shall be to your profit and worship.'[7]

As this advice reminds us, it was expected of a lord that he should gather men around him – his following was the outward and visible sign of his status. It was also expected of him that he should be generous, showing his people 'merry cheer', that he should feed and maintain them and reward them for their service with fees and gifts. And it was not only in his household that he needed to surround himself with his own people: it was even more necessary that he should make a good showing, attended by men clothed in livery with his arms or device, when he came to parliament, or appeared at a tournament, or answered the king's summons to serve him in his host. This sort of display cost money, but it was money worth spending. A lord needed to strike a high profile visibly, to uphold his 'worship' among his peers, and to demonstrate to lesser men that his good lordship and service were worth seeking. The prospect of his good lordship was what drew men towards his affinity, and so into the network of influences and common interests through which his territorial wealth was transmuted into social and political power in the regions of his dominance.

The size and precise shape of any given magnate affinity can be hard to pin down: the relationships involved could be so many and various. The affinity would include kinsmen of the lord; individuals retained in his service for life; counsellors, estate officials and others retained by an annual fee, and free tenants; these connections shading off into looser bound circles of association through regional family and neighbourhood interconnections. At the core of the affinity, and less difficult to identify, were those men of local substance, knights and esquires, whom the lord had retained for life by indenture. The indenture was a sealed contract recording the terms of their mutual relationship. The earliest such document that has survived bears the date 1287; there are quite a few that belong to the early fourteenth century, and by its later years a standard form had developed. A good example, somewhat late in date but on the usual pattern, is the indenture sealed on 26 May 1461 between Richard Neville Earl of Warwick (the 'kingmaker') and Sir John Trafford. For the sum of 20 marks per annum, assigned on the issues of the earl's lordship of Middleham, Trafford was retained for life by the earl, in peace and war, to be 'ready at the desire or commandment of the earl to come unto him at all such times and in such places as the earl shall call upon him . . . horsed, harnessed, arrayed and accompanied as the case shall require'.[8] He was to have wages of the earl when on his service – and no doubt he would also be fed and maintained when he was in his household. In war he and his men would get wages, and he was to hand over a third of his winnings of war (plunder and ransoms) to his lord. 'In witness whereof', the indenture concludes, 'the parties interchangeably to the presents have put their seals.' John Trafford in 1461 was establishing his position in a large retinue led by the most powerful peer in England. In many retinues the number of formally indentured retainers was probably not very great: they were a small, central group in the society that gathered about a lord and his household. But they were always there in such a society, and always significant.

Reading between the lines of Trafford's contract, we can see why indentured retainers were so important to their lords. The martial overtones of its vocabulary remind us of how traditional chivalrous and honourable values helped to underpin the relationship of loyal service and mutual obligation between lord and follower (the echoes of the old vocabulary of military feudalism in such documents explain one principal reason for the coining of the label 'bastard feudal'). But Trafford was retained not just as a soldier, but for life and in peace as well as war, and the kind of service that indentured retainers such as he might render in peace were very significant indeed. They were drawn from among the county gentry, and were not permanently resident in their lord's household. As substantial local men, they could keep an eye for him on his affairs in their neighbourhood. Theirs was the class that dominated local government, from whose ranks the sheriff, the under-sheriff and the justices of the peace in a county would be chosen, and who would represent the community of the shire in parliaments. The loyalty of his retainers could entrench their lord's influence solidly in a locality. As men of wealth and standing with tenants, kin and neighbours, they made their lord's formal retinue the centre of the web of connexions radiating outwards that made the lordly affinity a force in local affairs.

Since complaints about the abuse of their influence by retainers and of their disorderly behaviour were so frequent (for instance from the commons in parliament), it is worth stressing the positive aspects of the kind of ascendancy that, through his affinity, a lord might come to exercise in what he called his 'country'. Royal authority and the crown's servants and officers needed the buttress of locally powerful influence to make legal process and the protection of property rights effective at the regional level: and local genteel society valued the stability that good lordship and associations with a magnate's affinity could promote in a world where disputes were all too often pursued by violence. Land-owning gentry easily fell out with each other, usually over competing title to properties; and, since legal title could be difficult to establish, were easily prone to pursuing their quarrels by force. Magnate influence could be a major deterrent to their thus taking the law into their own hands. It might not be wise to evoke the intervention of a powerful patron to protect an otherwise challengeable rival's interest. A lord's arbitration (or perhaps the arbitration of two rivals' lords working together) could be a useful means toward compromise that would give something to both parties and restrain disorder from spiralling through their quarrelling: and the warrant of men of his affinity (or their affinities) might be useful in upholding the settlement. If parties went to law, a lord's influence with those responsible for its enforcement, the sheriff and the local justices, could help to ensure at least that those connected with him got a fair hearing. Stability and the maintenance of order in local society depended on a measure of interaction between public authority and private aristocratic power, and people expected that this should be so. That is what lies behind the seeming paradox, that the same kind of people – local gentry – who were most avid in the quest for the good lordship of a magnate patron were also the kind of people who were most vociferous in denunciations of the abuses of retaining.

In the military context of warfare against external enemies, the positive aspects of the 'bastard feudal' system of retaining were more straightforward and obvious, from a public point of view. A lord's indentured retainers formed a nucleus round which a fighting company of knights, esquires and archers could be rapidly enlisted for war or in a domestic emergency. Since in the late Middle Ages the main body of a royal host usually consisted of contingents recruited individually by captains, the leaders among whom were usually magnates, retaining by indenture was of service to the crown and to the realm at large in times of war. 'Trust it true', the chronicler John Hardyng wrote of the Percy Earl of Northumberland, 'there is no lord in England that may defend your realm against Scotland so well as he, for they (the Percies) have the hearts of the people by the north, and ever had.' Hardyng spoke from personal knowledge: 'I, the maker of this book, was brought up from twelve years of age in Sir Henry Percy's house, to the battle of Shrewsbury where I was with him armed, as I had been before at Homildon, Cocklaw, and at divers roads (skirmishes) and fields with him.'[9] It was not on the northern border only that the solidarity of magnate retinues proved their fighting value to the kingdom. Anyone who turns the pages of the Black Prince's *Register* may check for himself the connexion between the service of an extravagantly generous lord of the blood royal who happened also to be the most notable military commander of his age, and a national, martial achievement in the field in France. John Chandos, James Audley, Thomas Felton, the names of his followers that are familiar from Froissart's chronicles of chivalry are all there, together with notes of the rewards with which their leader saw fit to honour them; fees assigned on his landed revenues; warhorses with memorable names; captured armour, plate and jewels. The wars indeed gave a positive impetus to retaining; many men probably first made contact with the lords with whom they would one day be indentured for life, when they took service under them temporarily for campaigns in France.

The practice of retaining was regulated, in the late Middle Ages, by a number of statutes (not, it must be admitted, very effectively). The most important of these was Richard II's statute of 1390. This forbade all except peers (that is, men whose substance was not sufficient to guarantee their social responsibility) to retain men who were not their household servants by grants of fees and liveries. It also forbade peers to retain men of low estate, 'valets' and yeomen archers who were not permanently employed in the household, by grants of liveries. But it specifically permitted peers (and no others) to retain for life persons of substance, knights and esquires, who were not household men. Nobody wished to forbid this kind of retaining, because, as has been explained above, it was the best way that the king or anyone else knew of recruiting responsible men to perform essential services, and was the key to the mobilization of armies in time of war.

What inspired the inhibitions of the statute was the reverse side to those positive aspects of retaining that have so far been highlighted. Insufficiently restrained, retaining could be so abused as to enable peers to maintain what were effectively private armies, and gentry to gather about themselves bands of thugs, to the perturbation of the peace of the realm. Bastard feudalism was Janus faced: the kind of relationships between men that it fostered could play a vital part in the maintenance of social stability; they were equally capable of contributing to spiralling disorder. Genteel landowning families, as has been explained, fell out easily with one another. Force and favour were, in the conditions of the time, necessary adjuncts to a man's right at law, and the expectation, that his master's 'good lordship' would help him to fend off rivals' designs on his title and to advance his designs on theirs, was one principal reason why country gentry were anxious to enrol in the retinues of great magnates. Maintenance, the offence committed by the powerful when they upheld their followers' legal causes and quarrels by extra-legal means, was in consequence a besetting social problem. Maintenance might be more or less subtle: a corrupt sheriff might see to it that no jury was empanelled that would convict his lord's clients (who could then help themselves to their 'rights'), or a band of armed men in a lord's livery might convince a justice that it would not be worth his while to decide a case in a way that they did not like. The result was the same either way 'that true subjects . . . dare not for fear and doubt of their lives complain to your highness (the king) or sue for remedy after your laws'.[10] The disorder and disturbances consequent upon maintenance were thus cumulative. Retaining could too easily become a means to the systematic perversion of justice, in a particular set of associated interests. The obvious recourse of those disadvantaged in these circumstances was to look for a patron whose influence could be pitched against that backing their rivals. Lords thus became easily entangled in their followers' quarrels, and the resulting confrontations could become serious, politically loaded. In a region where two magnate families and their followers were competing for influence (as the Nevilles and Percies in the north, for instance) the cumulative consequence of their quarrelling and that of their retinues might fall not far short of a local civil war.

We shall deceive ourselves if we think of late medieval England in modern terms, with political coherence dependent on the smooth operation of relations between local and central government, and social tensions centring round the competing interests of classes divided politically from one another. Horizontal social and economic divisions, in this period, were less significant than the vertical ones which separated multi-class groups of men attached to different and often competitive interests, and which were led by the king and by individual magnates (for the king had his own retinue, the household men of his 'royal affinity'). These groups can be described in terms of 'solidarities', but there was a fluid side to their composition, which could be a factor of instability. There was nothing to stop a servant from taking the fees of more than one lord (and of keeping them, as long as those lords did not fall out). In the ebb and flow of the tides of political and social competition, most retainers were ready to desert the fortunes of a master whose star seemed to have passed the ascendant for one whose service promised more effective protection or greater reward, and there was nothing legally to prevent his doing so. Effective government, in these circumstances depended far less on the work of the central bureaucracy than it did on the ability of the king, the magnates and their principal followers to cooperate reasonably among themselves. This was the political reality behind the statement made early in this chapter, that the king's greater subjects were too powerful for him to control on the basis of authority alone.

'Bastard feudalism' was a version of the system of patronage and clientage which has been so important throughout English history, appropriate to the needs of an age in which influential protection was a prime social necessity, and in which the government could not afford to maintain standing forces against military emergency. A last point to be made must be to stress the strength of the military ethos that coloured the outlook of the leaders of the late medieval 'bastard feudal' world, the high aristocrats. As their sculptured effigies in full armour on their tombs remind us, these were in their own perception 'chivalrous' men, bred in a culture consciously knightly and martial. The natural training for youths of good birth was in a noble household, the chief subjects of their education horsemanship and the exercise of arms; 'as using jousts, learning to run with a spear and handle an axe, sword and dagger, wrestling . . . leaping, running, to make them hardy, free and well bred; so that when the realm in time had need of their service in deeds and enterprises of arms, they might be the more apt to do honourable service'.[11] The history that such youths learned and were taught to value was the story of the martial prowess of their ancestors, and of Christian champions such as Arthur and Charlemagne – and of the loyal followers of these heroes. The insignia (arms and other devices), which were the outward marks of the dignity and ancestry of lords and knights, were military. Livery, the granting of a heraldic badge to a follower, was a way of associating him with his lord in a relationship whose social traditions and ethic were soldierly.

This was why the fortunes of war were so important to the relations of king and magnates in the 'bastard feudal' age. Successful royal government depended on the capacity of kings to impress their leadership on the magnates who were their 'companions' sufficiently for all to cooperate together: to this end a degree of mutual trust and respect was necessary. This respect and confidence a king could obtain by proven martial ability more readily than in any other way. Edward III and Henry V, who won their battles, did not have much difficulty in canalizing the wealth and influence of their magnates and the manpower of their retinues to the service of their own military enterprises. There were material as well as psychological reasons for their success in doing so. Victory brought riches as well as glory to those who shared in it, loot and ransoms; and military service besides opened endless prospects of official advancement. By comparison with the fruits of office and domestic service these prizes were glamorous: Sir John Fastolf told his servant William Worcester that on the day of the battle of Verneuil in 1424 alone he won by the fortune of war 20,000 marks.[12] In the pursuit of such fortune, many were ready to lay aside, for the time being, their jockeying for favour and position at home. Edward III's reign, which witnessed the victories of Crecy and Poitiers and Najera, also witnessed the longest interlude untroubled by civil strife or aristocratic sedition in the whole of the late Middle Ages, and it was no accident.

A king who did not win victories could not obtain the confidence and respect of his powerful subjects with the same ease as one who could. He was likely to find it much harder to channel the ambitions and to control the naturally competitive interests and intrigues of great men and their followers. Worst of all was the fate of the king who fought a losing war. Defeat undermined respect for him and for his advisers; his borrowing and his taxes alienated his subjects at large; and, in the halls of the great, men began to murmur that it was time that someone took a hand to relieve the king of councillors who were serving him ill. Thus popular discontent and disaffection mounted towards the flashpoint of rebellion.

The object of this introductory chapter has been to highlight the significance of three strands running through the narrative history of England in the late Middle Ages; and whose interplay, as I see it, was formative. One is the impact of the ebb and flow of military fortune and misfortune in the wars in which England was engaged in the period. The second, related to the pressures of war, is the growing involvement in the political life of the realm of the genteel landowning class, and of the local communities; most obviously through their part in assenting to taxation through their representatives in parliaments, but also through the part they came to play in local justice and administration, and through service in the kings' wars. The third is the interaction between royal public authority and private noble power, the successful coordination of which, enduringly throughout the period, remained a key factor in holding the body politic together and on course. In tracing the story of the English polity from the age of Edward I to that of Richard III, the ways in which these three strands interacted, and interwove with other forces outside political control (notably the fourteenth century plagues) to shape its development, will be a constant focus of attention.

Notes

1 *Fleta*, ed. H.G. Richardson and G.O. Sayles (Selden Soc., 1953), Vol. II, p. 109. On parliament at the beginning of our period, see further Chapter 4 below.

2 J. Fortescue, *The Governance of England*, ed. C. Plummer (Oxford, 1885), p. 119.
3 *The Chronicle of Walter of Guisborough*, ed. H. Rothwell (Camden Soc., 1957), p. 216, note d.
4 See Fortescue, *The Governance of England*, p. 147.
5 On the literature, see the 'Note on Secondary Reading' below.
6 J. Smyth, *The Lives of the Berkeleys*, ed. Sir J. Maclean (Gloucester, 1883), vol. I, p. 304.
7 Household statutes, attributed to Robert Grosseteste, printed in *Manners and Meals in Olden Time*, ed. F.J. Furnivall (E.E.T.S., 1868), pp. 328–31.
8 This indenture is printed by A.R. Myers in *English Historical Documents 1327–1485* (London, 1969), p. 1126.
9 J. Hardyng, *Chronicle*, ed. H. Ellis (London, 1812), p. 351.
10 *R.P.* vol. V, p. 367.
11 *The Boke of Noblesse*, ed. J.G. Nichols (Roxburghe Club, 1860), p. 76.
12 See K.B. McFarlane, 'The investment of Sir John Fastolf's profits of war', *T.R.H.S.* 5th ser., 7 (1957), p. 95.

Note on secondary reading (post 1970)

Currently, the readiest introduction to late medieval English government is A.L. Brown, *The Governance of Medieval England, 1272–1461* (London, 1989). Also very useful generally are W.M. Ormrod, *Political Life in Medieval England, 1300–1450* (Basingstoke, 1995), and J.A.F. Thomson, *The Transformation of Medieval England, 1370–1529* (London, 1983). A very illuminating interpretive essay is G.L. Harriss, 'Political society and the growth of government in late medieval England', *Past and Present*, no. 138 (1993). R.W. Kaeuper presents an interesting (though controversial) interpretation of the impact of war on government in his *War, Justice and Public Order: England and France in the Later Middle Ages* (Oxford, 1998). Broad aspects of the impact of war are surely covered in M.C. Prestwich, *Armies and Warfare in the Middle Ages: the English Experience* (London, 1996).

On the law and the courts consult A. Harding, *The Law Courts of Medieval England* (London, 1973). On the developments in local justice and law enforcement, see W. Ormrod and A. Musson, *The Evolution of English Justice: law, politics and society in the fourteenth century* (Basingstoke, 1998). Two illuminating books by P. Brand examine the development of the common law and of the legal profession at the start of our period, *The Making of the Common Law* (London, 1992), and *The Origins of the English Legal Profession* (Oxford, 1992).

The essays on parliament in R.G. Davies and J.H. Denton (eds.), *The English Parliament in the Middle Ages* (Manchester, 1981) make an excellent starting point for its study. Most of the seminal and vital works of J.S. Roskell are collected in his *Parliament and Politics in Late Medieval England* (3 vols., London, 1981–3). On all that concerns parliament's fiscal role, G.L. Harriss, *King, Parliament and Public Finance to 1369* (Oxford, 1975) is vital: two important papers of his are 'Aids, loans and benevolences', *Historical Journal*, vol. 6 (1963), and 'War and the emergence of the English parliament', *Journal of Medieval History*, vol. 2 (1976).

On the nobility and their political role the starting point has to be K.B. McFarlane, *The Nobility of Later Medieval England* (Oxford, 1973). On the gentry, Part 1 of C. Carpenter, *Locality and Polity; a study of Warwickshire Landowning Society 1401–1499* (Cambridge, 1992) is illuminating (and much wider in range than the title implies): also very important, especially for the earlier part of the period, is P.R. Coss, *The Origins of the English Gentry* (Past and Present publications, 2003). There are two important papers on magnate arbitration in gentry disputes, by E. Powell, 'Arbitration and the law in England in the late middle ages', *T.R.H.S.*, 5th series, vol. 33 (1983), and 'Settlement of disputes by arbitration in fifteenth century England', *Law and History Review*, vol. 2 (1984).

On 'bastard feudalism' specifically, one must start from K.B. McFarlane's two seminal essays, 'Bastard feudalism', *B.I.H.R.*, vol. 20 (1945), and 'Parliament and bastard feudalism', *T.R.H.S.*, 4th series, vol. 26 (1944). Both are reprinted in his *England in the Fifteenth Century* (London, 1981), with an introduction by G.L. Harriss, reviewing the subject perceptively. Two other important works are J.M.W. Bean, *From Lord to Patron: lordship in late medieval England* (Manchester, 1989), and M. Hicks, *Bastard Feudalism* (London, 1995), the former for its in depth treatment and the latter interpretively. For the controversy over the roots of bastard feudal relations (largely related to the period pre-1290, but significant for interpretation), see P.R. Coss, 'Bastard feudalism revised', *Past and Present*, no. 125 (1989), and the 'Debate: bastard feudalism revised', between Coss, D. Crouch and D. Carpenter in *ibid.*, no. 131 (1991). *The McFarlane Legacy*, ed. R. Britnell and A.J. Pollard (Stroud, 1995) includes two important essays that are full of insights relevant to the discussion of the subject, 'The dimensions of politics' by G.L. Harriss, and 'Political and constitutional history before and after McFarlane', by C. Carpenter.

Section I

Edward I and Edward II
1290–1330

2 Outward war and troubles at home 1290–1314

On 26 September in the year 1290 Margaret, the seven-year-old queen of Scotland who was called the 'Maid of Norway', died in the Orkneys. She was the granddaughter and heiress of Alexander III, King of Scots, who had died in 1286; and for the last four years her kingdom had been governed by six 'guardians'. In 1290 she was at last on her way home from Scandinavia, where she had been born, and an agreement had that summer been reached for her marriage to the eldest surviving son of Edward I of England, the six-year-old Edward of Caernarvon. The Treaty of Birgham, which settled the terms of the match, had stipulated that Scotland should remain a kingdom separate from England, with her own laws and courts and parliament: but the young Edward and Margaret, and their heirs after them, would naturally inherit both crowns. Edward I of England was already lord of Ireland, and he had earlier in his reign brought the principality of Wales under his direct dominion. The treaty therefore promised in due course (if the children survived) to round off an *imperium* for the English royal house over the whole of the British Isles. It also offered a simple and peaceful solution to the problem of Anglo-Scottish relations, for the Scottish kings in the past had always contested the ill-specified superiority which the English kings claimed over their land. The death of the Maid of Norway was therefore a blow to Edward I, upsetting carefully prepared plans.

Margaret was the only surviving descendant of Alexander III, and when she died it was not clear who had the best claim to her vacant throne. The strongest competitors were John de Balliol, Lord of Galloway (and a substantial landowner besides in northern England), and Robert Bruce, Lord of Annandale. Both were descended in the female line from David, the brother of King William the Lion (1165–1214): Balliol was the grandson of his eldest daughter Margaret, Bruce the son of his second daughter Isobel. There were other important claimants also, notably the English nobleman John Hastings, who was descended from David's third daughter; and Florence Count of Holland, who was descended from Ada, the sister of William the Lion and David. The situation was confused, and as the news of the child queen's death spread, the supporters of Balliol and Bruce began to prepare for a possible war of succession. To cooler heads there seemed only one way out of the impasse, to refer the whole matter of the arbitrament of the succession to Scotland's powerful and hitherto friendly neighbour,

King Edward. The king of England was entirely willing to intervene, but on his own terms. The appeal to his judgement gave him a clear opportunity to gain, if not all that the Treaty of Birgham had promised for the future, at least some essential advantages. He could certainly clear up the old question of the superior right of the English crown over Scotland. It was in this spirit that he approached the question of arbitration, in May 1291, when he went north to meet the representatives of the Scottish kingdom at Norham on the Tweed.

By the end of June 1291 Edward had persuaded the Scots, pending a decision, to put the chief castles of Scotland into his hands, and the competitors had agreed to stand by his judgement. He had not managed to persuade the Scots to admit his feudal overlordship over their kingdom, but the agreement of the individual competitors to do homage to him, if they succeeded, secured the point in a way which was only a little less satisfactory to him. The great case proceeded slowly, and was considered with deliberation and impartiality. It was judged by the king of England's council, assisted by eighty Scots assessors, forty nominated by Balliol and forty by Bruce. Balliol argued that his right was best because he was descended from the royal house by the eldest line; Bruce in that he was a generation nearer in blood to a king than Balliol was. Florence of Holland claimed that David, William the Lion's brother, had resigned his right to the throne to William, who then assigned it to their sister Ada, Florence's ancestress; but he could produce no evidence for this assertion. Hastings claimed a third share in the kingdom on the ground that it was a fief of the English crown, and that therefore, as was the custom in England, co-heiresses (or their descendants) should divide the inheritance. This argument was rejected by King Edward and his advisers; the kingdom of Scotland, as a community entire in itself, could not be divided, they ruled. Proceeding on the principle of seniority in blood they finally, on 17 November 1292, awarded the kingdom, with all its appurtenances included, to Balliol. He was duly installed, and did homage to King Edward as he had promised.

Homage was the recognition of a formal feudal tenurial relationship, and it could be argued that the act implied acceptance by the vassal of the obligations towards his lord normally incidental to feudal tenure; that he must serve his lord in war and with counsel, and that his tenants had a right to appeal from his court to that of his superior. It was soon clear that Edward was quite determined to assert and establish his right to these incidents of feudal superiority with regard to Scotland, and that he would not regard himself as bound by assurances that he had given in the interregnum about the limits of his future demands. Only a week after Balliol's enthronement, he and his council heard at Berwick a case on appeal from the court of the kingdom of Scotland. Over the next year a series of further appeals from the Scottish king's court were heard by the king of England, and King John was forced to appear in King's Bench to defend his judgements. When, in the case of an appeal by MacDuff of Fife, Balliol questioned whether he was obliged to answer, he was declared to be in contempt of court, and condemned to lose three castles until he made amends. Edward clearly meant business, and not to allow the Scots to dodge what he considered to be their legal obligations. The attitude was typical of the man. In earlier years he had forced the Welsh by arms to acknowledge his jurisdiction. In England the *Quo Warranto* inquiries had firmly established the principle that no baron could exercise judicial rights except by the grant of the king, his superior lord and judge. A supremely successful ruler so far throughout his reign, Edward was confident that, when he was asserting legal rights, firmness would pay.

In this instance his judgement was questionable. In his confidence he was insensitive to the offence which his attitude gave, not just to Balliol, but to the lords and people of Scotland. John's Scottish councillors encouraged him to resist Edward, and finally took over resistance on his behalf. In June 1294 Balliol was summoned, as Edward's feudal subject, to perform military service in the war which had broken out between England and France, in company with the leading men of his kingdom. John agreed in principle, but delayed and made excuses, and to stiffen him into refusal his subjects in July 1295 imposed upon him a council of twelve peers, without whose agreement nothing affecting the realm was to be done. This meant that the summons would not be answered, if the twelve could help it. Edward's firmness thus failed to establish without cavil his feudal superiority over the Scots king. Instead it lost him, in the long run, all that he had hoped to gain in 1290 and 1292, and involved his realm in a war that outlasted his lifetime. The strains of that war taxed his resources to the limit and beyond, and undermined his authority over his own English subjects. It was to shake to its foundations the whole edifice of Plantagenet monarchy, which Edward had built to new strength in the first twenty years of his reign.

In fairness to Edward, it must be made clear that the problem of Scotland did not stand alone. If that had been the case, he might have had his way in the northern kingdom. But in 1294 he was faced with war on two other fronts, in Wales and in Gascony. This was why, in that year, he summoned Balliol to serve him in arms, and it was also why Balliol's subjects thought they had some chance of success if they resisted English demands.

The rebellion which broke out all over Wales at the end of September 1294 was a very serious affair. It kept Edward and his chief barons busy through the winter; and though its back was broken when the Earl of Warwick defeated the most important Welsh leader, Madog ap Llewellyn, in the spring of 1295, Edward had to remain in the principality until well past midsummer, re-establishing order and English authority. The trouble in his duchy of Gascony was still more serious, and this was what really gave the Scots their chance. In Gascony the English kings had stood in the same position *vis-à-vis* the kings of France as Balliol stood *vis-à-vis* Edward, ever since 1259 (when Henry III as Duke of Gascony had formally recognized the feudal overlordship of the king of France). Appeals from the ducal court had since then become so frequent that Edward had taken to maintaining permanent attornies to defend his causes before the French king's *Parlement* at Paris. In May 1293 an Anglo-Gascon fleet defeated a superior French Norman fleet off Cape St Mahé in Brittany, and afterwards sacked La Rochelle. Trouble of this sort was constant in the Channel and off the Biscayan coast, but King Philip IV of France took the particular incident seriously, demanding the delivery of the Gascon offenders to his courts, and full reparation for the damage done to his subjects. To back his demands, he summoned Edward to appear in person before the *Parlement*. Edward, who had no wish for war, reacted diplomatically, and despatched his brother Edmund to Paris to negotiate.

In Paris, Edmund was tricked. He was led to believe that a settlement could be reached – if Edward would permit the temporary surrender of Bordeaux and a number of other southern towns to Philip, for the sake of appearances. On the understanding that the cession would be temporary, and that the proceedings in the *Parlement* would be dropped, the towns were handed over. Notwithstanding this, on 21 April 1294 Edward was again summoned before the court, and on 19 May he was condemned for non-appearance and his duchy declared confiscate. Like Edward in Scotland, Philip had decided that firmness would pay when the right of an overlord had to be upheld. His decision led to the outbreak of a full-scale war.

King Edward's response to the sentence of confiscation was sharp. Orders were sent out immediately to array men for service in Gascony, and summonses were sent to the great men of the kingdom, John de Balliol among them, to be ready to serve with their followers. Abroad English agents went busily to work to recruit allies in the Low Countries and the Empire with the offer of pensions. The dukes of Bar and Brabant, both sons-in-law of Edward, were ready to help, and soon Count Florence of Holland and, much more important, the emperor elect, Adolf of Nassau, were drawn into the alliance. To raise funds for these and other war measures Edward took drastic steps. A threat to seize all wools and woolfells to his use forced the merchants to agree to a new and heavy customs duty at the ports (the *maltolte*). He demanded and, once again by means of threats, obtained a grant of one half of all clerical revenues from the clergy in convocation in September 1294. His commissioners seized to his use the proceeds of the crusading tenths, which had been imposed earlier by Nicholas IV and deposited in English churches and monasteries. In spite of all this frenetic effort, the king was however unable to send such forces to Gascony in 1294 as he had hoped. The rising in Wales intervened; men and money had to be diverted and the king himself was kept busy until the summer of 1295. Then the Scots took their opportunity to stiffen their resistance against English interference. They were in contact with Philip IV early in 1295, and on 23 October entered into a firm offensive and defensive alliance with him. Finally, in March 1296 John de Balliol sent his defiance to the king of England and renounced his homage. In the brief space of eighteen months Edward was thus faced with war on three fronts.

1295 saw the end of the war in Wales. In January next year Edward was able at last to reinforce John of Brittany, who had been sent to Gascony in 1294, with a respectable force under Edmund of Lancaster. In March 1296 the king was mustering a powerful army at Newcastle for the invasion of Scotland. At the end of the month Berwick was taken, and on 27 April the advance guard, under the Earl of Warenne, met and defeated the feudal host of Scotland at Dunbar. The earls of Ross, Atholl and Menteith were taken prisoner; and the English main-guard was now able to take Roxburgh, Edinburgh and Stirling without much trouble. Without an army, Balliol saw no alternative to capitulation. At Brechin castle, on 10 July, he resigned his crown and kingdom into Edward's hands, and was sent into England in custody, after being solemnly stripped of his dignities as king. Edward continued north, as far as Elgin, touring rather than conquering the country, and by the end of August he was back at Berwick. Thither he formally summoned the parliament of Scotland, and the great men of the kingdom did homage to him. The lands of those who had opposed him he restored; there were no great punitive measures. The government of the kingdom, however, was placed in English hands. The Earl of Warenne was left behind as 'keeper' of Scotland, and Hugh Cressingham as treasurer. Edward himself returned into his own kingdom.

Having now dealt with Wales and Scotland, Edward's plan for the next year, 1297, was to turn upon his third and most powerful enemy, the king of France. He would attack him on two fronts. One force, under the Constable (Bohun of Hereford) and the Marshal (Bigod of Norfolk), would go to Gascony; he himself would cross to Flanders, whose Count Guy had joined the English alliance, so as to make contact with his other allies in the Low Countries, and invade France from the north-east.

This plan was too ambitious: it overstretched Edward's resources which were already strained when it was formulated. In response to the complaints of the clergy both in England and France, that they were being plundered by the secular authorities in order to pay for the war, Pope Boniface VIII in 1296 issued his bull *Clericis Laicos*, forbidding clergy to contribute to taxation for secular purposes. On the strength of this bull, Archbishop Winchelsey for the English clergy refused the king's demand for a fifth in the parliament at Bury in November 1296. The king riposted by placing the clergy outside the law (30 January 1297), which action brought many to heel; and by the summer he had managed to achieve a reconciliation with Winchelsey and his bishops.[1] By then, however, Edward was heavily embroiled with a secular opposition to his military plans. In March, at Salisbury, Bigod the Marshal had flatly refused to serve in Gascony, unless in the personal company of the king. He and the Constable reiterated this refusal in London in July. By this time the scope of their opposition had widened: they challenged now the legality of the *maltolte* and of the summons that Edward had sent in May to all who held £20 worth of land to be ready to go with him to Flanders. Later, the two of them appeared armed in the Exchequer, to protest against the levy of an eighth, which had been granted to the king by certain nobles and knights assembled in his chamber (probably at some time in July). Although Edward did sail for Flanders, on

22 August, he went too late, with too small a force and inadequate funds at his disposal; and he left his kingdom on the verge of civil war.

Edward achieved nothing in Flanders, and he was glad enough, in October 1297, to make a truce with Philip IV. He was not able to return at once, since he had first to pay off some of the large debts that he had contracted with his allies. His presence was urgently needed in England, however, for events there were getting ahead of him. On 10 October the regent and his council came to terms with the opposition leaders, and agreed to confirm the Great Charter and the Charter of the Forest, with specific additional concessions which met contemporary complaints; the collection of the eighth was also stopped. What had forced the hand of the council was the rebellion against the new English government in Scotland. The success of the 1296 campaign had been too swift to be effective. Opposition gathered force all through the summer of 1297: William Wallace and Sir Andrew Murray emerged as leaders of the patriot party, with the backing of influential churchmen such as Robert Wishart, Bishop of Glasgow, and the connivance of some of the nobility. On 11 September at Stirling Bridge Wallace and Murray inflicted a bloody defeat on Warenne, the justiciar whom Edward had left in Scotland. Though the English garrisons held out at Edinburgh and Stirling, the whole country was in revolt thereafter; and in October Wallace and his men were raiding over the English border. In this situation the regent had no real alternative but to seek a reconciliation with the leaders of domestic opposition.

1297 saw the climax of Edward I's difficulties. After his return to England in March 1298, he never again had to cope with war on so many fronts, or with such determined opposition to his policies at home as he had done in that year. The truce that he had made with Philip IV proved to be the end of active hostilities in the war over Gascony. In 1298 the two kings agreed to refer their quarrel to the arbitration of Pope Boniface, in his private capacity as Benedetto Caetani; and though he did not succeed in resolving their differences, he managed to cement the truce by the arrangement of two important marriages, between Edward and Philip's sister Margaret, and between Edward's son and heir, Edward of Caernarvon, and Philip's daughter Isabella (the latter were not in fact married until 1308). After this Edward had to wait, for Philip would not brook any of his arguments that Gascony was not truly a feudal fief, nor would he restore the lands and towns that he had seized there. The king of France remained adamant until 1303, when, shaken by his recent defeat at Courtrai at the hands of the Flemings, he agreed to a final peace. Edward was restored to his duchy, and agreed to do homage for it; and Philip agreed at last to abandon his alliance with the Scots. Up to this point he had continued to recognize John Balliol as lawful king of Scotland, and had refused to make any peace in which the independent Scots were not included.

After 1297 the Scots were the one active enemy with whom Edward had to deal. As regards Scotland, his position was complicated by other factors besides purely military ones. Philip's support for his enemies placed one major obstacle in his way. In 1299 the Scots found another powerful diplomatic ally in Pope Boniface VIII. They had provided him with a well-prepared case to show that Edward had no right of superiority in Scotland, but that, in fact, the kingdom was in the special protection of the Holy See. In response to their appeal Boniface in 1299 by his bull *Scimus Fili* ordered Edward to desist from molesting them. The bull was presented to Edward in 1300 by Archbishop Winchelsey, and though he did not interrupt his military operations, he felt bound to make a long and carefully documented answer, while all the greater barons of his realm were persuaded to put their seals to another letter to the pope, in the same sense.[2] Boniface's attitude changed in Edward's favour a little later, when in 1302 his relations with Philip IV began to deteriorate very seriously. It was at this same point that Philip also, shaken by his defeat in Flanders, began to waver in his support for Scotland.

No diplomatic setback would persuade the Scots to submit. The initial success of Wallace and Murray in 1297 had solidified the spirit of resistance to the English among the ordinary free men of the kingdom, and most of the leading clergy pledged themselves firmly to the national cause. Though the secular aristocracy, who stood to lose most in the event of defeat, were not quite so united, a number of them helped to lead the resistance, and others failed to oppose it. Notable among the former were John Comyn of Badenoch and, until 1302, Robert Bruce Earl of Carrick, the grandson of the competitor of 1292 and the future King of Scots. In the absence of John Balliol, a caretaker government of guardians, acting in his name and that of the community of Scotland, was organized. The impressive number of documents which went out in the name of this government between 1297 and 1304 bears witness to its administrative effectiveness. Edward I thus found that nothing short of total military victory could make the northern kingdom his.

His strategy in Scotland seems to have been to overpower opposition by the sheer weight of superior force. This strategy had two major drawbacks. In the first place, after the ugly domestic confrontations in England in 1297, he never again felt able to put quite the same pressure on his people that he had before, to make them contribute towards the cost of the war in men and money. Secondly, there was the difficulty of the terrain in Scotland. With his superior army Edward might gain control of the principal castles, but there were not enough of these to hold down the country systematically, and he could not afford the money to build more (as he had done in Wales). Hills and forests provided his enemies with an easy refuge; even in southern Scotland their area was too wide to patrol, and he could never hope to control the land north of the Forth. All the same Edward's efforts in time seemed to be telling, because they were sustained. The English control of the sea, complete during the campaigning seasons at least, also worked in the English king's favour, and enabled him to keep his forts and forces victualled, admittedly at great cost.

Edward mounted a whole series of major campaigns in Scotland. When he returned to England in 1298, he moved the exchequer and the judicial bench north to York, so as better to concentrate the whole administrative force of his kingdom on reconquest. In the summer of 1298 he invaded Scotland with an army which included some 2400 horse, and which may have numbered 30,000 altogether. On 22 July his cavalry overwhelmed Wallace's pikemen at Falkirk, half way between Edinburgh and Stirling, after the archers and infantry had broken the ranks of the wedge-shaped 'schiltrons' of the Scots. But though he later took the castle of Lochmaben, Edward was not able to follow up this victory effectively. In 1299 he was too busy with other affairs to assemble a host, and so it was not until 1300 that he returned. Though the English army was perhaps as large as that of 1298, nothing was achieved beyond the capture of Caerlaverock, a castle which was not of great importance. The campaign of 1301 was not a success either, and though the king wintered in Scotland, early in January he agreed to a truce, to last until November. In 1303, however, it looked as if he would finish the job. At the head of another great host he swept north as far as Kinloss, beyond Elgin; and at the beginning of winter he took up his quarters at Dunfermline. John Comyn, the sole remaining guardian (Bruce had made his peace with Edward in 1302), could not field an army against him, and on 9 February 1304 he surrendered at Strathord in Perthshire. In March Edward was able to hold a parliament at St Andrews, to which virtually all the prominent men of Scotland came as his lieges. Scotland seemed once more, as in 1296, to have bowed beneath the English yoke.

In the peace that he now gave them, Edward treated the defeated leaders of the Scots leniently. Lands which they had forfeited for rebellion were to be redeemed, at the cost usually of two or three years' value. The ancient customs and liberties of the kingdom were guaranteed. From the peace, only the garrison of Stirling (which held out till May) and William Wallace were excluded. Wallace was in fact taken in the next year: he was sent to London where he was tried by a special commission and executed as a war criminal and a traitor. If Edward's claim that he was the rightful overlord of Scotland was just, a traitor is what Wallace technically was; but in the eyes of his countrymen he has always, and deservedly, been regarded as a martyr in their cause.

The pacification of 1304 was followed up, in September 1305, by a long ordinance which set out the manner of the future government of Scotland. It was approved by the English parliament, and was framed with the advice and help of ten Scottish representatives, who had been chosen for this purpose by the community of Scotland. A lieutenant was appointed, to govern the land on behalf of the English king; he was to be aided by a council mainly composed of Scotsmen and would preside over the Scottish parliaments. Four pairs of justices were assigned to four administrative districts: Lothian, Galloway, the land between the Forth and the Mounth, and the land north of that. Most of the sheriffs appointed in the ordinance to administer the counties were Scots; only the key castles were left in the hands of Englishmen.[3] A wealth of experience of the problems of government in strange lands, culled in Ireland and Wales, lay behind the provisions of this impressive and conciliatory document, which, while safeguarding the ultimate lordship of the English king, guaranteed to Scotsmen the major share in the administration of their country. But though it was designed as a lasting settlement, and does credit to its architects, it had no significance in the history of Scotland, or of England for that matter. It was a dead letter within a few months of its publication, long before its terms had come to mean anything in practice.

On 10 February, in 1306, Robert Bruce met John Comyn of Badenoch in the church of Dumfries; a brawl broke out, and Comyn was killed. It seems unlikely that this was a premeditated assassination; Bruce's first reaction seems to have been to seek a pardon from Edward I. When it was not forthcoming, he took the only step by which he could hope to defend himself, and asserted his claim to the Scots kingship. On 25 March he was crowned at Scone, in the presence of bishops Wishart of Glasgow and Lamberton of St Andrews, and of the earls of Atholl, Lennox and Menteith. A new chapter had opened in the history of Scotland.

The fury of the king of England knew no bounds when he realized that the work that he thought was done must be begun anew for a second time. On 5 April he appointed Aymer de Valence his personal lieutenant in Scotland, and gave him orders to hang and burn. When in June Valence defeated Bruce at Methven, the prisoners that he took received short shrift. David Earl of Atholl and Simon Fraser were sent to London and there executed as traitors; Christopher Seton was executed at Dumfries. Bishops Wishart and Lamberton, who failed to make their escape from the country, were sent to England and imprisoned there. As many of Bruce's family as the English could find were rounded up; three of his brothers were executed and his sisters imprisoned. This terrible ferocity served little purpose, however. For a few months after Methven Bruce had to wander as a fugitive, but in the spring of 1307 he was back in the field, and was strong enough to defeat Valence at Loudon Hill in May. Edward, irascible, old, and at last weakening physically, was by this time on his way north, but he was without an army comparable to the hosts of 1300 or 1303. On 7 July, after he had been carried with his soldiers for a few miles beyond Carlisle in a litter, he died. With him died the determination that had sustained the continuous English offensive in Scotland: the new chapter in Anglo-Scottish history had begun in earnest.

'I hear that Bruce never had the good will of his own followers or of the people generally so much with him as now. It appears that God is with him, for he has destroyed King Edward's power both among the English and the Scots.'[4] These words were written by a Scottish nobleman a few days after Loudon Hill; they may not have been quite true then, but they soon would be. Edward II had no option, when his father died at Burgh-on-Sands, but to turn his face south: he had a government to take over, a formal coronation to arrange, and other business of his own too. The trouble was that he did not return, as his father would certainly have done. Within a year of his accession, he was deeply embroiled in domestic confrontation with his leading magnates. So Bruce was able, in 1308, to consolidate himself against his Scottish rivals, the followers of the Comyns and of Balliol. In 1309 he held his first parliament at St Andrews, and reopened relations with Philip of France. By 1311 he was able to lead raids across the English border, and in 1312 he surprised Durham and ravaged Hexham. No effective effort was made to oppose him. In the autumn of 1310 Edward did, it is true, lead an army into Scotland, but his campaign was devoid of achievement, and it was suspected that his chief motive in going north had been to make things difficult for the commission of magnates who had been appointed in the spring to reform the realm and the royal household – the 'Ordainers'. One by one the great castles which had been in English hands since 1304 or earlier fell to the Scots. In 1313 and the early months of 1314 Perth, Edinburgh and Roxburgh were all taken.

It was in order to relieve the last major English stronghold in Scotland, Stirling, that Edward II at last put himself at the head of a royal host to campaign in earnest, six years too late. On 24 June, at Bannockburn on the way to Stirling, Robert King of Scots met this English army and inflicted on it a crushing defeat. The Earl of Gloucester was killed, and after the battle the Constable, Humphrey Bohun of Hereford, was taken prisoner, along with the Earl of Angus, Thomas Lord Berkeley, and many others of less note. Edward II saved himself by flight. The battle did not end the war, which was to last (punctuated by intermittent truces) through the rest of Edward's reign, but it finally dashed any remaining hopes that the English might shake Bruce's hold on Scotland. After twenty years of fighting, they were thus further than ever from establishing that lordship in Scotland which Edward I had originally sought. This failure was a heavy blow to English pride and to the reputation of the Plantagenet monarchy. Bannockburn capped all: no English host had been so humiliated by a foreign enemy since time out of mind.

Because the war had gone on so long, the consequences of Bannockburn were not merely in the military sphere. The full significance of the reverse can only be understood when it is viewed also in the context of the strains to which the long war had exposed the English community. It is to this aspect of events that we must now turn.

England was at war, more or less without a break, from 1294 to 1314 (and beyond, indeed). The armies which were set on foot in the period were very large: the force which invaded Scotland in 1298 numbered probably nearly 30,000 men, and the hosts of 1300, 1303 and 1314 were, if smaller, of comparable size. Between 1294 and 1297 Edward I also had to raise and pay large forces for service in Gascony, and in 1297 he sought to gather yet another army for the Flanders campaign. At the same time, his attempts to build up a system of continental alliances against Philip IV placed a heavy additional burden on his resources. He had besides to organize substantial fleets in connexion with both the Scottish and the Gascon wars (his reign saw the first official appointment of an 'Admiral of the Sea of the King of England'). These very considerable efforts posed collectively a threefold problem: of recruitment, of finance, and of war administration).

The department which had to bear the brunt of the exceptional administrative problems posed by the wars was the royal household, and in particular the wardrobe. The king took his privy seal (which was kept in the wardrobe) with him wherever he went, and its controller served as his military and diplomatic secretary. The household clerks played an important role on diplomatic embassies (though the negotiations over Gascony became so complicated that a special officer had to be appointed to look after its documentation, called the Keeper of the Processes). Whenever the king assembled a host, a large proportion of the forces that he raised were taken onto the payroll of the household, and the wardrobe staff had to act in effect as paymasters to the forces. Large sums were allocated to the wardrobe's use at the exchequer, but there was never enough to meet all its commitments, and the keeper, John Droxford, had to supplement his advances with loans – which he had to negotiate himself, as there was no one else to do it. The creditors were paid with debentures on the wardrobe, cashable at the exchequer (captains of soldiers were often also paid with these, when ready cash was not to hand). The wardrobe also had large responsibilities for victualling the army and castle garrisons. The strains of war thus swelled the king's itinerant household of normal times into a ministry of war, with national responsibilities for the duration of the emergency. Droxford and his clerks were overworked men, and it is not surprising that, in spite of their impressive ability in administration, by the end of Edward I's reign their accounts were getting out of hand. Attempts were still being made to settle them at the exchequer (to which the Wardrobe had to account) in the early years of Edward III's reign.

The recruitment of Edward I's armies posed legal and constitutional problems as well as administrative ones. The infantry was raised by commissions of array (in effect by impressment), which operated in each county. This system of compulsory service could be justified in terms of the ancient obligation on all able bodied men to serve at need in 'defence of the realm'; but it was not clear just how far this obligation could be made to extend. The foot soldiers were usually paid, in fact, from the point when they left their counties, which gives some hint as to where, strictly, their absolute obligation was thought to end. Edward also raised substantial forces of paid infantry in Wales and Ireland. The key arm, however, was the cavalry: it was the mounted knights who won the day at Falkirk and Methven and who lost it at Stirling Bridge and Bannockburn. They were also a very expensive force, requiring costly armour and a warhorse (the king normally paid for horses lost on campaign). They were recruited by a number of means, which require a little scrutiny.

The feudal obligation on tenants in chief to serve the king in war with a following of knights did not provide an adequate cavalry force in the days of Edward I, if it ever had done. This system of recruitment was obsolete, and the thirteenth century writs of watch and ward imposed the obligation to keep the arms of a knight ready for service not on those who held a knight's fee, but on those who held land to a certain annual value, £100, or £50, or £40 a year (£40 was the usual figure; the demand of 1297 that twenty librate landholders should serve as cavalrymen probably asked them to do more than they could afford). When Edward assembled his great hosts, a large number of these men, from the counties, were always taken into the pay of the household. This corps could be supplemented by further paid forces raised on the basis of a contract made between the king and a captain, who would subcontract with other knights to form a troop on a voluntary basis. The greater barons normally served the king in person (as was their traditional feudal duty), and they brought with them to his service their retinues, knights of their own households and other men recruited for the occasion. These retinues were usually considerably larger than the followings which feudal custom obliged the barons to bring, and the barons themselves usually served without pay, in Scotland at least. This was a considerable subvention for the king's forces, and suggests too that military service was not unpopular among the upper classes in Edward I's time. Unpaid service, however, could never be more than a subvention, whether it was voluntary or compulsory. The main body of the cavalry, those knights serving with the household and under contract, all had to be paid, as did the infantry also, and the expense was very high.

Pay apart, the king had to spend money on victuals, ships, siege engines, and on the replacement of mounts for his knights. Between 1294 and 1298 Edward spent something of the order of £730,000 on the war. This was the period of greatest strain, and Gascony proved easily the most expensive theatre of war. But expenditure remained high afterwards, though it is not so easy to calculate, because of the confusion of the accounts. Finance remained throughout the knottiest of the problems that war posed for the first two Edwards.

The ordinary revenue of the crown (from demesne lands, the profits of justice, the forest, and so on) was in Edward I's time about £19,000 per annum. The customs, before 1294, were bringing in between £10,000 and £12,000 annually. These revenues combined were clearly quite inadequate to meet the king's needs in a period of military emergency, and he had perforce in consequence to demand taxes from his people. In each year from 1294 to 1297 the king obtained lay subsidies from his subjects with their assent, and he did so again in 1301 and 1306. These usually raised between £30,000 and £40,000 (though the tenth and sixth of 1294 raised much more): perhaps nearly enough, that is to say, to pay for one host for a year in Scotland. In the same years 1294–7 Edward also obtained substantial grants from the clergy, but there was resistance to these levies, and the tenth granted by the clergy in 1297 was the last tax to which they gave assent in the reign. Edward raised more cash through extra levies on exports, over and above the customs. In the period of the *maltolte* on wool, again 1294 to 1297, the extra levy just about trebled the ordinary yield of the customs. The *maltolte* was abolished in 1297, but in 1303 Edward obtained the agreement of the alien merchants to an extra levy on their exports (half as much again on the customs) in return for the promise in his *Carta Mercatoria* of royal protection, freedom of movement in the kingdom, and immunity from the royal right of *prise*. This added some £5000 to the royal revenue annually, and Edward would have liked to extend the levy to the exports of native merchants also, but they would not hear of it. It was only a very inadequate substitute for the *maltolte*.

All these sources of revenue, over and above the customs and the issues of the demesne, depended in some degree on assent for their levy. Even the *maltolte* had had this in the first instance (though it was only under pressure, when threatened with the seizure of their wool, that the merchants had agreed to it). Edward I found other means of raising money which did not need assent at all from those who had to pay. Boniface VIII in 1301 and Clement V later allowed him to keep the greater part of the tenths which they imposed, for three and seven years respectively, on the spiritual revenues of the English clergy. The king also made use of his prerogative to raise revenue. In 1304, for example, he imposed a tallage on the royal boroughs and the estates of his demesne. The most important of his prerogative rights, from a fiscal point of view, was his right to *prise* or 'purveyance', to purchase compulsorily supplies for his household. This was not a very onerous burden on the subject in ordinary times, but when in war the king's household in arms expanded to comprise half and more of his host, it could become in effect a very important and burdensome tax. The officers of the household in these circumstances could not cope with the whole task of raising purveyance: the national administration had to help them. Writs were addressed to groups of counties, through their sheriffs, to supply goods to a quota fixed arbitrarily in advance. The price was also fixed in advance and payment was often made not in cash, but in tallies cashable at the exchequer. Purveyance was the secret of the success of the king and his household agents in organizing the supply of his great armies. It bore very hardly on the people, however, and though some effort was made late in the reign to spread the burden equitably, so that the poor should not be stripped of all they had to live on, it is not clear that this had much effect. Certainly it did not cool the general resentment at the king's extension of his ancient right to supply for his household into what amounted to a general tax.

With all the resources at his disposal, Edward I still never had enough to meet current expenses on his wars. In consequence he often had to borrow, and he raised some very substantial loans from the merchants of Florence and of south-western France, especially those of Bordeaux and Cahors. The Ricardi of Florence virtually bankrupted themselves in his service. Later the Frescobaldi became his chief agents, and virtually the whole of the customs revenue was pledged toward the repayment of their loans by the end of the reign. This meant that the exchequer saw little of this important revenue, for the Frescobaldi collected it themselves directly, at the ports. By this time the crown was also falling a long way behind on the repayment of other debts, to native lenders, to soldiers for their wages, to men whose goods had been compulsorily purchased (or purveyed) for the forces. This indebtedness may seem surprising, when we recall that the end of hostilities in the Gascon war and the breakdown of Edward's system of continental alliances had greatly reduced expenditure after 1297. Revenue, however, dropped even further than expenditure. Edward I obtained only two lay subsidies after 1297; and he also had to abandon the *maltolte*, which had brought in far more than the new custom granted with the *Carta Mercatoria* ever did. Above all, the king was constricted in all his fiscal expedients in his later years by his ardent desire never again to face an opposition as determined as that which his earlier measures had aroused in 1297.

Edward I never found more than *ad hoc* means of getting round the fiscal and administrative problems which his wars posed. Discontent, in consequence, was never allayed, and when Edward II, who had none of his father's talents, ultimately succeeded, he was faced with a situation with which he was not able to cope.

The troubles really began in 1297. In that year there was opposition to taxation (and to other royal demands too) from both the laity and the clergy. With the latter's special problems we shall deal elsewhere;[5] in any case, as regards the clergy Edward partly got round his difficulties by means of the share that he obtained in taxation imposed by the popes after 1301. The secular opposition was much more serious, and brought the country to the brink of civil war. It was led, as we have seen, by the Constable and the Marshal, the Earls of Hereford (Humphrey de Bohun) and of Norfolk (Roger Bigod).

1297 was the year when the strains that the wars imposed reached their peak. The country had been taxed heavily each year since 1294; the enormously expensive campaign of 1296 in Scotland was just completed and now the king was planning to send one army to Gascony, and to lead another himself to Flanders to cooperate with his continental allies. To make up the requisite forces, all who held twenty librates of land and upwards were summoned to do the king service overseas. The first sign of trouble came at the spring parliament at Salisbury, when Bigod flatly refused to serve in Gascony, unless he was in the personal company of the king. Before they next came to the king, he and Bohun had held a great meeting with knights of their followings in the forest of Wyre on the Welsh march. In London in July they refused to muster the host for Flanders, whose numbers were in any case pitiably below the expectation of the king when he sent out his summonses. About this time the king's opponents summarized their grievances formally in a celebrated document, the *Monstraunces*, which was drawn up not in the name of the two leading earls only, but of the whole community of the land.[6] Its opening protest was against the summons to those who held twenty librates or more of land to serve in Flanders. This summons had no customary precedent, and there was no promise that the service would be paid; besides, twenty librates of land was not enough to support a knight. It probably did more than anything else to solidify popular feeling on the side of the earls. The *Monstraunces* also protested against the burden of taxation, tallages, aids, and *prises* as a result of which 'many have no sustenance and cannot till the land'; and especially against the *maltolte* on wool, which struck at the chief source of personal wealth in the land. Magna Carta and the Charter of the Forest had been infringed, the *Monstraunces* claimed, and the ancient liberties of the subject 'arbitrarily put aside'. This long and varied list of grievances makes it clear that the earls were justified in claiming that the matters of which they complained affected not just themselves, but the whole community. The movement that they headed was broadly based: this was what made it both important and dangerous.

By the time that the king sailed for Flanders the earls had added another grievance to their list, the order for the levy of an eighth, which had been granted to the king 'in his chamber' by the loyal barons and household men who had assembled for service in Flanders. On 22 August the earls appeared in the exchequer and refused to pay the tax. Civil war seemed imminent, but in September, before things had come to that pass, the news of Wallace's victory at Stirling Bridge was known, and the government, in the king's absence, gave way. The charters were confirmed; the *maltolte* was abolished; and a promise was made on the king's behalf that he would never, in future, take any *maltolte*, or any unaccustomed aids, *mises*, or *prises* in his kingdom without the common assent of the whole kingdom. These undertakings, set out in the document known as the *Confirmatio Cartarum*, met the main points of the opposition. It did not, it is true, go anything like as far as the document called the *De Tallagio non Concedendo*, which seems to be a final draft of what the opposition hoped that the government would concede. This document is much more specific in its restriction of purveyance than the *Confirmatio*, and makes specific reference to the question of the service of twenty librate landholders. Constitutionally, the concessions of the *Confirmatio* were nevertheless very important. The clauses concerning taxation amounted to a formal agreement that the king would only levy extraordinary taxes with the consent of a body representing the community and summoned for that purpose (in effect, if not in name yet, a parliament). Or perhaps it would be more correct to say that this should have been the effect, if Edward had stuck to the promises made in the *Confirmatio* on his behalf, and which he explicitly confirmed himself on his return from Flanders in March 1298.

In 1298 Edward made some further concessions. He ordered a perambulation of the forests, to re-establish their ancient boundaries, and an inquiry into abuses of purveyance. But he had always been determined to be as little trammelled in his prerogative as he might be, and he soon showed that he did not mean to carry conciliation further than was convenient. When he confirmed the Forest Charter in 1299 the first five articles, which were crucial as regards boundaries, were omitted. The war in Scotland continued, and he was soon taking *prises* again on the old scale, without assent. The new customs levy of the *Carta Mercatoria* had the assent of the alien merchants, but not of the community of the realm, as it should have done if the *Confirmatio* had been observed properly. Because of the king's shifty attitude, thus evidenced, opposition was not allayed by the concessions of 1297 and 1298. It was never so fierce again, but strain continued to dog the relations of the king with his subjects over the ensuing years.

The years 1299 to 1301 were the period of greatest difficulty. Bigod protested sharply about the king's evasiveness in the matter of the Forest Charter in the spring parliament of 1299. In 1300 the charters had once more to be solemnly confirmed in parliament, and a number of further articles – the *Articuli super Cartas* – were established at the community's request, though with the exception to all its twenty clauses 'saving the right and prerogative of the crown'. In each county three knights were to be appointed to hear and deal summarily with allegations of infringement of the charters. *Prises* were to be taken in future only by the customarily authorized purveyors and for the use of the king's *personal* household. Writs under the privy seal were not to be used to initiate cases at common law, and the Court of the Household (the Marshalsea) must not try common law cases of debt or freehold, but only trespasses committed within the verge of the household. Each county should elect its own sheriff. The *Articuli* form an impressive document, and demonstrate the ability of the opposition to draft a statute dealing constructively not only with major fiscal grievances, but also with details of the everyday administration of the land.

A year later, at the Lincoln parliament of 1301, the opposition was still alert and active. A long bill was presented by Henry of Keighley, knight of the shire for Lancashire, in the name of the prelates and magnates. Its clauses returned to the attack on the questions of purveyance, of the keeping of the charters, and the perambulation of the forest; and the lords made the grant of a fifteenth conditional on the perambulation being finished by Michaelmas and on the acceptance of the boundaries it established. The king would not assent to a demand that the prelates should not consent to taxation of the clergy without the pope's leave. This was a significant demand, suggesting that Archbishop Winchelsey had by this time associated himself with the earls in the leadership of the opposition to the crown. Edward certainly later regarded him as his most important opponent; and there is a story that in 1302 there was even a plan to put him at the head of a council which would be imposed on the king.

In fact, after 1301, the opposition to Edward I seems to have slackened. It had won its point for the moment on the question of the forest, and Edward had the full support of his barons at the Lincoln parliament in his rejection of Pope Boniface's claim that Scotland was subject to the Holy See. The magnates had never opposed the war in Scotland, and in 1303 and 1304 their attention and energy, like Edward's, were concentrated on the final conquest of that kingdom. The remainder of the reign was comparatively untroubled domestically, and in 1305 Edward obtained from the new pope, Clement V, a release from all the undertakings which, under the stress of circumstances, he had made in 1297 and afterwards, except for his obligation to observe the charters (which were part of the ancient law of the land, established long before the recent troubles). His influence with Clement also secured the summons of Archbishop Winchelsey to Rome, to answer charges which the king had preferred against him. Edward seized the temporalities of Canterbury when he went, but, significantly, he did not make much use of the papal absolution from his oaths, except to annul the disafforestations of 1301. Edward, armed as he was with the pope's bull, knew that he must still move warily; the slackening of opposition did not mean that discontent was dead. The old grievances flared up again as soon as Edward himself passed from the world.

There was no real break in the history of the English king's domestic difficulties with his subjects at the accession of Edward II. Edward I bequeathed to his son a massive confusion in his accounts, a heavy burden of debt, and the war with Scotland. He bequeathed to him also a still more dangerous legacy, of widespread dissatisfaction with the manner of royal government. Bohun and Bigod were both dead before 1307, but others who had been prominent in opposition to the old king outlived him, notably Winchelsey, who was then still abroad in virtual exile. Edward II had no desire to keep alive private feuds of the past, and the archbishop was soon back in England at his invitation, but he and his like were as determined as they had ever been to curb what they regarded as misgovernment. In January 1308 a group of powerful men, who were on embassy to France in connexion with the new king's marriage and whose leader seems to have been Anthony Bek, Bishop of Durham, took an oath to stand together to 'redress and amend the oppressions which have been done, and still are being done from day to day, to the king's people'.[7] Bek had not long before seen his palatinate franchise, which had been seized into the king's hand at the orders of Edward I, restored by Edward II. He was to remain, until his death in 1311, on notably better terms with the young king than most of the magnates. What he and his companions at Boulogne had in mind were clearly the long standing grievances generated in the last reign, not the new distrust of royal capacity that was to build up rapidly in the course of 1308.

The continuity between the troubles of Edward I and Edward II is not always adequately stressed, but the evidences of it are clear enough. When Edward II was crowned, a new clause was added to the coronation oath, that the king should observe 'the just laws and customs that the community of the realm shall have chosen'. Though there has been much debate as to its meaning, the object of this addition seems clearly to have been to make sure that the new king should not, as his father had done, go back on enactments made with the assent of the community.[8] In July 1309, at Stamford, Edward II was forced to reissue the main clauses of the *Articuli* of 1300 (in particular that concerning purveyance) in a statute. In the next year, when opposition was mounting to a new climax and the magnates appeared armed in parliament, the king was forced to agree to the appointment of twenty-one 'Ordainers', with powers to draw up ordinances for the reform of the kingdom and the household. Their *Ordinances* are the most important constitutional document that emerged from the troubles of the years before Bannockburn.[9] They are also the most telling testimony that the unrest of the early years of Edward II had its roots in the troubles that Edward's father had experienced in the last ten years of his reign.

The theme of the observance of the charters, so strongly stressed in the earlier period, runs right through the *Ordinances*, which form a long document with forty odd clauses. The question of purveyance, the bone of contention that loomed so large in the *Monstraunces*, the *Confirmatio* and the *Articuli*, was taken up again, and dealt with sternly: those who took *prises* which were not lawful (i.e. were not for the king's own household) were now to be treated as common thieves. The *Carta Mercatoria* of Edward I was quashed on the accurate ground that it had not received the assent of the baronage (as the *Confirmatio* had ruled such levies should). The hold of the Frescobaldi on the customs, which dated from well back into Edward I's reign, was broken, and their proceeds rerouted to the exchequer. And though Edward II's campaign in the north in late 1310 was no doubt what the Ordainers had most prominently in mind, it is hard to believe that there was no connexion between the striking clause which forbade the king to go to war or to leave the land without the assent of his barons, and Edward I's departure for Flanders in 1297, which the earls who then opposed him had roundly and eloquently condemned in the last paragraph of their *Monstraunces.*

The insistence in the *Ordinances* on annual parliaments has sometimes been taken as one sign of a marked change of attitude since the days of Edward I. It is not clear that this view is justified. Parliaments had in fact been summoned more or less annually, and sometimes more often, since early in the 1290s. The insistence on regular parliaments seems not to reflect a grievance at their irregularity so much as a desire to have clear rules about the meetings of an assembly whose agency seemed necessary to implement a number of important reforms. The *Ordinances* laid down that the chief officers of state should be chosen with the assent of the barons in parliament (in this connexion it should be remembered that at the parliament of Lincoln in 1301 there had been an attempt to force Edward I to dismiss his treasurer, Walter Langton, which had not succeeded). It was in parliament that a commission (of one bishop, two earls and two barons) was to hear complaints against the king's ministers if they contravened the *Ordinances* (which seems to echo the demand of 1300, that the king should punish ministers whose actions contravened the charters, which Edward I refused to consider). Parliament, it should be added here, does not seem in the minds of the Ordainers to have in any sense necessarily included representatives of the commons. This does not mean that their attitude was a narrow, baronially exclusive one. It reminds us rather that what the Ordainers valued chiefly about parliament was its authority as a court which could set right what had been done ill, and could exercise a general supervision over the king's government. This was a natural attitude for men who could remember how, in the previous reign, efforts to limit administrative abuse and to restrain royal officials had been repeatedly thwarted by the unwillingness of the cunning and unscrupulous old king to cooperate.

There was, of course, much in the *Ordinances* which had nothing at all to do with events of Edward I's reign. This, however, is not so much a sign of discontinuity between the two periods, as a reflection of the differences of character between the two Edwards, which inevitably in an age of personal government affected their relations with their magnates. Edward I, in his later years, had a long and highly successful career of kingship behind him. He was a great warrior, who had served with distinction in the Holy Land, had conquered Wales and very nearly conquered Scotland. He was also a famous patron of the chivalrous sports and ceremonies which men of the magnate class enjoyed, a veteran of the tournament, an enthusiast for the cult of King Arthur who had been host to jousts of the Round Table at which knights from all over Europe had been present. He had outlived most of the companions of his earlier years, and the majority of the barons who attended his court and his parliaments were younger than he. Some of their fathers had learned by bitter experience how hard he could be when asserting his own right against others, and how terrible his anger was. To the young men who knew him in his late years he must have appeared both venerable and frightening. It is not surprising therefore that at the end of his reign resistance to his will slackened: it was plain common sense to postpone complaint until the formidable old king was dead, as he was soon bound to be.

The younger magnates, many of whom had been brought up with Edward II, must have known that he was of a very different calibre. Strong and tall, he was unproven as a soldier, and did not care for such martial exercises as the tourney. He enjoyed swimming, and country life, and the company of minstrels, but these were not preferences to earn him respect. He also had two vices from which his father did not suffer: a predilection for favourites, and an extravagant generosity in the patronage he extended to them and their cronies. He was not wise in his choice of intimates, particularly in the case of his first and most famous favourite, the handsome Gascon knight Piers Gaveston, with whom his relations may have been homosexual. Gaveston was anathema to the English magnates, who regarded him as an upstart; he retaliated by inventing scurrilous nicknames for them. To make things worse, he could beat them at the tourney. Worst of all was the way in which the grants of lands and offices, which his standing in the king's favour won for him, disrupted the normal flow of patronage between the monarchy and the magnates. But no one feared either him or his master, as they had feared Edward I, and it was this that made the great difference between the political circumstances of the two reigns, not a change in the constitutional ideas of the crown's opponents.

The *Ordinances* had a great deal to say both about Gaveston and about Edward II's over-lavish expenditure. The two subjects were related in the eyes of the Ordainers. As soon as he came to the throne Edward recalled Gaveston from the exile to which his father had condemned him, and made him Earl of Cornwall. In the coronation procession the new earl bore the sword of St Edward before the king, 'so decked out that he more resembled the God Mars than an ordinary mortal'. The lavish rewards that were showered on the favourite seemed to the other magnates unwarrantable, at a time when the crown was heavily in debt, when creditors were pressing for repayment of loans overdue years earlier, and when the whole land was complaining bitterly about arbitrary *prises* taken for the use of the king's household and soldiers, which were too often never paid for. The magnates besides could not but resent Gaveston's personal hold over the king. Without his private advice and assent nothing was done and nothing was granted. It was on the double charge, that he had impoverished the crown and alienated the king from his magnates, that the earls, led by Henry of Lincoln, demanded in the spring parliament of 1308 that he be banished anew.

In 1308 Edward bowed to necessity, and Gaveston left for the lieutenancy of Ireland. But he was no sooner gone than the king began to work for his recall, mollifying key opponents with grants of office and honour, and when he came back he was no less unbearable than he had been before. So, when the Ordainers were appointed to draw up reforms in 1310, with Henry of Lincoln prominent among them, the twin objectives of 1308, the removal of Gaveston and the curtailing of royal expenditure, retained high priority. As was to be expected, the *Ordinances* contained a long and formidable indictment of the favourite, who was said to have usurped royal power to himself, to have forced the king to part with lands to the impoverishment of his estate, and to have estranged the king's heart from his people. He was sentenced to banishment as an 'enemy of the king and the people' and forbidden to return. The *Ordinances* also imposed stringent limits on royal expenditure. No grants of lands, rents, escheats, wardship or office were to be made henceforward, without the assent of the baronage. In order to make sure that household expenditure was kept under control, the Ordainers insisted that the appointments of the steward of the household, the keeper of the wardrobe and the keeper of the privy seal should be vetted in parliament by the barons, as well as the appointments of such officers of state as the chancellor, the treasurer and the judges. It is unimaginable that Edward I would have tolerated for an instant limits such as these on his freedom of action as a monarch. But Edward II, in his obstinate attachment to his favourite, did; indeed he offered to accept any ordinances 'howsoever this may redound to my private disadvantage, as long as you shall stop persecuting my brother Piers, and allow him to have the Earldom of Cornwall'.[10] This is a measure of the differences between him and his father, and sufficient commentary on what differentiated opposition to the one and to the other.

Edward I in 1301, when he was faced with uncompromising opposition at Lincoln, conceded more than he wished to, but succeeded in uniting his barons in protest against the pope's demand that he should abandon the Scottish war. He then led them north against the enemy. Edward II could probably have done the same in 1311, but he would not abandon Gaveston. He went north and took the great seal with him, but this was so as not to be divided from his favourite, who had never left the country, and so as to rescind the *Ordinances* from a safe distance. The barons united, but against the king, not the Scots. On 19 May 1312, Gaveston surrendered to the earls of Pembroke and Warenne, on the promise that his life would be safe. He was being taken south by Pembroke, when he was taken from Pembroke at Deddington in Oxfordshire by the Earl of Warwick, who like Pembroke had been an Ordainer. Nine days later he was put to death, in the presence of Lancaster, another Ordainer, in direct breech of the promise of surety that Warenne and Pembroke had made.

Pembroke felt that his word of honour had been impugned and never forgave Lancaster and Warwick. Nor did King Edward.

In consequence of Gaveston's death an undying feud was born between Edward and his cousin, Thomas of Lancaster, who since the death in 1311 of his father-in-law Henry of Lincoln, had controlled no less than five earldoms – Lancaster, Leicester, Lincoln, Derby and Salisbury – and so enjoyed almost vice-regal wealth and influence. Lancaster and Warwick claimed that, in putting Gaveston to death, they had merely been enforcing the *Ordinances*. Not all their colleagues, however, saw it that way, and their action broke the unity of the magnates. Aymer de Valence of Pembroke, who had always been close to the court, rallied to the king, and so did Warenne and Gloucester. Humphrey de Bohun of Hereford stood uncertain between the two groups, between whom relations for a time completely broke down. In October 1313 the efforts of Gloucester and of the pope's representatives, Cardinal Arnold and the Bishop of Poitiers, effected a formal reconciliation, but there was no heart in it. The 'cold war' situation that Gaveston's death occasioned had not really ended when Edward in 1314 assembled his host to march against the Scots. Lancaster and Warwick both failed to join him, on the ground that he had not, as the *Ordinances* decreed, consulted with the barons before levying war and marching out of the kingdom.

On 24 June 1314 the cavalry of the great army which Edward had led into Scotland was bloodily overwhelmed by Robert Bruce's pikemen at Bannockburn near Stirling. The king was led away to safety by the Earl of Pembroke when it was clear the fight was lost: from Dunbar he took ship to Berwick, and from there reached York. His disaster became his English opponents' opportunity. Following his defeat, Edward had no option but to accept the counsels of Lancaster, the man who had killed Gaveston, and to reinforce the *Ordinances* at his request. But Lancaster came to power, now, not as the leader of a united baronage, but only of a party among them which, though territorially powerful, was not numerically impressive. The divisions among the great, which the circumstances of Gaveston's death (or murder) had engendered, had hardened to a point where they could not be easily allayed. A new chapter was beginning in the political history of Edward II's reign, in which the dominant theme was no longer the strains between the king and his greater subjects, but rivalries among the magnates themselves.

The quarter of a century from 1290 to 1314 was a crucial period in the political history of medieval England. Up to 1290, Edward I had ruled with unqualified success. Careful propaganda, to which the writs of summons to his great parliamentary assemblies are witness, had fostered a spirit of cooperation between crown and subject. This had enabled the king, in the earlier part of his reign, to take the initiative in reforming legislation and to control its direction. The great statutes of the years before 1290 cleared up a host of problems of land law and local government which had been fruitful causes of complaint among the king's subjects for three quarters of a century. In these circumstances the king was able to insist confidently on his rights. The great statute of *Quo Warranto* and the inquiries that preceded it firmly established the principle that all franchises in the land were dependent on the grant of the crown. The imprisonment of the earls of Hereford and Gloucester in 1291, for levying unauthorized war on the march, was a supreme demonstration of the king's power over even the highest. The royal authority had never seemed so clear of challenge as it did at that moment.

The strains of the long wars that followed called all this achievement into question. After 1297 the crown lost its control of the initiative in reform. The king's use of his prerogative rights was challenged, and his subjects demonstrated, notably in 1297 and again in 1301, that they could force him to make concessions by hard bargaining over financial supply. Accumulating debts limited the king's freedom of action, and increased his dependence on the cooperation of his subjects at a time when it was given less willingly than before. Order began to deteriorate, not only in the royal accounts but physically and socially in the counties. In 1305 Edward had to commission special judges of *trailbaston*, with exceptional powers, to deal with rising disorder at the local level; but their severity made them at least as unpopular as the abuses that they were supposed to put down. Heavy taxation, together with purveyance and the various other methods by which Edward sought to avoid having to negotiate with his subjects for assented taxes, were all bitterly resented. As events showed when Edward I died, men were at the end only waiting for him to be gone before making new efforts to curtail the burdens that royal government could impose.

Edward II's ineptitude, in particular his refusal to abandon Gaveston, ensured that, from the monarchy's point of view, the situation must deteriorate further. Dislike of Gaveston gave a new sharp edge to the baronial sense of grievance, and united the magnates in opposition. Edward II's failure, in his early years, to prosecute the war in Scotland, though it was not altogether his fault, also undermined confidence in royal leadership. The war with Scotland had never been unpopular, with the magnates or with the people more generally. Edward I had repeatedly proved able to rally support to the crown by the call to arms, very notably in 1298 and in 1301. In the eyes of the leading men of the kingdom victory in the field could compensate for a good deal of domestic tyranny. If the war could have been ended successfully, perhaps even Edward II might have found a way out of his trouble. But after Bannockburn it was clear that the kingdom could not be free either of the Scottish war, or of domestic tensions, for a long time.

Notes

1 On Edward's difficulties with the clergy see further Chapter 9, below.
2 For documentation see E. L. G. Stones, *Anglo-Scottish Relations* (London, 1965), pp. 81ff., 96ff.; and *P.W.* vol. I, pp. 103–4.
3 For the ordinance see Stones, *Anglo-Scottish Relations*, pp. 120ff.

4 Quoted by Barrow, *Robert Bruce*, p. 245, who conjectures that the writer was Alexander Abernethy.

5 See Chapter 9, below.

6 The text is given by J.G. Edwards, 'The baronial grievances of 1297', *EHR*, vol. 58 (1943), pp. 170–1.

7 See N. Denholm Young, *History and Heraldry* (Oxford, 1965), p. 130.

8 On the coronation oath, and the discussion that surrounds it, see Chapter 4, and the 'Note on Secondary Reading' appended thereto.

9 For text, see *Statutes of the Realm*, vol. I, p. 157 ff.

10 *Vita Edwardi II*, ed. N. Denholm Young (London, 1957), pp. 17–18.

Note on secondary reading (post 1970)

M.C. Prestwich, *The Three Edwards: War and State in England, 1272–1377* (London, 1980), now provides an excellent introduction to the whole Edwardian period. His major biography, *Edward I* (London, 1988), surveys that reign surely. Two important books cover the fiscal and financial history of the period, G.L. Harriss, *King Parliament and Public Finance to 1369* (Oxford, 1975), and M.C. Prestwich, *War, Politics and Finance under Edward I* (London, 1972). Important articles include K.B. McFarlane, 'Had Edward I a policy towards the Earls', *History*, vol. 59 (1965), reprinted in his *The Nobility in Later Medieval England* (Oxford, 1973); W.M. Ormrod, 'State building and state finance in the reign of Edward I', in W. Ormrod (ed.), *England in the Thirteenth Century* (Stamford, 1991); and M.C. Prestwich, 'Royal patronage under Edward I', in P.R. Coss and S.D. Lloyd (eds.), *England in the Thirteenth Century* I, (Stamford, 1986). Older articles that retain high value, by J.G. Edwards, B.C. Keeney, and H. Rothwell are listed in the main bibliography, section 2a.

On the problem of the Scottish succession, E.L.G. Stones and C.G. Hampson, *Edward I and the throne of Scotland* (Oxford, 1978, printing and discussing all the main texts) is authoritative. Two books that have offered a host of new insights into Anglo Scottish confrontation are F. Watson, *Under the Hammer; Edward I and the throne of Scotland* (East Linton, 1998), and C. McNamee, *The Wars of the Bruces: Scotland, England and Ireland 1306–28* (East Linton, 1997). G.W.S. Barrow, *Robert Bruce* (London, 1965) retains high value.

On the early years of Edward II (to 1314) J.R.L. Maddicott, *Thomas of Lancaster* (Oxford, 1970) is vital; also important are J.R.S. Phillips, *Aymer de Valence, Earl of Pembroke, 1307–24* (Oxford, 1972), and M.C. Prestwich's article 'The ordinances of 1311 and the politics of the early fourteenth century', in J. Taylor and W. Childs (eds.), *Politics and Crisis in Fourteenth Century England*. On Gaveston see J.S. Hamilton, *Piers Gaveston Earl of Cornwall, 1307–12* (Detroit, 1988); P. Chaplais, *Piers Gaveston, Edward II's Adoptive Brother* (Oxford, 1994), offers a new and very interesting interpretation of their relationship.

3 The reign of Edward II and its aftermath

The history of the years of Edward II's reign that followed Bannockburn is confused and anarchic. For convenience it may be divided into four periods. The first runs from the autumn of 1314 to the middle of 1316. After his great defeat at the hands of the Scots, Edward was in no position to resist the demands of his powerful domestic opponents, and in this period the influence of Earl Thomas of Lancaster was a decisive force in government. Partly on account of his own lethargy and incompetence, and partly because of misfortunes which it was beyond the earl's power to avoid, his influence was on the wane well before the end of 1316. By that time a new group of influential men was gathering at the king's court, who were opposed to the earl personally and to his policy of enforcing the *Ordinances* to the letter. The question during our second period, which extends from 1316 to 1320, was whether this hostility would degenerate into an open breach, or whether some *modus vivendi* could be established between the king's new friends at court and the king's greatest subject, Lancaster. Such a reconciliation was the object striven after by a group of moderate men, who included a number of bishops, the Earl of Pembroke, and perhaps the Earl of Hereford (though both these men had close associations with the court too). In 1320, the rapid rise to royal favour and influence of the two Despensers, father and son, upset the balance anew, and here our third period begins. The year 1321 saw a head-on confrontation between the king and the Despensers on the one hand, and a combination of Lancaster with the powerful barons of the Welsh march on the other. The defeat and subsequent execution of the king's chief opponents, including the earls of Lancaster and Hereford, at Boroughbridge in 1322, marks the end of this third period. In the fourth and terminal period from 1322 to 1326 the triumphant king and the Despensers abused their recovered power in England, and allowed themselves to be drawn into a confrontation with France which very nearly cost Edward his inheritance beyond the sea in Gascony. His deposition in 1327, however, solved nothing. In the depressing epilogue to his reign which runs to 1330, his Queen Isabella and her paramour Roger Mortimer were no more successful in their efforts to govern England than he had been.

Repeated reverses and failures in the north form an essential background to this sad tally of events. There, in Robert Bruce, Edward II faced an enemy who was as politically shrewd and militarily determined as he was neither. After Bannockburn Scottish raiding of northern England became organized, recurrent and systematic. The tactics of the Scots anticipated those of the English later, in France in the Hundred Years War. Their swift moving, lightly armed mounted forces made principally for soft targets, avoiding sieges for the most part and concentrating on the quest for loot and on inflicting economic damage, burning crops and villages and driving off cattle. The most valuable plunder of all came from the huge sums in money that the Scots were able to levy from the communities of northern England in return for being left unmolested: these made a vital contribution to the war chest of the comparatively impoverished King Robert. The quest for such plunder lured the Scots south, out of the already harried borderlands: in 1316, 1318, 1319 and 1322 they penetrated far into Yorkshire. In 1322 they virtually occupied the vale of York, and very nearly captured Edward II himself at Byland.

There was a political and diplomatic dimension to this military strategy. As is indicated by the negotiations which opened whenever truces punctuated the fighting, Robert Bruce's central objective was to force his adversary to recognize his title and the independence of his kingdom, and so to consolidate and stabilize the kingship that he had grasped by violence, after John Comyn's murder. To that end he encouraged and supported, between 1315 and 1318, his brother Edward's attempt to make himself a King of Ireland: and together they sought to stir up troubles for England in Wales at the same time. All this gives the story of the years from 1314 to 1330, viewed from the Scottish side, a coherence and direction that is sadly lacking over the same period in the domestic history of England, our chief concern and to which we must now turn.

We must begin, then, in 1314, at the beginning of the first of these periods. 'After this (the battle of Bannockburn) the king on the advice of his friends left a garrison at Berwick, and retreated to York; and there he took counsel with the earl of Lancaster and the other magnates': so says the *Vita Edwardi II.*[1] The measures of this York parliament of September 1314 set the tone for the next two years. Lancaster had always stood for the enforcement of the *Ordinances* to the letter, and this was given first priority. There were besides some important changes among the officials. John Sandale became chancellor, Walter Norwich treasurer; Ingelard de Warley lost his place as keeper of the wardrobe and was replaced by William Melton; and over the next months nearly all the sheriffs were removed and replaced. The next parliament, which met at Westminster in January 1315, took up the work of the York parliament and pressed ahead further with the enforcement of the *Ordinances*. A perambulation of the forests was promised, and a practical beginning was made in the business of reducing the expense of the king's household; Langton and Despenser were at the same time removed from the king's council. Still more striking, the business of the resumption of grants made by the king since March 1310 (the date given by the *Ordinances*) was taken in hand, and lists of lands to be resumed were despatched to the escheators north and south of Trent. This was a delicate affair: as Roger Mortimer of Chirk pointed out, his lands 'had not been given him to do damage to the king, but for the service that he had done for him'.[2] Lancaster consistently attached great importance to this matter of resumption: Mortimer's remark is a useful reminder that the justification or otherwise of the *Ordinances* in the matter of resumption and of economy generally could appear questionable. Lancaster was rich: Mortimer was not in the same street as a territorial magnate, and it seemed to him unjust that he should lose rewards that he prized highly, and that had been given for genuine service.

The Lincoln parliament of 1316 did not carry things much further than its two predecessors had. The most memorable event which it witnessed was the formal invitation to Lancaster to be the 'chief councillor' of the king. Lancaster in fact only agreed to be of the council on conditions: no matter was to be undertaken without the advice of the earls and prelates; any councillor who proffered advice which was not to the king's profit must be removed in the next parliament; and if his, Lancaster's, advice were not accepted, he reserved a right to withdraw from the council. What this last condition really meant was that the earl was to keep a freedom to dissociate himself from the government's actions if he did not approve of them, which was hardly a very responsible attitude for a chief councillor. He had not in fact had much to do with the day-to-day business of government over the last eighteen months. His influence had been a paramount one, but it was most often exercised from a distance. Decisions on important matters were constantly referred to him by letter, and he wrote back to the king and council with his comments from wherever he was staying on his estates. His new appointment did not change his practice. Persistent efforts to enforce the *Ordinances* suggest his continuing influence well into the summer of 1316, but he was not much at court after the spring parliament, and after April was no longer in active communication with the council. Lancaster's unwillingness to take a hand himself at the centre of affairs was one of the reasons why his dominance did not endure much longer after that.

There were other reasons too for his gradual displacement. A chief one was that, apart from formal efforts to implement the *Ordinances*, the period of his preeminence had singularly little to show in the way of achievement. This was by no means altogether Lancaster's fault, or anybody's; these were years of natural disaster. The heavy rains of the summer of 1314 ruined the harvests; and the famine that followed lasted for two years, for the summer of 1315 was no better. Prices of food soared; murrains broke out among cattle and sheep; exports of English wool fell steeply, and so royal revenue from the customs fell also. In these conditions governmental control at the local level, never very effective, inevitably deteriorated. Some of the outbreaks of local disorder reached serious proportions. In the autumn of 1315 a dangerous revolt broke out on Lancaster's northern estates, led by Adam Banaster, who sacked Manchester and Preston before he was brought to book and executed. In the early months of 1316 one Llewelyn Bren attacked Caerphilly castle, and it looked for a moment as if his movement might develop into a Welsh national rising. This was why many of the great lords of the marches were absent from the parliament of Lincoln that spring. In the summer of 1316 the townsmen of Bristol rose in open revolt against the constable of the castle.

These conditions and these disorders go a long way to explain why, in these years, so little attention was paid to what should have been the chief preoccupation of the government, the defence of the north. In 1315 the Scots had raided in County Durham, and besieged Carlisle, and in 1316 they penetrated further, into Yorkshire. Meanwhile another Scots force, under Edward Bruce, had invaded Ireland. For a time, until 1318 when he was defeated and killed at Faughart, Co. Louth, by an Anglo-Irish force led by John de Bermingham, it looked as if he might establish a Bruce kingship that would wholly undermine the English Lordship, which Edward II and his councillors were far too preoccupied to assist. Both in 1315 and 1316 English royal armies were summoned for a Scottish expedition; subsidies were raised to pay the troops, and supplies and transports were purveyed as usual; but in 1315 the host failed to assemble and in 1316 it disbanded without entering on any campaign. In prevailing conditions, the failure of the English to organize defence or reprisal against the Scots is not surprising. It is not surprising either that Lancaster's hold over affairs became more tenuous, in consequence of these failures and of his long absences from the centre of power.

In many respects, the conditions of 1317 were not very different from those of the preceding years. Dearth continued, prices remained high, and local lawlessness was unabated. Politically, however, the complexion of affairs was changing. A new group was gathering at court. From the autumn of 1316 on we find Edward II sealing a number of indentures with leading men, including the Earl of Hereford, Bartholomew Badlesmere, John Giffard and John Cromwell (and, later, Pembroke), retaining them for life in his personal service, in return for substantial fees. Also very prominent at court at this time, and especially for the rich rewards that favour earned them, were William Montagu, and the three men who had married the co-heiresses of the last Earl of Gloucester (Gilbert of Clare, killed at Bannockburn): Roger Damory, Hugh Audley and Hugh Despenser the younger. This new grouping, in which we find moderates like Badlesmere and established aristocrats like Pembroke combining with courtiers, was no doubt principally the result of the determination of all but Lancaster to see something done to defend the north against Scottish inroads, and their perception that to this end it was better to work with the king than in opposition to him. It also suggests that Edward was coming to realize how needful it was to his kingship to cultivate friends among his great men. The emergence of a more united front among the magnates brought into perspective Lancaster's growing isolation. The king had never forgotten, nor forgiven except in name, Earl Thomas's part in the death of Gaveston. His role in that business had divided him also from Pembroke and Warenne. Guy of Warwick, his erstwhile accomplice, had died in 1315. Because of Lancaster's wealth, his wide estates, and the political and military influence which his vast retinue constituted, he was still a power to be reckoned with; but by the end of 1316 he could no longer dictate policy from his castles by letter to the council.

Lancaster's obdurate stand on the *Ordinances*, in particular his insistence on the resumption of past grants and an embargo on new ones, set him and the courtiers totally at loggerheads. Through the year 1317, their mutual hostility drifted towards the verge of civil war. The courtiers did all that they could to make things difficult for Lancaster, and he responded in kind. On 9 May Lancaster's wife was abducted from Canford in Dorset by John Earl of Warenne, 'not in the way of adultery but for sheer spite of the earl' says the Meaux chronicle.[3] When in the summer the king ordered a muster at York against the Scots, Lancaster's retainers from Pontefract barred the way to the assembling forces. The earl, they declared, was Steward of England, 'whose business it was to look to the advantage of the kingdom', and 'if the king wished to take arms against anyone he ought first to notify the Steward'.[4] Before the end of the summer civil war had come so near that Lancaster made contact with the Scots, in order to secure his position. He and they appear to have connived together at the capture of Louis de Beaumont, Bishop of Durham and brother of the courtier Henry, by Sir Gilbert Middleton near Durham in September. In October Lancaster's retainer Lilburn seized Damory's castle at Knaresborough, and when the sheriff of Yorkshire came to besiege him, a Scots force appeared to the relief.[5] At the same time Lancaster's forces were attacking Warenne's castles at Conisborough and Sandal and wasting his lands in Yorkshire.

Thus by the end of 1317 the need for some measure of conciliation was becoming urgent. The king's most important subject had gone to the length of seeking an understanding with the king's chief enemy in order to secure himself against the court. The events of the spring of 1318 made conciliation still more necessary. In April Berwick fell to the Scots, and soon after they took the castles of Harbottle and Wark; all northern England was threatened. The task of mediation fell naturally to those moderates who were not committed entirely either to the court or to Lancaster. Prominent among these was Aymer de Valence, Earl of Pembroke, who had returned from abroad in July 1317, about the same time that the cardinals Anselm of St Marcellin and St Peter and Luke of St Maria arrived from Avignon, with a commission from John XXII to mediate both between the king and his magnates, and between the English and the Scots. Alongside Pembroke we must place his fellow the Earl of Hereford, who had been like him an Ordainer but never an extremist in opposition, and among the barons Bartholomew Badlesmere, who in 1318 became steward of the household, replacing William Montagu. These lay magnates all had close associations with the court, moderates though they were, so the guiding influence behind mediation had to be that of the cardinals and of a number of leading ecclesiastics: Reynolds the Archbishop of Canterbury, the Archbishop of Dublin, and the bishops of Norwich, Ely and Chichester were all prominent in negotiations. This whole group used to be dubbed, by historians of an earlier generation, as the 'Middle Party'. Conway Davies and other writers associated with them some other lay barons, Damory, Audley, even the Despensers, but, as Dr Maddicott has shown, these men were courtier favourites, not moderates.[6] Court connection, indeed, was one of the chief difficulties facing the new alliance of moderates, bishops and courtiers. The enforcement of the *Ordinances* was for Lancaster still the *sine qua non* of any settlement to which he should be a party. This would mean the resumption of grants made to the courtiers, whose new-found favour stamped them in Lancaster's eyes as 'evil councillors' of the kind that the *Ordinances* had condemned: but they, very naturally, were not eager to disgorge.

Negotiations towards a settlement occupied much time and attention late in 1317 and in 1318. The moderates' first success seems to have been with Damory, the courtier who stood highest of all in the king's favour at the time. On 24 November 1317, Pembroke and Badlesmere sealed a bond with him, whereby Damory promised to induce the king to follow the counsels agreed between him and the other two, and specifically to seek to prevent the king from making any grant of more than £20 worth of land without their consent.[7] This was certainly a move in a direction acceptable to Lancaster, and very much in the spirit of the *Ordinances*. The first agreement of the mediators with Lancaster, reached at Leicester in April 1318 (when the disasters in the north must have made agreement seem abnormally urgent) went further, however, than one can imagine Damory ever approving. The *Ordinances* were to be enforced, all evil councillors dismissed, and all lands granted contrary to the *Ordinances* were to be resumed. Lancaster was to be admitted fully to the king's peace, but significantly Warenne was not to be admitted to the peace of the earl: he must make his own terms with Thomas. Not surprisingly, these draconian conditions did not prove acceptable to the courtiers, though they were now prepared to meet concession with concession in the interests of conciliation. At a meeting in June at the exchequer, at which Pembroke, the archbishops of Canterbury and Dublin, and the courtiers Despenser, Damory and Audley were all present, Edward II's friends were willing to guarantee Lancaster safe conduct to come to the king, but pointed out that his refusal to cooperate had contributed in large part to the realm's misfortunes at the hands of the Scots. The *Ordinances* should be enforced, yes: but he must be prepared to work with others 'without accroaching sovereignty to himself'. It took two more months of hard bargaining, and big concessions from Lancaster, before a settlement was reached in the famous Treaty of Leake in August.

The observance of the *Ordinances* was the formal basis of this settlement: this had to be, if Lancaster was to be a party to it. There were, however, important modifications to the manner of their observance. The issue of evil councillors was solved by the appointment of a formal council: four earls were among its members, Pembroke, Richmond, Hereford and Arundel, but not Lancaster, whose interest was to be represented by a banneret whom he should name. Two bishops, one earl, one baron and this banneret were to be always with the king, and to authorize with him all that could be authorized (according to the *Ordinances*) without a parliament. This arrangement was a concession by

Lancaster, modifying his earlier position over evil councillors. In the crucial matter of resumptions the treaty was vague; in fact, grants were considered individually in the subsequent parliament, and on their merits were either cancelled or allowed to stand. Damory, Audley, the Despensers and Montagu all managed to retain some valuable assets. It was a major concession on Lancaster's part that he made no protest over this arrangement.

The Treaty of Leake was ratified in the parliament that was held at York in October 1318, in which the business of resumptions was initiated, and a committee was set up, once again, to consider reform of the king's household. The tenuous unity of king and magnates which the treaty established lasted nearly two years, and enabled Edward to mount a major campaign in the north in 1319, to which Lancaster led a large contingent. Signs of strains which could upset the settlement were, however, early apparent. Lancaster made a good thing out of his concessions at Leake, and in particular was able to maintain his insistence that Warenne should make his own peace with him. The price that Warenne had to pay for this was the release to Earl Thomas of all his lands in Yorkshire, and of certain estates also in East Anglia and Wales. It would seem that certain of the courtiers had besides to acknowledge large debts to the earl, as the price of conciliation with him. Thomas was still not fully content, even then: in October 1318 he demanded an investigation into his rights as Steward of England, and in May 1319 was claiming the right to appoint the steward of the household. This embroiled him in bitter controversy with the man who actually held the office, Bartholomew Badlesmere.

The courtiers were not satisfied either. In September 1319, when the royal host was before Berwick, Edward's promise that they should be richly rewarded, from the spoil that would be taken there, led to a renewed clash with Earl Thomas, who finally withdrew his forces. In consequence the siege had to be broken up. When, at the end of the year, a two-year truce was taken with the Scots, which seemed humiliating to the English, the courtiers blamed Lancaster (and vice versa). The earl refused to attend the January parliament of 1320. He seems to have been now retreating towards the position of isolated opposition that he had maintained in 1317. The king and the courtiers were beginning to think, as they also had in 1317, in terms of obtaining from the pope release from their oaths to observe the *Ordinances*. Nevertheless, when parliament met in October 1320 the *Ordinances* were still officially in force. Compromise endured, but it was wearing thin.

By the end of 1320 we are entering on our third period, of renewed confrontation. What destroyed the compromise finally was the rise in favour and influence at court of Hugh Despenser the younger, who by this time had eclipsed all others in the royal graces, as also in the rapacity of his territorial ambitions. His marriage to Eleanor, the eldest of the three daughters of the last Earl of Gloucester, made him co-heir in the great Clare inheritance with Audley and Damory. His desire seems to have been to concentrate all the Welsh territories of the Clares in his own hands, and to obtain in his own favour the revival of the Earldom of

Gloucester. Glamorgan was his share from the start; by a combination of force and persuasion he obtained the county of Gwynllwyg from Audley; to this he soon added Cantrefmawr and Dryslwyn in Carmarthen, and he began to cast envious eyes at William de Braose's barony of Gower, which marched with Glamorgan. De Braose's circumstances were straitened, and Despenser had all along been interested in the purchase of his inheritance; but when he died in 1320 John Mowbray, his son-in-law, entered on his lands on the strength of a grant executed by de Braose in favour of him and his heirs, with remainder to Hereford. Despenser now persuaded the king to order the seizure of Gower as an escheat, on the ground that this grant was unlawful, since land held in chief of the king could not be alienated except by royal licence. This rule had never been accepted as customary in Wales and the march, and the seizure thus constituted a direct challenge to marcher law. It was not only the privileges of the marchers that was in question, moreover: the territorial interests of some of the most powerful among them – Hereford, Mowbray, the Mortimers, Audley and Damory – were also involved. These men were soon the leaders of a confederacy sworn to uphold one another against the overbearing favourite of the king. It was unfortunate that, at this crucial point, Pembroke, who was more loyal, more moderate, and more experienced than most of his colleagues, was out of the country. In January 1321 Despenser was putting his castles in a state of defence, while the marchers were putting out feelers towards Lancaster: by April fighting had broken out in the marches.

The confrontation of the summer of 1321 was complicated by an absence of unanimity both among those who remained loyal to the king, and in the ranks of the opposition. Among the former Pembroke, perhaps Arundel, and the majority of the prelates had no desire to protect the interest of the Despensers, and were anxious to avoid civil war. On the other side, Lancaster's long standing ill will towards Damory and Audley made cooperation between him and these marchers difficult, and he was not prepared to have any dealings at all with Badlesmere, who had thrown in his lot with them. As a result, Edward felt strong enough to refuse to take the immediate action against the Despensers that the marchers demanded; but he was not strong enough to ignore the charges against his favourites altogether. Their consideration was postponed merely, to the coming parliament. In the meantime the marchers tried to consolidate with Lancaster a united opposition, while he sought to broaden its base with non-marcher elements, and so to strengthen the independence of his position.

On 24 May at Pontefract Lancaster brought together an assembly of the chief magnates of the north, who bound themselves to act together to preserve peace and to defend the realm; but they were not prepared to go further without the advice of the northern prelates, and there was no mention of the Despensers in their agreement.[8] So there had to be a second meeting at Sherburn-in-Elmet, at which, besides the northern magnates and prelates and a large number of Earl Thomas's retainers, some of the important marchers were present. A schedule of grievances for discussion was read at this assembly by Lancaster's retainer,

John de Bek, which included complaints about the Despensers but ranged more widely too, mentioning besides the new judicial eyres which the king had instituted, abuses of the staple regulations, and the need for united effort against the Scots. This attempt by Lancaster to unite opposition and broaden its base was not wholly successful. By indentures sealed at Sherburn, Lancaster and the leading marchers swore to act together against the Despensers, but the northerners who were present did not seal these agreements; and the clergy of the northern province, while ready to cooperate in any necessary action against the Scots, requested that the other matters be referred to the next parliament. The situation was thus still full of political ambiguity when parliament began to assemble at Westminster on 15 July.

As they marched towards London, says the St Paul's annalist, the opposition magnates, 'having taken counsel about what they could lawfully do, to displace and destroy the king's evil councillors, put together in writing a certain tract based on ancient custom, against the forthcoming parliament'.[9] This would seem to have been the famous tract which claims for the Steward of England the right 'to supervise and regulate, under and immediately after the king, the whole realm of England and all the officers of the law within the realm, in times of peace and war'.[10] Lancaster as Steward had made a claim not unlike this in 1317, but the tract went further: it was the Steward's duty also, with the Constable, to guard against evil councillors, and if the king would not act against them, to seize them as 'public enemies' and hold them for judgement in the next parliament. As far as is known, these claims to almost viceregal powers were never formally urged in the subsequent parliament, but they throw revealing light on the manner in which Lancaster's long experience of isolated opposition had developed his political thinking. In fact, when the parliament met, it was not he and his associates, but Pembroke who persuaded Edward to agree to the dismissal of his favourites, telling him that 'it was not worth his while for any living soul to lose his kingdom'.[11] On 19 August judgement was formally passed in parliament on both the Despensers: they were sentenced to total forfeiture and banishment as 'evil and false councillors, seducers and conspirators, and disinheritors of the crown, and as enemies of the king and the kingdom'.[12]

The judgement on the Despensers proved only to be a breathing space, at the brink of civil war. After the parliament, Edward's opponents returned to their estates, and Hugh Despenser the elder went into exile. But Hugh his son did not go further than the Channel, where he remained aboard ship, hovering off the English coast. He clearly knew the king was planning his recall and a *révanche*. Edward's chance came in early October, when Bartholomew Badlesmere was provoked into refusing Queen Isabella admittance to his castle of Leeds in Kent. Edward made this the pretext for raising an army at once to besiege the castle, and Pembroke, Arundel, Warenne and Richmond were ready to support him, as were also his two young half-brothers, Edmund of Kent and Thomas of Norfolk. Badlesmere's sworn allies of the summer, the marchers, began quickly to mobilize their forces to aid him, but Lancaster felt his grudge too deeply against the man whom he had sought unsuccessfully to displace from the stewardship of the household, and held his hand at the crucial period. He took certain steps to protect his own position, but he made no move outside his own estates while Leeds castle fell, and the king with his new army turned against the marchers.

Resistance to the king began to crumble. The Mortimers of Chirk and Wigmore surrendered into the king's mercy. Lancaster was at Pontefract when Hereford and the other dissidents of the Welsh march, who had retreated before the king's superior force, joined him. Thence they advanced to Burton-on-Trent, but then fell back north together, probably to seek refuge with the Scots, for Lancaster had been in close contact with Bruce and seems to have trusted in him more than in the English barons. At Boroughbridge in Yorkshire, on 16 March 1322, Lancaster and Hereford found their way barred by Andrew Harclay, the sheriff of Cumberland, with the levies of the northern counties. Hereford fell fighting at the bridge itself; Lancaster, Mowbray, Clifford and others surrendered to Sir Andrew, who turned them over to King Edward. On 22 March, after a summary trial, Lancaster was executed at Pontefract. Mowbray, Clifford and a number of other men, including Damory, were also condemned to death and forfeited their estates. The more prominent of their followers were proscribed as traitors and lost their lands. This was the first occasion on which summary sentences of death and forfeiture for high treason were passed on peers of the realm in England. It was an ominous precedent.

In so far as Thomas of Lancaster had had any consistent political programme, he had stood out for the enforcement of the *Ordinances*. His death settled the long dispute on this matter. 'Remember the following: first the statute about the repeal of the *Ordinances*: second, to embody the good points in them in a statute':[13] these are the first items of agenda which the king referred to the council before parliament met at York on 2 May 1322. In the parliament a large number of detailed points taken from the *Ordinances* and which were not offensive to royal dignity were embodied in a statute. The *Ordinances* themselves were condemned, and together with them the manner of their making:

> Henceforth, all manner of ordinances and provisions, made under any authority or commission whatever by the subjects of our lord the king or his heirs . . . shall be null and of no validity or force. But the things which are to be established for the estate of the king and of his heirs and for the estate of the realm and people shall be treated, granted, and established in parliament, by our lord the king with the assent of the prelates, earls, and barons and of the commonalty of the realm, as has been accustomed.[14]

The Statute of York here drew a clear distinction between reforms agreed and authorized in properly summoned parliaments with the king's assent, and reforms forced on the king by any committee or group of subjects outside parliament, whether the king had given them powers (as he had to the original Ordainers) or not (as in the case of the confederates of Sherburn-in-Elmet). The statute thus set a very difficult legal obstacle in the way of any who might seek to revive the *Ordinances*, or to impose restraints on the crown in the same way that the Ordainers and Lancaster had done. That extra-parliamentary mode of constitutional procedure became, as a point of fact, from this time on a thing of the past. For Edward II, that only helped to ensure that, when an opposition did reassemble, it followed a more drastic course.

Perhaps it would not have done if the king had exploited his triumph more wisely than he did. His victory over his old opponents had been satisfactorily complete. Lancaster, Hereford, Badlesmere and Damory were dead; so were a number of their more important followers, executed as traitors in the aftermath of Boroughbridge. Hugh Audley and the two Mortimers, of Chirk and Wigmore, who had surrendered, were the king's prisoners. With so many of his enemies eliminated or rendered powerless, the way could have been open for a policy of conciliation and consolidation. Instead, the twin hallmarks of the policies that Edward and the returned Despensers chose to pursue were revenge and rapacity.

The lands of those who had been killed in battle or executed were seized into the king's hand, as confiscate for treason. So were the lands of the king's prisoners, and of a number of prominent men who were known or suspected to have been adherent to the rebels. Most of these men (but not for instance the Mortimers, who remained prisoners) were permitted to ransom themselves and their lands, through the payment of large round figure fines to the crown. They were also obliged to take new oaths of loyalty to the king, supported by bonds in substantial sums to abide by their promises, and to find mainpernors to warrant payment in case of their future transgression. Commissions were sent out into the localities, to work with the sheriffs in gathering the names of less prominent 'contrariants', to ensure that their lands too were seized and fines fixed for their redemption. The administration of confiscated lands was entrusted at first to officials of the king's chamber; later it was transferred to the exchequer, whose records were massively swelled thereby. So was the royal revenue. The years 1322–1326 saw a major increase in the recorded annual take from royal lands; by 1324 the revenue coming in from confiscated lands alone had come to exceed the total of the ordinary farms of the shires. More generally, the same period witnessed a sustained and vigorous campaign to maximize crown income from all sources, by probing enquiry, by cutting waste and accelerating collection of sums due from contrariants. Edward II in his last years succeeded in making himself rich. When Bishop Stapledon handed over as treasurer to Archbishop Melton in 1325 he had some £69,000 in hand in cash; and Edward proved able to meet the expenses of the war with France of 1324–5 without recourse to extraordinary taxation and without substantially reducing this reserve.

Most of the lands seized from the contrariants of 1321–2 were kept in the king's hands. Of what was granted away, the lion's share, by a long margin, went to the two Despensers, father and son. Hugh the Elder obtained grants from the confiscated estates of Hereford, Damory, Badlesmere and Giffard. Hugh the Younger built up for himself a landed estate, with its principal focus in the Marches of Wales, which at the end of the reign was worth over £7,000 p.a., more than the last of the great Clare Earls of Gloucester had been worth at the time of his death at Bannockburn. To the new found riches that came to them by outright royal grant, the Despensers added ruthlessly by violence and fraud. By a mixture of duress and deceit Hugh the Younger prised from Elizabeth, Damory's widow, her lordship of Usk in exchange for Gower, and then proceeded against her for Gower, using the Braose claim on it as a stalking horse, and took that too. Alice Lancaster, Thomas's widow, was frightened by threats while under arrest into surrendering a major part of her own Lacy inheritance, including the important lordship of Denbigh, to Hugh the Elder. The Despensers even succeeded in securing (by sharp dealing) some substantial estates from the widow and heirs of Aymer of Pembroke (who died in 1324). The Despensers grew rich; they also made themselves objects of concentrated loathing, and undermined such trust as remained in the king whose favour they used as a tool in their depredations.

To do Edward and the Despensers justice, the period of their dominance, from 1322 to 1326, did witness attempts to institute some much needed administrative reforms. As chamberlain, Despenser the younger extended the system of reserving the issues of certain royal estates to the chamber and exempting them from exchequer jurisdiction. This helped towards providing funds for the expense of the royal household, and generally to give the crown greater freedom of action in financial affairs. Bishop Stapledon of Exeter, who was treasurer from 1322 to 1325, strengthened the staff of the exchequer, and improved its system of accounting. The number of escheators was also increased, from two to nine. The functions of the wardrobe were defined more clearly in new instructions, and the office of keeper of the privy seal was permanently separated from the keepership of the wardrobe. We should be careful of exaggerating the significance of these measures, however, important as they may seem to the administrative historian. The driving force behind them was not really better administration, but greed. They had little effect on governance in the wider sense. Ten years of perpetual civil insecurity had strained control at the local level to the point of breakdown. Lawlessness was rife in the 1320s; bands of armed men roamed at large and made a business of robbery. In 1326 a gang led by one Eustace de Folville ambushed the chief baron of the exchequer, Robert Bellers, near Melton Mowbray, and killed him. It is unlikely to be accidental that he was a man who had risen to prominence as a major agent in the handling of the contrariants' confiscated lands. This is a useful commentary on Stapledon's exchequer reforms: given conditions in which the chief baron might be surprised and murdered by bandits, the fact that the exchequer continued to function smoothly, even through the crisis of 1326–1327, loses much of its significance.

The story of England's external relations in the period 1322–6 is even more depressing than her domestic history. The truce which had been agreed with Bruce in December 1319 expired in the summer of 1322, and the Scots crossed the border again to raid as far as Preston and into Yorkshire. King Edward's effort at retaliation by leading an army into Lothian was a dismal failure; Bruce followed his retreat and came near to capturing the English king in a skirmish at Byland. Once again, the men of the north had to make terms for themselves with the Scots. To Andrew Harclay, the victor of Boroughbridge and now Earl of Carlisle, the situation after Byland seemed so desperate that he sought out Bruce himself, concluding, says the chronicle of Lanercost, that Edward II could not rule, 'and that it would be better for the communities of both kingdoms that each king should possess his kingdom freely and peacefully [i.e. without a feudal relation of superiority on the English side], rather than that every year there should be so much slaughter, burning and depredation'.[14a] Together, the earl and Bruce entered on a treaty, which, according to a version that the English court heard about, included a plan to bind the king and lords of England to abide by the counsel of twelve arbiters, chosen six from among the English and six from among the Scots, who would settle all issues between the two realms. Fortunately for Edward II, his friends got wind of Harclay's plan before anything could be done to implement it. The earl was arrested and brought to London where he was condemned and executed as a traitor. Though nothing came of it, the incident is significant. Within a year of Boroughbridge the loyalist Harclay had been driven by events to pin his hopes on plans for the constraint of King Edward and his council all too similar to those of Thomas of Lancaster, and was planning, like the dead earl, to use alliance with the Scots to force the king's hand.

The summer of 1323 saw a kind of settlement, it is true, in the north. On 30 May at Bishopthorpe a truce for thirteen years was agreed between the English and the Scots. But no sooner was the north quiet than troubles began to brew in Gascony. Up to this date, Edward II had been fortunate in that other preoccupations had inclined the kings of France toward conciliation in the south-west. But in 1323 tensions between the French king's officials and the English seneschal of Gascony led to the burning of the *bastide* which Charles IV was building at St Sardos, and war threatened. In 1324 Charles declared the duchy confiscated, and prepared to enforce his judgement by arms. There was no serious fighting; and in 1325 Queen Isabella, who had crossed to France to negotiate with Charles (who was her brother), obtained a truce on conditions: that Prince Edward be invested with the duchy and do homage to the French king, and that damages to the rights of the French crown and to French subjects in the course of the quarrel should be compensated. The agreement also saddled the English with responsibility for paying a relief of £60,000 for the duchy, and left the French in control of the Agenais, for the time being. Edward later formally went back on these terms. However, the only effort he made to restore the situation in Gascony itself was to summon a host in 1325, which never embarked. The infantry were not paid, and devastated the countryside around Portsmouth to make up for their wages. Thus the story of his failure in Gascony repeats the pattern of earlier failures in Scotland; and the result was that at the end of the reign the duchy was effectively in French hands.

Against this background of failures and disasters, it was natural that opposition to Edward and his ministers the Despensers soon began to consolidate once again. In 1323 the most troublesome men seemed to be bishops Orleton of Hereford and Burghersh of Lincoln (both of whom had been connected with the rebels of 1322). It was with Orleton's aid that in this year Roger Mortimer of Wigmore escaped from the Tower and fled to France. According to Le Baker's chronicle, it was the same bishop who was foremost in exciting Queen Isabella against the royal favourites, playing on her resentment at the sequestration of her estates (ordered in September 1324 with the assent of the Despensers, on the pretext of a threat of invasion from France).[15] Whether this is so or not, Isabella was soon to put herself at the head of the opposition. In 1325, as we have seen, she crossed to France to seek peace in the matter of Gascony: once safe at her brother's court she refused point blank to return unless the king got rid of the Despensers.

From this point the opposition began to crystallize as a party. The group which gathered round the queen in Paris was a powerful one. It included bishops Stratford of Winchester and Airmyn of Norwich; Roger Mortimer, whose mistress Isabella soon became; Edmund of Kent, who had been in charge of negotiations until her arrival, joined these, and so did the Earl of Richmond and Henry Beaumont. By September 1326 they were ready to take the initiative. Isabella, Mortimer and the young Prince Edward embarked with a force of Hainaulters at Dordrecht on 23 September; on 25 September they landed at Orwell in Suffolk. Thomas Earl of Norfolk and Henry of Leicester declared for them along with several of the bishops; in London there were riots in their support, in the course of which Bishop Stapledon was assassinated. The queen and her army headed west, in pursuit of the Despensers and the king, who had retreated from the capital and were making for Bristol. There a rising of the townsmen put the city into her hands, and the elder Despenser was taken. He was tried summarily before a tribunal of peers selected at random in the host, and executed (27 October). A few weeks later the king, the younger Despenser, the Earl of Arundel, and the chancellor, Robert Baldock, were captured at Neath Abbey in Wales. Arundel and Despenser were executed as traitors, while Earl Henry of Leicester, Thomas of Lancaster's brother, led King Edward away a prisoner to the castle of Kenilworth.

On 26 October 1326 the magnates who were at Bristol with Isabella had proclaimed her son Edward keeper of the realm. The writs which summoned parliament to Westminster in December went out, however, in Edward II's name. This was no sign of wavering intention: after all that had passed, there could be no question for his opponents of allowing Edward to rule any longer. The problem was how to be rid of him. There were no precedents for a deposition, and no one knew who could judge a monarch or whether anyone could. In so drastic a matter, it was essential to avoid as far as possible anything that might suggest that force was taking the place of law. Unless whatever was done achieved general assent the confusion which would result might be worse than anything which had gone before.

The first week after the parliament met (in January, as a result of a postponement) was in consequence devoted to consolidating a united front, not strictly in parliament, but among the king's lieges who were about the capital for its meeting. The first task for Isabella and Mortimer was to win over certain of the bishops, including notably Walter Reynolds of Canterbury, who were known to be hesitant. The excitement of the Londoners, who were solid in support of the queen, was probably instrumental in persuading them to bury their doubts about a deposition. On 13 January it was clear that a consensus had been reached, when a number of bishops and magnates, together with representatives of the clergy and the boroughs, took an oath at the Guildhall to maintain the queen's cause, 'to uphold all that has been ordained or shall be ordained for the common profit'.[16] Two days later the Archbishop of Canterbury, in a sermon preached in Westminster Hall before all who had come to the parliament (and probably others too) announced that the king was deposed by the unanimous consent of the magnates, clergy and people. His text was *vox populi, vox dei*. It is probable that it was on this occasion that the formal articles of deposition, which had been drafted by Bishop Stratford of Winchester, were read.[17] Next day a deputation set out for Kenilworth in which all the estates of the realm were represented. There were two earls, Warenne and Henry of Leicester, three bishops, four barons, a number of persons representing London, the Cinque Ports and other great towns, and representatives both of the clergy and the shire knights. They reached Kenilworth on 20 January. There Edward II reluctantly agreed that he would abdicate, if his son were allowed to succeed him. William Trussell, speaking for the delegation, renounced homage and allegiance to Edward 'on behalf of the whole kingdom'.[18]

There was thus no judgement on Edward II, and the fine point as to whether he was deposed by parliament or by some less official assembly of the whole people remains unclear. Though he was declared deposed before he abdicated, his agreement to do so rendered it unnecessary to clarify the situation further. Isabella and Mortimer had got what they wanted. They had forced him to withdraw from kingship, and had associated with themselves in the business not just a party, or the magnates only, but the people of the kingdom as a whole. They had achieved an appearance of communal unanimity in their action, and that was enough. There was no need to stir the dust of past controversy by the resurrection of the *Ordinances*, or by repealing the Statute of York, neither of which had much to do with their real object and that of their associates. That object was much more simple: to pay off the personal scores that had been left outstanding by the events of 1322 and their aftermath.

The deposition of Edward II ended a reign, but it did not end the conditions that had characterized it. In spite of all the attempts to create the appearance of consensus, the revolution of 1326–7 was of course a partisan triumph. The first acts of Edward III's first parliament make this clear: they were the reversal of the judgement of 1322 on Thomas of Lancaster (whose title and estates were therefore restored to his brother), and the reaffirmation of the judgement of parliament in 1321 against the Despensers. Mortimer, in power, proved to be as rapacious and overbearing as any of the late king's favourites. He acquired vast estates from the forfeitures of the Despensers and Arundel, and more was added by the queen and by grants of crown land. In the parliament of October 1328 he was created Earl of March, a new title which was to have a long history. By this time he was becoming as much hated as the Despensers had ever been.

The queen and Mortimer were not more successful in their dealing with the Scots than Edward II had been. The truce of 1323 had still a long while to run, but the new government in England wanted to show its strength, with disastrous consequences. Mortimer's campaign in the north in 1327 was expensive and ineffective; the English retreated before the Scots rather than offer battle, and afterwards there seemed no alternative to accepting terms virtually dictated by the Bruce. The Treaty of Northampton of 1328 formally recognized Robert Bruce as ruler of an independent kingdom, with no feudal ties with England. Thus he finally achieved, on parchment, what he had so long striven for. In England this was regarded as the shameful surrender of a just and traditional claim, a bitter and humiliating commencement to a new reign, to which the new king's subjects were by no means reconciled.

Domestic conditions in England remained unstable while Mortimer and Isabella were at the helm. The ex-king, as long as he lived, was an obvious focus of conspiracy, and there were two attempts to rescue him from prison in 1327. The rumour that a third attempt was planned precipitated his murder in Berkeley castle, on Mortimer's orders. His death did not change things any more than his deposition had. Mortimer's failures and his territorial greed had broken up the magnate coalition of 1326. Henry of Lancaster had so far broken with him that he refused to attend the October parliament of 1328 (where Mortimer was created Earl of March). They were reconciled, it is true, in 1329, but only after Mortimer had entered on Henry's Leicester lands with an armed force. In the spring of the next year, 1330, Edmund of Kent was detected in conspiracy against the government and executed. The chronic insecurity and the aristocratic feuding that had marked the whole reign of Edward II did not end until his son decided to take power into his own hands. Mortimer was arrested at Nottingham castle in October 1330; and the king's subsequent declaration that he intended 'to govern our people according to right and reason, as is fitting our royal dignity'[19] marks a break, at last, with these conditions.

England, during the reign of Edward II and its epilogue in the rule of Mortimer and Isabella, suffered twenty years of misgovernment, of chronic internal insecurity and repeated humiliation at the hands of external enemies. Why, we may ask, did these terrible conditions endure so long? Clearly, the magnates of the period must bear a heavy share of responsibility. They showed themselves incapable of sustained cooperation, even in face of the Scottish threat to northern England. None of those who enjoyed the royal favour showed an adequate sense of moderation. Mortimer displayed the same fault as a triumphant opposition leader. Thomas of Lancaster may deserve some credit for his stand on the *Ordinances* and his efforts to enforce them in detail; though it was not a very original or far-sighted policy, it earned him some popularity, both in his lifetime and posthumously. He never understood the need to cooperate with others, however; and the rancour with which he pursued personal grudges against men like Warenne and Badlesmere was ruinous to the cause that he espoused. Pembroke deserves more credit than most, but though he showed himself moderate, well meaning, and above all loyal to the king, he never succeeded in creating an effective political following, probably because he lacked the ability and force of character to do so.

The central and basic cause of the troubles was, however, without much doubt, Edward II himself. It is easy to overstate his incapacity: he was no cypher. He had a high sense of his royal dignity. On occasion (though too sporadically) he could show considerable energy, as he did in the crisis of 1321–2. His letters under the privy and secret seals show that he took a keen (but not always very perceptive) interest in the every day work of the officials of his exchequer. It has to be admitted, in his defence, that at his accession he inherited from his father a situation fraught with difficulties. But as Denholm Young succinctly put it, 'he sat down to the game of kingship with a remarkably poor hand, and he played it very badly'.[20] Faced from the outset with a Scots enemy as able and determined as Robert Bruce proved to be, there was a compelling need for Edward to impress himself on his magnates as their leader and to coordinate their aspirations and the English war effort. His consistent, obstinate and self-defeating loyalty to favourites who had achieved a personal ascendancy with him made sure that he would do neither. His determination to keep his friends by him and to honour them as he chose rendered it impossible to achieve that degree of cooperation between king and magnates, or among the magnates themselves, that was necessary to the successful conduct of domestic government, let alone to defeat the Scots. Bishop Stratford's indictment of 1327, justifying the deposition, sums up the ultimate despair and frustration with Edward's rule: 'throughout his reign he has been controlled and governed by others who have given him evil counsel, to his own dishonour and the destruction of Holy Church and all his people, without his being able to see what is good or evil or to make amendment . . . or to allow amendment to be made.'[21] In the final phase of the reign, the king and his two last favourites, the Despensers, showed by their reliance on confiscations, threats of disinheritance and bonds for good behaviour, that they trusted no one: in return, no one trusted them. It is hard to see that their opponents, when their time came, had much alternative to deposition.

The final humiliation, like most of the other catastrophes of Edward II's reign, is thus most readily explicable in personal terms, of the shortcomings of character alike of the king, of his favourites and of his domestic opponents. Perhaps the most damning indictment of them all, collectively, is their consistent failure to achieve anything effective in the war against the Scots, which should have been their chief preoccupation. Here it is worth reminding oneself of how far Robert Bruce's success was a contrasting, personal triumph. The difficulties that he had to contend against were very great. By comparison with England, his kingdom was impoverished, its administrative and governmental development backward. English influence at Avignon consistently denied him the papal recognition of his kingship that he sought, and he could never forget that his predecessor, John Balliol, had left a male heir, and that there were powerful men, in Scotland as well as in exile in England, who might be interested in a revival of the Balliol claim. The terms of the Treaty of Northampton of 1328 in the end seemed to secure for him what he had persistently striven for, recognition and independence, but when it was sealed he himself had a bare year to live and his heir was an infant. Bruce's triumph was to prove, after his death, personal, fragile and indecisive. That it so proved is telling testimony to the incompetence of the English leaders who through Edward II's reign and beyond it failed either to defeat him or to come to terms with him.

If Bruce's triumph was temporary, there was nothing temporary about the impact of the war in the north of his and Edward II's reigns. Though in the Yorkshire regions which had so suffered at the hands of Scots raiders economic recovery was quite rapid, in the border lands the scars left by the fighting took centuries, not generations to heal. In the comparative peace of the late thirteenth century the border counties had been an area of advancing prosperity, both in town and countryside; by 1328 only the signs of vanished prosperity remained, in burned houses and deserted countryside, and in the new power of Robert Bruce who had enriched himself with the plunder and tribute of the lands over which he had so constantly raided. Loss of livestock, and the burning of crops and homesteads had ruined agricultural prosperity, and there was a substantial exodus of poor folk who could no longer make a safe living from the country. Many landowners had been reduced to dire straits. Durham Priory's revenues, which in 1308 stood at £4500, had dwindled to a mere £1750 in 1335. Setbacks such as this were not a temporary phenomenon, moreover; the impoverishment was permanent.

These economic consequences of the Anglo-Scottish war had important political effects. In Edward's weakness, the lords of the north were left to organize defence themselves, or to make their own terms with Bruce. Behind the private treaties that they made with him in order to secure their own possessions, as too behind the reluctance of the northerners to throw in their lot with Lancaster in 1321, we can see developing an independent, northern attitude in politics, governed by considerations local to the Scottish border. In Harclay's conspiracy of 1323 we see the first effort of a border lord, with a military reputation and following, to direct the English political situation with purely northern ends in view. He was to have some formidable imitators later on, as we shall see, notably among the members of the house of Percy.

The Scottish wars did not end with Edward II, and the outbreak in 1337 of the great Hundred Years War between England and France meant that the lords of the north had to be left to fend for themselves, as they had done under him, more or less permanently. In consequence, the lines of development of the early fourteenth century set firmly. After Edward II's reign the border did not ever, in the Middle Ages, recover its prosperity. It became a land of herdsmen and cattle-thieves, of powerful but intensely local loyalties, where gentry like the Charltons and the Armstrongs lived in fortified dwellings, half as squires, half as bandits, and where men knew 'no prince save a Percy or a Neville'. To a southerner, it was almost a foreign country; it still seemed so to Camden in the sixteenth century when he visited it: 'over all the waste you would think you see the ancient nomads . . . a martial sort of people that from April to August lie in little huts . . . among their several flocks'.[22] The north acquired its own ways of thought and feeling, and its own literature, a balladry that turned its sorrows and violence into high poetry. Most important of all for the political historian, its conditions made the great lords of the border the most formidable, militarily, among the English magnates. This was why, in the later Middle Ages, their private feuds and rivalries were so often a threat to the stability not of the north only, but of the whole kingdom, and why their allegiances proved often to be the deciding factor in domestic politics.

Edward II's reign thus left a lasting mark on the political geography of England. Before his time the lords who had most often proved dangerous to the monarch had been the Welsh marchers, and in 1321 in the war against the Despensers they showed that their fangs were not yet drawn. It was the last occasion, however, on which their intervention, as an identifiable group, was decisive. In the later fourteenth century and afterwards the stormy petrels of English politics were not the men of the west, but the men of the north, above all the Percies – who had come into the north in the host of Edward I in the hope of gain and new lands, and who made it their homeland thenceforward, until in the end their unruliness brought final ruin upon the house.

Notes

1 *Vita Edwardi II*, ed. N. Denholm Young (London, 1957), p. 57.
2 *R.P.* vol. I, p. 305.
3 *Chron. de Melsa* (R.S.) vol. II, p. 335.
4 *Vita Edwardi II*, p. 81.
5 *Scalacronica*, ed. J. Stevenson (Maitland Club, 1836), p. 148.

6 See J.R. Maddicott, *Thomas of Lancaster* (Oxford, 1970), ch. 6, esp. pp. 195ff. Conway Davies, *The Baronial Opposition to Edward II* (Cambridge 1918), p. 433, described Audley, Damory and the Despensers as 'the raw material from which Pembroke had to build his middle party', which, as Maddicott shows, is misleading.

7 *P.W.* vol. II, Appendix, p. 120.

8 *Bridlington* (R.S.), pp. 61–2.

9 *Annales Paulini* (R.S.), p. 293.

10 The tract is printed in full by L. W. Vemon Harcourt, *His Grace the Steward and Trial of Peers* (London, 1907), pp. 164–7 (English translation, pp. 148–51).

11 *Vita Edwardi II*, p. 113.

12 ibid. p. 114.

13 J. Conway Davies, *The Baronial Opposition to Edward II*, Appendix, No. 93, p. 583.

14 *Statutes of the Realm* vol. I, p. 189. The constitutional importance of the Statute of York is discussed further in Chapter 4.

14a *Chron. de Lanercrost*, ed. and trs. H. Maxwell (Glasgow, 1913), p. 241.

15 *Chron. G. Le Baker*, ed. E. M. Thompson (Oxford, 1889), p. 18.

16 *Annales Paulini*, p. 323.

17 *Chron de Lanercost*, p. 258. The formal articles of deposition are given by Twysden, *Historiae Anglicanae Scriptores X* (1652), col. 2765.

18 *Chron. G. Le Baker*, p. 28.

19 *Foed.* vol. IV, p. 452.

20 *Vita Edwardi Secundi*, intro., p. ix.

21 Twysden, *Historiae Anglicanae Scriptores X*, col. 2765.

22 Quoted by E. Miller, *War in the North*, p. 10.

Note on secondary reading (post 1970)

Three books have dramatically revised perceptions of the reign of Edward II and its politics; J.R. Maddicott, *Thomas of Lancaster* (Oxford, 1970); J.R.S. Phillips, *Aymer de Valence, Earl of Pembroke, 1307–24* (Oxford, 1972); and N.M. Fryde, *The Tyranny and Fall of Edward II* (Cambridge, 1979). The seminal works of T.F. Tout, *The Place of Edward II in English History* (Manchester, 1914) and J. Conway Davies, *The Baronial Opposition to Edward II* (Cambridge, 1918) are in consequence interpretively out-dated. Valuable recent articles include N. Saul, 'The Despensers and the downfall of Edward II', *E.H.R.*, vol. 99 (1984); C. Valente, 'The deposition and abdication of Edward II', *E.H.R.*, vol. 113 (1998); and S.L. Waugh, 'For king, country and patron; the Despensers and the local administration, 1321–2', *Journal of British Studies*, vol. 22 (1983). Older articles that retain high value, by J.G. Edwards, E.B. Fryde and B. Wilkinson are listed in the main bibliography, Section 2a.

On the Scottish war in Edward II's reign, and especially after 1314, C. McNamee, *The Wars of the Bruces: Scotland, England and Ireland, 1306–28* (East Linton, 1997) is invaluable. Also very useful are A.A.M. Duncan's Historical Association pamphlet, *The Nation of Scots and the Declaration of Arbroath, 1320* (1970), and his 'The war of the Scots', *T.R.H.S.*, 6th series, vol. 2 (1992). E. Miller's pamphlet, *War in the North: the Anglo Scottish wars of the Middle Ages* (Hull, 1960) is eloquent on the consequences of the wars for northern England and the borders. On the war of St Sardos in Gascony, 1324–5, see M. Vale, *The Angevin Legacy* (Oxford, Blackwell, 1990), chapter 7.

There is no satisfactory in-depth study of the period of the dominance of Isabella and Mortimer, 1327–30. R. Nicholson, *Edward III and the Scots* (Oxford, 1965) is useful for the Weardale campaign of 1327; on the domestic side A. Verduyn, 'The politics of law and order in the early years of Edward III', *E.H.R.*, vol. 108 (1993) is of interest. The best resumé remains that in M. McKisack, *The Fourteenth Century* (Oxford, 1959).

Since the typescript of this book went to press, a new book has helped to fill the gap here: I. Mortimer, *The Greatest Traitor: The Life of Sir Roger Mortimer, 1st Earl of March* (London, 2003).

4 Politics and the constitution 1290–1330

The personal antipathies and rival interests of great men dictated the course of events through most of the long, sad reign of Edward II. Nevertheless, issues of general importance to the people at large were all the time involved. As we have seen, Edward II's difficulties had their origins in the later years of his father's reign, when the king and his magnates were divided on issues that were far from being merely personal. Two crucial problems were directly raised by the troubles of that time, the limit of the king's prerogative power, and the means of redress available to the subject against oppressive acts of the king and his officials. The second of these problems was bound to raise sooner or later a third issue, the question of the subject's right, in extreme circumstances, to resist the king's government. The events of the early years of Edward II brought this third issue squarely into the foreground. The period from 1290 to 1330 was in consequence a most important one in constitutional as well as political history.

The question of the subject's right to sue for lawful redress against the king was one which was raised early, and remained important throughout the period. In the 1290s it provided the central theme of the curious tract known as the *Mirror of Justices*, which provides an interesting illustration of the manner of argument on questions of political principle in the age. To the author of the *Mirror* it seemed quite wrong that the king should be above and beyond the law, as he effectively was, given the practice of the courts at the time.[1] The king's courts, he thought, ought to provide remedies even against the king himself. In the good old days of the first Anglo-Saxon kings they used to do so, he claimed. When the English first came to the land the earls, who were the king's companions, were each given a district to hold and defend, and it was agreed as law that these earls should hear and determine in parliament all writs and complaints concerning wrongs done by the king, by his family, and by his officials.[2] But now this custom is no longer observed, the *Mirror* laments, and the subject has no redress available against the king at law.

The point which the author of the *Mirror*, with his irresponsible invective and his entirely spurious history, was getting at had also troubled the *doyen* of English thirteenth-century lawyers, Bracton. Bracton stated quite clearly that the king was not beyond the law, but bound by it.[3] Royal authority came from God, and was an authority only to do that which was right and lawful, not to commit injury. But Bracton was much less clear when it came to the question of how the king may be constrained to obey the law. The king according to Bracton has no equal in his kingdom, still less any superior. His writ will not run against him and those who seek redress against the crown can only proceed by petitioning for grace, not by legal action. 'If he [the king] will not correct what is complained of, he must be left to the judgement of God.'[4] This was Bracton's own conclusion, but there were those, he admitted, who did not agree. In a passage where he is explaining that the assize of *novel disseisin* cannot be used against the crown he remarks thus: 'There are however those who say that the *universitas* of the kingdom and the baronage can make him correct his act, and that in the court of the king himself.'[5] This sounds reminiscent of the *Mirror*'s story of the right of the earls to hear complaints against the king in parliament. The reminiscence is much stronger in a passage which seems to have been interpolated into Bracton's text at an early date: 'The king has his court, that is his earls and barons, and earls are so called because they are the king's companions: he who has a companion has a master: if therefore the king is unbridled, that is if he act without the law, they [i.e. the earls] should put a bridle upon him.'[6] This is probably where the author of the *Mirror* got his ideas, though it need not have been: the subject was clearly one which was attracting a good deal of attention. Edward I's extension of such prerogative rights as purveyance to finance his wars gave it direct relevance to political issues of the day.

Another version of the same sort of idea is to be found in the tract called the *Modus Tenendi Parliamentum*, which was written, probably by a chancery clerk, about the year 1320. The *Modus* purports to record the custom of the days of Edmund Ironside, before the Norman Conquest; like the *Mirror* it is a record not of what parliaments ever did, but of what one writer thought they ought to do (though it should be stressed that the author of the *Modus* knew a good deal about parliaments, and offered a much more contemporarily relevant account of their purposes and procedure than the author of the *Mirror*). One important chapter of this tract is devoted to what are called 'difficult cases and judgements' in parliament – cases of the sort that may provoke discord between the king and his magnates. They should be referred, says the *Modus*, to a committee of twenty-five persons, to be chosen not by the king but by the Steward, the Constable and the Marshal (hereditary offices, all held by earls). These twenty-five shall choose twelve arbiters in the matter, the twelve six, the six three, and if necessary the three shall choose one (with the king's leave) and his judgement shall be final.[7]

As one might expect, there were attempts to achieve in practice something like what the author of the *Modus* and others suggested. The chronicler Langtoft has a story about the appointment, in the Lincoln parliament of 1301, of a committee of twenty-six discreet men, who should decide whether the king ought or ought not to yield to the petitions of his magnates. A year before this, in the parliament of 1300, the magnates had asked the king to promise that he would punish 'according to the law' officials of his who had contravened the charters. The *Ordinances* of 1311 actually instituted a committee, of one bishop, two earls and two barons, to be appointed in every parliament 'to hear and determine all plaints of those wishing to complain of the king's ministers, whichever they may be, who have contravened the *Ordinances*.[8] It looks, moreover, as though there was a genuine attempt to implement this clause in 1315, when, after Bannockburn, the *Ordinances* had been re-enforced.

Efforts such as these, to introduce the kind of legal procedures for obtaining redress against the crown that the authors of the *Mirror* and the *Modus* and the interpolator of Bracton wished to see, had little long-term chance of success unless the crown was prepared to acquiesce in them. Edward I was determined never to do this, and Edward II only approved the *Ordinances* under duress. A promise given by a king under duress was a bad guarantee. It seemed to give the *Ordinances* the force of law according to Bracton's authoritative definition: 'that is law which has been justly determined and approved, with the counsel and assent of the great men, the approval of the whole commonwealth, and the authority of the king'. Such laws could not be changed, in Bracton's view, except with the common consent of those who made them.[9] Edward I, however, had drawn a sharp distinction between laws that were made with the common assent and on the crown's initiative (as the charters which his father had freely granted in 1225, and the statutes of his own reign), and those which were made on the initiative of others, as the new laws which he promised to observe in the period 1297–1302. These promises, he told Pope Clement V in 1305, had been wrung from him unwillingly by men who had taken unfair advantage of him in a difficult time. Edward I, who even at the height of his difficulties had never allowed any hint of question about the Bractonian principle, that the king's writ does not run against the king, was determined not to be trammelled by the activities of parliament, which was his own court. As we know, Pope Clement released him from his promises, so setting a precedent that was obviously prejudicial to any future attempt to limit the king's action by the methods that the opposition had adopted in 1297 and afterwards. And Edward II did in fact attempt to follow his father's example, and to obtain from the pope an absolution from his promise to observe the *Ordinances*.

It looks as if the fourth clause of Edward II's coronation oath was drawn up with, among other things, a view to getting round the difficulty which the absolution of 1305 had posed. 'Sire, do you grant to be held and observed the just laws and customs that the community of your realm shall have chosen, and will you, so far as in you lies, defend and strengthen them to the honour of God?' – 'I grant and promise them.'[10] This was the text of the new clause. The magnates seem to have made use of it in 1308 to secure Gaveston's exile, claiming that since his banishment had been decreed by the people, for the good of the realm, the king was bound to enforce it.[11] The doctrine of the fourth clause, if thus interpreted, was not a comfortable one. Read in this way, it would seem to imply a transference of sovereignty from the king to the people too drastic to gain more than temporary acceptance. For this reason, many historians have doubted whether this was what the fourth clause really was intended to mean. We will only say this, that the magnates cannot have hoped that they could solve their problem for ever by binding the king for the future to accept rules propounded by the community. In an age in which it was widely accepted that the king had no superior in his kingdom and could not be sued, it was very unlikely that he would accept unwelcome dictates of the community, except under duress. Sooner or later the question had to be faced, whether and in what circumstances it could be lawful to use force against the king, in order to compel him to govern justly.

In connexion with this question of the use of force against the king, a very important declaration was made by the magnates, according to the Canon of Bridlington, in the year 1308. It is worth quoting in full:

> Homage and the oath of allegiance are stronger and bind more by reason of the crown than by reason of the person of the king, and this appears in that before the estate of the crown has descended to a person, no allegiance belongs to the person or is owed . . . Wherefore if the king by chance be not guided by reason, in relation to the estate of the crown, his liege subjects are bound by their oath made to the crown to guide the king back again by reason and amend the estate of the crown: otherwise the oath would not be kept. Then it is to be asked how they ought to guide the king in such a case, whether by form of law or by violence? He [the king] cannot be directed by course of law, for there are no judges except the king's. In which case, if the king's will be not according to reason, he will only have error maintained and confirmed. Wherefore it behoves in order to save the oath, that when the king will not redress a matter and remove that which is damaging to the crown and hurtful to the people, it is adjudged that the error be removed by violence: for he the king is bound by his oath to govern the people, and his liege subjects are bound to protect the people according to the law.[12]

Two points in this declaration are of particular interest. One is the clear distinction drawn between the crown (kingship as representing lawful authority), and the king in his personal, human capacity. The ability to draw this distinction has often been claimed to be a sign of precocious political thinking on the part of Edward II's opponents. There is nothing precocious about the other important point, however, the assertion that force is a legitimate means of seeking redress where the ordinary course of law cannot prevail.

In this last respect the declaration of 1308 had a sort of precedent in the sanctions clause of the Great Charter of 1215. That clause set up a committee of twenty-five barons, to whom complainants might resort if they believed their rights under the charter had been infringed; and who had the right and duty, if the king and his ministers would not amend the injury in question, to raise men and use every kind of force to distrain them to do so. The ideas of 1215 seem to have struck root, for they appear in another document of Edward II's reign besides the *Declaration*. This is the tract on the *Office of the Steward*, written by someone in the entourage of Thomas of Lancaster and probably in the year 1321.[13] According to this tract it was the Steward's duty to receive the complaints of those who had failed to obtain justice from the king or his courts, and to see that they were remedied in parliament. It also said that it was his duty, if the king followed evil counsel, to proceed together with the Constable and the Marshal against the king's evil counsellors 'with banner raised in the name of the king and the realm, and to take such a counsellor as the public enemy of the king and the kingdom'.[14] The reference to the raising of banners, a sign of open war, is striking. It reminds us of the connexion between the claims of the baronage and of such officers as the Steward in our period to a right to use force against the king, and the old feudal right of a vassal to make war on his overlord, if the overlord outstepped the customary and lawful limits of their contractual relationship.

In the political and legal literature of the late thirteenth and early fourteenth centuries, we have constantly found the same idea cropping up: that there are or should be persons with whom there lies a right to review the conduct of the king and his officials, and to constrain him to amend it, if necessary by force. This is a very interesting notion, suggesting strongly that men of the period were more concerned by the threat of too much government than its opposite. The persons with whom this right and duty to constrain the king was thought to lie were aristocrats, the earls according to some, the baronage or a committee of barons according to others, or the great hereditary officers of state, the Steward, the Constable and the Marshal (who were all earls, and who in fact played leading roles in opposition between 1297 and 1322). Their duty, however, was not viewed in a narrow, sectional way: it was to protect the entire community, not just the baronage, from governmental oppression. The opponents of the crown went out of their way to make it clear that their concern was for the community as a whole, through such propaganda documents as the *Monstraunces* of 1297 and the manifestos of the Lancastrian counter-parliaments of 1321.[15]

There were some seeds of responsible good sense in this approach to the problem of controlling and restraining at need the activities of a busy royal administration that was often oppressive and often corruptly directed. It was an approach that had no real future, however. By the time of Edward II it was already beginning to look antique in conception and unworkable in practice, too aristocratic and too redolent of the feudal past to afford a useful protection to the rights of the community of the king's subjects. This was in large part the result of two other developments of the period, the growth of a new legal concept of the crime of high treason, and the growth of the institution called parliament.

The ancient English idea of treason was an act of disloyalty to an individual lord. In the time of Edward I and Edward II ideas culled from Roman law, with which almost all common lawyers had at least a nodding acquaintance, were introducing into English custom the concept of high treason as a crime against the state, an injury to the majesty of public authority. Edward I and his judges, in proceeding against the leaders of the defeated Welsh and Scots, would not consider their actions in terms of the nobleman's feudal right to resist his overlord if the latter overstepped his rights. They judged armed rebellion to be high treason; and as traitors David of Wales in 1283, and later Rhys ap Mareddud, William Wallace, the Earl of Atholl and Sir Christopher Seton were judged and executed. In Edward II's reign this interpretation of armed resistance to the crown, as an affront to majesty and so high treason, was applied in the cases of Earl Thomas of Lancaster, the Earl of Hereford, Roger Damory, and a number of other rebels in 1322. The penalties of treason included forfeiture of all lands held in fee simple. It thus became very dangerous for a magnate to involve himself in actions which might be construed as treason, and specifically it became obviously dangerous to proceed against counsellors of the king, bad characters though they might be, 'with banners raised', in manner of war.

It should be stressed here that this idea of treason was not just a view of royalist judges: it was an interpretation of the law that was gaining wide acceptance. The opponents of Edward II proceeded against his favourites as traitors and public enemies. Gaveston, the Despensers and the Earl of Arundel were all charged with high treason. The particular treason that they were most often held to have committed was the offence of 'accroaching royal power': that is to say, of obtaining a hold over the king which enabled them to make illegitimate and abusive use of royal power, and so to injure its majesty and the public weal. There was an obvious and close connexion between this idea of treason and the view of the Roman lawyers that any exercise of imperial prerogatives by a subject was *lèse majesté*, high treason.

On the basis of the distinction drawn in the 1308 *Declaration* the opponents of Edward II's favourites could claim that their actions did not constitute armed resistance to the crown. They were only using force to make the king exercise the authority of the crown in a lawful manner, and to rescue him from those who were accroaching his power. This distinction was, however, too fine to be comfortably drawn in practice. The charge of 'accroachment' widened the scope of treason to the point where intimacy with the king might in itself be grounds of an accusation. Such extension of the meaning of treason endangered the stability of the realm, because the penalties of treason, death and forfeiture gave the heirs of a dead traitor a vested interest in the reversal of the political *status quo*.

Aside from the danger of facing a charge of treason, there was another reason to make magnates hesitate to implement the claims, put forward on behalf of the nobility, to a right to review the actions of the crown and if necessary to resist them. People in general were not sufficiently satisfied about the nature of this right. This was partly, no doubt, because people distrusted some of the men who claimed to exercise it, such as Thomas of Lancaster. It was also because its basis in custom was flimsy and unclear: no two authors ever described the right in quite the same way. The reaction to the counter-parliaments of 1321 is significant here. Lancaster and his allies went out of their way to make it clear that they were acting in the interests of the community as a whole. It was to provide 'suitable remedy' for the ills of the kingdom 'by common counsel and unanimous consent' that the meeting at Sherburn had been called, John de Bek told those who were assembled there.[16] But at Sherburn the northern magnates and prelates would not seal indentures to enter into confederacy with Lancaster and his marcher allies. The prelates, and probably the magnates too, wished to see the matters that had been raised dealt with not in an assembly of barons and their retainers, but authoritatively in a parliament summoned by the king in the customary manner.

The anxiety to see great matters dealt with in parliament is in fact a consistent theme of the years of trouble. The opponents of Edward I in 1297 insisted that taxes should only be lawful if granted by a representative assembly called for the purpose. The Ordainers built their scheme for reform round the authority of parliament. Lancaster, true to the principles of the *Ordinances*, told Edward II in 1317 that 'you ought not to wish to enact or treat outside parliament about anything which ought to be determined in parliament'.[17] Bishop Stapledon, a curialist on good terms with the Despensers, was insistent with the king late in 1321 that since the sentence which had been passed on them had been given in parliament, it ought not to be revoked elsewhere.[18] The York parliament of 1322 finally gave this view authority as constitutionally sound doctrine: 'matters which are to be determined for the estate of the king and his heirs, and for the estate of the kingdom and of the people, shall be treated, granted, and established *in parliament* by our lord the king with the consent of the prelates, earls, barons and of the commonalty of the kingdom as has been accustomed in time past'.[19]

Since a lawful parliament could only be assembled by the royal summons, this insistence on parliamentary authority was favourable to the crown. The Statute of York made it clear that counter-parliaments assembled by the Steward or the Constable or anyone else had no standing, and that it was unlawful for any assembly but parliament to seek to decide matters affecting the state of the realm. The York parliament of 1322 also quashed the *Ordinances*, and so the machinery that they had set up for the review of royal and official actions by a committee in parliament went by the board, and nothing took its place. This did not of course solve all problems for the king. Though the Statute of York was framed with a view to buttressing and protecting royal authority, its implications were by no means absolutist. The king might still find himself compelled by force of circumstance or duress to summon a parliament which he did not want to meet, and might there find himself compelled to agree to things which he did not like. The statute did not provide the king with any way out of this situation, and it could not stifle the sense, widespread even if vague and undefined, that the great men of the realm had a right, even a duty, to rescue the crown from evil counsel, by force if need be (we shall find this notion looming large much later, in Yorkist propaganda in Henry VI's reign). But it did deliver the king, and finally, from the bogy of 'companions' among his

subjects who could be his lawful masters, entitled to review official acts independently of any initiative on his part. Whatever might happen in parliament,
in the courts at large the Bractonian principles that the king had no superior
and that his writ would not run against himself were firmly retrenched.

In the last few paragraphs a great deal has been said about parliament, but we
have not said anything about what the word parliament meant to men in the
reigns of Edward I and Edward II. This is a subject which has given rise to a
good deal of controversy among historians in the past, and will probably
continue to do so in the future. It is a subject, however, on which something
has to be said, particularly given that the meaning of the word was shifting
importantly within the period in question.

Parliament has been described in the earliest stage of its development as 'rather
an act than a body of persons'.[20] This is a useful phrase. Certainly the composition of parliament was unfixed in the late thirteenth and the early fourteenth
centuries. Edward I summoned fifty-two parliaments; representatives of the
shires and boroughs attended thirteen of them only. On occasion, as for instance
in 1295 and the spring parliament of 1305, he summoned to parliament also
the representatives of the lower clergy, who later would have attended not
parliament but convocations. The number of those who received individual
summonses, the bishops, abbots, earls and barons, fluctuated very considerably
moreover. Ninety-eight lay lords were summoned in 1300, but four years
earlier, in 1296, only forty-three had been. Twenty important men, magnates,
bishops, judges and clerks, were all that Edward I summoned to the autumn
parliament of 1305, which drew up the ordinance for the government of
Scotland with the aid of ten representatives of that kingdom. No knights were
called from the English shires, no burgesses from the towns, and only a
handful of magnates, though the business that was in hand was of the highest
importance.

For this early stage, a definition of the occasions on which parliament might
meet is easier to find than a definition of its personnel. 'A session of the king's
council is the core and essence of every *parliamentum*,' Maitland wrote,[21] and
it is one of the few statements about the early history of parliament that stands
virtually unchallenged. The king's council was, of course, a body not more
easily defined in terms of personnel than a parliament. There were some efforts
to define the membership of the council in Edward II's time, in 1316 and
notably in 1318 in the Treaty of Leake; but they were not very successful and
things soon reverted to the usual situation in which the king took advice from
those whom he chose to consult. There was, however, a difference between a
parliamentary session of the council and a routine meeting of the royal familiars
in the king's chamber. When parliament met the courts were always in full
session, and its session brought together in a wider body of great men the
heads of the departments of state, the chancellor and treasurer, the judges, and
the leading officials of the household. A parliamentary session of the council
thus realized the royal authority at its fullest and most formal, and also at the

peak of its activity. It was a meeting in consequence which enjoyed a general competence to deal with all the affairs of the realm (except that it might be questioned whether it could grant a general aid, unless the shire and borough representatives were present, or at least a substantial showing of great magnates, lay and ecclesiastical).

The fact that parliaments met in the law terms and involved a plenary session of the king's courts may suggest that the chief function of parliaments at this stage was to deal with judicial business. Certainly pleas and petitions dominate the early records (or 'rolls') of parliament. Strictly speaking, of course, petitions, which normally came from individuals or corporations such as towns, request a remedy of the royal grace, not as of right. But it is reasonable to describe the parliamentary scrutiny of petitions as judicial business, since it concerned primarily the working of the law and of the courts. The usual process was that the council examined a petition handed in at parliament time, and then sent the petitioner on to the relevant court – the King's Bench, or the exchequer, as it might be – to seek a suitable remedy there. His petition was endorsed to this effect by the councillors who had examined it, and was recorded by a clerk of parliament before it was sent on to the lower court. Pleas of parliament were, in contrast, tried and terminated by the council in parliament. They were usually cases of first instance, that for one reason or another it was thought best to hear in parliament. A good example was the trial of Nicholas Segrave for treason in 1305. He was a baron of standing who had deserted the king's army in Scotland without the royal licence, and both his status and the gravity of his offence made it imperative that he should be judged in the most formal and authoritative forum available. There was apparently a good deal of discussion of his sentence, with the angry king bent on making an example and the worried magnates urging clemency. In the end Nicholas was released, on condition of finding seven good warrantors that he would hold himself ready at the king's will to surrender his person into prison and his estates into the king's hand.

Parliament was also a convenient forum for the announcement of new legal remedies. Most of Edward I's statutes were authorized in parliament, though this was sometimes done, curiously, after the main body of those summoned had gone home. This is a reminder that statutes did not need the assent of parliament; they were announced there because the king thought it a useful opportunity to give publicity to new legal remedies that he and his judges had devised. It was a time at which men did not yet draw a very sharp distinction between legislation and the judgement of pleas, as the author of the tract on the Steward's office makes clear: 'if it be found that the law is doubtful in an *individual* case', it says, the matter should be referred to a committee 'who shall there ordain, found, and establish remedy of law in all such cases for ever afterward to endure'.[22] Once again we find that parliamentary business is in the broad sense judicial.

The functions of parliament so far reviewed fit well with the famous definition of the law book, *Fleta*: 'the king has his court in his council in his parliaments, where judicial doubts are determined, and new remedies are established for new wrongs, and justice is done to everyone according to his deserts'.[23] They are functions, too, which received sharp emphasis in the *Ordinances* of 1311: 'in parliaments, pleas which are delayed . . . and pleas wherein the justices are of different opinions, shall be recorded and settled; and likewise those bills [i.e. petitions] which are brought to parliament shall be settled as heretofore in accordance with law and right'.[24] They are also, thirdly, the functions to which the early rolls of parliament give greatest prominence. They probably occupied more of the time of the counsellors and judges whose sessions were at the 'core' of parliament than anything else. That does not mean, however, that they were the only functions of parliaments, or the most essential, or the most important.

Edward I was in fact impatient at the amount of time that had to be spent on petitions. As early as 1279 he was complaining of the number of these, and the time that it took to consider them: henceforth, he ordered, only those which could not be answered without the king should be referred to him, 'so that the king and his council can attend to the great business of the realm'. It was to treat of the great business of the realm that men were summoned from far afield to attend parliaments, not to hear or for that matter to present petitions. The wording of the writs of summons to Edward I's parliaments makes this abundantly clear. This is how the king wrote to Edmund Earl of Cornwall in 1295:

> Because we wish to have colloquy and to treat with you and with the rest of the principal men of our kingdom, to provide for remedies against the dangers which in these days are threatening our whole kingdom, we command you, strictly enjoining you in the fidelity and love in which you are bound to us, that on the Sunday next after the feast of St Martin you be present in person to treat, ordain and act, together with us and with the prelates, and the rest of the principal men and the other inhabitants of our kingdom, as may be necessary to meet dangers of this kind.[25]

The evidence of the writs of summons throws the emphasis on different activities and functions of parliament to those highlighted in the rolls, with their records of pleas and petitions. To judge by the writs, the discussion of great matters of state was the prime purpose of holding parliaments.

Those whom the king summoned from a distance to treat and consult about the affairs of the realm by no means always stayed the whole length of a parliament. In 1305, for instance, the representatives of the shires and boroughs were sent home on 21 March, but the council continued to deal with business in parliament, some of it very important, until Easter (18 April). In fact, there was no special reason why the English kings should have summoned great men to treat on the affairs of the realm and representatives of the community to hear and witness what was done, at the same time that they and their counsellors were dealing with petitions and important judicial pleas. It was, however, highly convenient for them to do so, and lent added authority to both the political and the legislative decisions that were reached in great parliamentary assemblies. Had Edward I tried to keep such assemblies separate from the judicial sessions of the council, the English parliament might have developed into a professional judicial body like the *Parlement* of the French kings, and the representative assemblies into something like their *States General*. But he did not do so, and the result was that the political and legislative function of the court called parliament assumed in course of time far greater importance than its judicial authority.

The growing concern of parliaments with matters of more general import than purely judicial business helped to define its composition more clearly. Lack of confidence in Edward II and his intimate counsellors was here an important factor. The general preoccupation in the first part of his reign with correcting what the king and his ministers had done amiss shifted the emphasis of ideas about the authority of parliament. That authority was now to be esteemed, not because the king and all his judges and councillors were present at parliament time, but because other people were as well. The *Ordinances* labour, over and again, the need for matters of general import to be decided 'with the assent of the barons', not just of the council, in parliament. Thomas of Lancaster refused to recognize as 'parliamentary' assemblies to which the whole baronage was not summoned.[26] What precisely he thought this meant must remain in doubt, for it was not yet clear what entitled a magnate to an individual summons to parliament: the number of lords, lay and ecclesiastical, who received one fluctuated throughout the fourteenth century. Nevertheless, by the end of Edward II's reign it was clearly established that a council meeting could not be a parliament, unless a substantial body of peers had been summoned. A meeting such as that of the autumn of 1305, when a score of trusted councillors appeared to advise the king, would no longer have been reckoned a parliament.

In the Statute of York of 1322 parliament was clearly recognized as a body representing the whole community of the realm. That was why all matters affecting the 'estate of the realm and of the people' had to be dealt with in parliament. Earlier, in 1297, the *Confirmatio* had stressed the need for the assent of the community of the realm to all grants of extraordinary taxation. It is not clear from either document, however, who precisely had to be present in parliament for the whole people to be represented there. Evidence from Henry III's reign shows that, after the middle of the thirteenth century, the baronage alone or a part of it could be understood to represent the community. Parliament, according to the Provisions of Oxford of 1258, should be a meeting of the council with twelve barons chosen by their fellows to represent the community. The political tracts of the 1290s and the earlier part of Edward II's reign still assumed that the barons, or in some cases the earls alone, were the lawful guardians of the community's interest. The *Ordinances* again treated parliament as essentially a baronial assembly. This evidence makes it unfortunately impossible to associate the stress of the Statute of York on the representation of the 'commonalty' with the role of the commons in parliament, though the commons were present at York in 1322, as they had been in 1297 when the *Confirmatio* was granted.

If, however, the commons had not yet fully established their position in parliament in 1322, they had certainly come very near to it. After 1290 they were summoned to one in three of the parliaments of Edward I's later years. By the end of Edward II's reign a parliament to which they were not summoned was the exception. Time, the unsettled conditions of the period, and their increasingly regular appearance at parliaments, had made both king and barons aware of their usefulness as 'agents of propaganda and vehicles of public opinion' (to use Professor McKisack's phrase), and they had begun to find a part of their own to play in the redress of popular grievances. By the beginning of the next reign, in the early 1330s, we begin to find that commons' petitions (petitions, that is, which the commons as a whole had agreed to sponsor) were making a mark on the legislation that emerged from parliaments.

There is no doubt that the original reason for the growth of the influence of the commons in parliament was the part that they played in granting taxation. Even in the reign of Henry III doubts had been expressed as to whether the magnates alone, in a great council, could bind others who had not been present in that council to pay a tax that they granted. In this respect, the clause in the summonses to parliament of shire and borough representatives which insisted that they should come with full power to bind their communities (*cum plena potestate pro se et comitatu suo* in the case of the shire knights), and which became a regular feature of all writs of summons to them in the late years of Edward I, is clearly important. With the exception of the eighth of 1297, whose collection was abandoned because of opposition, Edward I never sought to collect a subsidy which had not received the assent of representatives armed with full powers to bind their communities. His writs ordering the collection of subsidies granted in parliaments normally referred to the assent which they had received. The principle that the assent of representatives was necessary to give lawful authority to a grant of taxation thus gained ground through regular practical application. In the *Modus* we find the lesson of practice translated into constitutional doctrine. 'Two knights who come to the parliament for the shire have a greater voice in parliament in granting and denying [an aid] than a greater earl of England' because, its author says, the knights of the shire with the burgesses and the proctors of the clergy 'represent the whole community of England', whereas a magnate comes to parliament 'for his own person, and for no other'.[27] The *Modus* is not of course a safe authority: but its author's opinion on this point is supported by the collective evidence of writs of summons to the commons, of writs authorizing the collection of aids, and of the asides of chroniclers.

The idea of representation that is so clearly expressed in the *Modus* had its origins in Roman law and canonical practice, which taught that a community of individuals, such as the chapter of a collegiate church (or a town corporation, for that matter) could act for legal purposes as a body through its proctors, appointed by the members of the community and with power to bind them all. The Roman and canon laws provided a full and elaborate theory of legal representation. Edward I in his summons to representatives of the lower clergy in 1295 actually quoted the canonical tag 'what affects all should be approved by all'. He was then thinking in terms of taxation, but the principle was one clearly capable of much wider application. At the end of Edward II's reign the procedures adopted at his deposition afforded a very startling demonstration of how far its application might be extended.

The deputation, which was appointed to go to Kenilworth to renounce homage and allegiance to Edward II in January 1327 was carefully constructed so as to represent the whole realm, as that realm was represented in parliament. It included two earls, three bishops, four barons, certain abbots and priors, two barons of the Cinque Ports, four burgesses of London, and some selected representatives of other boroughs and shire knights. At Kenilworth William Trussel, a knight, renounced homage and allegiance 'on behalf of the whole kingdom' (one authority adds 'and of parliament').[28] Though it cannot be proved conclusively that this deputation was appointed in or by parliament, there is no doubt about its representative capacity. The idea of a deputation seems to have originated when discussion was going on as to how King Edward could be forced to attend the January parliament, in which Archbishop Reynolds was much involved. He consulted his old and experienced friend, prior Henry Eastry of Christ Church, Canterbury, who advised 'that the king should be required to attend by an embassy of two earls, two barons, four citizens and four knights of the shire *elected to represent* the whole community of the realm'.[29] From the very beginning, the procedures followed at the time of the deposition assumed that what was to be done must be done with the authority of the whole realm. They also assumed that in order for this authority to be exercised all the estates, not just the magnates and the higher clergy, must be involved through representatives.

The procedures adopted at the deposition of Edward II are testimony to an important shift in perceptions of the balance of political authority in the English kingdom. They implied a significant retreat from the claim that had often been put forward in the past on behalf of the magnates, that they, on their own, could be regarded as in a special sense the guardians of the community and its rights. Even more notable, however, was the clear demonstration that, in the long run, the authority of the king was grounded in the assent of the community. It was shown that the customary laws, and the rights of the community, had an existence independent of the authority of the king, though not, perhaps, of the crown. The assertion of the representative authority of the people in 1327 exposed the flank of the royal prerogative, perilously. A means had been found to deal with a king who would not observe the customary limitations on his right or heed his subjects' demands for redress of legitimate grievances. It was not a tidy means, and it was not clear which was the crucial element, Edward's (forced) abdication, or the act of state, which was engineered to involve, through their representatives, all his people, high and low, in rejecting him. A precedent had nevertheless been set which, however dubious its constitutional interpretation, could never be forgotten.

It can reasonably be argued that what happened in 1327 is best viewed in political rather than constitutional terms. After as before 1327, English legal ideas and constitutional assumptions remained profoundly king oriented. Yet the fact remains that between 1327 and 1485 four out of nine English kings lost their thrones in their lifetimes; Edward II, Richard II, Henry VI and Edward V (that is without counting Edward IV, who lost the throne briefly but recovered it by force). In each case, moreover, means were sought and found of formally registering the people's assent to their being thrust aside. 'It is the way of the English', Jean Juvenel des Ursins observed in the fifteenth century, 'to think it of little account to change their kings whenever it seems good to them, even to kill them.'[30] Another French writer of the time believed he could trace twenty-six violent changes of dynasty in England since the Anglo-Saxon foundation of the kingdom. His tally depended on some substantial massaging of dark age history: but it is hard to deny that the late medieval story does suggest a radical difference between the relations of the English kings with the community of their subjects and the absolutist French tradition. France had her plentiful share of civil wars in the period, but there were no royal depositions.

Notes

1 *The Mirror of Justices*, ed. W. J. Whittaker (Selden Soc., 1893), p. 155.
2 ibid. pp. 6–7.
3 Bracton, *De legibus et consuetudinibus Angliae*, ed. G. E. Woodbine (Yale, 1922), vol, II, p. 33.
4 ibid.
5 ibid. vol. III, p. 43.
6 ibid. vol. II, p. 110.
7 *Modus*, ch. xvii.
8 *Chron P. de Langtoft* (R.S.) vol. II, p. 330: *Ordinances*, clause 40.
9 Bracton, *De legibus* vol. II, pp. 19, 21.
10 *Statutes of the Realm* vol. I, p. 168.
11 *Bridlington* (R.S.), p. 34.
12 *Bridlington*, pp. 33–4.
13 The text is given by L. W. Vernon Harcourt, *His Grace the Steward and Trial of Peers* (London, 1907), pp. 164–7 (English translation, pp. 148–51).
14 ibid. p. 150.
15 See above, pp. 36–7, 53–4.
16 *Bridlington*, pp. 62ff.
17 *Bridlington*, p. 52.
18 *Reg. Stapledon* No. 409, quoted by M. V. Clarke, *Medieval Representation*, p. 169.
19 *Statutes of the Realm* vol. I, p. 189.
20 F. W. Maitland, intro. to *Memoranda de Parliamento*, p. lxvii.
21 ibid. p. lxxxviii.
22 Vernon Harcourt, *His Grace the Steward*, p. 149.
23 *Fleta*, ed. H. G. Richardson and G. O. Sayles (Selden Soc., 1953), vol. II, p. 109.
24 *Ordinances*, cl. 29.

25 Wilkinson, *Constitutional History* vol. III, p. 178.
26 *Bridlington*, pp. 51–2; compare *Vita Edwardi II*, p. 104.
27 *Modus*, ch. xxiii.
28 *Chron G. Le Baker*, ed. E. M. Thompson (Oxford, 1889), p. 28: and MS chronicle quoted by M. V. Clarke, *Medieval Representation*, p. 185, note 4.
29 Clarke, *Medieval Representation*, pp. 177–8.
30 Quoted by P. S. Lewis, 'Two pieces of fifteenth century iconography', *Journal of the Courtauld and Warburg Institutes*, vol. 27 (1964), p. 319.

Note on secondary reading (post 1970)

Much of this chapter has been concerned with the early history of parliament. E. Miller's Historical Association pamphlet, *The Origins of Parliament* (1960) remains the best introduction to the topic. There is a wealth of further illuminating reading in two very substantial collections; E. Miller and E.B. Fryde (eds.), *Historical Studies of the English Parliament* (2 vols, Cambridge, 1970), which reprints F.W. Maitland's seminal introduction to the *Memoranda de Parliamento* of 1305, and two magisterial essays by J.G. Edwards, on the *plena potestas* of shire representatives, and on justice in parliaments; and R.G. Davies and J.H. Denton (eds.), *The English Parliament in the Middle Ages* (Manchester, 1981) which includes notable essays by J. Denton, G.L. Harriss, and J.R. Maddicott. G.O. Sayles, *The King's Parliament of England* (New York, 1975) is an important book; and J.G. Edwards' brief *The Second Century of the English Parliament* (Oxford, 1979) is also illuminating.

On the *Modus Tenendi Parliamentum*, the introduction to N. Pronay and J. Taylor, *Parliamentary Texts of the Late Middle Ages* (Oxford, 1980) has provided a new starting point; on this work see also M.C. Prestwich, 'The *modus tenendi parliamentum*', *Parliamentary History*, vol. 1 (1982). The older articles on the *Modus*, cited in the main bibliography Section 4c, by G.P. Cuttino, J.S. Roskell and V.H. Galbraith retain value, as does M.V. Clarke's dated but seminal *Medieval Representation and Consent* (London, 1936). On the statute of York there are new perceptions in W.M. Ormrod, 'Agenda for legislation, 1322–40', *E.H.R.*, vol. 105 (1990); older articles (main bibliography, Section 4c) by G. Lapsley and J.R. Strayer retain their relevance.

Among other topics treated in this chapter, see on treason J.G. Bellamy, *The Law of Treason in England in the Later Middle Ages* (Cambridge, 1970) and on the coronation oath the articles (all pre-1970) cited in the main bibliography, Section 4a, by R.S Hoyt, H.G. Richardson, and B. Wilkinson – and, of course, P.E. Schramm, *A History of the English Coronation* (Oxford, 1937).

The constitutional and legal implications of Edward II's deposition have been re-examined thoroughly and illuminatingly by C. Valente, 'The deposition and abdication of Edward II', *E.H.R.*, vol. 113 (1998).

Section II

The age of Edward III
1330–1360

5 The early years of Edward III 1330–1338

On the night of 19 October 1330, King Edward III, a young man of eighteen, entered Nottingham castle by a subterranean passage in the company of a group of youthful noblemen, the chief of whom was Sir William Montagu. In the castle he seized Roger Mortimer, the paramour of his mother Queen Isabella, who for the last four years had lorded it in England 'as if he were king over all'.[1] Mortimer was taken bound to London, where he was tried before his peers as a traitor: he was hanged at Tyburn on 29 November. The young king's *coup* had been carefully planned in advance, and the pope had had secret information about the sort of thing that was afoot. It had been a risky business, but the gamble paid off, and Edward in consequence at last began to rule the country of which he had hitherto been king in name only.

Few kings of England ever set out on their reigns with more intractable problems facing them than Edward III did. His father had reigned for twenty years, and for those twenty years nothing had been stable in English politics. In the long struggle between the king and the various groups of magnates that opposed him, order had declined steeply in the counties. In the countryside, marauding gangs wandered armed and unhindered. The final deposition of the king had utterly humiliated the monarchy. Edward III, if he was to make his authority respected, had somehow to recreate a confidence in royal leadership that had been totally lost in the years of trouble and misfortune. Those years had been marked by disasters outside as well as inside the realm. Among the charges levelled against Edward II by Bishop Stratford in his articles of 1327 was that his misgovernment had lost the kingdom of Scotland, and had come near to losing the lordships of Ireland and Gascony, and it was a charge that was justified. It must have looked, at the end of 1330, as if the most promising means whereby the newly independent Edward III might restore confidence in his leadership domestically, especially among his magnates, would be by asserting himself successfully at the borders of his kingdom or beyond them. That certainly seems to be how he saw it; but there were problems about where to make a start.

Gascony was arguably, from an English royal point of view, the most significant of the three theatres mentioned by Stratford in his articles. It was the ancient inheritance of the Plantagenet house, all that was left to it now of what had once been the Angevin 'empire' in France. The wine trade of Bordeaux was commercially important, and revenues from the duchy made a major contribution to English crown finances (calculated in 1324 at no less than £13,000 p.a.). The seamen and ships of Bayonne played a vital part in maintaining the lines of maritime communication between England and Bordeaux, and beyond with Spain. Among the Gascon nobility, traditional attachment to Plantagenet lordship was deep rooted: a number of them had served Edward I at the head of Gascon contingents in his Scottish campaigns. For all these reasons, the recurrent pressures of the French king's overlordship upon the English ruler's independence in his duchy were deeply unpalatable, and the outcome of the war of St Sardos had rubbed salt into the wounds. It had left the Agenais in French control, and the English saddled with responsibility for meeting a £60,000 relief for the duchy, as well as large financial claims for compensation for war damage. The problem for Edward III, when he seized the reins of power in 1330, was that he did not look in much of a position to shake off these obligations to the powerful new French king, Philip VI. An initiative to try to reverse the verdict of St Sardos did not promise much prospect of success.

Scotland was the issue that in 1330 was rankling most sharply with Edward's subjects. The recognition of Scottish independence in the Treaty of Northampton had been a very bitter pill. 'Accursed be the time when the parliament was ordained at Northampton,' the *Brut* chronicler declared, 'for the king by false counsel was fraudulently disinherited'[2] (by the recognition of Bruce as king). The trouble here was that with the Northampton Treaty so recently sealed, Edward's hands appeared diplomatically tied with regard to Scotland, for the time being at any rate: besides, the shambles of the Weardale campaign that had preceded it stood as a sharp reminder of the difficulties likely to be encountered in a new initiative in that direction. In the circumstances, it is not surprising that Edward's first ideas, at the beginning of 1331, seem to have turned toward a personal, major military intervention in Ireland. Fortunately for him and for the Irish, this project was rapidly abandoned when events in the north took a new turn, that altered the shape of the prospects there.

Robert Bruce, it will be remembered, had died in 1329, leaving as his heir his five year old son, David. For the heirs of Scottish families that had been driven into exile in consequence of their opposition to Robert in his early days, as for those English lords who had lost estates granted to them in Scotland by Edward I, the political uncertainty that David's minority generated seemed to offer a golden opportunity. The figure round whom this group, who came to be called 'the disinherited', now gathered was Edward Balliol, son of John Balliol, former King of Scots. In 1331 Edward Balliol was brought to England by two leaders of the disinherited, Henry Beaumont and David of Atholl. Using the Beaumont manor of Sandal in Yorkshire as their headquarters, they began to gather a little army. For Edward of England, the developing situation opened the possibility of testing the prospects of a renewed intervention in Scotland, without committing himself further than was safe or convenient. In formal loyalty to the terms of the Treaty of Northampton, the sheriff of

Yorkshire was instructed to forbid the assembly of men for the expedition planned by the disinherited and to arrest the leaders. It is virtually certain, however, that he was in fact told not to act on these orders; indeed, Edward III actually connived in the sale of English estates, by means of which the conspirators raised funds for their venture. They sailed from Ravenspur near Hull on 31 July 1332, and on 11 August won an unexpected but conclusive victory over the army of the guardian of Scotland, Donald Earl of Mar, at Dupplin Moor, not far from Perth. In the weeks following many Scottish nobles and churchmen flocked to seek Edward Balliol's peace, and on 24 September he was enthroned at Scone as King of Scotland.

In the autumn of 1332 Edward III travelled north to York, so as to keep a closer eye on events in Scotland. It was well for him that he did so. When the parliament that he had summoned there was fully assembled in January, Balliol was a fugitive suppliant for his aid. He had been surprised at Annan on 17 December by the Earl of Moray and Sir Archibald Douglas, who were faithful to David Bruce, and had to flee for his life. A firm decision on English policy was thus forced on Edward, and it had to be taken quickly; he must now either back Balliol, or back away.

Edward's reaction was unhesitant. In parliament, a council was appointed to attend and advise him on Scottish affairs, and the commons were then sent home. Three days after they had gone writs went out for the raising of troops. Within the week the Abbot of St Mary's York, acting as treasurer for the king, had made substantial advances to magnates who had agreed to serve in a forthcoming campaign, as well as to Edward Balliol and his followers. Orders were given for the exchequer and the Court of Common Pleas to be transferred from Westminster to York, where they were to remain for the next five years. In May Edward appeared at the head of his army before Berwick, and began to blockade the town. On 19 July, the Scottish army which had marched to its relief was crushingly defeated at Halidon Hill.

Halidon Hill was the first battle which fully demonstrated the potential of the English longbow. Among the Scots, who had charged uphill in the face of the archers' fire, the carnage was terrible. The deaths of five earls, of Sir Archibald Douglas, and of a host of other notable men made the victory seem complete, politically as well as militarily. Edward III left Scotland confidently on 29 July, while Edward Balliol marched forward to reduce the land and the fortresses of his surviving enemies. By midsummer of the next year, 1334, it looked as if Scotland was definitively his. David Bruce had left the country to seek refuge in France; and Balliol was able to leave his kingdom to come to Newcastle, where on 19 June he did homage to Edward III. The disinherited, and the Englishmen who had helped them, had meanwhile been richly rewarded by both king Edwards. John de Warenne was pardoned all his debts to the English crown and made Earl of Strathearn in Scotland; William Montagu was granted the lordship of the Isle of Man; Henry Percy was given custody of the castle of Berwick, and the lordship of Lochmaben and Annandale; David of Atholl received the grant of all the lands of Bruce's still living supporter, Robert Stewart. Edward III, of course, did best of all, by the terms of a treaty with Balliol which must be examined shortly. Bannockburn had been signally avenged.

The settlement of 1334 proved to be as short lived as all the previous attempts at an arrangement between the English and Scots kings. Before the summer was out Robert Stewart and the Earl of Moray, the leaders of the Bruce faction in Scotland, had turned the tables a second time on the new king. It was with difficulty that Balliol, deserted by his followers, managed to reach safety at Berwick. Two months had served to undo all the achievement of Halidon Hill and the year that had followed it.

Edward III's reaction to Scottish national resistance was the same as his grandfather's had been. Like Edward I, he put his trust in numbers. In the summer of 1335 he gathered the largest English royal host that had assembled for many years. Eight earls and twenty-three bannerets brought retinues to serve in his company. The Count of Juliers joined the king with a powerful troop from abroad; and a large contingent was brought over from Ireland. Edward also mobilized a substantial fleet, to guard the coasts and to help revictual his forces from the sea after they had entered Scotland. At the head of this great army Edward crossed the border, heading for Perth. There was no major battle; the appearance of the English awed those who could not avoid contact with them into submission. 'In the face of his might, none but children in their games would answer openly that they were the men of King David.'[3] The formal and temporary submission of the leaders of Scottish resistance was all that Edward gained, however. He could not keep his army in being for ever: even if he had been able to pay the men beyond September, few would have been willing to serve. When his back was turned, the risings began again. On 30 November David of Atholl, the most important of Balliol's Scottish followers, was defeated and killed. Edward in 1336 had to lead another English host into Scotland. Like his grandfather before him, he found that though he might keep his garrisons in the great lowland towns and castles, he could not conquer the countryside. He was back again in Scotland in the summer of 1337, though this time with a smaller force – and he could not stay so long. His relations with the king of France, which had been deteriorating for three years, were reaching breaking point, and the Hundred Years War was about to begin. Edward did not return to the north for five years, and by that time David Bruce was back in Scotland and secure on his throne.

Much the most illuminating document that has survived concerning Edward III's early adventure in Scotland is the treaty which, in 1334, he made with Edward Balliol. An understanding about the outline of its terms seems to have been reached some time earlier, indeed before the massive English intervention of 1333 – a fact which makes it quite clear that Edward III was in it with Balliol from the beginning. The treaty of 1334 was accordingly very generous to the English.[4] Balliol ceded to his friend and patron virtually the whole of the

Scottish lowlands, including Roxburgh, Jedburgh, Selkirk, Linlithgow, and Edinburgh itself. What was ceded here was demesne lordship, with no right reserved on the Scots king's behalf. For what was left of Scotland after this, Balliol recognized Edward III as his feudal suzerain, and to mark this dependence he swore to do him homage and to serve him in his wars with a stipulated following. In return, Edward recognized Balliol as king of Scotland, and agreed to abandon any claim to jurisdiction in Scotland, and not to entertain before his court appeals from the court of the King of Scots. Edward I's claim to hear appeals from the court of the Scots king had been the origin of the quarrel between him and Edward Balliol's father John. It is a sign of Edward III's originality that he did not think it worth his while to argue about this traditional right of a feudal overlord, if substantial territories were ceded to him in demesne lordship. He seems clearly to have preferred to be without the problem of overlapping jurisdictions in his relation with Balliol. Very significantly, his attitude in this matter with regard to the Scots anticipated the line which he and his advisers were to take up later in their dealings with the French kings over Gascony.

The treaty of 1334 was still-born: Balliol was a fugitive long before Edward III got possession of the land that it promised him. The English never reachieved the position of *arbitrage* that they seemed to have won for a brief moment in that year. It is in consequence tempting to write off Edward III's intervention in Scotland in the 1330s as an ambitious and expensive failure. It may not be right to do so. It is true that the expeditions of 1333 and of 1335 and 1336 were immensely costly; that this cost drove Edward to borrow heavily from Italian merchants; and that in consequence his financial position was already strained when the war with France broke out. It is true also that the English parliament complained a good deal about the way in which men were raised for his armies, and in which money was extorted to pay them, just as they had complained before in Edward I's time. Nevertheless Edward probably gained as much or more than he lost by his policy. The victory of Halidon Hill wiped out the memory of Bannockburn and the tale of reverses that had followed afterwards. To his English magnates, Edward had revealed himself as a capable military leader, and, in the aftermath of victory, a generous one. It is as well to remember here that it was a long time before it became clear that the cause of Balliol was hopeless; it certainly cannot have seemed so even in 1337. The English did not lose Edinburgh until 1341, and by then Edward had won another great battle, over the French in the Channel at Sluys, to which more attention was paid. The intervention in Scotland was not successful in the long run, but was sufficiently successful initially to set a new tone for the new reign.

It was a new tone to which Edward himself sought to give conscious expression, through the scenes and symbolism that chivalrous ritual afforded. There was a great ceremonial creation of knights when his host entered Scotland in 1333. The return from Halidon was celebrated by a great royal tournament at Dunstable; and heralds painted rolls of the arms of those who were present there, as they did of the Scots knights who came with Balliol to do homage to

Edward at Newcastle next summer. This event was the occasion for much feasting and minstrelsy. Edward III was clearly aware, very early, of the importance of making the most of success on the instant, in ways that would fix its memory gratefully in men's minds.

The history of Edward's relations with Scotland in the 1330s is perhaps most interesting for the way in which it fits into the pattern of his political apprenticeship in the early and formative years of his authority. It is worth briefly running over the outline of the experience to which this young king had at this stage been exposed. In 1326 he had been brought over from France in company with his mother and Mortimer and their mercenary bands, and had been a probably unwilling witness of their triumph, which toppled his father. In 1330 he himself had seized power by a daring and dangerous *coup*. He had then watched Edward Balliol and the disinherited gather a little army in secret, and all but win a kingdom. In the situation that their success created, the only sane course for him had seemed to be to ignore whatever legal and diplomatic obstruction the Treaty of Northampton put in the way of intervention in Scotland. In the aftermath of Halidon, he emerged as a victor and a hero in England, and was able to clinch a hard bargain with Balliol. This was a pattern that suggested that, where the advantages were sufficiently great, the niceties of legal and traditional relations were only one factor to be considered; that it was worth taking large risks; and that the manner of an action often mattered more, as far as men's responses were concerned, than its motive. It will be well to bear this pattern of experience in mind, when we have to consider other ventures on which Edward III embarked, in which the risks seem to have been greater than those he ran in the Scots War, and his objectives, viewed from a distance of time, more remote from the sphere of political reality.

The Scottish war can be regarded as a kind of prelude to the much more important war with France, which began in 1337. It was also directly connected with the chain of events which led to the outbreak of that war.

Anglo-Scottish and Anglo-French relations in fact presented from the very beginning problems which could not be separated. The Treaty of Corbeil (1327) had resealed the 'auld alliance' of France and Scotland more firmly than ever. It had even stipulated that, if a new war were to break out between the English and the French, the Scots would be bound to intervene on the French side, notwithstanding any treaty that they might make with the English.[5] The king of England was also Duke of Aquitaine, and as such a vassal of France; the French clearly realized that the Scots could be very useful if they wanted to put pressure on him in that capacity. One of the advantages that Edward stood to gain, if his client Balliol succeeded in making himself king of Scotland, was that it would render this part of the Corbeil treaty void and meaningless. A king of Scotland who had done homage to Edward and promised to serve him in his wars could not be party to the terms that Corbeil had arranged between the French and Scots.

These matters must have been very much in Edward's mind when he was considering whether to support Balliol. If he did so, he would inevitably give the French formal ground to come to the aid of their ally, David Bruce, probably by attacking Gascony. But in the crucial years 1332 and 1333 relations between France and England which had been tense in the immediate aftermath of Philip VI's accession in 1328, looked to have taken a turn for the better; and Edward had some sound reasons for hoping that they would remain so, whatever he did. King Philip was planning a crusade, and looked as if he would soon leave his kingdom; if he did, he would surely be anxious not to leave behind uncertain relations with the Duke of Aquitaine, who was his most formidable vassal. There was also another reason why Philip should have been anxious to remain on good terms with Edward; Edward was a possible claimant to his, Philip's, throne.

In 1328, the last Capetian king of France, Charles IV, had died without a male heir. The two men with the best claims to succeed him were Philip, Count of Valois, and the young Edward III. Edward was nearer in blood to the throne: his mother was the daughter of Philip IV, whereas the Valois claim came through count Philip's father, Charles, who was the younger brother of Philip IV. What stood between Edward and the French throne was the fact that his claim came through the female line, and precedent in 1316 and 1321 (when Louis X and Philip V had died leaving only daughters) had clearly established a rule that the crown of France could not pass to a woman. Edward could of course argue that though a woman could not succeed she might transmit her right to a male, and a claim was formally lodged on his behalf in 1328. But in the aftermath of Edward II's deposition he was not in much of a position to press his right, and it was Philip who was crowned at Rheims.

Following this, the advisers of Philip VI of Valois were naturally anxious that Edward should recognize and define his relation with the new monarch by doing homage for Aquitaine. Edward was as naturally anxious to avoid so doing, but in the unstable condition of England at the time he was in a poor position to refuse. In 1329 he crossed to France, and did homage to Philip VI at Amiens. Even with this the French were not quite content, and they pressed for a clear recognition that it was liege homage that Edward had promised. The performance of liege homage would imply a clear jurisdictional subjection to the king of France, and the obligation to serve him in time of war. In the fear once again that refusal might be met with force, Edward III gave in 1331 a written recognition that it was liege homage that he had sworn. Shortly after this he once more crossed to France, disguised as a merchant, and met Philip in secret at Pont St Maxence, where they agreed the outline of terms which should serve as a basis for a lasting peace between them.

Edward's recognition that he was the liegeman of Philip relieved, or seemed to relieve, the atmosphere of tension and suspicion that had prevailed between the English and French courts since 1328. In return for it he obtained the prospect of a formal peace settlement, and agreement that the issues outstanding from the recent war of St Sardos (including the question of the boundaries between his duchy and the land that was to be left directly subject to the king of France) should be sorted out by a 'process' – that is, by a tribunal of legal experts on which both sides had equal representation. The parity of the experts, implying a kind of independence in the relations between the parties, was a concession to Edward, calculated to take the sting out of the indignity of his recent recognition that he was Philip's liegeman. This concession, and the prospect of a formal peace, Edward seems to have interpreted as an indication that the French were anxious for conciliation and that he could probably intervene in Scotland in support of Balliol with impunity.

Edward III knew that the French were pressing ahead with preparations for the crusade. Philip was anxious to make his mark as a crusader, partly because, like Edward III, he was a new king, untried – and one also with a questionable hereditary title. Ever since the days of St Louis, his Capetian predecessors had felt that they had a special part to play in crusading, and a special place among European rulers on account of it. There was no better way in which Philip VI could impress himself on his subjects as the true heir to the line of St Louis than by leading an expedition to the East. Edward could well appreciate his position, because it was in many ways like his own; indeed, he himself considered taking part in the crusade. In March 1332 at Nottingham he formally announced in parliament his intention of doing so; but the idea was abandoned, for the moment anyway, when more inviting opportunities opened in Scotland as a result of Balliol's victory at Dupplin Moor. When he decided to seize his chance in the north he had to assume that Philip would be too busy to want to make trouble about the matter. It was a good gamble, and he took the precaution in 1333 to give careful instructions to his officers in the Channel ports that nothing was to be done which could offend the French while he was campaigning in Scotland. Unfortunately his assumption, reasonable as it was, proved incorrect.

Relations between France and England remained smooth through 1333, the year which saw Halidon Hill and the conquest of virtually all of Scotland by Balliol. The process of Agen had by now set to work and was making progress. In the spring of 1334 an English embassy crossed to Paris, and after an audience with King Philip they believed that the final peace was about to be settled. They were suddenly called back into his presence and were told by Philip himself 'that his purpose was, that King David of Scotland, and all the Scots, must be included in the peace'.[6] It was soon clear that the French king was in earnest in this unexpected and alarming demand. In May David Bruce landed with a small following in Normandy, where he was received by Philip 'very courteously' and lodged at Château Gaillard. From this point on, every English embassy to France was overlooked by the exiled court of England's open enemy, whom everyone knew that King Philip was sustaining.

The reasons behind the French attitude are easy to understand. The English kings had always been the most intractable vassals of the crown of France, and the Scottish alliance looked worth preserving for the hold that it gave the French over the English king. Philip was anxious to go on crusade, and he wanted to be sure that Edward would make no trouble in Gascony while he was away, and he therefore did not want to see Edward free of anxiety about his northern border. If he did not take action, it looked, in the spring of 1334, as if Edward would be free of anxiety there, with his friend Balliol on the Scottish throne. Philip moreover may not have realized quite what the reaction to his support for David Bruce would be. Certainly, if those authorities are right who say that he tried to insist on the acceptance of his own arbitration between the English and the Scots, he must have misread the situation.

Pope Benedict XII viewed the situation with a clearer eye than the French king did. From the moment that the king of France allowed himself to become directly involved, the Scottish succession war ceased to be a matter affecting the British Isles only: it assumed importance within the broad framework of European diplomacy, in the midst of which the papacy was working to make a crusade viable. Benedict saw that the English could not possibly accept French arbitration. He saw too that if Philip set out on crusade still nominally allied with Edward's enemies, and with Edward still nursing a grievance over the French retention of the Agenais, the prospects of the crusade, and perhaps for the peace of European Christendom, would be in jeopardy. Edward had important connexions in the Low Countries, on the borders of the French kingdom: his wife Philippa was the daughter of the Count of Hainault. If in Philip's absence Edward were to make a bid to regain lost land in southwestern France, he would find allies among these connexions, and also, no doubt, in France itself among those who, for whatever reasons, resented the new-made Valois monarchy. In a letter sent to Philip in the summer of 1335 Pope Benedict alluded pointedly to this danger, and warned the king to remember how powerful some of his enemies in his own realm were.

Benedict in fact foresaw the future with remarkable clarity. His difficulty was this, that though he could make sure that Philip's departure on crusade was delayed, by using his papal authority, it was very much harder for him to persuade Philip to moderate the position he had taken up as the committed ally of David Bruce, which he believed to be essential before he could allow the crusade to go forward. Finally, in March 1336, he decided to postpone the crusade *sine die*. Philip still stuck by the exiled king of Scotland. His reaction to the pope's decision was not to moderate his position, but to order the great crusading fleet that he was assembling on the Mediterranean coast to sail round to the ports of the English Channel. Edward III concluded that an invasion of his kingdom was projected.

Edward had suspected that an invasion might be attempted, ever since the day in March 1334 when Philip had declared that there could be no final accommodation over Gascony unless David Bruce's rights were protected in the same peace. This ultimatum was given at the moment when Balliol, Edward's client, was at the height of his fortunes, and David Bruce was a fugitive in hiding: the natural conclusion was that the French must mean to intervene in Bruce's support. This was why Edward III in 1335, though he was straining his resources to raise an outsize army for the invasion of Scotland, felt it necessary to incur extra expense to put the Channel ports and the southern counties into a state of defence. He had good reason to be worried at this moment. In a sermon preached at the French court in July 1335 the Archbishop of Rouen declared that Philip intended to send 6000 men to help the Scots. The draft of a scheme to send a French force to Scotland, which almost certainly belongs to this year or to 1336, actually survives. There was fighting in the channel in 1336. When Philip's great crusading armada appeared in the narrow seas, Edward was wholly justified in concluding that an invasion would be attempted.

Edward's reaction was swift and far more decisive than Philip's manoeuvres had been. In the summonses that were despatched for the parliamentary meeting at Nottingham at Michaelmas he made it clear that measures to resist the French menace would be the first item on the agenda. This parliament granted a tenth and a fifteenth; and the next one, which met at Westminster in March 1337 granted a tenth and a fifteenth for three years. This put the king's finances on a war footing. At the same time that parliament was summoned to Nottingham orders were sent to the seneschal of Gascony to put his fortresses in a state of defence, and to Bayonne requesting the townsmen to supply ships for service in the Channel. Still more significant was the embargo that was imposed on the export of wool from England by a royal ordinance of August 1336. This embargo cut off the weavers of the great Flemish industrial cities from their chief supply of raw wool. Edward's hope was that this would force Louis Count of Flanders into an alliance with England, in order to avoid the social confusion which the embargo would inevitably cause in his territories. Edward did not quite succeed in doing this, for Louis proved obstinately loyal to Philip, who had helped to put down his rebellious subjects eight years before; he did succeed ultimately, however, in persuading the Flemings to abandon their count and join his side (in 1339).

   The embargo on wool export was a first step toward carrying the war into the enemy's camp, and was followed up with a vengeance. On 6 December 1336 Edward gave Count William of Holland power to contract military alliances on his behalf in the Low Countries, and to offer fees to those who would promise service. In May 1337 his personal representatives, the Bishop of Lincoln and the earls of Salisbury and Huntingdon, appeared at Valenciennes, and set to work to build up, on the basis of the promise of pensions, a great coalition against France among the princes of the Rhineland and the Low Countries. They were prepared to pay almost any price to secure their master's interests. The counts of Gueldres, Limburg and Juliers, and the Archbishop of Cologne soon came to terms. John Duke of Brabant was less easily won, but he was brought in, hesitating to the end, at the enormous price of £60,000, and by the promise of commercial advantages in the wool trade for his territories. But the biggest prize of all (in spite of the fact that he was an excommunicated heretic) was the Emperor Louis IV of Bavaria, and his price was commensurate with his status, 300,000 florins. Thus Edward's counter-measures to the threat from France began to broaden his quarrel with Philip and the Scots into a European confrontation.

In August 1337 Edward III issued a proclamation which was to be read in all the county courts of the kingdom. Notwithstanding many offers of reasonable terms, it declared, 'the king of France, hardened in his malice, would assent to no peace or treaty, but called together his strong host to take into his hand the duchy of Aquitaine, declaring against all truth that it was forfeit to him'.[7] Philip had, in fact, declared the duchy confiscate on 24 May, and his Constable, at the head of an army, had entered the duchy to enforce the sentence. Edward's manoeuvres had convinced him that war was inevitable, and that he had better have the advantage of the opening move. The formal ground of his sentence was not aggression or misdemeanour on the part of Edward's officials in Gascony. It was that Edward, being a vassal of Philip's, had granted asylum at his court to Count Robert of Artois, whom Philip had stripped of all his honours and lands and had exiled from his kingdom. This was not a real ground for embarking on a war, so much as an excuse to bring matters to a head.

Even after the confiscation of Gascony, there was a moment when it looked as if war might be avoided, but the appearance was deceptive. In a desperate effort to prevent a head-on confrontation between two Christian kings which would be fatal to all crusading schemes, Pope Benedict despatched his *nuncios* to Paris and Westminster to try to reconcile the parties. Edward heard that they would be coming in the late summer of 1337, and wrote to the officials who were arraying men in Wales for a royal host that the muster scheduled for Michaelmas must be postponed. Just before Christmas, after difficult negotiations with the cardinals whom Benedict had sent to speak with him, Edward agreed to suspend hostilities until March; and later, in February, he extended this truce to midsummer. Edward acted, he said, out of reverence for the Holy See; probably his real reason for agreeing to delays was the difficulty of collecting the wool which parliament had granted him to help pay for a campaign in France. He was not really in earnest in seeking peace.

This is clear from a document that he sealed on 7 October 1337, the same day that he granted powers to the Bishop of Lincoln and others to confer on his behalf with the cardinals. It was of much more serious import. In it, he described himself as king of France and England, and appointed Duke John of Brabant his representative, to prosecute his right to the French throne in any way that he might see fit, and to accept on his behalf the homage of his French subjects.[8] Thus his riposte to Philip's confiscation of Gascony was to claim that he, not Philip, was the rightful king of France, and should have been ever since 1328. This deliberate reopening of the question of the French succession made it quite clear that Edward did not intend to compromise in any way on the issues of Aquitaine or Scotland. If he were pressed to do so, he would be likely to raise this larger and more dangerous issue.

Edward's claim, in this document of 1337, stands in isolation. He did not begin to use the style 'King of France' regularly and formally until three years later, in 1340; and it was only from then on that he took to quartering the lilies of France with the leopards of England on his seal. It is therefore not easy to be sure precisely how we should take the claim of 1337, at this stage. Many have doubted whether he can seriously have believed that he might be able to wrest their throne from the Valois, and have believed that his instruction to John of Brabant can be interpreted simply as a move in the diplomatic game, whose object was to make it difficult for the papal mediators to insist on concessions unwelcome to the English. It seems probable that Edward's motivation was more serious than this. A sentence which, a year after 1337, appears in an agreement between Edward and the Emperor Louis IV is here instructive. The agreement includes the grant to Edward of the powers of an imperial vicar: these are to last, it is said, 'until such time as he has conquered a substantial part of the kingdom of France'.[9] If Louis thought that Edward might make large conquests, why should not Edward himself have hoped so? Robert of Artois must certainly have encouraged him to think that way, and many at the time believed that his influence was decisive. Robert's only hope of regaining the influence that he had once exercised in France was through the triumph of Philip's enemies, since Philip was quite implacable towards him, so he may have been inclined to exaggerate internal dissatisfaction in Philip's realm. Wishful thinking may also have affected the attitude of some of Edward's allies in the Low Countries and the Rhineland, since recent attempts by the French to claim sovereignty beyond France's eastern border had roused ill-feeling. But even to impartial observers the condition of the new Valois monarchy did not look healthy. Benedict XII had warned Philip in 1335 that he should remember how powerful his domestic enemies were. Edward III probably had good reason to think he might make substantial conquests in France, whether or not a bid for the crown was realistic at this time.

There is another way of approaching the problem of Edward's deliberate reopening of the succession issue, which also helps to make it understandable. What he did in October 1337 is of a piece with the whole pattern of his direction of affairs in the early years of his reign. He had served a political apprenticeship which taught that fearless seizure of the initiative was the way to win in the game of power. The very boldness of questioning Philip's right to his throne was part of the advantage of doing so. There were obstacles in the way of pressing his own claim, it is true, the most serious being the fact that he had undoubtedly done homage to Philip in 1329, and had confirmed later that it was liege homage that he had done. By 1337, however, he had repudiated at convenience one agreement made in the first years of his reign, the Treaty of Northampton with the Scots – why not these others too? His dealings with the Scots foreshadow his French diplomacy in another way as well, and an important one. The terms of Edward's treaty with Balliol of 1334 suggest that he had then already grasped that, between kings, a feudal jurisdictional relationship could only be fruitful as a source of friction. The claim to the French throne offered a way of cutting the issues between him and Philip of Valois adrift from the old question of overlapping feudal rights in Gascony, which had caused so much trouble in the past. Henceforward, any territory that the English king could win or withhold from Philip in France by fighting he could call his own, because he could claim that he was king and sovereign there in his own right. If and when terms to end the fighting were proposed, moreover, he could hope to be able to trade his claim to the throne against recognition of his independent sovereignty in such territory.

The issue of the French succession promised to introduce a new element of inflexibility into the Anglo-French confrontation. It would take much more than stalemate in war to persuade the Valois to resign sovereignty in lands where they had once exercised it. It would also become very difficult for Edward to retreat from his claim to the French throne, if he once pressed it seriously. This probably explains why, in 1337, he took no more steps to publicize his position than those we have mentioned, and did not, as yet, adopt the style King of France in his ordinary correspondence. He wanted to leave himself as much room for manoeuvre as he could for the present. Nevertheless, it had begun to be clear that a war would be fought between France and England on issues more far-reaching than those of feudal right.

Notes

1 See *Chron A. Murimuth* (R.S.), p. 62; and *R. Avesbury* (R.S.), pp. 284, 285.
2 *Brut Chronicle*, ed. F. W. D. Brie (E.E.T.S., 1906), vol. I, p. 256.
3 A. Wyntoun, *Orygynale Cronykil of Scotland* (Edinburgh, 1872), vol. 2, p. 413.
4 *Foed.* vol. IV, p. 614.
5 *A.P.S.* vol. XII, p. 5.
6 *Les Grandes Chroniques de la France*, ed. P. Paris (Paris, 1837), vol. V, p. 357.
7 *Foed.* vol. IV, p. 805.
8 ibid. vol. IV, p. 818.
9 H. S. Offler, 'England and Germany', *E.H.R.*, vol. 54 (1939), p. 611, note 17.

Note on secondary reading (post 1970)

W.M. Ormrod's major biographical study, *The Reign of Edward III* (London, 1990) is very illuminating on the early years of the reign: his articles on 'Edward III and his family', *Journal of British Studies*, vol. 26 (1987), and 'Agenda for legislation, 1322–40', *E.H.R.*, vol. 105 (1990) are also helpful. C. Shenton examines Edward's seizure of power in 1330 in 'Edward III and the *Coup* of 1330' in J. Bothwell (ed.) *The Age of Edward III* (York Medieval Press, 2001).

Most of this chapter has been focused on relations with Scotland and France in the lead up to the Hundred Years War. For Anglo-Scottish affairs, R. Nicholson, *Edward III and the Scots* (Oxford, 1965) is a sure guide. M. Vale, *The Angevin Legacy and the Hundred Years War, 1250–1340* (Oxford, Blackwell, 1990) has enormously clarified the story of the Anglo-French tensions that culminated in the outbreak of the great war. Chapters 1–7 of J. Sumption, *The Hundred Years War*, vol. I, *Trial by Battle* (London, 1990) give a very full narrative, including a clear account of the French succession crisis of 1328. On this see also C. Taylor, 'Edward III and the Plantagenet claim to the French throne', in Bothwell, *The Age of Edward III*, cited above. On Edward's embargo on the export of wool, in the context of financial preparation for war, it may be best to look back to E.B. Fryde's article in *History*, vol. 37 (1952), 'Edward III's wool monopoly: a fourteenth century royal trading venture'.

On the cult of chivalry and ceremony in Edward's early years, see J. Vale, *Edward III and Chivalry: Chivalric Society and its Context, 1270–1350* (Woodbridge, 1982); and C. Shenton, 'Edward III and the symbol of the leopard', in P. Coss and M. Keen (eds.) *Heraldry, Pageantry and Social Display in Medieval England* (Woodbridge, 2002).

6 Edward III and the Hundred Years War 1337–1360

Edward III, at the request of the Pope's *nuncios,* agreed at Christmas 1337 to suspend hostilities against the French until March, and this truce was later extended to midsummer. In the meantime, however, fighting continued in Gascony, and in the spring of 1338 a French fleet appeared in the Channel, which attacked Portsmouth and ravaged the Isle of Wight. On 6 May Edward announced that he regarded the truce as no longer binding. The war which then began in earnest was to last more than one hundred years. Hostilities, of course, were nothing like continuous throughout that period, and this makes it possible to study the course of the war in phases. A first phase may be said to have ended when in 1360, at Brétigny near Chartres, a treaty was agreed between the French and English which came subsequently to be known as the 'great peace'.

This first phase of the war, from 1338 to 1360, may be further subdivided into three periods. The first of these witnessed, in the years 1337 to 1341, the attempt of Edward III to bring together a great coalition against the Valois, and its failure. The second saw new fronts opened up on French soil, in Brittany and Normandy, and ended with the capture by the English of the port of Calais in Picardy in 1348. The third period saw the great English victory at Poitiers, where King John of France was taken prisoner, and the campaigning which drew to a close when the peace was agreed at Brétigny.

In 1338 Edward's diplomats had already been at work for two years, building a network of alliances for England in the Low Countries. They had succeeded in making agreements with the Duke of Brabant, the Count of Hainault and Holland, and the Count of Gueldres, and most important of all, with the Emperor Louis IV. When Edward sailed with a host from Orwell in July 1338 he was able, therefore, to set up his headquarters immediately on landing at Antwerp, in the duchy of Brabant.

When Edward left England, the position in Flanders had already shifted in his favour. The disruption of industrial life which the embargo on the export of English wool, imposed in 1336, had caused in the great weaving centres of Ghent, Bruges and Ypres, meant that Count Louis's subjects could no longer afford to follow his example, and remain faithful to the French. At a great meeting in the monastery at Biloke their representatives agreed to adopt a scheme of armed neutrality put forward by Jacques van Artevelde of Ghent. In June 1338 they made terms with Edward's representatives, which won their merchants security in English ports and the towns of Holland and Brabant, and in return promised security to English ships in the ports of Flanders (provided they did not put soldiers ashore). Two years later, the exigencies of their commercial situation were to bring the confederation of Flemish towns, and Artevelde who was their 'captain general', into full alliance with Edward.

From Antwerp, Edward set out to meet his fellow ruler, the Emperor Louis, at Coblenz. A few days after their meeting on 15 September, Louis at Frankfurt formally appointed Edward his imperial vicar, with authority to exercise sovereign rights in the Empire and in any imperial land reconquered from the French, on Louis's behalf. This office also put Edward into an advantageous relationship with those of his other allies who were imperial subjects. As the emperor's representative he was their sovereign and, if they failed to fulfil the terms of their alliances, he could put them under the ban of Empire. Edward I in the 1290s had had difficulty in activating the support that he had been promised by the Rhenish princes, whom he had brought into a coalition essentially similar to that of 1338; Edward III could hope that he would not have to face quite the same problem.

Edward's relations with his allies, the emperor included, really depended, of course, on his promises to pay them pensions. If he could not pay them, all the agreements between them, the vicariate and everything else, would be null and void. Financial calculations were crucial to the whole scheme on which, at this stage, English hopes centred. In consequence, finance had far more to do with the course of the war in this phase than the largely abortive military operations that were undertaken. This means that in order to understand what happened to Edward and his coalition, we must start by examining the calculations on which his war finances were based.

The ordinary revenue of the crown at the beginning of the Hundred Years War was about £30,000 per annum, of which some £13,000 came from the customs. A lay subsidy would bring in about another £38,000, a clerical grant perhaps £19,000. These figures indicate a revenue position very comparable with that of Edward I, in the time of his wars. Like Edward I, Edward III initially found his subjects ready to be generous. At Nottingham in 1336 and at Westminster in the spring of 1337 he obtained ample subsidies; and the merchants granted him an extra subsidy (or *maltolte*) of 40s. on the sack of wool exported, over and above the customs. Edward III was, nonetheless, rather less well placed in 1337 than his grandfather had been in 1294. The Scottish campaigns had already faced him with very heavy expenses, and he had had to raise substantial loans. The biggest advances had come from the Bardi and the Peruzzi, bankers of Florence, and their loans were secured by assignments on the customs. Edward thus started at a disadvantage, and by September 1337 he was already pledged to pay pensions to allies, totalling over £124,000, by the end of the year. This expenditure, when added to the cost of maintaining the war in

Scotland, equipping a fleet and forces for service on the continent, and ordinarily recurrent items of expense, far outran the king's resources, even with the subsidies taken into account.

Edward's confidence in his ability to meet expenditure on a quite unprecedented scale was based on an ambitious and ingenious scheme to create and manipulate a royal monopoly in the export of wool. In the course of 1337 he struck a bargain with a syndicate representing the major English wool merchants, headed by William de la Pole and Reginald Conduit of London. This syndicate was granted a monopoly of export of wool, and powers of compulsory purchase from the producers (to whom a minimum price was guaranteed, but who were expected to allow the syndicate credit for payment until the wool was sold abroad). The embargo on the export of wool imposed in 1336 had stimulated demand in the continental markets, so that the syndicate was well placed to dictate the price as soon as the ban was lifted in their favour. A very handsome profit was to be expected, which the merchants agreed to share with the king. The wool was to be shipped to Dordrecht in Brabant, thus advantaging one of Edward's most valued continental allies, the Duke of Brabant. In order to make sure that the commercial *coup* envisaged was properly coordinated with the king's military diplomacy, a further agreement with the syndicate gave Edward's envoys in the Low Countries control over the disposal of the wool, and the right, if necessary, to buy it in from the merchants on the king's behalf. It was expected that this scheme would raise some £200,000 in cash for the king's war effort.

When the syndicate's first shipment of wool reached Dordrecht in November 1337, the king's envoys had already realized that he would not be able to pay the pensions due at the end of the year in full, and were negotiating postponements. The embargo on export was at this point just beginning to show signs of telling on the Flemings, so that it seemed desirable to maintain it. The merchants, on the other hand, naturally wished to sell their wool. After long and tricky negotiations, the king's envoys in the end exercised their right, and bought in the wool, paying the merchants a good price – but in notes of acknowledgement, to be 'cashed' by remission of duty on future exports. Most of these 'Dordrecht bonds' were in the end sold by their holders at a disastrous discount. The wool itself was sold by the king's representatives and raised a disappointing price. The merchants now refused to go forward any further with the scheme, which from their point of view had completely broken down. The king's envoys, having failed to realize enough cash, found themselves in a very ugly position, with clients whom they had no hope of satisfying seeking pay.

All this took place in the early months of 1338, before Edward set sail for the continent. In the spring parliament he obtained a grant of 20,000 sacks of wool, and on the strength of this raised new loans with the Bardi and Peruzzi. This cash, together with the proceeds of the sale of wool tided him over the crisis temporarily, and made it possible for him to go forward with his plans unchanged for the immediate future. But once he set foot on continental soil, his financial difficulties began to multiply again. The proceeds of the wool subsidy came in very slowly, and new loans had to be raised. In February 1339 Edward had to pledge the crown of England to the Archbishop of Trier. In May the Archbishop of Canterbury, the bishops of Durham and Lincoln, and the earls of Derby, Northampton, Suffolk and Salisbury made themselves personal sureties for a loan of 140,000 florins from the Bartolomei of Lucca. At about the same time Edward sent orders to the council in England to stop payment of all fees and pensions there, unless the recipients had no other source of income. So far, though Edward was having to pay his allies and his own forces, there had been no campaigning. In the late summer of 1339 they at last advanced, after much argument, into the Cambrésis, but the French would not meet the English and their allies in the field. In September the Count of Hainault abandoned both the army and his alliance. In the end Edward had to tell his allies to take their men home, and himself retired to Brussels, about £300,000 further into debt for a campaign, so called, that had achieved nothing.

Two events of the following year, 1340, were of considerable long-term significance. At the beginning of the year, the towns of Flanders finally entered into alliance with England. This meant breaking faith with their sovereign, King Philip, and it was partly to regularize their position that Edward at Ghent, on 26 January, solemnly assumed the arms and title of King of France. The implications of the step thus taken could not be confined to this immediate context, however. It made public and formal the claim that he had tentatively raised in 1337. From now on, it would be very hard to withdraw from that claim with honour, and from what it transformed into a dynastic confrontation, unless on highly advantageous terms. The second event took place in June, when Edward was returning from a brief visit to England to try to raise funds, and fell in with a great fleet of French and Genoese at Sluys. Though Edward's flotilla was heavily outnumbered, he decided to attack when the wind and tide turned in his favour. The English archers, firing into an enemy whose ships were crowded together, did terrible execution and the French fleet was virtually destroyed. The victory gave the English almost complete control of the Channel for years to come, and was long remembered by them as a notable judgement of God in their favour, in the quarrel with France. Neither event did much to alleviate the currently pressing difficulties for the English, however. The operations of Edward and his Flemish allies on land in the late summer were a disappointment. An attempt to besiege Tournai failed to take the city, and English, Brabançons and Flemings alike were all clamouring for pay. In September Edward found he had no option but to agree to a truce with Philip of France for a year, which was arranged at Esplechin through the mediation of Jeanne de Valois, the Dowager Countess of Hainault.

While Edward was abroad, the council that he had left to govern England in his absence was getting into more and more serious difficulties. Before he left, Edward had issued at Walton a series of ordinances concerning the administration of the realm. Their object was to reaffirm the royal prerogative, and to maintain the king's initiative in government in the military emergency while he was abroad, by subjecting the chancery and the exchequer to the stringent control of the privy seal; and also to ensure economy at the exchequer by careful audit and by disallowing exemptions from taxation and respites of debts to the crown. When Edward went abroad, taking the privy seal with him, the result was the opposite of that intended; the ordinances curtailed the initiative of the king's councillors in England, and their reactions were the less decisive in response to his needs because of them. The consequences of the economies that they imposed at the exchequer were besides highly unpopular, as was Edward's order to the exchequer in 1339 to stop payments of fees and pensions. Archbishop Stratford, who was sent home that year to explain the king's difficulties to the autumn parliament and to take over as chief of the council, found the estates ready to help the king, but insistent that his measures be modified, and that the *maltolte* on wool, which had been granted in 1336 without the commons' assent, should cease. On these conditions they would grant the king the tenth sheep and fleece and lamb in the land, provided a subsequent parliament would confirm the grant. In the spring of 1340 Edward himself was present in parliament, having obtained leave to be away from Brussels from the creditors to whom he was pledged (but he had to be back by midsummer). He was able to persuade parliament to increase its grant to a ninth for the years 1340 and 1341, and to continue the *maltolte* for fourteen months. But there were stringent conditions attached: that many debts and fines be pardoned; that purveyance be strictly controlled; that no aids should be taken in the kingdom without the assent of the commons in parliament. As Edward's debts mounted, the means to secure extra revenue from England were thus being steadily eroded. Even more galling, he had to consent to the appointment of a council, of which Stratford and the earls of Lancaster, Warenne and Huntingdon were to be members, with power to exercise the full royal authority in his absence. The Walton ordinances, one of whose prime objectives had been to maintain in the king's hands a tight royal control over the home government, thus became a dead letter; and Edward was probably not happy to see Stratford promoted to be virtually a chief councillor. The archbishop had already been encouraging his diocesans to resist royal demands for purveyance. But the commons were not prepared to make their grant unless the king met their conditions, and the appointment of this council was one of them; he had no option but to give way.

By the time that the truce of Esplechin was agreed, Edward III was bankrupt. He did not now dare to ask his creditors for permission to return again to England. As he could not stay on the continent as their virtual prisoner without serious damage to his prestige, he decided to slip away without consulting them. He arrived in England, unheralded, on 30 November 1340. He and those who had been with him in the Low Countries had put down their failures to lack of financial aid from England, and they put this down in turn to the ineffective reaction of the government at home. Edward in his anger was ready to lash out against all and any whom he believed responsible. The chancellor and the treasurer were removed immediately from their offices. Pole, Conduit and a number of other merchants were arrested; so were four judges of the common bench, and a general investigation into the conduct of lesser officials was ordered. Special commissions of *trailbaston* were appointed to make inquiries into all manner of misdemeanours and in particular to make sure that the ninth sheep, fleece and lamb granted by the spring parliament had been paid in full. Archbishop Stratford, who had been at the head of the council and against whom Edward and his intimates seem to have been specially incensed, was ordered to return to Brabant as a hostage for the king's debts.

Edward may well have had some justification for thinking that his servants in England had shown less energy than they ought to have done. But he made too little allowance for the difficulties against which they had to labour, and seriously misjudged the mood of his native kingdom. In the months before his return there had been something approaching a general refusal to pay further taxes. In Essex the sheriff had met armed resistance to the collection of the ninth. The council had feared revolt, writing to the king that 'the people would rise against them rather than contribute more'.[1] In these conditions, Edward's measures on his return only served to exacerbate bitterness, and to rouse popular sympathy for the victims of his purge. In London the inquiries of the justices of *trailbaston* were resisted with violence. The situation seemed to herald a return to the bad old days of Edward II.

Archbishop Stratford, the man against whom the king's rage was most bitter, had taken the measure of things far better than his master. He resolutely refused all summonses to appear before the king and his counsellors: he would answer charges against him before his peers in parliament, he said, not elsewhere. He replied to the broadsheet denunciation of his mismanagement as chief councillor which the king's men put out (the *Libellus Famosus*) in a series of letters which were aimed to broaden the issues between them, and which succeeded in putting across Stratford himself as the champion of all sectors of discontent.[2] He protested against infringements of Magna Carta by the king's judges of *trailbaston*. He insisted on the right of peers and ministers to have their offences examined in parliament. He stressed the privilege of the clergy of being taxed separately from the laity. These protests, which are full of echoes of the constitutional propaganda of Edward II's day, struck the chords of popular sympathy much more surely than the counter claims of the king and the little circle of advisers who had been abroad with him. Stratford succeeded in his object of broadening the issues involved in the crisis to the point where there was no alternative to summoning the parliament that he demanded.

What happened in this spring parliament of 1341 underlined the strength of Stratford's position and the weakness of the king's. Edward's intimates, William Kilsby the keeper of the privy seal, Sir John Darcy the steward of the household, and Bishop Orleton of Winchester were unable to swing the focus away from the issues of principle that the archbishop had raised. Edward wisely bowed before there was a storm. The commissions of *trailbaston* were withdrawn, and the king promised that infringements of the charters should be redressed by the peers in parliament. He promised too that peers should not be judged except in parliament, and that the officers of state should be appointed and sworn there. The statutes of the parliament of 1340 were confirmed and upheld, and the ninth was commuted to a grant of 30,000 sacks of wool. Finally, the charges against Stratford were sent for consideration to a commission of peers, including the earls of Arundel and Warenne who had spoken out on his behalf early in the parliament. Afterwards they were quietly shelved. The king and the archbishop were formally reconciled, and the other officials who had suffered in the recent purge were forgiven. The king withdrew on all the matters which had given rise to complaint, and the crisis was at an end.

The crisis of 1341, and the failure of the king's ambitious attempt to bring together a great confederation of continental pensioners against the Valois, must be viewed together. If the confederation was to mean anything in military terms it had got to be financed out of monies raised in England, from subsidies in wool or ready cash, and by means of the monopoly of the export of wool. It was in order to maintain strict control of these resources that Edward imposed such severe limits on the discretion of the exchequer in his Walton ordinances. When he found himself deserted by most of his allies and hopelessly in debt, and was forced to agree to the truce of Esplechin, Edward's angry reaction was to assume that his councillors in England had failed him. That this was not the real trouble was shown by the crisis that was already brewing before his return, and that climaxed in the confrontation with Stratford. What was really wrong was that Edward and his advisers had grossly miscalculated both the profitability of the monopoly of wool export, and the rate of taxation that his English subjects would tolerate. In consequence of these miscalculations he lost his allies; ruined his bankers, the Bardi and Peruzzi, on whose loans he defaulted; and very nearly provoked serious civil confrontations in his own kingdom.

Nevertheless, Edward weathered the storm surprisingly well. He did not worry overmuch about the fate of his bankers. The crisis at home passed over, and by October 1341 he felt so strong again that he repealed the statutes of the spring parliament on his own authority, on the ground that they had been made against his will and at a moment when he had no true freedom of action.[3] This was the same ground on which Edward I had sought absolution from his promise to observe unwelcome rules; Edward III, significantly, did not bother to refer to the pope as his grandfather had done but acted on his own authority. Nevertheless, he showed that he had learnt his lesson. He bore no malice against Stratford, who was readmitted to his intimacy and served the king loyally for the rest of his life. Edward never again sought to raise money in his kingdom on quite the scale that he had in the years 1336 to 1340, and he did not try to rebuild the continental confederacy of which he had hoped so much. He did not, of course, withdraw from his quarrel with the Valois, but prepared to prosecute it in a different way.

'In these days the king became very friendly with the men of Flanders, and he took to himself the title of King of France and England, and changed his seal, quartering thereon the arms of France with those of England. And the communes of Flanders made obedience to him as King of France, for they dared not do otherwise, because the pope had laid an interdict on all Flanders, to take effect if they should rebel against the King of France.'[4] This is how the chronicler Murimuth described Edward's formal assumption of the title of King of France, at Ghent in January 1340. He was not the only contemporary who explained Edward's action as motivated by the need to give some colour of legality to the alliance that the Flemings were making with him, but its implications were clearly much wider, as has already been suggested. Edward's following moves make it evident that he was fully aware of this, and intended to exploit his dynastic claim in a way that would carry the war into the enemy's camp with a vengeance.

On 8 February at Ghent he issued a proclamation, addressed to the bishops, peers, counts, barons and all the people of France. This proclamation was subtly worded, and contained the seed of a new diplomatic strategy for the struggle against the Valois.

Edward's proclamation was to the people of France at large, and told them that he had now resolved to take up 'the burden of government' of that kingdom, as the heir of 'Charles of famous memory, the last King of France'. Referring to the usurpation of his right by Philip of Valois, who had taken unlawful advantage of his youth in 1328, he was now ready, he declared, to receive into his homage all those who would follow the example 'of our beloved and faithful men of Flanders', and forget their past obedience to the intruder. As king, he promised, he would govern according to 'the good laws and customs which were observed in the time of our ancestor St Louis'. This, and other more specific promises, to strengthen the coinage, to limit the burden of taxation, to seek the advice of the nobles of the realm over its government, were the subtle parts of Edward's message. For this part of his proclamation echoes directly the demands for the maintenance of ancient rights and privileges, which the provincial leagues had made of King Philip IV in 1314, and of Philip V in 1317. To anyone in France, who, for whatever reason, was unsatisfied with the rule of the Valois, Edward offered here a justification, not just in terms of convenience but of principle, for changing allegiance.

Edward had good reason to believe that there would be those who would be willing to give ear to his promises. Robert of Artois, lately one of Philip's most influential subjects, was now his pensioner. In Flanders he had brought a whole province over to his side. Before the truce of Esplechin expired, he found another very important French ally besides these. In April 1341 John Duke of Brittany died, and his succession was contested between Charles of Blois, who had married a daughter of one of Duke John's brothers, and John de Montfort, the duke's younger brother. Both laid their claims before Philip's *Parlement*. De Montfort was in a difficult position, however; he knew that the custom of the duchy would favour his claim, but he knew also that the king had arranged the marriage of Charles of Blois, who was Philip's nephew, with a view to securing the inheritance for him. This situation was precisely of the kind that

Edward must have had in mind when he issued his Ghent proclamation. Before Philip's judgement in favour of Charles had been formally given, de Montfort had recognized Edward as King of France, and Edward had recognized him as Duke of Brittany.

John de Montfort himself had the misfortune to fall into the hands of his enemies at Nantes in November 1341, but his duchess Margaret rallied his supporters against the troops of Charles of Blois. By March of the next year a small force of English soldiers, led by Sir Walter Manny, was in Brittany. In the autumn Edward himself appeared there, with a host. Although the English did not achieve much in the field, Philip and Charles, with a superior army, failed to dislodge them from the duchy. They still held their foothold there in the spring of 1343, when a new truce for three years was agreed at Malestroit. The English were in consequence in a much happier position than they had been when the truce of Esplechin was sealed in 1340. In the three year interim now afforded them, both sides undertook to seek a final peace through the pope's mediation.

Edward had reasons to be glad of a truce in 1343. In England memories of the crisis of 1341 were still green, and he knew that many people had no relish for more costly campaigns. Domestic pressures demanded that he make at least the motions of seeking peace. The attitude of the papacy was also worrying; the new pope, Clement VI, was bent on a pacification, and some of the king's advisers feared that if Edward was not cooperative he might be excommunicated. This would be a diplomatic disaster, since it would give the French cause the standing almost of a crusade. Besides, it seemed a good moment to embark on serious negotiations. The situation for the English was more favourable than it had been in 1340, and they could set their price for peace high.

The confidence of the English was well demonstrated at the formal peace conferences which were held at Avignon in 1344, under the presidency of Pope Clement. So also were the diplomatic advantages which Edward's formal claim to the French crown had secured. The English negotiators had clearly been instructed to see, if possible, what the French would offer in the way of terms, and it took the pope a long time to draw them into making any suggestion of their own. In the end they agreed to do so, and stated that the surrender to the king of England of full sovereignty in Gascony might be a good start towards a peace. To the objection that this would mean that Philip must divest himself of an integral part of his royal inheritance, they replied that the French ought to be ready to consent to 'such a bisection, . . . seeing that the quarrel between the kings was about their right to the whole kingdom of France'.[5] They made it quite clear that, if their king were to compromise at all over his claim to the crown, it must be in return for sovereign rights in part of France at least. From this position the English only wavered to the extent of agreeing to send home for further instructions. This was at the end of November 1344, and by then the war was well on its way to reopening in earnest.

Much had happened to alter the diplomatic and military outlook since the truce of Malestroit had been agreed, and most of the changes played in Edward's favour. In 1343 Oliver de Clisson, of a famous and powerful Breton family, had been arrested in Paris and executed at Philip VI's orders. A group of Breton nobles who were captured later in the year suffered the same fate. Among them were two members of the important family of Malestroit. The effect of these executions was to reaffirm the spirit of provincial independence among the Breton nobility, not to crush it. Philip's victims had besides relatives and con-nexions outside Brittany, and disaffection from the Valois began to spread beyond the duchy. Godfrey, Count of Harcourt in Normandy, threw over his sovereign and came to Brittany to do homage to Edward's representatives. He was only one of a number of leading Normans who were suspected of being involved with the English at the time. It began to look as if the loyalty of a third French province, besides Flanders and Brittany, might be undermined.

In England too Edward felt more in control of the situation. The repeal of the statutes of the 1341 parliament had caused no repercussions. The mood of the people, and especially of the noblemen who were close to him, was not pacific. At the parliament held in June 1344 Edward was able to present the execution of the Breton *seigneurs* as a sure sign that the French did not mean to keep the truce. They were determined, he said, to destroy every ally of England. This propaganda had its effect, and the estates approved generous grants against the probable reopening of the war.

It had become clear by the end of 1344 that the peace conference at Avignon would not achieve a settlement. In the summer of 1345 Edward declared that he regarded himself as no longer bound by the truce, because the proceedings against his Breton allies had rendered it void. In the new conditions, which his efforts to detach leading Frenchmen from the Valois allegiance had created, he found himself able to operate against his enemy on exterior lines. Three English noblemen, Henry de Grosmont Earl of Derby, William de Bohun Earl of Northampton and Hugh Hastings, were appointed royal lieutenants in Gascony, Brittany and Flanders respectively. The armies they commanded were raised partly in England (largely by means of voluntary contracts, or indentures, and by the leaders themselves), and partly among the natives of the provinces in question. Henry of Derby's campaign in Gascony opened with notable successes; Bergerac, La Réole and finally Angoulême all fell into his hands.

These successes offset the effects of the deaths of two of Edward's allies in 1345: Jacques van Artevelde, who was murdered in Ghent in July, and John de Montfort, who died in September leaving an infant son heir to his claims in Brittany. In 1346 Edward determined to lead a host to France himself. Most of the greatest noblemen who were not already in France were with him when he sailed from Porchester in July. The destination of the expedition was not known until the last moment, and many assumed it would be Gascony; but it was in Normandy, at St Waast la Hogue, that the king landed.

'The people of Normandy have not been used to war; you shall find great towns that have not been walled, whereby your men shall have such gain that they shall be the better twenty years after.'[6] These are the words with which, according to Froissart, Godfrey de Harcourt urged the king to make a descent on the northern French coast. The form that the campaign took was a *chevauchée*, a large scale raiding expedition planned and conducted on lines that became a key element in the English way of waging war for the rest of Edward III's reign, and beyond. Penetrating deep into enemy territory, the host spread out across as broad a front as tactical prudence would allow and moved swiftly, destroying dwellings and plundering the countryside and town suburbs as it passed. There was no pausing to besiege walled cities or to garrison strong places taken, and the problem of victualling was solved by living off the land. With good fortune, plunder taken might make a substantial contribution to defraying the costs of the expedition; it also opened for the individual soldier alluring hopes of enriching himself through gains of war. Strategically, the objectives of a *chevauchée* were twofold, to undermine French morale, and confidence in their royal leadership, and to damage lethally the tax paying potential toward war expenditure of the provinces through which the expedition passed. If these two objectives were sufficiently achieved, the effect should be such as to bring the adversary to the negotiating table, in a mood to make concessions in order to halt the mayhem. There is debate as to whether the *chevauchée* strategy, as followed by the English in Edward III's time, had a further objective, to force the adversary to risk a pitched battle, defeat in which would increase the pressure on him to seek terms. In 1346, at least, there is evidence that Edward III was indeed hoping to force King Philip into a decisive engagement, provided he could do so on ground and in conditions that would advantage him.

That was how the campaign of 1346 turned out. Hurrying across Normandy, the English met only ineffective resistance at St Lo, Carentan and Caen: all these towns were sacked and an immense plunder taken. Pushing on toward Rouen, Edward found that Philip was waiting with a large force, and was turned south along the Seine. He managed to cross the river at Poissy, and made for the Somme; but when he reached it, Philip was close on his heels and it was clear that there would be an engagement. At Crecy, on 26 August, Edward halted to face his enemy on shrewdly selected ground. In the battle that followed that afternoon the French made the fatal error of attacking archers in a strong defensive position. Under a hail of arrows, the successive waves of their attack became entangled with one another. Their casualties were terrible; they included John, the blind king of Bohemia, the Duke of Lorraine, the counts of Blois and Flanders and Nevers; no one bothered to count the host of lesser men slain, says the chronicler Geoffrey Le Baker.[7] Philip himself escaped from the fatal field as darkness fell, and Edward was left in possession as victor, free to march on whither he would.

The *chevauchée* thus victoriously concluded, there was time now and the opportunity to further humiliate the enemy, by wresting from him an important maritime city. On 4 September Edward and his army appeared before Calais, and settled down to a siege that was to last nearly a year. It was easy here for the English to bring over reinforcements, and also to make contact with the Flemings, who held markets in the host twice a week and virtually supplied it. Philip made one effort to relieve the town, but retreated after reconnoitring the English position. On 4 August 1347 the town was surrendered unconditionally. Virtually all the inhabitants were evacuated, and Calais became, in a few years, an English military and mercantile colony. It remained so for nearly two hundred years.

While the king was busy about his campaign in the north of France, his lieutenants elsewhere were winning other notable successes in his cause. Henry de Grosmont was for a time in 1346 besieged in Aiguillon, but he was able to recoup his losses later and to take the important town of St Jean d'Angely. In the autumn of the same year, the Scots, true to their Valois alliance, attacked northern England, and were met at Neville's Cross near Durham by the Archbishop of York and the barons of the north. Their army was destroyed in the battle, and David Bruce their king was taken prisoner. Finally, in June 1347, Sir Thomas Dagworth, who had succeeded the Earl of Northampton as Edward's lieutenant in Brittany, defeated Charles of Blois at La Roche Derrien, and took him prisoner. When, in September at Calais, a new truce was agreed between the French and the English and all their allies, the English were triumphant in every sphere of the war.

By the autumn of 1347 the English had made just about as much effort as, for the time being, they were capable of doing. Edward, when he came home, had to face complaints of misgovernment in his absence, and against the means that he had used to raise men and money, just as he had done in 1340. But in the aftermath of so many English triumphs these troubles could not be as serious as they had then been. They had been triumphs of sufficient stature to alter the whole shape of the Anglo-French struggle. Crecy was an epic victory. Before the battle the French leaders had been so confident 'that each asked for particular Englishmen to be allotted them as prisoners',[7a] says Le Baker; after it, the pride of French chivalry was broken and ruined. At Calais Edward took one of the strongest and richest of the French Channel ports, after everyone had seen that the French king would not dare to try to break up his siege. The noise of these things went abroad through Europe. It is no accident that a year after the fall of Calais a party among the princes of Germany was trying to persuade Edward to interest himself in the imperial crown (which he wisely declined to do). The victories of 1346 and 1347 made Edward's name as a conqueror and a leader of chivalry: after them, there could be no more hopes – such as Pope Clement VI had entertained in 1344 – of reordering relations between the kings of France and England as they had been in the time of the last Capetian king.

The terms which in 1354 at Guines were proposed as the basis for a final peace and were accepted as such by Pope Innocent VI's mediator, the Cardinal of Boulogne, give a measure of the English achievement of the late 1340s. Seven years of desultory and occasional fighting had by then made no great alteration to the military situation of 1347. What was proposed was that Edward should renounce his claim to the throne of France; in return he should receive, in full sovereignty, Aquitaine and Poitou, Anjou, Maine, Touraine, and the march of Calais. Secret instructions that were given to Henry de Grosmont, now Duke of Lancaster, and the Earl of Arundel, as Edward's personal representatives to the pope, make it clear that Edward regarded the cession of these lands to him with full sovereignty in the light of compensation for resigning the title of King of France. The compensation was certainly commensurate with the magnificence of the title he was to lose; it would make him a king in France, if not of France. It entailed the virtual dismemberment of the Valois kingdom. That the pope and his cardinals, and even the advisers of John, who had succeeded his father Philip on the French throne, could contemplate the possibility of such a settlement is an index of how mightily Edward had advanced his cause since the early days of the war.

The treaty of Guines was in fact never ratified. It is not entirely clear what went wrong, but it seems that the English at Avignon became suspicious of the pope's good faith and thought that the French would not, in fact, renounce sovereignty in the lands they were to cede. In consequence, Henry of Lancaster refused on Edward's behalf to renounce the title of King of France. Instead of peace being made, the war reopened in earnest.

This was probably not unwelcome from the English point of view. People were already beginning to learn that they might make themselves fortunes out of the spoils of war, and young men were growing up, like Edward the Black Prince, who were anxious to make a name for themselves martially. New opportunities of exploiting domestic discord in France seemed also to be opening for the English. King John was repeating the mistakes of his father Philip. He had become involved in a complicated quarrel with Charles, King of Navarre, who was also Count of Evreux in Normandy and had great estates there and in Picardy. He and Lancaster had met at Avignon, and discussed plans which would virtually give the English control of Normandy. Nothing came of these discussions, and Charles and his sovereign were temporarily reconciled. Then on 5 April 1356, King John broke into the chamber where Charles was dining with the dauphin at Rouen, and took him prisoner. The Count of Harcourt and three or four others of Charles's intimates were executed on the spot. Though Charles remained a prisoner, his brother Philip immediately went over to the English and did homage to King Edward, who despatched forces to Normandy to his aid and that of the Harcourts.

The decisive action of the year 1356 was not in Normandy, but south and west. A year before, the Black Prince, now his father's lieutenant in Aquitaine, had led a great *chevauchée* into Languedoc, in which more spoil was won than in any previous campaign of the war. This summer he set out on another raid, north towards the Loire, probably hoping to effect a junction with Henry of Lancaster who was now commanding for the English in Brittany and lower Normandy. The appearance of King John at the head of a large army forced Lancaster to retreat, however. The Prince, falling back towards Gascony, found that John had turned to attend to him, and having outmarched him, was barring his way at Maupertuis near Poitiers. On Sunday 18 September Cardinal Talleyrand of Perigord failed to mediate terms between the two commanders, and on Monday a great battle took place. The Prince's archers were skilfully disposed in a strong defensive position, and as at Crecy, repulsed a cavalry charge with loss; the French then advanced against them on foot, with still more fatal results. They were overwhelmed completely. In the closing stages of the battle, 'when all around men were running and securing prisoners', King John himself was discovered in a throng of English and Gascons who were quarrelling for the greatest prize of all. He, and a host of other well-born prisoners, all worth great ransoms, were carried with the vast spoils of the expedition to Bordeaux. There a truce was agreed for two years, and the Prince and his royal prisoner sailed for London.

After Poitiers, it must have looked as if Edward would take all. His chief adversary was a captive in his hands. In kingless France government began to disintegrate. The royal council was bitterly attacked by the Estates General; the Parisians took arms and virtually held the dauphin a prisoner. They also released Charles of Navarre from John's prison, and the capital became the centre of a dangerous struggle for power between him and the dauphin. The truce of Bordeaux hardly gave a genuine respite from war. English soldiers in Normandy simply exchanged the banner and war cry of St George for those of Navarre and went on fighting. They found they could live well enough without pay by plundering, putting men to ransom, and levying tribute in the countryside round the castles that they held. 'Free companies' of soldiers in Brittany and in central France acted in a like manner. In these circumstances Edward came to the legitimate conclusion that he might, by a final effort at a crucial moment, be able to win the whole kingdom. A first attempt at settlement between him and John had broken down because the French could not even collect the first instalment of a ransom for their ruler. A second draft treaty was in such preposterous terms that it was probably meant to be refused by the French, and so furnish better excuse for taking to arms again. The English royal host assembled at Calais in the late summer of 1359, and was swelled with adventurers from Germany and the Low Countries who were anxious to be in at the death. Edward's objective was Rheims, and a gold crown, for use at his coronation there, was with his baggage.

Edward was baulked of his ultimate ambition. He reached Rheims, but failed to force an entry into the city and fell back in the spring towards Calais, harassed by French companies as he marched. Sickness also thinned the ranks of what had been a host twice the size of that which the Prince had commanded at Poitiers, and he must have known that another campaign on the same grand scale would be out of the question for the present. So, when the dauphin's agents proposed negotiations, he was ready to talk of peace in earnest. Within a week the envoys who met at Brétigny near Chartres had agreed the draft of a treaty between the two kingdoms.[8]

This treaty was ratified by the two kings, John and Edward, at Calais in October. John's ransom had been fixed at Brétigny at 3,000,000 crowns and the first instalment of 600,000 was paid before the ratification. Edward promised to renounce his claim to the throne of France. In return he obtained full sovereign rights in a new and broader Gascony, swelled by the addition to the ancient duchy of Poitou, Quercy, Limousin and the Agenais, and also in the march of Calais and in the counties of Ponthieu, Montreuil and Guines in the north. This was far from all that Edward had sometimes hoped for, and much less than he had been offered in 1358. It did not give him any right in Normandy, or the suzerainty over Brittany, both of which he had his eye on. But it made him sovereign in very large parts of what had once been France.

Edward was undoubtedly wise to accept the terms agreed at Brétigny as a settlement. He might have been tempted by the disarray of his enemies to press on in spite of difficulties, but he had learned now not to strain his resources too far. He had never, after the crisis of 1341, tried to raise taxation on the scale that he had in early years; and militarily, as the war went on, he had depended more and more for success on the support of allies in France, and on the free companies who wrought havoc in his enemies' lands without costing him anything. This strategy of waging war on the cheap enabled him to steer clear of dangerous domestic confrontations with his parliaments over issues of taxation and recruitment. But it also made Edward perforce an opportunist, who had to trim the horizon of his ambitions to the circumstances of the moment and the opportunities that they afforded. At Brétigny, he did just that.

There is one curious feature about the Treaty of Brétigny which, when one is considering what Edward had achieved in 1360, must not be overlooked. When the two kings met at Calais in October to ratify the Brétigny agreements, the clauses concerning the renunciations which they were to make, respectively of the title of King of France and of the sovereignty of the lands ceded to the English, were removed from the main treaty and dealt with in a separate document. This postponed the fulfilment of these clauses until November 1361.[9] This was a sensible step, as Edward naturally wished to be in actual possession of the lands in question before he formally renounced his title, and their transfer was bound to take time. When November 1361 came round, however, the renunciations were not made; indeed they were never formally exchanged. Technically therefore, Edward never renounced the title of King of France, and John never renounced sovereignty over Gascony. It was the English, apparently deliberately, who were responsible for delaying the exchange of renunciations. This has led some historians to suggest that Edward was not in earnest at Brétigny or Calais. He had done badly in the campaign of 1359–60 and knew he could no longer get what he had been offered a year before. But he had not given up hope, it is suggested, of pursuing his wider claim again one day under better auspices, and was therefore anxious not to renounce his French title. By delaying this issue, he managed, not very honestly, to keep his options open.

That Edward was pleased to leave himself some loophole which would allow him to resuscitate his claims some day is likely enough. The point, however, should not be stressed too far. Edward in fact ceased to use the title King of France after 1360, and did not employ it again for eight years, until the war began again. Through this period, he appeared quite content with the settlement he had achieved. It was the French king in the end who, by receiving in his court the appeals of Edward's Gascon subjects, the counts of Armagnac and Albret, took advantage of the non-fulfilment of the renunciations treaty. It was only when the French made it quite clear that they still claimed sovereignty that Edward revived his claim to the throne.

Privately, Edward in 1360 may have been disappointed that he had not won more from his adversary. Nevertheless, he had won what all contemporaries agreed was a signal triumph. 'When the noble Edward gained England in his youth', wrote Jean le Bel, 'nobody thought much of the English. . . . Now they are the finest and most daring warriors known to man.'[10] Edward had challenged the proudest kingdom in Europe and humbled her rulers in war. He had made himself sovereign lord in the lands in France where his father and his grandfather had been vassals, and in lands where they had never been lords at all. He had won control of the seas between England and France where Bretons and Picards had long preyed on English shipping. He had held the king of Scots his prisoner, and afterwards the king of France, and forced them (at Brétigny) to abandon their old alliance. He had achieved with all this the glamour of martial success in battles that had become famous wherever chivalry was honoured, Sluys, Crecy, Poitiers. If he modelled his court on that of Arthur, the British conqueror of long ago, it could seem only just and fitting for him to do so.

In Edward's time, the English chronicler wrote, 'to live was as if to reign: and his fame sprang so far that it came into heathendom and Barbary, showing and telling that in no land under heaven has been brought forth so noble a king.'[11] The commons in parliament were of the same opinion. 'Sire, the commons thank their liege lord as far as they know how . . . [and] from their hearts entirely thank God who has given them such a lord and governor, who has delivered them from servitude to other lands and delivered them from the charges suffered by them in time past.'[12] Looking back beyond his victories over the French and Scots to the disasters of the war of St Sardos and the years after Bannockburn, they might well speak thus. If Edward had died in 1360, he would be remembered as one of England's most successful medieval rulers – even though he had not won the French crown.

Notes

1   *The French Chronicle of London*, ed. G. J. Aungier (Camden Soc., 1844), p. 83; for the troubles in Essex see *C.C.R. 1339–41*, p. 536.

2   See *Foed.* vol. V, p. 225 (*Libellus*), and Birchington in *Anglia Sacra*, ed. H. Wharton (London, 1691), vol. I, pp. 27–36.

3   *Foed.* vol. V, p. 281.
4   *Chron A. Murimuth* (R.S.), p. 103.
5   K. de L. vol. XVIII, p. 243; see also pp. 242, 245–6.
6   K. de L. vol. IV, p. 381.
7   *Chron G. Le Baker*, p. 85.
7a ibid. p. 82.
8   *Foed.* vol. VI, pp. 178–96.
9   ibid. pp. 237–46.
10 Jean le Bel, *Chronique,* ed. J. Viard and E. Déprez (Paris, 1904), vol. I, pp. 155–6.
11 *The Brut*, ed. F. W. D. Brie (E.E.T.S., 1908), p. 334.
12 *R.P.* vol. II, p. 276.

Note on secondary reading (post 1970)

C.T. Allmand, *The Hundred Years War: England and France at War c. 1300– c. 1450* (Cambridge, 1988) and A. Curry, *The Hundred Years War* (London, 1993) provide useful general introductions to the history of the great Anglo-French conflict. J. Sumption, in *The Hundred Years War*, vol. I (*Trial by Battle*, London, 1990) and vol. II (*Trial by Fire*, 1999) provides detailed narrative of the period covered in this chapter. The Black Prince's career is described by R. Barber, *Edward, Prince of Wales and Aquitaine* (Woodbridge, 1978). Two books that are interpretively original and significant are A. Ayton, *Knights and Warhorses: Military Service and the English Aristocracy under Edward III* (Woodbridge, 1994), and C. Rogers, *War Cruel and Sharp: English Strategy under Edward III, 1327–1360* (Woodbridge, 2000); the latter greatly expands the themes outlined in his 'Edward III and the dialectics of strategy, 1327–60' in *T.R.H.S.*, 6th series, vol. 4 (1994): his *The Wars of Edward III: Sources and Interpretations* (Woodbridge, 1999) is also useful. The collection edited by Anne Curry and Michael Hughes, *Arms, Armies and Fortifications in the Hundred Years War* (Woodbridge, 1994) contains valuable essays, by A. Ayton on English armies, by M. Bennett on battle tactics, by R. Hardy on the longbow and by W. Ormrod on the domestic response to the war.

Two books that are useful on military topics are M.C. Prestwich, *Armies and Warfare in the Middle Ages: The English Experience* (London and New Haven, 1996) and K.R. De Vries, *Infantry Warfare in the Early Fourteenth Century* (Woodbridge, 1996). On archery specifically, see J. Bradbury, *The Medieval Archer* (Woodbridge, 1985), and C. Rogers, 'The efficacy of the English longbow: a reply to Kelly De Vries', *War in History*, vol. 5 (1998).

On the issue of whether Edward III really aimed and hoped to secure the crown of France, see the articles by J. Le Patourel cited in the main bibliography Section 3c; and J.J.N. Palmer, 'The war arms of the protagonists and the negotiations for peace', in K. Fowler (ed.) *The Hundred Years War* (London, 1971).

Edward III's efforts to build a grand continental alliance against France and the ensuing domestic crisis of 1340–1 constitute an individual section in this chapter. On the financial aspects consult G.L. Harriss, *King, Parliament and Public Finance to 1369* (Oxford, 1975), and E.B. Fryde, 'Parliament and the

French War, 1336–40', in T.A. Sandquist and M.R. Powicke (eds.), *Essays in Medieval History presented to Bertie Wilkinson* (Toronto, 1969), and see also Fryde's article in *History*, vol. 37 (1952). On the constitutional crisis, see N.M. Fryde, 'Edward III's removal of his ministers and judges, 1340–1', *B.I.H.R.*, vol. 48 (1975). On the continental alliances, see M. Vale, 'The Anglo-French Wars, 1294–1340: allies and alliances', in P. Contamine *et al* (eds.) *Guerre et Société en France, en Angleterre et en Bourgogne, xive-xve Siècle* (Lille, 1991).

7 England under Edward III 1330–1360

Twenty years of war had very important consequences for Edward III's subjects in England. The whole framework of their lives, their prosperity, the opportunities which could open for them, and their outlook, were all affected by the experience. Other factors too helped to make the period important in domestic history. The peers were acquiring new privileges, the commons in parliament a greater independence as a result of the part that they played in granting taxes. And in 1348 the Black Death struck England, with consequences which affected the lives of people at every social level. Its effects were in fact so far reaching that they will have to be dealt with in a separate chapter.

Edward deliberately sought to associate his people with his war policies, and his propaganda was both imaginative and effective. His war was given maximum publicity. Whenever parliament met, proceedings were opened with a speech from one of his officials, usually the chancellor or the treasurer, which was taken as an opportunity to remind the estates of the justice of the king's cause, and the need to support his exertions. On occasion veterans of the campaigns who were also intimates of the king were brought in to address them; thus Bartholomew Burghersh came into parliament in 1343 to talk about the campaign in Brittany, and in 1355 Walter Manny appeared to explain how the negotiations at Avignon had broken down because of the deceit of the French, and the king had had to go to war again. When the king was abroad, he kept in constant touch with his councillors, and sent home from time to time reports of his doings, which were to be read out in fairs and markets and other public places. In response to requests from the king, the archbishops and bishops were constantly instructing the clergy of their dioceses to offer prayers for the safety and success of the king's armies, or to thank God for his victories. In 1346 Edward wrote to the Prior Provincial of the Dominicans, explaining to him and to his order the justice of his claim to the French throne, so that they might preach of the matter at large.[1] Sermons and the prayers and intercessions that people heard in church kept the fortunes of the war constantly before their minds, and taught them to associate the king's victories with God's favour to the English.

The subject matter of the proclamations and speeches, through which the king and his advisers appealed for popular support, repays attention. The justice of his quarrel and his faith in God's favour were always to the fore: 'So we hope, by the aid of Jesus Christ our Lord, that we shall do battle shortly in the field, in this our just quarrel, to our honour and that of all our realm, and therefore we beg that you will pray for us devoutly.' Thus Edward wrote to his subjects from Calais in 1347.[2] In other documents one will find a good deal of careful explanation of the legal basis of the king's claims in France. There was much talk of the deceit of the French and their refusal to offer or accept terms reasonable and honourable to the English. One item in propaganda intended for domestic consumption is particularly striking – the labouring of the aggressive intentions of the French. In his letter of 1346 to the Dominican Prior Provincial, Edward described Philip VI as determined 'to root out the English tongue' from the face of the world. A genuine plan for the invasion of England, which was found at Caen by the king's host in that same year but which was undoubtedly drawn up at a much earlier date, was put to endless use. It was read aloud to the next parliament, and represented as a plan of that very year.[3] Of course the French did consider plans for invading England, more than once, but none of them came to very much. Edward and his advisers clearly appreciated the value of the advice that Hobbes later gave to rulers who wished to create solidarity of feeling among their subjects, to 'bring distant terrors near'.

The manner in which Edward sought to associate with his own cause the aspirations of the knights and nobles who were his captains shows his handling of public relations at its most positive, and also at its most imaginative. These were men who understood the same language as the king himself. Edward was careful to make sure that glory won in the field was for them as well as him. In the parliament of 1337, when it was known that war was imminent, six new earls were created, all men who were to be prominent among the king's military lieutenants. Henry de Grosmont became Earl of Derby; William Montagu, Earl of Salisbury; Hugh Audley, Earl of Gloucester; William Clinton, Earl of Huntingdon; William Bohun, Earl of Northampton; Robert Ufford, Earl of Suffolk. In 1346, when Edward landed at La Hogue, his first act was to make his son Edward a knight, and with him he knighted the lords Roger Mortimer, William Montagu the younger and William Roos. The prospect of winning fame in the field in France had a natural allure to an aristocracy brought up from youth to martial pursuits. Froissart tells a story that illuminates a typical attitude, of forty young knights of England at Valenciennes in 1339, who all wore a silk patch over one eye, because they had vowed among the ladies of England to see with one eye only until each had performed some deed of arms in France.[4] The making of knights in the field, the chivalrous ceremonial of the royal court, the great tournaments and feasts that Edward held, and such pageants as the torchlight procession of knights at Bristol in 1358, all served to encourage a martial and adventurous enthusiasm which could be channelled into war service.

It was after the great tournament at Windsor in 1344 that Edward laid the foundations for what was to become his Order of the Garter. His original plans were for a society of 300 knights, bound together as companions by their oaths to aid and support one another and the sovereign of the order, and modelled on the fellowship of knights of Arthur's round table. In the event, the order that he finally instituted (probably in 1349), was much smaller, twenty-six companions in all, and under the patronage not of Arthur, but of St George. The first companions were all men who had distinguished themselves in the campaigns of 1345–7; the Black Prince, the earls of Salisbury, March and Warwick, Sir John Chandos, and the Gascon Captal de Buch were all founder members. Other famous captains, as Walter Manny and Sir Thomas Felton soon joined them. The code of chivalry of the Arthurian fellowship of romance, which remained the ideal for Edward's order, taught that the first duties of a knight were to serve his lord loyally and to uphold the cause of right. The legendary heroes won their fame not by patriotic self-sacrifice, but rather in the vendettas of those who had been injured in their rights. This was the way in which Edward and his captains spoke and thought about their war too; it was his 'just quarrel', which he had 'undertaken', to recover his 'rights and heritage', in which he hoped with God's aid to do battle and to have a good issue of it. Much that would otherwise be puzzling about Edward's war and his aims in it becomes understandable if we remember that he and his companions thought in terms of chivalrous and honourable enterprise, rather than of modern national ambition.

Besides glory and adventure, the war held out prospects of more solid and material advantage to those who served actively in the hosts. There was the hope, for the leaders at any rate, of winning heritages for themselves overseas. Henry de Grosmont added to his estates the lordship of Bergerac in Gascony; John Chandos obtained fiefs in the Cotentin; Robert Knowles made himself a great *seigneur* in Brittany. For all, high and low alike, there was the prospect of loot, and plunder was always at least a subsidiary objective of even the great royal expeditions. 'In Normandy', Godfrey de Harcourt is said to have told Edward III, 'you shall find great towns that have not been walled, whereby your men shall find such gain that they shall be the better twenty years after.'[5] The gains which some men won lasted even longer: William Berkeley told John Leland in the sixteenth century that his house at Beverstone was built out of the ransoms that his great grandfather won at Poitiers.[6]

Ransoms provided the most startling profits which individual soldiers won in the war. Thomas Dagworth, who took Charles of Blois prisoner, got £4900 for him; Sir John Wingfield sold the Sire d'Aubigny, taken at Poitiers, to the king for 2500 marks; and Sir Thomas Holland got 20,000 for the Count of Eu, whom he took at Caen. It was not only the great captains who made fortunes in this way, but the ordinary men at arms too. 'The first time that I bore armour was under the Captal de Buch at Poitiers', a mercenary soldier told Froissart, 'and as it was my hap I had that day three prisoners . . . of whom I had one with another three thousand francs.' Even the very humble saw a share in the winnings of war: in 1358 we find the Black Prince ordering his treasurer to pay £8 12s. 6d. to a group of Cheshire archers, for their part in a silver ship, the property of the king of France, which also was taken at Poitiers.[7]

The wealth won in the war was sufficiently considerable to have a noticeable impact on social history. Gains of war made it possible for a good many noblemen to maintain a level of expenditure and to live in a style which would otherwise have impoverished them. The spoils that he made in 1355 and 1356 relieved the Black Prince of a heavy load of debt. Spoils also helped men of more humble origins to acquire solid fortunes which gave them and their descendants status outside the world of the camp and the battlefield. Many of Edward's most famous captains were not of the old nobility. John Chandos began his career as a poor knight of meagre estate. Robert Knowles's origins were even humbler, but he made an immense fortune, and we find him in his old age advancing substantial loans to the king. Ralph Salle, who became a considerable landowner in East Anglia, was said to be the son of a serf. These men of course were among the fortunate few, who outdid all the rest. But there were many county families for whose fortunes lesser gains of war provided a valuable subvention, and others who would have remained utterly obscure but for the chances that adventure abroad created. The doors of opportunity stood open to all. Even for the humblest in the army, the archers, the wage of 2d. a day was attractive by itself, in an age when a ploughman might hope to earn 12s. or 13s. in a twelvemonth.

Rates of pay and rules for the division of spoil in the king's armies were carefully detailed in the sealed contracts which the king made with his captains, and they with their subordinates, which are known as indentures of war. From soon after the beginning of the Hundred Years War these documents begin to survive in large numbers, and the conditions that they lay down become stereotyped. The daily rates of pay in Edward III's time were, for a duke, one mark (13s. 4d.); for an earl 8s.; for a banneret (a baron or knight of wealth and experience) 4s.; for a knight bachelor 2s.; mounted archers were usually paid 6d. a day and foot archers 2d. A captain promised to pay the king a third of all his ransoms and other gains of war, and took a third in turn from the men of his company. Indentures specified also the number of soldiers with whom the contracting captain had to serve, and the period of their service (normally six months or a year). These contracts were voluntary. The survival of war indentures in increasing numbers is thus an indication that service in the king's wars was becoming popular. Though commissioners of array were appointed to impress men more or less compulsorily for all the major expeditions, as those of 1339, 1346, and 1359, the proportion of men serving in the hosts of their own will was growing steadily. With their careful specification of terms of service and rules for the division of spoil the indentures reveal the business of fighting developing into a kind of joint stock enterprise of the king and his subjects.

The indentures are also evidence of a quiet revolution in the administration of war which the reign of Edward III witnessed. The captains who contracted with the king took on the responsibility of themselves recruiting and mustering their companies. They also, most significantly, took upon themselves the direct responsibility for paying the men who contracted to serve under them. The pay-masters who accompanied the hosts led by such magnates as the Black Prince and Henry de Grosmont were not clerks of the wardrobe but officials of the magnates' own households. They recovered the wages of their men directly from the exchequer; a first instalment was usually paid in advance but often they had to wait a long time for the rest of the money. In the meantime captains tided things over by paying soldiers from their own personal resources, and by crediting spoil to the account for wages. The fact that they were often prepared to leave their accounts at the exchequer outstanding for long periods is an indication of how profitable war was becoming.

In the old days the basis of a royal host had been the king's household in arms, and the wardrobe had looked after pay, commissariat and equipment. Those days were passing, and command in the armies, in consequence, became looser at the top. Commanders such as the Black Prince, Henry de Grosmont of Lancaster, and Sir Thomas Dagworth led their own troops and made their own plans of campaign. The scale of the war that Edward III was fighting made it necessary to give men such as these a wide discretion in their commands, and to rely on the administration of military finance through the exchequer, instead of the household. The readiness with which the king and his administrators adapted to the exigencies of new circumstances is striking, however, and fits, as we shall presently see, into a wider pattern.

One will find the names of almost all the great noble families of England among those who contracted to serve Edward III abroad. This is testimony to the success of his efforts to associate the aspirations and pride of the English nobility with his martial enterprises. This was not the only way in which he sought to fortify the loyalty of the peers to the monarchy, which his father's reign had shaken.

The king was generous to his noblemen. William Montagu, the intimate of his youth, was granted the earldom of Salisbury, the reversion of all the lands that the Earl of Warenne had held for life, and the reversion of the Montalt inheritance. Henry de Grosmont was created Duke of Lancaster, the first to hold the title of duke who was not a king's son, and was granted palatine rights for life in his duchy. William Bohun, another great captain in the wars and brother of the Earl of Hereford, was made Earl of Northampton and granted extensive estates in Oxfordshire and Berkshire. Especially striking are the pains that Edward took, over the years, to restore the fortunes of families that had suffered in his father's time and in his own early years. He looked after Joan, the daughter of his uncle Edmund of Kent, who had been executed in 1330, and when she married Thomas Holland he made him Earl of Kent. He allowed Arundel, whose father had been executed in 1326, to succeed in due course to most of the hereditary estates of his uncle Warenne, and the judgement on his father was solemnly reversed in the parliament of 1354. Also reversed in the same parliament was the judgement on Roger Mortimer, whose son was restored to his father's title of Earl of March. Edward took more pains to restore Mortimer than any other, perhaps because he himself had been the author of the father's undoing. To achieve his end he had to override the rights of the Montagus, the Berkeleys, the Beauchamps, and of others who had profited by the elder Mortimer's fall, but he did not hesitate to do so. These families had, after all, been rewarded well enough in other ways. None of them protested much, and March served Edward well, in his council, in his wars, and as a knight of the Garter.

In the later part of his reign Edward III did not raise many new families to the peerage. His most important new creations were in favour of his own children. The Black Prince was granted the earldoms of Chester and Cornwall (erected into a duchy in 1337), and later the principality of Wales. Lionel, born at Antwerp in 1338, was married to Elizabeth de Burgh, who brought him the honour of Clare, as well as wide lands in Ulster and Connaught. John of Gaunt, the next son, was married to Blanche, the heiress of Henry of Lancaster, and through her right became Duke of Lancaster, and Earl of Leicester, Lincoln and Derby. Edmund of Langley was created Earl of Cambridge in 1362. Thomas of Woodstock, the king's youngest son, married the elder of the co-heiresses of Humphrey de Bohun, Earl of Hereford. The magnificent inheritances which Edward's children acquired by marriage and paternal patronage set them apart among the English aristocracy. They had the wealth and status to aspire to play independent parts not only in English politics but in Europe. The Black Prince, after 1362, was Lord of Aquitaine. Lionel, after his first wife's death, sought a Visconti for his next bride; Edmund was betrothed to the heiress of Flanders (but did not marry her, because the pope at the French king's instance refused a dispensation). John of Gaunt, after Blanche's death, married Constanza, daughter of the deposed King Pedro of Castile, and so acquired a claim to a Spanish throne. Such a galaxy of princes, with ambitions in England and overseas which could easily become competitive, was a new feature of the English political scene. They added lustre to the ranks of the peerage, but lustre that was in the end to prove dangerous; the heads of the half-regal houses who fought one another in the Wars of the Roses were all descended from Edward III.

Families and individuals apart, the peers as a body gained advantages in this reign. As was shown by Edward's concession in 1341, that henceforward no peer should be arraigned or judged for any crime, except before his peers in parliament, the magnates were beginning to establish themselves as a class apart with special privileges. Even more important than legal privilege was the new freedom with regard to the administration and disposition of their estates which the nobility acquired through Edward's willingness to assent to legal devices which served to safeguard their family and territorial interests. The most significant development here was the growth of the device of 'enfeoffment to use' which before this time had been employed from time to time by feudal subtenants, but seldom by magnates (largely in consequence of the crown's determination to maintain a surveillance over the disposition of the lands of tenants in chief). This was the practice whereby a landowner alienated a part or parts of his estates to a group of his relatives or retainers (his 'feoffees'). At common law these 'feoffees' became the owners; the 'feoffor' retained the 'use' of the estates, and drew the profits during his lifetime. After his death his feoffees would proceed according to the instructions that he had left, which would usually be drawn up in a 'last will', a document originally separate from the testament. The owner was thus enabled to secure the integrity of his estates beyond his lifetime, to make arrangements for the settlement of his debts, and to make sure that there was provision after his death for his family and his followers. These for instance are the principal purposes for which, according to his will, Hugh Earl of Stafford made an enfeoffment of a large part of his property: that all his servants and retainers might be sure of enjoying the fees and rents he had promised them for the term of their lives; to provide a dowry for his daughter; and to provide an annuity for life of £100 for each of his younger sons. When all these beneficiaries were dead, the reversion of their interest was secured to the earl's heir.

Magnates who were going to the wars secured considerable benefits for their families through 'uses', in the event of their death abroad in the king's service. Uses also enabled men of the noble class to maintain a greater continuity in the administration of their estates and in their relations with their retainers, which in the past would have been broken when, at death, the crown entered on their estates (where crown officials might remain in charge for a long time if the heir was under age). The feoffees were now the owners at law, and so the enfeoffed estates remained in their hands when the feoffor died. Since few magnates enfeoffed all their estates to use, the crown retained wardship of the body of the heir, and of his lands held in fee simple, and the right to arrange his marriage, but there was a loss to the crown, consequent upon large parts of his estate escaping from wardship, which in the past had often proved a very valuable resource. The magnate who enfeoffed land to use ran a certain risk, of course, that his feoffees would disobey his instructions, and try to make the most of their position at common law as owners, but the advantages of the system greatly outweighed this relatively negligible hazard. In due course a jurisdiction over uses, outside the common law, developed with the chancellor, who judged cases brought by feoffors to use against defaulting or disloyal feoffees by equity, 'according to conscience upon the intent of . . . a feoffment'. This jurisdiction, of which the origins only can be traced back to the fourteenth century, was to be important in the history of the development of the court of chancery.

A royal licence was required before land held in chief of the king was enfeoffed to use. Edward III was, however, generous with his grants of such licences (and of course magnates could anyway enfeoff without licence parts of their estate which were not held in chief). Edward was also generous in granting licences to noblemen to entail their estates. This meant that although a number of great families failed during his reign to produce direct heirs (the earls of Warenne and Oxford are good examples), their lands did not, for the most part, revert to the crown. Since an estate 'in tail' was a life tenancy only for the holder, and inalienable, entail helped to protect the integrity of magnate inheritances.

'Tail male' – the entailing of an estate on the male heirs to the exclusion of all females – had the same effect; for it meant that if a landowner left daughters only, his estate reverted to the next male heir, instead of being divided, as was the rule of common law with regard to estates held in fee simple, between the daughters as co-heiresses. 'Tail male' (though only in due course, and after Edward III's time) came to affect the descent of titles, and so to give definition to the concept of a hereditary peerage. The effect of Edward's policy of meeting his magnates' wishes as far as was possible in such matters as 'uses' and entails has been described as 'a revolution in the law of real property'. The tight royal control which Edward I had preserved over the movement of the lands of his tenants in chief was undermined, together with the old simple relation between the crown and its feudal tenants. The crown lost valuable financial perquisites, to the advantage of the magnates; and the magnate families gained a greater degree of control over both the administration and the disposition of their inheritances. The pattern we here observe, of the decline of royal control over noble inheritances, echoes the pattern we observed previously, of the growing independence of the nobility with regard to the recruitment and terms of service of military contingents under their command. Edward III could still, of course, refuse licences to entail or to enfeoff to use, as he could still also summon his military tenants to serve him and array men for war in the counties. But once a new way of doing things has become normal practice, it ceases to be easy to make a break with it. By the end of Edward III's reign a return to the conditions and practices of Edward I's time had become impossible and unthinkable. A new balance had been created in the legal relations of the king and his magnates. Edward III gained by the loyalty which his generous policies fostered; he did not ever have to face the kind of difficulties in his relations with his magnates that his father and grandfather had.

The great Statute of Treason of 1352 was significant of the changed relations between the king and his magnates. In the reign of Edward II many peers, Gaveston, the Despensers and Lancaster among them, had been summarily convicted of treason on counts which included the wide and vague charge of 'accroaching' or usurping royal power. The new statute secured their successors against the threat of this charge, and of the terrible penalties that followed conviction, by defining high treason in the narrowest possible terms. It must be an 'open act', aimed to compass the death of the king, his chancellor, or his judges; or the violation of his wife or eldest daughter; or else an act of war done against the king in his kingdom. The statute specifically added that armed robbery, slaughter, and kidnapping were not high treason, but felonies or trespass. This last point was also important for the magnates. The goods of a convicted felon were forfeit to his lord, those of a convicted traitor were forfeit to the king, as were his estates if he possessed any. Robbery and kidnapping – crimes that were common enough – had on a number of occasions been construed by the judges as treason; the statute guaranteed that lords should not lose their forfeitures on a technicality of judicial interpretation.

Interestingly and in a way surprisingly, it was not the pressure of the lords, but of the commons that seems to have been behind the promulgation of the 1352 statute. It was they who asked for a clearer definition of both treason and 'accroachment', and they seem neither to have been responding to magnate promptings nor seeking any specific material advantage to the class that they represented. More simply, they disliked the construction, by which the judges in the 1340s treated highway robbery and riot as usurpations of royal power, because they suspected that the common law was thereby being pressed into the service of a prerogative absolutism whose legal limits were too vague. The fact that local disorder, in the period when the king was often abroad, had become a problem of alarming proportions did not seem to them as important as that men should know where they stood in law and be well protected against the oppression of ill-fettered royal power. This was typical of their whole attitude to royal government.

The commons were able, in Edward III's reign, to make their attitudes towards the king's government felt in an important way, because of the part that they played in granting taxation. Regular subsidies were the only resource adequate to meet the expenses that the French war involved. This put parliament in a commanding position, and the commons were clearly aware both of the advantage to them of formal association in all grants of taxation (a privilege not fully established at the beginning of the reign), and of the potential bargaining power which could stem therefrom.

This was made very plain by the events of the years from 1336 to 1341, when the king's financial demands were at their most strenuous. His obligations to allies, to whom he had promised pensions, and to the Italian bankers who had advanced him loans were getting him steadily into greater difficulties, and Edward and his ministers had no option but to bargain with parliament for what they could get. In 1339 the grant of a tenth sheep and fleece and lamb was made conditional on redress of grievances: exemption from prises and old debts; the grant of a new pardon for past offences; and the abolition of the *maltolte* on wool granted to the king by the merchants outside parliament in 1336. In the spring parliament of 1340 the grant of 1339 was increased to a ninth, but with new conditions, in laying down which it was the commons that took the initiative. Some of these conditions were very important. The king had to agree to confirm the charters; to cease taking any taxes to which parliament and the commons had not assented; and, most striking of all, to appoint a council which would have full and independent authority in domestic government while the king was overseas. It was the commons who wrung these concessions from the king (though prompted, probably, by Stratford). This was the first occasion ever on which they insisted on the appointment of named councillors.[8] They were learning rapidly that their newly established role in granting subsidies could enable them to make demands of a kind that in the past had never been made by any but magnates.

The parliament of 1341, which witnessed the famous clash between the king and Archbishop Stratford, saw still further concessions. The king's ministers and justices must be sworn in parliament to observe Magna Carta, the Charter of the Forest, and all the statutes of the land; and they must be prepared in each subsequent parliament to answer any complaint alleged against them. These radical articles, reminiscent of the *Ordinances* of 1311, did not endure as statutes; later in the year Edward, after consulting with his judges and magnates, declared that his consent to them had been unwilling, and repealed them on his own authority. Significantly, the commons in the next parliament (1343) entered a vigorous (though unsuccessful) protest against this action, on their own account and quite independently of the lords.

Other actions of the commons in this period have a distinct tone of self conscious independence. In 1339 they refused assent for their part to the grant of the tenth which the lords had proposed, insisting that they must first be given time to go back to their counties and consult with the communities that they represented. When the next parliament met, they retired to debate among themselves and to settle the conditions which they would attach to the grant that they would make. From 1341 onward the evidence that the commons were normally debating apart among themselves in parliament begins to be clear. They had established for themselves an independent role in the shaping of the 'common counsel of the realm'.

After 1341 the king's needs were still pressing, and he had to go through the process of bargaining for assistance many times. The commons did not grant taxes willingly; the cost of the great military efforts of 1346–7 and of 1359–60 caused serious discontent, and the conditions on which they agreed to assist the king were not easy. This was how the commons addressed him in 1348: 'Now we hear, that because of the new turn of events, the king is demanding a charge on his poor commons which is too great: may it therefore please his lordship to hear the burden of the charges and mischief which the said commons already endure.'[9] If they were to make a grant, they said, all judicial eyres must cease; there must be no separate grant made to the king by merchants; the king must undertake not to release the King of Scots or the other prisoners of Neville's Cross without consulting them; and all these conditions must be formally recorded on the parliament roll. A statement like this provides clear testimony to the commons' awareness of the strength of their bargaining position. Some of the demands, too, are very striking; the request for consultation before the King of Scots was released really asked for a right of review of the king's diplomatic negotiations.

The commons did not gain all they asked from the king in 1348, or on any other occasion. Even when the king did assent to their conditions, he did not always abide by them. Nevertheless, if one compares the rolls of the statutes of Edward III's reign with the listed petitions of the commons, one cannot but be made aware of the impressive influence of the commons on contemporary legislation. A very marked change has taken place since the days of Edward I. Edward I's statutes, it is true, were often framed with an eye to meeting public demand, but the initiative lay always with the king and his advisers; it was he and his judges who framed the statutes. The statutes of Edward III's reign do not reflect simply a response to public opinion; a great many of them stem directly from specific requests expressed in the commons' petitions. This is true of some very important statutes, those of 1340, for instance. Others, like the Statute of Treason and the first Statute of Provisors, were drafted by the judges, but in response to prompting from the commons.

The influence of the commons on legislation, which becomes such a notable feature of the parliamentary history of Edward III's reign, is symptomatic of the enhanced profile of local society, and of its dominant gentry class, in the wider community of the realm in this time. Three principal factors contributed toward the growing significance of the role of this estate in the polity, the pressures of war, public concern with the control of crime and disorder at the local level, and rising consumer demand for redress in the king's courts. The third of these factors is important in the parliamentary context, and is reflected in the preoccupation with matters of local justice and its administration which is a marked feature of the commons' petitions. The three taken together go a long way toward explaining why, despite the absence of constitutional crises as traditionally interpreted (outside 1341), the reign of Edward III has appeared to many historians as a key period in constitutional, parliamentary and administrative history.

In considering in this context the pressures of war, it is important to bear in mind that the demands of large scale warfare were a recurrent preoccupation for royal government not just through Edward III's reign, but over the whole period from 1294 on. From then on (as we have seen in an earlier chapter), it became necessary to summon more regularly parliaments in which the commons were represented, in order to obtain assent to subsidies for war purposes. Since the same men were often chosen as representatives in successive parliaments, on account of their prominence in their local communities, the commons gained experience of deliberation, and an awareness of their capacity for collective bargaining. When matters progressed to the collecting of a subsidy, and to arraying men in the shires for the campaign that it was intended to pay for, those best placed to carry out these duties (as collectors of subsidy, or commissioners of array) were once again the local prominent and influential landowners of the counties. The cooperation of county knights had traditionally been vital to the activities of central government at the local level: now they had to shoulder more tasks, more often, and this added to the involvement, and to the influence, of the county gentility in the affairs of the larger polity.

What was perceived as a rise in the levels of crime and disorder in the late thirteenth and early fourteenth centuries, was often identified then (as by some historians since) as a side effect of the wars. Purveyance and exorbitant tax demands caused resentment, and occasionally resistance; disbanded or deserting soldiers could turn easily to organized crime. The domestic confrontations of Edward II's reign also permitted and encouraged much violent disorder at the local level. In its efforts to tackle the problem of control, royal government experimented with various means, the revival of judicial eyres, the issue of general commissions of *oyer et terminer*, the *trailbaston* commissions of 1305. As time went by, however, more and more reliance came to be placed on those known as the 'keepers of the peace' in the counties. Recruited again from among the county landowners, they had first become prominent in the mid-thirteenth century, as assistants to the sheriff in local policing, with powers of pursuit, arrest, and indictment. What transformed them into the county commissions of justices of the peace was the addition to these powers (at first tentatively and experimentally) of the power to hear and determine cases of felony and trespass, in effect to act locally as the king's justices in these matters. Here Edward III's reign was the crucial period of development. In 1332 and 1335 the powers of the keepers, as justices, to determine cases were confirmed. The notion of the *quorum* (which meant that at least one justice learned in the law had to be present to hear important cases) first appears in a statute of 1344; a statute of 1362 required the justices of the peace to sit at least four times a year, the origin of their 'quarter sessions'. Their duties and jurisdiction, as defined by statute in 1368, had grown to include (besides hearing cases of felony and trespass) the maintenance of the peace, the enforcement of regulations about prices, weights and measures, and of the labour legislation imposed after the Black Death (this last a very important addition).

The significance of the jurisdiction of the peace commissions in cases of trespass deserves stressing. Pleas of trespass had been multiplying enormously from Edward I's time on: indeed, this is one of the most visible symptoms of that consumer demand for justice from the royal courts that was referred to earlier. The transference of the main burden of hearing them to the justices of the peace relieved a pressure on the central courts and the visiting justices of assize that had been threatening to become unmanageable. At the same time, it greatly enhanced the standing of the commissions of the peace, and of their members, in their regional worlds. In Edward III's time the peace commissions' personnel were named by the crown; they usually included at least one magnate, plus one or two professional lawyers, backed by resident county gentry. The early keepers of the peace had usually been county knights: in his reign gentlemen who were not knights, coming from established, sub-knightly families, begin to be more prominent, as they do on other commissions beside those of the peace, and in other offices, for instance that of collector of subsidy. More work had been generated in local administration than the limited knightly elites could manage: the growing weight and number of the tasks to be discharged here fostered substantially what Professor Peter Coss has called 'the emergence of the gentry'.

As the petitions of Edward III's parliamentary commons witness, there was a powerful general preference for the devolved, locally based authority of the peace commissions over that of centrally appointed special commissions, or the old periodic visitations by general eyres. The consequence of their pressure was a slackening of the central supervision of local justice and administration, which Edward I had striven vigorously to maintain and which Edward III, at the start of his reign, had made efforts to re-invigorate. The new influence that was devolved to the localities was thus in part concessionary. This prompts a question: why was so much conceded, apparently so easily? Does this represent the pliancy of a king who, in his preoccupation with external war, was prepared to barter central control in return for complaisance in assenting to the taxes that were needed to support his military adventures? Or does it rather reflect a realization on the part of Edward and his advisers, in the light of the difficulties that they had experienced (especially over the year 1336–41) of the wisdom of drawing a wider sector of the community into partnership in governance; and a perception of the ways in which that could positively buttress royal authority at the regional level? It is not easy to strike a sure balance between these alternative interpretations.

What the history of the bargaining between Edward III and the parliamentary commons, in the decades following 1341, does make clear is the commons' sense that they, and the kind of people that they principally represented, did have a part to play in the wider community of the realm, and had a right to do so. This is especially apparent from their sustained efforts to secure full control over all sorts of grant of taxation, not just over lay subsidies but over all other 'extra-ordinary' fiscal grants. It seems clear that they saw this as important, and as the key toward making headway in keeping the king to his side of the bargaining attached to their grants. The implications of their stance here were national, not local.

There were two very important sectors of the community which in Edward III's reign, as previously, often made grants to the king outside parliament. One of these, the clergy, succeeded until after the medieval period in maintaining their independent right to tax themselves, by means of grants voted in the convo-cations.[10] The other group in question was the merchants. Since the time of Edward I, English kings had periodically summoned representative assemblies of merchants, in which taxes which usually took the form of a 'subsidy' or *maltolte,* an extra charge on the export of wool over and above the customs, were negotiated. The advantage which merchants gained by their grants was a degree of monopoly in the export trade, usually organized through a 'staple'. A staple was a town or towns through which alone wool might be exported, and in which this monopoly of export was controlled by the merchants whom the assembly which made the grant represented (the 'King's merchants', or the 'Company of the Staple').

There was room in this system for serious conflict of interest. The agreed staple might be situated abroad; in 1338 it was at Dordrecht, in 1343 at Bruges, and after 1363 most often it was at Calais, which at the end of the four-teenth century was to become the permanent headquarters of the Company of the Staple. If the staple was abroad, the company operating it had of necessity to be a relatively small one: in 1343 for instance there were thirty-three members in the syndicate. This increased the potential for profit of the monopoly (these thirty-three members promised to pay the king, over and above the farm of the customs at the staple which they were granted, 10,000 marks a year), but excluded all except the favoured few from the advantages of the system. A series of staples, located in English towns, was preferable from the point of view of a larger body of merchants, but not so useful from the point of view of the king, who (especially after the failure of his Italian bankers, the Bardi and the Peruzzi, in 1345) relied heavily on the ability of the great English merchants to advance loans to him. Between the staple merchants and the producers (strongly represented among the shire knights of the commons) there was a still more serious clash of interest. The producers always suspected that the effect of *maltoltes* granted by the merchants was offset in the price that they offered for the wool. The producer thus would get no share in the profit, which a staple system ensured to the merchants by enabling them to control the price of wool on the foreign market.

In consequence, Edward and his ministers had to face a series of demands from the commons that *maltoltes* on wool should not be levied without their assent; that the staples abroad should be disbanded; and that the trade in wool and other 'staple' commodities (as hides, lead, and tin) should be entirely free. Thus in 1344, as a result of pressure from the commons, the Bruges staple was abandoned, and free trade permitted in England. The statute of 1353–4, which established a series of home staples and which the commons had a considerable hand in framing, went even further, prohibiting native merchants from exporting wool (the aim being to guarantee a competitive price to the producer, by making sure that alien exporters bought in the native market). The most bitter struggle of all was over the legality of *maltoltes* granted by assemblies of merchants. The view of the commons, clearly and strongly expressed, was identical with that of the magnates who had opposed Edward I's *maltolte* in 1297: *maltoltes* should not be legal, because their effect was felt largely by the 'people', not by the merchants who voted them. In 1339 and 1340, in 1343, in 1347 and in 1350, the commons petitioned for the abolition of *maltoltes* which had not received their assent. Edward gave way, abandoned the offending taxes (on condition, on occasion, that they be continued with common assent); but equally regularly he summoned assemblies of merchants again, with whom he negotiated new *maltoltes* and new staple arrangements.

By 1353, when plans for a system of home staples were being mooted, it was clear that the continued pressure of the commons was beginning to tell, on the merchants if not on the king. The system of home staples was planned and discussed in a great council in 1353, in which the mercantile element was domi-nant: there were present one knight only from each shire, and eighty-two burgesses from forty-three towns which had special interests in the wool trade. These representatives prepared an 'Ordinance of the Staple'. But they also requested that what they had agreed should be referred to the next parliament for confirmation, and that what was done in the great council should not be 'of record, as if it were done by common assent in parliament'.[11] The eighty-two burgesses clearly had no desire to get their arrangements into difficulties with the commons unnecessarily. Nine years later, in 1362, the position was finally regularized and defined: 'no subsidy or other charge shall be granted on wool by merchants or any others without the consent of parliament'.[12] The commons thus finally won full and effective control of lay taxation.

The statute of 1362 made sure that parliament would not share its fiscal role with another representative body. The implication of the request of the great council of 1353, that what was not done in parliament should not be 'of record' is perhaps even more significant. It was a sign of a recognition that parliament had a formal legislative role, and that its assent was needful to give authority to new laws of general importance. Here we see how the bargains which the commons struck with King Edward when meeting his requests for financial aid helped to define for parliament, and for the commons in particular, an essential place in the constitution.

The stresses of the war taught Edward III to take both the peers and the commons into partnership with the monarchy. After 1341, his plans for campaigns never again outran the limit of his subjects' willingness to serve him and to pay him in the way that they had done in the first four years of hostilities. He was always pressed, however, for ready cash, and had constantly to raise loans in anticipation of revenue. After the collapse of the Bardi and Peruzzi he had to look very largely to native merchants for advances. Of this situation another form of partnership, with another section of his subjects, was born.

The fate of the Bardi (whom he effectively bankrupted) was a reminder of the risks involved in lending to an ambitious king, and native merchants too had had ugly experiences in the early years. When in 1338 Edward's agents compulsorily purchased the wool which English merchants had shipped to Dordrecht, they paid in bonds which enabled the vendors to recover their money by relief from the customs. This was a very slow means of recovering debt, and most of the bonds were sold at a shattering discount. The merchants had also to contend with difficulties which the king's pliancy toward the commons created for them. The new merchant syndicate which was formed in 1343 was ruined because the commons in the next year forced the abandonment of the Flanders staple, from operating which the syndicate had expected to draw its profits. Nevertheless, for the really big merchants there were always attractions in lending to the king. The crown did not always default on its debts, and it seems clear that, to merchants at least, it was often prepared to pay interest on large loans. The crown could also offer a certain protection from the jealousy of fellow merchants and the commons, for instance by granting licences to export in the period when native merchants were excluded by the statute of 1354 from the export trade. William de la Pole of Hull, who was always prominent among the capitalists who lent to the king and suffered many adverse turns of fortune in consequence, nevertheless made an immense fortune. He and others like him understood finance so much better than the commons that they were always able to suggest ways of getting round inconvenient regulations or offsetting them.

The merchants who collectively did most for the king were those of London, which was easily the largest merchant city of England and was beginning to be a 'centre of national credit'. Acting together, the London merchants brought pressure to bear which persuaded the king to abandon the embargo of 1354 on natives exporting wool, and they were probably influential in bringing about the restoration of a foreign staple, at Calais, in 1363. Another way in which the greater London merchants secured rewarding benefits from the crown for their loyal financial assistance was by means of charters which were granted to a number of city companies. These secured to the companies virtual control within the city of the wholesale and retail trade in the products in which their 'misteries' specialized. The drapers in 1364 obtained the virtual monopoly of the city's trade in cloth, and were able to inhibit weavers, fullers and dyers from selling to any but themselves. The vintners' charter gave them control of the wholesale trade in England (except to the nobility), and in consequence over the activities of taverners who sold wine retail. The fishmongers acquired total control of their wholesale trade in the city. The great capitalists who obtained the maximum advantage from these charters were good friends to the king. The value of their friendship was appreciated, and though their privileges were often attacked, royal favour maintained their dominance in London through a long future.

Most of the great London merchants, besides plying their own trade, exported wool. They thus had a direct interest in the king's diplomatic policies, and, because the crown was heavily dependent on them for loans, could bring influence to bear in this quarter. This was to be very clearly demonstrated in 1382, when the preference, which the London merchants made a condition of lending, decided the council to abandon plans for an expedition to Portugal in favour of one to Flanders. The partnership of the crown and the city, whose foundations were laid in Edward III's reign, had an influence with a long future ahead of it; it tutored the monarchy towards the formulation of national commercial policies.

Partnership was the keynote of Edward III's domestic policies, and the partnerships that he formed were well calculated to achieve success in his aims for them, as long as fortune smiled on his enterprises abroad. Changed circumstances would reveal that there were difficulties inherent in some of the solutions he sought to the problems of his time, as is so often the case with new solutions. In particular the growing influence of the commons in parliament made public opinion more formidable to government than it had been. The control that the commons achieved over the granting of subsidies gave them a weapon that could be used to force the hand of a king and his councillors. This did not matter very much in the 1350s and 1360s when the commons, on the whole, approved the king's major enterprises. But if these did not justify themselves by prompt success, as they did in the age of Crecy and Poitiers, a more difficult situation might arise. The commons had acquired sufficient power, if they were not satisfied with the king's government or his policies, to obstruct them, to the point at which he and his counsellors might no longer be able to choose their own solutions to the problems facing them, let alone stick to them.

Other aspects of Edward's domestic policies also contained seeds of future discomforts that were not immediately apparent. Through the years from 1341 to the start of the 1370s relations between the king and his magnates were remarkable for their harmony. He took care to foster their sense of being his companions and trusted lieutenants in his great quarrel with France, and cemented the partnership by favouring their interests in other spheres and in other ways at the same time. The new freedom which magnates acquired in the management of their landed wealth enabled them to give a greater degree of cohesion to the organization of their retinues of followers and to the administration of their estates. This made it easier for magnates, through their retainers and feed men, to influence the course of local justice and administration. As long as there was harmony between the king and his great men over issues of policy and governance, this could facilitate cooperation between central and local government, and buttress royal authority at the regional level. But if that harmony were to come under strain, serious tensions between private power and public authority could develop. Even in the best of circumstances, it was not difficult for magnates to lean on local administrators in ways that would favour their private interests and those of their clients: in areas of their dominance, their feed men were likely to be well represented on, for instance, the commissions of the peace. If magnates fell out with the king, or with one another, the entrenched networks of private power, that Edward's politic concessions had allowed them to consolidate, could present formidable problems for royal authority. In Edward III's time, both locally and nationally, the dangers were not very apparent: they became clear enough in the troubled reigns of the two grandsons who succeeded him, Richard II and Henry IV.

Notes

1 *Foed.* vol. V, p. 496.
2 K. de L. vol. XVIII, p. 302.
3 *R.P.* vol. II, pp. 158–9.
4 K. de L. vol. II, p. 376.
5 K. de L. vol. IV, p. 381.
6 J. Leland, *Itinerary*, ed. L. Toulmin-Smith (London, 1909), vol. IV, p. 133.
7 K. de L. vol. XI, pp. 108–9; and *The Black Prince's Register* part IV, p. 254.
8 See G. L. Harriss, 'The commons' petitions of 1340', *E.H.R.* vol. 78 (1963), pp. 625–54.
9 *R.P.* vol. II, p. 200.
10 See further Chapter 9, below.
11 *R.P.* vol. II, p. 253.
12 *Statutes*, 36 E. III, I, c. 11.

Note on secondary reading (post 1970)

S.L. Waugh, *England in the Reign of Edward III* (Cambridge, 1991) concentrates on the domestic scene. W.M. Ormrod, *The Reign of Edward III* (London and New Haven, 1990) is particularly impressive on this side, and offers an interpretation significantly different to that I have given: see also his

'Edward III and the recovery of royal authority in England, 1340–60', *History*, vol. 72 (1987). My chapter is strongly angled toward the interaction between the progress of the war and domestic issues; on this subject R.W. Kaeuper offers an original and interesting interpretation (the 'law state' and the 'war state') in his *War, Justice and Public Order: England and France in the Late Middle Ages* (Oxford, 1988).

On propaganda and responses to it (and much else), J. Barnie, *War in Medieval English Society: Social Values in the Hundred Years War* (Ithaca, 1974) is illuminating; see also W. Ormrod, 'The domestic response to the Hundred Years War', in A. Curry and M. Hughes (eds.), *Arms, Armies and Fortifications in the Hundred Years War* (Woodbridge, 1994). On Edward III's exploitation of the cult of chivalry see J. Vale, *Edward III and Chivalry* (Woodbridge, 1982); also Barnie, cited above. For the significance of spoils of war, and their economic significance, see K.B. McFarlane, *The Nobility of Later Medieval England* (Oxford, 1973), chapter 1, section ii: and the articles by him and M.M. Postan in *Past and Present*, nos. 22 (1962) and 27 (1964). On pay, indentures, and administrative problems posed by war see the articles by N.B. Lewis and by A.E. Prince cited in the main bibliography, Section 3e, and H.J. Hewitt's invaluable *The Organisation of War under Edward III* (Manchester, 1966).

On Edward III's relations with the aristocracy, there are valuable articles by A. Ayton, 'Edward III and the English aristocracy at the beginning of the Hundred Years War', in M. Strickland (ed.) *Armies, Chivalry and Warfare in Medieval Britain and France* (Stamford, 1998); by J. Bothwell, 'Edward III and the "new nobility": *largesse* and its limitations in fourteenth century England', *E.H.R.*, vol. 112 (1997), and 'The English peerage and the 1337 Earls: estate redistribution in fourteenth century England', in Bothwell (ed.) *The Age of Edward III* (York, 2001): and by C. Given-Wilson, 'The king and the gentry in fourteenth century England', *T.R.H.S.*, 5th series, vol. 37 (1987). On enfeoffments to use and entails, see K.B. McFarlane, *The Nobility of Later Medieval England*, and J.M.W. Bean, *The Decline of English Feudalism* (Manchester, 1968).

On parliament, and on fiscal and financial history generally, see G.L. Harriss, *King, Parliament and Public Finance to 1369* (Oxford, 1975), and his brief and brilliant essay, 'War and the emergence of the English parliament', *Journal of Medieval History*, vol. 2 (1976). On issues raised during the crisis of 1340–1 specifically, see the works cited in the notes on further reading at the end of chapter 6, *ante*. On administrative developments, particularly in the field of local justice consult A. Musson and W. Ormrod, *The Evolution of English Justice: Law, Politics and Society in the Fourteenth Century* (London, 1998); also R.C. Palmer, *English Law in the Age of the Black Death; A transformation of Governance and Law* (Chapel Hill, 1993). H.M. Jewell, *Local Administration in the Middle Ages* (Newton Abbot, 1972) is a sound broad introduction to the subject.

Section III

The changing world of the later Middle Ages

8 Plague and economic change: an overview

The single most dramatic event of the fourteenth century in England was the onset of the plague which has come to be known as the Black Death. Its impact was horrific. In the course of its first visitation, in 1348–9, it is thought that more than a third of the population may have perished: some would suggest near a half. The demographic effect was not short-term, moreover: the population did not re-achieve its pre-plague level until long after the Middle Ages were past. Over the long run, the radical shift in the ratio of England's inhabitants to her resources had effects in virtually every aspect of economic and social life.

Ships' rats were what brought this bubonic plague, which had originated in Asia. The first English outbreak was at the port of Melcombe Regis in Dorset. From there it spread through the western and southern counties: in the winter of 1348 London was affected. The outbreak reached its peak in the early summer of 1349, when it struck the populous eastern counties. 'So great a pestilence before this time had never been seen, or heard of, or written of . . . so great a multitude was not swept away, it was believed, even by the flood that happened in the days of Noah'.[1] So wrote the chronicler of Louth Park abbey in Lincolnshire. Still more poignant, because more personal, comes the testimony of the Irish friar, John of Clyn, who watched the impact on prosperous Kilkenny:

> In scarcely any house did only one die, but all together, man wife with their children and household, traversed the same road, the road of death . . . And lest these notable events should perish with time and fade from the memory of future generations, . . . while waiting among the dead for the coming of death I have set them down in writing . . . and lest the writing should perish with the writer and the work with the workman, I leave the parchment for the work to be continued in case in the future any human survivor should remain, or someone of the race of Adam should be able to escape this plague and continue what I have begun.[2]

Though doubts have been expressed, and by medical scientists as well as some historians, it seems clear that the disease which struck in 1348 was bubonic plague. Guy de Chauliac, the papal physician at Avignon, described the typical symptoms, 'apostumes and carbuncles on the external parts, principally the armpits and the groin'; these are the buboes from which bubonic plague takes its name. Bubonic plague is carried by rats, and the infection is passed on by rat fleas. When the fleas become infected, through the blood of a diseased rodent, the effect is to glut their gullets: they become fiercely hungry, and in these conditions will leave the host animal and attack others, notably man. Rat fleas multiply best in warm weather, and therefore the onset of winter should put a term to a bubonic outbreak in northern latitudes. There is however a second variety of plague, pneumonic plague, which in more recent pandemics (for instance in Manchuria in the early twentieth century) has been associated with bubonic outbreaks: this appears to develop when humans with a pneumonic infection contract bubonic plague. This is a much more infectious version of the disease – it can be contracted by inhalation – and is relatively more fatal: it is not halted, moreover, by the onset of winter. The plague of 1348–9 was not so halted. Nor was the second visitation of 1361–2: the outbreaks of 1369 and 1375 were also very serious, nationwide. In all these instances it seems likely that there were pneumonic outbreaks, and certainly in the first two: later this variety of the infection seems to have died out. Bubonic plague had however become endemic. From 1348 to the end of the Middle Ages, chronicles record recurrent outbreaks at varying intervals; the last of this pandemic was the great London plague of 1665. Some of the later outbreaks were regionally limited, and confined principally to towns: an uncomfortably large number were of more general incidence, as those of 1399, 1407, 1413, 1434, 1464, 1471, 1479 and 1485.

We have said that the plague of 1348–9 may have killed more than a third of the population. The attempt to assess its mortality with any greater precision is beset with problems. It is clear, from manorial records, that in the countryside this was uneven. In some places it was very high, as for instance on some Crowland manors, and at Tilgarsley in Oxfordshire where the village was deserted after the plague; on the Bishop of Winchester's manor of Bishop Waltham, the death rate was a frightening 65 per cent. On some St Albans manors we find, however, that it was comparatively slight. Statistics have been compiled for various English dioceses of the institutions in the plague year to parish churches, which were vacant in consequence, arguably, of the plague. These produce some impressive figures: what looks like a 40 per cent mortality in Lincoln and York dioceses, and over 50 per cent in some others. Unfortunately these are not absolutely safe figures; episcopal registers do not usually distinguish between death from plague and from other causes, or state whether the incumbent was or was not resident when he died, and they sometimes do not even indicate whether a living was vacant through death or for some other reason. The percentages may err, perhaps, on the high side: they remain alarming.

If it is hard to be dogmatic about the effect of the first plague, it is harder still to generalize about the cumulative demographic impact of the plagues of

1348–9, 1361–2 and 1369. Russell has calculated, on the basis of the poll tax returns of 1377, that the total population was then about 2,250,000: he believed that in 1348, before the plague, it was about 3,700,000. Postan and others who believe that Russell's population figures are too low throughout, think it may have been nearer 3,000,000 in 1377, and about 6,000,000 in 1348. Most view the latter estimates as coming nearer to the truth.[3] On two points all parties are agreed. One is that the two centuries preceding 1300 had seen very significant demographic expansion; by 1300 perhaps a threefold expansion overall from a figure of *c.* 2,000,000 at the time of the Domesday survey of 1086. The second is that the population losses of the mid-fourteenth century were not made up. This is somewhat surprising: rapid replacement of lost population has characterized more recent plague pandemics, but that is not what happened after 1348. Though there are signs that figures were beginning to pick up a little a hundred and fifty years later, toward the end of the fifteenth century, for a very long period the replacement rate for the surviving population stood still, near one to one, occasionally even dipping below that. Various reasons have been put forward to explain this; for instance the high mortality in later outbreaks among young people who had not developed any immunity (the 1361–2 visitation is in some sources described as 'the plague of infants'), with the consequence that a heavily depleted cohort reached child bearing age. Modification of marriage customs has also been suggested as a factor: male mortality opened opportunities for women of paid work, which may have encouraged postponement of marriage, shortening the child bearing period. The principal factor, beyond much doubt, was the cumulative effect of recurrent plague and of other diseases that were rife in a society not well educated in hygiene. Whatever the balance of causes, the central significant consequence was the depletion of population, not just in the short term but over a series of generations. This was what upended the ratio of people to resources through the last century and a half of England's Middle Ages.

The true consequences of this demographic contraction can only be appreciated when they are considered over a much longer period than the decades either side of 1348. In order to understand their significance, we need to know about how things stood before, as well as about what happened after; and this means looking back beyond 1290, as well as forward into the fifteenth century. As doing so will make apparent, it is not possible to interpret the first onset of the plague, by itself and of itself, as a turning point in English social and economic history. It will also become apparent that there were other factors and forces besides demographic contraction that were working changes, and important changes, in these areas over the long period. Notable among these were the effects of the fiscal pressures on the economy of taxation to support the great wars with France and Scotland. Shifts in the pattern of external and internal commerce also have an important part in the story; so do monetary factors. All these strands, naturally, interacted with one another, which makes the economic story that we are seeking to trace a complicated one. For the sake of clarity (and inevitably with some consequent over simplifications) it may help to divide the story into three phases, the period before *c.* 1290, the years from 1290 to 1348, and the post plague period. Within each phase, three vital aspects of economic life will be the principal focus of our attention, trade and manufacture, conditions in urban society, and the agricultural economy. In the unfolding story, demography will be a thread running through each phase, but it will never be the only one on which we need to keep our eye. As we shall see, its significance is always at its clearest when we are looking at the life of the countryside, on which and by which three quarters of the population, at the least, lived and had their being.

Until its last decades, the thirteenth century was a period of marked demographic expansion and of economic development. By 1200 England had already established a secure niche in the system of European commerce, as an exporter of raw materials, hides, tin and above all wool. Wines, spices, cloth and salt fish (a staple of Lenten diet) were among the principal imports, together with various materials necessary in particular to cloth manufacture (for the domestic market), such as alum and dyes. Though most of the export carrying trade was in the hands of aliens, Italians and Germans of the Hanseatic towns, the balance of trade was on the whole favourable, with rather more money coming into the country than was taken out of it. This vigorous commerce, in combination with expanding population, fostered urban development. Towns grew in size and number, and in significance as distributive centres for both internal and external trade: a number of important new towns included Leeds, Liverpool and Kingston-upon-Hull. The great regular fairs, such as those of Lincoln, Boston and St Ives drew together merchants from overseas in quest of wool with English middlemen who had bought up wool in the countryside and brought it for sale (though the aliens also bought a good deal direct from such large producers as the abbeys of the north and west). Wool and the home cloth industry contributed to the growth and prosperity of a number of established towns, as Oxford, Winchester, Nottingham, Norwich and York. Thirteenth century London was already a major metropolis, a centre of international exchange and of manufacture of finished goods (especially luxury goods). Its population swelled enormously by immigration into the city, to a peak of perhaps 70,000. This made it the single English city comparable in size and economic activity with the great continental urban centres of Italy and Flanders.

Smaller towns, often villages promoted to borough status by a royal or seignorial landlord in return for a fee farm payment, grew in this period around local markets. It was a royal prerogative to grant the licence for a market, and over 3,000 were granted in the course of the thirteenth century. The grant of a market made a town a centre for the sale of agricultural produce from the surrounding countryside, and for the distribution of finished goods (the specialist occupations of the majority of its inhabitants constituting the clearest identifying mark of its urban way of living). Most boroughs enjoyed at least a degree of self government by charter from their lords, the town authorities collecting the tolls and rents which went to pay the fee farm, and regulating through the borough court the everyday lives and market dealings of the townsmen.

Local markets integrated town life and the wider course of commerce with the life of the countryside. Patterns of country living of course varied very greatly from region to region, on account of the variety of England's landscape and soils; nevertheless, some generalizations may be attempted. In the rural economy, conditions made the thirteenth century a good time for landlords. Growing urban populations needed to be fed, and the price of cereals kept high. In a heavily populated countryside, land for cultivation was in demand: rents and entry fines for tenant holdings could be pitched at a high level. Manorial lordship put the landlord at an advantage over his tenants, especially his unfree bond tenants, bound to the soil of his manor and owing him labour services on his demesne (or payment in lieu), and subject in their dealings with one another to his manor court. All these features favoured what has come to be called 'high farming'. Under this system, the lord cultivated his demesne lands directly, sending a substantial proportion of their produce to the market for sale, and profiting from the good prices for cereals and wool, the ample availability of cheap labour, and the competition for tenant land. Great land-lords did not usually exploit all their estates in this way: on some they would cultivate their demesnes directly, on others draw their profits from rent (the customary labour services being commuted for a money payment). Renting and commutation were indeed very widespread, because wage labour was so cheap and so plentiful: even on directly exploited demesne manors it could be more economic and more efficient than reliance on customary labour services. To make the most of high farming on a large scale careful supervision and accounting were necessary. For every manor of a great estate an account would be drawn up annually after Michaelmas (following the harvest), recording receipts from sale of produce, rents and profits of court, and showing the balance to be paid over to the lord after deduction for disbursements on wages, purchases of seed corn, and so on. These accounts would be carefully audited. The professional steward, entrusted with the supervision of a group of manors, riding round to survey and to preside over their courts on the lord's behalf, became an important figure in estate administration in the high farming age. Treatises on his duties, such as Walter of Henley's *Husbandry* and the anony-mous *Seneschaucie* bear witness to his developing professionalism.[4]

The good times for landlords were not good times for their peasant tenants. Well before 1300 reclamation, driven by land hunger and population pressure, had brought as much land into cultivation as at any subsequent point in English agrarian history. A good deal of the land most recently reclaimed was marginal in terms of productivity. Demographic pressure had besides promoted the fragmentation of peasant holdings: many customary tenants held only a quarter of a virgate or even less. Reckoning a virgate at a very rough average of 30 acres, this left them and their households perilously close to the margin of subsistence, even in good years, and a poor harvest could spell disaster. Here it should be remembered that the humble cultivator needed to meet more than the subsistence requirements of himself and his family: there were the calls of the lord too. He needed money to pay for necessities, pots and pans, cloth for clothing, perhaps for seed corn and for having his own corn ground at the mill, and very probably to meet a rent too. Wage labour, or perhaps involvement in a cottage industry, offered possibilities of augmenting the puny family income, but very much at the margin. Richer peasants, those with a virgate or more, could clearly hope to sell some of their produce; they were the kind of villagers whose peasant sheep flocks in some regions made a significant contribution to the market in wool. The stark facts remain that too many people were seeking to support themselves from the land available, and that landlords' demands, aimed at maximizing profits, sharpened the exposure to distress of too many of them. Those profits were largely expended in consumption, on building and life style: there was not much reinvestment, and no significant advance in the techniques of cultivation. In the overcrowded land there was thus for a period prosperity at one level, at another and infinitely more numerous level need that could easily become abject. It is not surprising that dearth years correlate with manor court records of brisk selling in the peasant land market, as poor men disposed of tiny parcels of tenant land in the attempt to raise money to pay for what they hoped would keep them alive.

Overall, England's economy in the thirteenth century was already, for its time, quite commercialized, and this goes for the rural world as well as for the towns. Even the very poor hoped to make some money from their produce or by the wages of their labour. Towns were, obviously, centres of specialization and of the division of labour, but both these were features of country life too. Every village had its specialists, in brewing, baking, milling, perhaps even in tailoring: cloth making flourished in the country as well as in towns, and mining was an essentially rural based industry. Communications were not as poor as is easily imagined: goods were carried to market over considerable distances, by pack-horse, cart, and where possible by water (the cheapest method of moving goods in bulk). Whoever drew the fourteenth century Gough map knew the main carrier routes of the kingdom well, the nodal points of their intersections, and the way in which they related to the river systems. Native merchants, in their dealings with aliens, were already using credit extensively: great wool producing abbeys, like Meaux in Yorkshire, were selling to Italian exporters futures in their wool crop. Commercialization did not make the balance of the thirteenth century economy, if balance it can be called, any less fragile. At all levels and in all sectors it was substantially under-capitalized. Any alteration in the prevailing pattern of conditions was likely in consequence to have destabilizing effects, and commercialization made sure that effects in one sector would impact on others too.

This is just what happened in the half century preceding 1348: conditions altered. They did so untidily, and unevenly across the sectors and regions; this makes it a hard period about which to generalize. Some historians speak in terms of an early fourteenth century 'crisis'; whether or not this term is justified, these were certainly years in which the English economy was encountering serious problems.

Three factors may be identified as helping to introduce a new uncertainty into the economic situation: natural misfortunes, the impact of royal taxation to meet the expenses of large scale campaigning, and the depression of price levels over a whole range of commodities, most notably wool and cereals. In addition, population seems to have peaked around 1300; thereafter it may have begun to decline. Town populations ceased to expand, and no more new towns were established. In a number of regions, there is evidence of marginal land going out of cultivation.

These last developments may have been the beginnings of a Malthusian reaction to over-population. Whether that is so or not, their effect was certainly exacerbated by natural disasters. The torrential rains of 1315 and 1316 caused harvest failure, and severe famine: the impact was compounded by an epidemic of enteric fever. The mortality rate may have been as high as 15 per cent; and indifferent harvests continued to characterize the next decade and more.[5] Weather wise things improved after 1330, but demand had slackened and wheat prices, which had soared in the famine years, were depressed. The years of poor harvests had added to the problems of the hard pressed peasantry: now low price levels made difficulties for the landlord too. A series of outbreaks, during the 1320s, of sheep murrain and of rinderpest among cattle (vital as draught animals) added to the problems of the agricultural sector. The one chink of light from the landlords' point of view was that rents remained high. The clear implication of this is that, though there may have been some contraction of population, it was not yet sufficient to ease the hunger for productive land. Nothing less than that could offer much prospect of amelioration to the peasant cultivator. The high yield of rents encouraged some landlords to reduce the cultivation of their demesnes and to lease out more land: Ramsey Abbey and the Bishops of Ely are examples. Most, however, continued to exploit their demesnes and the advantages of lordship in the traditional way, at a somewhat reduced profit and hoping loosely for the return of better times. Overall, there was not much change in the general course of agricultural life, although the bad years of natural misfortune were for many very bad years indeed.

Taxation for war purposes affected all sectors of the economy, including the agricultural. Here, once again, the peasantry in particular look to have been adversely affected. This was most clearly so after 1334: up to that date the poorest among them were formally exempt, but from then on the subsidies (tenths and fifteenths) were assessed on the locality and individual exemption for the poor ceased. So, as Michael Prestwich remarks drily, 'the number of taxpayers rose as the burden shifted lower down the scale'.[6] Purveyance, the compulsory purchase of foodstuffs for the royal forces, and the seizure of wools were even more sharply resented at the popular level than subsidy. 'Now the fifteenth runs in England year after year . . . the common folk must sell their cows, their utensils, even their clothing . . . still more hard on simple folk is the wool collection, commonly it makes them sell their possessions'.[7] It is true that the level of taxation was by modern standards low, in no sense crippling: but taxes had to be paid promptly and payment for goods compulsorily purchased was often long delayed – or forgotten. Tax moreover hit at the poor man's precious reserve of coinage, which he needed to meet such exigencies as his rent and the purchase of seed corn. Taxation and purveyance touched all, but landlords had larger reserves of produce and readier access to money: all the circumstances were such as to ensure that the poorer were hit harder than the better off.

In the commercial sector as in the agricultural, the first half of the fourteenth century was a period of difficulties. It was not a happy time for the trade in wool. There was a gradual, though uneven, downward trend in the number of sacks of wool exported; in 1307 some 47,000 sacks were taken out of the country, but in the 1320s the average was down to near 24,000. After this trough the trade picked up again somewhat, but it never again achieved the high levels of the early years of the century. This was, in part at least, the consequence of political disturbance and unrest in Flanders, the principal market for English wool, which had adverse effects on the Flemish cloth industry and so on demand. At the same time, prices to the grower were depressed. This was partly the consequence of exporters setting off high customs duties in the prices that they offered to the grower; scarcity of silver coinage, from the end of the 1320s, also helped to keep prices down. England's wool, as the protesting barons put it in 1297 (with some exaggeration, of course) amounted 'almost to the value of half the whole land';[8] hiccoughs in the export trade were bound to have very widespread repercussions, and not for merchants only.

The effect of war taxation on the wool trade is sharply marked. The repercussions of the extra levies, above the 'ancient' custom of 1275, that were imposed on wool exports were significant. The first of these levies was the *maltolte* of 1294, which at the rate of 40s a sack raised over the three years to 1297 a sum of *c.* £110,000 for Edward I. From 1303 to 1311 an extra levy was imposed on the exports of alien merchants only, which was renewed in 1322; in 1333 an extra levy was extended to English exporters, and the rate raised for aliens. These levies had two more or less direct consequences. One was the reduction, already alluded to, in the price merchants were prepared to pay to growers. The other was the capture by native merchants of the bulk of the export trade to Flanders, which the aliens had previously dominated. This in turn led to Edward III's attempt to fund the early campaigns of the Hundred Years War through a royal monopoly of the export of wool, with the aid of a syndicate of native merchants who would advance money to the crown and recoup from being permitted to export – in effect to share in the monopoly. A number of fingers were burnt in this experiment, as has been explained in an earlier chapter.[9] The consequent dislocation did not seriously damage the trade; but the sheer profitability of export that had once made it so attractive to aliens was gone, and the Italians after 1340 never again played the part they had formerly in the export trade, or in providing the crown with loans. Much of the money raised by Edward III through export levies and through taxation generally was, moreover, spent abroad, on pensions to foreign allies and the purchase of military supplies. More money was now leaving the kingdom than was coming into it, sharpening the scarcity of coinage with its deleterious effects on prices and the operation of markets.

For towns especially, as the market centres of commerce both external and internal, shifts and dislocations in the patterns of commerce had serious consequences. The picture that here emerges from the evidence is an uneven one, often less clear than one would wish. Depressed prices and the low velocity of the circulation of coin certainly did not make things easy for those small towns that acted as distributive centres for their surrounding locality. As has been noted earlier, in the first part of the thirteenth century a number of substantial towns and cities had flourished as centres of cloth manufacture: later in the century, the competition of imported cloth from Flanders together with difficulties (principally over wage levels) between merchants and the weaving craft gilds dented their prosperity. There was some consequential movement of the industry into the countryside, where wage levels were lower and there was no problem with organized labour. In this sector, the heavy taxation of wool exports and unrest in the Flemish industrial cities prompted in the fourteenth century a measure of revival, and not only in manufacture for the home market: English cloth exports began gradually to climb. In some old centres of production there was no recovery, not in Nottingham, nor in Northampton, nor in Winchester or Oxford: but Norwich, Beverley, Bristol and Colchester were all doing better again before the mid-century. Towns that were associated with the collection and export of the raw material, wool, like York with its port of Hull, continued to do quite well, in spite of the fluctuations in the trade; and as native merchants solidified their control of export, some, like William de la Pole of Hull, became very wealthy indeed. The city that most notably continued to flourish was London. Immigration from the countryside continued to replenish its population. Its accessibility to the merchants of East Anglia and the Midlands, the frequent presence of the royal household, and the location of the central government close by at Westminster all fostered its development as England's commercial and administrative capital. It had become the most important of all the centres of the vital export trade in wool, and the leaders of its merchant patriciate were among the richest men of the kingdom.

The first half of the fourteenth century was plainly a difficult time in the story of the English medieval economy. It remains nevertheless difficult to pick out clear trends. The gradual decline of the export trade in wool would probably have proved in the long run irreversible in any circumstances. But uneven as fortunes were in both the urban and rural worlds, it remains hard to pick out in the story of either overt signs that radical change was on the way. Had plague not struck in 1348, conditions might have stabilized in patterns very similar to those of the preceding thirteenth century, though with a somewhat reduced level of activity.

The immediate consequence of the mortality of the first visitation of the Black Death was a severe shortage of labour. 'By the winter' Henry Knighton wrote of the year 1349, 'there was such a dearth of servants and labourers that men were quite bewildered as to what they should do about it . . . beasts and cattle strayed everywhere, for none were left to tend them'.[10] The sharp rise in wages consequent on this shortage prompted the first governmental reaction to the plague, the famous Ordinance of Labourers of 1349 which, enlarged and amended, became a statute in 1351. The most important clauses of the statute pinned wages at the level of 1346, binding labourers to accept the rate of that year, and confirming to their personal lords (or to their masters in the case of apprentices) the first claim on their services. In order to control competition for labour, other employers were forbidden to receive workers before their customary obligations (or existing contracts) had been fulfilled.[11] Prices of manufactured goods were fixed at their pre-plague level: those of foodstuffs were to be 'reasonable'. The statute was enforced, from 1352 to 1359, by special commissions of justices in each county, who held their sessions four times a year and received payment. After this period the statute was enforced by the justices of the peace. For a time at least, perhaps down to *c.* 1370, the statute was not ineffective in restraining the rise of wages. In the long run it was doomed to failure because shortage of labour proved not to be a passing phenomenon: the population losses of 1348–9 were never made up. Scarcity of labour became consequently a constant of the economic conditions of the post-plague era, and wages could not be held back indefinitely: by the end of the century they stood at an average level which, in terms of purchasing power, was nearly double that of 1346.

The Statute of Labourers apart, one of the most remarkable things about the immediate aftermath of 1348–9 was how little was altered, despite the horrifying mortality. There was no sharp change in the pattern of government or of social structures. The war with France went on, and taxes to maintain it continued to be imposed. Profound changes did follow, but in the long term, not the short run. By no means all of them, when they did come, were attributable to the plague and the consequential demographic contraction, though some of the most important obviously were. Let us once again look in turn at the three fields of commerce and industry, urban developments and the agricultural economy, and try to figure out what ways things went in them and why.

In the middle of the fourteenth century England's prime export was still wool. Sheep farming is not labour intensive, so shortage of labour did not impact on it sharply. There were fewer people to clothe, at home and abroad, so demand slackened somewhat; productivity per capita did not fall at all. The decline in the trade, observable before 1348, continued progressively, but for reasons largely unconnected with demography. On the eve of the plague, in the 1340s, the average figure for export was 30,000 sacks a year: by the end of the century it had dropped to an average of 23,000 sacks. Later it sank much lower; over the period 1400 to 1500 the export average totals out at about 10,000 sacks a year, the mid century years, when relations with Burgundian Flanders broke down for a time, being particularly depressed. There were two principal reasons for the steady erosion of this trade's prosperity. One is already familiar, its continuing entanglement with Plantagenet crown finance. The other was the growing significance of the native English cloth making industry, and the impressive expansion of the export trade in finished cloth.

The public finance side of the story of the wool trade may be best guided through the history of the Staple. The first experiments with a staple town or towns through which all wool destined for export had to pass have been described in an earlier chapter.[12] Until the capture of Calais in 1347 the Staple, when abroad, was located in the Low Countries, in Brabant or at Bruges or St Omer: but Calais, so close to Flanders, was an obvious choice once it was in English hands. It was first formally established there in 1363, and after some temporary migrations, settled there permanently from 1392. These same decades saw the formal emergence of the Company of the Staple, the syndicate which operated its monopoly of export traffic. At its peak the Company had some 200 members: the rich London capitalists were its dominant partners. From the profits of operating the export monopoly, the Company was in a position to advance as a corporation substantial cash loans, which the crown recurrently needed in order to meet military (and other) expenditures. Repayment was secured by assignment on the customs duties on export. The Staplers' business was not without risk, and their monopoly aroused a good deal of resentment among growers, who suspected them of manipulating the foreign market in order to keep high profit margins to themselves. In spite of this hostility, their privileges were consistently maintained. They were too useful to crown finance to be dispensed with, though their capacity to lend naturally declined with the gradual decline of the wool trade. Edward IV finally tidied up the situation by handing over to the Company the collection of the export duties on wools (with the exception of wool being exported direct to Italy, by this time a negligible proportion), in return for which the Company undertook to meet the expenses of garrisoning Calais and of the convoy of wool fleets thither. They also agreed to pay into the Exchequer any surplus of their company profit over £15,000. They thus became in effect a nationalized company, with a responsibility for covering one item of the Crown's recurrent public expenditure. In that list of expenditures Calais was just one item, albeit a very important one; the Staplers' takings would not run now to covering more than that.

There can be no doubt that the way in which the Crown and the Staplers together managed wool export damaged the trade that the Staplers' handled. The Staple merchants, having bid down the price to the growers as far as they might, sought to offset their export duty obligations in the high price that, as monopolists, they could charge to foreign buyers. Given the continuing difficulties, political and commercial, of the Flemish cloth industry, the long-term effect was to depress sales and so to discourage export. Customs revenues which the Crown used as collateral, therefore shrank, and with it the Staplers' lending confidence. The Crown's bullionist regulations, designed to preserve specie in the kingdom, worked to the same effect. The export of specie was severely discouraged, and so was sale to aliens on credit. The bullion ordinances of 1429–30 insisted that all wool bought at the Staple must be paid for in bullion or coin, and that one third of the price must be delivered to the Calais mint by the seller, to be reminted into English coin. As English coin was of a higher standard than that of the Duke of Burgundy's dominions, this again drove the price of wool up to the foreign buyer, encouraging him to take his trade elsewhere and favouring the competition from Iberian and Scottish wools.

The decline of the export trade in wool and the monopolistic system of its management gave impetus, at its expense, to the native English cloth industry, which had already, as we have seen, been beginning to revive in the first half of the fourteenth century. Its rise meant that the quantity of home grown English wool that was exported reduced steadily as a proportion of the total crop. At first its recovery was based chiefly on the home market, but by mid century export was beginning to be significant. From 1347, when a custom duty was first imposed on native cloth exports, we can trace the rise of the trade systematically. There were fluctuations, sometimes acute, most of them the consequence of friction with Burgundian and Hansard shippers, but the overall pattern was of powerful growth. In the 1380s some 16,000 cloths were being exported annually: by the end of the century the average was near 40,000. By 1440 it was touching 60,000, outstripping at this point the value of wool exports. By this time the wool merchants who specialized in supplying the raw material to the native industry were acquiring a high commercial and social profile, men like John Thame of Fairford whose brass one may see in the church there and who commissioned the magnificent glass of its windows.

Among the reasons for the expansion of the cloth trade were several which present the reverse face of the circumstances that were affecting the wool trade adversely. Difficulties in the Flemish cloth industry, which reduced its need for raw wool, opened opportunities for English manufactured cloth: Gascony was at first the most important market, but other outlets in Spain, the Baltic, the Mediterranean and the Low Countries themselves soon became important. There were no staple limitations on exporting: in effect the trade was free. For that reason, aliens always maintained a major position as exporters, but native English merchants were in the business from the first and steadily increased their share of it. In 1391 the English merchant adventurers trading to Prussia secured from Richard II the right to govern their own colony there: those in the Low Countries (a still more important group) obtained the same privilege in 1407. The English side of the organization of the various companies of Merchant Venturers (founded with a view to keeping pace as exporters with foreign competitors) begins to emerge with clarity in the mid-fifteenth century, the most important being the London company. These Adventurers were general merchants: their share of England's import trade came to be greater even than their share of export, and their leaders grew very wealthy indeed.

Because the English export trade in cloth was directly linked to a domestic industry its economic significance was distinctly different from that of the wool trade. Notwithstanding some technological advances, such as the use of water power to drive fulling mills, it remained comparatively labour intensive. The higher wage levels of the post-plague period meant that the wealth that it generated was much more widely distributed than the profits of the wool trade, and the greater mobility of labour promoted by the new conditions meant that there was no shortage of workers. A number of the materials required for its processes had to be imported, such as alum and dyestuffs. Factors such as these affected importantly the locations of its development: in order to prosper a centre needed to have access to good supplies of the raw material, wool, and to a distributive centre for imports: proximity to a good supply of fast running water was also an advantage. This was why the Cotswolds, for instance, and the West Riding of Yorkshire were among the areas where it flourished. The Cotswold hinterland helped to foster the fortunes of Bristol, already a busy commercial port: Salisbury, with good communications with Southampton likewise did well as a distributing and collecting centre in the Wiltshire region with its downland sheepwalks and rural cloth industry. Some large cities were important as centres of production, Norwich and Coventry, for instance, and for a while York. But there was a tendency for manufacture to move into the countryside, where labour was cheaper, rents lower, and there were no restrictive gild practices to hamper the operations of the merchant entrepreneur, with capital invested in raw materials and equipment, who organized the workforce and sold the finished cloth wholesale. Small towns, hitherto insignificant, rose in consequence to new prominence and prosperity in the cloth producing regions, as did Lavenham in Suffolk, Wakefield in Yorkshire, Tiverton in the south west. The classic example is Castle Combe in Wiltshire. Here the manor, which had boasted a fulling mill in Edward III's time, came into the hands of the great soldier Sir John Fastolf early in the fifteenth century. From 1415 to the end of his military career, he clothed the men of his company in red and white cloth of Castle Combe 'purchasing yearly more than £100 [worth] of his tenants there'. So the manor began to prosper on a new scale: artisans, who paid 2s. a year *chevage* to live in its boundaries, arrived in numbers. Soon the reputation of the town's fine reds led clothmen like Roger Robins of Cirencester to send their cloths to be dyed there. By 1457 'Castle Combe' was a trade name known in London for fine reds. The profits of the manor lordship soared, and not of the lordship only. William Haynes, originally Fastolf's bond tenant and who had made himself a substantial producer, left chattels worth 3,000 marks to his widow when he died.[13]

The story of cloth making presents the cheerful face of late medieval England's urban history. The general picture is a good deal less happy, and here, at last, plague mortality looks to be at the root of what has been called the 'malaise'. Owing to their crowded, unhygienic conditions, towns were naturally particularly hard hit by the first plagues, and they tended to be more vulnerable to the later, bubonic visitations than were rural areas. In the post-plague age, shortage of labour, high wages and slackening demand all posed problems for towns. Empty houses spelt a drop in rental income for property owners. There was a marked reduction in the number of small but active market centres, especially in traditional corn growing regions in the Midlands: the shrinkage of population meant there was too little demand, in many places, to keep the craftsmen who had provided services to the surrounding countryside in profitable business. Though there was still immigration into towns, especially in cloth making areas, in too many places it was insufficient to balance the ravages of mortality. The burden of the fee farm of the city or borough, and of parliamentary taxation, fell in consequence more heavily on the surviving inhabitants, since these were assessed on the town in round sums and there were fewer to contribute. 'The city is impoverished by withdrawal of merchants and the great pestilence' the men of Lincoln pleaded in 1446, 'so that scarce 700 citizens stay there, of whom none can support the charge of the said farm'. Winchester, its citizens declared in 1440, 'through pestilence and loss of trade has had 11 streets, 17 parish churches, and 987 messuages in ruins during the last 50 years, and is so impoverished as to be unable to pay the fee farm'.[14] The fact that in the fifteenth century a good many fee farms were reduced, and tax assessments modified, is a clear indication that such distress was real, and undeniable.

Urban prosperity depended on production and distribution. As regards the former, competition from the countryside clearly affected some centres adversely; the growing rural cloth industry had much to do with the fifteenth century difficulties of York and Coventry, which down to the end of the four-teenth century had weathered trouble well. Craft gild restrictions here inhibited rationalization and maximization of production, which might otherwise have helped. Those towns that maintained a major distributive role fared best. This did not just mean those in cloth producing regions: Tavistock for instance did well because it was a major centre of collection and marketing for the rural based Cornish tin mining. The serious recession in import trade between 1450 and 1470, consequent on the loss of the French provinces, the outbreak of civil war at home and an interlude of particularly difficult relations with the German Hansards, caused discomfort almost everywhere.

The one city whose fortunes barely faltered over the long period 1350 to 1485 was, once more, London. There was a reduction in the overall population level, but not an acute one. The merchant capitalists of the city's greater guilds – the mercers, vintners, goldsmiths, skinners and grocers – profited by supplying the court, and a host of well off visitors drawn to the capital as the centre of national administration. They also dominated the export trades, both in cloth and wool. Something of the order of 60 per cent of all the kingdom's foreign trade flowed through London. London's consistent fortunes, however, were the exception to the generally uneven pattern of English urban history through this time.

It was in the countryside, without much question, that the demographic decline following the onset of the plagues made its sharpest impact on the economy, over the long term. The words 'over the long term' need to be emphasized. There was no great shift, in the aftermath of 1349, in the general pattern of the cultiva-tion and exploitation of agricultural estates. After some initial panic, landlords in the early 1350s found little difficulty in filling vacant tenancies (a telling indication of how sharp the pressure of population on the land had been beforehand). There was little serious dislocation of the demesne cultivation that had characterized the earlier 'high farming' age. A succession of poor harvests in the 1350s and 60s kept cereal prices high, and for the time being the enforcement of the Statute of Labourers was quite effective in pinning back wages. The consequences that might have been expected from the new shortage of labour and a drop in demand for produce did not, as a result, show very visibly. Landlords' incomes held up pretty well: Professor Holmes has calculated that on great lay estates seignorial income in 1370 was not on average quite 10 per cent lower than it had been in the 1340s.[15]

Part of the reason why such incomes had not fallen further was what has been called the 'seignorial reaction' of the decades immediately following 1348. At the national level this had an obvious symptom in the Statute of Labourers, approved in parliament where the lords and shire knights represented essentially the landowning interest. At the local, manorial level lords' stewards and auditors tightened up their accounting, and became more vigorous in the pursuit of arrears of rent and debts. Most lords sought at the same time to exploit more vigorously their legal advantages and their profits of court. Some renewed labour services which had previously been commuted, in order to ensure cheap labour on their demesnes: others charged highly for permission to employ their bond tenants. Dues such as *merchet* (the fine due from a bondman when his daughter married) were rigorously enforced, and more boon-works for the lord were demanded. Every endeavour was made to keep rents and entry fines at a high level. Efforts such as these, in combination with the vagaries of the weather, contributed to the considerable success of most landlords in minimizing the disadvantageous economic consequences of plague mortality over a period of some twenty years from 1348–9.

It was not possible to hold up the economic weather indefinitely, however. The 1370s brought better harvests: agricultural commodity prices fell and the attempt to hold back wages began to break down. Vacant holdings began to be harder to let, because it became harder to restrain discontented tenants from quitting their manors in quest of better conditions. Reaction had generated tension, and circumstances more favourable to the tenant stiffened resistance to it on their part. In 1377 a petition of the commons complained that 'in many lordships and localities in the kingdom of England the villeins and those who hold on villeinage . . . are refusing the customs and services due to their lords . . . by colour of certain exemplifications out of Domesday Book they claim that they are quit and utterly discharged of all manner of serfdom'.[16] Finally, in 1381, when tempers everywhere had been sharpened by the unjust incidence of the poll tax, resentment culminated in the Peasants' Revolt.

Significantly, given the pattern of seignorial reactions to the pressures of the post-plague period, the abolition of serfdom was in the forefront of all the demands made by the rebels in 1381. The men of Somerset concocted a charter freeing all men of their county from manorial bondage. Those of Essex were prepared to return home from London after Richard II, at Mile End, had promised them charters of manumission. Wat Tyler demanded that 'no man should be a serf, nor do homage or any manner of service to any lord, but should give fourpence rent for an acre of land, and that no one should work for any man but at his own will, and on terms of a regular covenant'.[17] Wherever they went the rebels made great bonfires of the records of manorial courts, and those who had helped to administer the Statute of Labourers were singled out for special persecution. The revolt of course achieved nothing; and when it was over charters of freedom granted in the heat of the crisis were revoked and old obligations reimposed. Yet there was no repetition of the events of 1381. Already by that time many landlords were beginning to realize that the struggle to maintain old ways would never be won, and were taking steps that in the long run (quite unintentionally) reduced to insignificance the grievances which had led to the revolt.

John Smyth, the historian of the Berkeley family, noted a great change during the time of Lord Thomas IV, in the mid 1380s:

> Then began the times to alter, and he with them . . . and then, instead of manureing his demesnes in each manor with his own servants, oxen, kine, sheep . . . under the oversight of the reeves of the manors . . . this lord began to joyst and tack in other men's cattle into his pasture grounds by the week, month, and quarter: and to sell his meadow grounds by the acre, and so between wind and water as it were continued part in tillage and part let out . . . for the rest of that king's reign: and after in the time of Henry the fourth let out by the year still more and more as he found chapmen and price to his liking . . . But in the next age that succeeded his nephew and heir male lord James who succeeded in these manors . . . let out [all] the manor houses and demesne lands, sometimes at racked improved rents according to the estimate of the time and sometimes at smaller rents . . . which is the general course and husbandry for far the most part to this very day [1618].[18]

The development that John Smyth so splendidly describes was a general one. Everywhere, in the late fourteenth century and the fifteenth, we find that lords were leasing out their demesnes, and that leases, with the passage of time, were becoming longer. Prior Chillenden of Canterbury between 1391 and 1411 leased virtually all the demesnes of Christ Church, taking food rents on some of the Kentish manors to supply the monastery. Crowland abbey had let most of its demesnes by 1430; Leicester abbey did the same over the period from 1408 to 1477. The process was not always fast but it was sure; every decade, as Miss Harvey writes of the Westminster Abbey estates, saw more leasing of demesne.[19] The result was nothing less than a complete change in the predominant role of the landlord in agriculture, from farmer to *rentier*. There were also very important results for customary tenants and labourers. The commutation of labour services became virtually universal, and wage labour, always important, became the pivot of all cultivation on any scale larger than that of the single peasant's family holding.

Gradually, in these changing conditions, we begin to see three groups emerging in the cultivating class, defined by new names, 'yeoman', 'husbandman' and 'hind', which now replace old terms with stronger manorial overtones, as villein, bondman, or cottar. The yeoman, who had put together parcels of leased land of up to 60 acres or more, employing labour and producing for the market, begins to look the recognizable ancestor of the future tenant farmer: the more prosperous yeomen could entertain hopes of rising into the gentility. The husbandmen were a much more numerous group. Typically, the husbandman was the cultivator of a rented small-holding, probably made up of strips in the still predominant open field system of farming, perhaps 15 to 30 acres in all. In the new framework, he was the nearest to the traditional customary tenant of the manor, tilling and harvesting first and foremost for his own household's subsistence; but working more land than his forebears would have done, and hoping to sell more of his produce. He was the classic working countryman of his age: for the author of *God Speed the Plough* he was the man 'whose labour maintains the world'.[20] The hind was the village worker who lived largely through the wages of his labour. He still had something of the old 'cottar' about him, but sharpened demand for his services and greater freedom of contract had opened prospects for him of a new level of humble prosperity. The literary sources are vividly explicit about the higher wages and better standards of living that labourers now expected: Gower complains that they will no longer take hire by the year or month, but insist on being paid by the day, and with good rations. Langland says much the same:

> May no penny ale them pay, nor a piece of bacon,
> But it be fresh flesh or fish, fried or y-baked,
> And that chaud or plus chaud for chilling of their mouths.
> But he be highly y-hired, else will he chide.[21]

For all, yeoman, husbandman and hind alike, agricultural life remained precarious, at risk from the weather, sheep murrain and cattle pests: but with the end of the old days of land hunger, high farming and low wages, times became a good deal better for those who lived on the land and tilled it.

Above all, the changed situation in the countryside rang the death knell of serfdom. It ceased to be practicable for lords to take advantage of the legal disabilities of villeins. To quote an example, a sum called a recognition had been paid traditionally by customary tenants on the Bishop of Worcester's estates when a new lord entered. In 1433, when the estates were in the king's hand in a vacancy it was reported that 'the customary tenants of the aforesaid manors were . . . in such great poverty that if these recognitions were levied from them they would leave the land, holdings, and tenures of the aforesaid lordships vacant, to the great prejudice of the lord king and the final destruction of the aforesaid manors'. The bishop's tenants in fact never paid another recognition; they shook themselves free, too, of seignorial tallage and a host of minor dues and 'pleas and perquisites of court'.[22] It was no good trying to bully tenants who would leave the land if they were pressed too hard; that would only reduce further the lord's already diminished customary rents. At the same time, as men of greater substance became involved more often in leasing customary holdings, and as anxiety began to rise about the depopulation of the countryside, the law at last began to offer greater protection to the manorial tenant. The council and chancery were upholding the customary terms of manorial tenures early in the fifteenth century, and in Edward IV's reign the common law began to entertain actions of trespass brought by customary tenants against their lords. Former villein tenures were now more often spoken of as copyholds. Under a copyhold, the tenant would, after paying his entry fine, receive a copy of the court roll entry admitting him to his holding, at a fixed rent. Normally copyholds were heritable, for a period of three lives (after which a new tenancy agreement would be struck). Copyholders were free to sell their holdings, provided the sale was recorded in the manor court and an entry fine paid by the purchaser. The comparative freedom of this form of tenure, compared with that of the former villein is striking. Villein status, though never abolished, had ceased to be relevant in the new conditions, and slid into oblivion.

As far as can be made out, the circumstances that favoured labourers and tenants late in the Middle Ages did not affect the fortunes of great landlords quite as adversely as we might expect. These were difficult times, but there was no real crisis for the seignorial class. Some ecclesiastical landlords found themselves in serious trouble, but mismanagement, or misfortune (as on some Durham estates, which suffered heavily in the fighting in the Wars of the Roses between the Yorkists and Margaret of Anjou), seem usually to have been involved. Enterprising abbots found means to maintain, even sometimes to increase their revenue: John Whethamstede at St Albans added to his rent roll by the purchase of substantial properties, and the Prior of Canterbury, seeing that rents for grazing were profitable, spent money heavily but intelligently to reclaim land from Appledore Marsh and to make it fit to let as a sheep pasture. The great secular landlords seem to have suffered even less than the religious. The tendency, among the greater nobility at least in the fifteenth century, was towards the concentration of ever greater acreage in fewer hands; what was lost in diminished rents was more than offset, for the successful, by a sheer increase of properties from which rents were drawn. Rent, besides, had its own advantages: it brought in a reasonably assured income, allowed better budgeting, and facilitated economies in administrative costs and household expenditure. For lay magnates there were, in addition, many ways of offsetting a decline in agricultural profits. Many enriched themselves abroad in the war with France, winning ransoms, booty, and estates overseas. For their services at home and abroad, lords expected and obtained rewards from the crown, new estates, offices of profit, annuities, wardships – and, of course, advantageous marriages for themselves and their heirs which would increase further the acreage of their inheritances. The effects of the plague in the long term caused a social revolution in the humbler strata of society, bringing to birth a new society of tenant farmers, copyholders and labourers, out of the debris of the old manorial community. They did not however seriously affect the position of landownership as the basis of the political, social and economic authority of the dominant element in society.

Country gentlemen, landlords and leaseholders on a lesser scale than the great lay aristocrats, do not seem to have fared badly either. Hard evidence about their fortunes and their management of their estates is not easy to come by, but it is indicative that their political influence and independence were steadily growing through the post-plague period. The same sort of opportunities to augment their incomes from land were open to knights and country gentry as were open to their superiors (though on a different scale), through annuities, fees, offices obtained as the reward of good service, and gains of war. Sir John Fastolf, as McFarlane has shown, was regularly sending home from France through the hands of his Paris banker, Jean Sac, moneys gained in war service, which his English agents invested in the purchase of manors. He had inherited lands worth £46 from his father, and he made a good marriage, worth £225 per annum to him; by 1446 he had accumulated lands to the astonishing value of £1,061 per annum.[23] Other men, who did not go to the wars, prospered likewise: Judge Paston, the founder of his family's fortunes, was a successful lawyer who built up his estate by shrewd purchases and the good marriages he made for himself and his sons. At a humbler level, Bartholomew Bolney, who got a start in life when he went to Winchester as founder's kin and later studied law, was able, as Steward to the Abbot of Battle, to build up for himself a comfortable holding in Sussex: the stout little book of his title deeds has left us 'the record of a small estate, acquired piece by piece, by an up and coming member of the administrative class'.[24] Significantly, gentlemen and aspirant gentlemen were prominent among those taking up leases of demesnes from greater landlords who had abandoned direct farming, and they did so with an eye to profit through good management at close quarters.

It is not surprising, therefore, to find gentlemen prominent among those who sought to make something of the shift away from arable farming toward pasturing that is observable in late medieval England. Pasture was less labour intensive than tillage, so less demanding in terms of the wage bill: sheep could be grazed for their mutton as well as their wool, cattle for hides as well as meat. Enclosure for pasture offered too a solution to the abandonment of customary holdings on indifferent land which was one of the consequences of demographic decline and more widespread internal migration of labour. In some places whole villages were emptied: nearly 70 were abandoned in Oxfordshire, for instance, between 1350 and 1485. Abandonment was particularly widespread in the old areas of intensive arable farming in the Midlands, and it offered an obvious opportunity to enclose. Landlords and lessors of demesne were not always quick in the uptake, but the potential to replace lost rents profitably was real, and the process over time becomes marked. At Compton Verney in

Warwickshire Professor Hilton has traced a steady tale of surrenders of holdings by customary tenants from the late fourteenth century on: by 1461 six large fields had been enclosed and were let for pasture, at nearly 20 marks each. John Brome of Baddesley Clinton in the same county, a rising gentleman, had 300 acres of demesne enclosed in the mid-fifteenth century: he was fattening cattle bought in the markets of Coventry and Birmingham which he sold to local butchers (and sometimes to London butchers too).[25] He and his like did not do badly. By the end of the century there were beginning to be complaints (not always well informed) about deliberate eviction of tenants by enclosing landlords who wished to convert arable into cattle and sheep pastures.

The picture of agriculture that emerges at the end of our period is thus one that looks more varied, both in economic and social terms than it did at its beginning. Much the same could be said of the whole economy whose fortunes we have been seeking to review. There was greater variety at the end of the period in export trade, an expansion of cloth making industry into new areas, and a very wide variety in urban fortunes. Behind these features there can be perceived another yet more important contrast, a shift in the distribution of wealth, both geographically and socially. Geographically, in the start of the fourteenth century, the richest region of England was the central belt, stretching from the Severn estuary in the west toward London in the south and up to the Wash northward, through the great corn growing counties. At the end of the fifteenth century wealth was concentrated in East Anglia, Wessex and the south west, and in the home counties. The correlation between this re-distribution of wealth and the growth of the cloth industry is clear; so is the significance of proximity to London with its large population that demanded to be supplied. Consequences of population decline and increased mobility of labour were among the contributory factors behind this redistribution, but they do not look like the principal ones. Socially, their impact is much clearer. Among the humbler, working sectors in society, wealth was now distributed more widely and less unevenly than in the past. That is where the great shift in the ratio of inhabitants to resources that followed the coming of the plagues is abundantly and impressively clear in its effects.

Notes

1 *Chron. Abbatie de Parco Lude*, ed. E. Venables (Lincolnshire Record Society, 1891), p. 38.

2 *Annals of Ireland*, ed. P. Butler (1849), p. 35.

3 J. C. Russell, *British Medieval Population* (Albuquerque, 1948), chapters 6 and 10: M. M. Postan in the *Cambridge Economic History*, vol. I (2nd edn., 1966), pp. 560ff.: and see now J. Hatcher, *Plague, Population and the English Economy, 1348–1530* (London, 1977).

4 D. Oschinsky (ed.), *Walter of Henley and Other Treatises on Estate Management and Accounting* (Oxford, 1971).

5   I. Kershaw, 'The great famine and agrarian crisis in England, 1315–22', *Past and Present*, no. 59 (1973).

6   M. C. Prestwich, *The Three Edwards* (London, 1980), p. 268.

7   Poem quoted by J. L. Bolton, *The Medieval English Economy* (London, 1980), p. 185.

8   From the *Monstraunces*: text printed in J. G. Edwards, 'The baronial grievances of 1297', *E.H.R.*, vol. 58 (1943), pp. 170–1.

9   *Ante.*, Chapter 6, p. 101.

10 *Chron. H. Knighton* (R.S., 1889), vol. II, p. 62.

11 25 Edward III, Stat. 2.

12 *Ante.*, Chapter 7, pp. 129–31.

13 On Castle Combe, see *V.C.H., Wiltshire*, vol. IV, pp. 129–33; and E. M. Carus Wilson, 'Evidences of industrial growth on some fifteenth century manors', *Economic History Review*, 2nd series, vol. 12 (1959–60).

14 *C.P.R. 1436–41*, p. 400 (Winchester); *1446–52*, p. 80 (Lincoln).

15 G. A. Holmes, *The Estates of the Higher Nobility in Fourteenth Century England* (Cambridge, 1957), pp. 114–15.

16 R.P., vol. III, p. 21.

17 *Anonimalle Chronicle*, ed. V. H. Galbraith (Manchester, 1927), pp. 144–5.

18 J. Smyth, *The Lives of the Berkeleys*, ed. Sir J. Maclean (Gloucester, 1883), vol. II, pp. 5–6.

19 B. F. Harvey, 'The Leasing of the Abbot of Westminster's demesnes in the later middle ages', *Economic History Review*, 2nd series, vol. 22 (1969), pp. 17–27.

20 W. W. Skeat (ed.), *Pierce the Ploughman's Creed* and *God Speed the Plough* (E.E.T.S., vol. 30, 1867), p. 69.

21 *Piers Plowman*, C Text, Passus VIII, ll. 333–6.

22 C. Dyer, 'A redistribution of incomes in fifteenth century England', *Past and Present*, no. 39 (1968), pp. 11–33.

23 K. B. McFarlane, 'The investment of Sir John Fastolf's profits of war', *T.R.H.S.*, 5th series, vol. 7 (1957), pp. 91–116.

24 M. A. Clough (ed.), *The Book of Bartholomew Bolney* (Sussex Record Society, vol. 63, 1964), p. xxviii.

25 R. Hilton, 'A study in the pre-history of English enclosure', in *Studi in Onore di A. Sapori* (Milan, 1957), pp. 675ff.

Note on secondary reading (post 1970)

J.L. Bolton, *The Medieval English Economy, 1100–1500* (London, 1980) is an excellent overall survey. Three books that are important and original interpretively are R.L. Britnell, *The Commercialisation of English Society, 1000–1500* (London, 1993); C. Dyer, *Standards of Living in the Later Middle Ages: Social Change in England, c. 1200–1520* (Cambridge, 1989); and S.H. Rigby, *English Society in the Later Middle Ages: Class, Status and Gender* (Basingstoke, 1995). On all that concerns the peasantry, R.H. Hilton, *The English Peasantry in the Later Middle Ages* (Oxford, 1975) is invaluable: on towns, the same goes for S.M.G. Reynolds, *An introduction to the History of English Medieval Towns* (Oxford, 1977). A very useful article by R. Schofield, with broad implications, is 'The geographical distribution of wealth in England, 1334–1649', *Economic History Review*, 2nd series, vol. 18 (1965).

On the plague, and its demographic impact, see J. Hatcher, *Plague, Population and the English Economy, 1348–1530* (London, 1977): on demography, J.C. Russell, *British Medieval Population* (Albuquerque, 1948) and M.M. Postan, in the *Cambridge Economic History* vol. I (2nd edn., 1966) p. 560–70, remain important. So does J.M.W. Bean, 'Plague, population and economic decline in England in the later middle ages', *Economic History Review*, 2nd series, vol. 15 (1962–3). G. Twigg is useful for the medical angle, *The Black Death: a biological reappraisal* (London, 1984); and R. Horrox, *The Black Death* (Manchester, 1994) is valuable for illustrative source material.

On export trade, the overall survey by E.M. Carus Wilson and O. Coleman, *England's Export Trade 1275–1547* (Oxford, 1963) remains important. On the wool trade, see T. H. Lloyd, *The English Wool Trade in the Middle Ages* (Cambridge, 1977); and on the cloth industry A.R. Bridbury, *Medieval English Clothmaking* (London, 1982). Other works are cited in the main bibliography, Section 5d.

Because the literature is very extensive, a selection of useful works on specific topics that have been treated in this chapter is best listed seriatim. (i) On the thirteenth century background, see E. Miller and J. Hatcher, *Medieval England: rural society and economic change, 1086–1348* (London, 1978), and *Medieval England: towns, commerce and crafts 1086–1348* (London, 1995). (ii) On the early fourteenth century and its 'crisis', see the papers collected in B.M.S. Campbell (ed.), *Before the Black Death: Studies in the Crisis of the Early Fourteenth Century* (Manchester, 1991); I. Kershaw, 'The great famine and agrarian crisis in England, 1315–22', *Past and Present*, no. 59 (1973); J.R. Maddicott, *The English Peasantry and the Demands of the Crown, 1294–1341* (Past and Present Supplement, no. 1, 1975); M. Mate, 'High prices in early fourteenth century England, causes and consequences', *Economic History Review*, 2nd series, vol. 28 (1975). (iii) On the Statute of Labourers, see S. Penn and C. Dyer, 'Wages and earnings in late medieval England and the enforcement of the labour laws', *Economic History Review*, 2nd series, vol. 43 (1990), and L.R. Poos, 'The social context of the enforcement of the Statute of Labourers', *Law and History Review*, vol. 1 (1983); and refer back to B.H. Putnam's invaluable *The Enforcement of the Statute of Labourers* (New York, 1908). (iv) On serfdom, and the Peasants' Revolt, see R.H. Hilton, *The Decline of Serfdom* (London, 1969): J. Hatcher, 'English serfdom and villeinage; toward a reassessment', *Past and Present*, no. 90 (1981); E.B. and N. Fryde, 'Peasant rebellion and peasant discontents', in E. Miller (ed.) *The Agrarian History of England and Wales*, vol. III (Cambridge, 1991), chapter 8; see also the studies of the Peasants' Revolt listed in 'Note on Secondary Reading' at the end of Chapter 10, below. (v) On landlords' estates and farming fortunes in the post-plague age see B.M.S. Campbell, *English Seignorial Agriculture, 1250–1450* (Cambridge, 2000); C. Carpenter, 'The fifteenth century gentry and their estates', in M. Jones (ed.) *Gentry and lesser Nobility in Late Medieval Europe* (Gloucester, 1986); E.B. Fryde, *Peasants and Landlords in later Medieval England, c. 1380–c. 1525* (Stroud, 1996); G.A. Holmes, *The Estates of the Greater Nobility in Fourteenth*

Century England (Cambridge, 1957) remains valuable. (vi) On towns, besides S. Reynolds cited above, see C.P.S. Platt, *The English Medieval Town* (London, 1976); on urban decline see R.B. Dobson, 'Urban decline in late medieval England', T.R.H.S., 5th series, vol. 27 (1977); D.M. Palliser, 'Urban decay revisited', in J.A.F. Thomson (ed.), *Towns and Townspeople in the Fifteenth Century* (Gloucester, 1988); and C. Phythian Adam's superb *The Desolation of a City: Coventry and the Urban Crisis of the Late Middle Ages* (Cambridge, 1979). (vii) On London and Westminster, see D. Keene, 'Medieval London and its region', *London Journal*, vol. 15 (1989): G. Rosser, *Medieval Westminster, 1200–1540* (Oxford, 1989); A.R. Myers, *London in the Age of Chaucer* (Oklahoma, 1974). (viii) On life cycles, women and gender, see the papers collected by R.M. Smith (ed.), *Land, Kinship and Life-cycle* (Cambridge, 1984), and by P.J.P. Goldberg, *Woman is a Worthy Wight: Women in Medieval Society* (Stroud, 1992); and the articles by Goldberg cited in the main bibliography, Section 5c.

9 Church and state in the later Middle Ages

The period from the end of the thirteenth to the end of the fifteenth century was a very important one in the history of the relations of church and state in England. It witnessed developments whose cumulative consequence was to establish, by gradual degrees, an effective royal supremacy in the English church long before that supremacy was legally enforced by Henry VIII. The spiritual authority of the pope and the general currency of Roman canon law in England were never challenged in principle, it is true, except by the heretical Lollards, in whose persecution the state took its part. Lyndwood, when he put together his great collection of the provincial constitutions of the English church (completed in 1430) assumed as the basis of their authority their conformity with the general canons of the church. The great volume of correspondence in the *Calendars of Papal Letters Concerning England* shows that Roman authority permeated the day-to-day administration of the English church at every level. Nevertheless the popes found, and increasingly as our period went on, that the effective exercise of their authority depended almost entirely on the willingness or otherwise of the English monarchs to cooperate and acquiesce in it. As Martin V ruefully put it, 'it is not the pope but the king of England who governs the church in his dominions.'[1]

Just before the beginning of our period, in 1279, Edward I's Statute of Mortmain pointed the shape of things to come. It had often given rise to complaint, the statute's preamble declared, that when laymen alienated estates to the church, the lords from whom they held these estates lost the prospect of ever again enjoying such feudal incidents as reliefs, wardships and marriages, because the church would never die or marry or leave an heir under age. Henceforward, therefore, no man was to alienate land to the church without the licence of the king. The church bitterly resented this intrusion into her relations with her patrons, but the statute stood. It had been carefully drafted. Edward I did not forbid men to endow collegiate churches with land; he merely brought endowment under royal supervision, and offenders against the statute were not prosecuted for giving land to pious uses, but for doing so without the king's permission. This was the way things were to work in the future in many more areas beside that of endowment.

The relations of church and state are a broad subject. For the sake of simplicity we may concentrate our attention on three important matters: clerical taxation, papal provisions, and the problem of church endowments which Mortmain has already raised.

Before the end of the thirteenth century the question of clerical taxation culminated in a crisis which largely decided things for the future. During this century, the popes had on a number of occasions imposed taxation, on their own authority, on clerical incomes, usually for crusading purposes. For this purpose incomes were assessed in each rural deanery by juries, which included laymen as well as clergy; the assessment made for Pope Nicholas IV's tenth of 1291 became the standard valuation for the rest of the medieval period. Henry III and Edward I acquiesced in this papal taxation, and were usually rewarded with a substantial share of the proceeds, which they employed for purposes of their own. The crown in consequence came to expect the church to make a contribution towards its extraordinary expenditure. When at the outbreak of war with France in 1294 Edward found himself in exceptional need, he expected exceptional assistance. The king summoned the bishops and clergy to Westminster in September, and gave them three days to make him an aid; their offer of two tenths was curtly rejected, and he asked for a half of their revenues. Those who demurred were warned that they would lose the royal protection if they did not pay, and the grant was made; something like £80,000 had been collected by September 1295. In November that year the representatives of the clergy were again summoned, this time to parliament along with the nobility, knights and burgesses; they granted a tenth and had to promise that they would give more if the need arose.

King Philip IV in France had at the same time been making heavy demands of his clergy, and complaints from disgruntled ecclesiastics in both lands reached Pope Boniface VIII. It was in response to these that he issued his famous bull *Clericis Laicos*. It was a trenchant restatement of the independent sovereignty of the pope over all that regarded the affairs of the clergy, and forbade ecclesiastics to contribute in any way to taxes imposed by the secular authorities, on pain of excommunication, unless the pope had given them leave to do so. It was issued in February 1296; when Edward in November again assembled the clergy at the parliament at Bury in order to obtain the further grant that they had promised, the new archbishop, Robert Winchelsey, had seen the bull. Edward wanted a fifth; he gave the archbishop and his clergy a delay till January to consider the matter, and when they then refused a subsidy, he put them outside the protection of his law. In face of this appalling threat to their security, the majority began to waver. Winchelsey for himself felt that he must stand firm and published the bull, but at the March convocation he agreed that others must be guided by their own consciences. Most clergy and religious houses were glad to come to terms with the king and buy his peace. Winchelsey stuck to his guns personally, but his position had been undermined. Edward, on his way to Flanders in August 1297, told the bishops, who assured him that they would seek the pope's leave to make a grant, that he would have his fifth right away, or a third of the clergy's temporalities if they preferred, and that he would permit no sentences of excommunication against those who paid.

Before there were any further developments the face, and probably the fortunes, of Winchelsey and the other papal loyalists were saved by Boniface's new bull, *Etsi de Statu*. This explained that *Clericis Laicos* should not apply when, in the opinion of the prince and his advisers, a realm was faced with an emergency. The archbishop thankfully accepted that there was an emergency, and both the southern and the northern convocations made grants in the autumn of 1297. In return the crown ceased to collect the earlier levy (the fifth), and the threat of excommunications dropped out of the picture.

Edward I in 1297 won a major victory. He demonstrated effectively that, faced with the threat of outlawry, the English clergy would not and could not take a stand against him, even with assured papal backing. He gained, from the pope and his Archbishop of Canterbury, the all important admission that, in an emergency, he had the right to ask for an aid from his English clergy without seeking papal permission (he was successful here, it must be admitted, largely because he was able to cash in on the firm line that Philip of France took on the same issue). Viewed in the light of the ancient claims for clerical independence of the secular authority, upon which *Clericis Laicos* was based, this was a crucial concession.

Edward himself used his success with wise moderation. He never again asked the convocations for an aid. Boniface, with equal wisdom, was agreeable to himself authorizing the levy of a tenth for three years in 1301, and letting Edward take the lion's share. His successors Clement V and John XXII followed his example when they imposed taxes on the English clergy. By the second half of the fourteenth century things had so far changed that, when Urban VI in 1388 sought to collect a twentieth in England, the response to his effort was a petition from the commons that anyone who levied such a tax without the assent of the *king* should be adjudged a traitor. The roles of king and pope were well on the way already to complete reversal; and the trend was to continue. In Winchelsey's day it had been the pope who claimed that he was protecting the clergy from uncustomary royal taxation; Edward IV claimed in 1463, when he persuaded Pius II not to levy a tax in England, that he was protecting the clergy from an uncustomary imposition that his ancestors had never permitted. A number of popes did try to collect subsidies in England on their own authority, but they were never successful. Henry VI, Edward IV and Henry VII all permitted the collection of taxes or voluntary gifts from the clergy, but that was a different matter: their permission had been sought and given in advance.

Long before the fifteenth century, the pope's right to authorize clerical taxation had ceased to be a lively issue. The issue that did remain alive was the right of the clergy to tax themselves independently through the two convocations. They objected to being summoned to make their grants in parliament, as they had been in 1295. Archbishop Stratford in 1341 succeeded in establishing that they should not be asked to contribute to taxes levied by parliamentary consent, but this did not protect the clergy from the threat of parliamentary authority in a more subtle form; namely from attempts by parliaments to make their grants conditional on the clergy also making a grant, of a stipulated size. In 1371 the bishops (who sat in parliament as well as in convocation) had to struggle to avoid their hands being tied. In 1385 the laity agreed to grant two fifteenths if the clergy would grant two tenths; but they met their match in the formidable Archbishop Courtenay, who was so incensed by the offence to clerical privilege as to insist that the request be erased from the roll. In the troubled reign of the needy Henry IV parliament returned to the attack and the clergy found themselves under still more severe pressure. The commons had come to suspect that a good many clergy were altogether escaping from the net, since stipendiary chaplains were not assessed to the clerical tenths. In 1406 the convocation of Canterbury was twice visited by a deputation of knights from the commons, and in the end agreed to a levy of 6s. 8d. on all salaried clergy not assessed to the tenth. We do not know what arguments were used on the occasion; we can only conclude that the clergy, who had resisted a similar demand in 1404, had concluded that more important privileges would come under threat if they held out.

The clergy had much to gain from maintaining their privileged position with regard to taxation. It enabled them to make their own conditions with their grants, to ensure that their complaints were forwarded from convocation to parliament, and to apportion the inevitable fiscal burden in the way that they chose. But the knowledge that, if they did not give to the king, parliament would make them give with the laity undermined any capacity they might have had to resist royal demands. The English kings of the later Middle Ages sometimes hesitated to approach the intractable commons in parliament, but they looked to the convocations with a contrasting confidence. We are accustomed to think of Edward IV as a king who sought to 'live of his own', and as far as parliament was concerned he had much success after 1471. In these years when parliamentary grants had all but dried up, he could rely, however, on obtaining at least some grants from the convocations. He and others did not think this was inconsistent with living of his own. That of itself is a sign of how, in one respect at least, a royal supremacy had grown within the framework of the English church, still linked though it was to Rome by ties of constant communication.

The question of papal provisions was a more important issue in our period than clerical taxation. The controversies to which it gave rise were more complicated, and it took longer for the dust to settle. In the end, the honours were not quite so unevenly divided.

As the universal ordinary, the pope could claim in canon law the right to collate to all ecclesiastical benefices. In practice he only 'provided' to those that he had reserved to his own collation. From 1265 onward, when Clement IV reserved all benefices whose holders died at the papal court, the classes of reserved benefices were greatly extended, especially in the fourteenth century.

Clement V reserved all benefices of cardinals, papal chaplains and *nuncios*, and benefices vacant by resignation, transfer or exchange at the papal court. John XXII added all benefices vacated as a result of provisions (when a great pluralist like William of Wykeham was promoted to the episcopate and had to resign his preferments these could be very numerous). Urban V in 1363 formally reserved the appointment to all archiepiscopal and episcopal churches (in practice in England all bishoprics were already before that normally filled by provision). The system was further extended by the frequent grants of bulls of expectation, assuring the grantee preferment in a particular church when a vacancy next occurred.

Provision was of course valuable to the popes as a means of extending papal influence, but it was much more valuable to them for financial reasons. Provisions (usually to benefices without cure of souls) afforded the popes a means whereby they could maintain the staff of the *Curia*, from the cardinals down to minor clerks and officials. Besides, a system of papal taxation was, as it were, built into the system of provision. The revenues of any benefice that was filled by provision, both for the preceding period of vacancy and for the first year of occupation, were due to the apostolic see (bishops and higher clergy paid what were called 'common services' on confirmation or provision by the pope, which were calculated on a slightly different basis to this one). These taxes, often lumped together under the general title of 'annates', were a rich source of income to the pope and were a considerable burden for those who paid. They went towards meeting the heavy expenses of the papal household and the households of the cardinals, and to paying for the defence and enlargement of the patrimony of Peter in Italy (which consumed more of the papal revenues in the fourteenth and fifteenth centuries than anything else did).

Explicitly the principal ground for the widespread objection of Englishmen to the system of provision was the way in which it interfered with the normal course of ecclesiastical patronage. Lay patrons were not much affected, since the pope did not as a rule provide to benefices that were in their gift. The king, however, could be, because he claimed among his *regalia*, when a bishopric was vacant and the temporalities were in his hand, the right to present to benefices to which the bishop ordinarily collated. This claim naturally brought his nominees into frequent conflict with papal provisors; but the king had the whip hand, because in England it was an established custom that cases involving advowson (the right to present to benefices) were tried in the lay courts. The real sufferers from provisions were ecclesiastical patrons, and above all the bishops.

> On the ides of October [Bishop Grandison of Exeter wrote to Clement VI in 1342] I was present in the council of the province of Canterbury in London, where among other things, if I may say so by your leave, no small wonder arose at the burdensome and hitherto unknown multitude of apostolic provisions. For it was said that from now onwards prelates, both greater and lesser, . . . will never be able to provide for the well deserving or necessary servants of their churches or of themselves.[2]

The bishops were afraid that soon they would not retain sufficient patronage to provide for the administrators of their dioceses and the clients of their households. Perhaps most of all bishops resented grants of expectancies; these could accumulate to the point where an incoming diocesan had little hope of using any of his patronage for years to come.

Other and wider interests besides those of the ordinaries were disturbed by the papal inroads into ecclesiastical patronage. Archbishop Romeyn of York put the point well, writing in the 1290s to Nicholas IV, to protest against papal plans to annex a prebend in his cathedral to a Roman hospital.

> This was not the intention of the catholic kings of England of famous memory or of those other faithful in Christ who founded not only our churches but the whole church in England for the spreading of the faith, and endowed her amply with temporal goods . . . they were thus generous to the churches for the saving of souls and the forgiveness of sins, that divine worship should be increased, that hospitality should be served and alms given to the poor, and that the churches should be served by good ministers, who would take their stipends for the time from the yield of the said temporal goods.[3]

Papal provisions and annexations thwarted directly the pious intentions of the founders of churches, Romeyn argued. His view was echoed by the community of the land in the parliament of Carlisle in 1307, by parliamentary petition in 1343, and in the preamble to the Statute of Provisors in 1351.

The view that Romeyn put forward, with its emphasis on the respect due to the intentions of founders and the right of their heirs, had deep roots in the old idea of the proprietary church, of the ecclesiastical benefice as the feudal property of a lord and patron. It also appealed to the principle, at first sight beyond challenge, that the English church was endowed to serve the needs of Englishmen. This argument does not look quite so sound when we consider what was the alternative to provision by the pope. The continuator of the *Flores Historiarum* praised John XXII, because his reservations saved the English church in Edward II's reign from a plague of illiterate and unworthy royal clients.[4] The maintenance of learning at the universities depended on provision of benefices for scholars; Oxford and Cambridge in the later fourteenth century were regularly sending lists to the *Curia* of those whom they wished to see preferred. Archbishop Romeyn's ideal vision of a church 'served in person by good ministers' was not the real alternative to provision that so many took it to be; that was rather a church in which the clients of the king and the aristocracy had a richer share of ecclesiastical plums. They would probably not have been at their posts any more often than the pope's clients. Romeyn's view nevertheless was the normal coin of criticism of papal provisions, and was held at large to enshrine a principle of self-evident validity.

Still stronger with people, but perhaps less heavily laboured in clerical correspondence with the *Curia*, were objections to the financial consequences of provision. When an alien resident at the pope's court was provided to an English benefice, its revenue was taken out of the country, an offence to the bullionist instinct of the late medieval commons. The collection of annates had the same effect, and everyone knew that whatever was done at the *Curia* cost gold, for there were fees to be paid for the writing, expedition and sealing of all bulls of provision. 'Thousands of pounds have been paid here to the Lombards for exchange [and transfer to Rome]', wrote Thomas Gascoigne in Henry VI's reign, 'to the impoverishment of the realm.'[5] In the Avignon period in particular there were suspicions that money from England was finding its way, by the medium of a francophile papacy, to the war chest of the French king. Opinion at large greatly exaggerated both the number of aliens provided to English benefices and the sums which were being carried out of England as a result of provisions. From our point of view the exaggeration is not so significant as the fact that Englishmen believed it, and believed that 'among the *curiales* of the apostolic see it has become a proverb that the English are good asses, ready to carry all the intolerable burdens that are put upon them'.[6]

The first formal attack upon the system of provisions was made in the parliament of Carlisle in 1307. Parliament returned to the charge in 1309, and still more bitterly in 1343, when the number of provisions had sharply increased with the coming of Pope Clement VI. In response to the commons' agitation Edward III put an embargo on the entry into the country of bulls prejudicial to the king and his people, and had the ports watched for them. When the mortality caused by the Black Death was followed by another wave of new provisions, the upshot of renewed parliamentary pressure was the Statute of Provisors of 1351.

The statute of 1351 ordained that henceforward elections to bishoprics and in collegiate churches should be free, and that clerical patrons should enjoy the free exercise of their rights of presentation. If any reservation or provision from the court of Rome interfered with these rights and processes the king would present to the office or benefice himself. If anyone presented by the king or by an ecclesiastical patron was disturbed by a papal provisor, the provisor and his agents should be arrested and imprisoned until he should renounce his provision. If the provisor could not be found he was to be outlawed. The effect of the statute was thus to impose the responsibility for defending the English church against provision on the king, by recognizing him as 'patron paramount' in his kingdom. Two years later the Statute of Praemunire tidied up the legal position by forbidding men to take abroad cases cognizable in the king's courts (as matters of ecclesiastical patronage certainly were).

The statutes of Provisors and Praemunire were not in practice the bulwarks against papal authority that they appeared to be on paper. The onus of implementing them fell to the king, and he in fact only enforced them when it was convenient for him to do so. Usually he found it more satisfactory to work with the pope rather than against him. In spite of the statutes the pope continued to provide English bishops to their sees and to translate them from see to see, taking annates when he did so. The men whom he provided were usually the crown's nominees. The king, lay patrons, and the universities continued to petition the popes for provision for their clients. But though the king did not enforce the statutes often, he found them a very useful weapon when the papacy proved either recalcitrant or demanding. In 1365, for instance, when Urban V renewed the demand for Peter's pence from England, which were long in arrears, the Statute of Provisors was reissued. There was a running battle between Edward III and the next pope, Gregory XI, which was not ended until 1375 when the king allowed the pope to resume provision, in return for a papal promise to confirm current royal nominees in their benefices and to moderate his provisions for the future. The Statute of Provisors was reissued yet again in 1390, after Urban VI had made difficulties about the translation (for political reasons) of a number of English bishops during the domestic crisis of 1388. Both sides, however, were by this time clearly playing for advantage, not victory. The same parliament that in 1393 approved a new and stiffer version of the Statute of Praemunire empowered Richard II to seek an accommodation over provision with Pope Boniface IX. And when, five years later, Richard and Boniface did agree to a formal *concordat*, which but for the revolution of 1399 might have become permanent, it effectively sold the pass on provisors, reserving the nomination to bishoprics to pope and king together, and allowing to the former the right to collate to one in every three important vacancies in cathedral and collegiate churches.

The Great Schism, which lasted from 1378 until 1417, greatly strengthened the hand of the king in his dealings with the pope, and there was not much trouble over provisions in this period. After the end of the Schism, Pope Martin V made a last great effort to obtain the repeal of the offending English statutes. In 1421 his collector in England, Simon of Teramo, discoursed to the Convocation of Canterbury on the pope's need to have provision in England, and Martin believed that he had persuaded Henry V, before his death, to do away with the statutes. A series of *nuncios* were despatched to England in the next few years, to work on the king's council and the convocations, and in 1426 Martin formally forbade the bishops to collate to any benefices that were reserved to the apostolic see. Things reached a climax in the next year when Martin suspended Archbishop Chichele, whom he suspected of sympathy with the opponents of provision, from his status as legate, and refused to reinstate him unless he, with the bishops, would formally apply to parliament for the repeal of the statutes. Chichele went through the painful and embarrassing process as ordered, in the spring parliament of 1428. With the bishops, he addressed both the lords and the commons separately, warning them of the possibility of an interdict if they were refractory. He made no impression, and he probably did not expect to. Martin V had to admit failure; a few months later he reinstated Chichele as legate. After this, for the remainder of our period, the vexed question of provisions remained quiescent.

The opposition to provisions secured, largely as a result of the weakness of the papacy in the period of the Great Schism, the virtual elimination, after 1400, of alien provisors from English benefices. This was of course very far from eliminating provision; Thomas Gascoigne half a century later was still fulminating against the 'disgraceful promotions of men in England who had licence . . . to sue out and accept provisions from the pope'.[7] That they still did so was largely owing to the connivance in the system of the kings of England. The crown was much less Erastian than the commons. The crown was also the real gainer both from cooperation with the papacy and from the anti-papal statutes; the two worked together to strengthen royal control over the episcopate and the composition of the higher clergy in general. Hamilton Thompson calls eloquent witness to this effect from the register of the Bishop of Hereford, Richard Mayhew, who was appointed 'by apostolic authority and by the nomination of the aforesaid most illustrious prince [Henry VII]'. Mayhew's successor, Charles Booth, was like him provided to the see, but the register did not in his case even mention the apostolic authority: he was 'nominated by the said most illustrious prince [Henry VIII] to the church and bishropric of Hereford, vacant by the death of the lord Richard Mayhew of honest memory'.[8] We see here the royal supremacy in action and almost acknowledged, long before the calling of the Reformation Parliament.

The act of supremacy apart, the most revolutionary step in the sixteenth century reformation was the dissolution of the monasteries. This too was foreshadowed, but much less clearly, in the late Middle Ages.

The impact, in the thirteenth century, of the order of St Francis with its claims for the special sanctity of holy poverty inevitably raised with new sharpness questions which had always been lurking about the justification for the endowments of the religious. The Statute of Mortmain, with its clear implication that no benefit to a church should justify injury to the legitimate interest of a lay overlord, was symptomatic of the altering outlook later in that century. Two events of the thirty years following its publication showed that the property of the religious was not so safe, nor held so sacred, as it had once been.

The more dramatic of these two events was the dissolution of the Order of the Templars. The charges that were brought against this rich and famous crusading order by Philip IV of France were largely unjustified, and, outside France at least, owed such confirmation as they obtained to confessions extracted under torture. But Pope Clement V was too weak to make a stand against the French king, and in 1312 he dissolved the order on his apostolic authority and transferred its property to the Order of the Hospital. Though this dissolution was not in any sense to the direct profit of the secular power in England, the royal officials had to play a major part in the process by which it was achieved. The Templars' lands were in the king's hands all the time that the charges against them were being investigated, and some never found their way out of them. More important than any material consequence of the dissolution was the impression that it made on people's minds. Langland, writing at the other end of the fourteenth century, had marked the lesson: he saw close at hand the time when others would go the same way as the Temple and for the same reason:

Both rich and religious that rood they honour
That on groats is engraven and on gold nobles.
For covetousness of that cross men of Holy Church
Shall turn as Templars did: the time approacheth fast.[9]

Langland did not expect the blow to other possessioners to come from the pope, but from the king and the lords. It is not at all surprising that he did so, especially in the light of the other event of the late thirteenth century to which we referred. In 1295, after the war had broken out between France and England, Edward I took the lands of the alien priories – those cells and priories in England that were dependencies of French monasteries, as Cluny and such Norman houses as Bec – into his own hands. The revenues were collected in each case by a royal official, who paid the proceeds into the exchequer and made the monks a bare allowance to sustain themselves. The lands were returned to their owners when the war ended, but the same thing happened again in 1324 when war with France broke out, and in 1337, and on the renewal of the Hundred Years War in 1369. As the war continued, what had begun as a temporary royal occupation began to wear an air of permanence.

The fate of the alien priories was decided in the fifteenth century. By that time many of the larger priories had solved their problem by purchasing from the crown letters of denization. Among the Cluniacs Lewes was the first to obtain this concession in 1351; Montacute was the last in 1407. Most of the non-Cluniac houses which were of sufficient size to be properly called conventual saved themselves in the same way. The case of the smaller cells, isolated properties where two or three or perhaps just one monk had resided to supervise the estates, was different. After 1369 most of them were farmed to the highest bidder, and some were sold; William of Wykeham thus obtained most of the lands of Tiron, which went to endow his colleges at Winchester and in Oxford. In 1408 the council agreed that the income from the farms of the remaining cells and priories should be earmarked toward the expenses of the royal household. Finally, by an act of 1414, the possession of all confiscated properties was taken into the king's hands, with a right of pre-emption to the existing farmers. Most of the estates in question were in the end transferred to religious and collegiate foundations; to Henry V's two houses (for the Carthusians and Bridgettines) at Sheen and Syon; to Henry VI's foundations at Eton and King's Cambridge; to the charterhouse of Mount Grace and the chapel of St George at Windsor.

As Knowles and others have stressed, the suppression of the alien priories did not directly anticipate the sixteenth-century dissolution. Most of their estates passed not into secular hands but to religious foundations, as the wealth of the Templars had. This was in line with the view that Archbishop Romeyn had voiced so strongly in another context, that the endowments of the church in England were for the sustention of religious life there, and for no other purpose. The real hostility that the petitions of the commons evinced with regard to the alien priories seems to have been based rather on suspicion of aliens, who sent wealth out of the land and probably betrayed the king's secrets to his enemies, than on enthusiasm for dissolution. Nevertheless the treatment of the priories showed what the lay power could do. As Professor McKisack writes, 'in the dissolution of religious communities at the bidding of the secular power, and not without profit to it, the historian may discern, albeit faintly, the shape of things to come'.[10]

Professor McKisack's words are reinforced when one looks at the pressures for that greater measure of disendowment that Langland thought was already impending in the late fourteenth century. The fiscal burdens of the Hundred Years War, and the suspicion among the aristocracy and gentry that the church was not pulling its weight in its financial contributions, brought the subject into the open in the parliament of 1371. This parliament witnessed a violent attack on the king's clerical ministers which led to the dismissal of bishops Wykeham and Brantingham, the chancellor and treasurer. Some of the lay lords apparently wanted to go much further. It was to this end that two Austin friars were brought into parliament, to expound and defend the view that, in a national emergency, the prince who has given property to churches may take it back, so as to use the revenues for national purposes. The friars argued their case with care and learning from the fathers of the church, but what it meant to the lords was something very radical: 'when war breaks out we must take from the endowed clergy a portion of their temporal possessions, as property that belongs to us and to the whole kingdom'.[11] This statement adds a new and startling dimension to the familiar view, rehearsed in the Statute of Provisors, that the wealth of the church endowed in England should stay where it belonged, in that kingdom.

Nothing came of the proposal of 1371, but the subject remained very much in the air for the next forty years. The events of 1371 sparked off a vigorous academic controversy, in which the Benedictines Ughtred Boldon and William Binham defended the sacrosanct nature of ecclesiastical property, while Wyclif came to the defence of the Austin friars and restated their case at greater length and with new ramifications. By 1381 these arguments were striking an echo at the popular level, as we see from the demand of the peasant rebels that 'the goods of Holy Church should not remain in the hands of the religious, nor of the parsons and vicars, and other churchmen; but those who are in possession should have their sustenance from the endowment and the remainder of their goods should be divided among the parishioners'.[12] It was only a few years before this that Langland had prophesied that possessioners would soon see 'Constantine's coffers' (as he called their endowments) broken open. Most alarming of all to churchmen (outside the crisis of 1381) was the extent to which talk of disendowment found sympathy among the higher ranks of the laity. Both in 1378 and in 1385 it was feared that proposals would again be aired in parliament; in the latter year laymen were already talking about what they should get for themselves, Walsingham says.[13] The advocacy of disendowment in the writings of Wyclif and his followers was by this time giving the issue new and sharp prominence. In 1404 a proposal to confiscate ecclesiastical temporalities was aired by the knights of the shire in the Coventry parliament; it was dropped after a sharp brush between Archbishop Arundel and the commons speaker, Sir John Cheyney, a knight of known Lollard sympathies. In the parliament of 1410 a similar bill was brought forward, with careful calculations as to how the funds released by confiscation might be used (based seemingly on those of an earlier Lollard tract).[14] Though this bill too got nowhere, its proposition, in itself, and the support it attracted gave the church hierarchy and the possessioners ample grounds for alarm.

The association of plans for disendowment with Lollardy in the end went far to discredit the whole idea, especially after Oldcastle's revolt in 1414 had shown that it was not clerical property holders only that it threatened. This was the main reason why so much less was heard of disendowment in the fifteenth century than in the fourteenth. It is hard to gauge how dangerous the threat to the possessioners really was before Oldcastle; probably the Benedictine chroniclers exaggerated it. But they were not the only ones who did so; there were also the men like Langland who foresaw something very like a dissolution in the proximate future. Ideas that would be familiar in the sixteenth century were in the air for a time at least, and at a moment when the lay farmers of the property of alien priories were in a very good position to imagine what advantage to their class could accrue from a major measure of disendowment.

Again and again in this chapter we have come across the same phenomenon, the growing authority of the king in the English church. It was to the king that patrons looked to protect their rights against papal provisors, and to the king that the popes looked to moderate the effect of parliament's anti-papal legislation. The king licensed the denization of the alien priories that were conventual, and organized the distribution of the properties of those that were not. It was to the king that the clergy appealed to protect the property of the church from Lollards and the privileges of convocation from parliaments. This is what we meant when we said at the beginning of this chapter that the fourteenth and fifteenth centuries witnessed the growth, by gradual degrees, of an effective royal supremacy in the English church.

The king, however, could not have withstood papal claims, in the matters of taxation and provision, or have laid hands on the property of the priories, if he had not known that he could rely on the full backing of the lay lords and commons in parliament. The kings took advantage of the groundswell of popular feeling in the background, anti-alien, anti-papal, and anti-clerical; they did not create it. If the English church was becoming recognizably a national church in the centuries before the reformation, it was because the people at large (without much precision in their ideas) wished it to do so, rather than as a result of conscious and premeditated royal policy.

This raises an important question. If we accept that anti-clerical feeling was a crucial factor in the history of relations between church and state in this period, then we are bound to ask how far its prevalence was justified by genuinely unsatisfactory conditions of contemporary ecclesiastical life. That it was prevalent, sometimes seemingly almost universal, we can judge not just from parliamentary petitions, but from a great *corpus* of anti-clerical satire and invective, both Latin and vernacular. There is no doubt about the cloud of testimony: Chaucer, Langland, Wyclif and Gascoigne are only the most famous names in the army of critics. But do they tell more than the truth?

Let us start at the top level of the hierarchy, and look at the episcopate. No one can deny that the English bishops of the later Middle Ages were, taken by and large, an impressive body of men. They were drawn from all walks of the clerical and the social world; from the professional administrators both of church and state, from the universities, from the religious orders; from among the cadets of noble houses and from the humble ranks of the middle and poorer classes. There was a steady rise, over our period, in the number of graduates among their number. Of those who owed their position to high birth or to the service of the crown, most showed themselves to be thoroughly fitted for their office both by their energy and their ability; one might instance Courtenay and Arundel among the aristocrats, and Thoresby, Wykeham, Chichele and Morton among the civil servants. Their registers reveal them as careful and conscientious ecclesiastical administrators. Many devoted their surplus revenue to enlarging and beautifying their cathedrals, to the support of poor scholars, and to the endowment of new foundations, some of which, like Wykeham's twin colleges of St Mary at Oxford and Winchester, were to have a long and important future.

Few bishops had any extensive pastoral experience before they were promoted to the episcopate, but in this sphere too the records of the best of them do them credit. The two Archbishops who had to face the crisis posed by the very heavy mortality among priests and clerks during the plague of 1348, Simon Islip of Canterbury and John Thoresby of York, had both risen through the administrative service of the crown. Both responded impressively to the difficult situation. Thoresby in 1352 set about a regular recruiting drive to the priesthood, and took vigorous action to reduce the problem of non residence among the parish clergy of his province. Both he and Islip also showed notable concern for standards of religious instruction and pastoral care among their clergy. The constitutions of Islip's synod, held at Ely in 1364, enjoined on every priest the duty to examine parishioners beliefs at confession, to make sure that children in the parish were being taught their prayers, and to preach often and in English. The short *Libellus* on ethical religious teaching that he composed and circulated to all the parish priests of his diocese is lost; but Thoresby's Latin *Catechism* is not. On his instructions, it was translated into English, and under the title of the *Lay Folk's Catechism* came to be circulated very widely. It was one of the most influential religious manuals for the laity of the late Middle Ages. Another primate with a very creditable record in the pastoral field was the aristocrat Thomas Arundel (York 1388–96; Canterbury 1396–1414). His early days as Bishop of Ely gave him connections with Cambridge, and he gathered round himself then a group of educated and very gifted clerks, including Walter Hilton, who was later to become the author of two of the most celebrated mystical treatises of the age, the *Scale of Perfection* and the *Epistle on the Mixed Life* (of ordinary activity disciplined by a regular routine of contemplation). Though Arundel is usually best remembered as a persecutor of the Lollards, his influence and that of men associated with him had much to do with the dissemination of some of the most important English religious writing of the whole late medieval period.

Nevertheless there were things amiss at the episcopal level. Too many bishops were absent from their sees for too long. They had duties elsewhere, attendance at parliaments and convocations; many were directly involved in royal administration. This did not, probably, much impair the day-to-day running of their dioceses. The diocesan administrative system in England was so developed that it could operate with complete efficiency in the bishop's absence. Suffragans, Irish bishops or mendicants with a see *in partibus infidelium*, could almost always be found to discharge such necessary episcopal functions as confirmations and ordinations. The bishop's vicar general in spirituals acted administratively and judicially as his deputy, with wide powers; he could take the oath of obedience to the bishop from incumbents, summon and hold diocesan synods, examine candidates for the priesthood. In the consistory court the bishop's official (often the same man as the vicar general) presided. The archdeacons in their jurisdictions carried out most of the routine administrative work and saw that sinners, when they were found, were fined. When, as often happened, the archdeacon was an absentee, his duties were usually discharged by one of the rural deans. The bishops' registers attest that most dioceses were run equally well by these people, whether the bishop was there or not.

What was too often lost by his absence was not efficiency but a sense of direction. Day-to-day business ran smoothly, most of the time, in the late medieval diocese, but the spiritual leadership that should have been expected from the top was too often insufficient, and was felt to be so. This was one of the reasons for very uneven standards among the diocesan clergy.

Chaucer was kinder to the parson, among the clergy of the prologue to the *Canterbury Tales*, than to any other. There were many incumbents who resided in their parishes and discharged their duties as this parson did, no doubt, but we cannot claim that they were the rule. Lack of diocesan supervision was only one reason for this, and probably not the most important. The prevailing attitude to benefices (the freehold of a church that carried with it the greater tithe) was not healthy; they were too often regarded as a kind of property. There were great pluralists, like Bogo de Clare and William of Wykeham in his early days, who drew a princely income from a multitude of benefices, including too many with cure of souls. Some rectories were attached to prebendal stalls in cathedral and collegiate churches; a great many were appropriated to monastic houses. In other cases livings helped to support clerks in the king's household or that of some aristocrat, or scholars at the universities; these men seldom had trouble in obtaining licences for non-residence. In these circumstances the greater tithe, the main revenue of the parish church, went to support the prebend or the monastery, the clerk or the scholar or the pluralist; the parish duties were discharged by a vicar on an often exiguous stipend. In effect, the income of benefices was being widely, almost systematically, exploited for purposes other than those for which they had been intended. The consequence of this was a low standard of literacy and life among the clergy who actually served parishes, their insufficient remuneration and perennial discontent.

There was no ready remedy for this condition of things. For a number of reasons, in the late Middle Ages it seemed to be growing worse rather than better. There was a steady increase in the number of churches appropriated to monasteries, as these found their revenues from estates diminishing in unfavourable economic circumstances. Literacy and bureaucracy, spreading hand in hand, increased the demand for clerical talent in the royal and aristocratic administrative services. A new factor was the growing number of chantry priests, who for a small stipend sang masses at a separate altar in the parish church, or in a collegiate church, or in a private chapel. Their life was easier than that of a parish vicar, and often financially more secure. The vision, which the heretic Wyclif and the orthodox Gascoigne shared, of a highly trained, resident parish clergy who could offer the intelligent among the laity a sound exposition of doctrine, was an impossible dream in the conditions of the time. Life as a vicar was too hard to attract men of talent; and too many vested interests stood in the way of rerouting the full incomes of parochial livings to their original and proper purposes.

There were lights as well as shades, however, at the parochial as at the episcopal level. A highly educated rector may not have been what most parishioners in most parishes felt they most needed. A vicar had to have sufficient Latin to conduct the liturgy; if he was not versed much beyond that in the language, there were plenty of aids in the vernacular available to him as a pastor and teacher. There was Thoresby's *Lay Folk's Catechism*; John Myrc's *Festiall*, a collection of sermons suitable for preaching on feast days and saints' days; and Myrc's manual in English for parish priests (which drew much from William of Pagula's *Oculum Sacerdotis*, a splendid Latin guide from the early fourteenth century to hearing confessions, to religious instruction, and to the administration of the sacraments). The readiness of parishioners to contribute toward the building, furbishment and vestments of their churches suggest a high price set on the ministration that their priests conducted in them; and their eagerness to endow charities and side altars and to maintain parish charities indicate a strong sense of the religious identity of the parish community. There seem to be few indications of any general or widespread feeling among the ordinary laity that they were seriously ill served.

For the monasteries, the later Middle Ages were a difficult time. The rise of the mendicant orders offered a rival vocation to theirs, and with the rise of grammar schools and universities they ceased to play an important role in education. The

Great Schism severed the connexion of the Cistercian monasteries with the general chapter of Citeaux (which was in the Avignon obedience) and a decline of standards and discipline followed. The Black Monks also suffered from the effects of the Schism, but less seriously; their real trouble was that they were being swept out of the main stream of religious life. Chaucer's picture of the monk is of a man often away from his cloister, richly dressed, who loved to dine off a fat swan and whose passion was the chase, nearer a celibate squire than a professed religious.

The records of the visitations of monasteries confirm Chaucer's picture and sometimes heighten it. There was too much comfort. Monks often had their own servants and in some houses had their own rooms and did not even take their meals together. There was often a good deal of drinking after compline. When Bishop Alnwick visited Bardney in 1438 he found that Brother Thomas Barton was accused of adultery with a washerwoman; that Brother Richard Partney had goods of his own and played dice; and that Brother John Hole had excused himself from his course in the saying of mass. Most of the brethren had been haunting taverns in the town.[15] This was a bad case but it was not atypical. The canons of Dorchester in 1441, we are told, were wont to sit down after compline, call for good ale and settle down to chess. At Peterborough 'religion was almost perishing', what with the incompetence of the abbot and the simplicity of the prior. A great many houses were in financial difficulties owing to mismanagement. As Hamilton Thompson wrote, 'the English monasteries in the fifteenth century needed spiritual quickening to justify their existence as a whole'.[16]

Not that the old vigour of the monasteries was entirely gone. In the late four-teenth century they contributed some notable leaders of the life of the church: scholars, like Ughtred Boldon; in Bishop Brunton of Rochester one of the greatest preachers of the age; in Thomas de la Mare, Abbot of St Albans, a leader of monks who was both an able administrator and an example of spiritual austerity. Benedictine graduates of Oxford and Cambridge were among the first in England to take an interest in the nascent revival of classical studies. There was besides, we should note, a fairly steady rise in the number of monastic voca-tions from the time of the Black Death right through to the reign of Henry VII. One order, moreover, the austere and recluse Carthusians, flourished in this last medieval age more than it ever had before. There were seven new foundations between 1370 and 1420. The most famous were the London Charterhouse, of which Sir Walter Manny, courtier and Garter knight, was an early benefactor, and Henry V's magnificent royal foundation at Sheen. The de la Poles were the chief patrons of the Charterhouse at Hull; Thomas Holland, Richard II's nephew, of Mount Grace in the Cleveland Hills. There was still, it is clear, some confidence in the value of the professed religious life, and especially in the upper ranks of society.

Of the whole clerical body, the friars were undoubtedly the most sharply impugned by the critics. 'A good friar is as rare as the phoenix', Wyclif wrote.

Chaucer's friar knew the taverns of the town and the houses of the genteel better than the hospitals, and could coax her last mite out of a widow. Langland scorned friars as fat with begging and for their easy confessions. Once, he admitted, he had seen Charity in a friar's coat, 'But that was far off in St Francis' time'.[17] Earlier Archbishop Fitzralph of Armagh, the great Oxford scholar and Irish metropolitan, had treated the whole structure of mendicant religion to a terrible trouncing in his *De Pauperie Salvatoris;* Langland and Wyclif are full of echoes of his denunciation.

It was natural that the friars should attract hostile attention. Beggars and scroungers are seldom loved, especially when they prosper, as the friars did. Because their orders were not enclosed and they wandered at large in the world, their backslidings were seen at large. There were too many friars, too many vocations, almost certainly, that proved hollow. Their competition with the parish clergy for the hearing of confessions and for burial fees aroused resentment in one ecclesiastical quarter, their independence of diocesans in another (this was what specially roused the anger of Archbishop Fitzralph). To severe moralists it looked often as if their ministrations, which had to be gentle to catch a clientele, were unhinging Christian discipline rather than revivifying the faith.

The view of the friars' critics was not the whole truth, however. They made a powerful contribution to the religious life of the fourteenth and fifteenth centuries. Duns Scotus and Ockham, the two greatest English scholastic philosophers of the whole Middle Ages, were Franciscans. It was the mendicants who took the lead in answering Wyclif's academic challenge to catholic orthodoxy. The friars were also the greatest preachers of the age, and the impact of their sermons is well attested by the popularity of such books as the *Summa Praedicantium* of the great Dominican, John Bromyard. Bromyard's homely anecdotes, drawn from everyday scenes of life to illustrate a profound moral teaching, had an impact that the exposition of sound doctrine, which learned seculars like Reginald Pecock and Thomas Gascoigne regarded as a first priority, could never have had. The bequests to the mendicant orders from all sorts of people, which recur over and again in late medieval English wills, show how their words went home; and that their intercession was prized, often more highly than that of any other religious, in the very age when Chaucer and Langland were denouncing them.

Taking the lights and shades together, the picture that we are forming of the clerical life and standards in the late Middle Ages is certainly not an entirely happy one; especially with regard to the regular religious, the facts go a long way to explain the strong anti-clerical feeling that is so marked in the writings of the great satirists and moralizers of the age. But we have not yet applied with any rigour the yardstick which is probably the most important measure of the value that men set on the life of their church: endowment. By this standard the fourteenth and fifteenth centuries did as well as most in the Middle Ages. True, apart from the Carthusians, the monasteries were not attracting patrons in the way that they once had. This, however, was because the foundation of collegiate churches, served by the secular clergy, and of chantries now took pride of place. Of the former an excellent example was the church at Higham Ferrers, founded in 1422 by Archbishop Chichele, for a community of eight chaplains, eight clerks and six choristers, who would pray daily for the lives and souls of King Henry V, Queen Catherine, the founder and all Christian people. There was annexed to the church a grammar school and a bede-house for old people. Edward Duke of York's great college at Fotheringhay and Lord Cromwell's at Tattershall were on very similar lines. Tattershall, like Higham Ferrers, had a grammar school attached. This should remind us, as should also the history of the foundations of colleges in Oxford and Cambridge, that this was a key period in the history of education, and one in which the church played, as it had traditionally, the leading role.

Chantry endowments, which supported a chaplain to sing mass either at an altar in a church or in a separate chapel, were also multiplying throughout our period. In the parish church of Newark-on-Trent alone there were no less than fifteen perpetual chantries at the end of the fifteenth century, each with its own chaplain. Most of these Newark chantries were endowed by gilds. Religious gilds, fraternities among townsmen or country parishioners subscribing to common funds to provide for masses and lights, for funeral rites and prayers for dead members, and for a feast on their patronal saint's day, proliferated enormously in the fourteenth and fifteenth centuries. These gilds were great founders of chantries; private benefactors too were very generous in endowing them. Masses for the dead and intercession for their safe journey through purgatory were the prime purpose, usually, of such endowments, but there was a very wide range to the charitable activities to which they might also contribute. Both gilds and individual patrons on occasion made provision, for instance, for a chantry priest also to teach a grammar school, for the children of the parish or locality. In social and spiritual service to the community, the church did not lag, and nor did its patrons.

No one, in fact, who knows the parish churches of England, and their buildings, wall paintings, tombs and glass which date from the last two medieval centuries, can doubt that the church remained at the very centre of communal life. The men who attacked the pope's right of provision, jeered at the friars, and questioned the monks' title to their lands, were proud of their English church and ready to dedicate their goods to its well being. The anger of Langland and the gentler satire of Chaucer are not symptoms of declining religious fervour; they are symptoms of the universal concern for religion, for the church, and for her standards.

Notes

1 Quoted by C. Davies, 'The Statute of Provisors of 1351', *History*, vol. 38 (1953), p. 133.
2 From Grandison's *Register*, quoted by Pantin, *The English Church in the Fourteenth Century*, p. 70.

3   Quoted by A. Hamilton Thompson, *The English Clergy and their Organisation in the Later Middle Ages* (Oxford, 1947), p. 10, note 2.
4   *Flores Historiarum* (R.S.) vol. III, pp. 175–6.
5   T. Gascoigne, *Loci e Libro Veritatum*, ed. J. E. Thorold Rogers (Oxford, 1881), p. 52.
6   *Chron A. Murimuth* (R.S.), p. 175.
7   T. Gascoigne, *Loci e Libro Veritatum*, p. 26.
8   A. Hamilton Thompson, *The English Clergy and their Organisation in the Later Middle Ages* (Oxford, 1947), pp. 36–7.
9   *Piers Plowman*, B Text, Passus XV, ll. 506–9.
10   M. McKisack, *The Fourteenth Century* (Oxford, 1959), p. 295.
11   Wyclif, *De Civili Dominio* vol. II (Wyclif Soc., 1900), p. 7.
12   *Anonimalle Chronicle*, ed. V. H. Galbraith (Manchester, 1927), p. 147.
13   T. Walsingham, *Historia Anglicana* vol. II (R.S.), p. 140.
14   A. Hudson, *English Wycliffite Writings* (Cambridge, 1978), pp. 135–7; *The St Albans Chronicle*, ed. V. H. Galbraith (Oxford, 1937), pp. 52–5.
15   See *Visitations of Religious Houses in the Diocese of Lincoln* vol. II, ed. A. Hamilton Thompson (Lincoln Record Soc., 1918), p. 11.
16   Hamilton Thompson, *The English Clergy and their Organisation*, p. 177.
17   *Piers Plowman*, B Text, Passus XV, l. 226.

Note on secondary reading (post 1970)

Two books that offer excellent general treatment of the subjects covered in this chapter are P. Heath, *Church and Realm, 1272–1461* (London, 1981), and R.N. Swanson, *Church and Society in Late Medieval England* (Oxford, 1988). M. Harvey, *England, Rome and the Papacy: the study of a relationship, 1417–64* (Manchester, 1993) is useful for Anglo-Papal relations in the later part of the period. On particular issues in church state relations, there is S. Raban, *Mortmain Legislation and the English Church, 1279–1500* (Cambridge, 1982): on other major issues raised in Edward I's reign see J.H. Denton, *Robert Winchelsey and the Crown, 1294–1313* (Cambridge, 1980). On provisions, besides the works by G. Barraclough, C. Davies and E.B. Graves cited in the main bibliography, Section 7a, there is R.G. Davies, 'Martin V and the English episcopate', *E.H.R.*, vol. 92 (1977). On taxation of the clergy, P. Heath, cited above, is a sure guide, reign by reign.

Much of this chapter has been concerned with the state of the clergy in its various orders. On the episcopate, R.G. Davies, 'The episcopate', in C.H. Clough (ed.), *Profession, Vocation and Culture in Later Medieval England* (Liverpool, 1982) is useful; on the pastoral activities of Archbishops Arundel, Islip and Thoresby see J. Hughes, *Pastors and Visionaries* (Woodbridge, 1988). On the parish clergy, there is P. Heath, *The English Parish Clergy on the Eve of the Reformation* (London, 1969); also helpful is R.N. Swanson 'Problems of the priesthood in pre-Reformation England', *E.H.R.*, vol. 105 (1990). On monastic life, B.F. Harvey, *Living and Dying in England, 1100–1540: the Monastic Experience* (Oxford, 1993) is original and important. On the friars, useful is C. Erikson, 'The fourteenth century Franciscans and their critics', *Franciscan Studies*, vols. 35–6 (1975–6). On chantries see K. Wood-Legh, *Perpetual Chantries in*

Britain (Cambridge, 1965); and on organized charity M. Rubin, *Charity and Community in Medieval Cambridge* is valuable. On all these topics, two out-standing older books have lost none of their value; A. Hamilton Thompson, *The English Clergy and their Organisation in the Later Middle Ages* (Oxford, 1947), and W.A. Pantin, *The English Church in the Fourteenth Century* (Cambridge, 1955).

The secondary literature on the church in England in the late Middle Ages is very extensive. On grounds of space, I have not attempted to list a large number of valuable works whose focus is locally limited – to a region, town or diocese. A number of useful biographical studies of leading churchmen are listed in the main bibliography, Section 7d.

10 Mysticism, Wyclif and Lollardy

Lollardy, at the end of the fourteenth century, brought the English medieval church face to face with the problem of a popular heresy for the first time. The Lollards were, or were claimed to be, followers of the doctrines of the great Oxford philosopher, John Wyclif. In order to set in perspective his career, his influence, and the significance of the heretical movement that he fathered, it will be useful to say a little introductorily about some general features of the religious climate of the times, and also about English scholastic learning in the years when he was still a young scholar, as yet unknown.

The tone of religion in fourteenth-century England was, by comparison with that of the preceding age, anti-sacerdotal and introspective. As we have seen, it was not a happy period for the established religious orders. The most respected among them were the austere and withdrawn Carthusians, who cultivated the solitary life. We hear much in the period of individual hermits and anchorites, as the recluse at Westminster and the monk solitary of Farne. The construction of chapels by great laymen in their own houses, and the popularity of the privilege of employing one's own confessor remind us of a new emphasis among laymen upon private devotions. The growth of a conscious, articulate and sometimes puritanical moral fervour among the laity was another marked feature of the age. This was partly, no doubt, the fruit of the great preaching and pastoral efforts of the friars. Above all, it was owing to the spread of literacy in the vernacular among the laity; that is, indeed, why we know about it. Quite humble people, in the fourteenth and fifteenth centuries, possessed 'primers', with the *paternoster*, perhaps the Hours of the Virgin, and the litany in English, and there were aids to following the church's services, such as the *Lay Folk's Mass Book*. Over and above these fairly elementary texts, a very substantial body of religious writings in the vernacular has survived from these times, which offer insights into English spirituality of the late Middle Ages that are simply not available for an earlier period.

Two aspects of this literature deserve special emphasis. One is its mystical bent, which we shall examine presently; the other is the popularity of sermons, whose prevailing tone was moral and puritanical. The sins of the rich, the idle and the luxurious, lay and clerical alike, were castigated with an eloquence firmly founded in Holy Writ. This was how the great Dominican preacher John Bromyard pictured the strong and wealthy of the world after they had passed from it:

> Their souls shall have instead of the palace and hall and chamber the deep lake of hell, with those that go down to the depth thereof. In place of scented baths the body shall have a narrow pit in the earth . . . instead of wives they shall have toads, instead of a great retinue and throng of followers, their bodies shall have a throng of worms and their souls a throng of demons. Instead of a large domain they shall have an eternal prison house, cramped for both body and soul.[1]

This sort of denunciation was typical. It was not of course the rich only that the preachers flayed with hot words; the terrors of hell were being prepared for all, high and low alike, who would not amend. Hence the parallel emphasis in the sermons on the things necessary for salvation, an understanding of the scriptures, of the Creed, and of God's commandments. To men eager for knowledge of the faith in which they walked the preachers pointed a hard way to salvation:

> As a child willing to be a clerk beginneth at the ground, that is A.B.C., so he who thus desires to speed the better beginneth at the ground of health, that is the Christian man's belief [i.e. the Creed] . . . for thus it behoves to climb up as it were by a ladder of divers rungs, from the ground of belief into the keeping of God's commandments, and so up from virtue to virtue, till he see the God of Sion reigning in everlasting bliss.[2]

'If I had gold enough I would give every day a noble to have every day a sermon, for Thy word is worth more to me than all the world,'[3] exclaimed Margery Kempe, the burgess's wife turned visionary from fifteenth-century Lynn. There can be no doubt about the way in which the sermons and the literature that they inspired reached right down among the people. The homilists' pictures of Bible scenes and of the day of doom were the basic source for popular dramas such as the miracle and mystery plays. The propaganda letters which circulated at the time of the Peasants' Revolt were full of saws drawn from sermons. It is a striking fact, but not in the light of the sermons surprising, that it is in the fourteenth century that we first come across religious treatises written by laymen. The most famous is the *Livre des Seyntz Medicines* written by Henry Duke of Lancaster about 1354: an allegory treating of the wounds that sin inflicts upon the soul, composed by one whose sense of his own moral backsliding was clearly vivid. The honour of being the first layman to write a homily in English seems to belong to Sir John Clanvowe, a knight of Richard II's chamber and one who was, interestingly enough, rumoured to be a Lollard. It is a stern, austere tract about the quest for the narrow way, in walking which a man may free himself of the 'foul stinking muck of this false fleeting world'.[4] In new conditions of wider literacy and armed with the weapon of the vernacular, laymen showed that they could now assume the homilectic mantle of the clerk.

Of all the works on which the influence of the homilists has left its imprint, the greatest is the *Vision of Piers Plowman*. It was written by an obscure, probably unbeneficed priest of the western midlands, William Langland. Its very structure, the personification in familiar contemporary dress of virtues, vices, and the qualities of the soul, reveals its deep roots in the sermon literature of the age. Because of the wonderful series of vignettes of contemporary life that it affords, it has most often attracted the attentions of social historians. But Langland's social gospel was essentially simple and scriptural:

> Such work to work, while we been here
> That after our death day Do-well rehearse
> At the day of Doom we did as he highte [i.e. commanded].[5]

Langland's eye was on the next world rather than this; and his way to salvation led by the familiar steps of sustained moral endeavour, knowledge of the faith, and keeping of God's commandments – 'all that the Book bids'. There is no message here that the homilists had not laboured a thousand times. What sets Langland apart is his instant sense of Christ's redeeming love, and his flashes of poetic religious insight:

> And if Grace grant thee to go in this wise,
> Thou shalt see in thyself Truth sit in thy heart:
> In a chain of charity as thou a child were,
> To suffer him and say naught against thy sire's will.[6]

The message of the mystics was not the same as that of the homilists, but they should not be set too far apart from one another. The mystical writers take as read the groundwork of knowledge of the faith and the commandments which are the sermons' recurrent themes. What they do is to add something more, and something which, as the circulation of their works among the clergy and devout lay people shows, had a profound impact on the religious life of the age.

The teaching of the mystics can best be illustrated through the works of four people: Richard Rolle, the Yorkshire hermit (d. 1349); the anonymous author of the *Cloud of Unknowing* (c. 1350); Walter Hilton, an Augustinian canon of Thurgarton in Nottinghamshire; and Dame Julian of Norwich (1343–c. 1420). All four, in differing ways, were concerned with the same matter, the mystic's experience of union with God in contemplation. This is an experience which, by definition, man cannot reach by reason or works, or hope to understand: to pierce the 'cloud of unknowing' that separates God from man is God given, an ecstasy vouchsafed only to His chosen ones. But those who have known it can point the way, through prayer and meditation and forgetting of the world. Both the author of the *Cloud* and Hilton were steeped in the *Mystica Theologica* of Dionysius, a Syrian monk of the sixth century, which was the basis of most mystical teaching in the western Middle Ages; the author of the *Cloud* translated it into English as *Deonis Hid Divinitie*. Rolle and Dame Julian were independent of this tradition. The former found his own way through reading and meditation: 'In searching the scriptures I have found that the highest love of Christ consists in three things: fire, song, and sweetness.'[7] Dame Julian's experience came by direct revelation, when she was sick, as she thought, to death, and saw the crucifix that the priest held before her changed: 'I saw the blood trickling down under the crown of thorns hot and fresh and right plenteously . . . like to the drops of water that fall off the eaves of a house after a great shower of rain.'[8]

Common to all four writers is their concern with a direct experience. Rolle, the *Cloud* and Hilton all discuss exercises preparatory to this experience, and two aspects of their instruction are striking. One is the private and personal nature of the devotions that they describe. The author of the *Cloud* and Hilton in his *Scale of Perfection*, his most famous work, were both writing for individual disciples. There is no sense, of course, in which their works are anti-sacerdotal, but they are not concerned with priestly mediation, only with the direct approach of the individual soul to God. Secondly, one is struck by their anti-intellectual bias. This is important because it is a reminder that the road to mystical experience is one that all may tread, not a private path for the priest and the learned. The monk solitary of Farne was the contemplative who, perhaps, put this point most eloquently: 'Let the meek hear and rejoice, that there is a certain knowledge of Holy Scripture which is learnt from the Holy Ghost and manifested in good works, that the fisherman knows and not the rhetorician, that the old woman has learned and not the doctor of theology.'[9]

The mystical bent of fourteenth-century religion was evinced in many ways, but most clearly of all in a new emphasis on the humanity of Christ. Behind this we can discern a widespread desire to find room, in the everyday life of the Christian, for direct contact with God. We find this emphasis in Langland, in his glimpse of Jesus going to joust in Jerusalem in Piers Plowman's arms: 'In his helm and his hauberk *humana natura*'.[10] We find it in Henry of Lancaster, the soldier with the rough experience of war setting his mind on 'the precious flesh, which was bound by its nature to shiver and shrink from this hard passion', and on the body on the cross 'with the heart split open and the blood all warm'.[11] Margery Kemp, when on her pilgrimage to Jerusalem she was shown the place where Jesus had suffered, 'wept and sobbed as plenteously as though she had seen Our Lord with her bodily eye, suffering his passion at that time. Before her in her soul she saw him verily in contemplation and that caused her to have compassion.'[12] In the round of the church's year this emphasis on Christ's humanity found expression in a new importance attached to the feast of Corpus Christi; in its rituals in the anxiety of the laity to see at the mass the elevated host, the true body of Christ under the likeness of bread.

There are reminders here of just how much Wyclif, the heretic who stepped out of the trodden way, was in religion the child of his age. He too longed to bring men face to face with the incarnate Christ, 'our true brother, a man with the rest of us'.[13] In another age, moreover, one less obsessed by the sacrament of the altar, he might not have found it so hard to dodge his conviction of the error of the church's eucharistic teaching, which was in the eyes of his opponents his central heresy.

John Wyclif was first and foremost a don, a figure of the schools in the Oxford that he loved. Oxford, when he came to her in the 1350s, was a university a hundred and fifty years old, an established and famous centre of European learning. Cambridge was a little younger. It was a great period for the endowment of colleges in both universities: at Oxford Queen's, Oriel, Exeter and New College were all founded in the fourteenth century, and at Cambridge Clare, Corpus and Pembroke. The colleges, with their endowed fellowships, were the home of a privileged *élite* among scholars. The majority of students (there were something like 1200 at Oxford at the beginning of the century) lived not in colleges but in private halls and inns under principals approved by the university, or in lodgings. The friars lived in their own convents, and the monks maintained halls of their own. Life was easier for the professed religious than for the secular clerks, who in order to maintain themselves had to find a patron – or a benefice. As a consequence of shortage of cash, most students proceeded no further than the degree in arts (compulsory as a prelude to higher studies for all except the friars, who read arts in their own *studia*, a privilege which others resented). Both universities were largely self-governing bodies: at Oxford the chancellor was elected from among the doctors of law and theology by the congregations of masters of arts, the ruling assembly of the university. The archbishops of Canterbury claimed a right of visitation, which was resented and at Oxford contested; but before the controversy over Wyclif's teaching arose it had not been used for a long time. To all intents the universities were independent administratively, and this independence was reflected in the freedom of academic speculation in their schools.

The artists and theologians were the men principally concerned in the great scholastic debates of the fourteenth century. Earlier, both Aquinas and Scotus had endeavoured in their teaching to hold together the two disciplines of philosophy and theology, to show reason and faith, philosophy and religion, working in harmony. In the fourteenth century the teachers in their tradition were faced with the challenge of the philosophy of the Franciscan, William of Ockham. Human knowledge, as Ockham saw it, was limited to what the intellect could apprehend, in the last resort through experience. There could therefore be no knowledge of the reality, outside the mind, of universal concepts, no means by which men could, in the strict sense, *know* God's ways and will or the workings of his grace. His will, unlimited and unknowable, Ockham concluded, must be absolutely free, in a manner beyond human comprehension. For this reason Ockham as a theologian concentrated on the human will and act, viewed in a context almost completely independent of the operation of divine grace. Ockham's supremacy as a logician won him a great following in the schools, both in Oxford and Paris. But teaching which set so far apart the worlds of faith and reason, and which seemed to imply that human action could condition grace, was bound to evoke a counter-challenge.

In the long run it was the disciples of Scotus, the most 'subtle' of all the doctors who had emphasized the divine will as the cause of all things, who made the best attempt at an answer to Ockham. Scotus was very widely read in Oxford in the fifteenth century. Earlier opponents of the Ockhamites, in particular Thomas Bradwardine, had stressed not God's will but his knowledge which, embracing all things, past, present and future, determined them. Bradwardine thus rescued the operation of grace from the semi-Pelagianism of Ockham; and he also reinstated the knowledge of the 'universal', because for him all knowledge was derivative from God's omniscient knowledge. The price of this new position was a rigid predestinarianism; God had to know, from before the beginning, who were the elect. The father of the church to whom Bradwardine owed most was Augustine, who was also a strong predestinarian. The most important thinker who was directly influenced by his *De Causa Dei* was John Wyclif.

In his very early years at Oxford Wyclif was apparently attracted by the teaching of Ockham; later he became the leader of the out and out opponents of the Franciscan's teaching on both knowledge and free will. His thought, like Bradwardine's, had its roots in Augustine. His other great debt was to the famous English master of the thirteenth century, Robert Grosseteste. Grosseteste's was a principal influence on his ideas on cognition. God's knowledge was for Wyclif the very foundation of existence; universals exist, he taught, not in the mind of man, but in the mind of God. God is not beyond knowledge, he is the source of all knowledge. God's reason and his will are not therefore beyond human comprehension. Wyclif, in rejecting experience of the singular as the key to human knowledge, advanced a theory of cognition that was avowedly Platonist; he did not reject Aristotle, the master of the logic *par excellence* to the Middle Ages, but he regarded his 'logic' as inferior to that of Augustine, which was founded in Plato. His new Platonist 'logic' won him a tremendous *éclat* in the Oxford schools, and he was early acknowledged as among her most renowned masters in the arts faculty.

When Wyclif proceeded from arts to incept in theology in the early 1370s, he had two principal duties in his new faculty: to lecture on the *Sentences* of Peter Lombard (the textbook of the theologian) and on the Bible. From the first he was determined to apply his philosophical system to the exposition of Christian doctrine and of Scripture. Here the implications of his metaphysics were far reaching indeed. His rigid predestinarianism coloured his concept of the church, which he elaborated in his *De Ecclesia*: the true church was not the church of priests but the body of God's elect, and those who were not elect, the 'foreknown' to damnation, were not part of it. It also led him to question the priestly powers to absolve, to impose penances and to excommunicate; the relation of individual souls with God was for him direct, beyond the control of any human agent. Predestinarianism further gave a special slant to the ideas on lordship which he took over, almost bodily, from Archbishop Fitzralph of Armagh, and which he expounded in his *De Dominio Divino* and his *De Civili Dominio*. True lordship, Fitzralph had taught, is founded in grace: therefore, Wyclif concluded, only the elect (who by definition are alone in grace) can enjoy true lordship. Lordship among men he regarded as the product of accidents of secular history (his biblical studies had taught him a sound historical insight). The temporal power of the popes, founded on the Donation of Constantine, had therefore no religious significance. If the Khan of the Tartars were to become lord of the world and make the Bishop of Cambalek in Cathay his universal patriarch, his grant would have an exactly parallel validity with Constantine's.[14] Following this lead, Wyclif turned to the Bible: the word pope was not used therein, he pointed out. The pope was a man; he might not be one of the elect, but of those predestined to damnation. There was nothing sacred about his lordship, or about the temporal endowment of any church; their origins were human. Human lordship was quite different from the 'evangelical' lordship of the elect who live in conformity with scripture's commands, which was the only true lordship for Wyclif.[15] Wyclif did not make very clear what he meant by this 'evangelical' lordship; he seems, though, to intend the right of the just to the use, in common, of what God has provided for men in the way of goods in this world – something very different from property in any ordinary sense. The implications of such teaching were radical indeed.

In the theology schools, Wyclif made Scripture his special mastery. He was the first English academic since Stephen Langton to comment in his lectures on the whole of the Bible. Here his philosophical system led him to take a rather peculiar view. Scripture was the foundation of faith, the truths in it were God given: therefore, Wyclif argued, they must be truths pure and timeless, known to God eternally. The Bible was more to Wyclif than words upon parchment. It was eternal truth, the will and testament of God the Father, containing in it all that was necessary to salvation. This conclusion led Wyclif, by the time he wrote his *De Veritate Sacrae Scripturae* (*c.* 1378), virtually to reverse the original relation in his thought of Platonist metaphysic to Holy Writ. The Bible, mirror of eternal truth, became the very centre of his theory of cognition now, the source of all genuine human knowledge; the logic of Holy Scripture was the only and all sufficient logic, he claimed, the rest mere sophistry. It was because of their plain conformity to Scripture that the 'logic' of the Neoplatonist Augustine and of Plato himself was superior to all other philosophy.

All the ills of contemporary Christianity now stood clearly revealed to Wyclif as attributable to a failure to grasp this central truth. Mahomet had taken the Bible and overlaid it with a veneer of human interpretation, which served mainly his own carnal ends, especially his greed for human lordship. In Christendom 'western Mahomets', the popes with their decretals and Ockham's disciples with their confidence in the human intellect, had done the same. The only hope for the future was 'evangelical reform', a return to the way of the Holy Book in its simplicity, stripped of all accretion. This was why Wyclif was insistent that the Bible must be translated into their mother tongue for laymen, and expounded to them in sermons by a learned priesthood. Since it had been the pope's church that sent the Bible along the path of the cross as a martyr by the promulgation of its 'carnal' decretals, it was to the lay power that he looked for the institution of evangelical reforms; it was the only power that he could look to. But Wyclif was more than another fourteenth-century apologist of the authority of the prince over the clergy in their secular lives. He was much more radical; in the long run the logic of his claims for the all sufficiency of the Bible as a law for men was not Erastian reform, but the holy democracy, anarchic in its practical implications, that was the ideal of the seventeenth-century sects.

The extremism of Wyclif's views naturally made him enemies. We know that, quite early in his career as a theologian, some of his critics were pointing out that there were difficulties about squaring his philosophical views with the teaching of the church about the eucharist. The matter was one that Wyclif could not leave on one side; to him as to his contemporaries, the eucharist was a central sacrament in the life of the church. Wyclif's critics were quite right; what he said would not square with the doctrine of transubstantiation. He himself found that he had common sense objections to it; he could not believe that what he saw in the priest's hand was no longer bread. There was also a philosophical difficulty. He could not accept the current Scotist interpretation, that after consecration the bread ceased to exist; according to his metaphysics, nothing that had existed could, in the Scotist sense, be 'annihilated'. Finally, Wyclif could find no authority in Scripture for the doctrine of transubstantiation. It was, it seemed, yet another human, carnal addition to the eternal truth, which was aimed to enhance the dignity of priesthood by a claim to semi-magical powers. Wyclif did not for a moment deny that Christ was really present at the mass, but his presence was, he said, sacramental, not the 'seven foot Christ'; and he was quite sure that the bread remained after consecration. Wyclif put forward his views on the eucharist publicly in the schools of Oxford in 1379. Next year they were condemned by a committee appointed by the chancellor, but he would not retract them. Soon after their condemnation he left Oxford for ever for his rectory at Lutterworth in Leicestershire.

From Lutterworth, a stream of angry works flowed from his pen. He restated his views on the eucharist. He furiously attacked the friars who presumptuously dared to follow an order which they called holier than that of the gospels, and who spread the new, idolatrous teaching on the eucharist (Wyclif believed that transubstantiation had only been the church's doctrine since the time of Innocent III). Harking back to the 'evangelical' conditions of the primitive church, he denounced the whole contemporary ecclesiastical hierarchy in resounding terms. His last work was his *Opus Evangelicum*. Its main theme was the sufficiency of the Bible both as a moral law and as a law for the church (in so far as it had a theme; anger at the end was diminishing his coherence). He never finished the work. As he was hearing mass on Holy Innocents' day, 1384, 'he fell down, smitten by a paralysis, especially in his tongue, so that neither then nor afterwards could he speak'.[16] Three days later he was dead.

Wyclif in religion was in many ways the child of his age. His concern for a clear understanding of true belief among the faithful and for a morality with a scriptural basis he shared with an army of eloquent homilists. But he turned their orthodox, if puritanical, pulpit oratory into a questioning of the whole structure of the contemporary church and its beliefs. His works do not reveal him as lovable: he was arrogant, wordy and censorious. Yet he remains impressive. He was consumed with a passion for the truth, and was intellectually undauntable. His readiness to thrust aside the pope, cardinals and all authority save that of Scripture was founded in a real religious conviction, which had drawn strength in long years of philosophical training and of exhaustive biblical study. The stern evangelical morality which was the positive side of his teaching brought him close to the doctrine of justification by faith. The three things necessary to salvation, he stated, were a belief in God, in his Holy Church, and a hope of glory.[17] Beyond that point the path must be that of Christ, who sent his disciples into the world to preach, not to build palaces and to keep the poor at the gate; who hated worldly pomp, and forbade his disciples to take to the sword; who came humbly to John to be baptized – not like the pope who calls men from the ends of the earth to his tribunal.[18] For all his limitations, Wyclif was a powerful intellect – he anticipated many of the fundamental positions of the sixteenth-century protestants – and he was a passionately religious man. That was what made him important and persuasive.

Wyclif, in his writings and sermons, repeatedly urged the need for lettered priests to preach and expound to the people the true, scripturally based faith. Around the time that he himself quitted Oxford, his injunctions were being taken up vigorously by a group of masters who had been drawn to his teaching there, among whom the most notable were Nicholas Hereford, John Aston and Philip Repingdon, canon of St Mary's, Leicester. We learn from Bishop Wykeham's register that in 1382 Hereford, with Aston and other Oxford colleagues, had been preaching errors (including errors concerning the eucharist) at Odiham and elsewhere in the Winchester diocese: and from Knighton's chronicle that Aston had been preaching errors in Leicester (almost certainly in company with and abetted by Repingdon).[19] This activity prompted a sharp reaction from Archbishop Courtenay, who summoned Hereford, Aston and Repingdon before a council at Blackfriars in London, where they were forced to abjure a list of their master's heresies. He followed this up with a visitation of the university of Oxford. Courtenay's measures of 1382 were only very partially and temporarily successful, however. Nicholas Hereford and John Aston soon returned to their heresy, though not to Oxford. Over the next five years both men were active preachers of Lollardy – the name by which Wyclifite heresy came to be known – among the people at large. The dioceses of Worcester and Hereford and the marches of Wales were the chief scenes of their ministrations. Aston died a heretic (*c.* 1387), but Hereford was arrested, in 1387, and in the end abjured his heresy for good. John Purvey, who had been Wyclif's secretary at Lutterworth, was another active preacher, and was the founder of the long lived Lollard community at Bristol. Apart from these, the most famous of the early Lollards was William Swinderby of Leicester. He probably acquired his Wyclifite views from the Oxford master, Philip Repingdon. Swinderby is a perfect example of the kind of devout, literate, religiously self-confident person to whom Wyclif's teaching, with its emphasis on Scripture and on the direct relation of the individual Christian and his God, had a strong appeal. He was prohibited, along with Aston and Hereford, from preaching in the diocese of Worcester in 1387; later he was a source of much disquiet to Bishop Trefnant of Hereford. After the early 1390s he disappears from history, but he had left his mark. Oldcastle, the later Lollard leader, whose patrimonial estates were at Almeley in Hereford, was almost certainly brought into contact with Lollardy through his evangelism.

The history of Lollardy after Wyclif's departure from Oxford is probably best considered in terms of two phases, before and after Oldcastle's abortive Lollard revolt of 1414. Between 1382 and 1414 Wyclifite teachings continued to command some sympathy and support in his old university, among lettered priests, and with knights and gentlemen of standing, some of whom can be identified. The connections between these groups were close enough to constitute a kind of evangelical network, operating at the radical fringe of the church's world. The revolt of 1414, however, discredited the movement decisively with the establishment, both clerical and lay. Thenceforward it became cut off both from fresh input from academia and from genteel patronage, and the secular arm was brought into active cooperation with the ecclesiastical authorities in its suppression. Lollardy survived, down to the Reformation, in regions and communities where the activity of the early preachers had enabled it to put down roots among the humble, in London, Bristol, and Coventry, for instance, and in parts of East Anglia and in the Chilterns; but now more or less surreptitiously, driven into the domestic circles and sectarian homes where little groups of pious, puritanical people met to hold unorthodox conventicles and to read, or be read, scripture.

Probably the most striking evidence of the vigour of Lollardy in the period 1382–1414 is the very large number of Wyclifite books and tracts, mostly in English, that have survived in manuscript from that period. The most important work, or at any rate the most widely disseminated, was of course the Lollard Bible. Wyclif had repeatedly emphasized the need for scripture to be translated, 'so that he who runs may read', and his disciples actually made two translations. The earlier was a literal version, following the word order of the Latin Vulgate so closely that it is often barely comprehensible. The second translation, completed in 1397, was in excellent, readable English. Over 200 manuscripts survive, and it is clear that it reached a far wider circle of readers than just Lollards; it is also clear that it provided the vital reading matter for the domestic conventicles of the later Lollard period. Besides the Bible, there is a very wide variety of further Lollard texts and tracts in English. A good many are simply vernacular paraphrases of passages from Latin works of Wyclif and his early academic disciples. Others are independent compositions, like the famous

Lantern of Light, with its theme of the contrasts between the fiend's church, headed by the Pope of Rome, full of mumbled prayers and the 'vain din' of music, and the true church of the chosen and saved, the church of the worship of the heart and of 'reading with mindful devotion'.[20] The language here has become tinged with populism; the puritan message reaches back to Wyclif.

Two further Lollard works of this period deserve particular notice. One is the great Lollard *Sermon Cycle*, of 294 sermons in English, appropriate to the major feasts of the church, to (some) saints' days, to successive Sundays, and to comment on the ferial gospels of the week, these making together a complete cycle for the liturgical year. This major collection was clearly put together with public instruction, very probably in church, in view. The other is the *Floretum* (or in an abridged version, the *Rosarium Theologiae*). Professor Hudson has described these two compilations as 'collections of authorities, biblical, patristic, scholastic and canonistic, on a range of moral and ecclesiastical topics arranged in alphabetical order, with cross references for ease of use by preacher or tract writer.'[21] Their distinctive feature is the number and length of the citations that they include from the works of Wyclif, which make them in effect handbooks of Wyclifite thought. Once again the purpose is instruction, to facilitate the task of the educated, Latin-literate Lollard preacher or author in relaying Wyclifite teaching to a wider audience. The range of references in these two works to other authorities, patristic and scholastic, besides Wyclif, is also significant. They could not have been put together without access to very ample library facilities. Almost certainly they must have been compiled by university men, working in Oxford. We know the names of quite a handful of Oxford scholars of Wyclifite inclination who were active in Oxford in the 1390s and 1400s: William James and John Gamylgay, fellows of Merton, Thomas Lucas, Robert Lychlade, John Mybbe, principal of Cuthbert Hall, and the two successive principals of St Edmund Hall, William Taylor and Peter Payne. Men such as these, and the compilation and circulation of texts such as the *Sermon Cycle* and the *Floretum*, were continuing to ensure, through the late years of Richard II and in Henry IV's reign, an active scholarly input into Lollard evangelism.

In this same period in which we continue to hear of Lollards in the university we come across a number of references in chronicles to Lollard knights. Walsingham and Knighton mention in particular a group of influential knights of Richard II's chamber; Sir Richard Stury, Sir Lewis Clifford, Sir John Neville, Sir John Clanvowe, Sir John Montagu. These were all rich and successful men, who had made careers for themselves in war and the royal service, and they had business interests in common. They were also educated: Stury was a friend of Froissart and Clifford of Chaucer; Clanvowe was the first layman to write a homily in English. Not all of them can be proved to have been Lollards, but Clanvowe's homily has Lollard overtones, and Neville certainly befriended Hereford in his heretical days, as Montagu is also said to have done. Closely associated with this group were two other knights, Sir Thomas Latimer of Braybrook in Northamptonshire, and Sir John Cheyney, another chamber knight. The Buckinghamshire branch of the Cheyney family, with whom Sir John was connected, was certainly in sympathy with Lollardy. There were clearly many more knights and gentry, whose names we do not know, who had Wyclifite sympathies and inclinations, besides these whose prominence attracted the chroniclers' notice. William Swinderby was able to come and go freely in his encounters with Bishop Trefnant, we are told, because there were gentlemen who were prepared to assure his safety. And in the parliament of 1410 members among the commons (alas, nameless) got as far as formally putting a disendowment bill, inspired by an earlier Lollard tract, which claimed that the confiscation of ecclesiastical temporalities could endow 100 almshouses, 15 new universities, and 15,000 additional pastoral clergy, as well as providing support for 6200 esquires for the king's service![22] Needless to say, nothing came of their proposition: what is remarkable is that it got all the way it did, to the king's high court of parliament.

Genteel patronage was clearly very significant to the story of Lollardy in its pre-1414 phase. Books were the life blood of Lollardy; aristocratic purses must have been important in meeting the expense of commissioning them. Protection offered by knights and gentlemen to Lollard preachers was crucial, too, in facilitating the preachers' dissemination of Wyclifite teachings to audiences among the common people. Knightly lay patrons could, and did, ensure to Lollard priests a public pulpit, by presenting them to parish benefices in their gift. Sir Thomas Latimer presented Robert Hooke (who lived to take part in Oldcastle's revolt) to his parish church at Braybrook: Sir William Beauchamp presented the Wyclifite Oxford MA Robert Lychlade to his living of Kemerton in Gloucestershire. Thomas Cheyney presented to the living of Drayton Beauchamp in Buckinghamshire Thomas Drayton, friend of William Taylor, the Lollard principal of St Edmund Hall. It is no accident that Northamptonshire and the Buckinghamshire Chilterns, where Latimer and the Cheyneys respectively had influence, remained infected with Lollardy long after 1414. Significant in another way is that when the Hussite scholars Nicholas Faulfis and George Knehnic came to England in 1407 to copy out *codices* of Wyclif's works and take them back to Bohemia, the three places that they visited were Oxford, Braybrook and Kemerton. A few years later, Sir John Oldcastle and the Lollard priest Richard Wyche, M.A., were in correspondence with Hus himself and his Prague followers. These connections of the early Lollards with the leaders of a theologically like minded movement in Bohemia are testimony to the coherence and sense of identity of the English Wyclifites of the generation following his death.

The features of the early Lollard movement that we have been describing all have parallels in the early history of protestantism in England, and go a considerable way in justifying Anne Hudson's title for her study of it, the 'premature reformation'.[23] What it lacked by comparison with the sixteenth century reformation was any sympathy or support from the episcopate and the high ranks of the ecclesiastical hierarchy, or from the greater secular magnates, let alone any royal favour. The Lollards expressly looked to the crown as the potential agent of church reform, but they looked in vain, and their hopes in their very first days of John of Gaunt (Wyclif's patron in the 1370s) proved vain likewise. They found sufficient support, and their evangelism was sufficiently successful, to greatly alarm the church authorities, but nothing like enough to mount the kind of challenge to them that the Hussites mounted in Bohemia.

The church leadership was quick to respond to what it saw as a serious danger, from the moment that Wyclif made public his unorthodox interpretation of the eucharist. Archbishop Courtenay acted vigorously in 1382, as we have seen, in order to stamp out heresy at what he perceived as its fountain head, in Oxford. But he and his colleagues found it hard to get effective backing from the lay power. Outside the lettered clerical world, it was not so easy to see how sharp the distinction was between Wyclif and the general run of radical anti-clericalism, and it was only gradually that the church succeeded in enlisting adequate support against Lollardy from the secular arm. As a result of pressure from Courtenay, a statute of 1382 ordered the sheriffs, upon certification from their bishops, to arrest unlicensed preachers and their abetters and to hold them until they cleared themselves in the ecclesiastical courts. This was not a very effective measure. The statute *de Heretico Comburendo* of 1401 was sterner stuff, forbidding upon royal authority unlicensed preaching, the holding of conventicles, and the dissemination of unlicensed books, and commanding that obdurate heretics who refused to abjure in the church courts should be handed over to the secular arm and burned. In fact, only two heretics were burned between 1401 and 1414; and it is interesting to note that there were parliamentary protests against the measures of both 1382 and 1401. This secular obstruction did not deter Archbishop Arundel, Courtenay's successor, in his determination to prosecute heresy with all possible rigour. His constitutions of 1409 placed newly tight restrictions on preaching by priests outside their own parishes, and generally on preaching, teaching and on the use of translations of scripture in the vernacular. In 1410 he appointed a committee of convocation to search Wyclif's works for errors and heresies (they came up finally with 267 opinions, which were formally condemned: there was a great bonfire of his books at Carfax in Oxford). In 1411 he made a visitation of the university, and a new oath was imposed on all taking a master's degree, not to uphold any of Wyclif's condemned views. Two years later, just after Henry V's coronation in 1413, Arundel commenced the actions in convocation which precipitated Oldcastle's revolt.

John Oldcastle, the leader of the Lollard revolt of 1414, was a prominent man. He had risen to distinction in the Welsh wars against Glendower; through Henry V's influence in the days when he was Prince of Wales he married Joan de la Pole, heiress of Lord Cobham, in whose right he came as a peer to parliament. He was also a recognized leader of the Lollards, and Archbishop Arundel knew from at least 1410 that his castle at Cooling in Kent was a resort of heretics. In 1413, soon after Henry V's accession, it was revealed in convocation that a search of a scrivener's shop in Paternoster Row had revealed a number of heretical books belonging to Oldcastle, and Arundel decided to act against him. His close associations with the new king made it necessary for the Archbishop to proceed carefully; they also made it particularly important that Oldcastle should be brought to book.

Oldcastle, if he had been less obdurate, could certainly have got off through royal influence. But his heresy was founded in a real religious conviction, and he would not take the easy way. He was arrested in the summer of 1413 and was brought before his ecclesiastical judges in October. Cross-questioned on his beliefs on the eucharist and confession, he denied the right of the pope, or of any other bishop, to define belief on these matters. Arundel provided him with a schedule in English setting forth the catholic teaching; he studied it and returned with still more uncompromising answers, denouncing his judges as traitors to God before all present. He was pronounced convicted, excommunicated, and was handed over to the secular arm. At Henry V's request, there was a stay of execution, to give the king himself a chance to reason his friend into abjuration.

On 19 October, during this delay, Oldcastle escaped from the Tower with the aid of outside supporters. By December, the court had wind of plans for a Lollard rising, and on Twelfth Night in the new year a number of London Lollards were arrested at the 'Sign of the Axe' in Bishopsgate. They revealed the details of the conspiracy, of a *coup* timed for the night of 7 January whose first object was to capture the king. Oldcastle must apparently have decided that it was too late to change his arrangements, for his followers were already converging on the capital from far afield. Their assembly point was in St Giles's Fields, and there in the darkness they stumbled into the strong professional forces that King Henry had ready. It is unclear how many Lollards had turned up: modern estimates have varied from a few hundreds to over a thousand. Some were killed, about eighty were taken prisoner, and the rest completely scattered. Oldcastle was one of those who escaped, but his rising was over. It was a complete fiasco.

Oldcastle's force was clearly not militarily impressive, an assorted throng of mostly very humble people, but they had come long distances. There were contingents from Buckinghamshire, Leicestershire, Warwick and Derby. Not all the known Lollard communities contributed; Norfolk, so far as we know, sent no one. It would seem also that by no means all the rebels were Lollards; of those who were executed for their part in the affair, only a handful were convicted of heresy as well as treason. Apart from those taken at St Giles's Fields, few paid the penalty of their lives. By 14 March it was considered safe to issue a pardon, from which Oldcastle and a few other notorious Lollards were excepted. He remained at large for another three years, a bogey to the authorities but not very dangerous; he was finally run to earth in Herefordshire in 1417, and the sentence passed on him was duly, if tardily, executed.

Oldcastle's revolt was the end of Lollardy as a movement with any political significance. Ever since the 1380s, its ecclesiastical opponents had been making determined efforts to discredit the sect with the socially respectable among the laity, by labouring the revolutionary implications for them of Wyclif's teaching.[24] His view that all true lordship was founded in grace could, these detractors pointed out, be turned against the secular prince and the aristocracy quite as easily as against the endowed religious. A rumour began to circulate that Wyclifite missionaries had helped to stir up the peasants against their lords in 1381. The revolt of 1414 seemed to demonstrate incontrovertibly that the churchmen were absolutely right, that Lollardy was a socially disruptive force that threatened lay lords and clerical ones equally. It completely discredited heresy with the upper classes. In the Leicester parliament of 1414 a statute was approved, assigning to the justices of the peace and of assize the duty of making searches for Lollards, arresting them and delivering them to the bishops, who would proceed against them in the church courts. The ordinary routine procedures of the civil authorities for the prosecution of crime were henceforward harnessed in support of the church for the suppression of heresy.

There were, it is true, plans for another rising in 1431, but no substantial people were involved; the only place where there was actual violence was Abingdon where Jack Sharp was ready to attack the abbey, but this did not pass the proportions of a riot. Though Lollardy survived right down to the sixteenth century it did so only as a religious movement among the humble, surreptitious and unorganized, which was no longer a serious threat to the church establishment.

The story of the Lollards in the later, post 1414, phase is not easy to put together. We catch glimpses of them from proceedings that were taken against them from time to time, but there is not much else to go on. Professor Thomson's exhaustive inquiries have shown that there were quite vigorous Lollard communities in a number of towns, and that they survived into the sixteenth century and maintained some degree of contact with one another.[25] In the countryside Lollardy seems to have gained its local vigour often (but not always) from the missionary activities of individual priests, like William of Thaxted in Essex and William White in East Anglia in the 1420s. It is virtually impossible to make any estimate of the numbers that may have been attached to the sect at any one time. The authorities in the fifteenth century clearly thought that Lollards were numerous; from the records that we have it would seem that their estimates were unnecessarily alarmist.

It becomes difficult, in this later period, to be sure just how much identity the Lollards had really retained as a sect, and to what extent their beliefs preserved significant connexions with the teaching of Wyclif and his first disciples. In the early days, when Purvey and others who had known the master were still alive, the links were often strong and conscious; William Thorpe counted himself proudly, he told Archbishop Arundel, among those who 'purpose to confirm their living to this learning of Wyclif'.[26] The case of Joan Boughton, an 'old cankered heretic' of more than eighty years who was burned at Smithfield in 1494 and held Wyclif to be a saint,[27] shows that this attitude long survived, but she may have been exceptional. William White's East Anglian followers were examined on a series of articles concerning their views on such matters as the obligation to pay tithes, the right of the faithful (ordained or otherwise) to preach – and the eucharist. From their answers one would certainly conclude that there was some distinct Wyclifite influence at work, for instance from the statement of his Beccles disciples that 'after the sacramental words (at communion) . . . there remains nothing but only a cake of material bread'.[28] But the master's original teaching has been crudely simplified. as Mrs Aston has put it, we 'observe heresy that was academic, more or less, in origin, passing through active proseletising . . . into the sometimes limited intelligences of glovers and skinners, and into the domestic talk of enthusiastic women. As it did so its content changed – and moved immeasurably further from Wyclif.'[29] The basis of charges against many later Lollards is a good deal vaguer than this, often merely the possession or study of English bibles. Bible reading and Bible study seem to be the main link between Wyclif's ideas and the proletarian heretics of the later period.

The best picture of Lollardy in its late, underground phase is that given in the mid-fifteenth century by Bishop Pecock, who by his own admission was well acquainted with 'the wittiest and cunningest men of thilk said sort'.[30] There was a good deal of variety in their beliefs, as he recognized, but essentially they were Bible men: their first and most general 'trowing' was that 'no governance is to be held the law of God save that which is grounded in Holy Scripture'.[31] 'They ween themselves to ken at full and substantially and pithily Holy Scripture', he says, 'for that they ken by heart the texts of Holy Scripture, and can lush them out thick at feasts, and at ale drinking, and upon their high benches sitting.'[32] Pecock's picture tallies with what the records of proceedings against Lollards tell us, of groups of simple people, not very dangerous and not very educated, meeting surreptitiously at one another's houses to read the Bible. Their naïve faith in their own knowledge of Scripture and their sense of belonging to the little band of God's chosen ones are their chief identifying features. There are echoes of Wyclif here, but they are only echoes. It is not the schools of the fourteenth century but the sects of the seventeenth that are recalled by these 'unlearned apostles and saints', as Jacob calls them, who were not 'graduate men, but the Holy Ghost inspired them and made them plenteous of heavenly lore'.[33]

Lollardy was long lived because, in the context of the religious feeling and attitudes of the late Middle Ages, it had a genuine appeal. In many respects this appeal had much in common with that of the mystics. Both teachings touched the religious aspirations of the lay and simple at sensitive points, in their desire for a closer contact with Scripture and with the life of Christ, for assurance of personal salvation, and for moral regeneration. Both had anti-clerical overtones. It is not so very remarkable that Margery Kemp, on whom the real religious influences were Hilton and Julian of Norwich, was more than once mistaken for a Lollard. But in the end, of course, mysticism and Lollardy led in opposite directions. At the popular level Lollardy was anti-sacramental, contemptuous of pilgrimage, image worship and spiritual direction. All the things that moved Margery Kemp to ecstasies, the scene of our Lord's birth, the crucifix, the elevation of the host at the mass, moved the Lollard who had lifted the latch of Wyclif's wicket to anger at superstition.

In fifteenth-century England, the influence of the mystics remained a stronger force than Lollardy ever was. The treatises of the fourteenth-century authors continued to enjoy an impressive vogue, and at the end of the century Caxton and Wynkyn de Worde early produced printed editions of them. Nicholas Love, the Carthusian prior of Mount Grace, rendered into English Bonaventura's meditative life of Our Lord, under the title *Mirrour of the Blessed Lyf of Jesus Christ*; it is a book to which we often find reference in wills of the period. Bequests do not only tell us who possessed books of this kind; they also give us a picture of how they were treasured. This is the colophon of a manuscript of Hilton's *Eight Chapters Necessary for Men that give Themselves to Perfection*:

> This book was made of the goods of Robert Holland for a common profit. [And let] that person that hath this book of the person that hath power to commit it have the use thereof for the term of his life, praying for the soul of the same Robert. And that he that hath the foresaid use . . . when he occupieth it not, lend he it for a time to some other person. Also [let that] person to whom it was committed for the term of his life under the foresaid conditions deliver it to another person for the term of his life. And so be it delivered and committed from person to person, as long as the book endureth.[34]

Robert Holland was a citizen of London who died in 1441. The spirit of Hilton's readers, devout and generous, shines through his words to remind us that it was the tradition of the mystics, much more than that of Wyclif, that coloured the religious life of the fifteenth century. More people read Hilton than ever read the *Lantern of Light*, and more people read the sermons in John Myrc's *Festiall* than ever listened to those of the Lollard cycle. The cults of the saints, the veneration of relics, pilgrimages and prayers for the dead, all anathema to the Wyclifites, remained among the most distinctive features of late medieval English spirituality. We are reminded here of the strength of an English catholicism, pre-Tridentine, insular and vernacular, which even the reformation never really succeeded in eradicating from English religion.

Notes

1 Quoted and translated by G. R. Owst, *Literature and Pulpit in Medieval England* (Cambridge, 1933), pp. 293–4.
2 *Pore Caitiff*, quoted by W. A. Pantin *The English Church in the Fourteenth Century* (Cambridge, 1955), p. 249.
3 *The Book of Margery Kempe*, ed. W. Butler Bowdon (London, 1936), p. 214.

4 V. J. Scattergood, 'The two ways – an unpublished religious treatise by Sir John Clanvowe', *English Philological Studies*, vol. 10 (1967), p. 45. Scattergood here prints the whole of this very interesting treatise with a brief introduction (pp. 33–56).

5 *Piers Plowman*, B Text, Passus VII, ll. 198–200.

6 ibid. Passus V, ll. 614–17.

7 *The Incendium Amoris of Richard Rolle of Hampole*, ed. M. Deanesly (Manchester, 1915), pp. 184–5.

8 Juliana of Norwich, *Revelations of Divine Love*, ed. G. Warrack (London, 1901), pp. 8, 16 (quoted by D. Knowles, *The English Mystical Tradition*, London 1961, p. 122).

9 W. A. Pantin, 'The monk solitary of Farne, a fourteenth century English mystic', *E.H.R.*, vol. 59 (1944), p. 178.

10 *Piers Plowman*, B Text, Passus XVIII, l. 23.

11 Henry of Lancaster, *Le Livre de Seyntz Medicines*, ed. E. J. Arnould (Oxford, 1940), pp. 163, 195.

12 *The Book of Margery Kempe*, p. 107.

13 Wyclif, *De Benedicta Incarnacione* (Wyclif Soc., 1886), pp. 28, 85.

14 Wyclif, *De Potestate Papae* (Wyclif Soc., 1908), pp. 215–16 (where he is following Fitzralph).

15 Wyclif, *De Civili Dominio*, Lib. I, ch. III, XIV.

16 H. B. Workman, *John Wyclif* (Oxford, 1926), vol. II, p. 316.

17 Wyclif, *De Veritate Sacrae Scripturae* vol. I, p. 243.

18 Wyclif, *Polemical Works* vol. II (Wyclif Soc., 1883), pp. 680–92.

19 *Wykeham's Register*, ed. T. F. Kirby (Hants Record Society, 1896–9), vol. ii, pp. 337–8; *Knighton Chronicle*, vol. II, pp. 176–8.

20 The text of the *Lantern* is edited by L. M. Swinburne (E.E.T.S., 1917).

21 A Hudson, *English Wycliffite Writings* (Cambridge, 1978), p. 7.

22 See A. Hudson, *English Wycliffite Writings*, pp. 135–7, for the full text.

23 Anne Hudson, *The Premature Reformation: Wycliffite Texts and Lollard History* (Oxford, 1988).

24 On this aspect of the campaign against Lollardy, see M. E. Aston, 'Lollardy and sedition', *Past and Present*, no. 17 (1960), pp. 1–44.

25 J. A. F. Thomson, *The Later Lollards* (Oxford, 1961).

26 *The Acts and Movements of John Foxe*, ed. J. M. Pratt (London, 1877), vol. III, p. 258.

27 ibid., vol. IV, p. 7.

28 N. Tanner (ed.), *Heresy Trials in the diocese of Norwich* (Camden Soc., 4th series, xx, 1977), p. 115.

29 M. Aston, *Lollards and Reformers* (London, 1984), p. 99.

30 R. Pecock, *The Book of Faith*, quoted by V. H. H. Green, *Bishop Reginald Pecock* (Cambridge, 1945), pp. 21–2. This is the most substantial modern study of Pecock and his work; see also E. F. Jacob, 'Reynold Pecock, Bishop of Chichester', *P.B.A.*, vol. 37 (1951), pp. 121–53.

31 *Pecock's Repressor* (R.S.) vol. I, p. 5.

32 ibid. p. 129.

33 E. F. Jacob, *The Fifteenth Century* (Oxford, 1961), p. 283; and *Lantern of Light*, ed. L. M. Swinburn, p. 5.

34 Quoted by R. W. Chambers, 'The continuity of English prose', intro. to *Harpsfield's Life of More*, ed. E. V. Hitchcock and R. W. Chambers (E.E.T.S., 1932), p. cviii.

Note on secondary reading (post 1970)

On the religion of the people and their observance, Part One of E. Duffy, *The Stripping of the Altars* (London and New Haven, 1992) gives a vivid account: also valuable, especially for the earlier, fourteenth century period is J. Hughes, *Pastors and Visionaries: Religion and Secular Life in Medieval Yorkshire* (Woodbridge, 1988). On preaching, see H.L. Spencer, *English Preaching in the Late Middle Ages* (Oxford, 1993). On two other important topics, see M. Rubin, *Corpus Christi: the Eucharist in Late Medieval Culture* (Cambridge, 1990): and M. Aston, 'Death', in *Fifteenth Century Attitudes*, ed. R. Horrox (Cambridge, 1994), with an excellent bibliography for further reading. On the English mystics, Hughes is again useful; the best introduction remains D. Knowles, *The English Mystical Tradition* (London, 1961). There are now for the specialist also the volumes to date of M. Glasscoe's *The Medieval Mystical Tradition* (Exeter/Cambridge, from 1980). On Margery Kemp there are M. Gallyon, *Margery Kempe of Lynn and Medieval England* (Norwich, 1995), and S. Bhattacharji, *God is an Earthquake: the Spirituality of Margery Kempe* (London, 1997).

Wyclif and Lollardy have, as always, attracted much attention. On Wyclif's Oxford, see J.I. Catto in J.I. Catto and T.A.R. Evans (eds.) *The History of the University of Oxford*, vol. II, *Late Medieval Oxford* (Oxford, 1992). On Wyclif see A. Kenny, *Wyclif* (Oxford, 1985): useful papers are collected in A. Kenny (ed.), *Wyclif in his Times* (Oxford, 1986).

On Lollardy, the key innovatory work is A. Hudson, *The Premature Reformation: Wycliffite Texts and Lollard History* (Oxford, 1988): her collected papers, out of which the book grew, are gathered in A. Hudson, *The Lollards and their Books* (London, 1985). Also very important are the papers of M.E. Aston, collected in her *Lollards and Reformers: Images and Literacy in Medieval England* (London, 1984). On Lollard knights and gentry see Part II of K.B. McFarlane, *Lancastrian Kings and Lollard Knights* (Oxford, 1972); also M. Aston and C. Richmond (eds), *Lollardy and the Gentry in the Later Middle Ages* (Stroud, 1997). Another interesting study is P. McNiven, *Heresy and Politics in the Reign of Henry IV: the burning of John Badley* (Woodbridge, 1987); and N.P. Tanner, *Heresy Trials in the Diocese of Norwich* (Royal Historical Society, London, 1977) gives good insights into later Lollard congregations. K.B. McFarlane, *John Wycliffe and the Beginning of English Nonconformity* (London, 1952) retains value (especially on Oldcastle's revolt): so does J.A.F. Thomson, *The Later Lollards* (Oxford, 1965).

Section IV

The uncertain years 1360–1415

11 Defeat abroad and unrest at home 1360–1381

For nearly nine years after the Treaty of Brétigny England and France were nominally at peace. In England these were carefree years, politically. Edward III, presiding over a magnificent court, felt that he had earned rest after his high deeds; 'I am growing old,' he told the king of Cyprus, who visited him to urge him to take the cross as a crusader, 'I shall leave it to my children.'[1] The Black Prince took his beautiful bride, Joan of Kent, to Aquitaine, which his father in 1362 granted to him as a principality, and at their court 'abode all nobleness, all joy and jollity, largesse, gentleness, and honour'.[2] Adventurous spirits meanwhile sought martial renown in wars overseas; on the crusade that the king of Cyprus led; in the Breton war of succession, which still continued; and in Spain. In their *insouciance*, the English seem hardly to have noticed the slow drift towards a new confrontation with France. When in 1369 the Hundred Years War reopened as a result of deliberate provocation on the French side, they were ill prepared. The pattern of events which followed this resumption of hostilities was, partly in consequence, in very marked contrast to that of the years which preceded the Treaty of Brétigny.

Peace did not much alter internal conditions in England in the 1360s. There was no great change in the approach of the king's advisers to problems of government. The general control over expenditure which Edington had established for the exchequer when he was treasurer in the 1350s was maintained. Peace did give the exchequer officials a chance, in 1363, to prepare something like a budget statement, a disappointing exercise which showed that even without the strains to which war exposed the royal revenues, they were hardly adequate to meet current expenditure. No special measures were taken, however, to improve the position: it was supposed that the ransoms of the kings of France and Scotland would make up for the deficit. The ransoms brought in some £268,000 in these years, but it was all quickly spent. When the war began again 'nothing was found in the king's treasury, but he was in such great poverty that he had to burden the clergy and commons with subsidies and loans'.[3] William of Wykeham, who had been the king's secretary, then the keeper of his privy seal, and finally became chancellor in 1367, was held by many to be chiefly responsible for the fact that, in the end, nothing was left of 'the great sums in gold' that the ransoms had brought in.

Abroad, in this period, England's most important involvement was in the affairs of the kingdom of Castile. The enlargement of the boundaries of English Aquitaine under the terms of Brétigny had made it more important than ever before for the English to take an interest in the affairs of the Spanish kingdoms. The Black Prince, who had just arrived with his wife in Bordeaux, was probably the chief architect of the treaty of alliance between England and King Pedro of Castile which was agreed in 1362. One of its stipulations was that the English would, if need arose, provide soldiers for service in Castile against Pedro's enemies. The threat of internal rebellion was what Pedro had in mind, and in particular the designs which his bastard brother, Henry, Count of Trastamara, entertained upon his throne. Henry at the time was in exile, and seeking aid at the French court in the furtherance of his plans. This was why the English alliance with Pedro, in due course, became a key factor in the chain of events which led to the reopening of war with France. In France, the Treaty of Brétigny had brought peace in name only. Great tracts of the countryside were still overrun by free companies of soldiers, who had nowhere else to go, and no means of living except as they were wont, by terrorizing the countryside and plundering merchants and travellers. Their activities presented the foremost of the formidable problems that Charles V had to face in 1364, when King John died in London (he had returned there as a prisoner when the Duke of Anjou, a hostage for his ransom, broke parole). Charles's position was eased in that year by the end of the Breton war. When Knowles and John de Montfort defeated and killed Charles of Blois at Auray, Charles V accepted the *fait accompli* and allowed de Montfort to do homage for the duchy. In 1365 the Franco-Navarrese war, which had also broken out anew, was ended by the victory of French forces at Cocherel over a largely English force led by the Captal de Buch and John Jewel. Charles thus obtained a free hand to deal with the problem of the free companies, and agreed to advance money to Henry of Trastamara, to take as many of them as he might into his pay and lead them out of the kingdom to make war on Pedro in Castile.

In the autumn of 1365 a great host of mercenaries began to assemble. Its chief captains were the Breton veteran, Bertrand Du Guesclin, and Arnold d'Audrehem, Marshal of France, and there was a powerful Anglo-Gascon contingent under Sir Hugh Calverley. In February 1366 their force was concentrated in Aragon, whence they crossed into Castile; and on 29 March Henry was crowned at Burgos. Pedro could muster no army capable of facing these tried soldiers, and fled from Toledo to Seville, thence to Portugal, and finally arrived in Gascony. He had already made contact with the Black Prince, to request him to implement the treaty of 1362 by providing forces which might restore him to his throne.

The Black Prince and his father were willing to do this, provided that Pedro would shoulder the expense. In the autumn of 1366, of course, Pedro was in no position to pay anyone anything, and the Prince agreed to be responsible for the payment of the army that was to be raised, upon promise of repayment from the king of Castile, once he was restored to his throne. He then began to assemble his army; the English and Gascons in the service of Henry were recalled, and a great host marched into Spain in 1367. At Najera this host routed the army of Henry, and took prisoner his two chief French captains, Du Guesclin and the Marshal d'Audrehem. It was the last of the victories that made the Black Prince famous in the annals of chivalry, and ended an age of martial success for the English.

Pedro was back on his throne after Najera, but it rapidly became apparent that he would not for a long time yet be able to raise funds to pay off the Black Prince's soldiers, who were clamouring for pay. Relations between the two rapidly deteriorated, to the point where Edward even began to consider foreclosing upon his creditor's realm, and making himself a king there. This dream did nothing towards satisfying the immediate problem of his unpaid army, however. The Prince seems to have regarded the claims of these his chivalrous companions as paramount, and decided that there was no option but to look to his subjects in Aquitaine for ready money. They had already borne heavy taxation at his hands, and the grant of a new hearth tax, which was agreed at Bordeaux in the autumn of 1367, raised bitter complaint. Two of the most important southern lords, the counts of Amagnac and Albret, refused to permit its levy in their domains, and appealed to Charles, king of France, to support them in their refusal. This gave the French king his chance to exploit the non-fulfilment of the famous renunciation clauses of his father's peace treaty with the English of 1360, and to reassert the traditional French claim to sovereignty over the duchy of Aquitaine.

Everyone knew that if Charles of France received the appeal of the Gascon lords in his *Parlement*, it must mean the renewal of the war. He moved circumspectly, consulting with his councillors and with experts in the law of nations and of treaties from the universities. But the Gascon lords knew that he would receive their appeal, and that hesitation was for form's sake. Charles had always assumed that the war would reopen one day, and prospects of concerting a Franco-Castilian offensive in Gascony had prompted him in the first place towards alliance with Henry of Trastamara. He believed the time for action was now ripe: Gascony was in ferment, and England unprepared. So he declared that he was bound to hear the appeal of the two lords, and summoned the Black Prince to come and defend himself against their complaints before the *Parlement* of Paris.

The Black Prince told the men who brought the summons to Bordeaux in January 1369 that he would come to Paris – at the head of 60,000 men. In England King Edward followed the advice of his parliament, that he might 'of right and in good faith' reassume the title of King of France, which he had not used since 1360. In the skirmishes that flared up all along the frontiers of Aquitaine, the banners of St Denis and St George were unfurled once more in engagement.

Over the years 1369 to 1381 the course of military operations in the war, which now began again in earnest, and the turns of English domestic politics were intimately connected. The story may be easier to understand if we follow first the course of the war, and then turn to examine the public reactions in England to the events that took place overseas.

The French, in this period of the war, were more fortunate than the English in their diplomatic alliances. A new treaty restored their old relations with the Scots in 1370. They were lucky in Spain also: by 1369 the Black Prince had abandoned Pedro, who was defeated and killed at Montiel, after Henry and Du Guesclin (who had paid his ransom) reappeared with a new French army. This meant that from the early 1370s, once Henry had established himself, the French enjoyed the important support in the Channel of the Castilian fleet. This enabled them, at least intermittently, to control the narrow seas, to prey constantly on English shipping, and to mount several alarming raids on the English coasts. Pedro's death had important consequences for the English also. When he died, his two daughters were at Bordeaux. In 1371, at Roquefort, Constanza, the elder of them, was married to John of Gaunt, Duke of Lancaster in right of his former wife Blanche, and the second of the surviving sons of Edward III. Next year, with the assent of the English council, Gaunt assumed the title of King of Castile. For the next sixteen years his influence in English politics made sure that plans for a Lancastrian intervention in Castile were always in the background of English military and diplomatic planning. This complication was not an advantage to the English war effort.

In France, the main sphere of operations, things did not go well for England after 1369. English councillors had no experience of the massive problems of maintaining a defensive war, and did not fully understand what they involved. They put their faith instinctively in the offensive methods which had paid off in the 1350s, and were no longer appropriate. A series of costly *chevauchées* were mounted, but achieved nothing. In 1370 Robert Knowles led an army through Picardy and past the gates of Paris, but he had little to show for it when he reached Brittany. Gaunt in 1373 led a more impressive host from Calais to the borders of Burgundy; but he lost more than half his men afterwards, marching to Bordeaux across the *massif* of central France in a freezing winter. In 1372, a year before, the Castilian fleet had caught and destroyed another expensive force which the Earl of Pembroke was shipping to Aquitaine, and destroyed it before it ever set foot on land. In 1375 an expedition to Brittany, where John de Montfort had again broken with his sovereign, started more promisingly, but had to be abandoned when the English negotiators at Bruges, headed by Gaunt, agreed a general truce with the French for a year. On all sides the English record was one of abject and costly failure.

The French had won notable successes in the years from 1369 to 1375, but by the end of them they were beginning to feel the strain. By 1372 they had recovered all Poitou, and, pressing further into the south west, had taken Pons, Taillebourg and St Jean d'Angely, confining the English effectively to the Bordeaux district. In 1373 Charles V's famous constable, Du Guesclin, and the Duke of Bourbon cleared most of Brittany of English troops. Du Guesclin's tactics, refusing to be drawn into engagement with the English on their long, destructive *chevauchées* and then massing troops to reduce the undermanned garrisons in English territory, were, however, expensive and only partly successful. The French never succeeded in clearing the central *massif* of the numerous free companies that operated in name for the English, and who were very hard to dislodge from their near impregnable hill forts in Auvergne and Limousin. There was little prospect in 1375 of administering a *coup de grace* either in Gascony or in Brittany, and that was why the French were glad of a truce.

The truce of 1375, initially agreed for a year, was later extended, to run until 24 June 1377. It represented the first concrete achievement of the papal mediators, who had been busy at the thankless task of peacemaking since 1369. During this two year interlude there was much discussion between the French, the English and the legates at Bruges about the terms of a possible final peace, but the mediators failed in the end to find any means towards a permanent accommodation. The French were willing to be generous in concessions of territory, but insisted that their king's sovereignty must be recognized through all Aquitaine. The English were prepared to listen to ideas for a partition of the duchy which would reduce the area of their authority, but they would not hear of admitting French sovereignty in at least part of what remained to them. The question of sovereignty defied resolution, as it was to continue now to do for the rest of the duration of the war. The experience of Brétigny had taught both the English and the French that it was the one thing that neither could totally abandon. By February 1377 the papal mediators had come to the conclusion that there was no way of postponing the recommencement of hostilities, as they explained in a frank letter to Edward III. When they left Bruges they could not know that theirs would prove to be the last effort at peacemaking by papal servants for many years. The Great Schism broke out in 1378, and peace ceased to be a priority with the warring popes of Rome and Avignon.

When the war reopened in the summer of 1377 Edward III had just died, after celebrating his jubilee. His government, during the truce, had had to face a serious domestic crisis and the English were no better prepared than they had been in 1369. The Duke of Anjou was soon threatening Bordeaux, and Burgundy moved up a force to besiege Calais. A Franco-Castilian fleet appeared in the Channel; Hastings, Rottingdean, Dartmouth and Plymouth all suffered, and Rye was burned. The late summer of 1377 was the darkest hour, however; stalemate was achieved much more rapidly between the two sides than it had been earlier, after 1369.

Charles V had in fact overreached himself in recommencing hostilities so soon. Riots in many cities and local revolts in the French provinces in 1378 showed that the strain of supporting the war was too severe. The king's attempt to annex Brittany, which his *Parlement* declared forfeit to the crown, was a major political blunder: too many Bretons saw it as a threat to provincial independence and rallied to de Montfort and England. The Duke of Anjou's designs on Majorca also proved an embarrassment. They drove his Aragonese rivals towards an English alliance, which the Navarrese were ready to join. In consequence

Cherbourg, Charles of Navarre's last stronghold in Normandy, was placed in English hands.

English fortunes in the field did not markedly improve, in spite of the difficulties of the French. John Neville, who came to Gascony as lieutenant in 1378, did manage in some degree to reactivate local resistance to the French. But the more ambitious expeditions which the government managed to organize and of which much was hoped were uniformly unsuccessful. In 1378 Gaunt sailed with a force that was supposed to be destined for Bordeaux; he stopped to besiege St Malo, without success, and returned empty handed. In 1379 a substantial force was mustered for a campaign in Brittany, under Sir John Arundel; it was caught by a storm at sea, and most of the ships were wrecked off the Irish coast. Sir John was drowned; the chroniclers saw in his fate a judgement of God, because of the disorders that his men had committed ashore while waiting for their transports. In 1380 Thomas of Woodstock, the youngest of Edward III's sons and Earl of Buckingham, crossed to Calais with a powerful host, which numbered many famous captains among its leaders, as Sir Robert Knowles, Sir Hugh Calverley, Sir John Harleston. Following the line of Knowles's march in 1370 they raided as far as the borders of Burgundy, before turning west with Brittany as their objective. While they were marching John de Montfort's bitter enemy Charles V died in Paris, and when the English arrived in his duchy he was already negotiating a peace with Charles VI's councillors. In April 1381 Buckingham was told that the French and the Bretons were no longer at war, and he had no option but to return, indignant and unvictorious, to England.

Despite these setbacks and failures, the English government by 1381 had become a good deal less prepared to consider peace than they had been in 1375. They believed, and with some reason, that new opportunities were beginning to open for them. In 1378 the Great Schism in the church had broken out, when the cardinals who in the spring had elected Urban VI in Rome deserted him, and elected in his stead in September Robert of Geneva, who became Clement VII, and made Avignon his seat. Charles of France recognized Clement as the true pope, but the English remained firmly loyal to Urban, as in the Empire did Wenceslas King of the Romans; so in France did the Flemings, who in 1379 had once again rebelled against their count. In these circumstances the old idea of a great continental coalition against the French was resuscitated. It would have the standing now of a crusade, in Urban's favour. It looked further as though Lancaster's Iberian diplomacy, which had already achieved an alliance with Portugal and an understanding with Aragon, might be tied in with the scheme. When the disappointed Buckingham got back to England in 1381 Simon Burley, Richard II's tutor, was on the point of leaving the realm to seek a bride for his master in Anne of Bohemia, the sister of Wenceslas; and Edmund Earl of Cambridge was assembling an army at Plymouth, destined for Portugal.

What Buckingham was in time to witness was not the successful foundation of an anti-French confederacy, however, but the Peasants' Revolt.

The Peasants' Revolt of 1381 was the climax of a crisis of confidence in govern-ment, which was largely generated by failures in the war. The effect of those failures was felt directly in England. The activities of the Franco-Castilian fleet and of French and Scottish privateers severely damaged English merchants and their commerce. The French carried out damaging raids on the Channel coasts in 1369, and again in 1377, 1378 and 1380. In 1377 Rye and Portsmouth were sacked; in 1378 Cornwall suffered severely; in 1380 Gravesend and Winchelsea were burned. The whole country had suffered as a result of the finan-cial burden which the effort to fit out substantial and uniformly unsuccessful military and naval forces imposed. Taxation was heavier and more sustained than it had been at any time since the 1340s. In spite of this, the English had lost control of the narrow seas, together with most of what they had once held in the south-west of France and their footholds in Brittany and Normandy.

Past experience did not help people in England in the 1370s to understand this pattern of events. Remote from the scene of the great campaigns, they could not comprehend that the new strategy of Charles V and Du Guesclin had rendered their previous methods of waging war obsolete, or that these were inappropriate to essentially defensive military objectives. Victories such as Crecy and Poitiers could not be won if the French would not meet the English *chevauchées* in the field; and *chevauchées*, in themselves, did nothing to protect under-defended territory. Because the English did not understand this, but knew that they were paying heavily to no apparent purpose, they attributed their failures to disloyal leadership, profiteering by captains and dishonest finan-cial administration at home. There was consequently continuous pressure, especially from the sectors of opinion represented in parliament, for more stringent control and audit of expenditure, for investigation into military and administrative incompetence and disloyalty, and for the displacement of dis-credited councillors (often in favour of inexperienced ones). Concessions to demands of this sort, always partial, did little to alter things. This fact, in itself, served to increase public bewilderment and distrust.

This situation was aggravated by lack of royal leadership. Edward III by 1369 was ageing fast. Happy in the ceremonious life of the court and with his mistress, Alice Perrers, he was content to leave the direction of affairs to others. The health of the Black Prince, his heir, had been permanently damaged in the Spanish campaign; in 1370 he had to resign the command in Aquitaine and came back to England, where he died before his father, in 1376. Lionel of Clarence, his next brother, had died earlier, in 1369. John of Gaunt, the Duke of Lancaster, was the most active member of the royal family, a powerful influence in council, often presiding on the king's behalf in parliament. But he had neither the political experience nor the military record to inspire general confidence. When Edward III died no regent was appointed for Richard II, the Black Prince's son who succeeded at the age of ten, probably because there was no one who commanded sufficient respect to fill the office. Throughout the years 1369 to 1381 there was thus no natural leader to focus the efforts and rally the loyalties of a frustrated and bewildered people.

By 1371 popular discontent had become vocal in parliament. The commons complained to the king that 'the government of the realm has long been in the hands of men of Holy Church, who cannot in all matters be brought to justice', and prayed that he would henceforth choose laymen as his ministers.[4] William of Wykeham, the Bishop of Winchester, had in consequence to resign as chancellor, and Bishop Brantingham of Exeter as treasurer. There were other troubles too in this parliament. Anti-clericalism, to which distrust of clerical ministers gave a sharp edge, encouraged suspicion that the clergy as a whole were not pulling their weight in the national emergency. The commons and lay lords tried to make their grant (of £50,000, to be raised by a levy of 22*s.* 3*d.* on every parish) conditional on the clergy making a grant of the same sum, and the bishops had to fight to maintain the fiscal independence of their convocations. More alarming still in the eyes of most churchmen, two Austin friars were brought forward to argue the case for impounding church lands for the king's use. Wyclif later recalled that their scheme for partial disendowment was supported by 'a certain lord wise in counsel'.[5] The monastic chroniclers believed that the leader of the anti-clericals was the Earl of Pembroke, and regarded the disaster which overtook his expedition at La Rochelle in 1372 as a judgement.

The rift between lay and clerical leaders of 1371 was not easily healed. The clergy were still touchy about taxation in 1373, when William Courtenay, the young Bishop of Hereford, protested sharply that the grievances of his clerics should be met before they paid any more to the king. The friars' scheme of disendowment had meanwhile stimulated a vigorous pamphlet warfare, in which Wyclif took a prominent part. It was this, probably, that first brought him to the attention of John of Gaunt. Meanwhile, the new secular leadership was discrediting itself. The parliament of 1373 was cooperative enough, but that was before it was known that Gaunt's great *chevauchée* of this same year would achieve nothing. As difficulties mounted over the next two years, the reaction of those directing policy was not deft. By entering into negotiations for the truce with the French that was sealed in 1375, they aborted the expedition that had been despatched to Brittany, and any hopes for its success. At the same time, they patched up an agreement with Pope Gregory XI (probably in the hope of securing better cooperation from the English episcopate), which permitted him to levy a tax on the English clergy, to help pay for his Italian war expenses, a move which was highly unpopular both with the laity and with the lesser clergy. The result was that when parliament next met, in 1376, the vocal public anger that was unleashed proved beyond the government's capacity, for the time being, to control.

The 'Good Parliament' of 1376 sat for longer than any previous parliament, and is exceptionally well recorded. Besides the official parliament roll, we have in the *Anonimalle Chronicle* what appears to be an eye witness account of the debates of the commons. The most striking point that this latter source reveals is the dominant part played by the commons in the proceedings that took place. No sooner had they returned to their own allotted 'chamber' in the chapter house at Westminster, after hearing the chancellor's speech which outlined the king's financial needs, than they took an oath to stand together as a single and united body to see through together all that should be proposed. Then, as they all sat round, a knight of the 'south country' came up to the lectern and spoke thus:

> My lords, you have heard the points put before this parliament, which are grievous matter, how the king demands a tenth and a fifteenth of clergy and commons . . . which to me seems a heavy burden, for the commons are enfeebled by the taxes and tallages of time past . . . and besides all we have given for the war for a long while we have lost, for it has been wasted and falsely spent . . . and as I have heard, there are certain persons who without the king's knowledge have got into their hands a great treasure in gold and silver to a great sum from him, and have concealed this wealth and gained extortionately for themselves by divers means, to the ill of the king and the kingdom.[6]

This was the opening round in a salvo of speeches attacking the administration of the last few years. Three days later, Sir Peter de la Mare, the steward of the Earl of March who had come as a knight for Herefordshire, was chosen to put the articles, which the commons as a united body wished to raise, to the lords and the king. Originally chosen simply for this occasion, he managed so well for the commons that he continued to act as their spokesman through the parliament, and became the first man to be recognized as a Speaker of the Commons.

De la Mare's first demand, which was duly met, was the appointment of a committee of lords to aid and counsel the commons. After this, he and his fellows made themselves very busy. They presented the longest list of petitions ever sent to the king by the commons in a medieval parliament. They conducted their own investigations into maladministration and examined witnesses in the chapter house. They demanded the appointment of a new council about the king, to be named in parliament, and got their desire. They had a series of meetings with the lords and with John of Gaunt, who was presiding in parliament on the king's behalf, and in their course made it plain that they would not proceed further in the matter of finance until the offences of the men whom they suspected of maladministration and peculation were investigated and punished.

The impeachment of these suspected individuals was the most important business of the Good Parliament. The people of whom they complained were, primarily, Lord Latimer, the king's chamberlain; John Lord Neville, the steward of his household; Alice Perrers, his mistress; and a group of rich merchant capitalists of London, Richard Lyons, John Pyel, John Pechey and Adam Bury. Latimer was charged with responsibility for the loss of the forts of St Sauveur and Becherel, of which he had been captain (it was alleged that money had changed hands for their surrender). He and Neville were also accused of buying up royal debts at a discount, and using their court influence to obtain full repayment to themselves. Alice Perrers was accused of wasting the king's goods and of maintenance and bribery in the courts. The charges against the Londoners all concerned illegal profiteering. The most serious was that against Lyons, that he, in conjunction with Lord Latimer and abetted by him, had arranged a loan to the king totalling 20,000 marks, for which a further 10,000 marks premium was paid (in effect concealed interest at the usurious rate of $33\frac{1}{3}$ per cent). As the details of the charges make clear, it was not, strictly speaking, the government as such that was under fire in the impeachments of 1376. The people that the commons accused were not the chancellor and the treasurer, but two soldier-courtiers, the king's mistress, and a group of corrupt financiers, who had used court connexions and influence to secure illegal profits to themselves from 'deals' with the government. This amounted, however, to a serious indictment of the government which had allowed these people and their 'covyn' to batten on the crown.

1376 was the first occasion on which charges were preferred against individuals by the commons as a body, and were tried before the lords in parliament (and convicted by them). This is the procedure which came to be known technically as impeachment, and much attention has focused on the question of its origin as a legal process. The lords in parliament had acted before as judges in state trials, in the cases of Roger Mortimer in 1330 and of Archbishop Stratford in 1341; what was new in 1376 was the role of the commons. Professor Plucknett believed that the model for their action was the old common law procedure of conviction based on notoriety. Miss Clarke believed that the whole commons acted as a jury presenting an indictment. Previously the only method they had found of proceeding against influential men was by petitioning for their removal from office and for their trial; by presenting an indictment the commons asserted their right to see justice done in the court of parliament. These arguments about the legal basis for the procedure are technical ones, and it may be doubted whether 'in the heat of the moment' (as John of Gaunt put it) the commons themselves were very sure of the technical status of what they were doing. What is clear, however, is that the precedent which was set in 1376 was constitutionally and politically of the highest importance. In impeachment, the commons found a means whereby any person of authority or influence (except of course the king in person) could be held responsible to the nation at large. Be he courtier, or captain, or councillor, or simply the holder of a patent of monopoly, the man with the king's commission could no longer regard himself as answerable to the king alone.

The secret of the effectiveness of impeachment was, of course, the ability of the commons to withhold cooperation in the matter of supply until their charges were heard. This was why impeachment opened to the commons a way to achieve what previously magnates had so often achieved only by force of arms, or the threat of it, the punishment of royal servants and agents whose malpractices had made them odious. It thus made a great breach in the theoretical defences of the system of personal monarchical direction which in practice was the day-to-day basis of national government in medieval England. It also, in 1376, gave a quite new significance to the force of public indignation.

John of Gaunt, who had acted on behalf of the king throughout the Good Parliament, clearly regarded its proceedings as an affront to the royal dignity and an unwarranted interference with royal freedom of action. No sooner had it dispersed, than he began to labour to undo its work. He suspected that the commons had had influential men behind them in their protests, notably William of Wykeham, the ex-chancellor who had been driven from office in 1371, and the Earl of March, the lord and patron of Peter de la Mare. Wykeham was the chief target of his anger; it was probably to prepare the ground for his disgrace that Gaunt brought Wyclif up to London from Oxford to preach against the over wealthy clergy; and in a great council at the end of the year the bishop was formally charged with administrative offences committed when he was chancellor and was deprived of his temporalities. March, about the same time, was relieved of the office of Marshal of England, and Peter de la Mare was arrested and imprisoned. In the spring parliament of 1377 the sentences on those impeached in the Good Parliament were quashed, at the request of the commons through their speaker, John of Gaunt's own steward Sir Thomas Hungerford.

This 'curialist révanche', if it may be so called, was not very effective. Gaunt's patronage of Wyclif involved him in a clash with the bishop of London, William Courtenay, which led to a more serious rift between him and the citizens of London. Some of his followers were roughly handled by the mob, and his political stock fell to a very low ebb. After Edward III's death in the summer of 1377 Wykeham was restored to his temporalities, with no protest on Gaunt's part, and de la Mare was released. Things were back by then very much to where they had been on the eve of the Good Parliament; what had happened since had served only to make the kingdom's governors a little less confident, and sharpen tensions among them.

This condition of things altered little through the years from 1377 to 1381, while the pattern of military failure set in the early 1370s repeated itself. There were many symptoms of domestic unease. In the autumn parliament of 1377 de la Mare was again speaker: he demanded that the commons should know the names of the members of the king's continual council, who had authority in his tender age and spent his money; that steps should be taken to ensure that they did not use their position to advance their personal interests; and that there should be more rigorous control of expenditure on the king's household.[7] In 1378 parliament was summoned to Gloucester instead of Westminster, because it was feared that it would be disturbed if it met in London, where the arrest in Westminster Abbey of two soldiers who had concealed a diplomatically important Spanish prisoner, Alfonso of Denia, had roused strong feelings. This incident, and rumours that plans for the dispropriation of church endowment would be mooted again, sharpened tensions between the secular and the ecclesiastical aristocracy. Relations were also tense between Gaunt and the court on the one hand and on the other the leading London merchants, who believed he was anxious to curtail their civic privileges. The Londoners were deeply suspicious too of the loyalty of the aristocratic military leadership, and their consequent unreadiness to lend to the crown added to the government's financial worries.

Despite these alarming signs of general uneasiness, the parliaments of this period were generous with their money grants. The commons approved, it would appear, of the government's reversion to a more aggressive military policy. The spring parliament of 1377 granted a poll tax of 4*d.* per head on the whole male population of the land between the ages of twelve and sixty. That of October in the same year granted a double subsidy, and in the spring of 1379 another poll tax was approved, with liability graded by rank, from 10 marks for the Duke of Lancaster down to 4*d.* for the labouring man. The commons showed much concern over the way in which their grants were spent. In 1377 they appointed war treasurers to supervise the expenditure of the double subsidy. In 1379 they asked for a full investigation of the state of the king's finances by a committee of lords. All was spent, however, and to little effect. In January 1380 Richard Le Scrope, the chancellor, had to explain to the commons that the continual council had nothing in hand to pay for the force which was to be sent to Brittany under the Earl of Buckingham.

In the spring of 1380 the commons granted a subsidy, but on the ominous condition that the continual council be dismissed, since their services were to no purpose and the officers of state could run the administration on their own at less expense. When in the autumn parliament at Northampton they were again asked for money their first reaction was that this demand was 'outrageous and insupportable'. There followed some long and angry wrangles between the lords and the commons as to how sufficient money could be raised. For a long time the commons were not prepared to make a grant unless the clergy would undertake to raise a third of the total sum needed, but in the end a grant was made without any important strings attached.[8] It was to be a poll tax again, as in 1377, spread over the entire male population; but the rate was now a shilling a head, three times its previous level.

This grant was to have a fateful history. The attempt to collect it led directly to an outburst of popular anger far more alarming than that of 1376, the great Peasants' Revolt of 1381. The poll tax fell most heavily on the poor, especially in those areas where there were no wealthy men resident to help them out with their contributions. Originally it was planned to levy the tax in two instalments, in January and June 1381. As soon as the first instalment began to come in, it became clear that there had been evasion on a massive scale. In consequence the government decided to collect the whole of the second instalment forthwith, and ordered inquiries into evasion and fraudulent collection in a number of counties, mostly in the south and east. When John Bampton arrived to collect cash at Fobbing in Essex on 30 May, the people of the township 'roundly gave him answer that they would have nothing to do with him nor give him one penny'.[9] He was driven away with force, and in consequence Robert Bealknap, Chief Justice of the Common Pleas, was sent down with a commission of *trailbaston* to punish the rioters. Meanwhile the men of Fobbing had called out their neighbours. When Bealknap came to Brentwood, his party was set upon, and expelled from the town with bloodshed. While he was hurrying back dismayed to London, the whole county was beginning to rise. The men of the Thames estuary villages were often in contact with their neighbours of the Kentish shore; and on 2 June, the same day that Bealknap was thrust out of Brentwood, Abel Ker of Erith and a party of rebels attacked the Kentish Abbey of Lesness.

From this point the revolt spread in Kent and Essex with a rapidity that argues a measure of preparation and organization. In Kent the rebels attacked Dartford on 4 June, on 6 June they were at Rochester, and the next day at Maidstone, where they 'chose as chief Wat Tyler'. What Wat's antecedents were is not known; one story is that he was an old soldier, another that he was later recognized as 'the greatest robber of all Kent' (the two are not irreconcilable). He was clearly an able captain, capable of instilling a sense of purpose and an impressive degree of discipline. The other important Kentish leader was John Ball, the revolutionary hedge-priest whose catchwords have gone down to history:

When Adam delved and Eve span
Who was then the gentleman?[10]

On 10 June, under Tyler's leadership, the rebel host entered Canterbury, where they sacked the Archbishop's palace. From there they set off for London. The Essex rebels meanwhile had taken Colchester and Manningtree. At Waltham they burned all the muniments of the Abbey of the Holy Cross. Then they too headed for the capital. On 12 June the main body of the Essex men was at Mile End; and the Kentishmen were at Blackheath, where John Ball preached to their assembled host.

The king was in London with his mother, Princess Joan, the chancellor (Archbishop Sudbury), the treasurer (Sir Robert Hales), the earls of Buckingham, Derby and Arundel, and other peers. It should have been easy to put the city in a state of defence, but no steps were taken, perhaps because the king's advisers feared that, in the event of an attack by the rebels, the mob would rise inside the walls. This fear was justified. On 13 June, with the help of friends within the city, the Kentishmen entered by London Bridge, and the Essex rebels by Aldgate. The king withdrew to the Tower, where there was a garrison. Once in the city, the first objective of the rebels was the Savoy, the great London palace of John of Gaunt. They threw the furniture out of the windows, tore down the curtains and rich hangings; the plate they broke and carried out to throw in the river Thames. Nothing was stolen; the rebels were insistent that they had come to punish and destroy, not to rob. A man who had stolen a silver goblet was lynched. Another group of insurgents made its way to the Temple, the headquarters of the legal profession, who were hated as the advocates of their oppressors, and there made a great bonfire of legal books. The hospital at Clerkenwell was also sacked, and the prisons at Newgate and the Fleet opened. As night fell discipline, which had been impressive at first, began to deteriorate, and there was much house-breaking and arson.

It was probably late on 13 June that the king held a council at the Tower, at which it was decided that he should agree to a parley with the rebels at Mile End. The object was, if possible, to persuade at least some of the rebels to disband, and to give Sudbury and Hales, whose heads the rebels were demanding, a chance to escape. So, on the morning of 14 June the fourteen-year-old king rode out from the Tower at the head of a little band of councillors. At Mile End they found the rebels, mostly Essex men, assembled; their demands were for the abolition of serfdom, that all tenants should be free and rents limited to 4*d.* an acre – and for the heads of Chancellor Sudbury, Treasurer Hales and other 'traitors' about the king (John of Gaunt, whom they were certainly after, was fortunately for himself in the north). All that they asked was granted – except the last point: Richard refused to let anyone be punished before he was tried. Thirty clerks were set down at once to commence writing charters of liberty; and the Essex rebels, leaving representatives to collect these when they had been sealed, began to go home.

Half the king's plan thus succeeded; the other half did not. While Richard was at Mile End Tyler and his Kentishmen broke into the Tower, where the guards put up no resistance (presumably for fear of endangering the king) and found Sudbury and Hales in the chapel, preparing for death. They were dragged out and beheaded, together with John Legge, serjeant at law, and William Appleton, John of Gaunt's physician. This was the signal for a 'carnival of anarchy' in the city, in which a great many lost their lives. There was a terrible massacre of Flemings, whom the London artisans hated for taking employment from themselves. Richard, returning from Mile End, found pandemonium loose; he did not try to press on to the Tower, but took refuge for the night at the Great Wardrobe, near St Paul's.

The climax came on the next day, Saturday 15 June, when the king summoned the Kentish rebels to Smithfield, to try if the tactics of the day before would succeed a second time. When the royal party, who had stopped to hear mass at Westminster, reached Smithfield, they found the rebels drawn up in orderly battalions, and Tyler with a single companion rode out to meet them. His demands were very like those of the Essex men, for the abolition of serfdom, for limited rents, that there should be no lordship save that of the king; to which was added a demand for the disendowment of the church's temporalities and their partition among the people (John Ball's inspiration, most probably, was at work here).[11] There was some heated argument; Tyler began to be abusive, and called for a drink. As he was remounting, after draining it at a draught, he touched his weapon; Mayor Walworth of London, seeing the king threatened cut him down on the spot. As they saw Tyler fall his followers were beginning to fit arrows to their bows, when Richard, with remarkable courage, rode forward: 'Sirs, will you shoot your king? I will be your chief and captain, you shall have from me what you seek. Only follow me into the fields without.'[12] As the king began to lead the rebels into the fields round St John's Clerkenwell, Mayor Walworth turned back into the city to raise a force for his rescue.

Loyalists must have had orders to muster earlier, for within the hour Walworth was back, with a strong force led by the veteran Sir Robert Knowles. These men now blocked their way home for the Kentishmen. The king wisely avoided an engagement; he simply gave the rebels leave to depart, under escort. By evening the main body of the dead Tyler's force had passed out of the city over London Bridge, where Tyler's head had already replaced that of Archbishop Sudbury.

After 15 June the king and his council were again in control in the capital and the climax of the revolt had passed, but it was by no means over. From London and the neighbouring counties it had spilled outwards. At St Albans the townsmen, led by one William Grindcobbe, had risen against their lord the abbot, and forced him to grant them a charter of liberties. In Suffolk John Wrawe, curate of Ringsfield, had put himself at the head of the country rebels, and the townsmen of Bury, long at odds with the abbey, called in his bands to pursue their vendetta. The prior, John of Cambridge, was executed; so was Sir John Cavendish, Chief Justice of the King's Bench, who was captured by Wrawe's men at Lakenheath. Wrawe made Bury his headquarters, and made a profitable business of pillaging the local gentry. From Suffolk the revolt spread into Norfolk, where it found a leader of Tyler's standing and ability in Geoffrey Lister, to whom Norwich opened its gates. There his followers crowned him 'King of the Commons'. Cambridge and Huntingdon were also affected by the revolt, and it seems clear that it might have spread further, into counties which saw no trouble or only isolated outbreaks, if the news of Tyler's death in London had not stiffened resistance. Geoffrey Lister and his men evacuated Norwich when her warlike Bishop, Henry Despenser, appeared with forces that he had personally raised. Lister attempted a stand at North Walsham, but his men were dispersed by a charge and he himself was killed. Wrawe surrendered without a fight to the Earl of Suffolk, who had come at the head of 500 lances from London. In Essex those rebels who remained under arms were defeated on 28 June after stiff skirmishing at Billericay by troops under the Earl of Buckingham and Sir Thomas Percy. In Kent the local gentry combined together to restore order. By the beginning of July the revolt had run all its course.

In the aftermath of the Peasants' Revolt, the measures taken against those who had joined in it were marked by clemency. Apart from those who fell at North Walsham and Billericay, few died for their part in it. Wrawe, Grindcobbe and some others were executed, but even among the leaders a good many were spared. On 30 August the king ordered that all proceedings pending against rebels should be transferred into King's Bench, and no new cases instituted. In December a pardon was published from which only a few individuals and towns (notably Bury) were excepted. Apart from the cessation of the poll tax, which was never again levied, the rebellion achieved nothing. The charters granted at Mile End were quashed, and the ancient bondage of the peasant was enforced again at law as if the charters never had been.

It is sometimes argued that the Peasants' Revolt is a misnomer for the rebellion of 1381. Certainly it was not just a peasants' revolt. The causes which led men and communities to join in the movement were multiplex. The grievances of the London artisans were not the same as those of the men of Kent and Essex; the townsmen of St Albans and Bury had particular quarrels with the abbeys which had denied them the chartered freedoms of other boroughs; at Cambridge, where the mayor led the rebels, the revolt gave the town its chance to strike at university privilege. Nevertheless, the traditional name seems to have fair justification. Deep seated and long-term factors, the consequences of recurrent plague and the slow decay of the manorial system, lay behind the demands of the rustic insurgents, who made the revolt so formidable, for the abolition of serfdom, and for fair rents and wages. Their discontent had been fanned by the insurrectionary preaching of friars and of poor priests like John Ball, who had taught them to doubt that the social order of the day could find any justification in the Gospels. These men were the revolutionary intellectuals of 1381. What united all, peasants, poor priests, artisans, and wealthy townsmen of Bury and Cambridge, was the common burden of the poll tax and a common surge of discontent with governors who had achieved nothing but the oppression of the people. The degree of organization of which the rebels showed themselves in the circumstances capable is impressive. In the countryside the basis of the rebellion was not the manor but a much larger unit, the shire; and around London, in Kent, Essex, and the capital the rebels managed to combine their efforts, for a time at least. This argues a greater degree of political awareness, and a greater capacity for corporate political action, than we might have expected from the fourteenth-century countryman. In this context, it is significant how many of those later indicted for their past in the rebellion were relatively prosperous by peasant standards, including men who had served, for instance, as constables or jurors in their local hundreds.

From our immediate point of view, the political aspects of the revolt of 1381 are particularly interesting. It was in political terms that many contemporaries explained it. Sir Richard Waldegrave, speaker in the commons in 1381, put the blame for what had happened on heavy taxation, the extravagance of the court, and illegal maintenance by lords and their retainers, 'in spite of which the common people have not been succoured against the enemies of the realm: for they and their homes have been pillaged and robbed and burned . . . for which no remedy has been or is yet provided'.[13] The rebels were, in fact, sharply conscious of the threat of French raids, ordering those in Kent who lived in coastal areas not to leave their homes in case there should be an attack. They were also clear about who, in their eyes, were responsible for the misgovernment of the kingdom, and were insistent in their demand for the heads of named traitors: Sudbury, Hales, John of Gaunt. Here their attitude was not very different from that of the commons in the Good Parliament, who had raised like them the cry of 'traitors about the king'. The rebellion is a remarkable demonstration of the way in which distrust of all concerned in government and administration had percolated right down to the grass roots social level.

Corruption in high places and among the powerful was the obsession of the peasant rebels, as it was of their betters:

> Truth is set under a lock
> And Falseness reigneth in every flock:
> No man may come Truth to,
> But he sing *dedero* [i.e. offer a bribe].[14]

This jingle, taken from one of a number of little letters which circulated among the rebels, couched in the obscure language of religious allegory, has direct echoes of Langland's *Piers Plowman*, in which Lady Meed, the personification of bribery, holds pride of place before the law, and has friends all about the royal court. Langland can have had no sympathy with the rebels, as the naïve and conservative social philosophy of his poem shows. Resentment of misrule and failure was no sectional feeling in the 1370s and after them, but a general one. Politically, the Peasants' Revolt comes in direct line after the parliamentary protests of 1371 and 1376: it was the flood tide of popular indignation.

Let us listen again to the words of Sir Richard Waldegrave, as the roll of the autumn parliament of 1381 records them: 'To speak the straight truth, the outrages and other things which the poor commons have suffered of late, and have suffered in common to a degree not before known . . . was the cause that moved them to do the riot and mischief that they did.' If matters were not remedied, he declared, 'the whole kingdom will be lost and utterly destroyed for ever, and our lord the king and the lords and the commons along with it'.[15] These are the most doleful words that were ever uttered by a speaker of the medieval commons. It is no accident that they were spoken when they were. In 1381 ten years and more of heavy taxation, political instability at home and defeat abroad had combined with the longer, cumulative effect of poor harvests and recurrent plague to foster a mood of desperation. The kingdom was a house divided, and seemed destined to fall. The fissures ran deeper than those that the rivalries of aristocratic houses so often engendered in late medieval England. The clergy believed they were threatened in their material interests by the lords and commons of parliament. The merchants of London thought their civic privileges and their mercantile monopolies were threatened by the lords and the country gentry. The common people felt themselves threatened on all sides, by economic oppression and legal corruption, and by lack of defence against the French. The cohesion of the body politic seemed threatened; mutual trust, the foundation of medieval government, had ceased to exist. Nothing so terrible as the events of the summer of 1381 ever occurred again, in fact, but long years of political instability and recurrent crisis lay ahead.

Notes

1 K. de L. vol. VI, p. 380.
2 Chandos Herald, *The Black Prince*, ed. H. O. Coxe (Roxburghe Club, 1842), p. 126.
3 *Anonimalle Chronicle*, ed. V. H. Galbraith (Manchester, 1927), p. 96.
4 *R.P.* vol. II, p. 304.
5 Wyclif, *De Civili Dominio* vol. II, p. 7.
6 *Anonimalle Chronicle*, p. 81.
7 *R.P.* vol. III, pp. 5–6.
8 *R.P.* vol. III, pp. 88–90.
9 *Anonimalle Chronicle*, p. 134.
10 *Chronicon Anglie* (R.S.), p. 321.
11 *Anonimalle Chronicle*, p. 147.
12 Oman, *The Great Revolt of 1381*, p. 76, and Chronicon Anglie (R.S., 1874, p. 297).
13 *R.P.* vol. III, p. 100.
14 *Chron H. Knighton* (R.S.) vol. II, p. 139.
15 *R.P.* vol. III, p. 100.

Note on secondary reading (post 1970)

The surest guide to the political history of the late years of Edward III is G.A. Holmes, *The Good Parliament* (Oxford, 1975), which ranges much more widely than its title implies: A. Goodman, *John of Gaunt* (London, 1992) is useful, and see also, on particular topics, M. Bennett, 'Edward III's entail and the succession to the crown, 1376–1473' *E.H.R.*, vol. 113 (1998), and J.W. Sherborne, 'The cost of English warfare with France in the later fourteenth century', *B.I.H.R.*, vol. 50 (1997). To the English intervention in Castile, the best guide remains P.E. Russell, *The English Intervention in Spain and Portugal in the time of Edward III and Richard III* (Oxford, 1955), but there are significant new perceptions in K. Fowler, *Medieval Mercenaries*, vol. I, *The Great Companies* (Oxford, Blackwell 2001); and see also R. Barber's *Edward, Prince of Wales and Aquitaine* (Woodbridge, 1978).

On the Peasants' Revolt, a major topic within this chapter, see firstly R.B. Dobson, *The Peasants' Revolt of 1381* (London, 1970, 2nd edn. 1983). The essays collected in R. Hilton and T. Aston (eds.), *The English Rising of 1381* (Past and Present publications, Cambridge, 1984) include valuable papers from C. Dyer on the social and economic background, by A. Harding on the peasants and justices, by A. Butcher on urban revolt, and by R. Faith on peasant ideology. Also useful are E.B. Fryde 'The English parliament and the Peasants' revolt of 1381' in his *Studies in Medieval Trade and Finance* (London, 1983); C. Barron, *Revolt in London, 11–15 June 1381* (London, 1981); N. Brooks, 'The organisation and achievement of the peasants of Kent and Essex in 1381', in *Studies in Medieval History presented to R.H.C. Davis*, ed. H. Mayr-Harting and R.I. Moore (London, 1985); and W. Ormrod, 'The Peasants' Revolt and the Government of England', *Journal of British Studies*, vol. 29 (1990).

12 The reign of Richard II

Richard II's minority ended effectively in 1380, when the last of the 'continual councils' which had been in charge since 1377 was dismissed.[1] There were nineteen more years left of his reign, after that, and it proved to be a stormy and unhappy one. It was also a crucial period in the history of England in the later Middle Ages. Events that it witnessed were to have a direct influence on English politics for the best part of a century after Richard was dead. The years of his personal rule may be divided for convenience into two periods. The first culminated in a crisis, which began with the impeachment of the chancellor, Michael de la Pole, in the autumn parliament of 1386, and ended with a purge of the royal court and the courtiers in the 'Merciless Parliament' of 1388. The second period also culminated in a crisis, which began in 1397 when Richard carried out a systematic purge of his enemies of 1388, and ended in 1399 when the most important of them to survive, Henry Bolingbroke, deposed him.

The early 1380s are, at first sight, a rather amorphous period in English politics. The attention of the chroniclers focuses largely on two matters, the alarms of the ecclesiastical authorities about the spread of Wyclifite heresy, and the stormy mayoralty in London of John of Northampton, a *protégé* of John of Gaunt whose efforts to break the control over city government of the oligarchy of great merchant capitalists ended in 1384 with his exile from the city. The tensions among the ruling classes observable in the 1370s endured, it is clear. Among the king's advisers, much time and attention was taken up with plans for the furtherance of the French war, but things did not go any more smoothly than they had in the preceding decade; and in the aftermath of 1381 money was harder to raise. Three of the four parliaments called between 1381 and 1383 refused to make any grant, and those of the years following were not generous. The London merchants, moreover, became more hesitant than ever over lending, especially during Northampton's term as mayor.

English military and diplomatic hopes tended to centre on the possibility of exploiting the Great Schism in the church to English advantage. Much was looked for from the marriage of Richard to Anne of Bohemia, sister of Wenceslas, King of the Romans, who like the English supported Urban VI against Clement of Avignon, but he proved incapable of offering effective alliance. Gaunt was anxious to further his own plans for an invasion of Castile, whose throne he claimed, under the guise of an Urbanist crusade. This plan was favoured by many among the peers, preferably in conjunction with a royal expedition, but money for that enterprise was not forthcoming. The commons and the mercantile interest preferred the idea of an expedition to Flanders, which had declared for Urban, and where the men of Ghent were in revolt against their count. After the defeat of Philip van Artevelde of Ghent at Roosebek in 1382 the wool route from Calais to Ghent was threatened and this decided the matter. There was insufficient cash for a royal expedition, and Bishop Henry Despenser of Norwich was allowed to recruit a force for Flanders, on which bulls from Rome conferred the status of a crusade. After some initial success in the summer of 1383, the bishop's campaign ended in ignominious defeat, and he and his captains were impeached in the autumn parliament. In the hurry of retreat they had sold out the places that they had taken to the French for cash down, though it is not quite certain that the bishop knew what was going on. Englishmen felt that, once again, the advantage which should have been bought with the money that they had laid out had been lost through treachery.

In 1385 Richard at last did lead a royal host to war; not to France, however, but to Scotland, where hostilities had been resumed after the arrival there of French troops under John of Vienne. The army of 1385 was a large one, and before entering Scotland Richard created his two uncles, Edmund and Thomas, dukes of York and Gloucester respectively, and made his chancellor, Michael de la Pole, Earl of Suffolk. He advanced as far as Edinburgh, but failed to bring the Scots to an engagement. The best news of the year for the English came in fact from Spain, where, with the aid of a small force of English archers, James of Aviz, the new king of Portugal, resoundingly defeated the Castilians at Aljubarotta. James was the champion of national, Urbanist and anti-Castilian feelings in Portugal, and his success suggested that the time was ripe for Gaunt to make his bid for the Castilian throne. In the spring of 1386, he made an agreement with Richard, whereby the king should pay for the transport of a Lancastrian army to Spain, and advance 20,000 marks to Gaunt for expenses, to be repaid when he had won his kingdom. On 8 July Gaunt sailed from Plymouth for Galicia. He was to remain abroad for over three years.

John of Gaunt departed at an ill moment for England. In the summer of 1386 a great French host was gathered at Sluys, and an invasion seemed imminent. After it had disbanded, a wave of indignation against the government whose repeated failures abroad had exposed the kingdom to such risk was unleashed in the autumn parliament, where chancellor Pole was impeached. The first great crisis of the reign had commenced.

In order to understand this crisis, we must try to peer a little behind the façade of events in the period 1381–6. Parliamentary and popular reactions to the government's lack of success, especially abroad, were reminiscent of the previous decade. In 1381 and 1382 there were demands in parliament for the investigation of the expense of the king's household. The commons hedged their grants for Despenser's crusade with conditions. Distrust of leading men was apparent; in the spring parliament of 1384 Pole was openly accused of bribery by one John Cavendish, a London fishmonger, and in the autumn parliament allegations of maintenance were raised against the king's intimate Robert de Vere, Earl of Oxford. The parliament of 1385 asked for an annual review of the expenditure of the household, and to know the names of the king's councillors, who, says Walsingham, were publicly reputed to be 'knights of Venus rather than Bellona'. He and other chroniclers confirm the impression given by the parliament rolls, of widespread distrust of those in high places. A number of aristocrats seem to have associated themselves with the general dissatisfaction, notably the Earl of Arundel, and the king's youngest uncle, Thomas of Woodstock, who until 1386 was denied much influence in politics. Arundel and Woodstock were both men with military ambitions and inclinations, and shared the suspicions of the commons that the king's advisers were preparing a 'sell-out' abroad to the French. There was some substance in these suspicions; the possibility that Richard might do homage for all or part of Aquitaine seems to have been mooted seriously in Anglo-French negotiations in 1384, and chancellor Pole certainly failed signally to organize succour for Ghent, which remained in revolt against its new count, Philip of Burgundy, until December 1385.

The reaction that criticism evoked from the government was strikingly different, in this period, from what it had been in the days of Edward III's wise pliancy. The men who charged Pole and de Vere in 1384 found themselves severely punished for defamation. The demand of the parliament of 1385 for an inquiry into household expenditure led to the drawing up of a new ordinance, but it was simply not implemented by the king and his advisers, and the names of the king's councillors were not made known. It looks as if the king and his circle were determined to make as few concessions to popular pressure as they could, and to establish a tighter control over the direction of events. In 1383 the initiative in the impeachment of Despenser was taken out of the hands of the commons, and the chancellor conducted the prosecution *ex parte regis*. The increasing use of the king's personal seal, the signet, as a warrant to the chancery, and complaints at the extension of the jurisdiction of the court of the royal household, point in the same direction.

Signs of the emergence at court of a political group close to the young king are also significant. Two figures in particular were notable. One was Robert de Vere, a close intimate of Richard's from 1383 onwards, who was created Marquis of Dublin in 1385, a title which set him apart from all the rest of the peers, except the royal dukes. The other was Simon Burley, an experienced soldier who had been long in the service of the Black Prince, and subsequently was Richard's tutor. He was made under-chamberlain for life in 1383 and chief justice of South Wales, and later became Warden of the Cinque Ports. His influence helped to gather in the chamber a group of knights dedicated to the curialist interest, many of them like himself old servants of the Black Prince, with a leavening of younger men, as the trio Beauchamp, Berners and Salisbury whom chroniclers mention with particular resentment. The fact that members of this group were visibly securing to themselves a disproportionate share of royal patronage did not add to their popularity. Two important additions to this court circle were Nicholas Brembre, the city merchant and financier who had replaced Northampton as mayor, whom Richard knighted; and Pole, the chancellor (whose original connexions had been Lancastrian). Pole's ancestry was mercantile; his promotion to the Earldom of Suffolk (with a grant of most of the inheritance of the previous Ufford earls) in 1385 was much resented by many among the older aristocracy.

Gaunt's departure from England in 1386 was important to this growing royal clique. With his immense wealth, his great following of retainers and his large experience of affairs, Gaunt's influence in politics was inevitably powerful, and the wilder among the young men close to Richard seem to have mistaken him for the chief brake upon their freedom of action. De Vere was almost certainly the moving spirit behind a plot to discredit Gaunt in 1384, when an Irish Carmelite produced a story that the duke was plotting against the king's life. In the spring of 1385 the king himself is said to have been privy to a plot to get rid of Gaunt. In 1386 Richard was no doubt glad to make his uncle's departure for Spain easy. Gaunt in fact seems to have been entirely loyal; the king and the king's cronies were wrong in seeing him as their chief enemy. They were meanwhile making for themselves other foes, less scrupulous than he, who would be formidable when he was gone.

Gaunt's departure for Spain, instead of freeing the hands of Richard's associates, brought them face to face with crisis. When parliament assembled in the autumn of 1386, the first demand of the commons was for the dismissal of Pole, whom they wished to impeach, and of the treasurer, Bishop Fordham of Durham. Richard, who had left Westminster for Eltham, replied that he would not dismiss a scullion from his kitchen at their request.[2] In defiance of what he must have known was the popular feeling, he elevated Robert de Vere, from Eltham, to a new dignity, to be Duke of Ireland, with viceregal powers there. But when a delegation appeared from parliament, headed by Thomas of Woodstock and Thomas Arundel, bishop of Ely and the earl's brother, he found his position would be hard to maintain. When he declared that their attitude amounted to rebellion and threatened to seek the aid of the king of France, they reminded him that there was past precedent, if a king would not be governed by the laws of the realm 'with the common assent of the people, for deposing the king himself from the royal throne, and to elevate some near kinsman of the royal line'.[3] Before the threat of Edward II's fate, uttered by the king's own uncle and a bishop of high birth who came as spokesmen for the whole parliament, Richard had no alternative but to bow.

So parliament was able to go ahead with its work, and Pole was duly impeached. The most important charge against him was his failure to succour Ghent; it is an index of the general determination to see the last of him, that when he cleared himself on this score, the prosecution was pressed forward to convict him on technical charges of maladministration and peculation. He was sentenced to forfeiture of a large part of his estates, and to imprisonment at 'the king's pleasure'. Worse offence to the royal dignity was to follow. A great and continual council was appointed, by statute, to govern for a year. It was given full control of all revenues and subsidies, and powers to survey the expenses of the household, inquire into all gifts of fees, land or office that the king had made, and to correct what had been done amiss. The composition of the council was not extremist; besides Woodstock, Arundel and his brother the bishop, there were men of more moderate leanings, the two archbishops, William of Wykeham and Bishop Brantingham of Exeter, Sir John Devereux and Sir Richard Scrope, who was a connexion of Pole himself. Richard's attitude was decided not by its personnel, however, but by the fact that it was appointed against his will, with offensive powers which effectively restored the situation of a minority. This was a weak point in the authority of the 'commission council'. Edward III, in 1341, had set a clear precedent for repealing, on his own initiative, statutes which in the king's view ran contrary to the royal prerogative and the law of the land. There was no clear reason why Richard should not do the same.

The council seems to have gone about its work conscientiously, but it had, from the outset, to contend with absolute non-cooperation from the king. Before parliament dispersed, Richard appeared in person before those assembled, 'and made public protest by his own mouth, that on account of any thing done in the said parliament, he was not willing that prejudice should be incurred by himself or his crown, and that his prerogative and the liberties of his said crown should be saved and guarded'.[4] Pole, whom parliament had condemned, had the fine imposed on him remitted by the king, and his 'imprisonment' took the form of house arrest at Windsor, where Burley was his gaoler. Then, early in February 1387, Richard quitted Westminster, where the commission council was sitting, taking with him Pole, de Vere, Burley, Sir John Beauchamp and a number of household men, and Sir Robert Tressilian, the Chief Justice of the King's Bench. These formed virtually a rival council to the one set up by parliament. Richard did not return to Westminster until the commission's year of authority was all but ended.

In the spring and summer of 1387 Richard was mostly in the midlands and the marches of Wales. There and in Cheshire the king retained archers and others in his service. On a visit to York he won over Archbishop Neville, who was a member of the commission, to his cause. He sounded out the sheriffs, about the forces that they could raise on his behalf, and about whether they could ensure that men favourable to the king's interest were sent to the next parliament. From them Richard got little change; all the commons, they declared, were favourable to the lords of the commission. He got more satisfactory responses from the city authorities of London, whom he consulted through the ex-mayor, Nicholas Brembre. But the most favourable response of all was from those 'old and trusted friends of the king', the judges of the common law who were Sir Robert Tressilian's colleagues.

At two great councils, at Shrewsbury on 21 August, and at Nottingham on 25 August, Richard and his advisers put a series of questions about the king's legal position to a group of judges who included (besides Tressilian) the Chief Justice of the Common Pleas, Robert Bealknap, with three of his colleagues, and the chief baron of the exchequer. The questions were subtle, the answers significant. It was first asked if the statute appointing the commission council 'derogated from the regality and prerogative of the lord king'. When this was answered affirmatively, two further questions and answers established that those who compelled the king to assent to such a statute ought to be punished 'as traitors'. So, in the judges' view, ought all generally who hindered the king in the exercise of his regality. The next two answers established that the king could in law dissolve parliament whenever he wished, and further that the lords and commons had no legal right to put forward articles of their own and insist on their discussion before dealing with the king's business (i.e. they had no right to insist on redress before granting supply). This cleared the way to the answer to a following question, which defined it as unlawful to impeach a minister in parliament without the king's assent. The judges further made it clear that in their view those who had claimed for the deposition of Edward II the status of a lawful precedent acted treasonably, and that the sentence recently passed on Pole was erroneous.[5]

The judges' answers branded the action of those who had forced the commission council on the king as a crime 'like treason'. The plan clearly was to arraign such of Richard's enemies as he thought fit on charges based on the answers, as soon as the commission's year of office had expired. The judges' answers were also constitutionally of great significance. They constitute the most clear and reasoned statement of the role of royal prerogative in government that was ever made in England in the Middle Ages. They made it plain that it was the king's prerogative to choose his councillors; that they were responsible to him, not to parliament; that parliament was dependent on his will for summons and dismissal; that it had no right to initiate business or impeach without his assent. Legally, the most doubtful point in the answers was that, in defining attempts to thwart the prerogative as treasonable, they ran counter to the definition of treason given in Edward III's statute of 1352, which limited the scope of treason to such acts as aiding the king's enemies, and levying war against him in his realm. Nevertheless, though the judges later were to claim that they responded under duress, they seem actually to have given their answers freely and even enlarged on certain points. According to the received canons of legal learning of the time, they were right in law. Their answers formed a decisive challenge to the power and authority which parliament had been quietly establishing for itself in its dealings with the crown over half a century past, and to the multiplying precedents for parliamentary insistence on redress preceding supply.

The challenge was both politically imprudent and badly timed. Common opinion was generally behind the commission council. The prospect of a new definition of treason brought with it the threat of large-scale forfeitures, to embitter the family relations and party alignments of the aristocracy as they had done in the reign of Edward II. The news of what the judges had told the king, with its implied threat to security of property, solidified support behind the king's opponents, and their leaders began to prepare for a show of force. When Richard returned to London, Gloucester (Thomas of Woodstock), Arundel and the Earl of Warwick were gathering their retainers. When they appeared before the king at Westminster on 17 November, they were ready to carry the war into his camp by 'appealing' five of his intimates, de Vere, Pole, Tressilian, Brembre and Archbishop Neville, of treason. The foundation of their charge was that these five favourites, by the undue influence that they had exercised over the king, were 'accroaching royal power'. This was a charge quite outside the limits of the 1352 statute, and harked back to the bad old days of Edward II, when it had been used against both Gaveston and the Despensers.

At Westminster Richard promised that his five friends should be kept under arrest until the next parliament, which was summoned for 3 February 1388, when the appeal against them would be heard. This gained him time; but after the army, which de Vere was leading out of Cheshire to his support, was dispersed by the appellants (now joined by Gaunt's son, Henry Bolingbroke, and Mowbray of Nottingham) at Radcot Bridge in Oxfordshire, all that time gained was a chance for his friends to flee the country. After Radcot Bridge the Londoners were not prepared to make a stand on the king's behalf. When the victorious appellants arrived in the capital, Richard at the Tower was entirely at their mercy.

On the day that the Merciless Parliament of 1388 assembled, the five appellant lords, Gloucester, Arundel, Warwick, Bolingbroke and Nottingham, entered the assembly together 'arm in arm, dressed in cloth of gold'[6] to uphold their appeal. Of the five men accused, only Brembre was there to stand his trial; the others had all fled, and proceedings against them were in absence. At the beginning, the appellants were in some difficulty over their manner of proceeding. The common lawyers declared that the appeal would not hold by their law (the treasons alleged were not among those defined in 1352 by statute), and the civil lawyers that their law would not apply to the case, since England had never been subject to Roman civil law. The problem was solved by a solemn declaration that the 'law and course of parliament' took precedence over the law of any other court in the kingdom, and that the lords of parliament, as the judges of its law, could hear the appeal. There was some legal justification for this claim. The statute of 1352 had stated clearly that new treasons, over and above those which it defined, should not be judged in the common law courts, but in parliament. Appeal was a method of criminal accusation recognized at common law, and there was precedent (in spite of what some historians have claimed to the contrary) for hearing appeals in parliament. Thus, in parliamentary appeal of treason, the appellants found a way of proceeding without overriding either the common law or the statute of 1352. They also provided a direct answer to the opinions which Richard's judges had expressed at Shrewsbury, by asserting the judicial supremacy of parliament over all other courts.

There is no need to examine the details of the trials in the Merciless Parliament; their results were a foregone conclusion. All five of the king's friends were convicted of treason. Only Brembre and Tressilian, who was found in hiding after he had been sentenced, were executed; the others were safe overseas. Their lands, of course, were forfeited. A number of Richard's other supporters were impeached: Simon Burley; the three chamber knights Beauchamp, Berners and Salisbury; and the king's confessor Rushook. Burley and the three knights were executed. The judges who had subscribed to the famous opinions, and Blake, the serjeant at law who had framed the questions, were sent into exile in Ireland. It is significant that the appellants had considerable difficulty in securing the conviction of Brembre, the only appellee who was tried in person. A committee of peers declared that they found nothing in the charges against him worthy of death, but they were overborne by pressure from the commons. Some of the peers also wished to spare Burley; again, it was the commons' insistence, and the determination of 'the undivided Trinity', Gloucester, Warwick and Arundel, that ensured the death sentence. Opinion at large was behind the most extreme measures of the parliament. If it had not been, the king could never have been so ignominiously humbled through the execution of his friends.

Having purged the king's intimates and censured the opinions of his judges, the Merciless Parliament had achieved what the appellants desired of it. To ensure permanence for its measures, they were formally declared irrevocable, binding on all future parliaments. At the same time, in order that the processes of the parliament should not be used against their inventors, it was declared that its procedures and convictions did not constitute a precedent. The appellants, at the request of the commons, were awarded £20,000 'for their great expenses in procuring the salvation of the realm and the destruction of the traitors'.[7] This was as far as the Merciless Parliament's achievement went, which reminds us sharply of the limited aims of the group of lords who dominated its proceedings. They wished to secure themselves, to get rid of the men who had been close to the king, to have a taste for themselves of the fruits of power and office, not very much more.

On behalf of the king's friends, it may be said that they at least, in the crisis of 1386–8, showed themselves capable of thinking in broad terms, about policies which, if they had been able to put them into practice, would have brought about a real change of direction in constitutional development. The judges' opinions outlined, by a series of legal definitions, a system of government which would rescue royal policy (and the officials responsible for carrying it out) from the constant and frustrating necessity of adjustment to meet the demands of public opinion, as expressed in parliament. In the mood of the kingdom of 1387, their plans were, however, simply unworkable. Nor were the royalists any more moderate than the appellants, in their human intentions. If fortune had gone their way, they certainly meant to purge their enemies, and would not have shown them more mercy, probably, than they were shown themselves.

The fact that the appellants had no new salve, apart from changes of governing personnel, was soon apparent. After initial success with a naval victory in the Channel in 1387, belligerence in foreign policy got nowhere. Before the end of 1388 negotiations with the French for a truce had been resumed, while in the north, English arms suffered a severe defeat at Otterburn at the hands of Douglas. When the autumn parliament of 1388 met at Cambridge, the commons were full of old and familiar complaints about the poor enforcement of the statute of labourers, misgovernment of the Calais staple, and the excesses committed by the liveried retainers of noblemen. By May 1389, the initiative had passed to Richard again. At a great council at Westminster he appeared in person, and declared that he intended to assume the rule of the kingdom himself, with the aid of councillors of his own choice. Without protest, Bishop Arundel, the appellants' chancellor, and his colleagues Gilbert and Waltham, the treasurer and the keeper of the privy seal, surrendered their seals of office.

The main consequence of the crisis of 1386–8 was the venom that it instilled into the feuds of the aristocracy. Such feuds were bound to involve not the principals only, but also the whole train of friends, relatives and retainers that constituted the 'affinities' of great noblemen. The revival of the charge of treason as a political crime was a particularly ominous feature, evoking unhappy memories of the days of Edward II. It was probably because they were aware of the terrible consequences which could stem from executions and forfeitures among the great that so many peers were anxious to restrain the vindictive anger of the appellants and the commons in the Merciless Parliament. They failed, as we have seen, and when that parliament dispersed, a crop of vendettas that would not be easily forgotten had been baptized in blood.

The men who in 1389 took over at the chancery and the exchequer were Wykeham and Brantingham; Master Edmund Stafford became keeper of the privy seal. All three were experienced administrators, who had been uncommitted in the recent troubles. Their appointment is one of the features that have led some historians to label the early 1390s a period of 'appeasement'. Certainly the tenor of politics was very different from that of preceding years. The parliaments of the period 1390–6 had none of the stormy quality of those of the 1370s and 1380s; they did not sit so long, and were summoned less frequently. There was a studied deference to parliamentary opinion; in 1390 the chancellor, the treasurer and all the lords of the council resigned their offices in parliament so that charges might be brought against them, and when none were forthcoming, were reappointed and resworn, in parliament. The commons were regularly consulted on such matters as peace negotiations with

France. There were numerous great councils, to which the appellant lords were regularly invited. The council records show that Gloucester, in particular, always received that respect which was due to him as an uncle of the king. When Wykeham and Brantingham, both ageing men, relinquished their posts, the men who replaced them were none other than the appellants' chancellor and treasurer, bishops Arundel and Gilbert. When Archbishop Courtenay of Canterbury died in 1396, Arundel was the man who succeeded him.

The return of John of Gaunt had much to do with the surface harmony in exalted circles of the years 1390–6. In 1388 he had come to terms with John of Trastamara the king of Castile, who could not expel him from Galicia even after he had lost most of his army through disease, and his daughter was betrothed to John's heir. In the autumn of 1389 he was back in England, and though he was in 1390 made Duke of Guienne for life, he did not spend much time there. In England he held a unique position among the aristocracy. He was the most experienced and easily the wealthiest of the peers, the father of one appellant, Henry Bolingbroke, and the elder brother of another, Gloucester. In the king's eyes he was uncontaminated by any association with the events of 1388. His views on the dignity of the royal office and prerogative were sympathetic to Richard's, as his conduct as lieutenant for his father long ago in the Good Parliament of 1376 had shown. Unquestionably loyal to the king, respected by most of his brother peers and feared by others, his influence was a powerful force to keep internal feuds in the background.

Bitterness, however, was very far from dead, notwithstanding Gaunt's influence and conciliatory policy, and there were plenty of signs of it. In 1392 Richard had to promise in council that 'he would do no harm to any lord or other his liege on account of things done in time past . . . nor would he seek to restore any of those who were condemned in full parliament in his kingdom'.[8] Richard never in fact tried to restore de Vere or Archbishop Neville (Pole had died abroad in 1389), but his old opponents were almost certainly right in thinking that he wished to do so. In 1393 there was a rising of the commons in Cheshire, and Richard had to deny publicly rumours that he was conniving at it for political ends of his own. Arundel thought the independence which Gaunt's intimacy gave Richard so dangerous that he even attempted to discredit the former by charging him with using undue influence on the king, in the parliament of 1394. The charge fell through, and he had to make a humiliating apology. In that same year Queen Anne died, and there was an ugly scene at her funeral when Richard struck Arundel across the face, because he was showing insufficient respect for the corpse. Arundel was so alarmed about his political position that he took the trouble to sue out for himself a formal pardon for all that he had been concerned with in 1387–8.

With the king wearing Gaunt's device in public, there was nothing that the ex-appellants could do to prevent him gathering about him a body of committed royal supporters far more formidable than the little group of curialists of 1387. Prominent in this new 'royal party' were a number of younger noblemen: John and Thomas Holland (earls of Huntingdon and Kent, and the king's half-brothers), John Montagu Earl of Salisbury, York's son Edward Earl of Rutland, and Sir Thomas Percy, who was steward of the household and represented the northern magnate interest. A number of clerks who had personal associations with the king were preferred to high ecclesiastical office: Medford, Bishop of Salisbury, and Walden, Dean of York, had both acted as secretary to Richard; Tydeman Bishop of Worcester had been his physician and Burghill of Lichfield his confessor; Merke of Carlisle was said to have been his boon companion. The king's knightly councillors, who discharged most of the routine administrative and judicial business of the council in these years, formed another group of supporters, able and experienced as well as influential. Baldwin Raddington (a connexion of Burley's), Richard Stury, William Scrope and Edward Dalyngryg, men with a martial background, were among the most prominent. The famous trio, Bushy, Bagot and Green, contributed experience of a different order. All three had sat in more than one parliament, and Bushy served as speaker in 1394. He and Green had both been in Lancaster's retinue, and continued to take his fees when they took the king's also. Meanwhile, outside and beyond the court, Richard in the 1390s was systematically working to buttress his position in the localities of the kingdom, by retaining for life knights and esquires of wealth and influence in their own counties. This effort to build up a royal retinue or affinity, comparable with the private retinues of the great magnates and recruited in the same way, was a novel initiative on the crown's part. It reveals Richard's alertness to the value for royal authority of a solid, interested core of royal supporters among the greater gentry, who could act as 'an informal network, linking the household and court to the out-lying regions of the realm'.[9] His inability to tap into such support had been a major factor in his undoing in 1387: he had learned his lesson.

Two important developments helped to alter the political situation of the 1390s. The first was Richard II's expedition to Ireland in 1394. The situation of the Anglo-Irish administration, centred on Dublin Castle, had long been unsatisfactory, and the king's chief justice now barely maintained control in the coastal towns of the Pale. The native chiefs, especially Art MacMurrough in Leinster, were pressing the Anglo-Irish so hard that many were leaving the country. Richard's first plan was to send Gloucester over as lieutenant, but his commission was revoked in 1393 and a royal expedition organized. The army that Richard raised was a very large one, and he marched at its head from Waterford to Dublin; this demonstration in force cowed the native chiefs into submission. The success thus achieved (very temporarily as it proved) gave Richard some cachet as a military leader. More importantly, it gave him and his officials an immensely valuable experience of military administration. The largest contingent in the army was raised and paid through the household. The process of raising large numbers of 'yeomen and archers of the crown', especially in Cheshire and north Wales, who received a fee and swore to stand by for service, pointed the way for the recruitment of a standing royal bodyguard, the famous 'Cheshire archers' of the last years of the reign. The badge of the white hart, Richard's personal emblem, was given as an outward sign that a yeoman had taken the king's fee. Thus, as Tout put it, 'the forces of autocracy began to be clothed in military garb'.

The other factor that dramatically altered the aspect of English politics in this period was the movement towards a *rapprochement* with France. A truce had been agreed in May 1389 for three years, and this was subsequently renewed while negotiations for a final peace went forward. Gaunt was very prominent in this business: he led the English deputation, which in 1392 was magnificently received at Amiens by Charles VI in person, and in 1393 and 1394 he and Gloucester were in charge of talks with the French (represented by the Dukes of Burgundy and Berry), which very nearly led to a settlement. The English appear to have at last become willing to concede on the issue of sovereignty over Aquitaine (though they were determined to resist concession over Calais), and a draft treaty was drawn up, under which Richard would have done liege homage to Charles VI for a territorially very substantial duchy. Opposition at home in England ensured that it was never ratified. Rumours that peace was in the offing sparked off a local revolt in Cheshire in 1393; and the parliament which met at Salisbury early in 1394 made clear the profound reservations of the commons about the proposed arrangement that their king do homage, which, as they put it, would place every Englishmen 'under the heel of the French king'.[10] Even if this English opposition could have been overcome, it seems likely that the draft terms would have been rendered unworkable by the Gascons, whose insistence that the duchy was inseparable from the English crown had led them by 1394 into open resistance to Gaunt's authority as their Duke. The final result, agreed in 1396, was, in consequence, short of a peace. It was a truce to last for twenty-eight years. This was a period long enough to relieve Richard of all concern about raising money for war overseas for the fore-seeable future. To cement the truce, Richard took a new bride, Isabella, the eldest daughter of Charles VI. She was only six, but Richard was not yet thirty: there was a prospect of an heir in due course, and in the meantime the new queen brought a dowry of 800,000 francs.

In special instructions, given just before the arrangements for his marriage were completed, Richard told his negotiators that they might reduce the sum demanded by way of dowry, if the French king and his uncles would promise to support him, if the need arose 'against all manner of folk . . . and to sustain him with all their power against any of his own subjects'.[11] No such agree-ment, of course, appeared in the final text of the treaty, but there was almost certainly a tacit understanding. When, at the end of 1396, Richard returned from Calais with his new bride, he was certainly in an immeasurably stronger position *vis-à-vis* potential domestic enemies than he had been ten years earlier. France was now an ally, not an enemy, and he was relieved of the dependence on parliament for war finance that had so long hampered the free rein of regality. He could afford to think again about putting into practice ideas about the way in which his kingdom ought to be governed that had been much in the minds of his intimates ten years earlier.

In the spring parliament of 1397 the commons presented the famous petition of Thomas Haxey: 'that the great and excessive charge of the king's household be amended and diminished'.[12] The subject of the petition was one that had sparked off Richard's anger before, and his reaction was the same as it had been in 1386. But his position was now different, far stronger; the consequence of the petition was Haxey's arraignment for treason. Not only was he convicted, but the lords in parliament declared further, on the king's behalf, 'that if anyone, of whatsoever estate or condition, shall move or excite the commons of parliament or any other person to make remedy of any matter which touches our person or our government or our regality, he shall be held a traitor'.[13] The echo of the judges' answers of 1387 is unmistakable.

Haxey's condemnation was the first warning of the gathering storm of the royalist *révanche*, which broke in the autumn parliament and swept away both the men of 1388 and their measures. Historians have been divided as to whether what happened was simply the fruition of the king's long laid plans, or whether it was triggered off by the discovery of a new plot by the old appellants, as Richard and his friends claimed in the summer when Gloucester, Warwick and Arundel were all arrested. Two facts strongly militate in favour of the first explanation. One is that in spite of the allegations that a new plot had been uncovered, the public charges which were brought against the three noblemen were, without exception, based on what they had done between 1386 and 1388. Secondly, Richard's actions were aimed just as much at the measures as at the men of 1388. This was not just a purge; it was an effort to force English government into conformity with doctrinaire principles of regality.

This intention was made plain at the opening of the parliament, when the chancellor, the Bishop of Exeter, preached upon the text from Ezekiel 'there shall be one king for all'. Kings, he explained, were sworn at their coronation to guard the regality and prerogatives of the crown, which were inalienable: 'Wherefore the king has caused his estates of parliament to be assembled on this occasion, to be informed if any rights of the crown are subtracted or diminished: so that by their good advice and discretion such remedy can be provided, as will make the king in his liberty and power as his ancestors were before him . . . there shall be one king for all and he shall govern all.'[14] The acts of the parliament were faithful to the spirit of the bishop's sermon. At an early stage the question of the statute empowering the 'commission council' of 1386 was raised by the commons (Bushy was their speaker), because 'it seemed prejudicial to the king and a usurpation of his regality'.[15] Not only was it struck off the statute roll, but it was declared that it would henceforward be high treason for anyone to 'pursue or purchase' any such commission. The finishing touches to this part of its programme were given when the parliament reassembled at Shrewsbury in January 1398. All the acts of the Merciless Parliament of 1388 were annulled. All and any who were involved in opposing the king in 1387–8 had in consequence to sue for pardon. The questions that had been put to the judges in 1387 were rehearsed, and their answers were formally pronounced good law with the assent of the whole parliament. Finally, the king's financial independence was strengthened by the grant for life of subsidies on wool and leather exports.

Careful plans had been laid in advance to secure the conviction of Warwick, Arundel and Gloucester, whose cases came before the first session of the parliament. In a great council at Nottingham in the late summer a group of eight lords, the earls of Rutland, Huntingdon, Kent, Somerset, Nottingham and Salisbury, with Lord Despenser and Sir William Scrope, formally appealed the three ex-appellants of treasons committed ten years before. In parliament, before the appeals were tried, the points of treason were formally rehearsed in a wording slightly different from the 1352 statute, to make sure that the charge would hold. Then the charter of pardon which Arundel had taken out in 1394 was solemnly revoked, as granted 'under duress' (a singular description of the so called period of appeasement). In order to leave no doubt about the legality of the forthcoming conviction, the spiritual lords, who would take no part in a judgement of blood, were forced to appoint a proctor, Sir Thomas Percy, the steward of the household, to act for them in the process. As a preliminary to the main trials, Archbishop Arundel was got out of the way; impeached by the commons, he was exiled, and a papal bull conveniently translated him to a see in the Avignon obedience. The appeals were then heard. Warwick broke down, confessed his guilt, and was exiled to the Isle of Man. Arundel took his stand on his pardon, but it was already revoked, and Gaunt, speaking as Steward of England for all the lords, sentenced him to execution. Gloucester did not stand his trial, because he had died in prison at Calais. It is virtually certain that he was murdered at Richard's orders with the connivance of Nottingham. Before he died he had written a confession, admitting his guilt in 1387 and that he had even withdrawn his homage from Richard, and he was condemned posthumously.[16] All the estates of the condemned men, including lands entailed as well as those held in fee simple, were forfeited.

Those who had helped in the undoing of the men of 1388 were amply rewarded. Henry Bolingbroke was created Duke of Hereford; Mowbray of Nottingham Duke of Norfolk; John and Thomas Holland dukes of Exeter and Surrey respectively; John Beaufort (eldest of Gaunt's sons by Catherine Swinford) became Marquis of Dorset; and Thomas Despenser, Thomas Percy, Ralph Neville and William Scrope became earls of Gloucester, Worcester, Westmorland and Wiltshire. These men got the lions' shares of the forfeited estates of Gloucester, Warwick and Arundel. The work of revenge was not yet complete, however. The lesser men who had abetted and aided the appellants in 1387 remained unpunished. Besides, in 1387–8 there had been five appellants, and two remained still, Bolingbroke and Mowbray, though now both seemed to be in the king's camp. Both these matters received attention in the Shrewsbury parliament.

The commons at Shrewsbury asked for and received a general pardon for past offences. From it were excepted, however, all those who in 1387 had 'ridden in arms and risen forcibly against the king'.[17] This exception was interpreted so widely as, in fact, to include no less than seventeen counties. In order to obtain full pardon, the proctors of these counties had to buy the king's grace, at the rate of 1000 marks per shire, and to take, in the name of their communities, a new oath of special allegiance to the king. Over and above this, they were forced to put their seals to blank charters, in effect pledging all the goods and persons of their communities to the king for loyal behaviour. One writer at least believed that the sealing of these charters, which put all seventeen counties at the legal mercy of the king, was 'the cause afterwards of the destruction of the king himself'.[17a] Besides these pledges from the counties, Richard took a personal oath from each of the lords spiritual and temporal individually, and from the commons collectively, to support and uphold all the judgements and statutes of the 1397 parliament. These oaths and pledges suggest that, even now, Richard and his closest advisers had little confidence in either lords or commons. Dread of the terrific consequences of straying from the path of obedience was to be the foundation of the new autocratic dispensation, not mutual love and regard between king and people.

It was at Shrewsbury, on 30 January, that Henry Bolingbroke appeared before the king in parliament, with a schedule concerning treasonable advances which, he alleged, Mowbray had made to him before Christmas. The king's intention, Mowbray had said, was 'to do with them [both] as he had done with the others already', on account of 'what was done at Radcot Bridge'.[18] Bolingbroke had gone to his father, who advised him to go to the king. There was, of course, no ready proof that the words really had passed, and Richard, in a hurry to complete the work of the parliament, had no desire to see the matter thrashed out in public on the spot. A committee of eighteen persons was about to be appointed, to examine and answer the petitions which the parliament's more pressing work had left outstanding. The same persons were therefore empowered to investigate Bolingbroke's allegations.

The committee met twice, at Bristol and at Windsor, in the spring of 1398. Since Bolingbroke's proofs were insufficient and Mowbray denied the charges, it was settled that the matter should be decided, as an issue touching the honour of noblemen, by a judicial duel. The combatants met at Coventry on 16 September. As soon as they appeared in the lists ready for combat, the king threw down his baton, and ordered them to disarm. He had decided (very likely at Gaunt's insistence) to avoid the shedding of blood by taking the quarrel into his own hands. He then pronounced sentence of banishment on both lords, on Mowbray for life, on Henry for ten years. Ten years is a long time, and Richard no doubt reckoned that the ex-appellant, on his return, would be a stranger and a spent political force; if, that is, he ever intended to permit his return.

Before they left England, both Bolingbroke and Mowbray were given permission to appoint attornies to receive the revenues of their estates while they were in exile. Just over four months after the aborted duel at Coventry John of Gaunt died, on 3 February 1399, and the question arose directly as to whether Bolingbroke should now be permitted to add to his already substantial estate the vast inheritance of Lancaster. It is not surprising, given their past and bitter experience of the power of overmighty subjects and Bolingbroke's record as an appellant, that Richard and his advisers were determined not to let him do so. Their difficulty was how to stop him inheriting with some colour of legal authority, especially since the grant of letters of attorney seemed to recognize and guarantee his full enjoyment of his right as a lord of lands. The expedient that they hit on was to make some significant alterations to the parliament roll of 1398. Where the original terms of appointment of the committee of eighteen had been to 'examine and answer petitions still outstanding', the words were now added 'and to terminate all matters moved in the presence of the king'.[19] Armed with this pseudo-parliamentary authority, the committee met again. They revoked the grant of letters of attorney of October 1397 as 'inadvertent', extended Bolingbroke's sentence of banishment to one for life, and took the whole of his inheritance into the king's hand.

Just a fortnight after the meeting of the committee that authorized the sequestration of the Lancastrian estates, instructions went out to mobilize the yeomen of the crown for a royal expedition to Ireland. Ten months previously Art MacMurrough had surprised and killed the king's lieutenant, the Earl of March, near Carlow. If English authority in Ireland were to survive in anything but name, intervention in force was necessary, and it was with a substantial army that Richard sailed from Milford Haven in May. Most of his closest associates among the aristocracy were with him; York was left behind as keeper of England, with Wiltshire, the treasurer, and the chamber knights Bushy, Bagot and Green. Pressing as the situation in Ireland was, the king's decision to leave the country was hardly wise. To many who were already alarmed by the novel courses of Richard's government, the seizure of the Lancastrian estates seemed the last straw. No man or family appeared to be secure in his property; the sacred right of inheritance was threatened. Lampoons and satires on the courtiers bore witness to a wave of popular resentment, and wild rumours were beginning to circulate. Richard was planning to make Dublin his capital and to tyrannize his English subjects from a distance; unheard of taxes were to be imposed; noblemen were going to be murdered and their estates farmed by Wiltshire for the king's profit. Richard's departure, taking with him most of his close associates among the peerage, together with their retinues and the greater part of his own, offered Henry Bolingbroke the ideal opportunity to attempt to retrieve his fortunes. Nevertheless, when he seized it, it seems to have taken both Richard and York as keeper of England by surprise.

Richard's confidence that he was in control of the situation when he sailed for Ireland, though misplaced, is at least in part explicable. He believed and trusted that he had finally secured his position and authority by the fears that his recent measures had inspired, and by the favours by means of which he had bound round himself what seemed a solid body of support. He had been careful, in 1398, to make sure that plenty of men profited by the fall of the old appellants, and he had been careful too to make sure that few suffered by the sequestration of the Lancastrian estates, confirming the pensions that Henry

.and his father had granted. Since the Shrewsbury parliament, he had continued to retain in his service more men of rank in the counties, and to ensure that his loyal supporters were prominent in local offices, as sheriffs and on judicial commissions. For all the *furore* over the confiscation of the Lancastrian inheritance, he might perhaps have been right in calculating that he could safely leave the land, but for two factors of which he did not take sufficient account.

One was the situation in France, where Bolingbroke was living in comfortable exile. Richard clearly believed that he could rely on the dominant influence in Paris of Philip of Burgundy to prevent any hostile move on Henry's part. Burgundy had been one of the chief architects of the 1396 *rapprochement* between the French and English courts, and it was in his interest as Count of Flanders to maintain good relations with the English government, on account of the dependence of the Flemish cloth weaving industry on English wool imports. But Burgundy had a bitter rival for power at the French court in the king's brother, Louis Duke of Orleans, whose ambitions looked as if they might be well served by a destabilization of the political situation in England. When Burgundy left Paris temporarily in June 1399, Orleans had his opening: he entered into a personal treaty of friendship with Henry, and connived toward making his preparations to intervene in England feasible. Richard had made a mistake in placing too much confidence in Burgundy, and of underestimating the fluidity of the political situation at the French court.

His other miscalculation, equally crucial, was with regard to the magnates of the north, whom he had left behind in England. Their attitude in 1399, and in particular that of the Percies, had a long history behind it. The Anglo-Scottish wars of the earlier fourteenth century bred feuds between the great families who held lands on either side of the uncertain border (as for instance between the Percies and the Douglases), which were pursued without much reference to the governments at either Westminster or Edinburgh. The difficulty of imposing any measure of control was, on the English side, the result partly of sheer distance, partly of the independence of northern society – an independence precious to its leaders because their fortunes and their standing so often depended on their freedom to prosecute vendettas against their private enemies. In these conditions the royal government had no option but to rely, almost entirely, on the local nobility for the safe-keeping of the land. When in the 1380s the problem of the defence of the northern border became acute again after the reopening of active war with Scotland, new experiments were made in the administration of the wardenships of the marches. They were made now the subject of formal indentures, the wardens contracting to serve for a period of years and to maintain forces for the defence of the border in return for stipulated wages. The rates of remuneration were princely (Henry Percy the younger in the East March in 1396 was assured of £3000 per annum in time of peace, rising to £12,000 in time of open war). This new system, which became permanent, offered opportunities to the magnates of the north, who normally controlled the wardenships, to consolidate their position locally by retaining what rapidly became, in effect, subsidized private armies. It also, naturally, accentuated their mutual competition for local office and influence.

Much the same period that witnessed the introduction of these new arrangements witnessed also the rise of the Percy family to new and spectacular prominence. The Percys had been lords of Alnwick since early in the century; in 1370 they acquired the Umfraville barony of Prudhoe, and a little later added to this the lordship of Cockermouth which carried their power into the West March. In 1377 Henry Percy was created Earl of Northumberland. In the late 1380s, when the new system of retaining wardens by indenture came in, the government from Westminster did its best to maintain a balance of power in the north, by ringing the changes among the wardenships between Percys, Nevilles and Cliffords, but between 1391 and 1395 the wardenships of both marches, East and West, were in Percy hands. Then in 1396, John Holland Earl of Huntingdon became Warden of the West March, and in 1398 he was succeeded by Edward, Duke of Aumale; both were courtiers, and lacked any family connexion with the border country. Northumberland, in 1381–2, had shown considerable resentment when Gaunt, also a magnate without border connexion, was for a time the king's lieutenant in the north, and his reaction now seems to have been similar. To add to the anxieties of the Percys for their new found dominance in their homeland, Ralph Neville in 1397 was created Earl of Westmorland. Royal favour, to which they owed their power, seemed bent on raising up rivals to them.

The Earl of Northumberland and his son Henry 'Hotspur' were both men of soaring ambition, and without much scruple when it came to maintaining the position of the family. Thanks to the crown's past generosity, in 1399 they disposed of military retinues of sufficient size to make their allegiance crucial in a political crisis. Richard believed that he had handled them with enough delicacy to keep them trustworthy (he had recently made Northumberland's brother Thomas, who was steward of his household and who had been very prominent in the proceedings against the old appellants in 1397, Earl of Worcester). But he was wrong in thinking so, as events proved all too soon after he had left for Ireland.

When Henry Bolingbroke landed at Ravenspur in early July he was accompanied by Thomas Arundel, the exiled archbishop, and a little band of his own faithful friends. Robert Waterton, John Leventhorpe, and others of his old officials and retainers were waiting to greet him. Near Doncaster he was joined by the Earl of Northumberland with his son Hotspur, by Ralph Earl of Westmorland, and other northern lords. On 2 August, by a commission under Henry's seal of the duchy of Lancaster, Northumberland was appointed warden of the West March, and thus both wardenships were again in Percy hands. As the price of their support, their restoration to an almost viceregal position in the north was well worth it to Henry; from this point forward the success of his intervention was assured by military power to which Richard's lieutenants proved unable to muster a sufficient challenge. Thus, in the hour of crisis, border polities proved decisive.

While Henry's host gathered strength York, as keeper of the realm, began to take belated steps to meet the mounting threat. Together with the forces that he had managed to bring together near St Albans, he withdrew westwards, making for Bristol, presumably hoping to link up with Richard on his return from Ireland. But Henry was before him, reaching Gloucester with more substantial troops on 25 July. Wiltshire, with Bushy, Bagot and Green, took refuge in Bristol, York himself in Berkeley Castle. There, on 27 July, he met Henry, and in effect capitulated to him. The constable of Bristol followed suit; Wiltshire, Bushy and Green were surrendered, and were executed on 29 July (Bagot had already fled further). Richard was by then back in the kingdom, having landed at Haverfordwest perhaps three or four days earlier.

He ought, for his own sake, to have got back from Ireland sooner. His difficulty had been that the ships that had carried him and his army over there had been dispersed to various harbours and he was unable, in consequence, to co-ordinate a concentrated return for his host. Salisbury sailed ahead with an advanced guard on 17 July, heading for North Wales: Richard followed from Waterford a week later, inadequately accompanied. He and his force reached Carmarthen, picking up bad news at every step; from there he rode away by night with a tiny following, to join Salisbury at Conway. Thomas Percy, Earl of Worcester and steward of his household, at this juncture deserted him, and so did the always unreliable Aumale. Everywhere and visibly, support in the crisis was melting away. Henry meanwhile had reached Chester, and had gained effective control of the city and county which ought to have provided the base for organized royalist resistance to him.

At Conway, on or about 10 August, Henry Percy, Earl of Northumberland, arrived with messages from Henry (accompanied, some sources say, by Thomas Arundel, the Archbishop). He assured Richard that his crown was not in jeopardy; all would be forgotten if he would agree to restore Henry to his inheritance, to summon a parliament, and to surrender five members of his council for trial therein. Richard, cornered without an army, accepted these demands after some deliberation, and agreed to go with Percy to meet Henry at Chester. There is good reason to believe that Northumberland, though he was later to deny it, had already agreed to Richard's deposition, and that Henry should succeed him. Before they reached Flint the party had been 'ambushed'. When Richard reached Chester, whence writs went out in his name to summon parliament, he was effectively Henry's prisoner. He was never free again. He resigned his throne on 29 September at the Tower of London, probably under some duress; on 30 September parliament assembled and the estates renounced their fealty to him.

Richard lost his throne partly through the weakness and treachery of men whom he had trusted, but principally through his own folly and misjudgement. We should, however, look circumspectly at the view that the autocratic tendencies of his later years may be explained in terms of mental unbalance. Richard did not and could not seek to impose autocracy on his own and unaided. His councillors were not, as his contemporary critics liked to suggest, a band of young and irresponsible upstarts. They were men of wealth and influence, and of wide and varied experience. Even on the notorious committee that licensed the sequestration of the Lancastrian estates the great secular magnates were well represented. Richard's advisers may have acquiesced in decisions that we can see to have been imprudent, but they were not the sort of men who could be browbeaten into submission to the will of a half-mad ruler. Nor was it just the desire for private gain that led them to cooperate in Richard's experiment in absolutism; it was a governmental policy that seemed to offer solider and more important advantages than that.

In the early 1390s there was widespread dissatisfaction with the way in which the country had been governed for more than twenty years. To seasoned councillors and administrators it must have looked as if there was much to be said for a retrenchment of the royal prerogative which would elevate the monarchy above partisan clamour. What they and Richard attempted was in many ways very like what Edward IV and the early Tudors were to achieve, the shaping of what historians have called a 'new monarchy'. Their methods anticipated those which were successful in these later reigns: the wider use of the prerogative courts; the effort to manoeuvre committed royalists into key positions in local government; above all the effort to secure the king a more ample income, and so relieve conciliar government of the most embarrassing brand of parliamentary pressure. In this respect the grant of the wool subsidy for life in 1398 was important. It was a concession entirely without precedent, and one which greatly enhanced the crown's freedom of financial manoeuvre; later it was taken as a sign of the culpable subservience of the commons at Shrewsbury, and of Richard's sinister determination to be free of all customary trammels on his regality. Henry VII and Henry VIII, moreover, would have had no difficulty in appreciating the motives of Richard's councillors for seeking, when an opportunity arose, to sequestrate a dangerous concentration of landed wealth in the hands of a single and not very trustworthy magnate. Richard's absolutism was perhaps a little more doctrinaire than that of later monarchs; some of his circle had almost certainly been influenced by the intellectual apologetic of French royal absolutism, especially that of the court circle of Charles V. But this did not much affect what they tried to do in practice.

The reason why Richard's experiment was a disastrous failure was that the basic principle of his absolutism was unsound. It was founded not on popular respect, but on fear. Richard and his familiars believed that they could make people obedient by frightening them. They bound men to take unfamiliar oaths, the breach of which would automatically be construed as treason. They excepted from the general pardon of 1398 all acts done in the 'eleventh year' of the reign (1387–8) with the deliberate object of making ex-opponents of the regime reveal themselves, and pledge themselves in the king's mercy for good behaviour. They really did frighten people thus; we know that some 600 people went to the length of sueing out individual pardons. Not only individuals but whole communities too felt their security threatened. London, which had seen its privileges seized into the king's hand once already in 1392 and had paid £10,000 to get them back, paid another 10,000 marks in 1398 for a surer recon-firmation. All these proceedings of Richard's were, when the time came, listed in the articles of deposition that were drawn up as evidence that he was a tyrant and unfit to rule.[20] Other sections of these articles, notably their account of his willing abdication, are barefaced tampering with the truth. In these particular matters, however, it is hard to quarrel either with the facts that they relay or with their conclusion.

The fines, blank charters, forced loans and conditional pardons through which Richard blackmailed his subjects into obedience proved self-defeating. In the fourteenth century the military, financial and bureaucratic resources of the monarchy were not sufficient to maintain royal authority without a basis of trust between sovereign and subject. Richard's methods undermined that trust and made his own weakness plain, for they revealed that he too was frightened. He did not sufficiently understand the need to woo his subjects, as did Edward IV and Henry VIII, and Henry VII too until avarice got the better of everything in his later years. Richard II was more like Richard III, who also relied on fear to secure his authority, and whose rule also crumbled in the face of an usurping invader.

There were flaws in Richard II's character, as well as his policies, that helped to bring about his fall. He could be arrogant, he could be wilful, and he showed himself on occasion both vengeful and treacherous. Yet he remains one of the most interesting of the kings of England of the later Middle Ages. His court was the most splendid and sophisticated that ever gathered about an English monarch in that period. He was the patron of Chaucer, and it was for him that the Wilton diptych, the finest product of medieval court art that has survived in England, was executed. Cultivated foreigners with a knowledge of the courts and chivalrous society of Europe, like Froissart and Philip de Mezieres, were impressed by the magnificence of his entourage. He had a sharper sensitivity to the cult of kingship than any other medieval king of England (the Wilton diptych shows him kneeling, with John the Baptist and the two English royal saints, Edward the Confessor and St Edmund, beside him, before the Christ child in the arms of the Virgin, amid angels who wear the badge of the white hart). He was a lover of fine things (witness his clasp showing a damsel carrying a parrot, and his white satin doublet embroidered with golden orange trees), and of richly illuminated manuscripts. His fancy for the colour of royal magnificence may have had much to do with the attraction of some of the wilder projects in which he became involved more than half seriously – his expensive efforts to get himself elected king of the Romans, for instance. There is a genuinely tragic irony in the fate which decreed that his reign should end dismally with a deposition. Its chief legacies to England in the next generation were ones that worked not for the glorification of monarchy which was Richard's dream, but to weaken it: a profound popular distrust of royal autocracy, and a line of kings with a questionable title to the throne.

Notes

1 *R.P.* vol. III, p. 73.
2 *Chron. H. Knighton* (R.S.) vol. II, p. 215.
3 ibid. p. 219.
4 *R.P.* vol. III, p. 224.
5 The text of the questions to the judges is given by the Monk of Westminster, printed in Higden, *Polychronicon* (R.S.) vol. IX, pp. 99–101.
6 T. Favent, *Historia Mirabilis Parliamenti*, ed. M. McKisack *(Camden Miscellany* vol. XIV), p. 14.
7 *R.P.* vol. III, p. 245.
8 *Prophet's Journal of the Council*, printed in J. F. Baldwin, *The King's Council* (Oxford, 1913), p. 495.
9 N. Saul, *Richard II* (London, 1997), p. 268.
10 Higden, *Polychronicon*, vol. IX, p. 282.
11 *Foed.* vol. VII, p. 811.
12 *R.P.* vol. III, p. 339.
13 ibid. p. 408.
14 ibid. p. 347.
15 ibid. p. 350.
16 ibid., pp. 378–9.
17 ibid., p. 369.
17a Kirkstall Chronicle, ms quoted by M. V. Clarke, *Fourteenth Century Studies* (Oxford, 1937), p. 111.
18 *R.P.*, vol. III, p. 382.
19 *E.H.R.*, vol. 40 (1925), pp. 323–4.
20 *R.P.* vol. III, pp. 417–22.

Note on secondary reading (post 1970)

The secondary literature on the reign of Richard II is very extensive, and a brief note cannot do justice to it. N. Saul's major biography, *Richard II* (London and New Haven, 1997), looks set to be the authoritative guide for a long while. Much attention has naturally focused on Richard II's relations with his magnates and here A. Tuck, *Richard II and the English Nobility* (London, 1973), and A. Goodman, *The Loyal Conspiracy; the Lords Appellant under Richard II* (London, 1971) are important. Goodman's biography of John of Gaunt is also useful, *John of Gaunt: the Exercise of Princely Power in Fourteenth Century Europe* (London, 1992), alongside which must be set S.K. Walker, *The Lancastrian Affinity, 1361–99* (Oxford, 1990). R. Du Boulay and C.M. Barron (eds.), *The Reign of Richard II* (London, 1971) contains useful articles by A. Tuck on Richard's patronage, by J.J.N. Palmer on his foreign policy, by C. Barron on Richard and London, and by R.R. Davies on Richard and Cheshire. J.L. Gillespie (ed.), *The Age of Richard II* (Stroud, 1997) includes essays by Gillespie on Richard, chivalry and kingship, by A.K. McHardy on Haxey's Case, 1397, and W. Childs on Anglo-Portuguese relations.

On the first major crisis of the reign, 1386–8, the following are helpful, in addition to the works of Saul and Goodman cited above; J.S. Roskell, *The Impeachment of Michael de la Pole, Earl of Suffolk, in 1386* (Manchester, 1984);

J.W. Sherborne, 'The defence of the realm and the impeachment of Michael de la Pole in 1386', in J. Taylor and W. Childs (eds.) *Politics and Crisis in Fourteenth Century England* (Gloucester, 1990); and S.B. Chrimes, 'Richard II's questions to the judges in 1387', *Law Quarterly Review*, vol. 72 (1956) remains crucial. On foreign policy and the French war see J.J.N. Palmer, *England, France and Christendom* (London, 1972); and C.J. Philpotts, 'John of Gaunt and English policy towards France, 1389–95', *Journal of Medieval History*, vol. 16 (1990) covers a key period. On Richard II in Ireland, see (besides R. Curtis's 1927 study of *Richard II in Ireland*) A. Tuck, 'Anglo-Irish relations, 1382–93', *Proceedings of the Royal Irish Academy*, vol. 69 (1970), and J. Lydon, 'Richard II's expeditions to Ireland', *Journal of the Royal Society of Antiquaries of Ireland*, vol. 93 (1963).

On Richard II's view of his kingship, see N. Saul, 'Richard II and the vocabulary of kingship', *E.H.R.*, vol. 110 (1995), and S.K. Walker, 'Richard II's views on kingship' in R. Archer and S. Walker (eds.) *Rulers and Ruled in Medieval England* (London, 1995); on the Wilton Diptych specifically, see D. Gordon, L. Monna and C. Elam (eds.), *The Regal Image of Richard II and the Wilton Diptych* (London, 1998). C. Given-Wilson provides useful material on the royal retinue in his *The Royal Household and the King's Affinity, 1360–1413* (London and Newhaven, 1986): see also J.L. Gillespie, 'Richard II's archers of the crown', *Journal of British Studies*, vol. 18 (1979).

On Richard's last years see, besides Saul's biography C.M. Barron's two papers, 'The tyranny of Richard II', *B.I.H.R.*, vol. 41 (1968), and 'The deposition of Richard II', Taylor and Childs (eds.), *Politics and Crisis in the Fourteenth Century*; C. Given-Wilson, 'Richard II, Edward II, and the Lancastrian inheritance', *E.H.R.*, vol. 109 (1994); J.W. Sherborne, 'Perjury and the Lancastrian Revolution of 1399', in his *War, Culture and Politics in Fourteenth Century England* (London, 1994; ed. A. Tuck).

13 The reign of Henry IV

It is not clear at just what moment Henry Bolingbroke decided to enlarge his bid for restoration to his Lancastrian estates into a bid for Richard II's throne. It may have been very soon after his landing, before or about the time the Percies joined him (in which case they were privy to his intention from the first, which they were afterwards to deny). Or it may have been later, perhaps at Chester. He had clearly made up his mind by 10 September, when he ceased to use Richard's regnal year to date his letters, and when arrangements to set the stage for his succession began to be put in train against the meeting of parliament at the end of the month.

On 30 September 1399 an assembly met in Westminster Hall that was not officially a parliament, since the summons to parliament had been in the name of Richard II, and had lapsed on his renunciation of the crown the day before. The throne stood vacant, covered with cloth of gold. First, charges against Richard were read out, and a commission representing all the estates of the realm was appointed, to renounce homage and fealty to him on behalf of the whole realm. Then Henry of Lancaster stood up and in his mother tongue claimed: 'this realm of England, and the crown with all the members and appurtenances, as I am descended by right line of the blood coming from the good lord Henry the third; and through that right that God of his grace hath sent me, with the help of my kin and of my friends, to recover it; the which realm was in point to be undone for default of government and undoing of the good laws'.[1] The lords spiritual and temporal, asked severally and together what they thought of this claim, gave their assent to it. For good measure it was reported to the assembly that Richard had approved that Henry should be his successor (which was probably not true). Archbishop Arundel, now restored to Canterbury, preached a sermon on the text *vir dominabitur in populo*, and dwelt on the ills which must overtake a kingdom governed by a child (the alternative claimant to Henry was the infant Earl of March). Subsequently the parliament, now formally summoned in the name of Henry IV, tidied things up by recognizing his eldest son Henry as his heir.

It is never easy to explain in constitutional terms the deposition of a monarch, but the Lancastrian lawyers and churchmen who drew up the lengthy articles against Richard II which were read to the parliament of 1399 made a very reasonable job of it. The theme was that Richard, by actions and statements which were rehearsed, had broken the fundamental rules which he had sworn at his coronation to uphold, and that this perjury demonstrably unfitted him for kingship. As we have seen, many of their specific charges had considerable substance. It was much less easy to explain why Henry should succeed Richard. Although Henry was, after Richard, the eldest descendant of Edward III in the male line, the young Earl of March, Edmund Mortimer, was hereditarily of a line senior to his, being descended in the female line from Lionel of Clarence, Edward's second son (John of Gaunt, Henry's father, was the third son). The way in which Henry and his advisers got round this child's inconvenient claim could not be straightforward, which is why historians have long argued about the exact nature of his title to the throne.

Henry himself would have liked to claim the throne by clear descent, on the ground that his ancestor, Edmund 'Crouchback' of Lancaster, had been older than Edward I, but was passed over because of his alleged physical deformity. The most diligent search of the chronicles failed, however, to unearth any evidence in favour of this Lancastrian fable. Henry's legal advisers were anxious that there should be some sort of recognition of his title by clergy and people, so that his royal right should not rest merely on successful conquest. The proceedings of 30 September combined all the possible lines of approach. Henry *viva voce* claimed the throne by blood and conquest, and the people assented; parliament ratified what had happened afterwards by recognizing Henry's heir as heir to the throne. The king's title was thus justified by descent, by conquest, by acclaim and by subsequent parliamentary recognition, without its being clear which, if any, of the ingredients was the crucial one.

Politically Henry's throne was not as secure as it looked at first sight. He had got the crown because he was the man of the moment; it was impossible to leave Richard on the throne, and a council of regency for the Earl of March could not have given the effective government that was needed. The Percies, whose support had been so crucial after he landed at Ravenspur, had everything to gain from his succession; so had Archbishop Arundel, the companion of his exile. He had plenty of committed aristocratic supporters, not just in the north where he could count on both Nevilles and Percies but in the south too, as the Earl of Stafford and lords Willoughby, Fitzwalter and Burnell. But Richard's old intimates, the Holland brothers and Salisbury and Despenser, were also powerful and influential men, and Aumale, the most important of them all, was the son of the Duke of York, whom Henry could not possibly afford to alienate. These men were not popular, but they had their own followings. They lost their new titles as a result of Henry's usurpation. One chronicle hints that Henry would have liked to proceed further against them, but that the commons urged him not to. The same chronicle makes it clear that some thought it would have been better for the people to hear from Richard's own mouth that he renounced the crown.[2] The official record of the change of dynasty that we have is an edited one, designed to make the operation look smooth; it omits all mention of murmurings such as these, as also of the public protest which the courageous Bishop Merke of Carlisle made on behalf of the ex-king. Henry did not succeed because the opposition to him was negligible, but because he had caught Richard and his friends hopelessly off their guard.

Henry had been king for barely four months, when he had to face his first revolt. It was organized by Richard's former friends, the two Hollands, Montagu of Salisbury, and Rutland (Aumale), and its object was his restoration. Thomas Merke, now deprived of his bishopric, and the Abbot of Westminster were also involved in the plot, and the plan was to seize Henry at Windsor, on the eve of the tournament arranged there for Epiphany, 1400. It failed, because Rutland revealed the scheme to his father, the Duke of York, who informed the king. Even so, Henry left Windsor in a hurry only twelve hours before the rebels arrived, and his son Henry was briefly their prisoner. The king at once began to gather forces in London and when the rebels decided to retreat their men began to melt away. Thomas Holland and Salisbury surrendered at Cirencester, and were lynched by a mob, as was Lord Despenser at Bristol; John Holland was taken at Pleshy in Essex, and beheaded by his captors. Some other leading rebels were executed at Oxford by the king's order. Among the lay leaders, Rutland alone was pardoned, because of his father's influence and because it was his information that had given Henry warning.

Very soon after the rising Richard II was dead, probably before the end of January. It was claimed that he had refused to eat, and died of starvation; but the date of his death seems too convenient, and he was probably killed at Henry's order. To allay any doubt of his death, his body was brought from his prison at Pontefract to London, and lay in St Paul's, with the head showing outside the lead coffin. The lands of his supporters were declared forfeit. The reflections of the council, after the new regime had thus weathered its first storm, were not very comfortable, however. Its members did not think it would be politic to call a parliament, because there would be too much opposition to any request for taxation. They were alarmed about the possibility of war breaking out with France and Scotland, and of the fiscal problem that that would pose. They were frankly frightened by the way in which Richard's friends had died; at this rate the judges would not be able to enforce order 'for fear of the unruliness and pride of the commons who do not wish to be under any governance'.[3] They advised the king to retain men in the counties by fee to aid in the keeping of the peace – an ugly reminder that they understood very clearly the part that Richard's Cheshire archers had played in sustaining tyranny.

Henry IV had seen plenty of martial service, and was an accomplished jouster; he had commanded the appellant army at Radcot Bridge, and had been on crusade to Prussia. He had a reputation as a warrior, and was expected to redeem the unmartial record of his predecessor. At the beginning of his reign his councillors felt, however, that to court war with France was too risky, and advised playing for peace by returning Isabella, Richard's queen, and her jewels. Scotland seemed a more promising quarter for aggression, partly, no doubt, because of the influence of the Percies in the council; and Henry's servants began looking into all the old records of the English kings' claim to the homage of Scotland. The flight from Scotland of George Dunbar, Earl of the March, helped to raise English hopes, and in August 1400 Henry, after summoning Robert III to do him homage, led a large army over the border. He reached Edinburgh, but achieved nothing of moment, and added no lustre to his name.

Bad news met Henry on his way south. In mid-September 1400, a quarrel between Owen Glendower, Lord of Glyndyfrdwy in north Wales, and Lord Grey of Ruthin, who was a stout supporter of Lancaster and a councillor, had blown up into an armed Welsh revolt. On 16 September Owen was proclaimed Prince of Wales by a group of Welsh landowners, most of them his relations; they and their followers descended on Ruthin, burned it and ravaged the English through Flint and Denbigh. Further afield, in Anglesey, the Tudors, who were related to Glendower and had had associations with Richard II, were also in revolt. Henry appeared from Scotland with his army at the end of September and carried out a punitive march through north Wales, which temporarily restored the situation. But none of the Welsh leaders were taken, and when he was gone the situation began to deteriorate again.

At the end of the first full year of Henry's reign, the situation looked shaky. Wales was in ferment. In the north the acquisition of George Dunbar as an ally was a double-edged benefit; the favours and influence that he achieved were not calculated to please the Percies, part of whose reward for 1399 had been an increased freedom of action in the marches. The Scottish expedition had proved costly both to the king and to the many peers who had made direct contributions in men and money, and after it, it was clear that parliament would soon have to be summoned and asked for a money grant. Henry at his accession had made much of his intention not to burden his people with taxes, but he could not fulfil his promises. Popular support for his regime at the outset had really been based on popular antipathy to the preceding one, and it was bound to wane once it became clear that the revolution of 1399 would not lead to greater stability in local government. The only men on whom Henry could count with complete confidence in 1400 were the tried servants and retainers of the duchy of Lancaster. The Lancastrian 'affinity' was the greatest private retinue in England, but in the circumstances of the day Henry needed support much more broadly based than that.

The events of the years 1401 and 1402 did not improve the situation. Parliament was critical of royal expenditure, of the royal council, and of the general lack of governance. In both years there were royal expeditions to Wales, neither of which achieved very much. The return of Isabella to the French court did not solve any problems; there was less now to hold the French back from war. In Gascony the situation of the English looked critical. The one ray of hope in 1402 was in the north, where in September Henry Percy (Hotspur) and his father the Earl of Northumberland overthrew the raiding Scottish host at Homildon Hill in Durham, and took prisoner the Douglas, Murdach of Fife, and the earls of Orkney, Angus and Moray. The lustre of the victory, however, went to the Percies, not to Henry. The king ordered that the magnate prisoners should not be ransomed, but put at his disposal. The earl handed over his prisoners in the autumn parliament, but Hotspur did not produce the Douglas. Relations between the king and the most powerful of all his late supporters were becoming uneasy.

'We hoped that at your wonderful entry into the realm of England you would have redeemed Israel', Philip Repingdon (the ex-Lollard, now a royal chaplain and a future Bishop of Lincoln) wrote to Henry IV in 1401, '. . . but now our joy is changed to sorrow, while all evils multiply, and the hope of healing has gone out from the hearts of men.'[4] It is not clear quite at what point general discontent began to foster rueful reflections about the justification of the revolution of 1399, but by 1402 they were beginning to be widespread. It was in this year that the Lady of the Isles produced the man whom some chose to regard as Richard II escaped from his prison: the 'Mommet' whose presence in Scotland was to be a long embarrassment to the house of Lancaster. Another rumour had it that Richard was alive in Wales. A number of Franciscans were involved in spreading pro-Ricardian propaganda, and convents as well scattered as Aylesbury, Northampton, Leicester, Nottingham and Stamford were affected. Friar Walton of Leicester, who turned informer, told the king's officers of plans to mobilize 500 men at Oxford, to go to join Richard II in Wales. The *Eulogium* gives a graphic account of the interview between Henry IV himself and Richard Frisby, chief of the conspirators whom Walton implicated. 'I do not say that Richard is alive,' Frisby told the king, 'but I say that if he is alive he is the true king of England.' He frankly did not believe the story of Richard's abdication: 'he would never have resigned had he been at liberty; a resignation made in prison is not a free resignation'.[5] The ugly truths about the manner in which Richard had been deprived of his throne, which the official record concealed, had somehow leaked out, and were being made public property through Franciscan sermons.

These signs of the impact of legitimist propaganda are significant, because they appear on the eve of very serious rebellions, in which Henry might easily have lost his throne. These rebellions involved a number of English magnates who had acquiesced in the revolution of 1399, with the Percies at the head of the list. Legitimism was not of course the reason for their rebellion, but aristocratic risings, in the later Middle Ages, had little prospect of success unless they could obtain a degree of popular support, and to this end needed the cloak at least of some general and readily understandable political objective. The rights of Richard, or if he was dead of the young Earl of March, provided just such a cover for the objects of ambitious men who had their own grievances against Henry IV, and thought it could be to their interest to overthrow him.

The first rebellion in point of time, that of Owen Glendower, cannot strictly be called a legitimist rising. Richard II, however, had always looked for support to Wales and Cheshire and certainly there was sympathy for his cause there; and as we shall see, Glendower's rising began to acquire in time a distinct colour of English legitimism. But in 1401 his appeal was to the Welsh nation, and the agents of rebellion were the bards, with their sagas of past independence and prophecies of a day when the Saxon yoke would be lifted. This was how the English saw the revolt too. In 1402 the commons petitioned that no Welshman should hold office in Wales, that gatherings to listen to the bards should be forbidden, and that Welshmen should not be allowed to be armed in public.

What was needed was not statutes, but money and reinforcements for Henry Prince of Wales and his council at Chester, who found their men constantly on the brink of mutiny or desertion for lack of pay. The situation was so serious that in 1401 both Hotspur and his father advised the king to offer Glendower terms, a pardon and the guarantee of his territorial rights, but they could not carry the council with them. In 1402 the Welsh leader felt himself sufficiently secure to suggest both to the Irish chiefs and to Robert III of Scotland a grand Celtic alliance against England. Two other events of the same year opened new vistas for him. In April his forces took Lord Grey of Ruthin himself prisoner. He was ransomed for 10,000 marks, which put Glendower in funds of a new order. A few weeks later he captured a still more significant prisoner, Edmund Mortimer, the uncle of the Earl of March. This time Henry would not negotiate with the rebels for a ransom. He was probably glad to have the eldest male member of the dangerous house of Mortimer out of the way, but the decision was not a wise one. Edmund's sister was married to Hotspur, and the king's refusal to allow a ransom created new ground for discord between him and the Percies. Glendower soon found he could exploit the situation by persuading his captive, since he could not be ransomed, to throw in his lot with him. Mortimer then married Glendower's daughter. On 13 December he wrote to his friends among the gentry and commons of Radnor to tell them that he would henceforward be fighting to secure Owen his right in Wales and to put the Earl of March on the throne of England.[6]

In 1402 the Percies were probably already considering breaking with Henry IV. Their support had been crucial to the success of his usurpation and they had been so amply rewarded for their part in it that it is not easy to explain their *volte face*. Northumberland had been made Constable of England and Warden of the West March; Hotspur Warden of the East March and justiciar of north Wales; Thomas, the Earl of Worcester, was made Admiral of England, and in 1401 steward of the household. A number of factors seem to have contributed to a steadily deteriorating pattern of relations between them and Henry. Affairs connected with the Scottish march were the most important: the new influence with the king of George Dunbar; the re-grant of the custody of Roxburgh castle (entrusted to them for ten years in 1399) to their bitter rival Neville, the Earl of Westmorland; their difficulties over obtaining full payment from the exchequer of monies owing to them as wardens. Henry's rejection of their offer to mediate between him and Glendower, his refusal to allow them to ransom the prisoners of Homildon, and his refusal to ransom Edmund Mortimer also must have played their part. Besides, the Percies did not trust Henry; their troubles over getting pay for their men, both in Scotland and in north

Wales, convinced them that he would leave them in the lurch at his convenience. If Dr Rogers is right in his suggestion that the Percies were deeply involved in the political crisis of 1401, when Henry was forced to name his council, their lack of faith in him must have been apparent from an early stage.[7]

By 1403, at all events, the Percies had decided that they would try their hand a second time at king-making. The main charge against Henry in Hotspur's manifesto, which the chronicler Hardyng has preserved, was his unjust treatment of the house of March, whom he had cheated of the inheritance to the throne.[8] Hotspur's claim was that at Doncaster in the summer of 1399 he and his father had promised to support Henry only in his claim to his duchy of Lancaster, not in any claim to the crown. He also charged the king with packing parliaments and levying taxes contrary to the promises of his accession. In May 1403, a month before the revolt, Henry already had wind of rumours that in the north men were preaching 'that the king had not kept his promises that he made at his advent into the realm'.[9] At the time Hotspur was already, almost certainly, in direct contact with Glendower. Nevertheless Henry was taken apparently by surprise on 12 July at Nottingham, on his way north with forces for the Scots border, by the news that Hotspur and Earl Thomas Percy were in revolt and had issued a manifesto at Chester, and that Northumberland was gathering men in the north to join them.

George Dunbar, according to the *Annales*, was the man who urged Henry to act swiftly, or all might be lost. It was sound advice. By 20 July Henry was at Shrewsbury, and Hotspur and his uncle withdrew from before the town, where they had hoped to capture the Prince of Wales before the king could help him. His speed brought him face to face with the main rebel army before there was any chance of either Northumberland or Glendower joining it. Before the battle there was a last minute attempt to negotiate, initiated by the king: the story ran after the battle that Hotspur would have accepted the terms offered, but that they were misrepresented by Thomas Percy, who actually spoke to the royal messengers. The battle was one of the hardest fought of the age; and little groups of combatants were still struggling on the field when darkness fell. But by that time Hotspur had fallen, and both Worcester and Douglas were the king's prisoners; on the next day, the rebel army had disappeared and the king was the clear victor.

Thomas Percy and a number of other notable prisoners were tried and beheaded at Shrewsbury. Northumberland, when he heard that his brother and son were dead, was ready to come to terms with Henry. He made his submission at York, and was placed in custody for the time being. He lost the office of Constable and his wardenship of the West March, which went to his rival Neville. His key castles were taken into the king's hand. The lands of Hotspur and Worcester were forfeited for their treason; George Dunbar was one of those who were well rewarded out of the confiscations.

The Earl of Northumberland was set at liberty, after the lords in the spring parliament of 1404 had decided that his conduct did not amount to treason, but to trespass only. His first step on being freed was formally, before his peers in parliament, to clear Archbishop Arundel and the Duke of York (the erstwhile Rutland, who had succeeded his father in 1402) of complicity in his rebellion. At the same time he was reconciled, before parliament and the peers, to both Neville and Dunbar. There were fears, it would seem, both that the recent revolt had had wider ramifications than had come into the open, and that border rivalry might, with Northumberland at large again, lead to the reopening of civil war.

The latter fear was well founded. The first sign that trouble was brewing again was an attempt by Northumberland to surprise Neville of Westmorland at the house of one of his retainers, Ralph Viners. The revolt of 1405 was in fact to reproduce all the elements of that of 1403, and potentially was quite as dangerous. Glendower had strengthened his position in Wales over the two years. In 1404 he had taken Harlech and Aberystwyth; most of west Wales as well as the north was now in his power, and he was solemnly recognized as Prince of Wales in a parliament to which men were summoned from every *cantref* obedient to his authority. As Prince he sent his envoys to the French court and received a promise of assistance, which materialized in 1405 with an expeditionary force under John de Hangest. Edmund Mortimer was still his ally, and two Welsh bishops, Trevor of St Asaph and Byford of Bangor, had thrown in their lot with him. These two men were probably the intermediaries between him and Northumberland. Their mutual alliance, together with Edmund Mortimer as a third party was sealed on 28 February in the famous 'tripartite indenture'. This proposed nothing less than a threefold division of the kingdom of England. Northumberland was to have all the north, as far into the midlands as Leicester and Northampton; Glendower a greater Wales, stretching into England as far as Worcester; Mortimer 'the whole of the rest of England'.[10] This was king-making with a vengeance.

One cannot be sure quite how seriously to take the tripartite indenture. One can be sure of the perilousness of the situation in 1405. Apart from the Welsh, the French and the Scots were ready to move, and the plans for revolt had strong backing in England. Thomas Mowbray the Earl Marshal, Lord Bardolf, and no less a man than Archbishop Scrope of York were all in the affair with Northumberland; Lord Clifford and Sir John Fauconberg were also apparently involved. Two manifestos survive which are connected with the revolt, and they make it clear that the tripartite indenture was not an agreed programme. One, to which Archbishop Scrope certainly gave his authority and which was 'posted in the ways and streets of York', complains of the lack of governance in the realm; of the taxes which weigh on clergy, secular men and merchants alike and undo them; and of the lack of defence of the realm against foes without (there had been a number of French raids on the Channel coasts). It also shows that Scrope had had contact with Glendower, directly or indirectly: 'if these matters be remedied', it declares, 'we have full information and promise from those now in revolt in Wales, that they will be content as they were in the days of King Edward and King Richard'.[11] The other manifesto is more extreme, charging Henry with usurpation, with the death of Richard II and the blood of his friends and the blood also of Hotspur, and of having brought nothing but misery and confusion to the land. It is not certain who framed this second manifesto; its tone is that of Ricardian 'Jacobitism' run wild.

As events turned out, the only formidable military danger in 1405 came from Glendower, who with Hangest's Frenchmen raided out of Wales up to the gates of Worcester. The northern revolt crumbled. A band of Percy retainers was defeated at Topcliffe; Scrope, who had drawn to his standard a substantial body of Yorkshire knights as well as clergy, was brought to parley by Neville of Westmorland, and tricked with a promise of support into dismissing his men. He, with Mowbray and his nephew Sir William Plumpton, were all then arrested. They were executed at York at the king's command, in spite of hot protest from Archbishop Arundel at the breach of Scrope's privilege of clergy. Northumberland and Bardolf, isolated in the far north, withdrew to Berwick, and thence into Scotland. The captains of Warkworth and of Berwick castle both attempted to hold out against the king for the earl; but Berwick could not stand the battering of the king's siege train, and William Clifford, captain of Warkworth, made terms and retired after his master into Scotland. A number of northern gentry were afterwards tried for their part in the rebellion, and put to death.

After 1405, Henry IV never again had to face a full-scale domestic rebellion. His troubles were not by any means over yet, for Glendower in Wales was still dangerous; Harlech and Aberystwyth were still in rebel hands three years later. It was not until 1409 that it was clear that the Welsh revolt was under control, and Glendower was still at large when Henry IV died. Henry had not finished with the Percies either. From Scotland Northumberland and Bardolf travelled into Wales in 1406; next year they were in France seeking aid for new moves from the Duke of Orleans; Adam of Usk met them at Bruges and was tempted to throw in his lot with them. Returning to Scotland, they made a last bid at invasion. Both died in battle, fighting the king's forces under the sheriff of Yorkshire at Bramham Moor in 1408. This was the last battle (outside Wales) to be fought on English soil in Henry IV's reign; but sentiment for the causes of Percy and Mortimer was not even now extinguished, and their names were still ones to conjure with.

The series of great rebellions in the first part of Henry IV's reign throws a very significant light on the revolution of 1399. They reveal how shaky the foundations of the Lancastrian succession were. It is a point too easily forgotten that the house of Lancaster, which was in the end displaced by the descendants of the March line, was very nearly extinguished in their favour in its infancy. The danger was not from northern and Welsh dissidents only. In 1404 the Lady Despenser was very nearly successful in a plot to abduct the young Earl of March, in which the Duke of York and Mowbray were both implicated. York had been suspected earlier, in 1403, of complicity with the Percies, and so had even Archbishop Arundel. According to the *Annales*, in that year the question of Richard's rights and the rumour that he was still alive were the talk even of the king's household.[13] We have seen how, in the same period, the Franciscans acted as agents of Ricardian and March propaganda. Two informers in 1405 accused a number of other religious orders of lending clandestine support to Glendower, including the abbeys of Ramsey, Crowland, Thorney and Woburn, all far away from Wales and the scene of action. It was impossible, in an age in which so much revolved about questions of inheritance, for people at large not to be troubled about what had happened in 1399. The usurpation injected into the political life of the kingdom a new and perilous force working in favour of disruption.

Legitimism was only one theme in the manifestos through which Hotspur in 1403 and Archbishop Scrope in 1405 sought to rally popular support. They both clearly believed that there was general dissatisfaction with Henry IV's record in government, and that it too could be exploited in their favour. It is time that we made the attempt to see how serious that dissatisfaction was, and what its roots were.

Finance was the foremost besetting problem for the councillors of the first Lancastrian king. The average annual revenue of Henry IV was lower than that of his predecessor (it has been calculated at approximately £90,000, compared with about £116,000 for Richard II), and there were more serious calls upon it than there had been in Richard's later years. Henry's treasurers were in a state of constant alarm. 'There is not enough in your treasury at the moment to pay the messengers who are to bear the letters which you have ordained to the lords and knights who are to be of your council', wrote Lawrence Allerthorpe in 1401; years later, in 1411, his successor was explaining to the council that the books still simply would not balance.[14] Something would have to go, he said; perhaps the budget for the defence of Aquitaine could be reduced. Councillors were frightened by the consequences of insolvency: Archbishop Arundel, speaking in 1406 on behalf of the lords named in parliament to be of the council, declared that they were ready to take up their duties 'if sufficiency of goods could be found to carry on government properly: otherwise not'.[15] The government found it a far from easy task to raise loans in anticipation of revenue. A letter from the council to the king in the early summer of 1405 gives a good picture of the kind of problem that Henry's advisers had to face. They have raised loans, they say, with great difficulty, which will cover the costs of Calais and of the fleet which is being fitted out under Prince Thomas, but they have nothing for Guienne at all. They have had to drive a hard bargain with the councillors of the Prince of Wales (who was defending the Welsh march against Glendower), who have only accepted an assignment on the subsidy due at mid-summer because there was nothing else to offer them.[16] This is a picture of a government which was simply not able to meet all the justified calls made on its pocket.

Parsimony, enforced by adverse circumstances, meant that Henry IV's government had to make demands on its aristocratic supporters which put a real strain on their sympathies. The Percies, before 1403, were constantly complaining that they had not been paid what was due to them for duties that they had performed. The same complaint that they made, that they were in constant danger of being deserted by their own men for lack of pay, and the same threat, that they would be forced to throw up their offices if there was no remedy, were echoed by many others, even on one occasion by the king's own son Prince Thomas. In 1405 Lord Grey of Codnor wrote that he was so embarrassed that even his harness was in pawn for wages to his own soldiers. The Duke of York in the same year obtained letters of privy seal to help him raise loans in the west country in order to pay his men at Carmarthen, but the men to whom they were addressed would lend nothing, because they had not yet been repaid earlier loans to the crown. His retainers had to be content with his personal promise 'as a true gentleman' that the revenues of his Yorkshire estates should be put into their hands from 1 August if no other way of paying them could be found.[17] Many lords were clearly advancing money of their own to pay their men in the king's service; this was quite normal, but repayment was so slow and inadequate that they were afraid of being faced with a choice between the alternatives of their own financial ruin, or of sacrificing the trust and respect of their own followers. The attitude of men thus placed could shade very easily from distrust and dissatisfaction with royal government into disloyalty.

In order to ease his financial difficulties, Henry had to look frequently to the commons in parliament for grants of taxes and subsidies. They usually gave him a good deal of trouble before they made their grants. Though they were not niggardly, they were determined that the king should stretch his own resources as far as was humanly possible. They were outspokenly critical of all forms of waste, demanding in 1402 and again in 1410 that grants for life, when they fell in, should be kept to the king's use; in 1404 they passed a stiff act of resumption, asking for a stop for one year on all fees and annuities from the crown. They made strenuous efforts, too, to make certain that moneys were really spent on the purposes for which they were voted; in 1404 they made the appointment of treasurers of war to supervise expenditure a condition of their grant; in 1406 they imposed the same duty on the council and appointed auditors at the exchequer. This is a record of sustained action with a consistent objective, and one not flattering to the king's dignity.

The commons of Henry IV's reign were sharply conscious of the strength which their control over financial grants gave their influence. In 1401 they went so far as to suggest that their grants should not normally be finalized until all their petitions had been heard and answered; the king did not concede the principle, but in practice he had more or less to observe it. They used their influence to some purpose when dealing, for instance, with the matter of the king's household and its expenses, constantly seeking to fix the source of its revenues, so that these could not be a charge on the grants that they made. Clearly they did not regard Henry's household with any more favour than their predecessors had that of Richard II. Their attitude towards the king's council was also significant. In 1404 they insisted that they should know the names of the king's councillors, in 1406 and 1410 that they should not only be named but also sworn in parliament. The object of the commons appears not to have been to control the composition of the council themselves; they simply wanted to be sure that the king was being guided by a representative group of the most substantial and experienced men of the kingdom, and not by a clique of *familiares*.

The best insight into the attitude of the commons towards the council is furnished by the lengthy series of articles which the commons in 1406 insisted that councillors should swear to observe. These stressed that all important decisions should be agreed by the whole council, not simply by those whom the king happened (or chose) to have about him. They also made it the duty of councillors to ensure that grants were not made under the great or privy seal unduly, out of favour; to make sure that persons about the king and queen did not use their position to maintain or further quarrels which could be decided at common law; to watch the expenditure of the household; to regularize the procedures for hearing petitioners for favour. It is unwise to read too much constitutional significance into these articles, which were only to remain in force until the next parliament. Their political significance is, however, important. They indicate a very considerable distrust of the king's personal intimates and *entourage*, strongly reminiscent of the attitude of past parliaments to the *entourage* of Richard II.

There was never, in the Middle Ages, so much plain speaking between king and commons as there was in Henry IV's reign. This was in spite of the fact that a number of their speakers were men high in the king's confidence, as Arnold Savage, Thomas Chaucer and John Tiptoft (the speaker of 1406). On occasion rather more than plain speaking was involved. In 1401 the commons asked the king not to listen to informers among their number, who to advance themselves might report debates in a manner which would 'grievously move the king against the said commons'.[18] In 1411 they referred to 'the great murmuring among your people, that your heart is heavy toward some of your lieges who have come at your summons to this your parliament, and to the last at Westminster', and asked for an assurance that there was no such ill will.[19] These remarks are entered on the parliament roll. A detailed account in a news letter of 1404 gives a stormy picture of the kind of wrangling that the roll must often conceal. Savage, the speaker, declared that the outrageous grants made by the king had brought the commons to the end of their patience. The advice of some of the king's councillors he pronounced frankly malicious. This letter also reveals, most significantly, that it was at the commons' petition that in this parliament Northumberland was allowed to appear to clear himself of the charge of treason, and that they even threatened to make no grant when the king tried to demur.[20] This was not the only occasion when the commons took an interest in high politics that was not pleasing to the king. The vote of thanks in 1411 to the Prince of Wales and other councillors who had just been dismissed (some of whom were rumoured to have suggested that the king should abdicate in favour of his eldest son) cannot have been much more welcome.[21]

There is no hint of direct sympathy with Ricardian or March legitimism in the records of any of Henry IV's parliaments. The attitude of the commons reflects rather an opposite feeling, anxiety that the succession should be unequivocally entailed on Henry's descendants. Their attitude seems to have been rather like that of the later Elizabethan commons, who constantly petitioned the queen to marry or recognize a successor. The motivation in both cases was the same: fear of the civil disorder that might follow a disputed succession. Disorder was a subject very much in the minds of the commons of Henry IV's reign, not surprisingly. It is interesting to note that their concern about lack of governance was not confined to the early part of the reign, the period of the rebellions. Nor were their complaints about other matters, as taxation, and the expenses of the household. Tensions between king and people underlay the comparative tranquillity of the later years of Henry IV, as they had the earlier years of open instability.

Despite the continued grumbling, there is a real contrast between the domestic peace of the years after 1406, and the civil confusion that reigned before. This contrast between the earlier and later periods of Henry's reign is interestingly repeated in the pattern of England's relations with external powers.

At the outset of the reign, Henry's uncertain circumstances posed two objectives, to maintain the truce with France, and to achieve recognition for himself and his dynasty in Europe. The latter object was complicated by the Schism in the church, which divided Europe ecclesiastically into two 'obediences', and by the parallel schism in the Empire, where both Wenceslas of Bohemia and Rupert of the Palatinate claimed to be the elected king of the Romans. The French, although they confirmed the truce with England in 1400, cleverly avoided formally acknowledging Henry as king of England. Henry did succeed in forging a series of dynastic connexions for his house: his daughter Blanche was married in 1402 to Lewis of Bavaria, King Rupert's eldest son; and Philippa in 1406 to the king of Norway. He himself married a second time in 1403; his new bride was the Dowager Duchess of Brittany, Joan. None of these marriages brought any material benefit for the time being. Henry's efforts to secure French agreement to the marriage of Isabella, Richard's ex-queen, to one of his sons, a connexion which would have had great political potential, were wholly unsuccessful.

It is questionable how much the successive confirmations of the truce with France in the early years were worth. The French court was constantly disturbed by the rivalries of the dukes of the royal house, who quarrelled and intrigued in Paris around the mad King Charles VI, and agreements were not always effective in binding all parties. Louis of Orleans, the king's brother, consistently urged hostile action against the English, and in 1404 his son Charles was betrothed to Isabella. Count Waleran de St Pol had married Richard II's sister and could not obtain her dowry; there was bitter fighting in the *pas de Calais* between the English and his men. There was also fighting in Guienne, and a privateering war in the Channel between English seamen and both the Bretons and the Flemings. Relations deteriorated with the years. There were numerous French raids on the Channel coast and islands, and in 1404 the French formally allied with Glendower, Henry's enemy. A French force marched with Glendower's men on his great raid into England in 1405. In 1406 there were plans for two simultaneous offensives against the English in France, in the Calais march and in Guienne. They came to nothing, but the reason why they did was not the firmness of the English; it was the quarrels of the French princes.

There cannot be much doubt that in the early years of Henry IV the French could have ended English dominion on French soil fifty years earlier than they actually did. The reason why they did not was the rivalry of the dukes of Orleans and Burgundy. Relations between these two were already strained when Henry IV came to his throne. Both had ambitions outside France: Burgundy, who was also Count of Flanders, in the Low Countries, and Orleans, who was married to a Visconti princess, in Italy. Both wished to use control of diplomacy and finance at Paris to further their own ends. After the death of Philip of Burgundy in 1404 and the succession of his son John the Fearless, mutual hostility became less restrained. It ruined the campaign plans of 1406. In 1407 Louis of Orleans was assassinated in Paris by retainers of John the Fearless, and France was brought to the brink of civil war. From this point onwards England no longer had much to fear from France; it was the turning point in her external relations in Henry IV's reign.

Another event, which took place shortly before this, strengthened Henry's position with regard to the old ally of the French, Scotland. In 1406 James, the heir of Robert III, was taken at sea by the English, while on his way to France. Robert III died shortly after this, and the man who was named as 'governor' of Scotland was Albany. His son, Murdach of Fife, was Henry's prisoner, and Albany was more anxious to see Murdach back in Scotland than the young James. With a hold over the Scots governor, and with France clearly on the verge of civil war, Henry at last began to look more formidable as a European monarch. The English were able to play a very prominent part, in consequence, in the negotiations which led up to the summons of the Council of Pisa, the first major European effort to end the Schism in the church. This made a considerable impression, both abroad and at home.

When in 1410 open war broke out in France between John of Burgundy and the princes who were allies of the young Charles of Orleans (the most formidable among them being his new father-in-law, Count Bernard of Armagnac), both parties were anxious for alliance with England. There seemed to be a real chance of securing from one or other at least the recognition of English sovereignty in the lands ceded to Edward III by the Treaty of Brétigny, an object which had dominated English diplomatic thinking ever since the 1370s. The question was, with which side should the English ally?

Henry IV's health deteriorated seriously after 1407, and in 1411 his son Henry Prince of Wales was at the head of his council. His choice was in favour of Burgundy. There was much to be said for this alternative. Because Burgundy's Flemish subjects were dependent on supplies of English wool, it looked as if it should be possible for the English to put effective pressure on him to steer any French government that he directed clear of intervention in Aquitaine. John was prepared besides to offer inviting terms: a marriage of one of his daughters to the prince, and to put certain important towns, Gravelines, Dunquerque, Sluys and Dixmude, into English hands. This satisfied Prince Henry, and in October an English force under the Earl of Arundel was despatched to Arras. They played a distinguished part in the campaign that followed, and entered Paris with Burgundy's army.

Before Arundel's force was back, the Armagnacs (the Orleanist party) had outbid Burgundy. Their negotiations commenced in the new year of 1412, and culminated in an agreement made at Bourges, by which the dukes of Orleans, Bourbon and Berry promised, in return for support against Burgundy, to restore to Henry IV the duchy of Aquitaine, and to do homage to him for their own lands in the duchy. As a first step towards implementing the English side of the bargain, a large host, under the command of Henry's second son, Thomas Duke of Clarence, was recruited. The Duke of York, Thomas Beaufort and Sir John Cornwall led important contingents. The muster was at Southampton, and Clarence landed at La Hogue in Normandy on 10 August 1412.

Clarence's expedition did not achieve the glory that was hoped for it, largely because the French parties had come to terms with each other, unknown to the English, when it landed. But it achieved enough to demonstrate forcefully the potential of English intervention in the disordered French kingdom. Clarence took St Rémy and Bellême, marched through Anjou, and crossed the Loire. The French had to buy him off, and showed their weakness by the sums that they agreed to pay: Clarence was to receive 120,000 crowns, York 36,000, and Sir John Cornwall 21,000. The Count of Angoulême was handed over as a hostage, and the treasures of Jean de Berry were ransacked for pledges for the sums due. Clarence passed into Gascony, and was at Bordeaux before Christmas, where plans were mooted for a campaign in 1413. Before they could mature, Henry IV was dead, and the whole aspect of things in England had begun to change.

The sudden *volte face* in English diplomacy in 1411, from alliance with Burgundy to alliance with the Armagnacs, was almost certainly the direct consequence of the dismissal, in November 1411, of the council headed by the Prince of Wales. This was the climax of a long period of tension among the groups close to Henry IV's throne. From at least 1407 onwards, the king had been often sick. Once his eldest son was free of military service in Wales, he in consequence assumed a dominating influence in the council. From the autumn of 1409 he was virtually its president. Always close to him were his half-brothers, the Beauforts; and the council named in the spring of 1410 was dominated by their party. Henry Beaufort, Bishop of Winchester, was a prominent member; Sir Thomas Beaufort became chancellor in succession to Archbishop Arundel; Lord Scrope of Masham, the treasurer, with the Earl of Warwick and Henry Chichele, who were appointed at the end of the parliament, were also associates of the prince. Archbishop Arundel, Lord Roos, and the Lancastrian knights who had been prominent in earlier councils were dropped; and it is clear that there were soon tensions between the new council and Prince Thomas, Henry IV's second son. The group that in 1411 forced its way to the front, with a consequent redistribution of offices, was headed by Archbishop Arundel, probably in alliance with Thomas; Arundel became chancellor, and Sir John Pelham replaced Scrope at the treasury.

The party divisions that lay behind this change seem to have been of a quite serious order. It was said later that at the time Prince Henry's court was always 'more abundant than the King his father's'.[22] Just before the autumn parliament of 1411 there was apparently a suggestion from the Beauforts that the king ought to abdicate in the prince's favour. In June 1412 in an open letter written at Coventry Prince Henry complained of malicious rumours that he was seeking to seize the throne, and that he had tried to thwart the expedition to Aquitaine. The reason why he would not sail with the expedition, he explained, was not that he was plotting sedition, but because he had been told to bring so small a force that it would not suffice for his own safety. It was the king's own familiars, according to Walsingham, who were so busy sowing rumour against him. Clearly a dangerous political situation was developing.[23]

A sick king, divisions among councillors and princes of the blood, open manifestos from persons maligned at court; all these things anticipate the symptoms of disarray that were later patent in the years when Henry VI's government was losing control on the eve of the Wars of the Roses. So do the tales from the end of Henry IV's reign of the disorders committed in London by the retainers of Thomas of Clarence and his brother John, and of Prince Henry 'coming to the council with an huge people' of followers. The situation when Henry IV died in March 1413 was, of course, infinitely less dangerous than that of, say, 1450; though the symptoms of disease in the body politic were similar, it had not yet taken hold as it was to later. Nevertheless we can see that Henry's victories over his opponents in the first part of his reign had failed to solve his problems. The shadow of civil discord was looming again in the last years, with party groupings among the nobility crystallizing into hostile factions.

Henry IV's record as a ruler should not be undervalued. In the days of his vigour he showed himself an able commander in the field. He managed his relations with the intractable commons in parliament with a skill that ensured that, for all their difficulties with one another, confrontation never reached the point where there was a real threat to royal government. The men whom he chose as counsellors and administrators showed marked ability, for the most part, and served him faithfully. Long before he died he had won over the greater magnates to acquiescence in his regime, in appearance at least. Yet no one regretted his days when they were over. The first request of the speaker in Henry V's first parliament was for 'more abundant government', which had been so often promised before; but 'how the promises were kept the king who now is knows well enough'.[24] Henry V did, in fact, provide better government than Henry IV had, but before the period of his great successes he had to deal with an ugly legacy of disaffection from his father's time.

The story of the Cambridge plot, hatched in 1415, is essentially an epilogue to the story of the reign of Henry IV. The chief architect of the conspiracy was Richard Earl of Cambridge, the younger brother of the Duke of York; his principal associate was the northern knight, Sir Thomas Grey of Heton. The Earl of March and Henry Lord Scrope of Masham were privy to the plot. Cambridge's fairly hare brained plan seems to have been to spirit March away to join a remnant of Glendower's rebels in Wales while the royal host was mustering at Southampton to cross to France, to raise the standard of revolt there, and to claim the throne for March as the rightful heir of Richard II. The scheme collapsed in disaster, because March, whose nerve was never strong and who had probably only been drawn half in through his resentment at the huge fine imposed on him (10,000 marks) for permission to marry Anne Stafford, revealed all to the king. Cambridge, Grey and Scrope were immediately arrested, and the first two made full confessions of their guilt. Grey's was crucial in implicating Scrope, who seems to have tried to dissuade the conspirators from their plans, and whose only real (and fatal) offence was his failure to disclose what he knew was going on. The three were tried by a rapidly assembled court of peers, and executed for high treason.

Financial difficulties, and resentment with what they felt to be mistreatment by Henry V, were probably what chiefly actuated the two principal conspirators (and March in his half involvement). The ramifications of their scheming, as revealed in their confessions, nevertheless all lead back toward the troubled early days of Henry IV's reign. Cambridge had been married first to Anne Mortimer, March's sister, and secondly to Maud Clifford, sister of Lord Clifford (whom he certainly sought to draw into his plot). Clifford was married to Elizabeth Percy. An important item in the conspirators' plan was to seize Murdach, son of the Scottish regent Albany and a prisoner in England, and to exchange him for Hotspur's heir, who was still an exile at the court of Scotland. This, they hoped, would enable them to draw old Percy supporters in the north into their revolt, with Scots backing. Scrope was the nephew of the Archbishop who had been executed at York in 1405 for his part in the second Percy revolt, and that was why he was approached. A whole network of connections that reflected the patterns of disaffection of 1403 and 1405 (and their focus on the March claim to the throne) was the foundation on which the conspirators of 1415 hoped that they could build.

The Cambridge plot points back, once again, to the significance of 1399. Sixteen years later it had not been forgotten that the Lancastrian title was better *de facto* than *de jure*. Henry IV never won the full loyalty and respect of the people whose government he had seized, and new aristocratic attempts at king-making never ceased to be a possibility while he was on the throne. With its long tale of civil war, sedition and popular dissatisfaction with government his reign gave England an ugly foretaste of the troubles of the time of his grandson, Henry VI, who was ultimately deposed by the heir of the line of March, Edward IV (who happened ironically also to be the grandson of Richard of Cambridge). Henry IV was of course infinitely abler than Henry VI, but there is not much to choose between the career as a king-maker of Henry IV's Earl of Northumberland, and the later and more famous king-maker, Richard of Warwick. What really made the difference between the two reigns was that Henry IV was lucky enough always to defeat his enemies in the field; his grandson was no soldier, and did not.

Notes

1 *R.P.* vol. III, pp. 422–3.
2 *Giles' Chronicle*, p. 5.
3 *P.P.C.* vol. I, pp. 107–8.
4 *The Correspondence of Thomas Bekynton* (R.S.) vol. I, pp. 151–4.
5 *Eulogium Historiarum* (R.S.) vol. III, p. 391.
6 H. Ellis, *Original Letters*, 2nd ser. (London, 1827), vol. I, pp. 24–6.
7 See A. Rogers, 'The political crisis of 1401', *Nottingham Medieval Studies* 12 (1968), pp. 85–96.
8 J. Hardyng, *Chronicle*, ed. H. Ellis (London, 1812), pp. 352–3.
9 E. F. Jacob, *The Fifteenth Century* (Oxford, 1961), p. 51.
10 For text see Ellis, *Original Letters*, 2nd ser., vol. I, pp. 27–8.
11 *Annales Ricardi II et Henrici IV* (R.S.), pp. 403–5.
12 *Anglia Sacra*, ed. H. Wharton, vol. II, pp. 362–8.
13 *Annales*, p. 391.
14 M. D. Legge (ed.), *Anglo Norman Letters* (Oxford, 1941), quoted by Jacob, *The Fifteenth Century*, pp. 75–6, who corrects the date of Allerthorpe's letter; and *P.P.C.* vol. II, p. 8 (statement of 1411).
15 *R.P.* vol. III, p. 573.
16 *P.P.C.* vol. I, pp. 259–63.
17 See *P.P.C.* vol. I, pp. 150–3 (Percies' complaints), pp. 263–4 (Prince Thomas), p. 277 (Grey of Codnor), pp. 271–4 (York).
18 *R.P.* vol. III, p. 456.
19 *R.P.* vol. III, p. 658.
20 See C. M. Fraser, 'Some Durham documents relating to the Hilary parliament of 1404', *B.I.H.R.*, vol. 34 (1961), pp. 197–9.
21 *R.P.* vol. III, p. 649.
22 *The First English Life of King Henry V*, ed. C. L. Kingsford (Oxford, 1911), p. 11.
23 *The St Albans Chronicle 1406–1420*, ed. V. H. Galbraith (Oxford, 1937), p. 65f.
24 *R.P.* vol. IV, p. 4.

Note on secondary reading (post 1970)

The reign of Henry IV has not attracted the same attention as that of his predecessor. The most recent biography is J.L. Kirby, *Henry IV of England* (London, 1970). The most penetrating appraisal is that offered by K.B. McFarlane in Part One of his *Lancastrian Kings and Lollard Knights* (Oxford, 1972). More recent, and useful, is P. Strohm, *England's Empty Throne: Usurpation and its Aftermath* (Yale, 1998). I have included in this chapter comment on the Southampton plot of 1415, although it took place in Henry V's reign: T.B. Pugh, *Henry V and the Southampton Plot of 1415* (Gloucester, 1996) traces back the connexions of this conspiracy with events of Henry IV's reign most illuminatingly. R.R. Davies provides a valuable study of Glendower's revolt, *The Revolt of Owain Glyn Dwr* (Oxford, 1995). Essays with a broad reference include A.L. Brown, 'The reign of Henry IV; the establishment of the Lancastrian regime', in S.B. Chrimes, C.D. Ross and R. Griffiths (eds.), *Fifteenth Century England* (Manchester, 1972); P. Morgan, 'Henry IV and the shadow of Richard II', in R. Archer (ed.), *Crown, Government and People* (Stroud, 1995); P. McNiven, 'The problem of Henry IV's health', *E.H.R.*, vol. 100 (1985); and A. Tuck, 'Henry IV and Europe; a dynasty's search for recognition', in R. Britnell and A. Pollard (eds.), *The McFarlane Legacy* (Stroud, 1995).

There are perceptive articles on the various risings and political crises of the reign. On the most important, the Percy revolts, J.M.W. Bean, 'Henry IV and the Percies', *History*, vol. 44 (1959) remains particularly valuable. On other revolts and crises see D. Crook, 'Central England and the revolt of the Earls', *Historical Research*, vol. 64 (1991); P. McNiven, 'The Cheshire rising of 1400', *Bulletin of the John Rylands Library*, vol. 52 (1970); A. Rogers, 'The political crisis of 1401', *Nottingham Medieval Studies*, vol. 12 (1968); P. McNiven, 'Prince Henry and the political crisis of 1412', *History*, vol. 65 (1980), and 'Rebellion, Sedition and the legend of Richard II's survival in the reigns of Henry IV and Henry V', *Bulletin of the John Rylands Library*, vol. 76 (1994).

Two useful papers on Henry IV's relations with parliament and its commons are A. Rogers, 'Henry IV, the commons and taxation', *Medieval Studies*, vol. 31 (1969), and A. Pollard, 'The "Lancastrian constitutional experiment revisited" Sir John Tiptoft and the parliament of 1406', *Parliamentary History*, vol. 14 (1995). On the royal household and retinue, see C. Given-Wilson, *The Royal Household and the King's Affinity 1360–1413* (London and New Haven, 1986).

14 Politics and society: parliament and the council

In tracing the turbulent political history of the reigns of Richard II and Henry IV we have repeatedly found it necessary to view the attitudes and the shifting alliances of the great magnates in the context of opinion in the country at large. We shall find in due course that, later in the fifteenth century, the view of the political classes continued to be an important factor in politics. 'Public opinion', 'political society' and 'the political classes' are good general terms, but ones whose connotations change with time. It will help us to understand our period better if we can explore a little more carefully what they mean with reference to the late fourteenth and fifteenth centuries.

In the *Prologue* to the *Canterbury Tales*, Chaucer has provided for us in a series of vignettes, drawn with poetic insight, a cross section of the society of his day. His best pictures, perhaps, are those of the clergy, whose calling laid them particularly open to his satire, but his lay figures are for our immediate purpose even more interesting. Here at one end of the social scale we meet the knight (almost certainly a banneret), who stands apart from all the rest, an aristocrat who has travelled far and wide in chivalry. At the other extreme there is the ploughman, a 'true swinker and a good'. Between these two in the social scale stand a group of people of middling rank, and one of the first things that must strike anyone who reads their descriptions is their comparative prosperity. This is true even of those who do not stand high in the scale. The miller and the reeve are manorial figures, but the miller has a white coat and a blue hood, and a sword and buckler at his side; and the reeve is a trusted, experienced steward, 'rich astored privily', with a fair dwelling shadowed with trees. The manciple, bursar to a society of lawyers, is another experienced steward, who can run business better than his learned masters. The weaver, the dyer and the carpenter, humble as their crafts are, are solid burgesses, with chattels enough to fit them for a seat on their guildhall dais. Even the ploughman, it would seem, is some way short of real poverty; he can afford to lend his neighbours a hand without hire. A second common factor among all these people is that they all, almost certainly, would be literate. The ploughman might possibly be an exception, but he has a brother who is a lettered parson: Langland's Piers the ploughman, a man of much the same standing, seems certainly, according to the poem, to have been able to read.

The most interesting figures, in the present context, are the merchants and the gentry. They are also the most notably prosperous. The wife of Bath, over-dressed on Sunday, has laid three husbands at the church door, and substantial men they must have been, for in her business of cloth making 'she passed them of Ypres and Ghent'. The merchant himself is a man playing for high stakes, changing currency, lending money and lading ships between Middleburgh and Orwell. Three men, the shipman, the man of law and the franklin, though they are not knights, all belong to what historians often call the 'knightly class', or the 'gentry'. The shipman, who knows every harbour from Gotland to Finisterre, might almost be John Hawley of Dartmouth, who in Chaucer's own time made a fortune largely through piracy, and prospered to be a man of wealth and landed estate. He sat in the commons for Dartmouth, was employed from time to time on commissions, and even acted as deputy to the lord admiral. The man of law is one of those successful barristers raised to the rank of serjeant-at-law, who were not only recognized as leading advocates in the central courts, but also often served as justices of assize, and from time to time attended the king's council to advise on points of law. Most interesting of all is the franklin. He is a 'great householder', a man of standing in his county, a justice of the peace, who has served as sheriff and represented the shire in parliament 'full oft'. Not a man of the knight's ancestry, he is a man of estate and authority, ambitious for the recognition of his kin as genteel. In him we recognize quite clearly the lineal ancester of Shakespeare's Justice Shallow, Robert Shallow esquire, justice of the peace, a 'gentleman born', who 'writes himself *armigero* in any bill, warrant, quittance or obligation'[1] – of a rising gentleman, that is to say, of the Tudor age.

Chaucer, of course, does not tell us anything about the political influence of his characters, or in detail of their economic status; that was not germane to him. We can get some way towards viewing the wealth and influence of the kind of men that he depicted in comparative terms, by looking at the instructions for the levy of the graduated poll tax of 1379.[2] In this very interesting social record we find the dukes of Lancaster and Brittany heading the list of those liable, in a class of their own, paying ten marks. Immediately after them come the earls, liable to £4. Barons, we shall find to our surprise, are not considered for the purpose of the tax as a class apart. They are lumped together with bannerets (knights of outstanding note, usually with a military background), and with knights bachelor who can 'afford the same style'. It is in this group, who pay 40*s.*, that Chaucer's knight would belong. There are bigger surprises when we look for the equivalent of the man of law and the merchant. The justices of the bench are taxed at £5, a higher rate than even earls paid; and serjeants-at-law pay at the same rate as barons and bannerets. Turning to the mercantile figures the Mayor of London of 1379 has to pay 'as an earl', and his colleagues the aldermen at the same rate as barons (this is near where Chaucer's merchant would come into line). It is hard to be sure where the shipman, the franklin and the wife of Bath would be, but all most likely in the group immediately following the barons and bannerets, which paid £1 and included all those whose estates would support knighthood, as well as successful merchants, and apprentices-at-law (junior barristers). They might have just fallen short of it, and certainly would have had connexions among the host of less influential people assessed at a mark, half a mark, three and fourpence, or one or two shillings, all of whom stood clear of the peasants and labourers who paid a groat, fourpence a head. That is probably what the ploughman would have paid, but perhaps even he might just have rated a shilling.

The men who devised the gradations of the poll tax of 1379 were of course seeking to tax wealth, not political influence. The two, however, can never stand far apart. That is why it is so striking to find the Mayor of London rated as high as an earl, and rich knights and serjeants-at-law set on a footing with barons who sat apart in parliaments and dressed retainers in their own livery. A London alderman, a knight banneret or a serjeant might be a man who had started from very small beginnings. Political society in the late fourteenth century, we are drawn to conclude, had broad parameters, and social barriers were far from inflexible.

It is useful to compare the poll tax assessment of 1379 with another fiscal source which can throw light on the distribution of wealth in England in the later Middle Ages: the returns to the tax on income from land and annuities of 1436. H. L. Gray, who studied the returns in detail, found fifty-one lay peers with an average income of £768 per annum, 183 greater knights with an average of £208 per annum, 750 lesser knights with an average of £60, 1200 esquires with an average of £24, and a further 5000 men with incomes varying between £5 and £20.[3] A good many of these 5000 would have called themselves esquires; others would have called themselves gentlemen. Gray's figures for the lords and knights tally well with the nearest available heraldic evidence, the Parliamentary Roll of Arms which was compiled in Edward II's reign; it lists over 940 armigerous lords and knights but is known not to be quite complete for its day[4] (it was only late in the fourteenth century that esquires began to be accepted as heraldically armigerous). Denholm Young, calculating on the basis of later heraldic evidence and using Professor Russell's population figures, reckons that perhaps one family in twenty might aspire to call itself genteel.[5] This figure probably gives an exaggerated impression of the size of a prosperous class; we know that there were plenty of rural communities, none of whose members could by normal standards have been rated a gentleman (though the word is, of course, elusive of definition). Cornwall, writing on the early Tudor landed gentry, suggests a proportion of one in fifty or so.[6] The difference between one in fifty and one in twenty is large, but a broad conclusion still remains. Given the substantial variety and number of men who stood, in terms of wealth and status, between the lords and knights and the humble ploughman or labourer, we get a picture of a remarkably wide distribution of wealth, with many gradations.

This conclusion is borne out by the explicit comment of a fifteenth-century observer. 'England is so thick spread with rich and landed men', wrote Sir John Fortescue, 'that there is scarce a small village in which you may not find a knight, an esquire, or some substantial householder called a franklin; all men of considerable estates. There are others who are called freeholders; and many yeomen of estates sufficient to make a substantial jury.'[7] Fortescue's emphasis here on landowning is significant. Land was the most important source of wealth in late medieval England, and it was also the most important source of power. Landowners of any standing, almost by definition, would have tenants and servants of their own: landowners were also the men on whom the king and greater magnates relied in local government and estate stewardship. This meant that landowners needed to be literate, if only so as to be able to read their accounts and to understand the implications of written instructions and legal instruments (title to land was the subject of perpetual litigation). A high proportion among them, it is clear, were a good deal more literate than that.

The letters of the Pastons, the Stonors, the Plumptons, and of other gentry families witness to the generally high standard of education of their class. John Paston I spent time at Cambridge, and trained in the Inns of Court. His son John went to Cambridge, to Trinity Hall, and his son Edmund was at Clifford's Inn. William Paston the younger went first to Eton, then to Oxford. It was becoming commoner in the fifteenth century for gentry to send their sons to board at school, and to the universities, even if they did not intend them to follow a clerical career. But the most important centres of lay education as the Paston's story suggests were the lawyers' Inns. There was scarcely an eminent lawyer in the kingdom, Fortescue reckoned, who was not a gentleman by birth, and the Inns offered a training not in law only, but in 'accomplishments suitable to their quality' too. 'The knights, barons, and the greatest nobility of the kingdom often place their children in those Inns of Court', he wrote proudly, 'not so much to make the laws their study (having large patrimonies of their own) but to form their manners.'[8] No doubt many gentlemen whose sons were at the Inns were actuated by a combination of snobbery with a sense of the solid value of a legal training to a landowner. William of Worcester, John Paston's contemporary, complained that the changing pattern of genteel education was eroding the traditional chivalrous values of the knightly class and that knights' sons lacked training in arms.[9] But the change that he lamented was one that was teaching the gentry a more sophisticated approach to politics than the old fashioned upbringing in a lord's household could inculcate, and to take a more informed view on general questions, political, legal and religious.

The growth of a professionally educated gentility was a factor of profound importance in late medieval England. It left a powerful mark on the king's council and service, in which laymen began to assume a steadily increasing share of administrative duties. From the beginning of the fifteenth century the treasurer of England, hitherto usually a high ecclesiastic, was more often a lay peer. Laymen also began to be prominent among the clerks of the Chancery and Exchequer, posts that had formerly been monopolized by clerics. Knights and esquires like Stury, Edward Dalyngrygg, Thomas Erpingham and John Norbury were among the men most regularly discharging business in the council in the reigns of Richard II and Henry IV. Laymen like Thomas Vaughan and William Alyngton were, in the Yorkist period, key figures in the new system for the administration of crown lands which helped to put the royal finances on their feet after the long disorder of the Lancastrian period. This growing preponderance of laymen in the administration of the kingdom was one of the distinctive features of the fifteenth century, and reminds us that in many respects it had more in common with the so called 'early modern' period than with the central Middle Ages.

Given their education and their material interests, the lively concern of the genteel and merchant classes with national politics is not surprising. Men like Erpingham and Norbury made a career out of politics and chivalrous war service. For a merchant trading on any scale, such political issues as the location of the staple, bullion regulations and the level of charges on exports were of vital concern. For county landowners such as the Pastons, with their many law suits and (in the Pastons' case) their interest in the contested inheritance of the great Sir John Fastolf, politics were something that they could not afford to neglect, because success at law was so often dependent on having friends who could bring pressure to bear in the right quarter. The bulletins of news from the capital with which their correspondence is rich reflect their constant and anxious endeavour to stand well with those whose fortunes were in the ascendant. It is clear, however, that they and their correspondents were interested in politics for more besides their effect on local and personal interests. They watched the collapse of the English regime in France with a sense of direct involvement in the national cause. To Friar Brackley, John Paston's friend who was with him at the making of Fastolf's last will, politics were deeply absorbing. A passionate Yorkist, who looked forward eagerly to the day when he should see Warwick the king-maker a duke, he had watched ever since the parliament of 1447 to see Jeremiah's prophecy fulfilled in the downfall of Henry VI's courtiers, he told Paston. He had a text for every turn of events, and longed to air his views at St Paul's Cross.[10]

The concern of Englishmen at large with politics and political issues is clearly reflected in the literature of the age. There is a very considerable body of ephemeral literary commentary on particular events and grievances: much of it has been edited in various collections of 'political poems'.[11] The broadsheet ballad, in the fifteenth century, was beginning to be a significant instrument of propaganda. Major poets whose prime concern was with social morality, like William Langland and John Gower, show a sharp eye also for what was going on politically. Langland's picture, in the prologue to his *Piers Plowman* of the rats' parliament appears to be directly related to the events of 1376,[12] and the recensions of Gower's works show clearly how, as he watched developments, his initial optimism about the government of Richard II changed to a bitter and critical hostility. Still more significant of active political interest are substantial works directly inspired by political events, such as *Mum and the Sothsegger*, a poetic treatment of events and issues of the years 1399–1402. Here we find a poet whose chief concern is with political personalities and institutions, the council and parliament, and who is anxious to discuss such matters as the justification of subsidies and the duties of members of the commons, who are

> . . . assembled for to show the sores of the royaulme,
> And spare no speech, though they spill [i.e. die] should![13]

Later, in the 1450s and 60s, we find writers like Fortescue and the author of the *Somnium Vigilantis*[14] seriously tackling, in vernacular tracts, the problems of English government and political obligation; the proper composition of the council, the nature of English law, and the right (or rather the lack of it) to resist the sovereign authority of the king.

One further literary *genre* with a political edge to it calls for particular attention, the advice literature that goes under the generic title of 'mirrors for princes'. There is a considerable corpus of treatises of this kind, in English, surviving from the late medieval period. Much, it is true, is translated or derivative from older works in the scholastic tradition; Hoccleve's *Regement of Princes*, for instance, largely derives from Giles of Rome's *De Regimine Principum* (*c.* 1280). For this reason, commentators on fifteenth century English political ideas have commonly given these works only cursory mention, but recent scholarship (notably the writings of Richard Green and John Watts) has given them much closer attention, and rightly. The dissemination of texts testifies to the contemporary interest that they commanded (no less than forty-five manuscripts of Hoccleve's *Regement* have survived); and knights and gentry are prominent among those who owned or commissioned translations of advice books. One of the three late medieval English translations of the pseudo-Aristotelian *Secreta Secretorum* was made, we know, for Sir Miles Stapleton: Sir John Fastolf got his nephew Stephen Scrope to do into English the collection known as the *Dicta Philosophorum*; Sir John Paston's 'grete book' includes a copy of Lydgate and Burgh's *Book of Governance of Kings and Princes*. Readers such as these clearly thought there was more in this advice literature than a heritage from the past of traditional moral maxims for rulers, and that it had things to say that had useful and relevant present applications.

The principal concern of works in the 'mirrors for princes' tradition was with the personal virtues needful to a prince, in order to discharge his proper political function of ruling his people in their common interest. The virtues on which they particularly focused were the four cardinal virtues, Prudence, Justice, Temperance and Fortitude. An important aspect of a ruler's prudence, they stressed, was his willingness to seek counsel. His choice of counsellors would therefore also be important. They needed to be the kind of men who would be well informed and experienced in the matters on which they gave counsel, and who would offer advice geared to the requirements of the common weal, not to the advancement of their own private ends. Here the advice literature became sharply relevant not just to the prince who should exercise virtuous rule, but also to the kind of men who might give him counsel, and to the kind of men who might counsel them in their turn. These are roles in which nobles, knights and gentlemen could have a part to play. Indeed, they clearly thought ought to have such a part, in bringing to their ruler's attention the needs of the community. This is plain from the interest they took in the two channels through which the community's needs could most effectively be represented to the king, the council and parliament. It is no accident that writers, such as Fortescue, who gave detailed and practical consideration to the working of these two bodies, also drew heavily on advice literature.

The Council and parliament can both be regarded, in their different ways, as representative institutions. Councillors, inevitably, were drawn from the dominant elite, of peers, bishops, and knights who had made their mark in one way or another in the service of the crown. Such men had counsellors of their own, servants, tenants, and clients: they were besides likely to be heavily involved in local government and administration in regions where their landed estates made them prominent. For this reason, such councillors could be expected to 'knowe the direction to be had moost expedient for the sad and politique reule' of the land:[15] they could speak not just for themselves but on the basis of their knowledge of the attitudes and concerns of their regional and county communities, with which their contacts were both close and multifarious. Parliament (which could still be regarded as an extension of the council, and to which peers who were councillors would of course receive with other lords individual summonses) was representative in a more formal sense. The knights and burgesses of the commons were present expressly on behalf of the communities that chose them. For this reason it will be convenient here to consider parliaments first, and to give particular attention to the role of the commons in them. What they as representatives had to say about the workings of government, about issues that needed to be tackled, matters that required redress, and about the measure of financial aid that the king's enterprises seemed to them to justify, promises to offer a fair reflection of the interests and involvement in politics of political society at large in the kingdom. On occasion, we will find, the commons saw fit to express, sometimes rather forcibly, their views about the council and the sort of counsel the king was receiving, so consideration of the one subject – parliament – will lead naturally into the other, the council and councillors.

The fifteenth century was an important period in the history of parliament. For as long as the war with France continued, royal requests for subsidy meant that it was summoned to meet pretty regularly (though the sessions were usually quite short, just a few weeks). The proroguing of parliaments became more frequent, so that the same commons members might return for two or even three sessions, returning each time more experienced in the handling of their business. No record survives of their debates (though they certainly did debate), but the range of interests reflected in their petitions offers powerful testimony to their sense of involvement with the common weal and their capacity for pressing their independent views in matters which they regarded as their proper concern. They displayed persistent vigour in their insistence that grants of taxation should be accompanied by measures which they thought (often wrongly) would lead to better government: in their efforts to force better economy on the king and the council, and in pressing the king to surround himself with 'sad and substantial councillors'. On one or two occasions, as we have seen, they even succeeded in impeaching councillors who, they believed, had betrayed the king's trust. This vigour so struck Stubbs that he believed it was deliberately fostered by the Lancastrian kings, and spoke of a Lancastrian 'constitutional experiment'. But the initiative was not from the king; the energy came from the members of the commons themselves, acting collectively, and the force behind it was their sense of obligation to the communities that had sent them to parliament.

Two aspects of the history of the commons in the fifteenth century deserve particular notice. One is the development, in the period, of the traditions and institutions of the commons house, and the sensitivity of its members about their privileges. The other is evidence of a quickening interest on the part of county gentlemen in election to parliament, and in elections and the electorate. We must look at each of these in turn.

The sense of corporate identity among the commons was developing fast in the late Middle Ages. In the fifteenth century we find the practice growing whereby private individuals and communities addressed their petitions to the commons, or to the commons and their speaker (as opposed to the king in parliament). When in 1407 the lords reported to the king on their own initiative what they thought was necessary in the way of a finance grant, the commons hotly protested that this prejudiced the liberties of their estate; and they obtained a ruling that nothing concerning grants should be reported until lords and commons were agreed, and that then it should be reported by the commons' speaker.[16] The development of the office of speaker was another feature of great significance. His function was to speak in parliament for the commons as a whole, before the lords and the king. The first speaker so to act for the duration of a whole parliament was Peter de la Mare in 1376. From the early years of Richard II's reign the commons were regularly electing their speaker and presenting him to the king, usually on the second or third day of parliament, when he made his 'protestation'. This was to the effect that he would say nothing of his own initiative, only what was the express will of all the commons, and that they should have the right to correct him if he misrepresented them in any way. Through the speaker, the commons found a means to give regular expression to their views as a body, independent of the lords.

By the middle of the fifteenth century it is clear that the speaker was doing a good deal more than just report the opinions of his house. He was becoming responsible for steering the commons through the *agenda* set out in the king's charge to parliament, and had acquired considerable influence over the passage of bills that were sent forward as common petitions. Abbot Whethamstede in 1454 spoke of him as having the *regimen* of the lower house.[17] In 1483 Bishop

Russell compared the speaker to the Roman tribune of the people: 'in the lower house, all is directed by the speaker, *quasi per tribunum*'.[18]

In the fifteenth century we begin to find among the speakers of the commons a predominance of men trained in the law, which was later to be still more marked. Such a training was obviously invaluable to a man who had much to do with the drafting of bills and with procedure. We also find that the speakers, who were always prominent men, usually had connexions with the government, or with some peer with major political interests. Thus in 1397 the chamber knight Sir John Bushy was speaker, and in Henry IV's reign a series of royal councillors, including Thomas Chaucer, Arnold Savage and John Tiptoft; in 1450 York's retainer William Oldhall was chosen; in 1453 Thomas Thorpe, who had close connexions with Somerset; and in 1461 James Strangeways, a Neville retainer. Is this a sign that the king and the great peers were using the office of the speaker to control the commons? Useful as the friendship of the speaker must often have been to the government (or on occasion to its opponents) it is hard to pursue this line of argument very far. The commons were quite prepared, if they thought themselves misrepresented, to disavow their speaker, and they took a real interest in his election, for which there was sometimes keen competition.[19] The choice of men acceptable to the king or to influential peers seems to have been inspired by the hope that this would help the commons to get their own business attended to, not that of the speakers' patrons. The speakers' connexions certainly do not seem to have hampered the free expression of the opinion of the commons as a whole. Very few speakers were ever as outspoken in their criticisms of the council, the king's household and the government's economy as Sir Arnold Savage was in 1404,[20] notwithstanding the fact that he was a royal councillor.

It is sometimes claimed that in the early days of parliaments, attendance among the commons was regarded as an onerous and unwelcome duty. This was certainly not the case in the fifteenth century. Though a good many of the smaller boroughs no longer sent resident burgesses to parliaments, they had little difficulty in finding instead gentlemen or lawyers who had property there and were more than willing to represent them, and as time went by they more and more often sent men who had no residence qualification at all but wished to go to parliament, and who can be broadly described as gentry rather than merchants. We come across a good many men among the knights of the shire of the fifteenth century who had sat in previous parliaments for boroughs. These developments helped to give the commons a more homogeneous social character and indicate clearly the widespread interest in obtaining a seat in parliament, as does the willingness of many borough members to waive, in part at least, their right to claim their expenses from their constituents. A new interest in the qualifications both of electors and members points in the same direction. In 1406 it was laid down by statute (in response to a common petition) that the returns of elections in the shires should be attested by all the electors (though it is clear that usually not all did so – only the most important men who were present on the occasion).[21] In 1429 the county franchise was limited to forty shilling freeholders, because of the disturbances that had been caused at elections by crowds of lesser men claiming the right to vote (this was to remain the county franchise until 1832). In 1445 it was decreed that no one of yeoman or lesser status should be eligible for election to parliament.

A fifteenth century election could be a tumultuous affair. In 1450 in Huntingdon, for instance, a group of no less than 124 freeholders complained that some seventy commoners, supporters of Henry Gimber, who was not 'of gentle birth according to your writ', appeared 'by labour of divers gentlemen of other shires and of this your said shire of Huntingdon' and disturbed the under-sheriff in his duty of examining the qualifications of electors. In consequence the petitioners, who had abandoned the field for fear of a riot, feared that the choice that they and 300 other electors had made in 'full shire' would be set aside and Gimber returned. As this story makes apparent, the votes of the humble forty shilling freeholders could have a significant impact on electoral calculations (that is the group to which those 124 freeholders who were frightened off clearly belonged). Simon Payling has shown that the list of attestors to the election indenture for Nottinghamshire in 1460 was almost certainly copied from a poll list; and, further, as is evident from the names of the large number of attestors (266), that the votes of the forty shilling freeholders from the northern wapentakes of the county were decisive in securing the return as members of Sir Robert Strelley and John Stanhope esquire. These two appear to have been standing on a 'ticket', and to have been more effective than two rival candidates in organizing their support.[22] There seems to have been no disturbance on this occasion.

There was often a good deal of jockeying for position, especially among the greater men of the shire, at an earlier stage than this, before the county court met to make the election. Peers with influence would write to their supporters and tell them who they wished to see elected. Thus John Paston in 1450 was told who York's candidates were and asked to help them; and in 1472 his son Sir John was warned that he had better give up his hope of being returned, as the dukes of Norfolk and Suffolk were agreed in advance as to who the Norfolk members should be.[23] Magnate influence, however, was by no means always able to get its way, for the leading gentry of the shires were not men easily overawed. 'I told my lord of Norfolk that I laboured divers men for Sir Roger Chamberlain and they said they would have him', John Jenny, who was working in the Norfolk interest in 1455, wrote to Paston, 'but not Howard, inasmuch as he has no livelihood in the shire.' 'It is an evil precedent for the shire that such a strange man should be chosen, and no worship to my lord of York nor to my lord of Norfolk to write for him', he wrote again later, 'for if the gentlemen of the shire will suffer such inconvenience, the shire shall not be called of such worship as it hath been.'[24] Sir John Howard was in fact returned and Jenny proved wrong, but for this occasion only. One of the Mowbray candidates for Norfolk was defeated in 1450; and in 1461 John Paston himself secured one of the county's seats in a hotly contested election, in spite of the efforts of the Mowbray interest.

Contested elections were far from the rule; most often, it seems likely, the names of those who would be returned, formally unopposed, had been settled in advance of the election in the county court, by consultation among the magnates and leading gentry in the shire (as in the case of Norfolk in 1472, mentioned above). The kind of persons that they would be likely to favour were those who would be able to speak independently and with authority on behalf of the community, and such persons were not hard to find. The greater gentry included, in almost all counties, a fair sprinkling of men who were in terms of wealth the equals of many peers. K. B. McFarlane, looking at the returns for the tax on landed incomes in 1412, found that in Dorset, out of fourteen landowners whose incomes were assessed at more than £200 a year, eight were peers and six commoners; in Sussex there were two peers and two commoners of this standing. All of the eight rich commoners in question sat at one time or another for their shires in parliament, and most of them a number of times. Men like Sir John Pelham (of Sussex) and Sir John Mautravers (of Dorset) were of a standing that made it quite as easy for them to influence peers as vice versa. The crown could of course always count on seeing a leavening of household men among the shire knights (eighteen counties had a 'householder' as one of their representatives in 1453, for instance), and every magnate hoped to see some of his retainers returned there (in 1422 Warwick 'topped the poll' with five clients among the county knights). Unless there was a very considerable degree of unanimity between king and lords, however, these connexions were nothing like sufficient to enable any single interest to control the commons. As a body, the lay lords were too irregular in their attendance in parliament to lead the lower house in any effective sense. The collective wealth, education and parliamentary experience of the commons put them in a position in which they were entirely capable of taking their own independent stand in their operative criticism of the working of the king's government, which, aside from their role in the making of fiscal grants, they regarded as their principal parliamentary business.

The key to the influence of the commons on government was their control over grants of taxation. They could use this to secure new legislation, which might be aimed to secure improved local governance, or to regulate prices, wages or commerce; but it was not easy to ensure that the resulting statutes were enforced. They were usually consulted formally about the making of treaties, and were in a position to influence foreign policy, but did not often seek to do so. What really decided the issue in the sorts of matters that most keenly interested the commons was the activity, or lack of it, of the king's council and of the royal officials answerable to it. One obvious way in which the commons could influence the day-to-day government of the realm was therefore by bringing pressure to bear on the king in connexion with the personnel of the council and the manner in which it discharged its functions. This they sought to do on a number of occasions, notably in 1376 and 1386, in 1401, 1404 and 1406, and in 1422.

In dealing with the council, one must be careful to distinguish between its different guises. The sources speak sometimes of the great council, sometimes of the privy council, or of continual councils; besides, parliaments could easily be described as councils. Stubbs long ago remarked that the great councils of the late Middle Ages may be regarded as 'either extra parliamentary sessions of the house of lords, or as enlarged meetings of the royal council'.[25] The former was the view of the lords themselves, as they gave it in the parliament of 1427. In a minority, they claimed, the king's authority was vested in the lords assembled in parliament or great council, and when these were not in session in the (continual) council.[26] Fortescue's description of the lords as *consiliarii nati* tallies with this opinion.[27] When the king was of age, what happened in practice eludes sharp constitutional definition. When he wanted weightier advice on matters of national importance, as issues of war or peace or relations with the pope, he summoned peers to counsel him, and sometimes others too, under privy seal letters, but he did not always summon all the peers, and by no means all those summoned attended. But the people who really mattered in everyday government were the continual councillors, the men in constant attendance who received the petitions of suitors, organized the raising of loans, and authorized privy seal letters, to move the great seal to authorize grants and appointments (this involved the council in the disposition of much valuable and important crown patronage). It was the composition of this body that from time to time agitated the commons. Significantly, their anxiety usually shows at times when it is clear that there was general unease about the undue influence on counsel of cliques at court and the sectional interests they were suspected of promoting.

This smaller, continual council in the later Middle Ages was becoming a steadily more professional body. It had a clerk and possessed its own rudimentary records. The administration of a special councillor's oath and the payment of salaries to councillors were beginning to be regular practice. In the 1390s, when Prophet's journal affords us a particularly close insight into the workings of the council, we find that some of Richard II's knights, like Stury and Sir Edward Dalyngrygg, were so regular in their attendance as to class virtually as professional councillors. The council had developed a jurisdiction of its own, dealing with the cases of petitioners who could not get redress at common law and with disturbances caused by great men and their followers (out of this jurisdiction the Court of Star Chamber later developed). This growth of professionalism helped to differentiate the administrators, who discharged conciliar business, from the court, the king's personal entourage. The personal influence of a strong king or a determined favourite could, and often did, blur the distinction, but not wholly. In the period of Suffolk's ascendancy over Henry VI, for instance, most important political and diplomatic decisions were taken at court and the signet, the king's personal seal, was often used to move the great seal; but the court did not assume the jurisdiction of the council. The fact that some at least of the council's functions were specific and identifiable made it easier for the parliamentary commons to discuss its methods and composition.

As has been said, the commons on a series of occasions insisted that the names of councillors should be declared in parliament. This might suggest that they were being used by interested parties among the lords, to help secure power in the hands of partisan groups. Analysis of the connexions of councillors who were named in parliament on such occasions as 1386, 1401 and 1406 does not support this view. The composition of these named councils tends to follow a pattern, including (besides the three officers of state who were regular members) the Archbishop of Canterbury, one or two of the greater lay peers, selected bishops and lay barons, and three or four distinguished knights. What the commons seem to have valued in this structure was that it brought together a council of really substantial men with the independence and experience to form their own views, whose standing was so secure that they would not need to use their position for self-advancement, and which would represent the interests of the realm and its component communities to the king as its governor. They regarded with suspicion anything that looked like the dominance of a household clique, particularly if the greater magnates, lay and ecclesiastical, were ill-represented (as was the case with the group that gathered round Pole and de Vere under Richard II, and was replaced by a named council in 1386; or the little nucleus of devoted Lancastrians, men like Erpingham and Norbury and Leventhorpe, on whom Henry IV relied heavily in his early years). Their preferences and anxieties here were entirely in tune with the teaching and advice in the matter of counsel of the 'mirrors for princes', discussed earlier, and clearly reflected views very broadly shared. Appeals to the king to take substantial men into his council could normally count on widespread support, as the manifestos of Cade, York and Warwick in the later fifteenth century remind us.[28]

The commons were not just interested in the composition of the council; they wanted to be sure that councillors did their job. Hence their efforts to ensure that there was always a quorum of officially appointed councillors in attendance (for example in 1401); to make those appointed take an oath in parliament (as in 1406 and 1410); and to regulate the manner in which the council dealt with bills presented to it. The most determined effort of the commons to overhaul the council's activities was made in 1406, and kept parliament in session for much of the time from March until Christmas. Two series of articles, the second very long, were produced, which the councillors appointed in parliament had to swear to observe. They were to act together as a body, a number were always to attend the king, and days were to be set aside for hearing petitions. They were to consider and approve all matters, except routine ones, that would eventually pass under the great and privy seals. Elaborate regulations guarded against the abuse of influence by suitors from the royal household and by councillors themselves. But the overriding concern that the commons evinced in 1406 was about the council's supervision of government finance. It was to review all grants made by the crown, to set aside revenues for the expenses of the household, and generally to check the expenditure of the king's money.

This was, in the eyes of the commons, the chief business of government, and to them good government meant government that was cheap to the subject.

It is interesting to compare what the commons wanted of the council in the Lancastrian period with Fortescue's ideal, set out in his *Governance of England*. Fortescue proposed that the council should be composed of four bishops and four peers, and twenty-four others, 'twelve spiritual men and twelve temporal men of the wisest and best disposed men that can be found in all the parts of this land'.[29] The numerical balance of this council is a little different from what usually satisfied the commons, but the basic assumption about its composition is the same, that it should represent the interests of the realm at large. All councillors should take an oath, and the twenty-four lesser councillors should be salaried. A book of regulations should be compiled, laying down hours of business and rules of procedure. The kind of affairs that Fortescue pictured his council weighing most carefully were 'how the going out of the money may be restrained, how bullion may be brought into the land, how also plate, jewels and money late borne out may be gotten again . . . and also how the prices of merchandise grown in this land may be upheld and increased, and the prices of merchandise brought into this land abated'.[30] Above all, he wanted to see very strict regulations to limit grants made out of the crown's revenues and lands, over which even the council's control needed to be limited by parliament, in order to reduce the need for taxation. This seemed to him to be the straight road to securing the prosperity not just of the king, but of the whole realm: 'for every man of the land shall by this foundation be the merrier, the surer, fare the better in his body and all his goods . . . this [land] shall be a college [i.e. a *real* community] in which shall sing and pray for evermore all the men of England, spiritual and temporal'.[31]

Fortescue's essay on governance thus concludes with a fine flourish of national spirit. The common national interest which he extolled was what bound together the commons of England in and out of parliament, and was at the root of their political involvement. Because it is still from time to time claimed that the growth of English national self-consciousness was a feature of the Tudor rather than the late medieval period, we may close this chapter with two quotations that illustrate the pride of fifteenth-century Englishmen in their country as a national community. One comes from the speech of the English representatives at the Council of Constance in 1417, protesting against the French claim that England should not rank in the council as a nation: 'As regards all the requirements for being a nation . . . whether a nation be understood as a race, relationship, and habit of unity separate from others, or as a difference of language which by divine and human law is the greatest and most authentic mark of a nation and the essence of it . . . in all these respects the renowned nation of England or Britain is one of the four or five nations that compose the papal obedience.'[32] The other comes from a sermon, preached by an anonymous clerk in the reign of Henry V, who was rejoicing that the new king had restored to the land the prosperity and honour that she seemed, before his day, to be in danger of losing:

> A great ship which sailed for many a day in the sea of prosperity is that plenteous realm, the realm of England. The forecastle of this ship is the clergy, prelates, religious, and priests; the hindcastle is the barony, the king with his nobles; the body of the ship is the commons, merchants, craftsmen and labourers . . . when our ship was full tackled, the three castles full apparelled with streamers and shields, it was a fair vessel to look upon, it was a fair ship! . . . The swift gallies of Spain, if they had sighted it upon the sea, would have wanted to take flight . . . the brave towered (vessels) of Scotland, as far as they might see her upon the sea, would have wanted to strike sail and honour her. The whole of Christendom feared and honoured the English for their bravery, their good realm, and the good life they led.[33]

This is the sort of way in which the men of fifteenth-century England were accustomed to thinking of their homeland. The sixteenth century may have celebrated English nationality with more eloquence, but not with any sharper sense of England's separate identity, or any clearer sense of the priority of the national interest over issues of local and political affinity.

Notes

1 *Merry Wives of Windsor*, Act I, Scene I.
2 *R.P.* vol. III, pp. 57–8.
3 H. L. Gray, 'Incomes from land in 1436' *E.H.R.*, vol. 49 (1934), pp. 607–39.
4 See N. Denholm Young, *History and Heraldry* (Oxford, 1965), p. 19.
5 N. Denholm Young, *The Country Gentry in the Fourteenth Century* (Oxford, 1969), pp. 1–8.
6 See J. Cornwall, 'The early Tudor gentry', *Econ.H.R.* 2nd ser., vol. 17 (1964–5), pp. 456–75.
7 J. Fortescue, *De Laudibus Legum Anglie*, ed. S. B. Chrimes (Cambridge, 1942), p. 69. I have retained the English of the older translation of F. Gregor (London, 1775), less accurate but to my mind more vivid.
8 J. Fortescue, *De Laudibus Legum Anglie*, p. 118.
9 *The Boke of Noblesse*, ed. J. G. Nichols (Roxburghe Club, 1860), pp. 76–8.
10 *P.L.* No. 355; see also No. 364.
11 See e.g. J. Kail (ed.), *Twenty six political and other poems* (E.E.T.S., original series, vol. 124, 1904); T. Wright (ed.), *Political Poems and Songs* (R.S., 1872).
12 *Piers Plowman*, B Text, Prologue, ll. 146–209.
13 *Mum and the Sothsegger*, ed. M. Day and R. Steel (E.E.T.S., 1936), ll. 1120–1.
14 Printed by J. P. Gilson in *E.H.R.*, vol. 26 (1911), pp. 513–25.
15 *R.P.* vol. V, p. 290.
16 *R.P.* vol. III, p. 611.
17 *Registrum J. de Whethamstede* (R.S.) vol. I, p. 136.
18 S. B. Chrimes, *English Constitutional Ideas in the Fifteenth Century* (Cambridge, 1936), p. 174.
19 J. S. Roskell, *The Commons and their Speakers in English Parliaments, 1376–1523* (Manchester, 1965), pp. 51–3, 63–4. The classic example of a contested election

to the speakership was 1420, when Roger Hunt was elected by a majority of four votes.

20 See Chapter 13, p. 253 above.
21 *R.P.* vol. III, p. 601.
22 S. Payling, 'The widening franchise', in D. Williams (ed.) *England in the Fifteenth Century* (Woodbridge, 1987), pp. 167–86.
23 *P.L.* Nos. 119, 701.
24 *P.L.* Nos. 249, 250.
25 W. Stubbs, *Constitutional History of England* vol. III, p. 262.
26 *P.P.C.* vol. III, p. 232.
27 Fortescue, *The Governance of England*, p. 147.
28 See Chapters 18 and 19, below.
29 Fortescue, *The Governance of England*, p. 146.
30 ibid. p. 148.
31 ibid. p. 153.
32 See Fillastres's diary of the Council of Constance, translated in L. R. Loomis, *The Council of Constance* (Columbia, 1961), p. 344.
33 G. R. Owst, *Literature and Pulpit in Medieval England* (Cambridge, 1933), pp. 72–3.

Note on secondary reading (post 1970)

In putting together the original version of this chapter, I drew heavily on older works which are cited in the main bibliography, Section 4a–c, by J.F. Baldwin, A.L. Brown, S.B. Chrimes, K.B. McFarlane, J.S. Roskell and R. Virgoe. Since then, a much closer attention has focused on the place of the gentry in political society: on this P.R. Coss, *The Origins of the Gentry* (Past and Present publications, London 2003, forthcoming) and the interpretive chapters of C. Carpenter, *Locality and Polity: a Study of the Warwickshire Gentry, 1401–1499* (Cambridge, 1992) are essential reading. Two papers that are of value in relation to popular involvement with politics are I. Harvey, 'Was there popular politics in fifteenth century England?' in *The McFarlane Legacy: Studies in Late Medieval Politics and Society* (Stroud, 1995), and C.D. Ross, 'Rumour, propaganda and public opinion in the Wars of the Roses', in R. Griffiths (ed.), *Patronage, the Crown and the Provinces* (Gloucester, 1981).

Literary treatments of politics and political ideas have been discussed in the chapter: here V.J. Scattergood, *Politics and Poetry in the Fifteenth Century* (London, 1971) is useful. On 'mirrors for princes' see J. Watts, *Henry VI and the Politics of Kingship* (Cambridge, 1996), chapter 2, and R. F. Green, *Poets and Princepleasers* (Toronto, 1980), chapter 5. There is a very substantial literature on Sir John Fortescue. Significant studies include A. Gross, *The Dissolution of Lancastrian Kingship* (Stamford, 1996); J.H. Burns, 'Fortescue and the political theory of *Dominum*', *Historical Journal*, vol. 28 (1985); P.E. Gill, 'Politics and propaganda in fifteenth century England: the polemical writings of Sir John Fortescue', *Speculum*, vol. 46 (1971): and J.L. Gillespie, 'Sir John Fortescue's concept of the royal will', *Nottingham Medieval Studies*, vol. 23 (1979).

Parliament and the council have been major themes of the chapter. On parliament, J.S. Roskell's introductory survey in vol. I of J.S. Roskell, L. Clark and

C. Rawcliffe (eds.) *The House of Commons, 1386–1421* (4 vols., Stroud, 1992) is essential reading: the volumes are invaluable, too, for their detailed biographies of M.P.s. The chapters by A.L. Brown (on 1377–1422) and A.R. Myers (on 1422–1509) in R.G. Davies and J.H. Denton (eds.), *The English Parliament in the Middle Ages* (Manchester, 1981) are very helpful. Important papers by H.G. Richardson and G.O. Sayles are brought together in their *The English Parliament in the Middle Ages* (London, 1981). On elections, valuable are P. Jalland, 'The influence of the aristocracy on shire elections in the north of England', *Speculum*, vol. 47 (1972); and on the same aspect with a wider compass, L. Clark, 'Magnates and their affinities in the parliaments of 1386–1421', in R. Britnell and A. Pollard (eds.), *The McFarlane Legacy* (Stroud, 1995); and on voting in shire elections, see S.J. Payling, 'The widening franchise: parliamentary elections in Lancastrian Nottinghamshire', in D. Williams (ed.), *England in the Fifteenth Century* (Woodbridge, 1987).

The best treatment of the council is now that given by J. Watts in his *Henry VI and the Politics of Kingship*, cited above; see also A.L. Brown in his *The Governance of Medieval England, 1272–1461* (London, 1989). The articles in the main bibliography, Section 4cii, by A.L. Brown, J.L. Kirby, J.R. Lander and R. Virgoe remain of value.

Section V

The rise and fall of the Lancastrian empire

15 The reign of Henry V

Henry V came to the throne determined, it would seem, that his reign should open a new chapter in the annals of his dynasty, and that the trouble of his father's time should be forgotten. One of his very first acts was to grant the Earl of March, the head of that house of Mortimer that had raised so much trouble for Henry IV, full livery of his lands. Just before Christmas in 1413 Richard II's body was brought by his order from Langley, where it had lain since death, and was buried with pomp at Westminster. The families that had suffered in the revolts against his father were progressively restored; in 1414 negotiations were opened that led to the restoration of Hotspur's son, the Percy heir, in 1416; Thomas Holland was restored in name and blood as the heir of his father John, who had been lynched at Pleshy in 1399; the process recorded on the 1399 parliament roll against the Duke of York (then Aumale) was quashed. The new king's intention to reconsolidate aristocratic loyalty around the throne and to have done with old feuds was patent.

The early years of the reign saw some significant creations of peerages with these same ends in view. York's youngest brother Richard was made Earl of Cambridge. Henry's own brother John was made Duke of Bedford, and Humphrey, the youngest son of Henry IV, was made Duke of Gloucester and Earl of Pembroke (Thomas, older than both of these, was already Duke of Clarence). In 1416 there was another important promotion when Thomas Beaufort, Earl of Dorset, was created Duke of Exeter. Later in the reign there were not many new English creations. This was no doubt wise, for the grants of land that usually went with such promotions had in the past been a sore point between kings and those who wished to see them husbanding their resources. Besides, by that time many English lords were winning new titles and lands on French soil. Henry's policy towards the aristocracy paid the intended dividend. There were, it is true, occasions early in the reign when revolt threatened. But John Oldcastle, Lord Cobham, was the only peer involved in the abortive Lollard rising of 1414. The Cambridge plot of 1415, which aimed to put the Earl of March on the throne, had wider potential ramifications among the peerage, but Henry chose wisely to proceed only against the principals, Cambridge, Lord Scrope of Masham, and Sir Thomas Grey. The affair had no sequel, and during the rest of the reign there was never a threat of aristocratic revolt.[1]

There was no important difference between the reigns of Henry IV and Henry V in the methods by which England was governed. The commons under Henry V played the same role in parliaments as they had in the past, without winning any new rights or privileges. The councils of the two kings tackled the same sort of tasks with the same sort of membership, except that, when Henry V was out of the realm along with many of his lay peers, the three officers of state had to transact most of the routine business on their own. Ecclesiastics were rather more prominent, perhaps, in Henry V's councils. Particularly influential were Henry Chichele, a trained lawyer and an experienced diplomat, who as Henry's personal choice succeeded Archbishop Arundel at Canterbury; Thomas Langley, Bishop of Durham, who had been chancellor to Henry IV and was chancellor again from 1418; Philip Morgan, doctor of laws and king's clerk, who rose to be chancellor of Normandy and Bishop of Worcester. Most important of all – until he began to entertain ambitions outside England in the European church – was Henry Beaufort of Winchester, Henry's uncle, his first chancellor, and the most generous source of loans to the crown through the reign. The Lancastrian knights, who had been so prominent under Henry IV, played an equally significant role under Henry V. Thomas Chaucer, John Tiptoft and Walter Hungerford all had long experience from the time of the father, and were the intimate, honoured and trusted servants of the son. His service, however, took most of his knights further afield, for longer periods, than that of Henry IV had ever done.

For it was in the field of foreign relations that the decisive change in the tempo and direction of English political history that came with the accession of Henry V was really apparent. The focus of concern shifted away early from the problem of domestic unrest to the chances of the Anglo-French war, in much the same way as it had in the fourteenth century after the accession of Edward III. The difference was that in this case the change was more abrupt, and that Henry achieved more than Edward III did, in a shorter time.

The accession of Henry V marked a clean break with the past in Anglo-French relations. The situation created by the civil war in France and the opportunities that it offered for the English were little different, it is true, from what they had been in 1411 and 1412, but the approach to them was new. English diplomatic thinking at the end of Henry IV's reign was dominated by the question of Gascony, as it had been ever since the 1370s, and by the hope of reestablishing something like the terms of the 'great peace' of Brétigny. Alliance with either of the French parties, Armagnacs or Burgundians, seemed to offer a prospect of achieving just this: the question was, with whom should the English ally? As Prince of Wales, Henry had favoured alliance with Burgundy; Arundel and Clarence preferred to treat with the Armagnacs. Henry V's initiative as king was much bolder. His diplomatic strategy was to negotiate with both sides simultaneously, an exercise that he developed in the course of the reign into a fine art. The object was to force them to raise their bids for English support (or neutrality); and besides, the negotiations helped to keep the two parties separate, so furnishing Henry with opportunities to improve his situation further by well-timed military interventions. In these circumstances, while keeping his claim to the crown of France always prominent in diplomatic exchanges, he was able to greatly extend the active discussion of those English territorial claims in France that were separable from that claim, to Gascony as a duchy, to Normandy, and to the one time empire of the Angevins.

Because the struggle between the French parties was the key to Henry's diplomatic and military strategy, it is necessary, if one is to understand English policy, to keep a constant eye on internal developments in France. When Henry came to the throne, Armagnacs and Burgundians were nominally reconciled, following the pacification of Auxerre, which had dashed the high hopes of the English for Clarence's expedition and the Anglo-Armagnac alliance of 1412. In 1413 disturbances in Paris, originally fomented by the supporters of John the Fearless, gave his rivals the chance to stage a *coup* against him. In August Duke John left Paris precipitately for his own dominions. With the return of the partisan Armagnac leaders to the capital the civil war was resumed, and the summer of 1414 saw hard campaigning in Picardy and on the border of Flanders. This campaign was ended by a new peace, agreed at Arras on 4 August. Duke John was not, however, readmitted to Paris, and so remained excluded from all direct influence on royal government.

These events in France dictated the pattern of English negotiations in the early years of Henry V. As was to be his wont, Henry talked with both sides simultaneously. On paper, it looked as if Burgundy had most to gain by alliance with the English, and some very interesting ideas were mooted with the duke's representatives during the parliament held at Leicester in the summer of 1414. The plans discussed included an offensive alliance, in which each party should share the conquests in proportion to their military contribution, and which would be cemented by a marriage between Henry and a daughter of the duke (this in spite of the fact that Henry had, in the previous January, promised representatives of the French court at Paris that he would not, for a year, consider marriage to anyone but Catherine, the daughter of Charles VI of France). The English thought at this stage that John would go further, and could even be persuaded to renounce his homage to Charles VI, but the peace of Arras was patched up between him and his French rivals before anything came of their suggestions along these lines. At Arras John promised that he would make no alliances with the English, but in fact he remained in close contact with Henry. There was so much duplicity on both sides that it is not easy to be dogmatic about the significance of their exchanges. John's hope was, probably, that he could get Henry to do some of his work for him without his having to commit himself irreparably to the English. Henry's calculation, that John at the least would not intervene if he made war on the other party, was in the event to prove surer.

The negotiations between the English and the Paris government of the princes and the Armagnacs are easier to interpret. In January 1414 a truce was agreed between them for a year, and the English appeared genuinely interested in the proposal for a marriage between Henry and Catherine of France. The Armagnacs were really anxious for a settlement with Henry; the question that had to be thrashed out during the year's truce was the price that they would have to pay for it. This was discussed at length in the summer of 1414 and in Paris in the early days of 1415, in formal negotiations. The French showed themselves prepared to offer something like the Brétigny terms with regard to Gascony, and under pressure were ready to enlarge their offers of territory in the south-west; they were also ready to offer a dowry for Catherine of 600,000 crowns (raised, under pressure, to 800,000). These were generous proposals, in any light except that of the English demands. Henry's envoys wanted a dowry of a million crowns. On the question of territory, they insisted that their king would not waive his right to the crown of France for less than the restoration, in full sovereignty, not just of Gascony but of the whole of the old Norman-Angevin empire: Maine, Anjou, Touraine, Normandy, with feudal superiority over Brittany and Flanders. This was much more than the French could contemplate ceding. In the spring of 1415 the English allowed an impression to be given that there might be concessions on their side after they had consulted with their king, and for this reason the truce, which ran out in February, was extended. This gave time for a last minute round of negotiations in July at Winchester, where the Agincourt host was assembling. The exchanges there were heated, and nothing was offered that the French envoys could accept as a basis for negotiations. When Archbishop Boisratier of Rheims and his colleagues returned to Paris an English invasion of France was clearly imminent.

It seems highly unlikely that the English meant these long negotiations to be anything but abortive. The Armagnac leaders had shown in 1412 that they were willing to offer what then seemed generous terms, and nothing had happened since to make the English think that they would concede as much more in the way of territory as was demanded in 1414 and 1415. The English were simply endeavouring, it would rather seem, to keep talks going until Henry was ready for powerful military intervention. Preparations for this began early. In the autumn parliament of 1414 the commons voted a double subsidy. By the beginning of the next year, 1415, the king was borrowing heavily on the expectation of what this grant would raise, pledging crown jewels and other valuables as security for repayment. At a great council at Westminster in April a large number of peers promised to serve at the king's wages with substantial contingents. Orders were given to impound ships, and envoys were despatched to the Low Countries to hire additional marine transport. The king was bent on raising a force of at least 10,000 men, and was putting himself heavily in debt to do so. Henry was not in earnest in his professed desire for a peaceful settlement; what he wanted was time to complete his preparations for massive military intervention.

Sedulous propaganda, both at home and abroad, paved the way for Henry's venture. There was much careful scrutiny of ancient records to establish to public satisfaction the legal basis of the English claims both to the crown of France and to a wide inheritance of territory there quite apart from that claim.

At Winchester in July 1415 Henry, in the presence of the assembled English nobility, treated Archbishop Boisratier to a learned (but partisan) disquisition on these claims, and on the duplicity of the French who had tried at every turn to dodge the issues. While he was on his way to Southampton, so the author of the *Gesta Henrici Quinti* tells us, 'he caused to be transcribed all the pacts and conventions made in the past between the serene prince his father, Henry IV, and certain of the greater princes of France, over divine right and the conquest of Aquitaine . . . and he sent off these transcripts to the General Council, and to Sigismund the Emperor, and to other catholic princes, that all the world might know what wrongs the duplicity of the French had inflicted on him'.[2] This labouring of the justice of the English claims in France, based in a precise antiquarian legalism, was to be a recurrent theme throughout Henry's reign, both in English diplomacy and in royal appeals for support from the community for the king's war.

Henry sailed with his army from Southampton on 11 August 1415. On 14 August he disembarked on the Norman coast, and settled down to the invest-ment of Harfleur. It took more than a month to reduce the town, which surren-dered on 22 September. Henry treated his new conquest in the same way that Edward III had treated Calais. The well born of the garrison were treated as prisoners of war, and the main body of the townsfolk were deported wholesale. A strong English garrison under the Earl of Dorset was then placed in the town, pending the arrival of colonists from England.

After the fall of Harfleur it was clear that the season was too late for any attempt to press on towards Paris or Bordeaux (as had probably been the original plan). The army was depleted by the necessity to garrison Harfleur, and had lost a good many effectives when dysentery broke out during the siege. A large French force was gathering at Rouen to oppose any further move. Many thought that enough had now been achieved, but Henry was determined to see something more of the country that he called his own. On 6 October he set out to march the 150 miles through upper Normandy from Harfleur to Calais, where his prisoners, released on parole, were bidden to meet him at Martinmas.

The sequel to his decision is too well known to need recounting in detail. At Blanchetaque the English found the crossing of the Somme barred by the French, and though they managed to ford the river much further south, at Béthencourt, the French meanwhile had got ahead of them, and blocked the way to Calais at Agincourt with a vastly superior force. If the French had followed the advice of their experienced commanders, Marshal Boucicaut and the Constable d'Albret, who did not wish to force an action, the English king might have been lost. But the marshal and the constable were overruled by younger men who were eager for glory, and the French forced on the engage-ment in which, with tremendous losses, their whole force was overthrown. The carnage was terrible, with great mounds of dead men piled on each other in front of the English position. The Constable of France, and the dukes of Bar,

Brabant and Alençon were among those killed. Among the prisoners who survived (a number were slaughtered when the rumour went round that a fresh French army was in the offing) were the dukes of Orleans and Bourbon, and the counts of Vendosme, Eu and Richemont (this last being the younger brother of the Duke of Brittany). The English losses were not heavy. The Duke of York and Michael de la Pole, Earl of Suffolk, were the only prominent men killed, among a total of perhaps 400 men.

Agincourt was fought on St Crispin's day, 25 October; the news of the victory reached London on 29 October. Six days later the parliament met at Westminster, and heard the chancellor, Bishop Beaufort, dilate on the trinity of divine judgements that now stood in the English favour in their king's quarrel with France – Sluys, Poitiers and Agincourt. The reaction of the commons is a telling tribute to the impression that the news made. They voted a new subsidy, and agreed to accelerate the collection of the second of the two subsidies granted a year before; and they granted the king a subsidy on wool for life. Such a life grant had been made before once only, to Richard II in 1398. Contemporaries regarded that grant as symptomatic of the helpless subservience of the Shrewsbury parliament. In Henry IV's reign the commons consistently refused to extend grants of a wool subsidy beyond the term of a few years. The grant of 1415 is therefore the clearest possible demonstration of the extent to which Henry V's great victory won him a new, full confidence from the people that he ruled.

After Agincourt, the question of the right of the Lancastrian dynasty to sit upon the English throne ceased to be an issue in English politics. The focus of interest henceforward, until 1420, was on the prospect of new offensives and further victories. The mood of the moment was well expressed by the chaplain who presented an address to the king just before the meeting of convocation, after his return to England in November 1415:

> The winter is gone, . . . flowers have appeared, the flowers of vigorous and warlike youth: and flourishing vines, whereby I understand that noble progeny of kings of England which formerly spread their branches throughout the world, have given forth odours of fame and worthiest probity. . . . And you, dread prince [he concluded], receive not the glory of God in vain, but in the prosecution of your right, casting away the lust of power, go forward manfully.[3]

This was what was now expected of Henry, to press forward until a just peace should be established, that would guarantee the ancient rights of the English royal house in France.

Henry V's victory at Agincourt placed him in a very favourable bargaining position with regard to the parties in France. The Duke of Orleans, the nominal leader of the Armagnacs, was his prisoner; so were the Duke of Bourbon and

Arthur de Richemont, the brother of the Duke of Brittany. John of Burgundy, who had taken no part in the Agincourt campaign, was still excluded from the government of Paris, and so Henry could entertain high hopes of making him a useful ally. He could also hope for generous offers from Paris to induce him not to ally with John.

These diplomatic advantages were complicated and to some extent compromised in 1416 by the intervention in Anglo-French politics of the Emperor Sigismund. Sigismund had been the prime mover in bringing together the general council of the church at Constance in order to end the Schism, and like many others at the council he believed that the duration of the Schism was being perpetuated by 'the discords among the kingdoms' of Europe. Late in 1415 he had succeeded at Narbonne in persuading the Iberian kingdoms to abandon Pope Benedict XIII and adhere to the council. From there he travelled to Paris, where he arrived in March 1416. The councillors of Charles VI, shaken by Agincourt and anxious about the possibility of an alliance between Henry of England and the Duke of Burgundy, were very ready to let him try his hand as a mediator between them and the English. Henry, as a Christian prince who had given his adherence to the council and who was represented there by a powerful English delegation, could hardly refuse to entertain the proposals of a mediator, whose prime avowed purpose was to restore unity to the church. On 1 May Sigismund landed at Dover, and was received with a lavishness of display fitting to his high position.

The visit of the emperor posed a problem for the king of England. Henry had already in 1415 drawn the attention of both Sigismund and the council to the English claims arising out of the Treaty of Brétigny, and to the recognition, by the Armagnac princes in the Treaty of Bourges of 1412, of the justice of the English claim to Gascony. After his victory at Agincourt, he was in a good position to insist that the Brétigny terms at least must be accepted as the minimum basis for a definitive settlement. As a mediator, Sigismund was likely to press him to waive higher claims. But Henry wanted more; and in order to get more without appearing to disadvantage at the international level he knew that he would have to proceed with great delicacy. No expense needed to be spared on the entertainment of his imperial guest. Hence the lavish ceremonial and heraldic welcome that was prepared for him; his admission to the order of the Garter at Windsor; the presentation to the emperor of the gold collar of SS, the Lancastrian emblem; his state visit to parliament, which had been kept in session specifically for the purpose.

During the first stage of the negotiations that were conducted under Sigismund's auspices, it began to be clear that the French would not raise their offers, nor the English lower their demands to a point which could be the foundation of an immediate peace. By mid June 1416 the hopes of Sigismund and the Count of Holland (who was the dauphin's father-in-law and also an imperial vassal and had been associated with the emperor as a mediator) had come to centre on proposals for a three year truce, and for a personal 'summit' meeting between Henry, Sigismund and Charles VI, probably on the Calais march. The French royal prisoners were enthusiastic for this scheme, and the envoys from Paris thought it should be acceptable; when they left England in late June it was to arrange a preliminary meeting to discuss the terms of the truce. They had been preceded to Paris by an embassy from Sigismund, commissioned to represent there the advantages of his plans. Unfortunately, the two embassies arrived to find the council in Paris divided. Though Anjou and a number of other leading men were in favour of the truce, there was also an influential 'war party', headed by Count Bernard of Armagnac. Recalled to Paris after Agincourt and granted the constable's sword, his first act had been to organize the investment of Harfleur. In March 1416 he had caught Dorset's garrison in the open on an extended sortie, near Valmont, and inflicted severe losses on them. He believed that the proposals for the truce were, on the English side, simply a device to save their new won town. In a crucial meeting on 15 July his views carried the day, and it was agreed to spin out dealings with the English until Harfleur should fall, with the prospect of being then able to negotiate from a new position of strength.[4]

Militarily, there was no doubt much to be said for Armagnac's views; diplomatically they were blundering. The count's martial policy was in itself a direct affront to the emperor's mediation, and the affront was aggravated by the undignified treatment and the evasive answers that the English envoys, who had been sent to discuss the details of the proposed truce, received from the French at Beauvais in July. At this point the pressure on Harfleur was being increased. Henry could thus point out to Sigismund direct evidence of the duplicity of the French, and of the insincerity of their professed desire for a peace. Sigismund took the point. In consequence Henry was able to change the whole tenor of Anglo-Imperial relations, which had commenced in an effort at mediation, and to turn them into the foundation of a series of important diplomatic victories for the English cause at the expense of Valois France.

The first open sign of the new direction that events were taking was the treaty which was agreed between Henry and Sigismund at Canterbury on 15 August 1416. This completely altered the position of the emperor. In the preamble to the formal terms he gave an account of the course of his mediation, retailing his efforts to achieve a reasonable settlement and the way in which the French king had spurned them and, by doing so, had proved himself to be a promoter of discord in Christendom. It was time for the pride of the French to be punished, the emperor declared. He and Henry, 'his brother', had therefore made a treaty of perpetual friendship, binding themselves and their heirs (note here the recognition of the dynastic legitimacy of the house of Lancaster) each to support the other in the prosecution of his just rights in France. Detailed clauses of the treaty provided for free commercial exchange between England and the Empire; that neither sovereign should harbour or assist the enemies of the other; and it was clearly understood that the emperor would be prepared to give Henry direct military support in France.[5] On the same day that the treaty was sealed, an English fleet under the Duke of Bedford defeated the Franco-Genoese squadron that was blockading Harfleur from the sea, and revictualled the town. By this time feelers had already been put out with a view to bringing into the Anglo-Imperial alliance a third party, none other than John the Fearless of Burgundy himself. Armagnac's policy had rebounded with a vengeance.

As early as July, the Earl of Warwick had met Duke John at Lille, and had conveyed to him an invitation to be present at the conference between the English, the French and the emperor that it was planned to hold at Calais in October. After the sealing of the Canterbury treaty, the possibility of bringing John to the conference assumed greater importance for the English than any putative negotiations that there might be with the Paris government. The new plan of Henry and his ally Sigismund was for a majestic alliance of England, Burgundy and the Empire, which would overthrow the Valois and reunite strife-riven France under Henry's kingship. Under the aegis of Henry and Sigismund the council would then be brought to a triumphant conclusion, the Schism healed and the church reformed. Perhaps then they would join in a crusade against the Turk. The hard material advantages of this scheme were to the benefit of the English specifically, and their enthusiasm for it is written clear in the tremendous efforts that they were prepared to make to get Duke John to Calais. Henry was ready to shoulder the whole cost of the meeting. A plethora of carefully worded instruments were drawn up to guarantee the duke safe conduct to Calais with a vast retinue, and Henry's own brother, Humphrey of Gloucester, was placed in Burgundian hands as a hostage for his security.

Henry and Sigismund were waiting for Duke John when he reached Calais on 4 October. An embassy from Paris had just left, having concluded a truce until the following February. The duke remained in Calais until the 13 October, engaged in a continuous round of ceremonial meetings and secret negotiations, and departed on apparently affable terms with the king of England and the emperor. What precisely passed between the parties is not easy to tell. It is known that John at Calais did homage to Sigismund for the counties of Burgundy and Alost, and so formally reinforced his relations with one member of the Anglo-Imperial alliance, but what he said to the other is unclear. 'It passed not beyond the royal breast or the silence of the council', says the author of the *Gesta*.[6]

A text that purports to be an agreement with Henry in Duke John's name does indeed survive, and a very remarkable text it is. The gist of it is that the duke has come now to accept the justice of Henry's claim to the throne of France; he promises that he will do Henry homage as king, not directly, however, but as soon as 'he shall have conquered a notable part of the kingdom'; and he assures Henry that if, in the meantime, he appears still to recognize Charles VI as his sovereign this is but 'dissimulation for the sake of a greater good'. There is too an explicit, if undated, promise to help Henry with men and arms. The trouble with this text, which in the past has often been accepted as the record of a formal agreement, is that no copy of it survives that is in John's hand or sealed with his seal (as it is supposed to be). It seems very unlikely indeed that John put his name to the terms of this 'infernal pact'.[7]

This does not mean that it is not a very significant document. Even if it is, as most scholars now accept, merely a draft of what the English hoped John would agree to, it still reveals what was under discussion at Calais. John, we should remember, had come to the town of his own free will to debate personally with two sworn enemies of his liege lord, the king of France. He compromised himself simply by going there; he did homage to Sigismund for his Imperial lands, and the fact that, two years later, the English still thought that he might decide in certain circumstances to do homage to Henry for his French fiefs[8] does not suggest that he excluded the possibility at all clearly. It seems safe to conclude, in short, that John said and did enough at Calais, without coming to any formal terms, to satisfy Henry that, unless the French political situation altered radically, he would not oppose an English invasion, and that he might support it. From the point of view of Henry's plans, that was what was crucial.

John of Burgundy was not the only French prince with whom Henry was in contact at this stage. John of Brittany, the other great duke of northern France, had long had close connexions with England (he was the son of the queen dowager, Joan of Penthièvre, by her first marriage). There is some evidence that he may have actually visited England in April 1417, though no chronicler says anything about the matter or what the purpose of a visit would have been (not that there can be much doubt about that). We are on surer ground about Henry's relations with the French princes who were his prisoners. For their prospects of freedom and future influence in France, the failure of Sigismund's mediation and the Anglo-Imperial alliance could bode no good; and Henry had hopes that he could gain much by playing on their anxieties. It was with the Duke of Bourbon that he had most success, as he confided in a letter written in January 1417 to John Tiptoft, his personal envoy to Sigismund, who after the Calais meeting had returned to Constance. Bourbon had agreed, the king wrote, that the English suggestions about what they would accept as the basis for peace terms were 'great and reasonable'; the duke had further agreed that if he were freed on parole to urge acceptance of these terms and the French refused them still, he would renounce his homage to Charles VI and acknowledge Henry as king of France. He had hinted that others among the prisoners might follow suit.[9] It was beginning to look as if the whole structure of loyalties on which the Valois monarchy depended might be pushed towards collapse.

Henry's letter to Tiptoft mentioned that Bourbon had insisted that he must be allowed to conceal his change of allegiance at least as long as he was on French soil (a condition parallel to that of the draft 'infernal pact' between Henry and John the Fearless). This remark shows that Henry understood that diplomacy alone could only undermine his rival's authority, not unseat him. The last words of his letter indicate how he intended to finish the job. 'But Tiptoft, . . . I will not leave my voyage for any treaty that they make.' The time was ripe for a second military intervention, with the prospect this time of support from the Empire and perhaps from Burgundy.

The last months of 1416 and the spring of 1417 witnessed, as had the spring of 1415, a great burst of administrative energy channelled into military prepara- tions. The autumn parliament of 1416 granted a double subsidy, but there was soon an urgent need for ready money, and the spring saw the government indulging in much short-term borrowing. Commissioners were sent into the counties to raise loans; and some very large sums were advanced by individuals, notably by Bishop Beaufort. Parliament, in June 1417, ratified the agreement by which the customs of Southampton were pledged to him as security for the repayment of a great loan of 14,000 marks. Certain features of the proposed expedition involved more careful advance planning and heavier expenditure than two years earlier. Henry's plans in 1417 were for the conquest of territory, and it was therefore desirable that his army should not have to live off the country. This meant making arrangements to supply the army from England. The force which was in fact brought together numbered about 10,000 men, and carried a powerful siege train, so this was no mean task. A large fleet had also to be assembled to transport the army across the Channel. Among the captains of the host were two dukes and eight earls; among the lay peers John of Bedford (who was named as lieutenant in the king's absence), the Duke of Exeter and the Earl of Westmorland were almost the only really prominent noblemen who remained at home.

Henry sailed from Southampton, and landed with his army at Touques, close to Harfleur in Normandy, on 1 August 1417. By the beginning of September the important town of Caen had been taken by assault, and Henry made it his headquarters for the time being. No field army appeared to oppose his siege, nor was there any attempt by the French to save Argentan, Verneuil or Alençon, which also fell during the autumn. Falaise was taken just before Christmas. After the fall of Alençon, which put the English in a position to threaten Maine, John of Brittany came to meet Henry at Caen, where in November he made a truce with him both for his own duchy and for the lands of his young son-in-law, Louis of Anjou. Henry was thus secure for the time being as far as the great French feudatories of the west were concerned, and could consolidate his hold on lower Normandy. In the spring of 1418 he was able to detach forces under Gloucester and Huntingdon to reduce the Cherbourg peninsula, and another task force under Warwick to besiege Domfront. Domfront fell early in July, Cherbourg not until September. By then Henry himself with the mainguard had pressed forward along the Caen–Paris route; they took Louviers on 20 June and Pont de L'Arche on 20 July, thus severing communica- tions between Paris and Rouen, the ancient, prosperous and populous capital of Normandy lower down the Seine.

The English, when they began to settle down to the siege of Rouen in August 1418, were in effective control of the whole of lower Normandy. This con- quest had taken them just a year, in the space of which the political situation in France had altered dramatically. Almost at the same moment that Henry landed at Touques in August 1417, John the Fearless led a host that he had been gathering at Arras out towards Paris. Early in September, when he had taken Beaumont and Pontoise, he could threaten the capital directly; this was why the Armagnac government was unable to attempt to relieve Caen or any of the other towns that the English besieged in the autumn of 1417. Up to this point, the Burgundian intervention lived up to all the hopes which, after the Calais meeting of 1416, the English must have entertained. But in November near Tours, Burgundy 'captured' Isabella the queen of France, who had been banished from court since the preceding April. From Chartres, she issued a manifesto declaring that she now took upon herself the regency on behalf of her husband Charles, and that she would support the Duke of Burgundy in his efforts to 'save' the country. At Troyes she and the duke began to organize a new 'national' government in opposition to that of Paris. The hopes of Burgundian sympathizers in the capital began to revive, and in May 1418 the gates were opened to the Burgundian captain, the Lord of l'Isle Adam. A number of leading Armagnacs were taken prisoner; most of them, including the count himself, were later lynched by the city mob.

John the Fearless thus recovered what he had always sought, control of the government of France and its capital. There was only one drawback to his victory and the queen's: Tanneguy du Chastel, the Breton who had been Provost of Paris for the Armagnacs, succeeded in getting the heir to the throne, the dauphin Charles, safely out of Paris. The Armagnacs had strong military forces in the Loire valley, and behind their protective screen they were soon busy organizing a new government of their own around the dauphin at Poitiers. The Duke of Brittany, in September 1418, made an effort to bring the parties together, but the dauphin and his councillors repudiated his so-called Treaty of St Maur-les-Fossés, because it gave them no share in the control of affairs in Paris. Henry V, therefore, as his army settled down to besiege Rouen, was in an excellent position to play his old game of keeping the French parties at logger-heads by negotiating with both simultaneously, pushing ahead meanwhile with his own military operations.

To do John of Burgundy justice, he did try to bring together an army to relieve Rouen. It encamped at Beauvais and supplemented its inadequate wages by living off the country. South and west of Paris the Armagnacs remained formidable, and the duke's stock, which had stood high in the summer, began to fall in the hungry capital city. He knew that his rivals were meantime discussing at Alençon projects for alliance with the English against him. In the circumstances he did not feel it safe to leave the Paris area, and Henry was able to press forward the siege of Rouen without hindrance.

Henry called Rouen 'the most notable place in France save Paris'.[10] The high walls were more than 5 miles in circumference, with a deep ditch before them; and there were more than sixty towers at intervals between the five great forts at the city gates. From these the garrison's artillery and engines kept the besiegers under fire. The English lay before the town from August until January, and there was some fierce fighting in the course of the numerous sorties. But what really won the city for the English was not deeds of arms, but the commanding diplomatic position that Henry had achieved with regard to the parties in France, coupled with the security of his financial position. Henry's army was paid regularly, firmly disciplined, and victualled by fleets which plied between England and Harfleur; one single shipment in September conveyed from London thirty butts of wine, 1000 pipes of ale and 2500 cups 'for your host to drink of'.[11] He was therefore able at the same time to maintain his siege, and to make sure that Burgundy was too concerned about the possibility of an Anglo-Armagnac alliance to attempt to relieve Rouen.

By the new year of 1419, famine had done Henry's work for him in the city. It had been crowded with refugees from the countryside when the siege commenced, and at Christmas a crowd of poor men, driven out of the city to save rations, were fed by the English. A week later negotiations for a surrender opened. It was finally agreed that, if no relief came by 19 January at noon, the English should take possession; all who would take the oath of allegiance to their king should remain in enjoyment of their property and privileges, but the citizens must pay an indemnity of 300,000 crowns, for having kept the king out of a city that was his own inheritance. On that date, with cries of 'Welcome, Rouen, our King's own right', the English entered.

After the fall of Rouen, resistance in Normandy crumbled. By the end of January Longueville, Arques, Nesles and Torcy were in English hands; Mantes capitulated on 5 February and Dieppe on 8 February. Virtually the whole of the ancient duchy was in English control by the spring.

In Normandy, as elsewhere later, Henry took practical steps to make his rule acceptable to his new subjects. From a very early stage of the conquest he showed himself anxious to guarantee the freedom and privileges of all who would take the oath of allegiance to him. This meant maintaining a very strict discipline in his host, to restrain soldiers who were avid for plunder and ransoms. As the conquest proceeded, the basic structure of provincial administration was taken over unaltered: the old *baillages*, the administrative districts, were maintained, and so was the sovereignty of the exchequer at Rouen, the highest judicial authority in the duchy. Certain measures seem to have been aimed to enhance Norman pride in provincial individuality, as the reassembling of the Norman estates (which had not met since the 1390s), and the revival of the ancient Plantagenet office of seneschal of the duchy. Some high offices were naturally granted to Englishmen: in 1419 the seneschal, the president of the exchequer, all the *baillis*, and of course the captains of castles were all English. The president of the provincial *chambre des comptes*, whose headquarters were at Caen, was however a Frenchman, Louis Burgeys, and so were nearly all the local *prévots*. Henry made no attempt to introduce Englishmen into high office in the church, moreover, and typically showed special anxiety that the pastoral clergy should not leave their posts and people – this in spite of the fact that the clergy generally were among those least willing to recognize the new regime.

There was, however, another side to Henry's Norman policy. As at Harfleur in 1415, at Caen and at Cherbourg steps were taken to encourage English settlement. To those Frenchmen who left the country, and to towns that did not open their gates to him, the king became progressively sterner. Louviers and Rouen both had to pay substantial indemnities for excluding him. After the fall of Rouen, there was a very considerable enfeoffment to Englishmen of lordships that had been deserted by their Norman seigneurs: in the first five months of 1419 something like 250 fiefs were granted to Englishmen. Some of the peers and captains in Henry's service received very large estates. Clarence was granted the three *vicomtés* of Auge, Orbec and Ponteaudemer; Salisbury became Count of Perche, and Exeter (who had come over in 1418) Count of Harcourt; Lord Roos became the lord of Braqueville and Sir Walter Hungerford the lord of Homet. But the great majority of those enfeoffed were lesser men, who were not captains even of small contingents. 'From this we may infer', Professor Newhall writes, 'a policy seeking to create in Normandy an English petty nobility which would be chiefly interested in the duchy.' The fiefs that Henry granted carried, of course, an obligation to help in the defence of the duchy, but they also promised their new owners a considerable potential of profit as landowners.

Here are the outlines of a remarkable attempt to provide a settlement of Norman affairs, which would preserve the duchy's ancient customs, its provincial identity, and its Frenchness, but would at the same time forge special ties with England, through a leavening of English settlers both in the commercial towns and among the landowning classes, and also in the higher ranks of the administration. Henry's policy guaranteed security and their traditional way of life to those Normans who would accept him, and also ensured a share in the benefits of the conquest to the Englishmen who carried it out. A constructive balance of firmness and conciliation was made the basis of an effort to engender, with the least possible friction, a new spirit and new conditions in the province. Henry did not quite succeed in achieving this ambitious object, it is true, but he laid strong foundations. Normandy remained in English hands for thirty years after the fall of Rouen.

After the fall of Rouen, the English were militarily in a position to threaten Paris directly. It therefore became clear that neither of the French parties could hope to master the other, without first reaching some sort of agreement with Henry. When the siege began, alliance with the dauphin had seemed to offer the most interesting possibilities, but the long exchanges between his representatives and the English at Alençon in November 1418 ended abortively, and in 1419 hopes refocused on an accommodation with Duke John of Burgundy. On 30 May he and Queen Isabella came to meet Henry face to face at Meulan, bringing with them the princess Catherine. Two days later Henry saw her for the first time, kissed her, and was instantly in love.[12]

These were very serious negotiations, and at their start there were men on both sides who thought that peace must come of them. The Meulan conference was also the last occasion on which Henry appeared to be willing to consider terms that fell short of promising him the crown of France. The English demands, given the military and diplomatic circumstances, were realistic: the hand of Catherine with a fitting dowry, together with the cession in full sovereignty of the duchy of Normandy and all the lands in the south-west that had been ceded by the Treaty of Brétigny. Yet the negotiations soon ran into difficulties, over the terms on which Henry would renounce his right to the French crown, and his right to the Angevin lands which he claimed separately therefrom. The real trouble seems to have been that Queen Isabella and John were afraid that, if they ceded so much to France's ancient adversary, their own followers would desert them. While the conferences with Henry continued, they therefore opened negotiations with the dauphinists on the side. On 3 July the French did not turn up for the talks that had been projected for that day with the English. On 11 July the queen and the duke were reconciled with the dauphin at Pouilly.

All that was arranged was a formal, personal reconciliation between the principals: detailed terms between the new allies had still to be arranged. This was why the English met with little resistance when they began to push toward Paris again, after the truce that had covered the conferences at Meulan ran out on 29 July. Negotiations were then going forward busily for a further meeting of the dauphin and the Duke of Burgundy. It took place at Montereau, on 10 September 1419. They met in an enclosure on the bridge over the Yonne. When the gates were closed on the duke's party, he was cut down by Charles's retainers. In consequence, as the prior of the Charterhouse at Dijon later put it, the English entered France 'through the hole in the Duke of Burgundy's skull'.

The prior spoke truly, for the murder left the French totally disorganized in face of the advancing English. There could now be no hope of reconciliation between the dauphin and the old Burgundian party, to whom fell as a dire debt of honour the task of avenging their dead leader. The Burgundians were, however, in confusion; John's heir, Philip, was in Flanders, without an army, out of contact with both the queen at Troyes and the Burgundian garrison in Paris. The dauphin, after the murder, had even less chance than before of re-entering Paris. There was only one man who could be master of the situation, and that was Henry of England.

Henry knew that he was in charge as soon as he heard the news. To the Count of St Pol, who was captain of Paris and knew that the alternative to a truce with the English would be siege and starvation, he made it clear that the French could not hope to resume talks where they had broken off at Meulan; he was fighting for the crown, not for 'the duchies', though he would be prepared to allow Charles VI, old and mad, to keep the throne while he lived. This was in

September; in the ensuing weeks he made it clear to Duke Philip, who was seeking time to gather an army and to concert a policy with his relatives and with the towns and nobility of northern France, that the Burgundians must accept his terms. Otherwise he would press on alone and seek alliance with the dauphin. By December the duke had come to the conclusion, in spite of serious misgivings, that he had no option but to meet Henry's demands, and to try to persuade the French court to follow suit. On Christmas Day, the English and the Burgundians became allies. At this stage, the queen at Troyes was still hoping to reconcile the court with the dauphin, but she had no forces and no money and in the new year she gave way. A proclamation in the name of Charles VI declared the dauphin guilty of treason for his part in the murder of Duke John, and Duke Philip was granted the powers that he needed to arrange things, on the king's behalf as well as his own, with Henry.

A formal draft of a treaty of peace between France and England was drawn up early in April; on 21 May it was ratified at Troyes in the presence of Henry V, Charles VI and Philip of Burgundy. Its terms were substantially those that Henry had stood out for when he allied with Philip in December. Henry was to marry Catherine; Charles VI would keep the throne for his lifetime but at his death it must pass to Henry, and to his heirs for ever. Between France and England there should be peace and perpetual alliance, but the two kingdoms would be kept entirely separate, to be ruled in accordance with their own ancient laws and customs. Henry promised that France should be ruled by Frenchmen, that her great lords and churches should be maintained in their estate, and likewise the *Parlement* and other offices. Normandy, it was stipulated, should remain under English government until Charles VI's death, when it should revert to the crown of France. The Duke of Burgundy gained by the treaty valuable territorial concessions, and Henry's promise of aid in avenging his father's murder. The treaty bound the parties to it to make war to reduce to the obedience of Charles VI (and so of Henry, who was to be regent for him) all those lands and towns held by the dauphin and his supporters. At the time this included Languedoc and most of the country south of the Loire, besides much of Champagne and a good many strong places both in Picardy and the Paris area itself.[13]

These military facts bring out one point which sharply differentiates the Treaty of Troyes from the other great settlement of the Hundred Years War, the Treaty of Brétigny of 1360. Its chief clauses enshrine a settlement about the succession to the throne of France and the government of that kingdom, and concern one nation only. The clauses about the dauphin, and the obligation to make war upon him and his followers, emphasize another respect in which the Troyes treaty differed from that of Brétigny; it was not in the same sense a treaty of peace. Other Frenchmen besides the dauphin were not parties to it. The position of such great feudatories as the Duke of Brittany and the Count of Foix was not clear: the decision, whether to take the oath to observe its terms, had to be left for them to sort out themselves. This meant that the success of the treaty, as a settlement, must depend in large part on the speed and effectiveness with which Henry and Duke Philip could deal with the dauphin Charles. The longer that fighting continued, the less likely such great men as Brittany and Foix would be to commit themselves to the Lancastrian succession. One of the great weaknesses of the treaty was that, while in name it established peace between England and France, in reality it only established peace between the English and a party in France.

The fact that the Treaty of Troyes established a formal peace between the kingdoms of France and England was in one way very important, however. The English commons, in the parliament of 1420, petitioned for confirmation that in the future the crowns of England and France should be kept strictly separate.[14] They attached importance to the terms of the treaty in this matter for good reasons. The clear separation of the kingdoms meant that, now that the two countries were at peace, the subjects of the king of England had no obligation, as such, to aid Henry in the war that he was waging as regent and heir of France. The custom, clearly recognized, that the king had a right to demand subsidies from his parliaments to support his wars did not bind his subjects to contribute to a war in which he was not engaged as king of England. The commons in fact only once more made a grant of subsidy in Henry V's reign, in the second parliament of 1421, and that grant was significantly, in name, for the defence of the realm. After his death, they did not make any grant for the war for six years. By 1420 England, it is clear, was beginning to feel the strain of the war. We are reminded how formidable the task was with which Henry saddled himself at Troyes, and how desirable it was that serious fighting be brought speedily to a successful close.

Henry himself understood the need for speedy and determined action. It is hard for the historian to regard the last two years of his reign as anything but an epilogue, but for him they were probably the most active years of all. He gave himself no respite. The Treaty of Troyes was finalized on 21 May; on 2 June Henry was married to Catherine in the cathedral there; two days later she was following her husband to the siege of Sens. By the end of the month that town and Montereau were both taken and Henry was pressing on to invest the formidable dauphinist stronghold at Melun. That siege occupied him until mid November. In December he was in Paris for the meeting of the Estates General which ratified the Treaty of Troyes. He was able to find time to supervise measures for raising new taxes and for strengthening the coinage before he left, a bare two days after Christmas, on what was to be his last visit to England, pausing on his way to be present at the meeting of the Norman estates at Rouen in January.

Henry landed at Dover on 1 February 1421, and gave himself no more rest in England than he had in France. On 23 February Catherine was crowned queen in Westminster Abbey. Immediately afterwards the royal couple set out on a lightning tour of the kingdom, which took them to Bristol, Shrewsbury, Coventry and Leicester before Easter; then on to Nottingham, York, Beverley,

Lincoln and Norwich. A tour of holy places, Walsingham called it, but there was sterner business to the fore all the way; wherever he went the king was busy pressing men to promise loans for the war, or service in arms. He did not want to mar the impression that he had made in his homeland by his triumphs by asking parliament for a subsidy, but he was determined to find men and money. He was back in London for the opening of parliament on 2 May. By June he had collected large sums (Beaufort, admittedly under pressure, lent no less than £17,666) and reinforcements for his host to the number of some 4000 soldiers. It was at their head that he landed at Calais on 11 June.

It was time for him to be back. On the Saturday before Easter, his brother the Duke of Clarence had been defeated and killed in a bloody engagement at Baugé in Maine by a combined force of Scots and Armagnacs. Militarily Baugé had no decisive consequence, for Salisbury with the main English field army eluded the victors' pursuit. Politically, however, it was a significant setback for the English. Within a few weeks the Duke of Brittany negotiated a formal truce with the dauphin, and there was a temporary panic in Paris when the news of Clarence's death came through. Henry's return steadied the situation, but the task ahead of him had become more formidable. The dauphin's forces fell back from Chartres, which they were besieging, at his approach, and the English followed them to the Loire; but there was no battle. With the coming of winter, Henry and his tired army settled down to invest Meaux on the Marne, the most formidable dauphinist stronghold now left in the country south of Paris. They were seven months at the siege, for the fortified market of Meaux did not surrender until 10 May 1422. By then dysentery had thinned their ranks terribly, and the king's own health was broken.

Meaux was the last of Henry's conquests. He started out in July for the siege of Cosne-sur-Loire, but he was so sick that he had to be carried in a litter. After a few days he could go no further, so they brought him back as far as Bois de Vincennes, and there, in the small hours of 31 August 1422, he died. So he was never king of France after all. Charles VI did not die until nearly two months later, on 21 October. It was not Henry V, but the infant son whom Catherine had borne him in England on 6 December 1421, who inherited the two crowns of France and England, and the war in France to which his father had pledged him.

Henry V's reign is the record of a tremendous English achievement. There can be no need to labour the victories in the field, which speak for themselves; but the work and the sacrifices, at home and in the background, that made victories possible do deserve particular emphasis. Before this reign, no English royal host had ever been kept in continuous service, in the pay of the crown, for anything like the period that the army of 1417 was. This army was, further, largely supplied from England, at least until 1420. To finance campaigning on such a grand scale and for so long was a major fiscal and administrative triumph. In order to meet Henry's needs taxation had to be heavier than it ever was before or afterwards. Yet Henry did not have to listen to plain speech from the commons about lack of governance or the mismanagement of royal expenditure, as his predecessor had so often been compelled to. There were of course complaints. Before Henry's return from France in 1421 the commons were becoming patently fretful about the inconveniences arising from his prolonged absence. On the whole, however, there seems to have been agreement that in spite of all the strains, the country was better governed than it had been, or would be, for many a long year.

More was needed to make Henry's campaigns financially feasible than the complaisance of the commons. His government also found it necessary to raise large sums by borrowing, to tide over delays while subsidies were still unpaid. The business of raising loans and seeing to their repayment, as well as the business of overseeing the collection of subsidies and of recording the indentures that the king sealed with his captains, fell on the council and the exchequer – the same exchequer whose processes have often been described as too slow and cumbersome to meet the needs of government in the fifteenth century. The council also had much to do with raising the reinforcements that were constantly needed for Henry's army. It could be just as strenuous to raise men as it always was to raise taxes. Both men and money were, however, consistently and successfully levied, and that without the load of crown debts getting out of hand. The whole achievement triumphantly demonstrated that the English administrative machine was up to any task that could be imposed on it.

What made the difference between the reign of Henry V and those of other medieval English kings before and after him was the directing mind of the ruler, and his personality. Henry possessed in a remarkable degree those qualities that contemporaries looked for in a monarch: piety, chivalrous courage and devotion to justice. His religious conviction was personal to a degree that reached beyond ordinary conventions. He was ready to try his own hand at wrestling with the unregenerate Lollards, Oldcastle and Badby. He directed himself the quest abroad for religious staff for his foundations for the Carthusians at Syon and the Bridgettines at Sheen. In 1421 he summoned the chapter of the English Benedictines to meet in his presence, so as personally to impress on them the need to put their houses in order. His courage and chivalry were the theme of many stories told of him, as of his sleeping in his armour on the night before Agincourt, and of his sparing the life of the seigneur de Barbasan, because they had fought hand to hand in a mine under the walls of Melun. Above all, men were impressed by the quality of his justice, stern and impartial. 'He was the prince of justice,' Chastellain wrote, 'he gave support to none out of favour, nor did he suffer wrong to go unpunished out of regard for affinity.'[15] This quality won him appreciation not only from English and Burgundian writers, but also from otherwise hostile dauphinists, like Perceval de Cagny and Juvenel des Ursins.

Henry displayed other, more individual qualities as a ruler besides these traditional ones. He gave himself so fully to the business of government and warfare, attentive to every detail, as to leave little time for relaxation; he may even have lost the taste for it. The records of his diplomacy are evidence not only of his skill and knowledge, but also of a ruthless and single minded determination to have what he was convinced was his own. His letters, many of them written in English (the preference for the native tongue was his own) give more personal glimpses of an imperious will: 'but Tiptoft, know that I will not leave my voyage for any treaty that they make'. With his reserve, his enormous ambition, and his conviction of his right to have things his own way, his is not a character that can command wide sympathy with the present generation. It is therefore the more important to remember how deeply he was admired, even venerated, by contemporaries who knew and served him. He was certainly the most successful king of England of the later Middle Ages, and probably the ablest.

The unity of purpose and the unprecedented effort that Henry was able to evoke in England make it possible to argue that, had he lived, he might have completed the conquest that he began. The tragedy was that no one else could, and yet that no one could afford, when he was gone, to retreat from the labour that he left unfinished. His victories convinced not only the king himself that God was on the side of his right, but also his subjects. No one could understand, when he died, that the will that had sustained success had died with him. Much later Lancastrian history is only explicable in terms of the bewilderment of people who felt sure that Henry's conquest could and ought to be maintained, but could see the edifice of his achievement crumbling before their eyes.

Notes

1 On the Cambridge plot, see Chapter 13, pp. 258–9.
2 *Gesta Henrici Quinti*, ed. B. Williams (English Historical Soc., 1850), p. 10.
3 *The Letters of Margaret of Anjou . . . and Others*, ed. C. Monro (Camden Soc., 1863), pp. 2–6.
4 See *Chronique du Religieux de St Denis*, ed. L. Bellaguet (Paris, 1852), vol. VI, pp. 24–6.
5 For text see *Foed.* vol. IX, pp. 377–81.
6 *Gesta Henrici Quinti*, p. 103.
7 For text see *Foed.* vol. IX, pp. 395–6.
8 *P.P.C.* vol. II, p. 354.
9 *Foed.* vol. IX, pp. 427–30.
10 J. Delpit, *Collection générale des documents français qui se trouvent en Angleterre* (Paris, 1847), p. 223.
11 ibid. p. 225.
12 This reaction appears to have been quite genuine: see J. Waurin, *Chronique* (R.S.) vol. II, p. 286.
13 For text see *Foed.* vol. IX, pp. 877–82 (preliminaries of April) and 895–904 (final treaty).
14 *R.P.* vol. IV, p. 127.
15 G. Chestellain, *Chronique*, ed. K. de Lettenhove (Brussels, 1863), vol. I, p. 334.

Note on secondary reading (post 1970)

The major biography by C.T. Allmand, *Henry V* (London, 1992) gives very full coverage. The essays in G.L. Harriss (ed.) *Henry V: the Practice of Kingship*

(Oxford, 1985) are especially useful on the domestic side (by Harriss on the king and the magnates and on financial policy, by J. Catto on the king's servants and on religion, by E. Powell on law and order). Harriss's biography of Henry's uncle, *Cardinal Beaufort* (Oxford, 1988) is also helpful (chapters 3–5), and so is T.B. Pugh, *Henry V and the Southampton Plot*. K.B. McFarlane offers a brilliant portrait of the king in Part One, chapter 7 of his *Lancastrian Kings and Lollard Knights* (Oxford, 1972).

On the military side, A. Curry, *The battle of Agincourt: sources and interpretations* (Woodbridge, 2000) is useful: the two older books, by E.F. Jacob, *Henry V and the Invasion of France*, and R.A. Newhall, *The Conquest of Normandy*, retain high value (see main bibliography, Section 3d). See also the essays by C. Allmand and by M. Keen in Harriss, *Henry V: the Practice of Kingship*, cited above. On law and order in England during the reign, see E. Powell, *Kingship, Law and Society: Criminal Justice in the Reign of Henry V* (Oxford, 1989).

16 Henry VI and France
1422–1453

Henry V's death left his successor with a very intractable problem in the relationship of the two Lancastrian kingdoms, of England and France. English interests and aspirations were at once tightly associated with his French conquests, and insufficiently so. Up to 1419 it had always seemed likely that Henry would be content with Normandy and with the re-establishment of the boundaries of 1360 in Gascony. Englishmen, who were well aware of the advantage of such conquests to their commerce, shipping and defence, were prepared to pay for them. The advantage to them of the conquest of the whole of France was not so obvious, and they were not keen to shoulder the fiscal burden that it might involve. But Henry, through the terms of the Troyes settlement of 1420, had (probably deliberately) made it difficult to separate the two objectives. The Treaty of Troyes accepted that Normandy was part of France and should revert to the French crown at Charles VI's death. This made it difficult to distinguish between limited English objectives in northern France and Henry's own objective of complete conquest.

Henry's success in the war up to the time he died had besides complicated matters, by introducing a new element into the material interests of the English overseas. A number of English lords and knights had been rewarded with conquered land, and now held extensive estates on both sides of the Channel. Englishmen had been settled deliberately in some Norman towns, as Cherbourg, Caen and Harfleur, and had acquired property in many others. Normandy and the conquered lands in France had become for them a country of opportunity, and, as the records show, considerable numbers crossed the sea in quest of fortune there, the soldiers apart. To consolidate the English element, which promised to constitute a nucleus of Lancastrian loyalism in Normandy at least, it was laid down that Englishmen must pass on their properties, if they disposed of them, to Englishmen. Thus an English 'presence' in France was created which was more than just military, the preservation of which had to rank as a national commitment. Yet Englishmen in England were no less anxious than they had been before to be relieved of war taxation. The commons in parliament had insisted that, as in the Troyes terms, the two kingdoms of England and France should remain clearly separated, so that there should be no doubt that the obligation to pay for the reduction of the dauphin's supporters should fall on the

French. When Henry V died and the will that had driven men forward was still, the English parliament ceased to contribute to the war. No subsidy was granted for nearly seven years.

Parliament only resumed its contribution to the war when the conquests of Henry V seemed to be threatened. The result was that in the interim, though the house of Lancaster retained its commitment to making its kingship a reality in all France, Bedford (Henry's brother who directed the government there) was unable to pursue more than limited military objectives. The Norman estates made generous grants towards the war, and he was able to keep the garrisons there and in conquered France up to strength, and by withdrawing men from them to put armies in the field. But he could not contemplate ambitious schemes for further conquests without straining his limited resources dangerously. He did not get adequate support from England until the moment of opportunity was passed.

The arrangements that were made for the government of the two Lancastrian kingdoms when Henry V and Charles VI were both dead aggravated the problem that the uncertainty of English war aims created. In France Bedford became regent. In England Humphrey of Gloucester, Henry V's younger surviving brother, was made protector and chairman of a regency council.[1] The only proviso in these arrangements which could help to coordinate policy in the two realms was the stipulation that Bedford, when in England, should take over as protector; but he could not do this without leaving his charge in France. There was thus no longer a single personal direction behind both governments, and the separation of the Lancastrian realms on which the Troyes terms had insisted was sharpened. It became possible, in these circumstances, for Henry VI's two governments to pursue policies that were not just separate but conflicting.

This in fact was to happen at an early stage, and with serious consequences. The trouble arose out of the continental ambitions of the protector of England, Humphrey of Gloucester. Henry V, in 1421, had given asylum to Jacqueline, countess in her own right of Hainault and Holland, who was estranged from her husband, John of Brabant. The couple were childless, and John's heir was Duke Philip of Burgundy, whose hope was to absorb the inheritance of both parties into his own dominions. Some time early in 1423, however, Gloucester, having obtained from the schismatic Pope Benedict XIII a dissolution of Jacqueline's former marriage, married her. The parliament of 1423 naturalized her as an Englishwoman, and in the next year he was able to set about raising money and an army in England to recover his wife's inheritance. Though the council, led by Bishop Beaufort as chancellor, was unsympathetic to the venture, it was not without support in influential quarters. The possibility of making conquests that would consolidate English influence in the Low Countries had long had a place in English military and diplomatic speculation, and there were significant interests and significant men who distrusted Burgundy, including, unfortunately, some very prominent English captains in France. Burgundy at once prepared to aid John of Brabant. Gloucester's campaign in

Hainault of 1424–5, luckily, proved something of a fiasco, and in the spring of 1425 he was back in England, leaving his wife and an English garrison behind in Mons. Bedford succeeded in smoothing over the anger of Duke Philip, for whom the quarrel with Gloucester had acquired an acutely personal edge, but not before Philip had begun to entertain overtures from the adversary of England, the dauphin Charles. Though he remained formally the ally of Lancaster, from this point forward he never lost contact with the other side. The Burgundian alliance, which had been the cornerstone of the settlement of 1420, was thus unduly strained very early in Henry VI's reign.

The dauphin, at the beginning of Bedford's regency, was not an adversary to be despised. He had settled his capital at Bourges, and his administrators, if lethargic, were highly competent. All south of the Loire, except Gascony, was his, and his financial resources were more ample than those of the regent. After the arrival of substantial forces from Scotland, under the command of the Earl of Buchan, he had a formidable field army at his disposal.

In spite of the dauphin's apparent strength and Bedford's difficulties, the English were remarkably successful in the field in the early years. In 1423 the Franco-Scottish forces took the offensive, in an attempt to cut across Burgundian held territory to join forces with the pockets of dauphinist resistance in Champagne. At Cravant the Earl of Salisbury, hurrying by Auxerre with an Anglo-Burgundian force, threw his men across the Yonne in sight of the enemy and defeated them. The next year saw an even more important victory. Bedford, having assembled a field army at Rouen, was preparing to invade Maine; at about the same time Buchan, whose army had been reinforced both from Scotland and with Italian mercenaries, began to advance from Le Mans. The two hosts met at Verneuil on the borders of Normandy, on 17 August. The battle was hard fought, but at the end of it the English had won a victory almost as decisive as Agincourt. The Scots, caught in a pincer between the corps of Bedford and Salisbury, were virtually eliminated. Buchan and his lieutenant Douglas were both killed; so were the counts of Aumale, Narbonne and Ventadour. The Duke of Alençon and Marshal Lafayette were taken prisoner. The dauphin's field army had been completely destroyed.

In the aftermath of Verneuil, Bedford was able to settle down to consolidate the English position north of the Loire. In 1425 Salisbury, after 'tidying up' in Champagne and capturing Rambouillet and Étampes, took command in the west and captured Le Mans; by the end of the year all Maine was in English hands. Sir Thomas Rampston was despatched to the Breton border, after the duke had in 1424 allied with the dauphin, and more than held his own there. Things looked bright for the English when in 1428 Salisbury, who had gone home to raise men, arrived in France with much needed troops. The plan at first agreed was to use these forces for the reduction of Angers, but the earl had more ambitious ideas. His objective was to seize a bridgehead on the Loire much nearer Bourges, at Orleans, preparatory to carrying the war into the heart of the dauphin's 'kingdom'.

It was with considerable reluctance that, after debate, Bedford agreed to acquiesce in Salisbury's strategy. Between 1422 and 1428 he had concentrated consistently on consolidating the English position north of the Loire, by steady reduction of land and strongholds. He followed here the example that Henry V had set in Normandy. This military strategy was combined with efforts to make the most of the diplomatic possibilities, by maintaining the Burgundian alliance and putting pressure on the French royal dukes who were prisoners in England, the Duke of Bourbon (who had agreed to take the oath to the Treaty of Troyes if released) and the Duke of Orleans (who by 1427 had begun to show signs that he might be induced to do so). An attack on Orleans, in the heart of its Duke's territories, would be bound to compromise this manoeuvring, something Bedford was naturally anxious to avoid. It was Salisbury's proposed strategy that carried the day, however, and one can see why it did. It was endorsed by Gloucester and by the Council in England. To many Englishmen and to others too, it looked as though a major military success offered, in 1428, the best chance for the English of a rapid conclusion to the fighting, in their favour; also, that they needed to make the running now, and themselves. It was becoming arguable that the Burgundian alliance was proving a good deal less reliable than Bedford hoped it to be; and there were other reasons too for concluding that time was not on the side of the English cause in France.

With every year that the dauphin retained control south of the Loire and outside Gascony those great French feudatories who were not prisoners of the English became more unwilling to commit themselves to one side or the other, and more anxious to keep the game in their own hands. Brittany hovered between Lancaster and Valois; in 1423 at Amiens he entered into a personal alliance with Burgundy and Bedford; in 1424, when Burgundy's relations with England were becoming strained as a result of Gloucester's activities, he allied with the dauphin; in 1427 he came back to the English side as a militarily non-effective ally. The Count of Foix was out for what he could get. Before Henry V died, he had virtually settled with England on terms which would give him the lieu-tenancy in Languedoc and the direction of the offensive against the dauphin in the south-west. When he learned that Henry was dead he held his hand, spinning out negotiations, and early in 1424 (before Verneuil) he allied with the dauphin on terms which gave him the lieutenancy but did not commit him to hazardous and expensive military operations. These two reactions, self-interested and noncommittal, were typical.

Still more important, delay in pressing forward the English advance laid bare the artificial nature of the Anglo-Burgundian alliance. Forced on Duke Philip in the intractable political circumstances of 1419 when the duty of avenging his father seemed paramount, it offered few enduring advantages to Burgundy. It did not give Philip the control in Paris that his father had so long sought, and his part in the war cost money which he could only raise with difficulty from his own dominions. It exposed them to much incidental devastation, while the strain of their defence interfered with his pursuit of more interesting ambitions in the imperial Low Countries and the Rhineland. Gloucester's ill-judged bid for the inheritance of Hainault and Holland hurt him here, and reminded him sharply that his family's natural and traditional connexions were with the French and the Rhenish nobility, not the English.

Yolande of Aragon, Dowager Countess of Anjou, the dauphin's mother-in-law and a dominant personality at the court of Bourges, was able to turn the strains which were becoming apparent in the Anglo-Burgundian alliance to Charles's advantage. In 1423 the alliance of Bedford, Burgundy and Brittany had been cemented by the marriages of Anne (a sister of Duke Philip) to Bedford, and of Margaret (another of Philip's sisters) to Arthur of Richemont, John of Brittany's brother, who had accepted the Treaty of Troyes. In 1424, when before Verneuil things looked difficult for the English, Yolande succeeded in winning the Duke of Brittany round to her side. Then after Verneuil, she persuaded Arthur of Richemont to desert the English too, and to accept the constable's sword of France, which Buchan had held. Burgundy, significantly, was agreeable to his taking the office. Henceforward one of the marriages that had been intended to forge a family league on the Lancastrian side was therefore a bond working the other way – through Margaret of Burgundy, Richemont's wife, Yolande could hope to put pressure on Duke Philip. Another marriage reinforced this connexion between the dauphin's court and Burgundy – that of Charles of Clermont, Bourbon's heir, to Philip's third sister Agnes. The first effect of this new series of alliances, coupled with Gloucester's intervention in Hainault, was that Philip of Burgundy in 1424 agreed to make a truce with the dauphin.

Thanks to Yolande's efforts, the dauphin's party at the end of 1424 looked ahead of the game in the complicated diplomatic manoeuvring among the great in France. Two things made it impossible for them to exploit their advantage further. One was the destruction of Buchan's field army at Verneuil. All that the dauphin could count on thereafter were the unreliable companies, commanded by old Armagnac freebooters, like La Hire and Poton de Xaintrailles; these were ill paid and conducted themselves not much better than brigands. They were no match for Bedford's English soldiers, regularly paid and mustered, well disciplined and accustomed to coordinated operations. The other difficulty that beset the dauphin's party was the atmosphere of intrigue and instability at the court of Bourges. Some of Charles's advisers were able men, but their greed outran their talents. With the rise to favour of the ex-Burgundian Georges de la Trémoille the old Armagnac counsellors, Louvet and Tanneguy du Chastel, were at last eclipsed; but confusion became worse than ever when a furious quarrel broke out between the new favourite and Richemont. The constable was driven from the court, and a private war broke out between his partisans and those of La Trémoille, with the dauphin taking the favourite's part. This internecine strife cost the dauphin all the advantage that Yolande's diplomacy had promised.

Thus, by 1428, the internal political situation in France had become very complicated. That, no doubt, is one of the reasons why Salisbury's advocacy of a major frontal assault on dauphinist power, directed at Orleans, carried the day. The English in 1428 still had the military initiative, and it is just possible that, if Salisbury had lived, he would have taken the city and carried the war successfully into the kingdom of Bourges. But a stray cannon ball carried away the victor of Cravant, and Suffolk who succeeded him in command at the siege was not taking any risks, seeing that the garrison was quite as large as his own force. The English were still before the city on 28 April 1429, when a relieving host appeared, with Joan of Arc at its head.

> At the which time, after the adventure fallen to the person of my cousin of Salisbury, whom God assoil, there fell, by the hand of God as it seemeth, a great stroke upon your people that was assembled there in great number, caused in great part as I trow of lack of sad belief and unfaithful doubt that they had of a disciple and limb of the fiend, called the Pucelle [i.e. the maid], that used false enchantments and sorcery: the which great stroke and discomfiture not only lessened in great part the number of your people there, but as well withdrew the courage of the remnant in marvellous wise, and couraged your adverse party and enemies to assemble them forthwith in great number.[2]

That is how Bedford later described the advent of Joan of Arc. He may have exaggerated the impact of her appearance on the English, but there is no doubt about its effect on the French. The peasant girl of Domrémy, who arrived at Chinon early in 1429 with the story of her 'voices' which had told her of her mission to deliver the dauphin and his kingdom from the English, had caught the imagination of the soldiers of France. She succeeded where no one else had since Verneuil, in welding the scattered forces that passed for the dauphin's army into an effective field force, and in firing the troops with confidence. At Orleans the English had for the first time to face an army that was superior to theirs not only in numbers, but in determination and morale as well.

Joan's army entered Orleans on 3 May 1429; by 8 May she had driven Suffolk from his lines before the city. On 12 June at Jargeau she defeated Suffolk's own corps, and took him prisoner. On 18 June her troops, now joined by Richemont with a Breton contingent, met Lord Talbot and Sir John Fastolf with the main-guard of the Orleans army at Patay and completely overwhelmed them. This left no substantial English force between her and Paris, and she might have pressed on to the capital. Bedford, regarding his forward position as untenable, withdrew into Normandy and made Rouen his headquarters.

But Joan's plan was different. Instead of advancing on Paris, her army swept north-east in a wide arc, and into Champagne. The towns on the route opened their gates to her with monotonous regularity. On 17 July, only a month after Patay, the dauphin was solemnly crowned, with Joan looking on, at Rheims, the ecclesiastical capital of France and the traditional place of coronation, by the Archbishop Regnault of Chartres. This was no empty ceremony. A crowned and anointed king's title was something very different from the claim of a dauphin. Moreover, though he did not come himself, the coronation was witnessed by representatives of the Duke of Burgundy. In a European context, the position of Charles VII had been immeasurably strengthened.

The remainder of the campaign of 1429 continued gloriously. Laon, Soissons, Senlis, Château Thierry and Compiègne all fell to the French. None of this achievement was followed up in 1430. The fighting in 1429 had emptied Charles's treasury, and La Trémoille, jealous of Joan's success, was determined to keep her as inactive as he could. Burgundy, with the generous addition of Champagne to his apanage, re-entered the war as an active party on the English side. It was in Champagne, at Compiègne, whither she had marched to raise the Burgundian siege, that Joan of Arc was taken prisoner by the troops of Jean de Luxembourg.

Joan was bought by the English for 10,000 crowns, and was tried for heresy at Rouen in 1431. For them, it appeared to be a political necessity to discredit her. There was not much savour of justice about the proceedings against her: conviction was what the presiding judge, Pierre Cauchon, Bishop of Beauvais, was aiming for. The reports of the case were doctored at his orders. L'Oiseleur, the priest who heard Joan's confessions, played the part of a stool pigeon. In the end, worn out by the hardship and loneliness of captivity, she gave way and abjured her 'voices' as lying impostures. Her sentence was imprisonment for life. Joan, before she 'confessed', had been led to suppose that she would be transferred to an ecclesiastical prison; when nothing was done to change her gaol she reassumed men's clothes (wearing male attire had been a principal charge against her) and withdrew her confession. As a relapsed heretic she was brought before her judges again and handed over by them to the secular arm. On 30 May 1431 she was burned as a witch and a heretic in the market place of Rouen.

By the time that Joan was burned her existence had ceased to matter in the world of high politics. No effort was made to save her by the court of Bourges, where La Trémoille was still supreme. Burgundy had got his hands full with a new concern, the struggle for the succession of Lorraine between his vassal Anthoine de Vaudemont and René of Anjou. To the English, in 1431, what mattered was not to ruin the maid but to undo the effect of her victories. Substantial forces were raised at home, and, at last, English money to pay them. There was hard fighting in 1431 and 1432, but not much to show for it, and in 1433 Bedford went home to raise more men and report on the ominous military situation. In 1434 the record was brighter, in spite of risings in Normandy against the English; Arundel restored some losses in Maine and Talbot campaigned successfully in the valley of the Oise. Given a little more time, the situation might have been restored to the *status quo ante* of 1428, but the English were not going to be given time.

In 1433 Richemont returned to Charles's court and at last toppled La Trémoille. With his return, there was a return to the diplomacy of Yolande's day, with its object of wooing Burgundy out of the English alliance. This diplomacy was furthered by the efforts of the papal mediators, who under the leadership of

Cardinal Nicholas Albergati were working to bring all the parties in the war to the conference table. It was their efforts and Richemont's that persuaded Philip of Burgundy at Nevers, early in 1435, to agree to the calling of a peace conference, and to agree also with Richemont that if peace could not be made and if he could do so without dishonour, he would leave the English alliance.

The great peace conference which was held in the abbey of St Waast at Arras in August and September 1435 was a turning point in the diplomatic history of the war. Cardinal Beaufort was the nominal leader of the Lancastrian embassy (for there were representatives of both Henry VI's kingdoms), but the real work was done by John Kemp, the Archbishop of York, and Pierre Cauchon. The leaders of the French embassy were the Archbishop of Rheims, the Duke of Bourbon, and the Constable Richemont. Burgundy was treated as an independent third party and his chief negotiator was his chancellor, Nicolas Rolin. The presidents of the congress were two cardinals, Albergati the papal legate, and Hugh de Lusignan, cardinal of Cyprus and legate of the Council of Basle. Since the English and French never met face to face but relayed their offers and counter offers for a settlement through the mediators, the cardinals were key figures. They were also key men because only the church, which had jurisdiction over oaths and perjury, could decide whether Philip of Burgundy was bound for all time to the English by the oath that he had undoubtedly taken in 1420 to uphold the Treaty of Troyes.

The exchanges between the English and French at Arras show clearly how the English commitment to the claim to the French throne, coupled with their inability to put into the field forces that could do more than hold their own against the French, had put the Lancastrians in a false position. The English would not recognize Charles's kingship; they would not even countenance a formal peace, insisting that nothing could be settled finally while their king was under age. They were prepared to offer a truce for twenty or even fifty years, and to go with it suggested a marriage alliance between Henry's line and Charles's; that the Duke of Orleans who had been a prisoner since Agincourt should be released; and that they would 'leave a part of the King's realm in France to his adversary'. Charles equally would not recognize his rival's kingship. He was prepared to offer him all Normandy, Guienne, and perhaps more land west of the Seine, but insisted that Henry must renounce his title of King of France, and must hold any lands ceded to him as a vassal of the French crown. The French were prepared, it is true, to let him postpone his homage until he came of age, or for seven years. This was as far as they would go, and Cardinal Albergati declared that it must be regarded as a sufficient offer. From the point of view of the English it was hard to agree with him. They still held Paris and land south of it, much more of France than the French were even offering them as an apanage. The military balance in the war was very undecided. Not surprisingly, the maximum French offer was rejected by the English envoys on the spot and by their government when it was later reported to them. The English therefore left Arras, *re infecta,* on 6 September.

Up to the last moment the English would not let themselves believe that Burgundy would desert them. But they were no sooner gone than he and the French began to move towards their *rapprochement*. Philip and Richemont were closeted together nightly; and the final ceremony took place in St Waast's abbey on 21 September. The cardinals absolved Philip from the oath that he had taken at Troyes on the ground that it was legally invalid, endangering his soul by committing him to war and bloodshed, and founded on an illegal transaction, since Charles VI had no power to alienate his succession. Philip in return for this absolution remitted his rancour against his father's murderers, and recognized Charles VII as his king. He thus extricated himself from the English alliance publicly, and with his honour intact, which was what he had intended all along to achieve through the conference.

Since Burgundy did not immediately commit himself to fight the English but only to make further efforts to bring them into a peace, the gain to the French from Arras, great as it was, fell short of being decisive. For the English the outcome was a major disaster. Without the Burgundian alliance, the Lancastrian dual monarchy ceased to be viable. There could no longer be any prospect of conquering new territories from Charles, and with Burgundy now a liegeman of the adversary, the line of communication to Paris was endangered. It could only be a matter of time now before they would have to retreat into Normandy. To fill the cup of England's sorrows, the Duke of Bedford died on 15 September 1435. His first wife Anne, Philip of Burgundy's sister, who in her lifetime had done much to keep the alliance with her brother in being, had predeceased him by two years. With him the English lost the only leader who, after Henry V's death, had succeeded in achieving a measure of true respect among the French of the conquered lands.

The English reactions to their declining fortunes in the war over the period 1429 to 1436 are very interesting. The need to redress the balance after the victories of Joan of Arc evoked a determined response. The niggardly finance of the preceding period was abandoned, and parliament voted a double subsidy in 1430, followed by single subsidies in 1432 and 1433 and by a subsidy coupled with an income tax in 1436. In 1430 Henry VI himself was taken to France with substantial reinforcements. Bedford raised more men and money when he came over to England in 1433. The English were in consequence of these efforts able to reconsolidate their military position and to restore the headquarters of their government to Paris after its temporary withdrawal to Rouen. But after this they could do no more than hold their own, and there was no question of further increasing the effort. Financial *insouciance* in the 1420s had allowed the government to accumulate a serious backlog of debt. The result was that what was achieved in 1430 and 1433 increased the backlog of bad debt, in spite of parliament's generosity. The difficulty of the situation was clearly revealed in 1434 when Gloucester declared that he would restore the situation in France, if he could be granted £48,000 to fit out a new army. In terms of military logistics, he was right about the scale of forces that he would need to regain the initiative, but as the treasurer made plain, it would not be possible, given the current load of debt, to make available half the sum.[3]

Another English reaction to the success of Joan of Arc was of a different order. 'If the king might with God's grace obtain his crown within the obeisance that he hath in his city of Paris, it were a great confirmation of obeisance of all his subjects there.'[4] So the English lords concluded after they had heard of Charles VII's coronation at Rheims. In 1430 Henry VI, a boy of eight, was taken over to France, and he was crowned the next year with due pomp in Paris. The decision to crown Henry in France was a very natural one, aimed to show his kingship as no less divinely sanctioned than his rival's. Nevertheless, it was not in all respects a very judicious step. A coronation at Paris inevitably lacked in French eyes the lustre of a ceremony at Rheims. Henry's coronation was not, in consequence, a full answer to that of Charles, but at the same time it committed him, and Englishmen, more seriously than before to sustaining his French kingship. An uncrowned Henry might, eight or ten or fifteen years after 1431, have been able to accept terms comparable to those that the uncrowned Edward III had accepted in 1360, when he promised to renounce the style of King of France. For a crowned and anointed king to abandon a God-given charge was much harder. The reaction of the Lancastrian government to mounting military problems was here incautious, committing the king more seriously than ever to a claim that was becoming all the time harder to uphold.

The reaction of the English to the Burgundian *volte face* of 1435 was in the same spirit as their coronation of Henry. In the heat of the moment, anger at betrayal drowned all thoughts of peace. Unless the king was to be asked to strip himself of the 'name, style, title and honour of King of France', the English must throw themselves into the war effort with renewed vigour, the chancellor told parliament;[5] and the commons responded with the grant not only of a subsidy, but also of a graduated tax on incomes from land and office. Envoys were despatched to the Empire, to Gueldres, Liège and Cologne, in the hope of forming an alliance against Burgundy. The mood of belligerence was well summed up by Sir John Fastolf, in a minute of advice to the king's council in France:

> Therefore it seemeth, under the noble correction aforesaid, that the king with all his might and power should sustain that right and title that he hath in France, of which he standeth this day possessed, not taking regard for the clamour of people, nor for wasting of the country, for better is a country wasted for a time than lost: and he should not depart from his right by any treaty and wilfully disinherit himself, his heirs and all his successors, but rather should abide the adventure that God should like to send him in the defence and pursuing of his right.

As to practical steps to achieve his end, Fastolf's recipe was a powerful raid, with a scorched earth policy of deliberate destruction, into Artois and Burgundy, which would frighten the duke and cost little, as the men would live off the land. 'And it may be thought', he concluded, 'that the king may and ought to make all this cruel war without incurring a charge of tyranny, seeing the terms he as a good prince has offered his adversary, the which are utterly refused.'[6]

Once again, as the threat of defeat became more apparent, the Lancastrian reaction was not strategic withdrawal, but to retrench the English commitment to the war. Their reaction to the Burgundian *volte face* was a deadlier struggle on more fronts. Betrayal only made them the more determined to go it alone.

There were of course those in England who saw the necessity of seeking some sort of compromise with the adversary. Parliament, in 1431, was agreeable to the opening of negotiations with Charles; and Hugh de Lannoy, a Burgundian ambassador to England, wrote in 1433 that 'from what we can perceive they know very well that the affairs of France cannot long continue in the state in which they are now'.[7] Lannoy visited the Duke of Orleans, who was much excited about the prospect of peace, and the Earl of Suffolk, Orleans's guardian. Suffolk may by then already have been converted to the idea of a settlement, as he certainly was in the years following Arras. Cardinal Beaufort, who after 1435 and into the 1440s remained a principal influence on English policy making, was of the same mind. It was natural that he should be alive to the advantages of peace, since as a prince of the church he was expected by the pope to employ his influence in the church's quest for an accommodation. With his long diplomatic experience and his Flemish contacts, Beaufort had also a clearer understanding than most English councillors of the vital role of the Burgundian alliance and the likely consequences of the end of it. He saw clearly the need to seek for terms that would preserve the honour of England and of Henry VI, before the English position weakened further.

Beaufort and Suffolk were both men with their own political followings, and their influence was destined, in the years following Arras, to become successively dominant in the councils of Henry VI. Unfortunately support for the approach that they favoured, founded in real diplomatic understanding and a sense of the limits of English resources, was not sufficiently widely shared. In the council they had to face the uncompromising opposition of Humphrey of Gloucester, the king's uncle, his heir apparent and the old enemy of Burgundy, who made himself the champion of war to the utterance. Gloucester was trusted and respected among the people to a greater degree than either Beaufort or Suffolk, both of whom spoiled their reputations by their too open quest for self-advancement. Gloucester, besides, was far from alone in his opposition to concessions to the French. As Fastolf's memorandum clearly witnesses, the English captains and men at arms in France were whole heartedly on the side of belligerence, and they were not men whose views were to be lightly disregarded.

Because the diplomatic realism of Beaufort and later of Suffolk had to contend both with the opposition of powerful critics in council and of popular nationalistic chauvinism, it proved of no advantage to England. In the years after Arras her war efforts and her diplomatic quests for settlement were bedevilled by divided and uncertain counsels. The bitter personal rivalry between the leaders of contending groups in the council, especially of Beaufort and Gloucester, introduced an element of unreason into their disagreements over policy. As the leading men of the realm became more concerned to worst one another than to save the fast deteriorating situation in France, the auguries looked always darker.

From 1435 onward, Charles VII was becoming steadily more formidable as an adversary, even though Burgundy did little to help the French war effort. He had put aside now the lethargy of the days of his sorry dauphinate. His ordinance of 1439, organizing a standing military force and the regular channelling of taxation to the war exchequer, put his army on a newly effective footing. Richemont's fidelity and Burgundy's refusal to risk a confrontation with his new liege lord led to the collapse of the aristocratic rebellion of 1440 known as the *Praguerie*. Militarily, the French kept the initiative in the war for most of the time. Early in 1436 Richemont's men retook Paris. In 1438 the French were able to resume the offensive in the south-west. In 1442 Charles himself appeared in Gascony at the head of an army and Bordeaux seemed directly threatened. It was only the hardness of the winter which put an end to the campaign and saved the English there.

In the north, which was the chief theatre of the war, the English nevertheless put up a startling resistance. In 1436, when Burgundy made his one effort on the French side by moving up a Flemish army to besiege Calais, Gloucester relieved the town and led a glorious raid unopposed into Artois. In the same year Talbot and Lord Scales routed La Hire at Ry; in 1437 the former took Pontoise from the French and threatened Paris; in 1440 he defeated Richemont at Avranches. But the most glorious moment of all was 1441, when York took command in Normandy for the second time since Arras. He and Talbot in a brilliant campaign crossed the Oise, broke up the French siege of Pontoise, and drove Charles and Richemont helter skelter before them in their anxiety to avoid a pitched battle. Had York had more men there is no knowing what he and Talbot would have done. But their army was not half the size of the French, and when their exhausted men got back to Rouen, there were no reserves to go to succour Pontoise, and the French came back and took it.

1441 showed what the English could still do; shortage of money was what held up the despatch of reinforcements which were necessary if they were to do more. In 1442 and early in 1443 the council was feverishly trying to raise it; both in Gascony and Normandy the need for troops was becoming desperate. But the crown's credit was no longer good; money was not readily forthcoming; and by March 1443 the logic of looming insolvency was all too clear: 'it is unfeasible to make two armies'.[8] With the aid of a very large loan from Beaufort there was just enough to put together a single expeditionary force. The cardinal's financial stake enabled him to dictate the choice of its commander; it was to be his nephew John Beaufort, recently promoted to be Duke of Somerset. John's younger brother, Edmund Beaufort, was titular Count of Maine for the English; this indicated a direction for Somerset's offensive, once he should have crossed the sea. Altogether, Beaufort family ambition was given a disproportionate place in the mounting and planning in this late attempt at a fresh, major English military initiative in France.

The fate of this expedition was the saddest fiasco for the English in this period of the war. The campaign strategy for it, which Garter King of Arms was sent to explain to York, was not unsound: Somerset should work on York's western flank, in Maine, and lure the French away from Normandy. With luck and good cooperation, the two commanders might, it was hoped, then be able to combine to force the enemy into a major field engagement in adverse circumstances.[9] There was, however, a sting in the tail of Garter's message: York had asked for £20,000 for arrears of pay, but he was told he must wait, since all that was available had gone to fit out Somerset's force. The cardinal's influence had secured for Somerset's expedition priority in the matter of pay, and also, no less importantly, a commission for its leader which made him independent of York, the king's lieutenant in Normandy. This might not have mattered if, once in France, he had been ready to coordinate his operations effectively with York, as a colleague. But after he had crossed to Cherbourg he never made contact with the Norman lieutenant. He conducted a plundering raid of his own into Brittany (nominally at truce with England), and engaged in some desultory fighting in Maine, which signally failed to draw out a French host to challenge him. His captains pressed him to reveal his plans, but he would not, he said, divulge his 'secret'.[10] It remained a secret when his force disbanded and he came back to England, where he died shortly afterwards. York in Normandy, meanwhile, managed to hold his own, more or less, but with no margin for counter attacks like that of 1441.

Negotiations with a view to a peace had been going on continuously from the moment that the English recovered from the initial shock of the Burgundian change of allegiance. The first notable effort in this direction was a second major conference, on the lines of Arras (though the manner of proceeding was different), held near Calais in the summer of 1439. The English by this time were much more ready to make substantial concessions than they had been in 1435. In the way of territory they would accept the lands which the English could claim separately from the crown of France – in effect, what they still held. Beaufort and Kemp, who led the English negotiators, were personally prepared, it seems, to concede Henry's title of King of France, but Gloucester's influence in the council prevented them from doing so. So they suggested that both Henry and Charles should be called king, referring to Carolingian precedent: 'so hath been seen before this time that such have been kings of France or part thereof, that have each called themselves Kings of France'.[11] The French were not interested. As at Arras, so at Calais they were not prepared for any settlement unless the king of England agreed to renounce his claim to their crown, and to hold what he should have in France as their king's liegeman.

After it had become clear that acceptable terms for a peace were not likely to be forthcoming, the Duchess of Burgundy who was representing the French as a mediator put forward a suggestion which, it seemed at first, might prove acceptable and which Beaufort was initially ready to consider. There should be a long truce, perhaps for thirty years; without prejudice Henry should cease to use the title of King of France, and Charles, without prejudice, should raise no claim to sovereignty in the lands that the English held. All those who had been put out of their property by one side or the other should be reinstated. The English studied this proposal carefully, and sent home for new powers, but in the end rejected it. They could not get round the question of face; even if Henry only dropped his title for the truce's duration 'it would discolour and put in great suspicion and doubt his title and claim . . . and all the wars and labour done in and for the said title'.[12] They were also worried about the practical implications of the restitution of French owners. It would mean putting out the king's loyal subjects, and this could not be considered unless compensation was paid, and the French king would have to pay this, or at the least the greater part of it. It was beginning to be clear that the English settlement in France was nearly as serious a stumbling block in the way of peace as the issue of sovereignty and the claim to the throne. It was not a matter which diplomatic equivocation could hope to get round.

The question of the release of the Duke of Orleans was much discussed at Calais. After the conference there had proved abortive, this seemed to Beaufort and the peace-makers on the English side to be the only further step open to them which might produce concrete results. In the council the suggestion that he should be freed was bitterly opposed by Gloucester; he refused point blank to be a party to it, and put out a broadsheet giving his reasons and denouncing the diplomatic conduct of Beaufort and Kemp in 1439. Nevertheless the arrangements went forward in the spring of 1440. It was made a formal condition of the duke's release that he was to devote all his influence to bring about a peace. Diplomatically, this promise was something of a forlorn hope. It was long odds against Orleans, after his long captivity a stranger to France and to French politics, persuading his countrymen to alter their adamant stance of 1435 and 1439. The duke, to do him justice, did his best to prosecute a pacification. He soon found his personal influence would not be enough, but he hoped he might prevail with the backing of other peers of France, and this drew him into the edge of a renewal of the *Praguerie* in 1442. Armagnac was toying with the same plan of rebellion, and Orleans suggested that the possibility of a marriage between Henry VI and one of the count's daughters might be explored. The proposal, which the English and Gloucester in particular were ready to take seriously, unhappily coincided with Charles's appearance in the south-west with an army in 1442 and the count, who knew how unwelcome the match would be to his king, was in no position to commit himself. Nothing definite had come of the English discussions with him, when in 1443 the French came up with an offer to re-open negotiations, and with a different suggestion for a bride for King Henry. The bridge suggested now was Margaret, the daughter of René Duke of Anjou, and Charles VII's niece by marriage.

The French, apparently, specifically expressed the hope that Suffolk would lead the negotiations on the English side. His influence in King Henry's court had been steadily growing for some time, and with the withdrawal of Beaufort from centre stage after the dismal failure of Somerset's campaign, he was now the dominant influence in the king's counsels. He was at first hesitant about leading an embassy, fearing, he hinted, that he might be charged with being a francophile, and with selling out English interests and honour to the French. As he must have seen, there were obvious difficulties about the Angevin marriage proposal. Margaret was not René's heiress, and it was unlikely that he could offer anything substantial in the way of dowry. His brother Charles was the titular French count of Maine, and alliance with his house would almost certainly lead to demands for concessions in that region (which Gloucester, and perhaps especially the Beauforts, were likely to oppose). Nevertheless, there looked to be some off-setting advantages. For a long time now the best hope of persuading Charles VII toward concessions over territory and sovereignty had looked to be through the influence of princes about his court with an interest in accommodation with the English. Alliance with René's house might do just that, and if he personally could be drawn into a long truce he would likely be keen not to expose his territories that marched with English occupied lower Normandy to renewed warfare. Besides, the English acutely needed a breathing space from military operations. After some persuasion, Suffolk accepted the leadership of the mission which negotiated what has come to be called the Truce of Tours.

What Suffolk accomplished at Tours fully justified his misgiving that men might 'sow rumour' on him for not being tough enough in his dealings with the French. Henry was affianced to Margaret, but on terms that were not satisfactory. The French remained adamant that the sovereignty over all the English possessions in France must be reserved to their king. This Suffolk could not possibly concede, and all that he gained with Margaret in May 1444 was a truce for two years, with the armies halted at the points that they had reached on the day that it was sealed. Two years of truce were not enough. Given the indebtedness of the English crown and the impoverishment of war-weary Normandy, such a brief interval could only work in the interests of Charles VII, to whom it offered a welcome opportunity to consolidate his domestic authority in France. Suffolk in fact had committed himself to a position in which he had no option but to try to make Henry's marriage the foundation for working toward a settlement in further negotiations, but in which it was not likely to be any easier than before to insist on honourable terms.

From 1444 until the end of the war, English policy abroad was inextricably entangled with domestic politics. This was because Suffolk's position at home depended upon the Truce of Tours opening a way to a lasting settlement with France. It was with such a settlement in view that an impressive French embassy, led by the Archbishop of Rheims and Louis de Bourbon, arrived in England in the summer of 1445. Their negotiations bore no fruit, however, because as in the previous year the French were not prepared to offer terms that the English could accept. The furthest that the negotiators got was a general agreement that it was desirable to arrange a meeting of the two kings, on French soil, in the next year. How this prospect was regarded at large in England was clearly seen when, with the meeting (which never took place) in view, Henry sought from the spring parliament of 1446 a release from the obligation which his father had entered into, not to make any terms with Charles without the assent of parliament. The release was granted, but the chancellor, on behalf of all the lords, made a formal declaration that they regarded the whole summit meeting plan as Henry's private affair: 'which said motions and stirrings, only our Lord has been pleased to arouse and instigate in you, as He knows; you have not been aroused or instigated by any of the lords or any other subjects of this your realm'.[13] The lords could hardly have made it plainer that they suspected that the meeting would be a prelude to concessions of which they did not approve and for which they would not be held responsible.

What the English lords did not know in the spring of 1446 was that Henry had already agreed to one very major concession to the French, the surrender of Maine. In 1445 the French had several times indicated that they would regard this as an excellent first step towards a settlement, and they must always have reckoned that once Henry was married to Margaret of Anjou, he could be persuaded to return Maine to her father, its ancestral count. Margaret, from the moment of her arrival, had been pressing Henry hard, and on 22 December 1445, in a personal letter to Charles VII which quoted no authority but his own, he undertook to deliver Maine and all the towns and castles there to Charles and René, 'in good faith and on our kingly word'.[14] It is impossible to be sure how far this letter reflects an essentially personal decision on the king's part. It seems, however, very difficult to believe that Suffolk, the 'priviest' of the king's advisers, did not at least know what was happening. It is understandable that he (and any others who were in the know) should have been anxious to be as little involved as might be. The matter was not made public, and presumably he and they acquiesced in the hope that the cession would help to set the proposed meeting of the two kings going in a cordial atmosphere.

The decision to cede Maine was not one that could be long kept secret. The bitter anger with which it was greeted when it became public, both in England and among the English in France, posed a problem for Henry's advisers. Suffolk was so alarmed by the 'slanders that were put on him in this regard' that he got the king to make a formal declaration in council exonerating him from any guilt (but not from any part) in the affair.[15] Though the truce was renewed, the meeting of the two kings was postponed and postponed again, while French pressure to proceed with the cession intensified. In Maine itself, the commissioners appointed to hand over the castles, Matthew Gough and Fulk Eyton, connived with the garrison commanders to postpone for as long as possible fulfilment of the king's promise. To old campaigners like these it was almost impossible to reconcile themselves to the loss, without a blow, of lands which English arms had conquered and defended. They stuck vainly out to the end in demanding compensation for the departing English, of which Henry's letter unhappily had made no mention. Le Mans was in fact only surrendered by them in March 1448, when Charles had made it clear that he would not renew the truce unless it was given up, and had moved up an army to besiege the town. The English who marched out mostly laid their humiliation at Suffolk's door.

At home, Suffolk felt it necessary to obtain other guarantees of his security besides the king's declaration in council. The man from whom he believed he had most to fear was Gloucester, the old apologist of vigorous war. The spring parliament of 1447 was summoned to Bury, safely remote from the capital where the duke had always been popular. Humphrey arrived late, on 18 February; he had just taken dinner in his lodgings when a deputation arrived, consisting of Buckingham, Dorset, Salisbury and Viscount Beaumont, who placed him under arrest. A charge of treason, of having planned a rising that would coincide with the parliament, had been prepared, but it was not needed. Within a week, Humphrey had died in confinement, probably of a heart attack brought on by the shock of arrest. Popular surmise naturally concluded that he had been murdered. There seems no reason to doubt that Suffolk was behind the move against Gloucester, prompted by fear of the advantage that the duke might take of dismay at the cession of Maine. At all events, it was he and his clique who were popularly blamed for Humphrey's death.

With Humphrey dead, the nearest male heir to Henry VI was the Duke of York, and here was another problem. York had clearly hoped that, in the wake of the Truce of Tours, he would be re-appointed lieutenant of Normandy for a further term. The cession of Maine had however meant that something needed to be done to secure the cooperation of Edmund Beaufort, its titular English count and the successor to his brother John as Duke of Somerset, and it was he, not York, who was appointed lieutenant in 1447. York probably interpreted a report, the previous year, that Adam Moleyns, keeper of the privy seal, was accusing him of embezzlement of soldiers' wages as intended to hinder his reappointment. Instead of going back to Normandy he found himself named as lieutenant of Ireland. He had great estates there and the office was a prestigious one, but not quite so prestigious as the Norman lieutenancy. He crossed to Ireland in 1449, to take up his new charge, but the manoeuvring which had brought it to him had probably not endeared him to Suffolk, and certainly not to Somerset. As heir presumptive to the throne, he was one who had the potential to be dangerous to both of them.

It might have been expected that Suffolk, in the delicate position in which he now found himself, would try to make the cession of Maine the stepping stone to a final peace with France. What he did was the complete opposite. It is not easy to understand why he embarked on the reckless course that he now chose. The most reasonable explanation seems to be that he was hoping to restore his reputation with those who thought that he, with Margaret of Anjou, had sold out England and Henry VI totally to the French. Perhaps he may also have hoped that the moves he was now contemplating would alarm Charles VII into a return to the negotiating table; if so, he was miscalculating, disastrously.

Brittany was the pivot of the plans now hatching in the mind of Henry VI's chief councillor. The duchy was one with which the English had traditionally friendly relations. Though Duke Francis was a French liegeman, his youngest brother Giles had been brought up at the English court and was the king's pensioner; he was also, in the right of his fiancée, Françoise de Dinan, heir to the richest inheritance in the duchy after the duke's. Unfortunately, he was on bad terms with both Charles VII and his brother, at whose orders he was arrested and imprisoned in 1446. His imprisonment was much resented among Englishmen, especially the captains in France, and Suffolk must have known that if he could obtain his release it might do much to restore his waning prestige. He may even have dreamt of substituting Giles for his brother on the ducal throne, and of so securing a *quid pro quo* for Maine in Brittany.

The trouble was that Giles was in prison, and that any attempt to rescue him must involve armed invasion of the dominions of a French liegeman, Duke Francis, which would endanger the truce with France. Nevertheless Suffolk was not deterred. When the English evacuated Maine, the troops from the garrison were redeployed in forts on the Breton border. When the truce was renewed in 1448, Suffolk took a daring step: in the text which was handed to the French, in other respects exactly similar to that of the previous truces, the Duke of Brittany was quietly listed among the allies of England, instead of France. The French failed to notice the alteration, verbally slight but diplomatically crucial. On paper this altered by a stroke of the pen the whole legal situation. With the duke listed as an English liegeman, Charles VII had no longer any right to intervene in his relations with Henry VI, which became a domestic issue between sovereign and subject. The English insisted on the point in negotiations later in 1448: 'in the said truces Brittany is included as being of the English obedience'.[15a] Finally, on 24 March 1449, François de Surienne, a famous *routier* in the English service and a knight of the Garter, was unleashed on the duchy and took the rich town of Fougères by escalade.

The immediate reaction of Duke Francis was to demand reparations – or the disavowal of de Surienne. When both demands were ignored, he appealed for aid to his liege lord, Charles VII. There seems no doubt that Suffolk and Somerset (Dorset had now been promoted Duke of Somerset) were involved up to the hilt in François's adventure, though this was never admitted; and they paid no more attention to Charles than they had to Francis, sticking doggedly to the line that Brittany was in the English obedience. In consequence, on 31 July, when three months of negotiations had got the Franco-Breton demands for indemnity nowhere, Charles VII declared himself formally discharged from the truce, and his forces began to enter Normandy.

Suffolk's diplomacy, wildly rash on the most charitable view, now rebounded with a vengeance on his country and himself. The English were quite unprepared for the French offensive. Somerset, the lieutenant in Normandy, was caught in a position in which, if he withdrew garrison troops to form a field army, he must lose more towns than he could afford to. The French were in superior numbers, operating on exterior lines, and were abundantly supplied with artillery; no town, once besieged, stood much chance of relief. First Evreux and Louviers, then Coutances and Alençon and Argentan all fell. By 16 October Charles and Dunois had appeared before Rouen, where Somerset had assembled a substantial army. He might have made a serious show of resistance if the inhabitants had not risen and opened the gates to the French. Somerset had to parley from the citadel, and agreed to withdraw his men to Caen, but Charles would only allow him to do so on condition that Arques and Caudebec were also surrendered, and that Talbot, Somerset's ablest commander, was handed over as a hostage for good faith.

The critical situation was well understood in England. What was needed was a 'great puissance'; 40,000 men would be enough, John Fastolf thought (his attitude had not changed much since 1435).[16] That 'puissance' ought to have been in Normandy six months earlier, however; and when an army was at last equipped, it was not of 40,000, but of some 3000, under Sir Thomas Kyriel. Kyriel landed at Cherbourg in March 1450, and after retaking Valognes began to march to join Somerset's mainguard at Caen. When he advanced there was only the inferior force of the Count of Clermont across his path, but he moved too slowly and was caught at Formigny between the corps of Clermont and the Constable de Richemont. His army was annihilated in the one pitched battle of the whole campaign, on 15 April – all save the troop of Matthew Gough, who cut his way out and got safely to Bayeux.

This was really the end. In June the French columns closed in on Somerset at Caen. After three weeks of bombardment he came to terms again; he would quit if he was not succoured by 1 July. There was not the slightest prospect of succour coming, and the condition only served to save face. The last town remaining to the English fell less than two months after Somerset had fulfilled these terms; on 19 August John Paston's agent wrote to him from London 'this morning it was told that Cherbourg is gone, and we have now not a foot of land in Normandy'.[17]

In the next year, 1451, it was Gascony's turn. There were virtually no English forces in the duchy. In England there were plans to make an army of the men who had come back with Somerset, but in the domestic crisis that followed the Norman collapse arrangements once again proceeded too slowly. Lord Rivers (who was to command) and his men were still in England when Bordeaux surrendered to the great French armies that were closing in upon the town.

In the south-west of France there was an epilogue. An English army did arrive, in 1452, in answer to the appeals of the Bordeaux townsmen and those Gascon leaders who did not much care for their new French lords. It was some 3000 strong and was led by Talbot. On 20 October he fell on Bordeaux; the inhabitants rose in support and it was quickly his. Libourne, Castillon, Cadillac and other towns followed suit, and early in 1453 Talbot was reinforced. Even so, he had not much more than 6000 men with which to face Charles's great army. Following the strategy that had won the day in 1450 and 1451 the French advanced in separate columns, and Talbot's only hope was to divide them and defeat them in detail. But he seems to have misunderstood the nature of Jean Bureau's position when he attacked him at Castillon; his army was destroyed and he himself left dead on the field. After Castillon, there were neither men nor a captain to oppose the French when they appeared a second time before Bordeaux. The great war of the French and the English had drawn at last to its close.

The impact of the final disaster that overtook the English cause in France between 1449 and 1453 needs to be stressed. It is often understated by British historians. Material interests as well as the royal and national reputation were at stake in the maintenance of the overseas possessions of the house of Lancaster. 'Control of Normandy', as Richmond writes, 'gave the coastal shires of England about thirty years of security: no one wanted a repetition of the enemy raids of the 1370s. It was a wise strategy that kept the war as deep into France as possible.'[18] Control of the sea, we should note also, was almost certainly one important factor in the development, on the very eve of the final collapse, of English designs on Brittany. One warmonger in 1449 was even talking of forcing the Bretons (by a victory on land) to use English ships for all their carrying trade.[19] It is true, of course, that the author of the *Libel of English Policy* (*c.* 1437) did attach more importance to the navy and to the defence of Calais than to the retention of Normandy, but this was not a typical view.[20] It was certainly not that of Gloucester, for whose patronage of his policies the author hoped. The more general view was that the retention of the French provinces was a vital interest, the key to the safety of the Channel coasts and of English shipping in the Channel. Thirty years of occupation had taught Englishmen to set a high value on their control of the Northern French littoral.

The most important single factor that is neglected by those who under-emphasize the importance of the loss of the French provinces is the nature of the English presence there in the fifteenth century. It has been alleged that, after Henry V's reign, the English governing classes were losing interest in the war and were not as ready to serve abroad as they had been. There is some evidence to support the latter point, but if fewer men who held important local offices or represented their shires in parliament served in this period than before, there is a ready explanation. The English involvement in France in this period was different from what it had been in the days of Edward III, or even at the time of Agincourt; the forces that fought abroad in Henry VI's time were not, for the most part, expeditionary armies, but a standing garrison. The Englishmen whose names are so familiar in the annals of the war – men like John Fastolf, William Oldhall, William Glasdale and Matthew Gough – made their careers in France, and not in England, for the time being at least. Permanent service, as part of a standing garrison, was not the kind of service that it was either easy or appropriate for noblemen or the heads of county families to discharge in person. Significantly, however, in the 1430s and 1440s the aristocracy continued to monopolize the prestigious and potentially rewarding high commands (there was even rivalry over them, as York's relations with the two Beauforts, John and Edmund of Somerset, remind us). There was not so much a loss of interest in the maintenance of the war in this period, but modification and alteration of the interests involved in its maintenance.

Soldiers apart, there were a considerable number of Englishmen who had settled in Lancastrian France, and had acquired property there, or trading interests, or administrative office. Together with the soldiers, these people constituted what was virtually a colonial presence. Twenty years after the English defeat (in 1472) the memory of the opportunities which the occupation of Normandy had offered to the enterprising was still green: 'many gentlemen, as well younger brothers as others, might there be worshipfully rewarded, and inhabit that land for the sure guard of the same'.[21] In the late 1440s the interests and opportunities of the war in Normandy and of Englishmen there were not a memory; they were a living concern, which their kinsmen at home could not ignore. Besides, these Englishmen in Normandy were men engaged in the defence of interests which those kinsmen at home regarded as important.

There was a great deal of anxiety about the men in France at the very end of the war. 'Consider', says a memoir of the year 1449, 'what inhumanity it would be, what lack of charity to one's neighbour, to desert now those gentlemen, and common people too, who for these thirty two years have borne such burdens in the king's cause.'[22] And think too, its author adds, of the problem that they may pose if they come back to England, where there is no occupation for them. This was no idle aside: 'and then', Bale wrote in his chronicle under the year 1450, 'were all the Englishmen driven and sent out from France, Normandy, Anjou, and came into this land in great misery and poverty by many companies and fellowships, and went into [the] several places of the land to be inherited with and live upon the alms of the people. But many of them drew to theft and misrule, and noyed sore the commonalty of this land spiritual and temporal, and many of them afterward hanged.'[23] The distress of the returning soldiery was visible proof of the damage that defeat abroad had inflicted on Englishmen; it was also an ugly reminder that England's enemies were now just across the Channel, that she was destitute of allies, that the harbours of Normandy, and, still more important from a commercial point of view, of Gascony, were not safe for her ships and merchants any longer; and finally, that the nation had been humiliated.

The psychological effect of the collapse overseas was naturally very great. For more than 100 years Englishmen had been fed sedulously with propaganda about their kings' rights in France; now all the blood and treasure that had been spent in pursuit of those rights was revealed to have been wasted. The fact that, at the last, all was over so quickly heightened the sense of shock, anger and bewilderment among the people, as they woke to the fact that a tremendous defeat had dishonoured the crown and the whole land. When Cade's rebels marched on London in the summer of 1450, they were demanding the blood of the traitors, by whom 'the realm of France was lost, Normandy,

Gascony, Guienne and Anjou, and our true lords, knights and esquires, and many a good yeoman . . . lost and sold ere they went'.[24] Suffolk had then already been impeached by the commons, and murdered on his way abroad into exile. His friend Adam Moleyns had been lynched by mutinous soldiers at Portsmouth. The confusion had begun, which a few years later would plunge the country into civil war. The issues that were at stake in the Wars of the Roses were, it is true, embedded in the domestic history of England in Henry VI's reign, which we must presently examine, and had only indirect connexions with the events of the French war. If, however, Henry VI's councillors (and above all, Suffolk and Somerset) had not totally discredited the king's government by their mismanagement of his affairs in France, the domestic strains, which culminated in civil war, might never have become so acute that only arms could resolve them.

Notes

1   See further Chapter 17, below pp. 325–6.
2   *P.P.C.* vol. IV, p. 223.
3   ibid. p. 214.
4   ibid. p. 92.
5   *R.P.* vol. IV, p. 481.
6   *L. and P.* vol. II, pt II, pp. [577], [579]–[581].
7   ibid., pt I, p. 239.
8   *P.P.C.* vol. V, p. 229.
9   ibid. pp. 259–63.
10   T. Basin, *Histoire de Charles VII*, ed. J. Quicherat (Paris, 1855), vol. I, p. 150.
11   *P.P.C.* vol. V, p. 361.
12   ibid. p. 392.
13   *R.P.* vol. V, p. 102.
14   *L. and P.* vol. II, pt II, pp. [639]–[641].
15   *Foed.* vol. XI, pp. 172–4.
15a   A. Bossuat, Perinet Gressartet François de Surienne (Paris, 1936), p. 327.
16   *L. and P.* vol. II, pt II, pp. [598ff.], [723]–[725].
17   *P.L.* No. 103.
18   C. F. Richmond, 'The keeping of the seas during the Hundred Years War 1422–1440', *History* 49 (1964), pp. 283–98.
19   *L. and P.* vol. II, pt II, p. [724].
20   G. Warner (ed.), *The libelle of Englysche polycye* (Oxford, 1926).
21   *Lit. Cant.* (R.S.) vol. III, p. 282.
22   *L. and P.* vol. II, pt II, p. [726].
23   *Six Town Chronicles*, ed. R. Flenley (Oxford, 1911), p. 128.
24   *Three Fifteenth Century Chronicles*, ed. J. Gairdner (Camden Soc., 1880), p. 97.

Note on secondary reading (post 1970)

There is no overall, in depth study from an English perspective of the fifteenth century phase of the Anglo-French war. The relevant chapters in R.A. Griffiths, *The Reign of Henry VI* (London, 1981), and in B.P. Wolffe, *Henry VI* (London, 1981), are helpful, the former offering fuller treatment. C.T. Allmand's study of *Lancastrian Normandy, 1415–50* (Oxford, 1983) explores a central topic. Two biographies, G.L. Harriss, *Cardinal Beaufort* (Oxford, 1988) and A.J. Pollard, *John Talbot and the War in France, 1427–53* (London, 1983) are very useful, the former on diplomatic and the latter on military aspects especially. On diplomacy see further J.K. Ferguson, *English Diplomacy, 1422–61* (Oxford, 1972). Two important papers that look set to shift perceptions of diplomatic relations 1422–35 are M. Warner, 'The Anglo-French dual monarchy and the house of Burgundy, 1420–35', *French History*, vol. 11 (1997) and M.K. Jones 'Immunity from war and the lands of a captive knight: the siege of Orleans revisited', in M.J. Arn (ed.), *Charles of Orleans in England* (Woodbridge, 2000). Two slightly older studies that retain high value are J. Dickinson, *The Congress of Arras: a study in medieval diplomacy* (Oxford, 1955), and C.T. Allmand, 'The Anglo French negotiations, 1439', *B.I.H.R.*, vol. 40 (1967).

On the fighting in France to 1445, two essays by M.K. Jones are of particular interest; 'The battle of Verneuil, 1424; Towards a history of courage', *War in History*, vol. 9 (2002), and 'John Beaufort, duke of Somerset and the French expedition of 1443', in R. Griffiths (ed.), *Patronage, the Crown and the Provinces in Later Medieval England* (Gloucester, 1981). Also useful is A. Curry, 'The first English standing armies? Military organisation in Lancastrian Normandy, 1420–1450', in C.D. Ross (ed.), *Patronage, Pedigree and Power in later Medieval England* (Gloucester, 1979). Essays relating to the very last years of the war include M. Vale, 'The last years of English Gascony', *T.R.H.S.*, 5th series, vol. 19 (1969); M. Daniel and M. Keen, 'English diplomacy and the sack of Fougères in 1449', *History*, vol. 59 (1974); and M.K. Jones, 'Somerset, York and the Wars of the Roses', *E.H.R.*, vol. 104 (1989).

17 Henry VI and England 1422–1450

The opening of the long minority of Henry VI in England was not very auspicious. At the very outset there was disagreement as to how the country should be governed. Under the terms of a codicil in Henry V's last will,[1] Humphrey Duke of Gloucester, who had been acting as Guardian of the Ream in the king's absence, claimed the *tutela* (that is the legal guardianship) of his eldest son. Gloucester's interpretation of this codicil was that it in effect conferred on him a regency, the guardianship not only of the infant king but of his realm, its government and administration, with a wide discretion in the distribution of royal patronage. The magnates in England who met in council on 28 September took a different view: that whatever arrangements were made should be approved in parliament, to summon which writs were accordingly sent out in the name of king and council. Before it met, things had been further complicated by the receipt of a letter from John Duke of Bedford, Humphrey's elder brother, written from France and reminding the council of the pre-eminence that fell to him 'by the laws and ancient custom of the realm', as the senior male of the royal house after the king. The stage was thus set for some uncomfortably tough talking.

When parliament met on 9 November the commons were prompt to ask 'who should have the governance of the realm under our sovereign lord the king by his high authority?' The question took time to settle; though Bedford was out of the country, shouldering his new burden as regent of France and could not press his claim, Gloucester could and did. The lords of the council stood firm, however. With the advice of the crown's lawyers behind them, they rejected the codicil of Henry V's will; the dead king could not, by will or otherwise 'without the assent of the three estates commit or grant to any person the rule or governance of this land longer than he lived'.[2] They upheld the precedent of 1377, when Richard II's minority began, as showing that at the accession of a minor authority must rest with the peers as councillors until new arrangements were made in parliament. Gloucester had to give way, and on 5 December it was decided by the assent of both lords and commons that Bedford should be 'Protector of the realm' whenever he was in the kingdom, and that when he was overseas Gloucester should be.[3] On 9 December the council over which the protector should preside was named in parliament. One of the conditions on which this council took office was that wardships, marriages, escheats and such great patronage should be in its disposal, as also the appointment of sheriffs, justices of the peace, escheators and customs officials. Thus only the lesser patronage of the crown was left in the free disposal of the protector.[4]

These arrangements had some unsatisfactory features. Of one something has been said already, that there was absolutely no formal provision for liaison between the English council and Bedford as the regent of France. The provision that when Bedford was in England Gloucester must automatically give way to him was not calculated to promote harmony between the brothers. The fact that, at the very beginning of the minority, the peers of the council and the man who as protector was to preside over them had already found themselves at loggerheads boded ill for the future. A schedule of provisions concerning the council approved in parliament in 1423 suggests that further difficulties were appearing early. The first of them declared that 'neither my lord of Gloucester, nor no other man of the council, in no suit that shall be made to them, shall no favour grant, neither in bills [petitioning] for right, or office, or benefice, [whose decision] belongs to the council; but shall only answer that the bill shall be seen by all the council, and the party suing so have answer'. Still more disturbing was the sixth provision: 'forasmuch as it is too great a shame that unto strange countries our sovereign lord shall write his letters by the advice of his council . . . and singular persons of the council to write the contrary: that it be ordained that no man of the council presume to do it, on pain of shame and reproof'.[5] What precisely was in the mind of those who drew up this provision is not explicit, but almost certainly they were moved by Gloucester's determination to pursue his wife Jacqueline's rights in Hainault. This he could not do without straining the Anglo-Burgundian alliance, and we know that this danger was brought to the attention of the English council.[6]

One of the men who probably drew the council's attention to the dangers implicit in Gloucester's continental ambitions was Henry Beaufort. According to Hardyng, he was also prominent among those who in 1422 resisted Gloucester's claim to a virtual regency.[7] Between these two men a feud was developing which would shortly come out into the open, and which rumbled on, distracting and sometimes dominating the conciliar government of the kingdom, through the remainder of Henry's minority and beyond it. In order to appreciate the significance of the great quarrel, a brief examination of the careers and influence of the two protagonists becomes necessary.

Duke Humphrey is deservedly remembered by posterity as the great patron of scholars and writers, both Italian and English, whose influence did much to introduce Englishmen to the thought and scholarship of the early Renaissance. But it was not until the 1430s that Humphrey began to make his mark as a patron and collector of manuscripts; in the early 1420s his experience was largely military. He had been created Duke of Gloucester and Earl of Pembroke in 1414, when he was twenty-three. At Agincourt he distinguished himself and was wounded. He served in France from 1417 to 1419, again with distinction, and commanded at the siege of Cherbourg. From the last day of 1419 until Henry's return to England in 1421, and again from May 1422 until his brother's death, he was 'keeper' or 'guardian' of England. His government was as far as we know entirely creditable, and established a firm place for him in the affections of the citizens of London, an important sector of opinion. After Henry's death, though, as we have seen, he had to accept unwelcome limits on his powers as protector, his opportunities for pursuing independent and personal policies were greatly extended. He was powerful enough to engineer the quasi-banishment of the Earl of March, one of his most significant potential opponents, to Ireland. When March died in 1425, leaving as his heir a minor, the young Duke of York, he obtained the wardship of his estates, which further strengthened his territorial influence. Early in 1423 he married Jacqueline Countess of Hainault, although she was not formally divorced from John of Brabant (she and Gloucester held that this first marriage was invalid). The parliament of 1423 recognized them as wed, and Gloucester was able, with his large resources, to raise an army in England for a bid to recover for her from John of Brabant the government of her county, with himself as consort. He sailed from England on 16 October 1424.

When Gloucester left England leadership in the council fell naturally to Henry Beaufort, Bishop of Winchester and chancellor of the realm. The second of John of Gaunt's sons by Catherine Swynford and the great uncle of the king, Henry in 1422 had a long career in the church and in politics behind him. He had been chancellor of Oxford University in 1397; in 1398 he was consecrated Bishop of Lincoln, and in 1404 was translated to Winchester. The great estates of this rich diocese secured him a princely income, and his exports of wool brought him into contact with the merchant aristocracy. He was prominent in the council over which Henry V, when Prince of Wales, presided between 1409 and 1411, and with his accession as king he became chancellor. He was then already a quite substantial government creditor, and in the course of Henry V's reign he was to lend the crown over £35,000. The loan that he made in June 1417, of £14,000, was much his largest to date, however, and was made in rather special circumstances. Beaufort was at the point of resigning the chancellorship to embark on a pilgrimage to Jerusalem, which took him by Constance at just the crucial moment when the fathers of the Council were about to elect a new pope. It looks as if he had bought the freedom to play a hand for himself in the international politics of the church. At Constance he was able to be instrumental in bringing about the smooth and undisputed election of Martin V, and his reward was a red hat and a legatine commission to England. This commission was obtained in breach of praemunire and, as Archbishop Chichele pointed out, of the customs of the English church. Henry V made it clear to Beaufort that if he tried to implement his bulls it would mean the loss of the temporalities of his see and the forfeiture of his goods. It took the bishop two years to make up his mind to settle definitely for his English wealth in preference to an international ecclesiastical career; and the latter ambition was, as events proved, only postponed. The price of his restoration to royal favour was another enormous loan to the crown (£17,666), and a postponement of repayment of his previous one. These loans were secured on the customs; after Henry V's death Beaufort foreclosed, and was permitted to appoint one collector in every port in the country. He had established what McFarlane called 'the beginnings of a stranglehold over the royal finances'; this gave him a very powerful political voice in the minority council.

Both Gloucester and Beaufort sought to put their dominant position in England when Henry VI's minority began to the service of their private ambitions. Their rivalry was not only personal, moreover. When Martin V made Beaufort a cardinal he was hoping that he would be the means of restoring 'the pristine liberty of the church' in England through the repeal of the offensive Statutes of Provisors and Praemunire. With his Flemish mercantile contacts, Beaufort also understood better than most how vital the Anglo-Burgundian alliance was to maintaining the settlement that Henry V had achieved at Troyes. Gloucester's ambitions in Hainault cut clean across that alliance, since Duke Philip of Burgundy claimed that John of Brabant and Jacqueline were lawfully married and that he was their heir. Gloucester also, probably quite genuinely, sympathized with the English protectionist instinct which was behind the reduction, approved in 1422, of the customs for native merchants, aliens still paying at the higher rate; this was contrary to the interests of Beaufort's Flemish friends and favourable to Gloucester's London contacts. As protector, Gloucester was inevitably involved in the enforcement of the anti-papal statutes, which many saw as the bulwark of English ecclesiastical liberties and interests, and he soon learned to pose as their champion. Though Gloucester's political sympathies were less coherent and more insular than Beaufort's, they were at once more popular in England and quite incompatible with the bishop's.

Duke Humphrey cannot have been sorry to witness an outbreak of anti-Flemish agitation in London in 1424, just before he sailed for Hainault. Bills against the Flemings were circulated: 'some were set upon the Bishop's gate of Winchester, and some on other bishops' gates', and Beaufort, so he claimed afterwards, began to fear a serious insurrection 'in destruction of divers estates of England'.[8] Once Gloucester was fully occupied abroad, he placed Richard Woodeville in charge of the Tower with a strong company and instructions not to admit anyone without orders from the council. He also had a number of London citizens arrested. After Gloucester's return in the spring of 1425 the citizens naturally turned to him as their protector; people began to get excited and Woodeville apparently refused Humphrey admission to the Tower, acting on Beaufort's orders as chancellor. Through the summer matters rose towards a climax, which came at the end of September. Beaufort had assembled a force of retainers from as far afield as Lancashire and Cheshire at Southwark, and prepared for a surprise *coup* in the city, intending further, Gloucester alleged, to seize the young king at Eltham. The *coup* failed, because the mayor raised the city in the protector's interest. There was an ugly skirmish at London Bridge on 30 October before a truce was arranged by Archbishop Chichele of

Canterbury. Next day Beaufort decided that Bedford must be called in if a show-down was to be avoided. 'As you desire the welfare of the king our sovereign lord and of his realms of England and France, and your own weal and ours also, haste you hither', he wrote, 'for by my troth if you tarry we shall put this land in adventure with a battlefield. Such a brother as you have here!'[9]

It was high time that someone took charge of events. There had been other ominous signs in 1425 besides the skirmish at London Bridge; there had been 'much altercation' between lords and commons over tonnage and poundage in the summer parliament, which witnessed also a fierce dispute over precedence between the Earl Marshal and the Earl of Warwick: 'there was much trouble and heavyness in the land'.[10] When Bedford arrived his efforts to reconcile his brother and Beaufort at first met with little success; Gloucester was not prepared to make any move towards peace before parliament met, hoping no doubt that his cause would find favour with the commons. The estates were summoned to Leicester, so as to be out of range of London violence, and after a good deal of argument Beaufort and Gloucester were persuaded to accept arbitration. A committee of peers decreed that they should shake hands and admit each other to peace according to a prescribed form of words, promising to show good lordship and favour to one another's men. Beaufort's set speech was longer than Gloucester's, virtually a public explanation of his conduct. He had the worst of it and resigned the great seal on 13 March 1426 in favour of Bishop Kemp of London, preparatory to going abroad.

As long as Bedford remained in the country there was no further threat to the tranquillity of the government, and when he left he took Beaufort with him. They parted at Calais in the spring of 1427, and Beaufort, having received at last his cardinal's hat at the duke's own hands, proceeded for Bohemia as legate of the Roman *Curia*. Before Bedford left England, the lords of the council had taken the precaution of obtaining from him a confirmation that he accepted their interpretation of the proper relations of the protector and the council. They had clearly come to regard Gloucester with some distrust. A loan was made to him for a further expedition to Hainault, but it never sailed, because pressure from Bedford prevented it. Soon Gloucester began to lose interest in the affair; he accepted Martin V's decision upholding the marriage of Jacqueline and John of Brabant and left his ex-wife abroad friendless. He meanwhile regu-larized his relations with her former lady-in-waiting, Eleanor Cobham. This cost him popularity with the commons; and his attempt to obtain a redefinition of his powers as protector in the spring parliament of 1428 was successfully resisted by the lords.

There was trouble again later in 1428, when Beaufort returned once more to England, armed now with a legatine commission to preach the crusade against the Hussites. Initially Gloucester had conciliar support in protesting against Beaufort's using a legatine commission in England without royal licence, and in questioning whether, now that he was a cardinal, custom could permit him to continue as Bishop of Winchester. But in 1429 the military situation began to look very ugly after the relief of Orleans, and Beaufort was recalled to the council. He and the men whom he had in the end been allowed to recruit for his crusade had to be diverted to serve in France.

In 1431 Gloucester returned to the attack. Henry VI had been taken to France to be crowned and he was now in the king's absence keeper of the realm (the protectorship had lapsed following the English coronation). In November, under his instructions, the law officers presented a petition demanding that Beaufort be deprived of the see of Winchester on the ground that it was legally incompatible with his cardinalate. The petition was heard before the great council, and writs under the Statute of Praemunire were subsequently made out against the bishop. At the same council Gloucester's salary as chief councillor was increased to 5000 marks per annum, in spite of sharp opposition from Chancellor Kemp.

Affairs were once again moving towards crisis. The charges against Beaufort were postponed until he should be in England to answer them (in the event until the May parliament of 1432), but as soon as he landed from France certain jewels and plate that the bishop was holding as security for his loans were seized, probably on Gloucester's orders. About the same time a number of changes were made in the personnel of the court and the council. Kemp and Lord Hungerford left the chancery and treasury respectively and were replaced by Bishop Stafford and Lord Scrope; Lords Cromwell and Tiptoft were replaced as chamberlain and steward of the household by Sir William Phelip and Sir Robert Babthorpe. Cromwell was later to complain that his dismissal was improper. It looks suspiciously as if Gloucester was trying to get awkward individuals out of office in preparation for a showdown with his rival.

When parliament did meet Beaufort took the initiative by declaring his readiness to answer the charges of treason, which he had heard, so he said, that men were making against him. No one charged him with treason, and the commons petitioned that, in view of 'the many great and notable services that he had done', he should be free of any charge under the anti-papal statutes.[11] He was in consequence formally authorized at last to hold his English preferment notwithstanding the cardinalate, but he had to pay for the privilege. He agreed to postpone repayment of 13,000 marks of old loans, to lend £6000, and to deposit a further £6000, which would be treated as a loan if on inquiry it proved that the jewels that had been seized from him earlier really were held as securities. Once again he had bought himself out of a difficult situation.

In the year 1433 Bedford was again in England. On his return Lord Cromwell returned to influence and replaced Scrope as treasurer, and Suffolk replaced Babthorpe as steward of the household. It would probably be wrong to read much partisan significance into these changes. What is significant is the evidence of real anxiety about the effect on government of factious rivalry among the great, and the attitude of the commons towards Bedford who in their eyes stood above the party strife. In the second session of the parliament of 1433 the speaker came forward with a petition to the duke personally. 'The said commons consider', he declared, 'that the presence and being of my said Lord of Bedford in this land, since his coming into it, hath been full fruitful, and that the restful rule and governance of this land hath greatly increased and grown thereby.'[12] In consequence the commons prayed that the duke would not go back to France but would remain with them. Bedford, in reply, made it clear that he could not consent unless he was given, as chief councillor, a really free discretion in government, such as none had enjoyed since 1422, especially in the matter of patronage. All that he asked was granted, without cavil. This shows how deep distrust of divided counsels had bitten, for it was the abandonment of a ten year effort to keep limits upon the influence of Henry VI's uncles, Bedford as well as Gloucester.

As events turned out, Bedford was not able to stay in England after all. Affairs in France were in too parlous a state. On 14 June 1434 he told the council that he must leave, and made some suggestions for raising finance to strengthen his forces as far as was feasible: 'For God is my witness, how great a pity it were . . . to lose that noble realm for the getting and keeping of which my lord that was your father, to whose soul God do mercy, and other many noble princes, lords, knights and squires and other persons in full great number have paid their lives.'[13] On 1 July he left England for the last time; just over a year later, in September 1435, he was dead. At the time the great congress at Arras, which proved a decisive turning point in English fortunes overseas, was about to close. A year after that, Henry's long minority came to an end, so that there was something of a turning point in domestic history too. Before we follow further the course of political events, it will be useful to look back over conditions in England in the minority; to see what substance there was behind the alarm at deteriorating order at home which led the commons to press Bedford to stay, and to examine the financial situation which by 1435 was beginning to look critical.

The cost of maintaining the war in France in the 1430s was not in principle beyond the resources of the crown and the taxpayers, for the time being at least. Henry V's reign had shown that it was possible to maintain military expenditure at a considerably higher level than that of this period, without the crown's debts getting out of hand. The difficulty of doing so had, however, since then become greater than it ought to have been, on account of the financial insouciance of the early years of Henry VI's minority. Besides, since the commons did not have the same confidence in the government of the 1430s as they had had in Henry V, they were not prepared to respond to its demands with the same generosity.

Englishmen had always assumed that, once a notable part of France was conquered, their king's French subjects ought to shoulder the fiscal burden of the war. There was in consequence no grant of extraordinary taxation after Henry V's death until 1428. In the autumn parliament of 1422 the customs were reduced for English exporters. King Henry's death also gave the high born and influential among the crown's creditors their chance to insist on payment of long standing debts, and to gain other financial advantages too.

Thus we find that Sir John Cornwall made sure of the compensation due to him for his prisoner the Count of Vendosme, taken at Agincourt, whom he had surrendered to the crown; that the Earl of Huntingdon was promised payment of arrears of wages of war and obtained a grant towards his ransom (he had been taken by the French at Baugé); that Bishop Beaufort secured his hold on the customs, so that by 1425 virtually all his loans to date had been repaid. Gloucester was able to make sure of a princely salary of 8000 marks as protector. Nearly all the new councillors in fact used their position to their own benefit in one way or another (some petitions for favour were endorsed by the very men who presented them). The overall consequence was that through the early years of the reign, when there were no subsidies granted in parliament and no unduly heavy expenses to meet, the issues of the exchequer nevertheless regularly exceeded its net receipts. The failure to balance the account was not dramatic, averaging out at about £1600 a year; but the book-keeping totals are deceptive, concealing the true situation. By 1430, when it became clear that there would again have to be major expenditure on maintaining the war abroad, the exchequer was already carrying an uncomfortable load of accumulated debt; by 1433 the debts for which provision needed to be made had reached the frightening total of £164,815.

In the new military situation after Joan's relief of Orleans the commons were in the first instance generous. The parliament of 1429 granted a double subsidy, that of 1430 a subsidy and a third, together with a graduated land tax on all estates of a whole knight's fee or more, or worth upwards of £20 per annum. But the parliament of 1432 granted only one half subsidy, and quashed the land tax (which, as the commons rightly complained, was too complicated). In 1433 the commons granted a whole subsidy but reduced the total assessment by £4000 'to the release and discharge of the poor towns, cities and boroughs, desolate, wasted or destroyed, or else to the said tax greatly overcharged'.[14] This reduction became a regular feature of subsequent grants. The result of this growing niggardliness might not have been so very serious if, in 1429, the exchequer had not been carrying an accumulated deficit. But that was what it was doing, and there now arose heavy expenses quite apart from military expenditure, in connexion with the king's two coronations and with renewed diplomatic activity.

When he was appointed treasurer in 1433, Lord Cromwell decided on a full-scale investigation of the financial situation. The picture that he had to paint in the parliament of October was a gloomy one. His figures showed a deficit of £21,000 for the current year; over and above this there was a total of £164,800 of bad debt outstanding at the exchequer which had to be paid off in instalments, term by term. One major trouble, clearly, was that the king's ordinary revenues were overburdened with fees and annuities: 'now daily many warrants come to me of payments, as well for lords as for other divers persons, of much more than all your revenues would come to . . . the which warrants if I should pay them, your household, chamber and wardrobe, and your works should be unserved and unpaid: and if I pay them not, I run in great indignation of my lords, and great slander, noise and spite of all your people that bring me any warrants'.[15] Cromwell, a treasurer making a new start, wanted to be free of blame for past extravagance, and may have exaggerated a little. The real trouble was not the annual account, but the backlog of debt; until that had been cleared, even when war expenditure was discounted, something like an annual subsidy was needed if the government was to pay its way. This meant that even if the commons were to be as generous as they had been in the middle years of Henry V's reign, the council could not consider expenditure on the war on a scale approaching that of, say, 1417 and 1418. In fact, the commons were not inclined to be anything like as generous.

The last sentence in the terms of the commons grant of 1429 reveals one of the major reasons for their lack of confidence in Henry VI's minority government. 'We trust fully', they declared, 'that through such comfort as we have conceived by our lords on your behalf, that we shall have knowledge of good and sad government in every part of this your said realm, ere you dissolve this your present parliament.'[16] Ever since Henry V's death order had been deteriorating; now lack of governance was undermining confidence between governors and governed, in just the same way as it had in the reign of Henry IV. In this same parliament there was a strong plea from the commons for the better enforcement of the statute against liveries. In new articles governing the conduct of conciliar business, a special commitment was imposed on councillors to refrain from maintenance at law, 'by word, by message, or by writing to officer, judge, jury or party, or by gift of clothing or livery'. In 1433 the commons asked that this article should be read again, and an oath taken to observe it not only by the dukes of Bedford and Gloucester, and the other lords of the council, but by all the prelates, peers and magnates present individually.[17] As a supporting measure, it was ordered that lists be prepared in each county of influential persons, who should be required to take an oath to uphold the peace. The commons' request to Bedford to remain in England, because his presence was 'the greatest surety that could be thought' of the 'restful government' of the land, was made in the same session, and shows how serious was the loss of confidence in the continual council and its capacity to govern.

The anxieties of the commons were amply justified. We have seen earlier how the quarrel of Beaufort and Gloucester brought the country to a point where civil war seemed to threaten in 1425. The example of the two leading councillors was inevitably infectious. In 1428, a dispute between the Duke of Norfolk and the Earl of Huntingdon caused serious rioting in East Anglia, and very nearly developed into a private war. They were at loggerheads again in 1430, and now the Earl of Warwick had become involved as well. Norfolk and Huntingdon significantly were among a group of peers who were warned not to bring more than their normal retinues when they attended the parliament of 1432, along with Salisbury, Stafford and the disgruntled Cromwell. It was naturally difficult for the council to control these quarrels among the great; their protagonists were its members. This was what made them so dangerous. From the households of the great, moreover, disorder naturally radiated outwards. The consequence was that disturbances quite unrelated to the quarrels of the magnates, such as the abortive Lollard rising of 1431, caused more alarm than was really justified: people saw in them further signs of the inability of the council to maintain order, and feared for the whole social fabric.

At this point it is very important to stress that we are talking about fears rather than facts, about a decline in public confidence and not a breakdown of government. There are heavy charges that stand out against the council that sought to govern England in Henry VI's minority, of insouciance, of self-seeking, of the inability of the members to obey the rules that they prescribed for themselves. It was with the council of this period in mind that Fortescue was later to write:

> The king's council was wont to be chosen of the great princes, and of the greatest lords of the land, both spiritual and temporal . . . which lords and officers had near hand as many matters of their own to be treated in council as had the king. Wherethrough, when they came together they were so occupied with their own matters that they attended but little, and other whiles nothing, to the king's matters. . . . Then could no matter treated in the council be kept privy. For the lords oftentimes told their own counsellors and servants, that had sued to them for those matters, how they had sped in them and who was against them.[18]

Fortescue's words have been widely remembered. It is therefore the more important to remind ourselves that the record of the minority council was by no means wholly discreditable. In the early years its members no doubt did spend too much time on private business. But when things became harder, from 1429 on, the records show them devoting themselves commendably to effort in the national cause, investigating the crown's finances and seeking remedies for their inadequacy, raising loans and reinforcements for the field in France, planning diplomatic overtures and looking for avenues towards an honourable settlement with the enemy. In the deteriorating military situation most of the great showed themselves ready to make personal sacrifices; Beaufort to stretch his resources to make further loans, Bedford and Gloucester to accept substantial cuts in the chief councillors' salary. If sufficient solutions to the multifarious problems facing it eluded the council, it was not for lack of trying.

What perhaps stands most of all to the credit of the councillors of the minority is that in spite of all their difficulties they managed to continue to work together. They refused to acknowledge Gloucester's right to a regency in 1422, but they cooperated with him first as protector and then as chief councillor. They would not let the pope or Beaufort browbeat the Archbishop of Canterbury; equally, they would not tolerate Beaufort's permanent exclusion from the council. Bedford and the council imposed peace between Gloucester and Beaufort; Gloucester and the council imposed peace between Norfolk and Huntingdon. There were times when it looked as if control was on the point of breaking down, but it never did; and the credit must go to the sense of responsibility, collective and individual, of council and councillors.

After 1435 there was a gradual quickening of the tempo of English domestic politics. Party strife among the great became sharper, the signs clearer of declining order in the country and of declining trust in the king's government. The change was partly related to the alteration in the English position abroad after the collapse of the Anglo-Burgundian alliance. The demise of Bedford, the man who had been most successful in keeping the rivals of the council table at arms length from one another, and who was better trusted by the commons than any of the other great men of the kingdom, was another factor. Most important of all, however, was the king's coming of age in 1437. The job of the minority councils had been to form decisions on the king's behalf: an adult king was expected to take counsel, but to form his decisions himself. In the circumstances in which Henry VI emerged from his minority, it was inevitable that competition should develop to have the ear of a young and inexperienced ruler, and so shape his decision making.

The failure of the Arras peace congress had important domestic consequences, because it sharpened divisions of policy within the council over the conduct of the war. The need to achieve some sort of settlement with the French was now apparent to a number of councillors, notably Beaufort. His unique capacity (and readiness) to advance major cash loans, which the government could not do without, ensured that his remained a very powerful influence in framing diplomatic policies. Gloucester, on the other hand, had never appreciated the importance of the Anglo-Burgundian alliance, and stood forward as the champion of vigorous military action. He was now easily the most prominent aristocrat among those who had fought in the campaigns of Henry V, in which he had distinguished himself more often than either of his brothers, Bedford or Clarence. He was the natural person for the survivors of those great days to look to, in their disappointment at recent setbacks and their confidence that reinforcements and vigorous campaigning could still restore the situation. A third figure who after 1437 began to be very prominent was William de la Pole, Earl of Suffolk. Already experienced and influential as a councillor, his office of steward of the royal household gave him particularly ready access to the king's person, and special opportunities to shape his preferences in policies and patronage.

When parliament met early in 1437 the commons went out of their way to commend the noble service that Gloucester had performed at the relief of Calais the year before. Later in the year, when the king appointed a council to advise him in his majority, Gloucester's was the first name on the list, with a salary of 2000 marks per annum. In 1439 the peace conference at Calais brought him to the fore in discussions in the council about the terms there proposed. By his own account it was largely owing to his intervention that the English were adamant in refusing to waive the title of King of France: 'I answered and said I would never agree me thereto, and that I would rather die.'[19] After Calais, the next move of those who believed that the quest for a settlement with the French remained a first priority was to open negotiations for the release of the Duke of Orleans. This brought about a showdown over policy between Gloucester and the king's other advisers.

When arrangements for the release of Orleans were first mooted, early in 1440, Gloucester entered a public protest to the king, against his 'enlargisement and deliverance'. As its text makes clear, this was really a political manifesto against Beaufort, whose dismissal from the council he formally demanded (together with that of his colleague, Archbishop Kemp of York).[20] Beaufort, naturally, was the chief target. The whole story of the cardinal's offences against the provisors legislation was rehearsed again, together with all the objections to the introduction of a red hat into the kingdom. His loans, Gloucester alleged, had always been to his own profit, and to the king's ultimate loss; he had established a stranglehold on the customs; he had foreclosed fraudulently to secure crown jewels that he held in pledge; and was now beginning to force the sale of crown lands, to the impoverishment of the king's heirs to all time. Particularly interesting are Gloucester's remarks about Beaufort and the council; he had achieved, he said, such mastery of the king 'as no true liegeman ought to usurp' and was calling the council to meet at his own house and on his own authority. Thus he had cut off and estranged 'me your sole uncle, together with my cousin of York, my cousin of Huntingdon, and many other lords of your kin from having knowledge of any great matters that might touch your high estate and realm'.[21] Government had fallen into the hands of dishonest brokers, who would defraud the king of his wealth and abandon his titles in France, this was the theme of the manifesto; the excuse for its publication was that the cardinal and his clique had established such a hold over policy that a loyal councillor had now no option but to appeal directly and publicly to the king to have done with them.

Negotiations for the release of Orleans went ahead notwithstanding. After it had been agreed, Gloucester entered a second protest. This was in form a sober and quite accurate critique of the policy decision,[22] which, he argued, would be interpreted abroad as a symptom of English weakness. The combined effect of his two manifestos was to stir Henry VI's advisers to a reply, a counter-manifesto to quiet the 'noise and grouching' that it had stirred among the people.[23] That the king's council should feel so vulnerable as to need to justify their policy by public broadsheet is an ominous sign, indicative of real instability. Their manifesto was ably drafted, but in difficult times it is always easier to criticize than to defend official policy, and it lacked the bite of Gloucester's attack. The next step of the king's intimates seems to be a recognition of the political weakness of their position, and the impossibility of securing themselves against popular dissatisfaction that his protests had stirred by mere argument.

Their new answer to Gloucester's intransigence was an effort to discredit him by public scandal. In the summer of 1441 two clerks, Roger Bolingbroke and Thomas Southwell, were arrested on the charge of practising against the king's life by sorcery. Roger abjured his black arts publicly on 16 July at St Paul's; a few days later it was noised abroad that he had admitted, under examination, that he had been instigated to his acts of sorcery by none other than Eleanor

Cobham, Gloucester's second duchess. She was arrested, and was tried in October before the bishops of London, Lincoln and Norwich. Suffolk himself had had a hand in the trial of her accomplices, and the man who now conducted her prosecution was Adam Moleyns, the clerk of the council, who was intimately connected with the clique which, under Suffolk's leadership, was becoming dominant about the king. They, rather than Beaufort, may have been the prime movers in the affair. Eleanor admitted her traffic in sorcery and with sorcerers and submitted herself to the correction of the bishops; but the charge of plotting to destroy the king by magic she flatly denied. Her sentence was to perform full and public penance, going on foot through London with a taper in her hand to offer at the altars of St Paul's, of Christchurch in Aldgate, and of St Michael's Cornhill, on the three next market days in the city. After that, she was committed to prison for life. Of her accomplices, Southwell died in prison and Bolingbroke was hanged; and Margery Jourdemain, the witch of Eye who, it was said, prepared the potion that ensnared for Eleanor Humphrey's love, was burned at Smithfield.

Eleanor was undoubtedly guilty of dabbling in witchcraft; that the main object of her trial was political is suggested strongly by the composition of the court, the publicity of her penance and the public fate of her accomplices. Gloucester himself was not involved, and the affair did not completely destroy his influence, but for the time being it discredited him sufficiently for his rivals' purpose. It was not the first time that English politicians of this period had employed this rather unattractive type of manoeuvre. The whole episode is strongly reminiscent of the deliberate English effort to discredit Joan of Arc at her trial as a sorcerer and a heretic. Beaufort, however, had never employed this sort of means in domestic political infighting, and the business smacks more of the methods of the Earl of Suffolk, who had been steward of the household since 1433 and was now beginning to emerge as a dominant figure at court. His rise seems to have been a consequence of the achievement of his majority by Henry VI, and of subsequent changes in the role of the council in government.

When Henry came of age in 1437 there was no sudden change; the council that he appointed in November was virtually identical in composition with that of the preceding years. There were of course some changes in its powers; the king now reserved to himself control over collation to benefices in his gift, appointment to office, and the grant of charters of pardon. The new council was, however, intended to play a meaningful part in government (the regulations for the council of 1406 were reissued for its guidance), and in the first instance it certainly did so. But attendance began to decline early, and from 1438 on the warrants drafted by the council's clerk show a small group of persons constantly in attendance, Bishop Stafford the chancellor, Bishop Ayscough and the Earl of Suffolk being the most regular, with, of course, the clerk, Adam Moleyns. These men all had easy access to the king; that was the secret of their growing influence. As it grew in the early 1440s, so the influences of both Gloucester and Beaufort, the great rivals of so many years, began to wane. The scandal of the arrest and conviction of his duchess effectively rendered Gloucester a spent force. The last occasion when Beaufort was a decisive influence in council was during the preparations for Somerset's French expedition of 1443. Between 1441 and 1443 the council continued to meet formally and regularly, but the intimacy of Suffolk and his associates with the king was steadily undermining its significance. By 1444 the old rule, that all major grants should be scrutinized by the council, was a dead letter. Moleyns's endorsement of a bill was accepted as adequate warrant by the privy seal, which moved the great seal; and a new ordinance that the privy seal should accept all warrants with the king's sign manual or under the signet (which Moleyns kept) merely regularized the position.

The king's new friends did very well out of their position of influence. Suffolk's promotions are the most dramatic witness to this: in 1437 he became high steward of the duchy of Lancaster, north of Trent, and in 1438 chief justice of south Wales; in 1442 he was granted the reversion of the Earldom of Pembroke if Gloucester should die childless; in 1444 he was created a marquis. Later he was to get still more; in 1447 he was appointed Lord Great Chamberlain of England, Constable of Dover and Warden of the Cinque Ports, and in 1448 he became a duke. Ordinary people were naturally soon aware of the way that influence was going, and came to know that their petitions for favour were most likely to be met if they were sponsored by one of the curialist group. This, and Suffolk's capacity for the time being to cooperate reasonably with leading peers (Gloucester excepted) had the effect of strengthening his hold and that of his associates on government. In public policy, especially in relations with France, he continued to follow broadly lines laid down in the day of Beaufort's high influence. The measure of consensus that he managed to achieve was fragile, however: it needed visible successes to hold it together. In the years following 1444 these were becoming hard to come by.

In order to appreciate the difficulties facing Suffolk, it will be helpful to say a little of three matters which by the mid 1440s had been giving rise to popular disquiet for more than a decade. There was widespread concern about the state of public order. The state of the royal finances was moving from the problematic toward the alarming. The third matter was, of course, the need to find some way out of the impasse of the French war, about which a great deal has been said already, to which a little must be added from the domestic angle. Let us look at each of these matters in turn.

Lack of governance was no new complaint, and it is no surprise to find after 1437 continuing evidence of the kind of aristocratic misdemeanor that had troubled the minority. The earls of Salisbury and Westmorland came near to blows over a disputed inheritance in Yorkshire; the followers of the Earl of Devon and Sir William Bonville were involved in armed clashes in the west; in Gloucestershire a running fight of long standing between the heir male and the heirs general for the Berkeley inheritance continued to disturb the peace. In Bedfordshire, rivalry between Lord Fanhope and Lord Grey of Ruthin culminated in an ugly fracas in 1439, during the session of the justices of the peace. But there was alarming evidence now of more general disorder. From the march of Wales came stories that in Hereford outlaws and evil-doers were coming openly into the market towns, no officer preventing them, so that 'they do not fear to kill and burn and rob in the said county'. The counties of the south coast complained of 'murders, mayhems, and batteries' and of the despoiling of goods by soldiers passing on their way to France.[24] In 1439 the commons in parliament took the remarkable step of petitioning for the penalty of total forfeiture against certain notorious criminals, if they could not be brought to book. One of these was the colourful Piers Venables, gentleman, of Derbyshire, who gathered a band about him, and 'in manner of insurrection, went into the woods in that county, like as it had been Robin Hood and his meiny'.[25] His band had ridden raiding into Cheshire, where another band from Shropshire under Philip Egerton had also gone raiding. The demand for extra-ordinary penalties for this sort of banditry shows that people felt things were getting out of hand. There was no longer sufficient confidence in the county officers; and the commons believed that they were as often as not in league with criminals. They denounced bitterly the misdemeanours of sheriffs and under-sheriffs, which threatened 'importable hurt, open disinheritance, suppor-tation of manslaughter and great oppression to many of the liege people of our sovereign lord'.[26]

Government finance over the period 1436 to 1445 is a parallel story of the steady deterioration of an initially unsatisfactory situation. Late in 1435 the commons, nettled by what they regarded as the Burgundian betrayal of England, were generous, granting a whole subsidy and a graduated tax on all incomes from land and annuities of over £5 per annum. But afterwards they only granted in 1437 a subsidy, in 1439 a subsidy and a half, and in 1442 again a subsidy – all to be paid by instalments, and all subject to the now regular deductions. The king's advisers were very busy in these years in their efforts to raise new forces for the defence of Normandy and Gascony, and these grants did not meet the full cost of the troops that they needed to equip. The exchequer therefore found it harder than ever to meet its commitments, and the burden of accumulated debt grew more and more alarming. Even Beaufort found difficulty in obtaining adequate security for new loans, and satis-factory terms for the repayment of old ones. It is not surprising to find that the circle of those ready to lend to the crown was a dwindling one, and that arrears of pay owing to magnates and others in the king's service were accumulating. At the same time purveyance for the household began once more to attract uncomfortable attention, always a sign that the king was short of cash. Certain revenues of the duchy of Lancaster were in consequence of complaint earmarked for the expenses of the household, but this did not solve the problem; in 1442 the commons asked the king to appoint a committee of lords to ensure that 'good and sad rule be had in your said household'.[27] This was the same familiar request that had been heard so often in the days of Henry IV, and, now as then, was a symptom of growing strain between the governors and the governed.

The difficulty of finding a solution to the growing financial problem was greatly complicated by the heavy load of fees and annuities that were assigned on the crown's regular revenues. In Henry IV's day this too had been a pressing problem, but then at least there was some attempt to curtail expenditure: there had even been a stop on annuities in 1404. In the 1440s there was not much serious attempt at parsimony. Henry VI from the time that he attained his majority was very free with grants of land, office and fee. Apart from his two great foundations at Eton and King's College Cambridge, those who gained most from his largesse were his intimate advisers and their clients. It was a case of the governors conniving at the impoverishment of the government, and did not enhance the reputation of Henry's friends.

Financial difficulties and the problem of Anglo-French diplomacy were intimately inter-related. Unless some sort of settlement could be reached with the French there was not much chance of finding a solution to the problem of mounting royal insolvency. But it was difficult in practice to find an avenue towards settlement, because of the domestic political danger involved in conceding enough to the adversary to bring him to terms. Gloucester had made all too public in 1440 his suspicion that the king's advisers were intending to betray the national interest and all the achievement of the past by signing away the king's crown and title in France. He had made it clear too that in his opinion, if the king would take other advisers they would press his war abroad more successfully. The success that York and Talbot did achieve in Normandy with slender support from England lent colour to this suggestion, and it was in any case what most people wanted to believe. If Suffolk was to survive politically he had got to achieve not just peace, but peace with honour; if he visibly failed in that endeavour, public indignation was likely to spin affairs out of his control. In 1443–4 Suffolk's hopes were centred, as we have seen earlier, on the Angevin marriage as a step on the way to an Anglo-French settlement, but his hopes were not well founded. Though the two year truce agreed at the same time as the marriage was welcome in the short run as affording a respite to the hard pressed Norman garrisons and from taxation for war purposes, in the longer run the marriage merely aggravated suspicions that a sell out to the French was in the offing.

For a little more than five years after the Truce of Tours was sealed, until the beginning of 1450, Suffolk strove not very competently to ward off the crises that were threatening. The underlying pattern of domestic history in this period was not sharply different from that of the preceding years. Nothing was done that offered any serious promise of better governance at the local level. In the financial sphere, the sealing of the Truce of Tours obviously eased the strain of military expenditure, but the accumulated debt from the past meant that little relief was felt immediately. The costs of a now enlarged (and enlarging) royal household and of a new household for the queen substantially offset such saving as was made. Bishop Lumley of Carlisle, the new treasurer appointed in 1446, did make a brave attempt to bring assignments to crown creditors, on royal revenues at source, under exchequer control, and so get a grip on the management of government finance; but his efforts were greatly hindered by the host of men and interests seeking exemption from the restrictions he imposed, through court or personal influence. He succeeded in staving off crisis, but there were plenty of large debts outstanding when he left office in 1449, and some of them were long-standing.

The successes of those with household connections in obtaining priority for repayment of their loans, payment of their fees, and in the distribution of royal patronage generally did not endear others to what had come to bear the appearance of a court clique, headed by Suffolk, dominating the king's government. His regime's partiality and its lack of achievement fostered a mood of disillusion and distrust. Rumours began to circulate that the king was 'not so steadfast in his wits as other kings have been before'.[28] Numerous popular ballads circulated which inveighed against the clique with influence at court in a style ominously reminiscent of the adverse satires directed against Richard II and his household supporters in the last years of his reign. The most constant refrain of this literature, as in that earlier time, was the evil of livery and maintenance, particularly of maintenance by members of the royal court and household. The ballads reflect a widespread suspicion that the whole administration of the kingdom was being controlled by a small group of individuals and their clients, for purposes of personal advantage and regardless of the common weal.

Such suspicions had ample foundations. The careers of men such as the household knight John Say or the civil servant Thomas Thorpe, both objects of the poets' scorn, fully justify the suggestion that men in favour were doing well for themselves in spite of the crown's poverty. Accusations of maintenance against the courtiers and their protégés were equally well founded. Margaret Paston in 1448 declared that in Norfolk none dared be so hardy as to say or do anything against Suffolk and his clients.[29] Indictments presented after Suffolk's fall bore her out all too clearly. Three men closely associated with the earl (promoted duke in 1448) through the duchy of Lancaster administration in East Anglia, Sir Thomas Tuddenham, John Heydon and John Ulveston, had been rigging the legal administration of the county for years. The sheriff had been a tool in their hands; juries were packed with their men: 'there can no man indict him, for Sir Thomas Tuddenham maintaineth him' had been a typical record.[30] In Kent, the associates of James Fiennes, Lord Saye and Sele, chamberlain of the household from 1447 and a close associate of Suffolk's, conducted themselves in much the same way as Tuddenham and Heydon in Norfolk. The activities of men such as these built up dislike of the courtiers of Henry VI toward a climax of resentful bitterness. But for the time being nothing could be done, because they had the ear of the king from whom all authority stemmed, and protest seemed hopeless.

The principal political events of the years 1444 to 1450 were nearly all in one way or another bound up with the problems of Anglo-French diplomacy, and have been discussed in an earlier chapter. There is no need to go over the ground again in detail. Suffolk's efforts to avoid or deflect the wave of public anger that followed the decision to cede Maine to the French were not very happy. Gloucester's death in confinement after his arrest at Bury in February 1447 labelled him in the public eye as the murderer of the 'good duke' Humphrey. Moleyns's attempt to discredit York by charging him with embezzlement of soldiers' wages sowed distrust between the court and the major peer whose support might have done most to shore up the government's eroded reputation. Finally, the folly of the attack on Fougères in Brittany – in which both Suffolk and Somerset, the Beaufort who had replaced York as lieutenant in Normandy – were implicated, plunged the kingdom back into the war with France unprepared. Suffolk's miscalculations finally culminated in the military debacle of 1449–50 in which Normandy was lost for good, and from the consequences of this neither the king's favour nor anything else could save him.

On 7 February 1450 the commons in parliament impeached Suffolk who, as they put it, had been for so long 'priviest and best trusted' with Henry VI. Two sets of charges were brought against him, the first mainly concerned with his mismanagement of the war and of diplomacy, the second (thrown in for good measure when proceedings seemed to be hanging fire) with frauds, peculations and maintenance committed at home in England.[31] He was accused of being responsible for the release of the Duke of Orleans, the surrender of Maine, the inadequate safeguard of Normandy and the alienation of England's old allies, as Brittany and Armagnac. He was also charged with using his influence to secure for himself rich grants from the crown (as the wardship of Margaret Beaufort and the reversion of the earldom of Pembroke); of embezzling the proceeds of subsidies; of making sheriffs of his own choice 'so that they that would not be of his affinity in their counties were overset'; of being privy to a murderous attack on Lord Cromwell and sheltering his assailant, Suffolk's own retainer William Tailboys. There were some very wild allegations besides, even that Suffolk had plotted with Dunois and other Frenchmen to invade England, and depose Henry VI in his own favour.

This remarkable medley of indictments demonstrates very clearly how closely men associated Suffolk's mismanagement of affairs abroad and his misgovernment at home. Hurriedly put together, the charges were in no sense exhaustive, but they were enough to secure his dismissal. They were never fully tried, because Henry intervened personally to save his favourite from a worse fate by banishing him from the realm for five years, on his own authority. This did not in fact save Suffolk; the ship on which he was embarked for France was run down in the Channel by a vessel called the *Nicholas of the Tower*, and by order of its captain Suffolk's head was struck off. The sailors who executed him claimed that they were acting on behalf of the 'community of the realm'. He had made himself so hated in England that to put him to death appeared to them to be a patriotic service.

No one knows who the captain of the *Nicholas of the Tower* was, or whether he had any reason or backing for a special animus against Suffolk. The incident was just one of a series of clear indications that control was slipping from the hands of the government in England. When Suffolk died one of his recent associates had already met a violent end, Bishop Adam Moleyns, who had been lynched by a mob of malcontent soldiers at Portsmouth. This was an ominous beginning; much worse was to follow before the summer of 1450 was out.

In the early spring there had been a number of serious riots in Kent, which grew in May into a full-scale rebellion, the revolt of Jack Cade. The rising spread to Essex, which sent a contingent to join Cade before London, and areas further afield were affected too. Superficially, this revolt of the 'commons of Kent' bore a resemblance to the movement of 1381; but it was really very different. It was not a peasants' revolt. A good many artisans of the Kentish towns were involved, but it also found support among men of higher status. Prosperous yeomen, and men who were notables in their local communities, were prominent among those later pardoned for their part in the rising. Over seventy persons who described themselves as gentlemen were involved, and Cade's lieutenant, Robert Poynings, came of lordly blood. Cade himself claimed that his name was Mortimer and that he had connexions with the Duke of York (who he really was we do not know). The concerns of the rebels, as revealed in the three manifestos that have come down to us, were a mixture of the social and the political.[32] The longest of the three is much preoccupied with social and economic grievances, some of them specifically Kentish, with maintenance and extortion by local officials in the county, with purveyance and the administration of the statute of labourers. Politics, though, were very much to the fore in all three. The rebels demanded the punishment of the traitors who were about the king, 'the false progeny and affinity of the Duke of Suffolk', in consequence of whose counsel the good Duke Humphrey was done to death, and 'the realm of France was lost, the duchy of Normandy, Gascony, Guienne and Anjou'. The rebels demanded that the king should 'take about his noble person men of his true blood from his royal realm', to wit the Duke of York, and the dukes of Exeter, Buckingham and Norfolk. 'We say that our sovereign lord may understand this,' Cade's men concluded: 'His false council has lost his law: his merchandise is lost: his common people are destroyed: France is lost. The king himself is so placed that he may not pay for his meat and drink.'[33]

The reaction of Henry VI's government to the crisis of popular revolt compares unfavourably with that of Richard II and his advisers in 1381. Cade's men withdrew from Blackheath, where they were assembled, in the night of 17 June, after exchanges with a delegation from the council, headed by the two archbishops, to whom they handed in a petition for redress. When, two days later, a group among the retainers of the lords with the king virtually mutinied, and demanded action on the rebels' requests, the kingdom's governors panicked. Lord Saye (treasurer, and chamberlain of the household, particularly detested by the Kentishmen) was arrested and sent to the Tower, and a proclamation issued that all 'traitors' should be taken, wherever they might be. Then, on 25 June, Henry and his councillors made off for the midlands, leaving the Mayor of London and Lord Scales, in charge at the Tower, to face the music if the rebels should reappear before the capital. On 29 June Cade's men did reappear at

Blackheath, and on 2 July advanced to Southwark; on 3 July, after a brief skirmish, they crossed London Bridge into the city.

Cade's rebels were in control of London on 4 July. Lord Saye, was taken from the Tower, subjected to the mockery of a trial, and executed, along with his retainer William Cromer who had been sheriff of Kent. A third member of the recent governing clique, Bishop Ayscough, had been assassinated at Salisbury a few days before. Both in London and the suburbs, there was a good deal of disordered looting and pillaging. The rebels were only dislodged from the city when Lord Scales brought out his professional troops from the Tower, and after a fierce fight which raged all the night of 5 July on London Bridge. A free pardon in the end dispersed them, though Cade himself and some others remained in arms; he died soon after, mortally wounded in an attack on Queenborough castle. The government did not even then feel strong enough to take repressive steps, and despatched instead a judicial commission into Kent to hear the grievances of the county. The momentum of rebellion died down only gradually: the threat of large-scale disturbance rumbled on in Kent for five years.

Cade's revolt, and the deaths of Suffolk, Moleyns, Ayscough and Lord Saye demonstrate clearly the degree to which, in the year 1450, the governing council had lost control of the kingdom. In the years preceding, Suffolk had maintained himself only by his personal influence with the king and queen, and by total unscrupulousness when it came to eliminating such potential opponents as Humphrey of Gloucester. In fairness to him, it must be admitted that he came to influence at a time when public confidence in government, shaken by financial mismanagement and by reverses in the war in France, had long been declining, and that he inherited a well nigh impossible diplomatic situation. But he succeeded only in making confusion worse. The misdoings of his period of ascendancy, at home and abroad, built up popular resentment to flashpoint. When Englishmen suddenly saw what was left to them of Henry V's famous conquests in the process of being engulfed, the structure of central authority proved too fragile to stand the shock. The collapse of government that ensued brought popular unrest to the surface in the volcanic eruption of Cade's revolt, and sowed the seeds of new tensions among the great. Out of these grew the struggles which we call the Wars of the Roses.

Notes

1 See P. and F. Strong, 'The last will and codicils of Henry V', *E.H.R.*, vol. 96 (1981), pp. 89–98 (this last will was long thought to be lost).
2 *R.P.* vol. IV, p. 326.
3 ibid., vol. IV, pp. 174–5.
4 ibid., vol. IV, pp. 175–6.
5 ibid., vol. IV, p. 201.
6 *L. and P.* vol. II, pt. II, pp. 386–7: see also K. H. Vickers, *Humphrey of Gloucester* (London, 1907), pp. 130–1.
7 J. Hardyng, *Chronicle*, ed. H. Ellis (London, 1812), p. 391.

8 *Great Chronicle of London*, ed. A. H. Thomas and I. D. Thornley (London, 1938), p. 136.

9 ibid. p. 137.

10 J. S. Roskell, *The Commons and their Speakers in English Parliaments, 1376–1523* (Manchester, 1965), p. 186.

11 *R.P.* vol. IV, p. 392.

12 ibid. p. 423.

13 *P.P.C.* vol. IV, p. 225.

14 *R.P.* vol. IV, p. 425.

15 ibid. p. 439.

16 ibid., vol. IV, p. 337.

17 *P.P.C.* vol. IV, p. 64, and *R.P.* vol. IV, pp. 421–2.

18 J. Fortescue, *The Governance of England*, ed. C. Plummer (Oxford, 1885), p. 145.

19 *L. and P.* vol. II, pt. II, p. 446.

20 ibid., vol. II, pt. II, pp. 440–51.

21 ibid. p. 442.

22 *Foed.*, vol. X, pp. 764–7.

23 *L. and P.* vol. II, pt. II, pp. 451–60.

24 *R.P.* vol. V, p. 61 (south coast shires), p. 106 (march of Wales).

25 ibid., vol. V, p. 16.

26 ibid., vol. V, p. 108.

27 ibid., vol. V, p. 63.

28 See Storey, *H. of L.*, pp. 34–5.

29 *P.L.* No. 56.

30 ibid. No. 144.

31 *R.P.* vol. V, pp. 177–9, 179–82.

32 I. M. W. Harvey, *Jack Cade's Rebellion of 1450* (Cambridge, 1991), Appx. A, pp. 186–9, for texts.

33 See *Three Fifteenth Century Chronicles*, ed. J. Gairdner (Camden Soc., 1880), pp. 96–7.

Note on secondary reading (post 1970)

Two major studies give ample coverage of the domestic history of Henry VI's reign, to 1450, R.A. Griffiths, *The reign of Henry VI* (London, 1981) and B.P. Wolffe, *Henry VI* (London, 1981). J.A. Watts, *Henry VI and the Politics of Kingship* (Cambridge, 1996) presents a penetrating and innovatory interpretation. The relevant chapters of C. Carpenter, *The Wars of the Roses: Politics and the Constitution, 1437–1509*, and of R.L. Storey, *The End of the House of Lancaster* (London, 1966) are extremely useful. G.L. Harriss's *Cardinal Beaufort* (Oxford, 1988) traces the career of a figure who was a dominant political payer through most of the period. His great rival, Humphrey of Gloucester, lacks a modern reassessment; on the disgrace of his duchess, Eleanor Cobham, see R.A. Griffiths 'The trial of Eleanor Cobham, an episode in the fall of Humphrey Duke of Gloucester', *Bulletin of the John Rylands Library*, vol. 51 (1969), and on his humanist patronage S. Saygin *Duke Humphrey of Gloucester and the Italian Humanists* (Lerden, 1997). H. Castor, *The King, the Crown and the Duchy of Lancaster* (Oxford, 2000) is illuminating in relation to the career of the Duke of Suffolk. On the early political career of Richard Duke of

York see P.A. Johnson, *Duke Richard of York, 1411–1460* (Oxford, 1988). Among many valuable essays on the political history of the time, especially useful are B.P. Wolffe, 'The personal rule of Henry VI', in S.B. Chrimes, C.D. Ross and R.A. Griffiths (eds.), *Fifteenth Century England, 1399–1509* (Manchester, 1972): J. Watts, 'The Counsels of King Henry VI, *c.* 1435–1445', *E.H.R.*, vol. 106 (1991), and 'When did Henry VI's minority end?', in D.J. Clayton, R.G. Davies and P. McNiven (eds.), *Trade, Devotion and Government: papers in Later Medieval History* (Stroud, 1994); and G.L. Harriss, 'Marmaduke Lumley and the Exchequer crisis of 1446–9', in J.G. Rowe (ed.), *Aspects of Late Medieval Government and Society: Essays presented to J.R. Lander* (Toronto, 1986).

On the crisis of spring 1450 and Cade's revolt, topics which conclude this chapter, see I. Harvey, *Jack Cade's Rebellion of 1450* (Oxford, 1991); and R. Virgoe, 'The death of William de la Pole, Earl of Suffolk', *Bulletin of the John Rylands Library*, vol. 47 (1964/5).

18 The Wars of the Roses
   1450–1461

The aristocracy and gentry of the fifteenth century were always inclined to use force when they could have gone to law: after Cade's revolt they had less hesitation than ever about putting their private quarrels to the issue of arms. The early 1450s witnessed recourse to violence in a whole host of disputes. Summonses of the offenders before the council, which was usually the only effective authority when the great were involved, now simply went unheeded. Lord Cobham's men clashed with those of Lord Wiltshire, those of Lord Cromwell with the men of the Duke of Exeter. In the west September 1451 saw the Earl of Devon formally besieging his old enemy Lord Bonville in Taunton castle. The worst troubles were in the north, where the long-standing feud of Nevilles and Percies threatened to achieve the stature of a full-scale private war. The Percies viewed with understandable dismay the rising fortune of their rivals. Richard Neville had married the heiress of Salisbury and had acquired important estates in Yorkshire and elsewhere from his mother, Joan Beaufort; his son Richard had married Anne Beauchamp, and in 1449 succeeded in her right to the earldom of Warwick and its magnificent inheritance. The younger Percies, in particular the Earl of Northumberland's tempestuous third son, Baron Egremont, saw no means of checking an influence which threatened to swamp their power in their traditional homeland, short of force. Many historians have regarded the battle at Heworth in 1453 between the followers of Nevilles and Percies as the first battle of the Wars of the Roses, 'the beginning of the sorrows of England'.[1]

The most important of all the aristocratic quarrels that threatened the peace in these times was that of the dukes of York and Somerset. It was different from the others. Theirs was not just a quarrel over lands, or inheritance, or local influence; it was a political feud. In order to understand the quarrel between these two men, which in the end drew into its orbit all the other vendettas of the aristocracy, it is necessary to remind oneself of the salient facts in their careers up to about the year 1450.

Edmund Beaufort succeeded his brother John Duke of Somerset, who died in 1444, leaving no male heir. The Beauforts were descended from John of Gaunt, by his third wife Catherine Swinford, so Somerset was the senior male

member of the house of Lancaster after the king. But for the statute that barred
the Beauforts from the line of succession, he would have been Henry VI's male
heir in 1450 (Margaret, the daughter of his brother John, was in fact the
mother of Henry VII). Edmund had a distinguished record as a military leader
in France in the early 1440s, and although his wealth was negligible by comparison with York's in terms of land, he had done well for himself in the way of
title and office. He had been created first Earl, later Marquis of Dorset; and in
1446 it was he who was appointed to succeed York as lieutenant in Normandy.
As lieutenant he had been intimately concerned in the cession of Maine and
knew of the moves that led up to the capture of Fougères; and he was the
commander immediately responsible for the disasters of 1449 and 1450. But
though he was, after Suffolk, the man most obviously to blame, he was not
called to account when he came back to England with his bedraggled army
after the fall of Caen, just after the collapse of Cade's revolt. Instead he was
called to the council table and promoted constable of England; he was soon to
become also captain of Calais, the most important remaining military command
overseas. It was to him now that the court turned, as did householders like John
Say and John Trevilian, who had been Suffolk's associates and felt the need now
for a new leader and protector.

Richard of York's career and position were different. After the king, he was the
greatest landowner in the realm, with property in many English counties and in
Wales, as well as vast estates in Ireland. The most important concentration of
his properties was in central Wales and in the English border counties. He was
of the blood royal on both sides. His father was that Richard of Cambridge
who was executed for treason at Southampton in 1415, and who was the
younger son of Edmund of Langley, Edward III's fourth son. Richard became
the heir of York when his uncle was killed at Agincourt. His mother was Anne
Mortimer, and when the last Earl of March died in 1425 he was his heir also.
In the legitimate line of succession he was closest to Henry VI's throne in
1450; and through the Mortimers his line went back to Lionel of Clarence,
who was the second son of Edward III and older than Gaunt; and so he inherited
the Mortimer claim to the throne which, if dormant, was technically senior in
blood to that of the house of Lancaster. In the early 1440s he had been abroad
too much to be close to the court and its circle. He had twice been lieutenant
in Normandy; and in his second term there had been slighted first by the grant
to John Beaufort in 1443 of a lieutenancy independent of his, and secondly
when Edmund Beaufort superseded him in 1446. As lieutenant he had incurred
heavy expenses which the exchequer had been slow to meet; in 1450 he was still
owed more than £38,000. His appointment to the lieutenancy of Ireland in
1447 meant that he was again out of the country in the critical period from
1449 to the summer of 1450. In France, where he had been comparatively
successful, he had attracted to his circle a number of distinguished military
figures such as John Popham and William Oldhall, men of a class to whose
pride and interests the collapse of the English cause abroad was particularly
painful. He thus had numerous grounds for resentment against the government

in general and Somerset in particular. He had suspicions, in 1450, that Somerset might use his influence with the childless Henry VI to quash the act barring the Beauforts from the succession, so disappointing York and his heirs of their hopes of a throne.[2]

The propaganda of Cade's revolt with its demand that Henry take York into his council, showed that Duke Richard was in 1450 one of the few magnates who still enjoyed an untarnished popular reputation. For just that reason, he was a man whose potential influence the courtiers and household men whose reputations were tarnished felt that they had cause to fear. The confusion following the revolt and the English collapse abroad gave him a clear opportunity to intervene in England, and secure a commanding position for himself. At the beginning of September he came across from Ireland and landed in Wales. The king's current advisers very foolishly revealed their hostility by attempting to impede his landing. He nevertheless reached London safely, with a retinue, to demand his place in the council and the trial of those popularly accused of treason – to wit, chiefly, Somerset. The stage was set for the confrontation from which the Wars of the Roses directly sprang.

The years from 1450 to 1461 witnessed dislocations of government which were often total, the outbreak of a ferocious civil war, and the ultimate supplanting of the Lancastrian dynasty by that of York, in the person of Duke Richard's son Edward IV. The political events of the period are confused and complicated, and historians are widely disagreed about the factors that conditioned their troubled pattern. For the sake of simplicity it seems easiest to recount first what happened, as briefly as may be consonant with coherence, before attempting to analyse the underlying reasons for disorder.

York's protest to the king, on his arrival in England in 1450, had no very visible effect. He was soon busy, 'labouring' to ensure the election of men sympathetic with his views to the parliament which was summoned for November 1450. He had some success at least, and the man whom the commons elected as their speaker when they assembled was William Oldhall, a veteran of the French wars and a key figure in York's council. The popular mood was very bitter against Somerset, who was threatened by the London mob during the parliament; there seems besides to have been an attempt to have him put under arrest, and the commons petitioned the king to dismiss him from his court together with a number of other courtiers associated with the late Duke of Suffolk, including Lord Hoo, John Say, John Trevilian, and Alice, Suffolk's duchess. The commons also made demands for reforming measures, which resulted in a new and stringent act of resumption, and in an act to ensure that all future royal grants should be scrutinized by a committee of the council. On personal issues, however, the government would not be stampeded. The king agreed to ask those courtiers whom the commons had named and who were *not peers* to withdraw, but that was as far as he would go, and the crown would not entertain a posthumous act of attainder against Suffolk. In the second session of the parliament the court was confident enough to take the initiative, and when Thomas Yonge, the member for Bristol, petitioned that York be recognized as heir apparent the parliament was dissolved, and Yonge was sent to the Tower. A little before this Somerset had been appointed captain of Calais, and Abbot Bowlers of Gloucester, whose dismissal from court the commons had requested, was named for provision to the see of Hereford.

York's attempt to shake the government through parliament thus failed. His next effort was based on a show of force. It was well prepared in advance. In the autumn of 1451 letters in his name were circulating, soliciting armed aid; Oldhall and others were busy stirring popular support. Further letters to various towns, such as Canterbury, Colchester and Oxford, inciting them to support an armed movement for the common weal, were sent out early in 1452. On 3 February, at Shrewsbury, York in a great manifesto denounced the misdeeds at home and abroad of Somerset, 'who ever prevails and rules about the king's person, by which means the land is likely to be destroyed'.[3] Marching southward with his retainers, he was joined by allies from the west, the Earl of Devon and Lord Cobham with their followers. His hope probably was that this show of armed force, coinciding with a series of civic risings over southern England, would, without a battle, cause such panic among his opponents that he would be able to dictate terms to the king. His principal aims seem to have been to secure for himself a chief position in council, and to see Somerset put on trial on charges of treason (based on his misconduct and cowardice as Norman lieutenant). Once again, however, these opponents acted more firmly than he expected. The king mustered an army, and though York slipped past them into Kent, he found himself at Dartford facing a superior force, whose captains included most of the greater peers.

There could have been a pitched battle, but there was not; both sides agreed to negotiate. The bishops of Ely and Winchester and the two Neville earls of Warwick and Salisbury, kinsmen of York, acted for the king; and York finally agreed to disband his force. Yorkist inclined sources suggest that he was tricked into doing so, with a promise that Somerset would have to face his charges; a more convincing version is that, seeing himself inadequately supported, he agreed to disband on condition of his own admission to the king's good grace and of the reference of the issues between himself and Somerset to arbitration. Even so, when he reached London with the king, he found himself effectively under arrest in his city house at Baynard's Castle. In the end he was released, on the council's advice, on promising that he would never again proceed against any subject of the king by force, or raise forces without the king's licence. After that, on 7 April, a general pardon was issued for all who had been concerned in the late disturbances.

Somerset in the next few months consolidated his position. He seemed at last to be doing something to restore the court's tarnished reputation, and there was much activity to set on foot the force which in the autumn sailed under Talbot for Bordeaux. There, as we know, it won initially dramatic success. The parliament that assembled at Reading in March 1453 proved almost as sympathetic to the court as its predecessor had been hostile. Its speaker was Thomas Thorpe, a baron of the exchequer, who had associations with men who had been close both to Suffolk and to the Beauforts. With the war in Gascony in mind, the commons voted generous subsidies, and granted the king the wool subsidy for life. It further made a grant to enlist 20,000 archers for service in 'defence of the realm', in effect as a reservist bodyguard for the king, reminiscent of the White Hart retainers of Richard II. Besides this, the commons demanded that all grants to persons 'who were assembled in the field at Dartford' be revoked, and attainted William Oldhall of treason.[4] The triumph of the court seemed complete when parliament went into recess for the summer, but before it reassembled the situation had changed out of recognition.

Violent disorders had broken out again in the north in the summer of 1453, and Nevilles and Percies had called out their men. Somerset had managed to embroil himself with the powerful Neville Earl of Warwick by an attempt to poach off him the wardship of his relative George Neville's share of the Beauchamp inheritance in Wales. Talbot's army in Gascony had been annihilated at Castillon. Worst of all, in August, King Henry VI lost his senses and memory. This was the first attack of a mental disease whose periodic bouts would prostrate him at intervals through the rest of his life. Its onset saved York from the threat of complete political isolation. In blood and wealth he was the greatest of the peers, and in this new crisis his colleagues could not do without him. They insisted on his summons to the council.

When York returned to the centre of affairs, he was no longer next heir in blood to Henry VI. On 14 October 1453, after eight years of barren wedlock, Margaret had borne the king a son, Edward. It was soon clear that she would claim, in his name and her husband's, the regency, and this may be the reason why a number of influential peers began to draw closer to York, for Margaret had never been trusted. York's old ally Devon was back now at the council, and the Nevilles, having been threatened by Somerset's influence, were friendlier than in 1452. In December Somerset was put under arrest in the Tower. But when the commons, prorogued in November and again in February, finally reassembled in March, the question as to whether Margaret should be regent, or York protector, was still unsettled. It might have been referred to arms, if the death of the chancellor, Archbishop Kemp, had not precipitated matters. Someone had to have authority to appoint a successor to the office which was the lynchpin of royal administration. On 27 March York was named protector and chief of the council, on terms almost precisely similar to those on which Humphrey of Gloucester had held the office in Henry VI's minority.

York's first protectorate on the whole does his reputation credit. He of course took certain steps to secure his position. His brother-in-law Richard Neville, Earl of Salisbury, became chancellor. He himself replaced Somerset as captain of Calais, whose garrison was the most important standing military force in the crown's service. In these appointments he acted with the assent of a powerful and not notably partisan council of peers, and, significantly, no extreme steps were taken against Somerset. York's main claim to credit rests on measures taken to ensure better government. He made a genuine effort to get a better attendance of peers at the council. Moneys were earmarked for the keeping of the seas, for the expenses of the king's household, and for the cost of Calais, in an effort to ensure better accounting and economy of resources. In the summer of 1454 York personally headed a judicial commission to the north, where a thoroughly dangerous situation had developed. Thomas Percy, Lord Egremont, had succeeded in drawing into confederacy with himself Henry Holland, the young Duke of Exeter, who was in violent dispute with Lord Cromwell (whose heiress niece had recently married a Neville), and who may also have considered himself a rival with York (now allied with the Nevilles) for the protectorate. The two peers had assembled substantial followings, and seemed to be on the point of revolt. York's coming, strongly attended, frightened the pair into disbanding their men. Exeter fled to London, where he was arrested, and later placed under custody in Pontefract. Egremont remained at large, but was taken later in the year after another fracas with the Nevilles at Stamford Bridge, and imprisoned in Newgate. Perhaps York would have got further still with the pacification of the north if he had been given time, but he was not. At Christmas in 1454 Henry VI recovered his senses, and after that York's commission as protector lapsed.

Somerset's release from the Tower followed Henry's recovery, and he once again replaced York as captain of Calais; orders were given for the release also of the Duke of Exeter. Salisbury and Worcester, the chancellor and treasurer, gave way to Thomas Bourchier, Kemp's successor at Canterbury, and the Earl of Wiltshire. York and his friends read these changes as a sure sign that, if they did not act, Somerset would move to get his own back for a year and more of imprisonment, with charges of treason hanging over him. In May 1455 a great council was called to Leicester, to 'provide for the King's safety',[5] and from all shires knights favourable to the court were summoned to attend. York and the Nevilles concluded that the object of the meeting was to set the stage for their undoing. So they mustered their men, and began to march towards London.

From Royston in Hertfordshire, on 20 May, York and his allies despatched letters to the Chancellor, Thomas Bourchier Archbishop of Canterbury, explaining their purpose and demanding an audience. These reached him just as the court was about to set out for Leicester; later, the Yorkists would allege that Somerset prevented their being shown to the king. Two days later, on 22 May at St Albans, Henry, his court and Somerset, with a hastily mustered force accompanying them, found the Yorkist lords and their followers across their way.[6] They had come, they told the king's herald, 'to have the traitors that were about him punished, and in case he [York] could not have them with good will and fair consent, he would have them by force'.[7] The Duke of Buckingham, to whom Henry had entrusted command on his side, at first attempted to gain time by parleying, but it was soon clear that, since neither he nor the king would sacrifice Somerset, the chief 'traitor', the issue would be decided by arms. In the engagement that followed, the Yorkists carried the day and captured the king. Very few lost their lives, but among them were Somerset, the Earl of Northumberland and Lord Clifford. A new and terrible element thus entered into the quarrels of the great in England, the blood feud. 'By God's blood,' Lord Clifford was to cry to York's son at Wakefield in 1460, 'thy father slew mine, and so will I do thee and all thy kin.'[8]

The Yorkist lords who had shown so little moderation in rebelling, showed wise moderation in their victory. The letters that they had sent to the king through the chancellor before the battle at St Albans, proclaiming their intentions, were read in parliament, and all responsibility for the engagement was laid at the door of Somerset, Thomas Thorpe and William Joseph, of whom the first was conveniently dead and the other two unimportant. A general pardon, excluding only these three, was proclaimed. The archbishop carried on as chancellor, and his brother Viscount Bourchier became treasurer; Warwick now became captain of Calais. In the parliament's second session, in November, York at the request of the commons again became protector. He remained so until 26 February 1456, when Henry came into parliament in person and relieved him of the office. From a partisan point of view York's brief second protectorate secured for his party one tremendous political advantage, the control of Calais and its garrison; Warwick was able to remain unshaken in command there for the four crucial years following, and it was from Calais that, in 1460, the Yorkist *révanche* after the rout of Ludford was organized. In other respects the second protectorate was less remarkable. York showed the same anxiety for better government as in his first, and he was still high in esteem with many sectors of the people at the end of it, but he did not have time to achieve anything of note. His dismissal did not mark a complete eclipse from power, for he remained a member of the council. It did, however, demonstrate that all power was still insecure. The death of Somerset at St Albans had solved nothing; the rivalries of great families remained as sharp as ever, and embittered now by bloodshed. No consensus that could steer the realm toward stability had emerged among the peers who had found themselves armed on opposing sides at St Albans.

Moderate men, like the Bourchiers and the Duke of Buckingham, who was head of the great house of Stafford, seem to have hoped at the end of York's second protectorate for a political compromise, whereby the court and the Yorkist group should work together in council. The party that was centred on the queen's household and the heirs of the men who had died at St Albans was bent not on compromise with the Yorkists, but on their elimination. Their alliance was a natural one: the Yorkist resort to arms had aroused in Margaret fears that her son's rights, perhaps even his succession, might come under threat. Her leadership ensured for her party ready access to Henry VI personally; and so they steadily gained ground. The outbreak of private war in the Welsh marches between York's followers, led by Sir William Herbert, and Edmund Tudor, Earl of Richmond (regarded by the queen as an important prop to her son's authority as Prince of Wales), must have strengthened their argument that compromise was not possible; and the removal of the two Bourchiers from the offices of chancellor and treasurer late in 1456 was a sign of their growing dominance. Bishop Waynflete of Winchester became chancellor, and the treasurer was the Earl of Shrewsbury, now becoming an important figure in the court party; the queen's chancellor, Laurence Booth, became keeper of the privy seal about the same time. The last major effort towards compromise was made by the king in person in March 1458. York, Warwick and Salisbury agreed to pay for the foundation of a chantry at St Albans, in which prayers should be said for the souls of all who had fallen in the battle there, and to make compensation to their families. There followed a ceremonial reconciliation of the parties. The vast retinues that peers brought with them to London for the meeting of the great council that prepared the way for this 'love-day' (Northumberland is said to have brought 1500 men south with him) suggests that a good many of them feared that its discussions would prove the flashpoint for renewed violent confrontation. It also suggests that the reconciliation was a form of words only, in which no one had much faith. So it proved to be.

In 1459, the tensions that the love-day had failed to still escalated into renewed crisis. The Yorkist lords did not attend a great council at Coventry in June, from which rumours emerged that charges were being prepared against them. They decided on a pre-emptive strike. Warwick crossed from Calais in September with an armed company, and marched toward Worcester to join up with the followings raised by his father Salisbury and by York. Salisbury, hurrying out of the north, defeated at Blore Heath a Lancastrian force under Lord Audley which sought to bar his way: its leader was killed in the fighting. The Yorkists effected their junction, but by that time the king and Margaret had assembled an army considerably more substantial than their combined forces. When the two hosts came face to face at Ludford Bridge, in Shropshire, morale among the Yorkist troops began to crack. Their leaders had been outmanoeuvred, militarily and politically. Many of them were unwilling to fight with their sovereign personally present among their opponents and Andrew Trollope, with a large party of the soldiers from Calais, took his men over to the king's side. On the night of 12 October the Yorkist lords slipped away under cover of dark and fled, York to Ireland, Salisbury and Warwick, with York's heir Edward Earl of March, to Calais. Their army capitulated next day, and disbanded.

Before the 12 October, writs had already gone out to summon the parliament which met at Coventry in November. Unsurprisingly in the circumstances, few of the representatives who came to it had Yorkist sympathies or connections. The mood of Margaret and her advisers is well summed up in the tract called the *Somnium Vigilantis*, put out by one of their clerical supporters, in order to impress on any waverers among those assembled the need for condign punishment of those who had so recently challenged the royal authority and dared to confront in arms the king in person.[9] Mercy and pardon would now be only folly; as their repeated rebellion demonstrated, 'they been incurable'. A wholesale act of attainder convicted York, the Nevilles and their supporters of treason, and legalized the seizure of their lands. The distribution of the major part of the forfeitures to Margaret's loyal supporters eliminated for the future any room that may have remained for compromise or conciliation between the parties. The Yorkists had now to return to the fight or lose all. If the *Somnium* is any guide there were those who thought this was going too far,[10] but their voices were not much heeded in the 'parliament of Devils' at Coventry.

Those courtiers who received grants from the forfeited estates of the Yorkist leaders did not enjoy them for long, for in the summer of 1460 the wheel of fortune turned again. At the end of June Warwick and Salisbury, with March, slipped across from Calais. London opened its gates to them, and marching north they met and defeated the royal host at Northampton. The Duke of Buckingham, the Earl of Shrewsbury, Lords Beaumont and Egremont all fell in the battle, and the king was taken. York was still in Ireland when it was fought, and he did not cross to England until the eve of the parliament that opened on 7 October. Three days later he arrived with his host in London. On 16 October his counsel came into parliament, and submitted on York's behalf a claim to the crown of England.

Up to 1460 York and his followers had always stuck to the claim that their sole aim was to secure the dismissal and punishment of those who had advised King Henry VI traitorously, and so to ensure the better government of his realm. Now, when York brought the rival royal right of the house of March into the open, no one seems to have been anxious to hear about it. This seems surprising as far as the Nevilles are concerned, since they must surely have known of his intentions: perhaps they had concluded, in the months between their victory at Northampton and York's arrival from Ireland that it would be impolitic to press it. The lack of enthusiasm on the part of other peers is readily understandable. York's claim was based, quite simply, on the assertion that he was the heir of a line senior by descent in blood from Edward III to all the kings of the house of Lancaster.[11] To admit his claim would therefore mean, for these great men at least, admitting that they and their ancestors had for sixty years lived under usurpers, conniving at the exclusion from the throne of the rightful heirs. It would also mean war *à l'outrance* against any of their fellow peers who remained loyal to the house of Lancaster, for everyone knew that Queen Margaret would never abandon the fight for her son's rights while he lived. It is not surprising therefore that the lords did not want to answer York's counsel, that they tried to pass the question over to the judges of the common law, or that the judges passed it back, declaring that such matters were beyond their science, being governed not by the common law but by the law of God and of nature. In such a matter, they averred, the lords of the blood and the peerage of the realm must be the judges.

This evident desire not to open up the question of the Lancastrian royal title makes it the more remarkable that the peers found such difficulty as they did in answering York's submission. Of all the arguments that they advanced against it, based on prescription, on the statutes, on York's own long acquiescence in Henry's rule, the only one in which they seem to have placed real confidence was the unquestionable fact that they themselves had all sworn personally to be Henry's true and faithful liegemen. A stand on this point was inevitably only a partial answer to York; it clarified the situation as regards Henry VI, but not for the future. In all other respects York's arguments seem to have carried a measure at least of conviction, and the peers decided to take the same way out of the dilemma as had the Treaty of Troyes for France, to recognize the reigning king for his lifetime and to entail the succession upon the claimant – York – and his heirs. Like the French lords who were parties to the Treaty of Troyes, the peers took oaths individually to uphold the new settlement. Thus the lords admitted that, however unwilling they might be to go back on their allegiance to Henry VI, they had no real answer to Richard of York's proud claim, based on seniority in blood, that 'though right for a time rest and be put to silence, yet it rotteth not nor shall not perish'.[12]

Before the year 1460 was out, Queen Margaret, with the Duke of Somerset, the Earl of Devon and the Earl of Northumberland, had gathered a new army in the north. On the last day of the year, this army overthrew York's at Wakefield. Duke Richard died fighting, and his ally the Earl of Salisbury, who was taken prisoner, was beheaded on the field. Later, both their heads were displayed on the walls of York, the duke's crowned with a paper cap. When Margaret advanced south in February she had promises of aid from both France and Scotland. On 17 February she defeated Warwick's forces at St Albans. King Henry, whom the Earl had brought to the battle, was freed to join his wife, but even with him at her side, the Londoners would not open their gates to Margaret. She withdrew north, and Warwick was able to join York's son Edward, Earl of March, who had just defeated the Earl of Wiltshire's Lancastrian army in the borders of Wales at Mortimer's Cross.

After Mortimer's Cross, as after St Albans, prisoners of distinction taken in the field were executed. Gregory's macabre description of the death of Owen Tudor brings home vividly the way in which such summary processes were introducing a new and demoralizing vindictiveness into English political strife:

> And in that journey was Owen Tudor taken and brought unto Haverford-west, and he was beheaded at the market place, and his head set upon the highest grice of the market cross, and a mad woman combed his hair and washed away the blood of his face, and she got candles and set about him burning more than a hundred. This Owen Tudor was father unto the earl of Pembroke, and had wedded Queen Katherine, King Harry the VI's mother, weening and trusting all alway that he should not be headed till he saw the axe and the block; and when that he was in his doublet he trusted on pardon and grace till the collar of his red velvet doublet was ripped off. Then he said 'That head shall lie on the stock that was wont to lie on Queen Katherine's lap' . . . and full meekly took his death.[13]

At St Albans the Yorkist–Neville alliance had lost the advantage that had been crucial to them in 1460, their possession of the king. They now in consequence really had no option but to accept the logic of events, and to make a new king of their own. Acclaimed by the citizens of London, Edward of March was installed as king (but not as yet formally crowned, of course) in Westminster Abbey on 4 March, before he set out to follow Margaret's troops. He found them on the 29 March at Towton in Yorkshire, and won an overwhelming victory. Though Margaret, Henry and their son escaped in the rout, Edward was left king of England for the time being; a new reign had begun and a new dynasty had been founded.

There has been a great deal of debate among historians as to how we should try to explain the civil disorders, in the course of which the house of Lancaster was ultimately displaced. Traditionally the Wars of the Roses have been regarded, as they were by Shakespeare, as a straightforward struggle for the throne, a more or less direct consequence of the usurpation of 1399. Some have sought to connect the civil wars with the earlier struggles of Gloucester and Beaufort, the old apologists respectively of warlike and pacific policies abroad; the English collapse in France according to this view (which now looks rather dated), set their political heirs, York and Somerset, at one another's throats. Professor Robin Storey has argued very cogently a view which explains the outbreak of the civil wars in more domestic terms, as a consequence of the mounting rivalries of aristocratic houses, and of the social disorder to which maintenance, the chief abuse of aristocratic patronage, gave rise. Others would explain the outbreak of the wars as resulting from the individual unfitness to rule of a single under mighty king, Henry VI, who was too weak and too mad to restrain his over ambitious magnate subjects. K. B. MacFarlane argued forcibly for this interpretation, to which John Watts has added additional and important refinements.

Storey's explanation does not disregard the importance of the king's incapacity, but does not make it the key factor. If Henry's unfitness to rule was so patent, how comes it, he asks, that York could only muster a minority and partisan group among the peers to rescue the kingdom from it? For him, maintenance and lack of governance were what brought conflict to a head, rather than, simply, the under-mightiness of the king. The Wars of the Roses were, he writes, 'the consequence of an escalation of private feuds. Gentry, with understandable lack of confidence in the processes of law, attached themselves to lords who could give them protection against their personal enemies, and in return supported their patrons in private wars with their peers. These baronial hostilities similarly resulted in the contestants aligning themselves with the major political rivals, and thus drawing their retainers into the conflict.[14] Storey has backed his thesis with an impressive body of evidence, drawn from an intensive study of the local and family rivalries of both the gentry and the peerage in the 1450s. He has shown, firstly, how the disorderly conditions of the age made it imperative for the gentry to find powerful patrons and how those who were successful used the influence that they so acquired to further private ends, as Tuddenham and Heydon, for instance, did in Norfolk. He has shown, secondly, how the influence of the peers who were patrons depended on their standing with the court and the king, which could secure for peers themselves lucrative offices, grants of crown land and the prospect of advantageous marriage, and for their clients control of local offices, as those of sheriff and justice of the peace, which were the key to county influence. He has shown, thirdly, how the allegiance and the switches of allegiance of aristocratic families were conditioned by their own standing at court and that of their chief rivals. The key moment, according to Storey's thesis, came when the old family feud of Nevilles and Percies became aligned with the rivalry of York and Somerset, the protagonists on both sides being from then on too powerful to resign themselves to eclipse without an armed struggle.

There is clearly a great deal of force in this interpretation, especially in the significance it attaches to the convergence, in 1453–4, of the quarrel between York and Somerset with the clash of Nevilles with Percies. Nevertheless, it does not quite satisfy as an overall explanation. The webs of influence that bound together the fortunes of peers and their retainers were not a relatively new feature in the 1450s, but a constant of the late medieval social and political scene (a point which McFarlane, whose work, more than that of any other, first brought home their importance in the disorders of Henry VI's reign, emphasized particularly). The ramification of private feuds may explain a great deal about the Wars of the Roses, but not why they happened when they did. It does not explain why, in southern England at least, the Yorkists enjoyed a general popular sympathy which their opponents did not. Perhaps still more important, contemporaries, though they were aware that the civil wars were closely bound up with struggles for private influence among the great, believed that other and more serious issues were at stake as well. It is unlikely that contemporaries were entirely wrong.

The view which singles out the under-mightiness of the king as the central problem behind the crisis of the Lancastrian dynasty in the 1450s clearly has much to recommend it. There can be no doubt that Henry VI's personal inadequacy as a monarch was a crucial factor in English politics in the 1440s and 1450s. It is not easy to find traces of any political decisions that were indubitably his own, and those that have been claimed for him, as the decision to cede Maine to the French in 1446, do not enhance respect for his judgement. Normally, the evidence suggests, he was ruled by other men or by his wife and their unscrupulous *coterie* of clients. The long minority had destroyed the coherence of the body of faithful Lancastrian retainers and servants, on whom Henry IV and Henry V had depended so much. This was not Henry's fault, but he failed signally, after he came of age, to reconstitute a body of loyal supporters committed to him personally among the nobles and gentility, which was essential to maintain kingship in the fifteenth century. Those who were about his court owed their influence and position, for the most part, to others. The authority of royal command ceased to be respected, because men did not believe that it was Henry who gave the orders. So in the end war broke out, McFarlane argued, 'because the nobility were unable to rescue the kingdom from Henry's inanity by any other means'. Arms had to be the solution, because inevitably only a section of the nobility was ready to act; the king's incompetence had divided the aristocracy, setting those who profited by it fatally at odds with those who did not, and nothing short of force would remove the former.[15]

Watts refines this general interpretation in a very illuminating way. As he ably illustrates from contemporary theoretical writing on royal government, it was the common assumption in fifteenth century England that the king's personal authority was the sole legitimate basis of command. Wise counsel aiming at the common weal could only be made authoritative by a royal judgement extrinsic to the body or group counselling. For counsellors to be heeded, they needed therefore to have easy access to the king. This created no problems in normal circumstances, under a king who would listen to various counselling voices, and then make a decision which drew authority from his personal directive will. In Henry VI, however, after he came of age, his counsellors found themselves faced with a ruler who was spectacularly lacking in any sort of directive will. The only possible way for them out of the consequent constitutional dilemma was to somehow endow him with what Watts calls a 'surrogate' will. His personal authority, that is to say, must be associated with decisions made for him by others, rather as in a minority but without the official sanction that arrangements for a minority would give.[16]

For a leading counsellor to thus 'forge' a royal will, and so generate a flow of sensible and acceptable governmental decisions, directed at the common weal, two things were necessary: ready and regular access to the king whose will needed to be identified with the decisions he was advocating, and a measure of consensus from other great men of the kingdom in those decisions, as being consistent with the common weal. This combination, Watts argues, was in essence what successively Suffolk, Somerset, York and Margaret of Anjou were all trying to achieve; all failed to do so. York in his first protectorate succeeded in fulfilling the second requirement, of carrying sufficient consensus with him: but outside the period of the king's insanity he never had sufficient court influence and support to identify his policies with the king's will. Suffolk, Somerset and Margaret all more or less achieved that first requirement, but all failed with the second; Suffolk, because his disastrous foreign policy (and his greed for favours) undermined consensus and left him isolated; Somerset because York's implacable resentment (and, once again, his own acquisitiveness) meant that he could not control the situation when Henry VI lost his wits; Margaret because her hostility to York and the Nevilles was too open and unrestrained, given their wealth, standing and records (and because she lost, ultimately, when it came to fighting). Henry alone was in a position which should have enabled him to restrain these contenders for his surrogate will, by imposing his own; but he had no will of his own to impose. In the end, there was no alternative to looking for another king, with a will and a readiness to make his own decisions, and so break the vicious circle of escalating violence.

The broad thrust of this explanatory approach of McFarlane and of Watts, focusing on the unfitness of Henry VI for the role of monarch, is clearly very persuasive. It helps to clarify why Lancastrians and Yorkists respectively took the political stances that they did, and the kind of support bases that they could look to. Lancastrian propaganda emphasized the unique quality of royal authority, emanating from the king personally and vital to good governance. Influence centred in the royal household and radiating outward from it, easy access to the king and benefits from his patronage were the forces that held together the core association of courtier peers and ecclesiastics, household knights and esquires, royal and duchy of Lancaster officials that made first Somerset and then Queen Margaret politically formidable. With the passage of time their stance began to bear an appearance that might be dubbed ultra royalist (and was so depicted by their opponents). From 1456, when Margaret was keeping the court as much as she could away from London (where York was popular), the household provided the way round the problem of loosened contact with the chancery and exchequer. By 1458, if not earlier, the treasurer of the household, Sir Thomas Tuddenham, was drawing financially directly on the sheriffs (at least sixteen of whom, that year, had pensions in the household). The treasurer was the Earl of Wiltshire, another entrenched Lancastrian, who was quite willing to acquiesce in this bypassing of the exchequer. The direct association of the household with the county administration proved invaluable again next year, when a royal host had to be mobilized to face the challenge of York, Salisbury and Warwick, and opinion massaged in the November parliament at Coventry. In the last years of Margaret's dominance the administration seems to have been developing into a household tyranny strongly reminiscent of that of Richard II's last years; it had indeed hit on some expedients which Richard II's courtiers did not think of.

York's answer to his rivals' control through court and household was to take his stance on the common weal and its needs, and to question publicly any association of their policies and practices with the king's will. He made no attempt to act the constitutionalist, in the sense that old fashioned English historians understood, and play on the institutional limits to royal authority, demanding rather that it be freed from corrupt influences. There was a strong populist note in his appeals for support. Proclamations, manifestos and open letters were the instruments of his propaganda, and they were skilfully worded to show his devotion to the public good. It was the 'great complaining and rumour that is universal throughout this realm', he explained in 1450, that prompted his return from Ireland to take a hand in affairs.[17] Everything that he proposed to do, he assured men at Shrewsbury in 1452, would promote 'the ease, peace, tranquility, and safeguarding of the realm'.[18] In 1455 his letters declared that it was for the 'restful, politic rule' of the land that he was labouring.[19] His last great manifesto, put out in 1460, ranged over the whole history of a decade and more to charge the courtiers with all that had gone amiss: with the death of Humphrey of Gloucester; with responsibility for the loss of Normandy and Gascony; with embezzlement of subsidies and unscrupulous private profiteering on all sides;

with the determination to make away with their rivals and have their lands. The queen's friends were openly aiming, he declared, at a tyranny, so that 'the king's subjects and their heirs and successors will be in such bondage as their ancestors never were'.[20]

York's propaganda struck a chord because the grievances that it aired were genuine popular grievances, and because a great many people supposed York to be entirely honest in his professed desire to remedy them. 'The common people of the land hated Duke Edmund (of Somerset) and loved the Duke of York, because York loved the commons and preserved the profit of the land.'[21] Even the author of the Lancastrian *Somnium Vigilantis* had to admit that popular sympathy was with the other side.[22] This went a considerable way to make up for York's exclusion from both the court and the council through long periods, and for the comparative weakness of his following among the peers, which was always his most serious disadvantage, though it did not go quite far enough. As we have seen, his place in popular esteem frightened his enemies, to the point where in the end they felt it prudent to keep the court that they controlled away from London, where popular feelings could be violently expressed. These facts have an important bearing on the dynamics of politics in mid-fifteenth-century England. Public opinion was a powerful political force. It needs to be remembered that the first major rebellion of Henry VI's reign was not a rising led by aristocrats, but the popular revolt of Jack Cade. Control of the court and of royal patronage, even with local support woven round household connexions in the counties behind it, was never enough, on its own, to ensure successful dominance. Emphatically it was not enough, if it could not be squared with what general opinion perceived as the demands of the common weal.

This should remind us forcibly of the relevance of the disasters of the English in France to the outbreak of the civil wars in England. The loss of the English provinces was a tremendous blow to national pride. For the thirty-five years before 1450 their conquest and defence had been consuming blood and treasure, and the shock was traumatic. 'Hey alas we dolorous persons', wrote William of Worcester in his *Boke of Noblesse*, 'suffering intolerable persecutions and misery, as well in honour lost as in our livelihood unrecompensed, what shall we do or say? God forbid that such great wrongs should go unpunished, so great a loss unrepaired.'[23] The damage, moreover, was not merely psychological, as we have seen. The loss of the French provinces harmed trade. The Channel became less safe than ever to English shipping, and the long cherished English dream of controlling all commerce that passed through the narrow seas stood revealed as an empty wish. Mercantile interests were by no means the only ones to suffer. Soldiers apart, there were a good many Englishmen who had a direct stake in the retention of the overseas territories, because they held lands or houses or offices of profit there. The records show clearly that Englishmen were still interested in acquiring property in Normandy and Maine, even in the 1440s. The attitude of these sorts of people is well expressed in a petition of 1452, asking for compensation: 'here follows the sorrowful lamentation for the loss of Normandy of your most true, humble and loyal subjects, of late dwelling in the towns and county of Maine . . . which is your right and proper inheritance belonging to you since the time of King Henry II after the conquest'. If they did not get some indemnity, these men declared, they would be forced to 'spend their lives in a different manner from what true Christians and loyal subjects ought to do'.[24] And we must not forget fighting men like Oliver of Kattersby, who had commanded at Domfront in 1450: 'and the said Oliver remained a prisoner, and afterward he returned out of the enemies' prison into England, and for want of comfort and relief he died of grief of heart at Westminster in very great poverty, in the year 1457'.[25] In the 1450s the individual ruin of those who had made the war in France their honourable livelihood was visible, and visible misfortune has a way of making those who see it angry.

It is not surprising, therefore, that the culpable loss of Normandy and Guienne was a recurrent theme of Yorkist propaganda. York knew that what he said on this subject would strike home, for he could read clearly between the lines of Suffolk's impeachment and Cade's proclamations. So in his Shrewsbury manifesto he called on men to consider 'first the worship, honour and manhood asserted of all nations to the people of England, whilst the kingdom's sovereign lord stood possessed of his lordship in the realm of France', and then to compare with this the 'derogation, loss of merchandise, lesion of honour, and villainy, reported generally for the loss of the same, namely unto the Duke of Somerset, when he had command and charge thereof'.[26] His ally Mowbray, when he charged Somerset with treason in the council in 1453, took up the same theme of 'the overgreat dishonours and losses that be come to this full noble realm of England'.[27] In 1460 York's manifestos were still labouring the point, charging the courtiers who had suffered 'all the old possessions which the king had in France and Normandy . . . to be shamefully lost and sold'.[28] By then York's one time success as lieutenant in Normandy was passing into the mythology of his party. 'Regent he was and governor of France', an anonymous supporter wrote: 'Normandy he guarded from danger. He passed over the river at Pontoise and drove away the King [Charles VII] and his Dauphin in flight.'[29] This sort of half accurate memory of better days past inevitably had a powerful emotive force amid the calamities of the late 1450s.

Because it can be shown that by no means all those who had fought in France were Yorkists, and because only a limited number of Englishmen were directly affected by the loss of the English provinces, the defeat of the English is often neglected in explanations of the outbreak of the English civil wars of the 1450s, which ended by bringing down the Lancastrian dynasty. It should not be. In 1450, the sense that the country's interests had been damaged and its honour outraged, and that those responsible should be held to account, was genuine and widespread. The collapse in France shattered confidence in the king's government and the counsels informing it, and at the same time propelled the furious York, former lieutenant in Normandy, into passionate confrontation with Somerset, the lieutenant who had lost the duchy. It was a double misfortune that, in this dire pass, the king on the throne should have been the inane Henry VI, and that York was sufficiently ambitious and arrogant to believe, as other ambitious magnates had in the past, that it could be justifiable, if other means could not prevail, for a great lord of the blood royal to take it on himself to right the wrongs of king and country by force. Without the defeat abroad, and without the sense that the common weal had been gravely damaged by the misconduct of the king's counsellors and chief captain, his first attempt at armed intervention, in 1452, would have been very hard to justify. Virtually all the charges that he had then prepared against Edmund Beaufort related to his mishandling of affairs in France. When he took to arms the second time, in 1455, it was still Somerset that he was after. The debacle that under Somerset engulfed English Normandy, where York was himself a significant land-owner, was what launched Richard of York in the first instance along the path that led to armed clash at St Albans with a company which included the king personally. After that, the chances of re-establishing consensus and orderly government without more battles and more bloodshed became much slimmer.

A final word must be said about the question of the succession. It is fashionable nowadays to regard this issue as something that only really became important after 1460. It is true, certainly, that up to 1460 York made no mention of his right to Henry VI's throne, but was, on the contrary, careful to stress that he was actuated by loyalty to his sovereign, seeking to save the crown from false councillors. The reaction of the peers to York's claim in 1460 shows how wise he had been to avoid this dangerous topic in earlier years. This does not, however, mean that in earlier years it was not important. The question of the succession had been much in men's minds from the beginning. York was thinking about it in 1450, when he complained that Somerset was seeking to 'corrupt' his blood and to 'undo' him and his issue – that is, to secure to the Beaufort family the succession which, since Henry was then childless, looked likely to pass to York or his heirs. Yonge was sent in the Tower in 1451 for demanding that York be recognized as heir apparent. Somerset and the court party moreover gave the succession issue deliberate prominence in the hope of thereby discrediting York as a traitor. Their packed juries in East Anglia in 1452 charged William Oldhall, York's councillor, and others with 'proposing to depose the king and put the Duke of York on the throne'.[30] York's claim to the throne was too much talked about to be kept out of sight at any time in the 1450s. As political events polarized the rivalries of the great amid the collapse of government, it became virtually certain that it would one day be advanced. Abbot Whethamstede, discussing the motives for the rebellion of the Yorkist lords in 1459, said that some thought they had risen because they were excluded from the council; others, that it was in order to rid the kingdom of the familiars of the king: 'a third group said that they had risen chiefly for this reason, that the lord Duke of York might sit on the throne of the lord king . . . and that this should be confirmed and strengthened in him and his heirs by hereditary succession, from now on and for ever'.[31] Eighteen months later Edward IV was king, but he would not have been if a Yorkist succession had not seemed on the cards for a long time before.

Notes

1   *L. and* P. vol. II, pt. II, p. [770].
2   *P.L.* Intro., p. lxi.
3   *P.L.* Intro., p. lxxiii.
4   *R.P.* vol. V, pp. 230 (archers), 265–6 (attainders).
5   *R.P.* vol. V, p. 280.
6   The complicated course of events leading up to and surrounding the first battle of St Albans are examined in detail in a long and authoritative article by C. A. J. Armstrong, 'Politics and the battle of St Albans', *B.I.H.R.* 33 (1960), pp. 1–72.
7   ibid. p. 63.
8   E. Hall, *Chronicle*, ed. H. Ellis (London, 1809), p. 251.
9   Printed by J. B. Gilson, 'A defence of the proscription of the Yorkists in 1459', *E.H.R.*, vol. 26 (1911), pp. 512–25.
10 ibid. pp. 514–15.
11 *R.P.* vol. V, pp. 375–80, sets out York's claim and gives the record of the discussion and the final settlement.
12 *R.P.* vol. V, p. 377.
13 *Gregory's Chronicle*, p. 211; quoted by J. R. Lander, *The Wars of the Roses* (London, 1965), p. 119.
14 R. L. Storey, *The End of the House of Lancaster* (London, 1966), p. 27.
15 K. B. McFarlane, 'The War of the Roses', *P.B.A.*, vol. 50 (1964), pp. 87–119.
16 J. Watts, *Henry VI and the Politics of Kingship* (Cambridge, 1966), esp. Chapters 2 and 4.
17 *P.L.* No. 114.
18 *P.L.* Intro., p. lxxiii.
19 *R.P.* vol. V, p. 280.
20 *English Chronicle*, ed. J. S. Davies (Camden Soc., 1856), p. 87. The bogy of tyranny was very much to the fore all through the period 1450–60; see for example Cade's proclamation in *Three Fifteenth Century Chronicles*, ed. J. Gairdner (Camden Soc., 1880), p. 94.
21 *English Chronicle*, p. 71.
22 *E.H.R.* 26 (1911), p. 521: 'As for the favour of the people, there is no sure ground of argument [in that] . . . it is a shrewd consequence: the people favoureth them, *ergo* they be good.'
23 *The Boke of Noblesse*, ed. J. G. Nichols (Roxburghe Club, 1860), p. 49. I have slightly paraphrased the original.
24 *L. and P.* vol. II, pt. II, p. [598].
25 *L. and P.* vol. II, p. [633].
26 *P.L.* Intro., pp. lxxii–lxxiii.
27 *P.L.* No. 191.
28 *English Chronicle*, p. 87.
29 *Political Poems and Songs* (R.S.) vol. II, p. 257.
30 See Lander, *The Wars of the Roses*, p. 63.
31 *Registrum J. Whethamstede* (R.S.) vol. I, p. 337.

Note on secondary reading (post 1970)

There has been much writing on the years 1450–61. They are well covered in the studies of Henry VI's reign cited in the bibliography to Chapter 17, by R.A. Griffiths and B.P. Wolffe (both 1981). J. Watts, *Henry VI and the Practice of Kingship* (Cambridge, 1996) is important, offering a new interpretation, which has much in common with that of C. Carpenter in her *The Wars of the Roses: Politics and the Constitution, c. 1437–1509* (Cambridge, 1997). R.L. Storey, *The End of the House of Lancaster* (London, 1966) remains valuable, and K.B. McFarlane, 'The Wars of the Roses', *Proceedings of the British Academy*, vol. 50 (1964) is seminal (reprinted in his *England in the Fifteenth Century*, London, 1981).

On Richard Duke of York, a central figure in these years, see P.A. Johnson, *Richard Duke of York, 1411–1460* (Oxford, 1988). Important articles on aspects of his career and fortunes include two papers by M.K. Jones, 'Somerset, York and the Wars of the Roses', *E.H.R.*, vol. 104 (1989), and 'Edward IV, the Earl of Warwick and the Yorkist claim to the throne', *Historical Research*, vol. 70 (1997): two papers by R.A. Griffiths, 'Richard of York's intentions in 1450 and the origins of the Wars of the Roses', *Journal of Medieval History*, vol. 1 (1975), and 'The King's council and the first protectorate of the Duke of York', *E.H.R.*, vol. 99 (1984); T.B. Pugh, 'Richard duke of York and the rebellion of Henry, Holland duke of Exeter in May 1454', *Historical Research*, vol. 63 (1990); G.L. Harriss, 'The struggle for Calais: an aspect of the rivalry between Lancaster and York', *E.H.R.*, vol. 75 (1960); and J.M.W. Bean, 'The financial position of Richard Duke of York', in J.C. Holt and J. Gillingham (eds.), *War and Government in the Middle Ages* (Woodbridge, 1984). On Queen Margaret of Anjou, from 1455 York's most determined opponent, see the relevant section in A. Gross, *The Dissolution of the Lancastrian Kingship* (Stamford, 1996); D. Dunn, 'The Queen at war: the role of Margaret of Anjou in the Wars of the Roses', in D. Dunn (ed.), *War and Society in Medieval and early Modern Britain* (Liverpool, 2000); and M. Kekewich, 'The attainder of the Yorkists in 1459; two contemporary accounts', *B.I.H.R.*, vol. 55 (1982).

On the first pitched battle of the wars, C.A.J. Armstrong, 'Politics and the Battle of St Albans', *B.I.H.R.*, vol. 33 (1960) remains vital. On rivalries of individual magnate families, see M. Cherry, 'The struggle for power in mid-fifteenth-century Devonshire', in R.A. Griffiths (ed.), *Patronage, the Crown and the Provinces* (Gloucester, 1981); R.A. Griffiths, 'Local rivalries and national politics – the Percies, the Nevilles and the Duke of Exeter', *Speculum*, vol. 43 (1968); and S.J. Payling, 'The Ampthill dispute: a study in aristocratic lawlessness and the breakdown of Lancastrian government', *E.H.R.*, vol. 104 (1989). On Humphrey Stafford, Duke of Buckingham, an important 'moderate' figure, see C. Rawcliffe, *The Staffords, Earls of Stafford and Dukes of Buckingham, 1394–1521* (Cambridge, 1978).

On military aspects, A. Goodman, *The Wars of the Roses: military activity and English Society, 1452–97* (London, 1981) is useful: this book and those under the title *The Wars of the Roses*, by J. Gillingham (London, 1981) and by A. Pollard (London, 1981) provide helpful reading on topics covered in this chapter, and in the next two also.

Section VI
The Yorkists

19 Edward IV and Richard III

Between 1461 and 1485 four kings sat upon the throne of England: Henry VI, Edward IV, Edward V and Richard III. All four were driven from the throne by force, one (Henry VI) twice, one (Edward IV) only temporarily. Edward IV was the only one of them who did not meet a violent end. As these dismal statistics witness, the political history of the twenty-five years of Yorkist rule was confused by kaleidoscopic changes of fortune, in which little else was at stake besides the power and influence of individual men. Their history is for us confused further by the fact that events in England were always closely connected with the turns of fortune in another power struggle which was going on simultaneously across the Channel, between the kings of France and their great vassals, the dukes of Burgundy.

Two issues were in consequence constantly to the fore in the high politics of this quarter of a century. One was the straightforward question, who should sit on the throne of England, and by what right? After the Yorkist triumphs of 1471, which inaugurated Edward IV's 'second reign', it looked for a time as if this question was settled; with Henry VI and his son Prince Edward both dead (the one murdered, the other killed in battle), there was no longer any obvious potential Lancastrian challenger to the Yorkist king. But the usurpation by Richard III in 1483 of Edward V's throne threw all back into the melting pot, and brought the shaky (and hitherto largely ignored) claim of Henry Tudor into new prominence. The other issue was the direction of English alliances on the continent. To the rival parties across the channel the question of who ruled England, and of how he could be manipulated in their interest, was a matter of obvious significance. These two issues were thus closely connected, but unfortunately for purposes of clarity, not in any entirely consistent way. It will be wise to say something about both, by way of introduction to the history that revolves around them.

The contending parties in England were already more or less inextricably entangled in continental power politics when Edward IV became king in 1461. This was inevitable. Henry VI's queen, Margaret, was a French princess, the kinswoman of King Charles VII and the daughter of Duke René of Anjou. The Yorkists had therefore natural ties with those who were the enemies of her family. Warwick, when in the late 1450s he was captain of Calais, established friendly contact with the dauphin Louis, who was at odds with King Charles and in exile from his court. In 1460 he and York made fruitful use of the friendliness of the papal legate, Francesco Coppini, who was also the agent of the Sforza of Milan; the Milanese were anxious to prevent Charles VII from helping René to press his claim to be king of Naples, and hoped a Yorkist government would keep Charles occupied by an attempt to invade France and recover the lost English provinces there. This past history apart, at just about the time when Edward IV became king certain events abroad helped to make the entanglement of the English succession struggle with continental politics more important.

It had always been clear that the kings of France could not indefinitely tolerate the position of near independence which Philip Duke of Burgundy had been able to establish in his French territories as a result of his sovereign's preoccupation with the war with the English. In 1461 Charles VII of France died, and his son Louis, Warwick's one time friend, succeeded. There was a change of tempo, with a new king determined to assert himself, and a confrontation of France with the Duke of Burgundy, and perhaps with the Duke of Brittany also, became likely. It seemed certain that, in the event of such a confrontation, English support for one side or the other would affect the outcome – provided of course that whoever was king of England was in sufficient control of his own kingdom to be capable of intervening effectively.

The question of the English succession was therefore of great significance to others besides Englishmen, including powers who at times might be interested in keeping the issue uncertain. Among the English themselves it was debated hotly, not only on the field of battle but on paper also as a question of law and right. Lancastrians and Yorkists concurred in making heredity central to the debate. John Fortescue, in the long years of exile to which his loyalty to the Lancastrians condemned him, defended Henry VI's title at length. His chief argument against the Yorkist claim was that, by 'the laws of God and of nature', no woman could succeed to the throne or pass on a title to it. He also sought to prove that Philippa, the daughter of Lionel of Clarence from whom the Yorkist title derived, was illegitimate.[1] There were apparently other tracts besides Fortescue's put out by the exiled Lancastrians in the 1460s, perhaps many more than have survived. Yorkist broadsheet propaganda engendered a whole historical mythology of its own. The troubles that had smitten England in Henry VI's time were God's punishment upon the people who in 1399 deserted their true born king, Richard II, in favour of a race of usurpers. The Lord had shown his wrath first when he struck Henry IV with leprosy, afterwards through the misfortunes that had dogged all Henry's progeny.[2] The justice of the claim of the true blood of York, the right heirs of Richard II, was attested by the victories that God had given them over their adversaries in the field. Yorkist kingship thus sought a martial, chivalrous glamour, such as that of Henry V and Edward III had enjoyed, which associated its claims with past prosperity and victories (an uncomfortable proportion of them fought, it must be admitted, on English soil), and with popular hopes for the recovery of the English cause abroad.

Caution is required in assessing the significance of the apparent preoccupation of the English parties with the question of hereditary royal right. Was it laboured in their propaganda because they knew that men felt the matter to be important, or because they wished to give the colour of a great legal issue to what was, in reality, not much more than a struggle for personal power and influence? The latter, it would seem, is probably nearer the truth, though a dispute over succession could never seem a light matter in an age when most individual and family fortunes stood or fell on issues of inheritance. Much noble blood was shed in the field in the Yorkist period; many men of fame and family were executed, and others whom the axe could not reach were attainted in parliament and lost lands and title. For all this the wars were not fought out in a spirit of implacable vendetta. A few families, bound by interest or loyalty to the house of Lancaster, proved irreconcilable to a Yorkist regime: the heirs of Somerset, the earls of Oxford, the Tudors. But even among the peers the majority could usually be counted upon to rally to the king *de facto,* if he could hold his own, without too much regard to his title *de jure.* Among the influential gentry families of England's regions, the overriding anxiety, it seems clear, was for stability. The domestic quiet of Edward IV's second reign and its governmental achievements offer testimony to their readiness to accept a monarch who seemed able to assure it to them, whatever some may have thought in private about his title. Conversely, the sudden violence of Richard III's usurpation shook their confidence in his ability to do so, and that rather than doubts about his right, was the fatal flaw in his regime. These facts seem to make clear what was the true significance of the concentration of propagandists on hereditary right; it drew a thin veil of principle over the fact that what was in dispute in the English civil wars was not the manner of government of the country, but more simply, what persons should govern it.

It will be wise here, before we embark on the confusing history of the wars themselves, to say a word about the chief protagonists in them. These were Queen Margaret of Anjou, Richard of York's old enemy; Richard Neville, Earl of Warwick, who had been York's most important supporter; and York's three surviving sons, Edward IV, George Duke of Clarence, and Richard Duke of Gloucester, who later became Richard III.

After Edward IV's victory at Towton on 29 March 1461, Queen Margaret, with her husband and her son Prince Edward, retreated into Scotland. Many of the peers who had been prominent as her supporters in the closing years of Henry VI's rule were now dead, slain or beheaded; the earls of Wiltshire, Shrewsbury, Devon and Northumberland, and Lord Beaumont (though of course they had left heirs). In England she now had to look for support mainly in the north and in Wales. In Northumberland her supporters held the Percy castles of Alnwick and Bamburgh (Berwick had been surrendered to the Scots early in 1461); they included Henry, the new Duke of Somerset, Lord Roos and Sir Ralph Percy. In Wales the one time followers of the Beauforts (Somerset) and the Talbots (Shrewsbury) provided the nucleus of a Lancastrian group, now headed by the Earl of Pembroke, Jasper Tudor. Outside England, Margaret looked for support to James III of Scotland and to her relative Louis XI, the new king of France. It was from Scotland that she renewed contact with the French court. Neither James nor Louis was to be much relied on, now that Margaret was no longer a queen regnant, for Edward IV could make himself dangerous to both. She, however, was indomitable, ready to meet any and every hardship and adventure to which exile, flight or poverty might condemn her, and determined to fight on for as long as her son remained alive and capable of inheritance. Early in 1462 she sailed for France; by the autumn she was back, with a small force of French troops under Pierre de Brézé, to continue the struggle.

Richard Neville, Earl of Warwick and called the king-maker, was in 1461 undoubtedly the man of the moment. His support and his father's had been vital to Richard of York, and after Edward IV's succession Warwick was easily the most powerful territorial subject of the new king. His grandfather, Earl Ralph of Westmorland, had acquired wide lands by his second marriage, to Joan Beaufort; and though the earldom went to Ralph's eldest son by the first wife, a great part of the family inheritance (including wide lands in Yorkshire) went to Joan's eldest son, Richard, the king-maker's father. He married Alice Montagu, heiress of Salisbury, and their son, the king-maker himself, married Anne Beauchamp, who became the heiress of Warwick and Despenser. Joan Beaufort's other children had been well married too: William to the heiress of Fauconberg and Cicely to none other than Richard Duke of York himself. Warwick could therefore, in consequence of his family's connexions, fairly call himself a lord of the blood royal, and he held land in more than half the counties of England. He was besides chamberlain of England, Warden of the Cinque Ports and captain of Calais. The style of his living accorded with his rank and wealth, and earned him popularity. 'The earl was always held in great favour by the commons of the land, because of the exceedingly great household which he kept daily in every region wherever he stayed or passed the night. When he came to London he held such a household that six oxen were eaten at breakfast, and every tavern was full of his meat.'[3]

Warwick was not a wholly attractive character. His temper was short, and when thwarted he was sullenly unforgiving. His ambition knew no bounds: 'his insatiable mind could not be content . . . there was none in England who was before him or who owned half the possessions that he did . . . yet he desired more'.[4] His position, moreover, was one of great difficulty, especially after Edward IV's accession. Earlier, when he and Richard of York still professed to be loyal to Henry VI, he knew he could get what he wanted from York because his support was vital. Besides, if he could not get it, he could always abandon York, who was only a fellow peer. He could not hope to part so easily with Edward IV, because he himself had made him king. Yet he was bound to have difficulties with him. As a Milanese observer shrewdly remarked, it must be questionable how long Edward would endure Warwick's tutelage. Once Edward began to have a will of his own, in policy and about his court, Warwick would no longer be 'everything in the kingdom'.[5] It is never easy for an ambitious man who has been successful to relinquish power; Warwick's temperament made it, for him, virtually impossible.

Edward IV, who came to the throne in 1461 very much as Warwick's protégé, was the eldest of three surviving sons of Richard of York. Of the other two it is not necessary to say much now (both were still minors); events will bring their characters into perspective. George, the elder, who was created Duke of Clarence after his brother's coronation, was to entertain high ambitions, but lacked political skill; untrustworthy, his career fully justified Shakespeare's epithets 'false, fleeting, perjured'. Richard, who became Duke of Gloucester in 1461, was to be an able soldier and administrator; but there were flaws in his character which came out very clearly when his brother Edward was dead. Edward IV, the eldest, was probably also the ablest, all round. Handsome, affable (especially towards ladies), he was not quite twenty in 1461, a largely unproven youth. Time was to reveal him a great soldier and a successful ruler. From his father he inherited lands and the service of loyal and able counsellors, the most notable of whom was William Hastings, created Lord Hastings in 1461. At the beginning of the reign, however, the new king stood necessarily in the shadow of his great follower Warwick. He was not yet married, and it was clear that his marriage, and those of his brothers, must have in due course significant relevance to the policy and connexions of the new regime.

The natural match for Edward would have been a foreign noblewoman, probably a French princess (as Warwick would have wished) or a Burgundian lady (as others would probably have preferred). Edward decided to make his own choice, and a very surprising one it proved to be. On 1 May 1464 the king, while on his way to the north, rode to Grafton Regis and there secretly married the Lady Elizabeth Woodeville, the eldest daughter of Lord Rivers and the widow of Sir John Grey, who had been killed fighting for Henry VI at the second battle of St Albans. The secret was revealed a few months later, at a great council at Reading, and the match created a new territorial interest in English aristocratic politics. Elizabeth's advancement brought fortune to her family on a dramatic scale. Her brother John married the ageing Duchess of Norfolk, and her son by her first marriage the heiress of the Holland duchy of Exeter; her sisters married into the families of Buckingham, Arundel and Herbert.

Politically Edward's marriage was a serious mistake, straining relations dangerously between the king and the Nevilles, and sowing seeds of jealous discord among his other followers. We should beware, however, of exaggerating its folly. It is often said of Elizabeth Woodeville that she was a *parvenue*, that marriage to her demeaned the king in the eyes of his great subjects, and that the advancement of her relatives alienated them from Edward. The first of these assertions is certainly not correct. The new queen's father had only been created Lord Rivers in 1449, but her mother was Jacquetta of Luxembourg, a daughter of the great Burgundian Count of St Pol, and had been the second wife of the Duke of Bedford. Her brother Anthony had married the Scales heiress and assumed the title. Lack of reliable contemporary records makes it impossible to assess precisely the reaction of Edward's councillors at Reading to the news of the match, but it cannot have been quite the traumatic shock to the social exclusiveness of the peerage that it is often said to have been. Some may have resented the fortune that the marriage brought to the Woodeville family, but Edward was careful not to lavish on his new relations grants of office under the crown, and so their political influence was limited. The Woodevilles never quite became the focus of a dominating clique, like that which Suffolk and, later, Margaret of Anjou had gathered about Henry VI; to the end they remained only one interest among a number that jostled one another for influence around the Yorkist throne. To Warwick, admittedly, the marriage of Anne Holland to a Woodeville must have been specifically galling, for she had been earlier pledged to his nephew George. The king was careful, however, to placate the Nevilles, promoting Warwick's brother George to the vacant archbishopric of York, and his other brother John to the earldom of Northumberland, in the same year as his own marriage. If the marriage of the king put a period to his friendly association with Warwick – and it did – this was not initially, it would seem, because of its domestic repercussions, but because it was a direct challenge to Warwick's continental diplomacy. Of this more must be said in due course.

We are beginning in fact to anticipate. It becomes necessary now to give some sketch of the events of the years before Edward IV's marriage in 1464, which led up to an open breach between the king and Warwick, and so to the first crisis of his reign.

When Edward IV was crowned in June 1461, the Lancastrians were still formidable in the north, and it was not until November that he was able to meet his first parliament. By then most men were rallying to the rising star of York, and there was a gratifying attendance of peers; the commons, with James Strangeways, a Neville retainer, for their speaker, were very amenable. Edward's title to the throne was solemnly rehearsed and recognized, and all the acts of the Coventry parliament of 1459, which had attainted so many Yorkists, were reversed. A new crop of attainders disinherited the outstanding Lancastrian supporters. In a spirit of doctrinaire legitimism, the process against the Earl of Cambridge, the king's 'noble predecessor' who had been condemned to death in 1415 for his plot to unseat Henry V, was quashed.[6] Parliament thus set a seal of formal legality on what Warwick and Edward, in the course of the year, had already achieved by force. No formal action, it is interesting to notice, was taken against Henry VI. Yorkist legitimism did not demand a formal deposition, like that of 1399; it was enough that the old blood royal had returned at last to its right.

Through the first three years of Edward IV's reign the military activity of the Lancastrians in the north and west and the threat of Queen Margaret's diplomacy kept the king and Warwick together. The fighting was at times severe. In 1462 Warwick seemed to have triumphed in the north; he forced the lords in Bamburgh (Somerset and Sir Ralph Percy) to surrender into Edward's allegiance, on condition that their lands were restored. Margaret herself had by this time already left Scotland. But in 1463 she was back again; Percy let her French captain, Pierre de Brézé, into Bamburgh, which Henry VI made his capital. Though Warwick succeeded in checking the Scots allies of the Lancastrians at Norham, and Margaret left again for the continent, things were still uncertain in the north at the end of the summer. In the winter Somerset went back to the Lancastrian side, and Jasper Tudor raised their standard in Wales. His rebellion was contained by Lord Herbert, and the most serious fighting was in the north. There the Lancastrians were defeated in two engagements in the spring of 1464, at Hedgeley Moor and Hexham, by Warwick's brother Lord Montagu; at the latter field Somerset, Roos, Hungerford and a number of gentlemen were taken and summarily executed as traitors. After this Alnwick and Dunstanborough surrendered without resistance, Bamburgh after a short siege. When, a year after this, the unhappy Henry VI was finally taken prisoner in Lancashire near a ford across the Ribble, the Yorkist victory was complete.

Edward IV might have found the task of holding the throne that he had seized in 1461 much harder if Margaret had been luckier in her quest for allies abroad. In 1462 it looked as if she would succeed in making a firm agreement with Louis XI, in return for the promise in her name and Henry's that Calais and its march would be ceded to France when they were back on their thrones. A direct move against Calais was difficult to stage at this point, however, because it lay close to the dominions of the Duke of Burgundy, with whom Louis was simultaneously negotiating for the return of the Somme towns, and with whose court Warwick was in close touch. Warwick was in the circumstances able to insinuate skilfully that the French king might find alliance with the house of York more profitable than the support of its enemies. In October 1463 their communications bore fruit in a convention at Hesdin, where, with the Duke of Burgundy acting as mediator, a truce was agreed between Louis and Yorkist England, and Louis promised to give no further aid to Henry VI, Margaret, Prince Edward her son, 'or any other enemies of the King of England'.[7]

It was unfortunate for Warwick that he allowed his personal interest and national diplomacy to become very closely entangled at this important stage. The seigneur de Lannoy, who was in England as the special envoy of Louis in the spring of 1464 succeeded quite remarkably in charming the earl into a belief that between him and Louis there could be a special, personal relationship. Well before the truce was agreed, the suggestion had been mooted that the new Anglo-French *entente* might be cemented by a marriage between Edward and Bona of Savoy, the sister of the French queen, and Lannoy had sounded Warwick about the possibility of a secret alliance of France and England against Burgundy. Hints had been dropped that all this might pave the way towards a territorial title and apanage for Warwick himself in France. Thus already, in 1464, prospects for an English royal marriage to a French princess, for an

Anglo-French combination against Burgundy, and for a European role for the house of Neville had all become associated in negotiations in which Warwick personally was heavily involved. In the summer of this same year the earl was looking forward to a personal meeting with Louis XI at Calais, scheduled for October, where he hoped to push these plans a stage nearer fruition. The news that Edward was already married, revealed to the council at Reading in September, was for him a thunderbolt, therefore. It dashed the hopes that his soaring ambition had fostered. From now on he knew that his ascendancy over Edward and in England was insecure at best, and that the prospect of gains for himself and his house from an Anglo-French *entente* had become suddenly tenuous.

At the time when the secret of Edward's marriage was made public, relations between France and Burgundy were openly deteriorating. Louis in fact knew during the summer of 1464 that Edward IV was in contact both with Charles Count of Charolais, the ageing Duke of Burgundy's heir, and with the Duke of Brittany, who were soon to be the main leaders of rebellion against Louis in the 'War of the Public Weal'. The king of England, independent of Warwick and in opposition to his diplomacy, was veering towards the traditional English ally, Burgundy, whose friendship offered the surest protection for England's commercial ties with Flanders and Brabant, and could pave the way towards a bid for the reconquest of Normandy and Guienne. If Warwick had now been prepared to acquiesce in Edward's personal assumption of control over diplomatic initiative, the course of both French and English history might have been altered. To Louis XI's delight he was not. For the next four years he instead continued to pursue with Louis's encouragement what was in effect a private diplomacy of his own, independent and opposed to that of the king. An open breach between him and Edward was inevitably drawing nearer.

In 1466, the English council debated, hotly and at length, the arguments for and against two important diplomatic marriages, both aimed to cement Anglo-Burgundian friendship. One was projected between Charles of Charolais (who became Duke of Burgundy next year) and Margaret of York, Edward's sister; the other between Clarence and Mary, Charles's daughter. In spite of Warwick's opposition, Edward seemed determined to push ahead with both arrangements. Margaret's marriage came off, but the other did not. There was a difficulty, it proved, over Clarence's matrimonial future, and one that brought a showdown between Edward and the Nevilles another step nearer. In 1467, Edward discovered that Warwick's brother George, Archbishop of York, was working to secure a dispensation from the pope to enable Clarence to marry Isabel Neville, Warwick's daughter, instead of the Burgundian lady. He reacted strongly. On 8 June George was relieved of his post as chancellor, and the great seal was entrusted instead to Robert Stillington, Bishop of Bath and Wells (about a year earlier Lord Rivers, the queen's father, had replaced Walter Blount as treasurer, apparently to Warwick's considerable chagrin, and had been made an earl).

Edward thus took the initiative a second time, but he was soon running into difficulties. Encouraged by the prospect of alliance with Burgundy to revive English continental ambitions, he had obtained a double subsidy from parliament for an expedition to France, but the project did not seem likely to materialize. People were beginning to murmur that none of the promises of prosperity and good government that the Yorkists had made in the past had been fulfilled. Warwick had acquired meanwhile an influence over Clarence, whose ambitions for political influence were so far unsatisfied. Louis XI, all the time, was encouraging the earl towards sedition, holding out glamorous prospects of a pension and a great lordship in the Low Countries, to be carved out of territories that would be conquered from the Duke of Burgundy.

The crisis came in the summer of 1469. In the spring there was a serious rising in the north, led by one Robin of Redesdale. Robin's manifesto, behind which the hand of Warwick looks clearly apparent, adapted all the old Yorkists' complaints against Henry VI to the damage of his Yorkist successor. The king, it was alleged, had estranged the lords of the blood (Warwick and Clarence) from his council; he had taken about him a 'meiny' of evil counsellors (the Woodevilles, William Herbert Earl of Pembroke, Sir John Fogge) who had plundered his estate and 'would not suffer the king's laws to be executed upon whom they showed favour to';[8] he had oppressed and grieved the poor commons with taxes and purveyances. Edward prepared to move north against the rebels in July, but found that their forces were more formidable than he had expected. Meanwhile, on 11 July, at Calais, in Warwick's presence, Archbishop George Neville joined Warwick's daughter Isabel in marriage to George Duke of Clarence. After this, their party crossed to England and marched on London, which opened its gates to them. Edward had not the time to gather an adequate force. William Herbert, marching to join him, was defeated at Edgecote near Banbury, and was beheaded by the rebels on the field as a traitor. After this the king decided, wisely, to make no resistance, and allowed himself, with Richard of Gloucester and Lord Hastings, to be taken prisoner at Olney in Buckinghamshire. Lord Rivers and his son John, the queen's father and brother, were captured at Bristol and executed.

Warwick was to learn, and very soon, that to capture a king and kill his friends was only half a victory. All that he had really achieved was to recreate the turmoil and insecurity of the last miserable years of Henry VI's reign. In the wake of his *coup*, a wave of disorder spread through the counties, as men who anticipated a return to the bad old days took the law into their own hands. A parliament was summoned to meet at York, but it had to be countermanded because of 'the great troubles in this our land not yet appeased'.[9] Warwick's original intention had almost certainly been to use this parliament's authority to put George of Clarence on Edward's throne, but he could not risk going that far in the condition of spreading confusion that he now faced. He found that he could not, after all, do without the support of Edward's recognized authority. He could only get it by releasing Edward from custody, and, once Edward was free, men, even great men, began to rally to him. The authority of a crowned king was preferable, in the eyes of all except committed rebels and Lancastrian irreconcilables, to the uncertainty which was all that Warwick had to promise.

Warwick had brought back the bad old days, to his own cost, with a vengeance. With Edward at liberty again and in the saddle, what could the king-maker and Clarence do but spin fresh plots against the inevitable recon-frontation? The confusion that they had unleashed anew proved their undoing when, in the spring of 1470, Lord Welles, who was embroiled in a local quarrel in Lincolnshire, released a manifesto in their names.[10] Edward was on the alert; Clarence and Warwick could not muster men with sufficient speed, and took to the sea. Calais closed its gates to them, and in the end they dropped anchor off Honfleur. They had no one now to fall back on, except Louis XI, and had lost their independence even in their dealing with him.

From this point forward, effective direction of the English situation more or less passed out of the hands of native English leaders for a period, into those of their respective continental allies. Just as Warwick had found himself unable to con-solidate a partial victory, so Edward was to prove unable to consolidate a partial recovery. Everything had been thrown out of joint. Warwick was out of England, but he still had important potential allies there, notably his brother John Neville. John had not moved against Edward in 1469, but the king, when he was free again, felt bound to try what conciliation could do in the north; Redesdale had demanded the restoration of the Percy heir, and restored he was in March 1470 to the earldom of Northumberland. John Neville, who had been created earl in Percy's place in 1464, after his victory at Hexham, was compensated for the loss of this title with a new Marquisate of Montagu, and substantial west country estates, once the attainted Courtenays'; at the same time, his son and heir George was married to the king's daughter Elizabeth and created Duke of Bedford. The loss of the Percy lands and earldom neverthe-less rankled with him, and Edward's move was not entirely astute. He gained the nominal allegiance of an ex-Lancastrian on whom he could not count in a crisis, and turned John Neville from an unreliable ally into a malcontent, who was soon to serve him a particularly ill turn.

So Edward found himself in 1470 in possession, for the time being, of a restive kingdom. Warwick's position was worse, for he could not hope now to be more than a pawn in the schemes of Louis of France. Ever since 1467, or perhaps even earlier, Louis had hoped that he might somehow be able to yoke Warwick with Margaret of Anjou, in a bid to restore Henry VI. The alliance would be an unnatural one, for Warwick had upon his hands the blood of Somerset, Northumberland, Clifford, Roos and half a score of other late sup-porters of Margaret; and it would almost certainly break down in some new confrontation, but Louis did not care for that. He would only offer the earl support in a new adventure in England on condition of his reconciliation with

Margaret, and on the promise of English support, once Warwick and Margaret were in control, in his own war against Burgundy. Warwick was prepared to put himself in this false position, and Margaret was brought round to it for her son's sake. The two strange allies of the future were reconciled at Angers, and Louis thereon undertook to find money to pay the forces which Warwick and Clarence were gathering in Normandy. When a storm broke up the English fleet which was watching the coast, Warwick embarked at La Hogue, and on 13 September 1470 he landed in company with Clarence, the Earl of Oxford, and Jasper Tudor at Dartmouth.

Edward was caught off his guard, as Warwick himself had been earlier in the year. Marching south from York, he had reached Doncaster when he learned that John Neville had gone over to his enemies, and was only a few miles away, coming to take him with a far larger force than his own. He had to move quickly. Crossing the Wash with great difficulty, he reached King's Lynn, and there, with a few followers, notably his brother Gloucester and Lord Hastings, he embarked for the Low Countries. So Edward was thrown back on Charles of Burgundy, as Warwick had been on Louis XI, and the autumn of 1470 became formally the forty-ninth year of the reign of Henry VI.

The 'readeption' of Henry VI was a sorry and short lived affair. There does not even survive a roll recording the acts of its single parliament, though we know that it did not vote any subsidy for the war against Burgundy which Warwick, bound to Louis XI, had to embark upon. The king-maker's power had been shaky a year before when he had tried to seize the reins of government; now it was much less secure. Neville retainers apart, there was no one upon whom he could rely, or who wanted to rely on him. Clarence, now no longer in a position to conspire for the throne, was discontented, and was soon in touch with his brother abroad. Margaret did not trust Warwick sufficiently to come from France, or let her son cross to England, until it looked as if things might be settling down. The most faithful Lancastrians, those who had endured exile, posed a further and dangerous problem for the king-maker; what was to be done, for instance, about the young Henry Tudor, whose earldom of Richmond had been conferred on Clarence, who was outwardly loyal to the new regime that he had helped to build? Henry Tudor was too young as yet to cause serious trouble, but the heirs of Somerset and Holland were old enough, when they arrived home from exile. They had no love for Warwick, and probably meant to do him harm if they could.

The deep division between Warwick and the true Lancastrians was the ruin of both when Edward reappeared. He arrived at the Humber with a fleet and 2000 men, equipped at Flushing in the dominions of Charles of Burgundy, on 14 March 1471. The Percies made no move against him, and when he got to York the city opened its gates. As his army began to swell, the story which he put about on his first arrival, that he had come only to claim his duchy of York, was forgotten. Clarence, seeing the way things were going, threw in his lot with him. He reached London ahead of Warwick and a number of peers there joined him, Norfolk, the Bourgchiers, Lord Mountjoy. At Barnet, on 14 April,

Edward and the king-maker finally met in battle; the earl's host was defeated, and both he and his brother the marquis fell on the field. On the same 14 April, Margaret and her son Edward at last landed in England, too late. Edward caught the army that she and Somerset gathered in the west at Tewkesbury on 4 May, before they could join Jasper Tudor in Wales, and overthrew them. Prince Edward was killed, and Somerset was taken and executed. Margaret was captured a few days later at Little Malvern Priory.

Soon after Edward IV returned victorious from Tewkesbury to London, Henry VI was dead, murdered in the Tower of London. With Warwick dead also, Margaret a prisoner, and Edward on his throne again, the allies of Charles of Burgundy had carried the day everywhere in England against those of Louis XI.

The pattern of English involvement in continental politics, which had been set in the years between Edward's marriage and his recovery of his throne in 1471, remained unaltered for another four years. For Louis XI, the triumph of Edward was a major setback. Barnet and Tewkesbury cost him the control of English affairs which before he had all but achieved, and his only hopes of regaining influence now were either to persuade Edward to alter his alliances, or to stir up Clarence once more against his elder brother. Neither alternative was promising. Clarence was hardly in a position to try his hand again, and Edward's clear purpose was to turn his alliance with Charles of Burgundy from the dependence of exile into the opportunity for an English come-back in France, at Louis's cost.

It could be argued that, after his victories in England of 1471, Edward was unwise to embroil himself as fully as he was to do in continental politics. There was no longer any realistic rival for his throne, about whom Louis XI or irredentist Lancastrians in exile could weave conspiracies. The strength of his domestic position was in fact to enable him, in the course of his second reign, to consolidate his royal authority with notable success (by means which will be discussed in the next chapter). In 1471, however, the measure of that strength cannot have been fully apparent. Edward, in the aftermath of his misfortunes in 1469 and of Henry VI's readeption, must have felt acutely the need to be able to point to some tangible success, which would endow his regime with the lustre of achievement in his subjects' eyes. The events of the last two years had shown that he had failed, in the first years of his reign, to engage their loyalty fully, and had nearly cost him the throne for ever. The prospect of intervention abroad, with a fair chance of success, was therefore most attractive to him. As a speaker on the king's behalf pointed out to the commons in parliament in 1472, ever since the Norman Conquest England had been most secure and prosperous in the times when her kings made 'outward war' on their enemies. Even Henry VI had 'stood ever in glory and honour while the war was continued beyond', so the speaker said.[11] Why should not massive intervention in France do the same thing for the Yorkists as it had done for the Lancastrians in the reign of Henry V – when likewise the quarrels of a Duke of Burgundy with a French king's councillors had given England her opportunity?

The responsibility of Henry VI's ministers for the loss of the English territories in France had been a traditional theme of Yorkist propaganda, and already in his first reign, in 1468, Edward had been toying with the possibility of attempting their reconquest. Through 1472 and 1473 we find him, therefore, busily negotiating with all Louis XI's enemies with this object in mind, with Francis of Brittany and with John of Aragon, as well as with Charles of Burgundy. Surprisingly, it was with the last that he had most difficulties, for Charles was preoccupied with ambitions in the Empire, and was already showing signs of that defective judgement in politics which was to be his ruin. In 1474, however, a firm agreement was at last concluded. In a treaty sealed in London on 25 July Edward promised to invade France with an army of 10,000 men. Charles undertook, in return for this aid and the promise of the future cession of a vast bloc of territories in eastern France (including Rheims in Champagne, the traditional site of the French royal coronation), to recognize Edward as the rightful King of France.[12]

The army that Edward assembled in order to fulfil his part of the London treaty was, says Commynes, the largest and the best armed that any English king had ever led into France. It numbered perhaps 11,000 men, with a magnificent artillery, and among its captains were a great many of the highest nobility of the land. The campaign of martial propaganda that preceded the expedition met with an enthusiastic response: 'all applauded the king's intentions and bestowed the highest praises on his proposed plans.'[13] Parliament was persuaded to approve the collection of substantial subsidies. A great deal of money was also raised by way of benevolences, and commissioners were sent busily about the counties to persuade men to make 'gifts': 'The king goeth so near to us in this county, both poor and rich, that I wot not how we shall live, but if the world amend', Margaret Paston wrote from Norfolk.[14] Edward himself backed the efforts of his servants by personal application to wealthy donors, bringing the rich and unwilling 'by fair words up to the mark'.[15] The efforts of the government to make adequate military and financial preparation were of the same scale of seriousness as they had been in the old days of Henry V, and seemed to portend a similarly determined military venture.

Edward IV crossed to Calais with his host on 4 July 1475. Thither Charles of Burgundy came to meet him, but he did not bring his army; indeed, until just before Edward's crossing he had refused himself to quit the unsuccessful siege that he had laid to Neuss, and he left his men behind there, in Lorraine. From Calais Edward advanced, with Charles in his company, to St Quentin, which the duke told him would be surrendered, but it was not. When the two princes parted in August, Louis had already gathered a powerful army to oppose any further English advance. Now totally disillusioned about the prospects of effective support from either Burgundy or Brittany, Edward, in mid-campaign, decided to reverse his policy completely, and to enter into negotiations with

Louis. On 29 August the two monarchs met, at Picquigny on the Somme. The treaty that they sealed there established a truce for seven years between their kingdoms. Their respective claims to the crown of France were referred to a court of four arbitrators (which in fact never sat). Edward abandoned his alliance with Charles, and agreed to evacuate his army in return for 75,000 crowns in cash down, and – most important of all – on the promise of a French pension of 50,000 gold crowns annually.

The Treaty of Picquigny was a dramatic *volte face* in late medieval English diplomacy. It had its disadvantages, of course. By retreating without striking any serious blow in France, the king clearly ran the risk of losing face in the eyes of his soldiers and his subjects. The expenses that the expedition had involved were bound to seem more grievous when it proved empty of achievement; and the excesses of the disappointed and disbanded soldiery in England were to add to the public dissatisfaction. Nevertheless most of the councillors who were with Edward abroad were in favour of the treaty (Richard of Gloucester was one of the very few significant exceptions). The main advantage of the agreement, from the English point of view, was that it offered a respite from continental entanglements, which was much needed in the interest of organizing more secure government at home. Together with this it guaranteed a more than welcome subvention to the crown's financial resources. It is an index of the confidence of the Yorkist councillors in their ability to contain the domestic situation, now that the threat of 'outward war' and its pressures were removed for the time being, that they were willing shortly after Picquigny to agree to release Margaret of Anjou, in return for a ransom, and to let her go free into France.

The diplomatic turnabout of Picquigny proved, in the event, more important and more decisive in English history than anyone at the time can have expected. Edward, when he made the treaty, by no means abandoned his dreams of continental conquest; he merely postponed them. Yet when he died in 1483 the serious chances of restoring an English presence on the continent had become infinitely more remote, and the traditional Anglo-French rivalry, which had dominated north European politics for more than a hundred years, had ceased to matter. This was because, in the interval, events had developed far more rapidly than could be foreseen in 1475.

Two years after the Treaty of Picquigny was sealed, Charles the Bold of Burgundy was killed at Nancy, fighting the Swiss and Austrians who were supported by subsidies from Louis XI. His heiress Mary, and his wife Margaret of York were left virtually at the mercy of the French king. Margaret's first and natural hope was to save herself by an English alliance, to be cemented by the marriage of Mary to Clarence (whose first wife had died), but Edward, determined to preserve his French pension, would not hear of this. Louis, in consequence, was soon in control of ducal Burgundy, and seemed likely to succeed in absorbing the whole Burgundian inheritance by marrying Mary to the dauphin. Unfortunately for him, he tried to move too fast when he attempted to take over the direct government of Flanders; Flemish distrust of the French hardened into hostility, and Mary was married instead to Maximilian of Austria, the son of the Emperor Frederic III. Maximilian claimed all the lands that Mary should have inherited, and he and Louis were soon at war.

Maximilian's hopes of success were continually centred on alliance with England, while Louis XI's object was to keep Edward out of the war. Edward did not alter the policy he had adopted in 1475, and continued to play for time. He listened politely to Louis's proposals for an increase in his pension as a condition of closer alliance, for a marriage for one of his daughters with the dauphin, and for a combined offensive against Maximilian which would gain for England crucial trading privileges in the Low Countries. He listened also, more than politely, to Maximilian's proposals for joint action which would recover for himself Burgundy, and for England her lost French provinces, perhaps even the French crown. But though by 1480 Edward IV was veering towards Maximilian, he would not commit himself fully. He kept just sufficiently clear of involvement to draw annually his pension from Louis XI, which he was finding infinitely useful.

Edward's delays permitted Louis in the end to outmanoeuvre him. In 1479 English relations with the Scots were deteriorating, and the French king made the most of his chances to foster ill-feeling. In 1481 full-scale war broke out. In this year and again in 1482 Richard of Gloucester, acting as lieutenant for the king in the north, led armies across the border; and though he did not succeed, as Edward hoped he would, in displacing James III in favour of his brother Albany, he took Berwick and wasted the country as far as Edinburgh. While Edward was fighting this war with some success on a shoestring (for he deliberately avoided asking parliament for a subsidy until 1483), he was naturally unwilling to engage in any major commitment on the continent, and eager to keep his French pension. Louis was in consequence able to undermine the confidence of Maximilian's hopes for help from England, by judiciously informing him about the rival negotiations which he, Louis, had been conducting with Edward, behind Maximilian's back. The latter, already hard pressed, in consequence decided in 1482 to agree to terms with the French.

The Treaty of Arras, sealed on 23 December, ended their war, and provided for a future marriage between Maximilian's daughter and the dauphin. England was wholly excluded from their arrangements, and the pension of 1475 ceased to be paid. All present hopes of a profitable English intervention abroad were dashed; and it looked as if English influence in the councils of Europe could for the time being be discounted.

Thus, just over seven years after Picquigny, Edward found that he had missed the last opportunities that an English king would be offered of intervening in France with any real hope of re-establishing the English presence there. The memory of past triumphs was so potent, it is true, that many did not realize this for a long time. Henry VIII could still dream of reconquering part, at least, of what had once been the Lancastrian empire. But it was an empty dream; between the years 1477 and 1482, with the collapse of the great power that Burgundy had once been, the traditional English ambitions had ceased to be realistic.

Edward, when he made peace with Louis XI in 1475, played for time, in order to consolidate himself at home. He needed the respite, for the years following his return in 1471 had not been easy. Though his conciliatory policy after Tewkesbury (there were no attainders) had paid dividends, bringing into his service such able ex-Lancastrians as Sir John Fortescue and Morton, there were still some irreconcilable Lancastrians at large (notably the Earl of Oxford and Jasper Tudor) who might prove troublesome, especially if they could obtain French military assistance. Oxford actually attempted a descent on Cornwall in 1473, and seized St Michael's Mount where he held out successfully for a considerable time. Even more dangerous were the divisions in the king's own family. Clarence, in the right of his wife Isabel Neville, had a claim on the vast inheritance of Warwick the king-maker. But Richard of Gloucester had his eye on the same lands, and secured a claim by his marriage, in 1472, to Warwick's younger daughter, Anne Neville. The wrangling between the two brothers over the partition of the estates became extremely bitter, and the king had to intervene. In the final settlement Clarence did well enough, securing the Beauchamp lands of Warwick's countess, but the great northern estates of the Nevilles went to Gloucester. The brothers remained on poor terms, and Clarence deeply dissatisfied. He had once aspired to Edward's throne; in 1470, when Henry VI was restored, the succession had been entailed on his heirs if Henry's line failed; and he had not forgotten these things. He had his own contacts with Louis XI. There was plenty, in fact, to make Edward uncomfortable about his closest kinsman and richest subject, especially if Louis XI tried to fish in troubled waters. After 1475 he could feel easier, on that score at least.

In 1477 Edward took a chance, when it was offered, to deal with Clarence. Their relations had deteriorated after Edward refused to entertain his sister Margaret's plan for a marriage of Clarence to Mary of Burgundy (a refusal understandable enough in the light of Clarence's past conduct). In the summer Clarence seems to have been privy to a minor rising in Cambridgeshire, and Edward heard of it. Things came to a head before the end of the summer, as a result of a curious intrigue whose details remain obscure. John Stacey, an Oxford clerk, had been accused of attempting to compass the king's death by necromancy, and implicated as his accomplice Thomas Burdett, a member of Clarence's household. The two men were executed. On the day following their execution Clarence appeared unheralded at Westminster, to protest their innocence over the king's head before the council. Edward had had enough, and a few weeks later riposted by placing Clarence in custody. In 1478 parliament, at the royal instigation, proceeded against Clarence by bill of attainder. He was not heard in his own defence; and the Duke of Buckingham, as seneschal of England, passed sentence on him as a traitor. The commons pressed for execution, and he was put to death in the Tower of London – by what means it is not quite clear – on 18 February.

The death of Clarence cleared from Edward's way the one figure who might still threaten him in England. Clarence's heir was a minor. With every year that Edward reigned, the significance of the surviving Lancastrian exiles dwindled. The best pretender that they could now raise was the obscure Beaufort claimant to the earldom of Richmond, Henry Tudor, who was in Brittany; and the Beauforts were statutorily debarred from the succession anyway. Edward's own surviving brother, Richard of Gloucester, did not seem dangerous; he had an impressive record of loyalty, and was the king's most trusted councillor, directing affairs for him in the north. Edward rewarded Richard amply for his successes in the Scottish war of 1481–3 (notably the recapture of Berwick), with grants which directly associated his interests with further conquest in the north. Gloucester and his heirs were granted the wardenship of the west march in perpetuity, together with the castle of Carlisle, and permitted to hold and exercise palatine rights in all lands they might acquire in Lidderdale, Annandale and Clydesdale in Scotland. These lands, if conquered, would give Richard an apanage fit even for a king's brother.

So when at the end of 1482 Edward's continental diplomacy collapsed and he found himself no longer allied to either Louis or Maximilian, there was no need for undue fear that either would now be able to disturb the domestic political situation in England. There was no one left on whose disloyalty to the regime either could hope to play. Edward seemed to have secured himself and his dynasty; he was only forty, and his son Edward was growing fast in his thirteenth year. Time, however, was once more not on Edward's side. In April 1483, he died suddenly, after a short illness. The country in consequence had to face all the tremendous problems which, in the political conditions of the age, inevitably attended a minority. England was probably lucky that Louis XI died only a few months after Edward, like him leaving an heir under age; he also left counsellors who understood very well how to make trouble for an English king, as events would soon show.

Edward V was twelve in 1483; so his formal minority was going to be short (Henry VI had been deemed of age when he was fifteen). The shape of his future regime was likely therefore to be determined by the influences dominant about his person during the minority and as he emerged from it. Edward IV, in his (lost) will, had apparently named his brother Richard of Gloucester to be protector of the realm on his son's behalf. Edward V, when his father died, was at Ludlow, in the charge of the Queen's brother, Anthony Woodville Earl Rivers, his 'governor' who had now for some time been the most prominent figure in his princely council. In the new situation, it was very natural that the Queen and the Woodvilles should hope to maintain and consolidate their influence about the new king. Though there is slight evidence of any serious competition between the Woodvilles and Gloucester before Edward IV died, there was now, therefore, a clear conflict of interest, with potential for serious tensions. It was out of that conflict of interest that the story of Richard III's seizure of his nephew's throne developed.

In London, the Woodvilles had in April 1483 the immediate initiative. Under their influence the council (following the precedent of 1422) insisted that Edward IV's testamentary nomination of Gloucester as protector must be subject to its confirmation, and fixed an early date for the coronation (in Henry VI's reign, Humphrey of Gloucester's protectorate had formally ended when the king was crowned). Rivers was instructed to bring the king to London, in all haste and well attended. These moves appear to have alarmed Lord Hastings, Edward IV's chamberlain and closest councillor, who was not on good terms with the Woodvilles, and probably suspected them of planning a *coup* that would thwart his former master's intentions. On his insistence, and with the Queen's agreement, a second letter was despatched to Rivers, dropping the emphasis on haste and setting a limit of 2000 men to come to London with him in the king's company. It seems likely that about the same time Hastings or some other councillor wrote to Gloucester in York, apprising him of the situation and of the need to be in the south to look after his own interests.

The next move took the Woodvilles, and more or less everyone else in the capital, completely by surprise. On 29 April Rivers and the young king reached Stony Stratford in Northamptonshire to meet (apparently by agreement) the Dukes of Gloucester and Buckingham, who were now also bound for London with their followings. Next morning Rivers found himself arrested, together with Sir Thomas Vaughan and Sir Richard Grey: Gloucester and Buckingham took control of the king, and Rivers' company was disbanded. The two dukes, with the king, then pressed on for London. The Woodvilles made an attempt to organize resistance there, but found themselves unsupported. Sir Edward Woodville, the Admiral, put to sea with his fleet: the Queen, with her younger son Richard and her daughters, took refuge in Westminster Abbey's sanctuary. On 4 May Edward V, Gloucester and Buckingham reached the capital, and the king was lodged in the Tower.

Developments between 4 May and 13 June are unfortunately not as amply recorded as we could wish them to be. The council confirmed Gloucester in the office of protector, and the coronation was postponed, to 22 June. Buckingham, Richard's partner in the *coup* at Stony Stratford, was dramatically rewarded. He was already the most substantial noble landowner in Wales and the marches: he was now made chief justice of north and south Wales, with control of the principal royal castles there and the authority to array men in the western counties of England. The effect was to make him virtually a royal viceroy in Wales. Once confirmed as protector Richard also made some changes of office. Bishop Russell of Lincoln became chancellor, and John Woode, an associate of Gloucester's, became treasurer.

These were not changes calculated to disturb the Yorkist establishment left behind by Edward IV, but Richard's next moves were. On 10 June, he wrote to the north, to summon a large armed force to London. Then, on 13 June, in a council meeting, he unleashed another thunderbolt. Lord Hastings, he declared, had been in contact with the Queen in Westminster sanctuary, and was party, with others, to a treasonable plot to undo him. Hastings was led out, and beheaded with no trial. Bishop Morton and Lord Stanley were placed under arrest, and taken to the Tower (Stanley, curiously, was soon freed, but not so Morton).

It is likely enough that Hastings was beginning by this time to be alarmed at the way the protector seemed to be proceeding; whether he was really involved in a plot is unclear. No more is it clear when it was that Richard first contemplated seizing the throne for himself. It could be that it was when he first heard of his brother's death: it could be that it was when he and Buckingham agreed their plan for Stony Stratford; it could be that he was still hesitating in early June. After Hastings' execution, it became the only logical step, if he was to keep control of developments. Events from this point moved rapidly. On 16 June the Queen was persuaded to release Edward V's brother out of sanctuary, pending the coronation; later that day the coronation was postponed. About the same time, on Richard's instructions and without trial, Rivers and Sir Thomas Vaughan were executed at Pontefract, where they had been held since the end of April. Then, on 22 June, Ralph Shaw at St Paul's Cross preached a public sermon, in which he set out the right of Richard to succeed to the throne of England: and on 24 June Buckingham at the Guildhall addressed the mayor and citizens to the same effect. Edward V, his brother, and all Edward IV's children were born out of wedlock, he told them, since, when King Edward married Elizabeth Woodeville, he was already under contract of marriage to Lady Eleanor Buder (a story which, as far as it can be checked, seems to be without foundation). Clarence's heir was excluded from the succession, on the ground of his father's attainder. The crown must therefore pass to Richard of Gloucester, the sole representative of the old and true blood royal.

On 25 June Buckingham made a second address, to an assembly of lords and commons (not strictly a parliament, since the summonses for that day in Edward V's name had been cancelled). He returned from it with a petition to Richard to take the crown that was his by right. Richard had plenty of troops in London, and the petition was probably not spontaneous. He accepted the request that it contained, and dated the beginning of his reign from 26 June.

Edward V and his brother Richard Duke of York, who was with him in the Tower, were last seen for certain during the mayoralty of Edmund Sha, which ended in October 1483. Everyone soon believed that they were dead – indeed the Italian Mancini thought they were as good as dead before he left England at the end of June.[17] There is no absolutely firm evidence that Richard III was responsible for their ends, but there is no good reason to doubt that he was. Their lives could not be anything but a direct threat to his throne. Though he was crowned in great pomp, and though he had organized successfully for himself a claim in blood and as the elected choice of the three estates, what had really made him king was his military control of the capital in the crucial weeks of May–June 1483 – and the support of Buckingham. His subjects' acceptance of him was skin deep. If either of the princes had lived, he must inevitably, sooner or later, have become the focus of conspiracies to unseat Richard.

In a century in the course of which four kings (or five if one includes Richard II) lost the throne of England in consequence of rebellions, the usurpation of 1483 managed to be particularly shocking. Never, even in recent years, had so many powerful men been hurried out of the world with so little reason, or so little ceremony. Rivers, a pious, upright, apolitical peer, who wore a hair shirt and dreamed of going on crusade, had committed no crime with which he could be charged, and no more had Grey or Vaughan. The charges levelled by Richard against Hastings were unproven when he was beheaded without trial. Edward V had patently never been in a position to do anything to deserve to lose his throne. The reaction of Richard's subjects was what might have been expected. It was not respect which his actions inculcated, but fear, insecurity and distrust. Resentment and bewildered impotence are the dominant emotions in most contemporary accounts of events in London in the crucial days of June 1483: 'I have seen many men burst forth into tears and lamentation when mention was made of him [Edward V] after his removal from men's sight', wrote Mancini.[18] No one had said anything quite like that when Richard II or Henry VI lost their thrones, because the men who rose against them were actuated in part at least by resentment at genuine misgovernment. The usurpation of 1483 bore no such justification.

The first challenge to Richard began to develop within weeks of his coronation. Militarily the movement that has come to be known as Buckingham's rebellion was a fiasco (there were no battles), but it could have been very dangerous if things had gone only a little differently. It began with plans for a rising, in the home counties and southern England, aimed to rescue Edward V and his brother from the Tower before it was too late. A particularly ominous feature was that the leaders of this movement included, in virtually every affected region, prominent knights and gentlemen with careers and connections in the personal service of Edward IV and in his household, that is to say leaders of the old Yorkist establishment. Such were, for instance, Sir John Fogge and Sir Thomas Brown in Kent, Sir John Cheyne in Wiltshire, Sir William Stonor in Oxfordshire, Sir Giles Daubeny in Somerset. The influence of men such as these had in Edward IV's time been a vital prop, at regional level, to stable royal authority. Only two major peers, it is true, became involved. There is nothing surprising about finding the fugitive Thomas Grey, Marquis of Dorset and Queen Elizabeth's Woodville's son by her first marriage, among the leaders of rebellion in the west. What motive drew in Henry Duke of Buckingham, architect with Richard of the usurpation and so richly rewarded for his part in it, is on the other hand very hard to fathom. The influence and persuasive tongue of Bishop Morton, a prisoner in his care at Brecon, no doubt played an important part, but it is hard to see what Buckingham hoped to gain from deserting his partner in crime of the spring. Drawn in he was, however, and his involvement had one very crucial effect. Buckingham almost certainly knew that the princes in the Tower were dead, and he made contact with Henry Tudor in Brittany – probably through Morton. Henry's Lancastrian claim to the throne, through his mother Margaret Beaufort, was a very weak one, since the Beauforts had long ago been statutorily debarred from the royal succession: but he was now prepared, if he should become king, to undertake to marry Elizabeth, Edward IV's eldest daughter. Thus what had begun as a movement of the old Yorkist connection was transformed into a bid for a Tudor succession, keeping its Yorkist colour through a prospective Tudor marriage to the princess who, with the princes gone, looked to be Edward IV's nearest heiress.

The rebellion, which ran its course, through October, was a complete failure. From London John Howard, newly created Duke of Norfolk brought the Kentish rebellion under control. Buckingham, in the marches of Wales, found himself unable to raise any significant support, and was captured in Shropshire. Autumn storms dispersed the ships with which Henry Tudor had hoped to reach the west country, and he was back in Brittany by the time Richard appeared there with an army. Dorset, Morton, and a number of other leaders succeeded in getting away to France before he could catch them. A few, less fortunate, were taken and executed (including, of course, Buckingham), but there was not much bloodshed, either in the field or on the scaffold. On the other hand, no less than 104 named persons were attainted in the January parliament of 1484 for their part in the revolt. Its ramifications had, it is clear, proved to be perilously wide.

Despite its failure, Buckingham's revolt had two consequences that were of decisive impact on the political pattern of what was left of Richard's brief reign. It brought home very sharply to the king that he could not rely on the loyalty, especially in the southern and midland English localities, of the old servants of the house of York, who he had at first perceived to be prepared to accept the *fait accompli* of his succession. He must rely on men there who would be his own, if he was to keep control. The fact that so few peers had been involved in the 1483 revolt was a promising sign, and Richard took care to promote the local influence and authority of those he trusted most, Francis Lord Lovel in the south midlands, Howard of Norfolk in East Anglia. But the southern counties, where magnate territorial influences had long been less powerful, demanded a different approach. Already by the end of 1483 a number of knights and esquires from the affinity that he had built up in the north in his brother's reign were being moved into important southern offices: Halnath Mauleverer became sheriff of Devon, Thomas Huddleston of Cumberland sheriff of Gloucestershire, Edward Redman of York sheriff of Somerset. The distribution of forfeited lands after the attainders of January 1484 enabled Richard to push forward a policy of positive 'plantation' of northerners into southern landed societies. Thus, for instance, Sir Robert Brackenbury of Durham obtained wide estates in Kent that had once been properties of Rivers, Buckingham and Cheyne, and Sir Richard Ratcliffe of Cumberland profited similarly in Devon from confiscated Courtenay estates: Rosemary Horrox and Charles Ross have compiled impressive lists of other northerners who profited similarly from grants of confiscated land and vacant offices.[19] This 'plantation' policy was understandable, and in its way sensible enough; the difficulty was the resentment generated by the intrusion of newcomers with no local roots among the established gentry of the local communities. It introduced a new, uncertain and so unwelcome factor into their calculation of family interest, their cultivation of friendships, and their aspirations to local office (newcomers were very prominent in the commissions of the peace). Richard and his advisers no doubt hoped that assimilation and absorption would do their work in time. Assimilation does take time, however; the year 1484 proved full of alarms and rumours of sedition and projected risings, and about Tudor plans for invasion.

The new significance that Henry Tudor's claims acquired as a result of Buckingham's overtures and Morton's intrigues was the other important consequence of the 1483 revolt. From that point on, a steady trickle of malcontents began to swell the group of exile Englishmen about him in Brittany. When, late in 1484, John Lord Mountjoy (an old Hastings connection) not only allowed his prisoner the Earl of Oxford (a veteran Lancastrian) to escape from Hammes Castle near Calais, but went with him to join Henry, there was real concern. Richard's reaction to this growing Tudor threat was again, in principle, a sensible one, to put pressure on Brittany to abandon support for his potential rival. Duke Francis in 1484 was on the edge of being drawn into an alliance with Louis of Orléans and Maximilian that would confront the regency council of Charles VIII of France, and Richard was prepared to offer military aid, on condition of Francis putting Henry Tudor under strict surveillance. Henry however was forewarned (probably by Morton from Flanders), and made his escape just in time from Brittany into France. In France, Richard's overtures to the duke of Brittany had helped to rouse fears of renewed English designs on French territory (very likely Richard did have that idea in the back of his mind, as his brother had had before him). His policy thus backfired. The hope of getting Henry Tudor under safe, friendly surveillance evaporated, and French interest in the destabilization of the English political situation was re-generated.

So matters moved forward, to the final crisis of the reign of Richard III. The French were cautious, unwilling to commit themselves too far: they allowed Henry freedom of movement, but were not prepared to offer much in the way of military or financial support. All he could obtain was a loan, and permission to recruit soldiers. When he, Oxford and his uncle Jasper Tudor sailed from Harfleur with a force of perhaps 1000 French troops, they were therefore embarking on a very risky adventure. They landed at Milford Haven on 7 August, 1485.

It is hard not to conclude that, in the ensuing confrontation, the odds were in Richard's favour, despite all his difficulties. Henry in Wales was joined by Rhys ap Thomas and Sir John Savage, and later, in Staffordshire, Sir Gilbert Talbot came in, but no major peer stirred for him. His stepfather Lord Stanley, the most powerful lord of the north west midlands and of whom he had probably hoped much, made no move. Richard, on the other hand, had been on his guard and was at Nottingham, ready to mobilize, when news of the Tudors' landing reached him. The army, largely recruited in the north, with which he faced Henry at Bosworth in Leicestershire on 22 August was certainly larger than his rival's (perhaps 8000, to 5000 in Henry's company). Among its aristocratic leaders Howard of Norfolk, John de la Pole, Earl of Lincoln and Lord Lovel were all entirely committed and trustworthy. Northumberland was less so (his troop never in fact engaged in the battle), and Sir William Stanley, who appeared at the field with a force, was even less so. The issue was decided when Richard, with his household troops, attempted to charge the group round Henry Tudor, and Stanley's men moved in on Henry's side. Richard was killed in the mêlée. At the end of the day Stanley placed the crown, which had been knocked from Richard's helmet, on Henry's head.

Bosworth decided who should sit on the English throne: it did not decide much else. Had Richard killed his enemy and triumphed, it is probable that his rule would not have proved radically different in style from that of Edward before him or Henry after him. He had considerable administrative ability and energy, and England would no doubt, over time, have settled down under him, as it did under Edward and under Henry. He was not given time, however, and that this was so was his own fault. It seems highly unlikely that Henry Tudor would have ventured as he did in 1485 if he had not been well aware of how widely Richard was resented and mistrusted. Richard's summary executions of Rivers and Hastings, the disappearance of his nephews, the confiscations of 1483–4, his favour to northerners and his plantations of strangers in the south, all combined to undermine confidence in him as a man and as a king. It did so crucially and especially among those who had once been committed to the house of York, and who would surely have maintained that commitment to Edward V, if Richard had not usurped his throne.

William Collingbourne of Wiltshire, whose rhyme, pinned to the door of St Paul's cathedral, cost him his life, was a former gentleman usher of Edward IV's household. His famous couplet

> The cat, the rat, and Lovel our dog
> Rule all England under the hog[20]

summed up succinctly what a great many men like him felt about Richard's regime, and what a great many who unlike him raised no protest felt also. Richard's great failure was in winning sufficient hearts, and his actions were ill calculated to win them. It was a failure that proved the death warrant of his dynasty.

Notes

1   See J. Fortescue, *Of the Title of the House of York* and *Defensio Juris Domus Lancastriae* in his *Works*, ed. Lord Clermont (1869), vol. I, pp. 497–502, 505–10; and his *Governance of England*, ed. C. Plummer (Oxford, 1885), Appx. C and D, pp. 353–6.
2   *Political Poems and Songs* (R.S.) vol. II, pp. 256ff., 267ff., 271ff.
3   *Great Chronicle of London*, ed A. H. Thomas and I. D. Thornley (London, 1938), p. 207.

4   *A Remarkable Fragment of an Old English Chronicle*, ed. T. Hearne in *T. Sprotti Chronica* (Oxford, 1719), p. 299.
5   *C.S.P. Milan* vol. I, pp. 76, 100.
6   *R.P.* vol. V, p. 484; for 'noble predecessor' see *Warkworth's Chronicle*, ed. J.O. Halliwell (Camden Soc., 1839), notes p. 39.
7   *Foed.* vol. XI, pp. 508–9.
8   See manifesto in *Warkworth's Chronicle*, pp. 46–51.
9   See C. L. Scofield, *The Life and Reign of Edward IV* vol. I (London, 1923), p. 502.
10 *Chronicle of the Rebellion in Lincolnshire* in *Camden Miscellany* vol. I (1847), p. 6: S. Bentley, *Excerpta Historica* (London, 1831), pp. 282–4.
11 *Lit. Cant.* (R.S.) vol. III, p. 282.
12 *Foed.* vol. XI, pp. 804–14.
13 Continuation of the *Croyland Chronicle*, in W. Fulman, *Rerum Anglicarum Scriptorum Veterum* (Oxford, 1684), vol. I, p. 558.
14 *P.L.* No. 758.
15 *C.S.P. Milan* vol. I, p. 194.
16 *Foed.* vol. XII, pp. 14–21.
17 See *Great Chronicle of London*, p. 234, and Mancini, *The Usurpation of Richard III*, p. 93.
18 Mancini, *The Usurpation of Richard III*, p. 93.
19 R. Horrox, *Richard III: a Study of Service* (Cambridge, 1989), pp. 187–200; C. Ross, *Richard III* (London, 1987), pp. 119–24.
20 i.e. The northerners William Catesby and Sir Richard Ratcliffe, and Francis Lord Lovel; Richard's badge was the white boar.

Note on secondary reading (post 1970)

C.D. Ross has written biographies of both Yorkist kings, *Edward IV* (London, 1976), and *Richard III* (London, 1981). R. Horrox, *Richard III: a Study of Service* (Cambridge, 1989) is illuminating for Richard's career under his brother as well as for his reign, with a fresh angle of approach. C. Carpenter, *The Wars of the Roses* (Cambridge, 1997) surveys effectively the whole Yorkist period; and J.R. Lander, *Crown and Nobility, 1450–1509* (London, 1976) is perceptive and interesting. Northern England was very important in the politics of the Yorkist period, on which see A.J. Pollard, *North Eastern England during the Wars of the Roses* (Oxford, 1990).

Very useful for the reign of Edward IV are M. Hicks' two biographies, *False, Fleeting, Perjur'd Clarence* (Gloucester, 1980) and *Warwick the Kingmaker* (Oxford, 1998). On Clarence, C. Carpenter, 'The Duke of Clarence and the Midlands: a study in the interplay of local and national politics', *Midland History*, vol. 11 (1986) is also valuable. On the king's marriage, and the Woodvilles, see M. Hicks, 'The changing role of the Wydevilles in Yorkist politics to 1483', in C.D. Ross (ed.), *Patronage, Pedigree and Power in Later Medieval England* (Gloucester, 1979); J.R. Lander's older article, 'Marriage and politics in the fifteenth century: the Nevilles and the Wydevilles', *B.I.H.R.*, vol. 36 (1963) retains value. Lander's article on 'The Hundred Years War and Edward IV's campaign in France', in A.J. Slavin (ed.), *Tudor Men and Institutions: studies in English Law and Government* (Baton Rouge, 1972) is useful for the

Piquigny expedition; and his 'Attainder and forfeiture, 1453–59', *Historical Journal*, vol. 4 (1971) is valuable on crown/magnate relations. On the royal affinity, see D.A.L. Morgan, 'The King's affinity in the polity of Yorkist England', *T.R.H.S.*, 5th series, vol. 23 (1973).

A great deal has been written on Richard III, much of it of uneven quality. Besides the books by C.D. Ross and R. Horrox, cited above, there are some valuable articles and monographs. Three useful papers relating to the usurpation are W.H. Dunham and C.T. Wood, 'The right to rule in England: deposition and the kingdom's authority', *American Historical Review*, vol. 81 (1976); J.A.F. Thomson, 'Richard III and Lord Hastings: a problematical case reviewed', *B.I.H.R.*, vol. 48 (1975); and C.T. Wood, 'Richard III, Lord Hastings and Friday the 13th', in R. Griffiths and J. Sherborne (eds.), *Kings and Nobles in the Later Middle Ages* (Gloucester, 1986). Also valuable are L. Gill, *Richard III and Buckingham's Rebellion* (Stroud, 1999), and, on the personal side, J. Hughes, *The Religious Life of Richard III: Piety and Prayer in the North of England* (Stroud, 1997). M.K. Jones, in his *Bosworth 1485: Psychology of a Battle* (Stroud, 2002) suggests exciting, but to my mind unconvincing, new interpretations.

The studies of the *Wars of the Roses* by Gillingham, Goodman and Pollard, cited in the bibliography to chapter 18, all remain useful for the Yorkist period.

20 England under the Yorkists

The Yorkist kings have been often acclaimed as the authors of new ways in government, who laid the foundations upon which the despotism of the Tudors was built. It is doubtful whether their practices were in fact startlingly original, and nowadays it is questioned whether there ever was a Tudor despotism. In addition, there are difficulties about discussing Yorkist kingship in terms of consistent and coherent trends because the political circumstances of Edward IV's first reign were so different from those of the second, and those of his second reign so different from those of Richard III's. It is none the less true that Edward IV was more successful in governing England than any king had been for a hundred years, except for Henry V. It is also true that there were significant similarities between his and his brother's governmental style and approach, and those of Henry VII. The Yorkists did solve problems where the Lancastrians had failed lamentably to cope, and in ways that set important precedents.

There was nothing obscure about what was wrong with the government of Edward IV's Lancastrian predecessor in its last days. Sir John Fortescue, Henry VI's famous chief justice, made a clear and penetrating diagnosis of its shortcomings in his *Governance of England*. Three evils stood out for him: the insolvency of the crown, lack of prudent and disinterested counsel with the common weal as its objective, and the disordinate influence of great men and their retainers. He attributed the insolvency of Henry VI to inadequate control of expenditure, on the household and on fees and pensions granted with too free a hand; and to overlavish patronage which had substantially reduced the crown demesnes. This had driven the crown to borrow, and to borrow again to meet its creditors, in consequence of which they 'alway grouch for lack of their payment and defame his highness of misgovernment'.[1] The overgreat riches and ambition of the greater nobility had been in itself dangerous: 'there may no greater peril grow to a prince than to have a subject equipollent to himself'.[2] The private interest of the lords had made them bad counsellors. They had used their influence to obtain the appointment of their dependants to key offices in local government, to the end that they might 'be more mighty in their countries to do what they list; and the king in less might and [to] have the fewer officers to repress them when they do amiss'.[3] To this analysis of the broad causes of Henry VI's difficulties (his personal inadequacies apart), we would only wish to add one item: the discredit that military failure abroad brought upon the king himself and his advisers.

Fortescue had his own ideas about how the ills that he diagnosed should be remedied. There were those in his day, he tells us, who looked for a solution in a wholly different style of government, more like that of absolutist France, but for himself he had no desire to see the king's rule over England brought closer to despotism.[4] It was his special pride that, in his native land the king ruled according to laws chosen by his people (statutes made in parliament) and could take taxes only with their assent.[5] This mixed constitution in which authority was shared between the king and his subjects (what Fortescue called *dominium regale et politicum*) was made workable by the prosperous independence of the commons of England, which was the glory of the land and made it strong.[6] Fortescue believed that constitutional change in an absolutist direction could only weaken the kingdom, and looked therefore for a solution to her troubles in practical administrative improvements, which would strengthen the monarchy, and yet preserve intact the virtue of the political laws. Measures should be taken to increase the king's revenue by acts of resumption, with parliament's assent; by a careful calculation of his needs and the provision of a regular revenue to meet his recurrent charges;[7] by careful scrutiny of grants of pensions and an embargo on the grant of demesne lands in fee without parliamentary consent.[8] He wished to see the wealth of the magnates kept within limits by a sharper insistence on the king's right to control their marriages and to vet all alienations of their estates, which ought not to be demised without a royal licence.[9] He also wished to see a very close scrutiny by the king's council of all petitions for office, and a limit set on the number of offices under the crown which any one man might hold; and to make all office holders swear that they would take no fee or livery from any man but the king for the term of the offices to which they were appointed.[10]

The most original, but also arguably the least realistic of Fortescue's suggestions for better government was for a new kind of council.[11] In the past, he complained, great lords had abused their position as councillors to further their own interests and those of their kinsmen, servants and tenants, and had neglected the king's business. He therefore proposed the appointment of a council of twenty-four persons, twelve clerks and twelve laymen, wise and discreet men of middling means who should be salaried, and should swear to take no fee or livery of any but the king. These men would act together with eight of the great lords (four bishops and four secular magnates) whom the king would name annually to serve along with them. By this means Fortescue believed prudent counsel would be ensured, and that private interest and corruption could be effectively eliminated from its heart and centre in the king's council.

To judge by their acts, the Yorkist kings saw eye to eye with Fortescue in his diagnosis of what was amiss in the government of England. Their remedies were not always the same as his, but they were often very reminiscent of what he wrote. This does not mean that he influenced them (he wrote for the Lancastrians in exile), simply that the lines of approach that he suggested were those which common sense and past experience suggested as most likely to restore things to a better frame.

The Yorkists, needless to say, did not adopt anything like Fortescue's plans for the reform of the council; these were too tidy and impersonal to be practical. But their councils were very different from the continual councils of Henry VI's early years. Their composition was fluid, the personnel depending on the king's choice (though in the 1460s, of course, there was always a group of Neville supporters). We know of a great many men who were called councillors (124 names have been traced). A large proportion were men of middle standing, including professional administrators and lawyers, such as Sir William Alyngton (speaker in parliament in 1477), Sir Thomas Vaughan (treasurer of the chamber), Sir John Fogge and Richard Fowler (king's solicitor and later chancellor of the duchy of Lancaster); and under Richard III William Catesby (speaker in 1484), Sir Richard Ratcliffe (knight of the body) and Thomas Lynom (the king's solicitor). A number of clerics did good service too, the most notable of all, after 1471, being the ex-Lancastrian exile and future cardinal, John Morton. There was a close association between the council and the royal household, especially through those knights and esquires of the body who were also councillors. This meant that the council always had a leavening of men directly dependent on the king, who had fees and robes from him and had made their way in his service.

This does not mean that the Yorkists sought in any way to eliminate the aristocracy from their councils. There were always some peers present at its meetings; and under Edward IV William Lord Hastings, the chamberlain, was a dominant figure among the crown's advisers. John Tiptoft Earl of Worcester was twice treasurer of England in his first reign, and as such was normally present at council meetings. Lord Audley, Lord Stanley and, in the reign of Richard III, Lord Lovel also gave much advice. The reason why the very great among the magnates, men like Warwick in Edward's first reign and Gloucester in the second, were often absent when only routine business was in question was that they had plenty of affairs of their own – and indeed of the king's – to attend to, far from the court and Westminster. They and other peers were always summoned when major political decisions were to be taken. Great councils, at which a substantial body of peers were present, were summoned frequently enough by the Yorkists. It was to a great council at Reading in 1464 that Edward announced that he was married; to a great council that he expounded his plans for his sister Margaret's marriage in 1468. When the news of Charles the Bold's death reached England in 1477, a great council was immediately summoned to review the diplomatic implications of the new and unforeseen situation.

Though the Yorkist councils were very different from the continual councils of the 1420s and 1430s, there was nothing new about them. The lack of definition of the personnel of the small council in the Yorkist period, its close connexions with the household, and indeed its activities, were all reminiscent of the councils of Henry VI in the period of Suffolk's dominance, and later of that of Queen Margaret; and also, for that matter, of the council of Richard II's later years. With a king on the throne who was able bodied and of sound mind, the composition of the council always tended to reflect in large degree royal eclecticism; and what such a king looked for was ability in combination with personal commitment to his royal interest.

What was especially notable about the Yorkist council was its assiduous attention to business. The fact that there are few surviving enrolments in the chancery which quote conciliar authority for the issue of letters under the great seal does not mark a decline in its influence. It is clear that, in the case of a good many warrants under the signet and the king's sign manual, the council had in fact been consulted. And it was not just the traditional routine business that kept councillors occupied. They were continuously busy coordinating the work of officials charged with, for instance, the management of royal estates, which was an important new side to their activity. Appointments to office were brought under closer scrutiny than in the past: 'As for the labour for the baileyships and farms', Godfrey Green wrote in 1475 to his patron Sir William Plumpton, 'your worship understands what labour it is to sue therefore: first to have a bill enclosed of the king, then to certain lords of the council (for there is an act made that nothing shall pass from the king until such time as they have seen it), and so to the privy seal and chancellor.'[12] Here is an 'act' that would have warmed Fortescue's heart. Calais was another matter which, in the early 1460s, took up a good deal of time, and it was to the credit of the councillors that at length measures were taken which both secured the regular payment of the garrison and offered the staplers the prospect of seeing their loans to the crown more rapidly repaid. The councillors were hard at work, day in, day out; when the king was away from his capital some went with him and some stayed at Westminster to dispatch business there. Their energy and activity was one major reason why the kingdom was better governed under the Yorkists than it had been for many years.

In Fortescue's advice on the governance of England, measures to improve the crown's financial position took pride of place. Indebtedness had been the bugbear of the Lancastrians, and had much to do with both Henry VI's military failures in France and his political misfortunes in England. In this sphere the efforts of the Yorkists to set things to rights were impressive.

A very substantial enlargement of the crown's revenue from land was a major achievement of the Yorkist period. The accession of Edward IV considerably increased the royal estates, adding to the old crown lands and those of the duchy of Lancaster his two great private inheritances of March and York. Edward IV also made better use of his right of wardship than his predecessor had, and held some very important inheritances in hand in this way at times, including those of Buckingham and Shrewsbury. Between 1461 and 1473 there were too a number of acts of resumption, though it must be admitted that the effect of these, as of previous Lancastrian acts, was substantially reduced by the very large number of exemptions from them (besides, Edward was himself generous, sometimes beyond the point of policy). Attainders added further to his properties. Though many of these were ultimately reversed the additional revenue that they brought in meantime was considerable, and the Clarence estates, which included much of the great Warwick inheritance, were a really golden prize when they came in in 1478. This was the most important gain of the whole period; before it Edward had never come quite up to Fortescue's ideal of a king who had no subject near 'equipollent' with himself,[13] but afterwards he undoubtedly did.

The crown profited not only because it had more estates than before, but also as a result of their more efficient administration. The Yorkists extended to a much larger proportion of the crown lands than their predecessors had what have been called 'the normal methods of contemporary large scale estate management'.[14] The great private landowner employed professionals to oversee his estates – usually a surveyor, a receiver and an auditor to look after manors that were grouped regionally. Among the crown lands, until Edward IV's time, only the duchy of Lancaster lands had been administered in this way, most others being farmed out through the exchequer. Starting in 1461, the first year of his reign, Edward regrouped a series of complexes of estates, and put them under the management of professionals in the royal service. John Milewater was appointed receiver for a group of estates in the Welsh border counties, some belonging to the earldom of March, some to the duchy of Lancaster, and some to the Stafford inheritance which was in wardship; his accounts were audited at Hereford by John Luthington. Other groups of estates in other areas were treated similarly, and when Clarence was attainted the system was further extended. Peter Beaupie, clerk of the greencloth, took initial control of the forfeited estates (an enormous accretion to the crown's landed wealth) which were divided into a series of local receiverships: thus the Clarence estates in the western midlands were entrusted to the management of John Harcourt, those in the central midlands to John Luthington, and those in the west country to John Hayes. A general supervision over all these officials was exercised by Sir Thomas Vaughan, the treasurer of the chamber, with a commission working under him. Richard III followed his brother's example in management when he seized the throne; John Fitzherbert was made responsible as receiver for most of the lands of Queen Elizabeth Woodeville, and Edmund Chadderton for those of the Earl of Buckingham when they were forfeited after his revolt.

The headquarters of this system of estate management was the chamber. The treasurer of the chamber (from 1465 Sir Thomas Vaughan) received a good proportion of the issues of the estates in cash; some was paid out in accordance with warrants under the signet, the king's private seal. Vaughan, with others of the council's professionals, usually audited the accounts before they were passed on to the exchequer, before which the receivers were not answerable. The exchequer was thus largely bypassed as far as accounting was concerned, and entirely as regarded the handling of the issues of the estates. As long as the household men to whom estate management was entrusted were faithful in discharging their duties, this made for speedier and more efficient collection of revenue. Most important of all, it relieved the revenue of the crown estates in question from the burden of assignments made at the exchequer, with which the issues of crown lands had always been heavily loaded in the Lancastrian period. This did not really diminish the importance of the exchequer as a financial department; it continued to supervise the collection of subsidies, the customs, and some farms, and to meet major national expenses. It did mean that the king gained an independence in the control of a valuable proportion of his revenues which his predecessors had never enjoyed.

Edward IV took some other measures to improve the crown's income from estates and rights over landed property. In 1462 the exchequer was ordered to omit from the Pipe Roll accounts farms and fee farms of 40s. and above in annual value, and officials were appointed in eight regions to collect the issues and pay them over to the treasurer of the household. This does not seem to have resulted in a substantial increase in revenue. But the case was different with the commission appointed in ten counties in 1474 to inquire into feudal tenures and the king's rights arising therefrom; some of the fines imposed for evasion of incidents were very heavy. These measures are interesting because they help to illustrate how the whole Yorkist system of management anticipated, often in detail, that of the early Tudors. The task of the commissioners of 1474 was essentially the same as that which the hated Dudley and Empson discharged for Henry VII. By 1485 the idea of something very like a court of general surveyors was already envisaged. We learn this from a signet memorandum of 1484 on royal estate management: all auditors, it stipulated, were each year, between Candlemas and Palm Sunday, to make declaration of the livelihood in their charge, 'by which the king's grace should know all the lordships that pertaineth to his crown'.[15] Declarations such as these were what the general surveyors of the future were to be concerned with, but their records do not begin until 1503–4.

Edward IV, like Henry VII, acquired in the end a reputation for avarice. Perhaps it was deserved. But it needed constant economy and careful accounting for his measures to have any effect at all. We can see this anxiety for economy written very clear in, for instance, the famous Ordinance of 1478 for the household (whose expenditure had been a constant source of complaint for a century) which made sharp restrictions on allowable expenses. Many of its regulations are directly related to passages in the *Black Book of the Household*, compiled a little earlier, and whose chief object was to ensure careful account of all moneys that the household spent.[16] Edward IV's household in fact cost less to run than that of either Henry VI or Henry VII, though he certainly lived with more magnificence than the former.

By the 1470s the effects of overall economy – of better management, better accounting, and cuts in unnecessary expenditure in all areas of crown finance –

were such that the king was able to start paying off old debts. Between 1471 and 1476 debts owed to Gerard Caniziani, the agent of the Medici, were reduced from £14,390 to £3000. In 1478 the king was able to assign revenues to pay off the whole of his debt of over £12,000 to the city of London. In 1466 he had owed nearly £33,000 in Calais, mostly to the staplers; by 1483 this was reduced to a mere £2000. Edward died solvent, which none of his Lancastrian predecessors had done. He had broken the vicious spiral of mounting insolvency which in their day, as Fortescue noted, had brought the king's name into disrepute and estranged his subjects from him.

The issues of crown lands and the profit of feudal rights were not the only sources of revenue that made Edward IV a newly wealthy king. The pension that Louis XI agreed to pay him at Picquigny in 1475 was a very important subvention, and so determined was Edward to keep it that he was prepared, as we have seen, to sacrifice the coherence of English diplomacy to this single end. Two other sources of revenue which were significant demand special attention.

During the fifteenth century revenue from the customs fell, largely because of the decline of the trade in wool on which the duty was heaviest. Rather than raise the rate on other exports, Edward preferred himself to engage in commerce: 'like a private person who lived by trade, he exchanged through his agents merchandise for merchandise with both Italians and Greeks'.[17] As early as 1463 his agents shipped more than 300 sacks of wool, to be sold for the king's profit. In 1464 James de Sanderico took charge as his factor of the shipment of 8000 cloths, from Southampton. In 1466 Alan de Monteferrato was commissioned to ship 6000 sacks of wool, 20,000 cloths, 16,000 blocks of tin and 10,000 'barrels' of vessels of pewter via the straits of Gibraltar to Italy. Ventures such as these brought a handsome profit. Edward's mercantile enterprises besides brought him into much contact with foreign merchants (the larger part of his exports were shipped in foreign vessels) and he was able to borrow more money more often from alien merchants than any king since Edward III. Caniziani, the Medici agent, was particularly serviceable in this regard; he became a trusted intimate, and on occasion acted for the king in diplomatic business.

Benevolences were the other source of finance that Edward exploited with particular success. Notionally a benevolence meant a free gift, usually in lieu of obligatory military service, and it was not strictly a new source of revenue, for Richard II and the Lancastrians had from time to time obtained similar 'gifts' from their subjects. But Edward was more systematic, especially with the benevolences that were raised to pay for the Picquigny expedition and for the Scottish war at the end of the reign. The benevolence of 1475 was solicited throughout the kingdom and the king took a personal hand in raising the money: 'he handled the people so graciously that he got more money than he would have got by two fifteenths', says the chronicle of London (this is an exaggeration).[18] The cash was collected by receivers appointed for the purpose and paid not to the exchequer but into the household. In effect, it was a national tax on incomes over £10 and movables of the value of £40 and upwards, and it certainly tapped fortunes (especially some commercial fortunes) which subsidies did not. Its incidence indeed was probably more equitable than a subsidy's. Edward's benevolences raised a great deal of money. Though Richard III in 1484 tried to make political capital out of condemning them, it would seem that they were not in general very sharply resented.

An important point about benevolences was that, as 'free' gifts, they were not subject to parliamentary assent. This was true also of all the other sources of revenue that we have been examining in this chapter, and it is no accident. These are the words that Edward addressed to the speaker and the commons of parliament in June 1467: 'the reason why I have called and summoned this my parliament is that I intend to live on my own, and not to charge my subjects except for great and urgent causes, which concern rather their own welfare, and the defence of this my kingdom, than my own pleasure'.[19] Edward was quite determined to live as far as he could without parliamentary grants, and after 1475 he was remarkably successful in doing so. In the last years of the reign, in spite of the war with Scotland, he did not summon parliament and ask for a subsidy; and he only did so in the spring of 1483 when, after he had been outmanoeuvred in continental diplomacy by Louis XI, there was a clear possibility of war with France. This does not mean that Edward IV wanted to rule without parliament in some sort of despotic manner. He knew well the value of the support of the commons in parliament, and exploited it skilfully; as his speech of 1467 makes plain, his object was to woo his subjects, not to over-awe them. But he knew too that the independence of the commons could make parliamentary meetings awkward, especially at any moment of tension. The fact was one which all intelligent political managers of the age understood; the Lancastrian courtiers, preparing to move against York in 1455, thought it wiser to summon named knights from the counties to a council, rather than a parliament, and Warwick in 1469 cancelled the parliament that he summoned (probably to witness the deposition of Edward in favour of Clarence) because he was not sure that he could control it. By summoning parliament less frequently, and by avoiding as far as he might requesting grants that could be hedged with conditions, Edward enlarged the freedom of royal initiative in government and his subjects were grateful for being asked for aid less often.

The other great problem, besides finance, which Yorkist government had to face was that of public order. Fortescue outlined the difficulties aptly. The great nobles of the realm disposed of so much wealth and influence that men were more willing to put their trust in their favour than in the king's law. They were able to use their influence to infiltrate supporters who had taken their fees and liveries into key positions in local government, as sheriffs and on the commissions of the peace, which offices they proceeded to abuse in the interests of their magnate patrons – and of their own. The consequent perception was that the common law was failing to offer the protection that it should; its officers were venal, its juries packed or easily intimidated. Maintenance had so distorted the effect of the law that force or the favour of a lord who had force at his beck offered a better protection than it did. This state of affairs imposed two priorities: better control of the influence of the magnates, to ensure that it worked with and for the crown and not against it, and the strengthening of royal authority over local government.

Edward IV had a threefold problem in his dealings with the aristocracy. He had not only to restrain their misdemeanours; he had also to make sure that loyal friends were well rewarded; and he had further, since he had taken the throne by force, to secure the allegiance of men who might doubt that he was the rightful king. Towards the last end his policy was a judicious mixture of terror and conciliation. Great men who were taken in arms in the field against him were tried summarily as traitors under martial law, and executed; his constable, Tiptoft, who presided over many such trials, earned himself the ugly nickname of 'the Butcher of England'. Those whom the king could not touch, because they escaped his power, were attainted. Edward IV, however, made it clear early that he was willing to reverse attainders in favour of Lancastrians who would reverse their allegiance, and that he had no wish to see heirs of good family lose their inheritances. In 1462 he was prepared to take even Somerset back into favour, and in 1469 he positively created danger for himself by restoring the Percy heir. In the 1470s there were more reversals of old attainders than there were new ones. This policy paid off, and in his later years he was well served by ex-Lancastrians, including even Sir John Fortescue himself, who had spent ten years in exile for Henry VI.

To those who served him well and loyally Edward was not less generous than his royal predecessors. He built his brother Richard of Gloucester into a subject powerful enough to prove over-mighty, as after Edward's death he did. Wisely, he did not grant many offices to his wife's relatives, the Woodevilles, but they did spectacularly well in other ways, especially through advantageous marriages. To others he was very generous with grants of profitable posts, and his chamberlain, William Lord Hastings, did as well in this way as any courtier of Lancastrian times. Hastings had started out on his career as a knightly retainer of Edward's father, Richard Duke of York, and he was only one of a substantial group of men promoted to the peerage for their good service in the Yorkist cause. Among such were Walter Devereux, Lord Ferrers, who had been with Duke Richard at Ludford; Robert Ogle, Lord Ogle, a veteran of the border struggles who had fought for him at St Albans, and who was appointed in 1462 constable of the Percy castles of Alnwick and Warkworth; Walter Blount, Lord Mountjoy, who had been York's treasurer of Calais in 1460 and became treasurer of England in 1464; John Lord Wenlock, once a Lancastrian but attainted as a Yorkist in the Coventry parliament of 1459, who was killed at Tewkesbury; Thomas Lord Lumley; John Lord Dinham; Humphrey Lord Stafford. Two men rose much further than these through their services, to glamorous dignity: William Herbert in Edward IV's first reign, created Earl of Pembroke in 1468; and John Howard, one time knight of the shire for Norfolk who under

Richard III became Duke of Norfolk in 1483, and died fighting for him on Bosworth field. The Yorkist peerage was very much an aristocracy of service (as the Lancastrian peerage had also been in later days when families like the Hungerfords and Tiptofts, descendants of old retainers, arrived in the lords). Edward's promotions had their price, in terms of grants of lands, reversions and offices, because peers had to be rewarded in a manner fitting their rank; but the loyal support that he engaged by them made it worthwhile.

Edward's efforts to place limitations on the aristocratic abuse of livery and maintenance were to some extent compromised by his lavish new creations and his need to count on the support of retainers dependent on loyal peers. His statutes on this subject did not go much further than those of Richard II. As the substantial collection of retaining indentures made with knights and squires by his intimate Lord Hastings shows, he did not seek any more than Richard had done to prevent peers from retaining men for lawful purposes. His inhibition, in the statute of 1468, on the granting of liveries and badges by peers (or anyone else) to men who were not their household servants was not observed, and no peer was prosecuted under the statute for giving liveries, so far as is known (though three peers, the Earl of Shrewsbury, Lord Grey and Lord Mountjoy, were prosecuted for giving liveries, probably to yeomen, shortly before the statute was passed). Edward was pleased, rather than the reverse, to see the retainers of loyal men like Hastings well entrenched in local office and influence, and did not mind much whether they showed their badges or no.

Nevertheless, Edward was determined that his justice should restrain aristocratic violence and rivalry better than his predecessor's had. The ordinary common law courts, which enforced statutes, were not up to this task; speedier and more arbitrary procedures were needed. In Henry VI's reign the Statute of Riots of 1453 had looked to action by the council to solve the problem, and had laid down dire penalties for peers who failed to answer summonses under the privy seal to appear before it.[20] This was the right answer, and anticipated the practice of the Tudor Court of Star Chamber; the trouble in the 1450s was that the summonses were ignored and the penalties not imposed. Yorkist action on the same lines seems to have been more successful, though it has not been very adequately studied. Edward's remark when John Paston failed to answer a summons suggests determination: 'we will send him another, and by God's mercy if he come not then he shall die for it. We will make other men beware by him how they shall disobey our writing'.[21] Paston, who was in fact flung into gaol, was of course not a peer, only a very substantial landowner. But Lord Grey was a peer, and in 1471 he found himself before the council in the Star Chamber, to be ordered by the king personally not to molest the mayor of Nottingham, and to refrain, under heavy penalties, from retaining a party in the town by giving men his livery. In the 1470s there is evidence of very heavy fines being imposed on a number of noblemen who were not considered trustworthy. The king was also skilful in persuading the powerful to accept his arbitration, backed by bonds to keep the peace, in their family rivalries, as for instance that of the Harringtons and Stanleys in Lancashire. Edward in his second reign was making his authority effectively felt by the great men of the realm, and he was doing so by the very same means that Henry VII was to adopt later.

In two regions where there was a particularly dire history of aristocratic and gentry unruliness, the Yorkists took steps to reassert their authority which had important implications for the future, the north, and Wales and its marches. In the Lancastrian period the kings had relied largely on the local magnates, in particular on the Nevilles and Percies, for the keeping of the peace there. These families usually controlled the wardenships of the marches, and they were also granted special commissions of the peace, to hear and determine cases that arose in the north with the assistance of lawyers and knights of their own house-holds. Their rivalries had, however, often made their powers as much a menace as a benefit. Since the Percies through the last years of Henry VI had been con-sistently loyal to the house of Lancaster, Edward IV in his first reign relied principally on the Nevilles, Warwick and his brother John, who became Earl of Northumberland and acquired thereby most of the confiscated estates of Percy. After 1471 and the fall of the Nevilles, Edward tried an approach that was slightly different, building up the position in the north of his brother Richard into what was virtually a northern viceroyalty. The Neville Yorkshire estates came to him, as a result of the agreement brokered by the king between him and Clarence, by his marriage, and he was granted all the lands of the manor of Richmond in the county. He became warden of the West March, and was entrusted with control of the duchy of Lancaster's northern estates and officers. There were some initial difficulties with the restored Percy Earl of Northumberland, warden of the East March, but another agreement brokered by Edward, in 1474, established a mutually satisfactory con-dominium, in which Richard was clearly the senior partner. In 1480 he was made king's lieutenant in the north. After he became king, Richard carried the delegation of royal authority in the region one step further by setting up a council in the north. At its head he placed the Earl of Lincoln, whose headquarters were at Sheriff Hutton in Yorkshire, and its personnel included both noblemen and professionals. It was formally the king's council in the north; it could exercise the same equitable jurisdiction outside the common law that the king's council in London did in the south, and had complete authority in all matters of rebellion and riot. Richard here went a step beyond past reliance on the support of loyal magnates and their household men in a remote area; he brought direct royal authority into the troubled north and set it on a permanent footing.

The Yorkist assertion of royal authority in Wales and its marches followed comparable lines. Here in his first reign Edward IV relied heavily on the terri-torial influence of William Herbert, created by him Earl of Pembroke, who was beheaded by Warwick after the fight at Edgecote in 1469. After his recovery of the throne in 1471, Edward did not turn to Herbert's heir; he created his new born son Edward Prince of Wales, and appointed a council to act for him. Over the ensuing years, the powers and personnel of this council were steadily strengthened. From a body originally mainly concerned with the administration of the estates of the Principality and the earldom of Chester, it grew into an authority with considerable powers, to appoint to judicial commissions in Wales and the marches, to inquire into the misdemeanours and negligences of officials, and to array men in pursuit of criminals and to maintain order. The crown's territorial influence through the estates of the earldom of March helped to buttress its authority: to these were added in 1479 those of the earldom of Pembroke which the king compelled William Herbert II to surrender in exchange for the earldom of Huntingdon. Ludlow castle became the residence of the Prince and the headquarters of his council, under his 'governor' Anthony Earl Rivers and Bishop Alcock of Rochester. Richard III, after Buckingham's rebellion, abandoned this conciliar experiment, for the time at least: maybe he would have revived it for his son, had he lived. The seed had been sown, however, for the future council in Wales and the marches of Tudor times.

The important point about these Yorkist solutions to two particular regional problems was that they brought direct royal authority appreciably closer to their local societies. There was a significant difference, in the north, between the authority of a royal duke, the king's brother and visibly his representative, and the influence of a Percy or Neville earl who was at the same time warden for the king of one of the marches. Much the same was true of the authority of a princely council in Wales, as compared with the influence of a Herbert or a Stafford. Fortescue put the point nicely (though what he had in mind were the powers that he hoped for, for a Lancastrian Prince of Wales); 'the offices, . . . that my lord the prince gevyth . . . I reken the officers as the kynges officers'.[22] Encouraging those with judicial or administrative offices to discharge to regard themselves as servants of the crown, rather than of some lord whose influence had gained them their office, was an important route toward restraining the level of local disorder that the family feuding of aristocrats and their retainers could so easily promote, especially in regions remote from London and Westminster.

Against men of lesser status than the nobility and the very great gentry, Edward took steps to make the common law prevail. If no peers were prosecuted under the 1468 statute against livery and maintenance, this was not true of others; the King's Bench rolls show that a great many lesser men were prosecuted. We should remember here that some of the worst symptoms of lack of governance in the 1450s were the consequence of the gangsterism of lesser men and their followers, like Charles Nowell and Robert Ledham of whom the Paston letters complain; and that, in the eyes of Edward IV and his councillors at least, the granting of liveries casually to men of yeoman status was probably the one genuinely anti-social aspect of the customary practice of retaining. Early in his reign, in 1462, Edward himself sat in King's Bench for three consecutive days, 'in order to understand how his laws were prosecuted'. In 1476, when a wave of disorders had followed the disbanding of the Picquigny army, he himself went on tour in the counties with his justices; 'and he spared none, even of his own household . . . and by the execution of this stern justice everywhere, highway robbery soon ceased'.[23] Highway robbery of course did not cease for many years, but Edward's comparative success stands in sharp contrast to the failure, in the Lancastrian period, of the special commissions of justice sent into the counties (for example after Cade's revolt) to achieve anything of note.

The use that the Yorkists made of these same special commissions of justices of *oyer* and *terminer* was in fact a notable feature of their government. Here, once more, they were not original, but used tried methods to new effect. Their commissions were often large, with perhaps as many as a score of names; since two justices constituted a quorum to hold pleas, this made it possible to conduct a number of investigations simultaneously. The scope of the commissions was wide too, sometimes covering several shires at a time. A nobleman of high standing was usually in overall charge (Clarence, Gloucester, Hastings and, earlier, Warwick all served in this way on a number of occasions), and at least one justice of one of the benches was always included; the remaining members would be noblemen and gentry who were considered reliable by the regime. As Professor Bellamy writes, 'in any matter of vital importance, the special commission must have looked very much like the royal council in another guise'. The difference of guise was significant, however, as he points out, since these justices judged cases by common law and could give judgement of life and limb, which the council normally did not. They were probably the most important instrument that the Yorkists used for disciplining lawlessness at the local level, which, as everyone recognized, had got out of hand in the 1450s.

In ordinary conditions, of course, the key men in the system for the enforcement of local order were the justices of the peace. Their responsibilities had been growing steadily since the mid fourteenth century, as the additions to the commissions of the peace testify. They were responsible now for enforcing not only the peace, but also the statutes of labourers; the statutes of livery and maintenance (upon lesser men and in the first instance); the statute against the Lollards; and the statutes against clipping and counterfeiting coin. They could hear and determine cases of felony and trespass, armed conventicles, maintenance, and labour offences. They could take surety from those who threatened bodily harm, and could inquire by sworn inquest into felonies and trespass, breaches of the assize of weights and measures, and the negligence of officials in enforcing statutes. They fixed maximum wages, and vetted gild regulations. Two statutes, of 1388 and 1390, made provision for their payment out of the penalties that they imposed, and for the payment of the clerk who kept their records. They were thus by the beginning of the Yorkist period well-established officials with very wide powers to supervise criminal justice and economic regulations, and this period saw still further additions to their powers. An act of 1461 transferred to them the petty criminal jurisdiction previously exercised by the sheriffs in their tourns, and an act of 1483 empowered them to admit to bail prisoners arrested by the sheriffs on suspicion of felony.[24] These two acts were among the latest steps in the long history of the decline of the sheriff, once the key figure in local justice. Though he was still responsible for empanelling the juries whose verdict as to fact decided most of the cases heard before the justices of the peace at their quarterly sessions, the justices had become the all important men.

The problem of making these justices effective in the local enforcement of the common criminal law was directly related to the problem of livery and maintenance. The justices of the peace were recruited largely from the gentry of the shires (with a leavening of lawyers and the occasional magnate), and the gentry were the class which, as the clientele of noble patrons, was most deeply involved in disorder, maintenance, and the packing of juries and commissions in the localities in the Lancastrian period. The Yorkist kings, as a result of their success in making the crown a greater landowner than it had ever been before were able to some considerable extent to counter the forces of maintenance with their own weapons. Partly this was achieved through the delegation of royal authority – or perhaps it would be better to say royal influence – through trusted peers who were locally well endowed and had strong court connections. The best example, under Edward IV, is probably Lord Hastings. Created a baron in 1461, Hastings was not among the greater magnates in terms of territorial possession; but the authority which the king gave him through his stewardship of Duchy of Lancaster lands in the north midlands, and of other estates there recovered to the crown by the resumption of 1473, made him in Edward's second reign the most powerful man across the counties of Derby, Nottingham, Stafford and Leicester. He was able to build up in the area a strikingly powerful and numerous affinity, counting even peers, Lords Grey of Codnor and Lord Mountjoy, among his retainers. Because Hastings was the king's chamberlain, a dominant figure in his household and among his most intimate counsellors, to be of his affinity was little different from being of the king's own affinity. Thus his influence became a force drawing the gentry of his region into the orbit of direct royal authority and of personal allegiance to the crown.

The royal household grew under Edward IV: in the 1470s there were perhaps thirty to forty knights of the body (compared with ten near the start of his reign), and as many esquires. In regions where the greatly enlarged royal estates made the crown the principal landowner, and especially in those where magnate territorial influences were comparatively slight (as was the case, for instance, in a good many southern counties), these men and others with household connections contributed significantly as landowners to making the impact of royal authority more direct. The council took a close interest in appointments to the commissions of the peace; and the links between the royal household (that is to say, in effect, the private retinue of the crown) and local government were systematically developed. Thus in Kent, under Edward IV, Sir John Fogge and Sir John Scott, squires of the body, were both often on the commission of the peace, and both served as sheriff; in Somerset Sir Giles Daubeny, squire and afterwards knight of the body, was sheriff in 1474–5, sat for the shire in parliament in 1478, and was a justice of the peace from 1475 to 1483; Avery Cornburgh, yeoman of the chamber, was sheriff of Cornwall and later of Essex and justice of the peace in Essex. The advancement of household men to important local offices is equally a marked feature in Richard III's reign, the only difference being, as we have seen, that so many of them were drawn from his northern affinity, and strangers to the localities in which their advancement was intended to subvent royal authority. To the end Yorkists remained far short of ever hoping to reach the position that Fortescue wished to see, where none held office who had clothing and fee of any but the crown, but they made a start towards his goal. In doing so, they began to forge that close connexion between the crown and the gentry of the localities, which was a marked feature of the Tudor period, and their household men, with their strong personal associations with the court and its circles, were instrumental agents in the process.

It should be stressed that there was nothing very new about this policy (Richard II and Henry IV had been keenly aware of the importance to the monarchy of committed support in the counties); and, once again, that Yorkist reliance on gentlemen was in no sense inimical to aristocratic interest, and was not intended to be. It was inimical only to the abuse of aristocratic power. The line of division between the peerage and the greater gentry was not a sharp one. Most of the peers promoted by the Yorkists were drawn from the gentry class, and many had performed locally the same sort of function that the knights and squires of the household were so useful in discharging. Lord Dinham had been sheriff of Devon when he was a knight; Lord Wenlock had represented Bedfordshire in six parliaments under Henry VI; John Howard, Duke of Norfolk, had been sheriff there and John Jenny had intrigued with the Pastons to keep him out of parliament in the days when he was plain Sir John. The secret of Yorkist success in government was not restraint of the aristocracy by means of a new alliance of the crown and the middle class, a notion far too modern for them to comprehend; it was the harnessing of all the forces of patronage, private interest and good lordship – of 'bastard feudalism' – to the support of the monarchy. This meant relying on peers as well as gentry, and on others too, citizens and yeomanry; on all and any whose trust could be personally engaged.

In order to foster that loyalty and pride of service which gave psychological strength to 'bastard feudal' relationships, the Yorkists took pains to make their kingship prestigious in their subjects' eyes. They nursed carefully the mythology of Yorkist legitimism. The attainders of the Earl of Cambridge and his fellow conspirators, who had plotted to unseat Henry V and crown Edward IV's 'noble predecessor' of March in 1415, were solemnly reversed in 1461. Pamphlets and ballads laboured the theme that the misfortunes of the house of Lancaster were a judgement of God upon the race of Henry IV, who had seized the throne of an anointed king. This emphasis on hereditary right and legitimate succession subtly magnified the dignity of kingship, whose inheritance was governed by the laws of God and nature, laws beyond and above the common law and even parliament. This was why there was no parliamentary deposition of Henry VI; that would have demeaned the dignity both of kingship and of legitimacy. This theme culminated in Richard of Gloucester's claim in 1483 that he should be king because he alone represented the old and true blood royal, sacred and unadulterated.

In spite of their attention to economy, the Yorkists were careful to make their state magnificent. Henry VI's too obvious poverty had lost him respect; when he appeared in London in 1470 it was 'more like a play than a showing of a prince to win men's hearts', an observer wrote, 'for by this means he lost many and won none or right few, and ever he was showed in a long blue gown of velvet, as if he had no more to change with'.[25] Edward in contrast was the height of fashion, 'frequently appearing in a great variety of most costly garments, of a quite different cut to those which had usually been seen in our kingdom'.[26] A king ought to be magnificent, wrote the author of the *Black Book of the Household*, 'which means superabundant liberality'.[27] Edward sought advice from the Burgundian court as to how to organize his own with duly opulent ceremony. He showed what he could do on such occasions as that when he welcomed to England the Seigneur de la Gruthyse, who had been his host in exile in 1470. Gruthyse was presented, on his arrival at Windsor, with a gold cup set with precious stones and 'a great piece of an unicorn's horn'. He was lodged in chambers 'hung with white silk and linen cloth and all the floors covered with carpets', and undressed by the lord chamberlain. He was feasted, slept in a bed of state, and had a kind of pavilion erected over his bath.[28] To a modern ear this sort of reception can sound like excess blending into absurdity. In the fifteenth century respect for dignity and authority was not to be had without display and the Yorkists, wisely, did not spare expense to this end.

Edward IV sought to woo his people by address as well as magnificence. He was handsome, and could make himself familiar, especially with the ladies. The *Great Chronicle of London* tells a pleasant story of how, in 1475, as 'he passed through a town of Suffolk, he summoned a rich widow before him, amongst others, and asked her what her goodwill would be towards his great expenses. She liberally granted him £10. He liberally thanked her, and then drew her to him and kissed her. Which kiss pleased her so much, that for his great bounty and kind deed he should have had £20 for his £10.'[29] The shrewd Milanese ambassador noted his skill in dealing with people: 'I have frequently seen our neighbours here who were summoned before the king, and when they went they looked as if they were going to the gallows. But when they returned they were joyful, saying they had spoken to the king and he had spoken to them so benignly that they did not regret the money they had paid.'[30] The Londoners were Edward's special favourites. In 1481 he entertained the mayor and aldermen at a great hunting party in Waltham forest, and sent some of the game to their wives. Nothing, says Thomas More, had for many a day 'got him more hearts or more hearty favour among the common people, which oftentimes more esteem and take for greater kindness a little courtesy than a great benefit'.[31] Edward was adept at winning men, especially common men. The Yorkist cause in its old days of opposition had always drawn its greatest strength from popular support; he as king made this one of the props of his monarchy.

The conscious effort to make royal rule popular was a very important aspect of Yorkist kingship. In so far as Yorkist policies were in any way systematic, they were not very original. The clearest precedents for their methods, however, were not those of periods of successful government, but those of the least successful reigns of the later middle ages in England, Richard II's and Henry VI's. Edward IV succeeded in applying solutions to governmental problems formulated by these unpopular monarchs and their advisers without thereby alienating opinion at large, and it was the secret of his success.

Almost all the expedients of Yorkist government had been tried before. Richard II had seen, quite as clearly as Edward IV, how desirable it was to reduce the crown's dependence on parliamentary subsidies. He and his councillors had worked to create connexions between the court and the local ministers of government, by recruiting men with county influence to the household and by advancing householders to shrieval office. Suffolk, in the period of his dominance, had done the same, and so had Queen Margaret and her associates in the late 1450s; the Yorkists merely followed their example. The Lancastrian statute of riots of 1453 aimed to control aristocratic misdemeanour by the same conciliar jurisdiction that the Yorkists employed more effectively. Richard II had sought to enlarge the crown's regular revenues, including those from land (which was one important object of the confiscation of the Lancastrian estates). In the late 1450s, when Margaret's supporters the Earl of Wiltshire and Sir Thomas Tuddenham were treasurer and treasurer of the household respectively, an attempt had been made to route royal landed revenues direct to the household, bypassing the exchequer, with the connivance of householders among the shrievalty. Wiltshire and Tuddenham were no less aware of the value to the crown of funds outside exchequer control than the Yorkists and their chamber officials, though it looks as though they would have made the wardrobe rather than the chamber their headquarters of private royal finance.

There were of course many differences in detail between Edward's Yorkist practice and these earlier efforts to solve the same sort of problems by the same sort of means. The most important difference, however, was a very simple one. The servants of Richard II and Henry VI were hated and they knew it. They were frightened of the people and kept away from their capital in times of trouble. As Fortescue's book on *Governance* shows, it did not take any very startling originality to propound administrative proposals for strengthening the authority of the crown, which in the fifteenth century was clearly recognized as needful for the better government of the kingdom. But administrative solutions had no real chance of succeeding unless they could be made acceptable to opinion at large. Richard II and the advisers of Henry VI failed totally in this respect; Edward IV, determined to engage his subjects' support for their government, was much more successful. The combination of popular address, of which Edward III and Henry V had in the past shown themselves masters, with the administrative expedients of kings who had been labelled 'tyrants', made his monarchy impressive, and is the key to why historians, looking back to the failures of Henry VI, have sometimes labelled it 'new'. Edward IV, at an early stage, grasped what the right priorities were; and though he also made political blunders (notably the Woodville marriage) survived to give his regime the air of greatly increased solidity that it wore in the 1470s.

Richard III, in his royal propaganda, denounced the corruption and luxury of Edward IV's court, his abuses of the law and the oppressive nature of his benevolences, promising his people surer governance and better justice than they had enjoyed in his brother's time. But in reality there was little difference between their approaches to the problems of ruling. Richard was guided by the same principles as Edward in his choices of counsellors and servants, in the means by which he sought to make royal authority felt in the localities, and in his attention to the management of the crown's landed estate and of its financial resources more generally. He understood quite as well as his brother the need to court public opinion (though he was not so successful in winning it over). If he had triumphed at Bosworth, he would almost certainly have succeeded in making his position no less stable than Edward's looked to be at the start of 1483, by the same means. It was his political actions, that made it hard for him to win his subjects' trust, not his administrative policies. The route that he took to gain the throne shook the sense of stability that Edward's successful rule had nourished, and reawakened fears of the kind of disorder that had dogged the 1450s and 60s. In 1485, as in that time and in the last years of Richard II, too many people felt insecure. That opened the way for Henry Tudor's bid for the throne. Bosworth decided that it should be he, not Richard, who restored the stability that the civil wars had taught Englishmen to prize above most things, by means largely adapted from Yorkist practice.

Notes

1 J. Fortescue, *The Governance of England*, ed. C. Plummer (Oxford, 1885), p. 118.
2 ibid. p. 130.
3 ibid. p. 152.
4 ibid. pp. 137–40.
5 J. Fortescue, *De Laudibus Legum Anglie*, ed. S. B. Chrimes (Cambridge, 1942), pp. 40, 86.
6 *Governance*, ch. I and II; see also *De Natura Legis Nature* (in the collected *Works*, ed. Lord Clermont), Lib. I, ch. XVI.
7 *Governance*, ch. VI and XIV.
8 ibid. ch. XIX, p. 154.
9 ibid. p. 134.
10 ibid. pp. 143–4, 153.
11 ibid. ch. XV.
12 *Plumpton Correspondence*, ed. T. Stapleton (Camden Soc., 1839), p. 33.
13 Fortescue, *Governance*, p. 130.
14 The quotation is from B. P. Wolffe, 'The management of English royal estates under the Yorkist kings', *E.H.R.* vol. 71 (1956), pp. 1–27.
15 Quoted by Horrox, *Richard III: a Study of Service*, p. 302.
16 The text of the ordinance is given by A. R. Myers, *The Household of Edward IV* (Manchester, 1959), pp. 211–28; for the relation between it and the *Black Book* see his introduction, pp. 39–44.

17 *Croyland Chronicle*, in W. Fulman, *Rerum Anglicarum Scriptorum Veterum* (Oxford, 1684), p. 559.
18 *Great Chronicle of London*, ed. A. H. Thomas and I. D. Thornley (London, 1938), p. 223.
19 *R.P.* vol. V, p. 572.
20 *Statutes*, 31 Henry VI, c. 2.
21 *P.L.* No. 417.
22 *Governance*, p. 151.
23 *Croyland Chronicle*, p. 559.
24 *Statutes*, I Edward IV, c. 2; 1 Richard III, c. 3.
25 *Great Chronicle of London*, p. 215.
26 *Croyland Chronicle*, p. 563.
27 Myers, *The Household of Edward IV*, p. 86.
28 *The Record of Bluemantle Pursuivant*, in C. L. Kingsford, *Historical Literature in the Fifteenth Century* (Oxford, 1913), pp. 386–7.
29 *Great Chronicle of London*, p. 223.
30 *C.S.P. Milan* vol. I, p. 193.
31 Thomas More, *History of King Richard III*, ed. J. R. Lumby (Cambridge, 1883), p. 3.

Note on secondary reading (post 1970)

Three books that include wide ranging discussion of Yorkist government are C. Carpenter, *The Wars of the Roses: Politics and the Constitution* (Cambridge, 1997); J.R. Lander, *Conflict and Stability in Fifteenth Century England* (London, 1974); and A. Goodman, *The New Monarchy: England, 1471–1534* (Oxford, 1988).

On individual topics treated in the chapter, see on the council A.L. Brown, 'The King's councillors in the fifteenth century', *T.R.H.S.*, 5th series, vol. 19 (1969); and the earlier articles by Lander in *E.H.R.*, vol. 73 (1958) and *B.I.H.R.*, vol. 32 (1959), cited in the main bibliography. On Richard III's role in the north of England while Duke of Gloucester, see R. Horrox, *Richard III: a study of service* (Cambridge, 1989); and on the Council in Wales and the marches D.E. Lowe, 'Edward IV, the Wydevilles, and the Council of the Prince of Wales', *Bulletin of the Board of Celtic Studies*, vol. 29 (1982). On the administration of crown lands, the key work is B.P. Wolffe, *The Crown Lands: an Aspect of Yorkist and Early Tudor Government, 1461–1536* (London, 1970). On restraints on magnate retaining, see M. Hicks, 'The 1468 Statute of Livery', *Historical Research*, vol. 64 (1991): W.H. Dunham, *Lord Hastings' Indentured Retainers* (New Haven, Conn., 1955) remains of value. On justices and law, see J.R. Lander, *English Justices of the Peace, 1461–1509* (Gloucester, 1989), and J.G. Bellamy, *Crime and Public Order in the Later Middle Ages* (London, 1973); Bellamy's 'Justice under the Yorkist Kings', *American Journal of Legal History*, vol. 9 (1965) remains valuable. On the household and the royal affinity, two useful articles by D.A.L. Morgan are 'The King's affinity in the polity of Yorkist England', *T.R.H.S.*, 5th series, vol. 23 (1973), and 'The House of Policy: the political role of the late Plantagenet Household', in D.R. Starkey (ed.) *The English Court from the Wars of the Roses to the Civil*

War (Harlow, 1987); R. Horrox, cited above, is also valuable. On propaganda and the presentation of Yorkist kingship articles of interest include A. Allan, 'Royal propaganda and the proclamations of Edward IV', *B.I.H.R.*, vol. 59 (1986), and R. Barber, 'Malory's *Le Morte Darthur* and Court culture under Edward IV', *Arthurian Literature*, vol. 12; C.A.J. Armstrong's study of 'The inauguration ceremonies of the Yorkist Kings and their title to the throne', *T.R.H.S.*, 4th series, vol. 30 (1948) retains its value.

Epilogue

The year 1485 marks no break in constitutional, social, economic, nor yet in religious history. In political history, however, it remains a useful dividing line. The government of the first Tudor was not, it is true, very different in its methods or its objects from that of the Yorkists. If, however, we look at things from the point of view not of the ruler but of the subject, then a change is apparent, and an important one. The political side of the human experience of an individual who lived through his adult life under Henry VII was different in quality from that of a man who reached maturity in 1450 or 1460. The humiliation of the English defeat in France, which up to 1460 and beyond was kept vivid by Yorkist propaganda and Yorkist continental ambitions, was for most of Henry VII's subjects only something in the memory of their fathers and grand-fathers. Henry VII's reign, moreover, saw only the last flickerings of the civil Wars of the Roses. In 1500 it could not be said, as it was in 1472, 'every man of this land that is of reasonable age hath known what trouble this realm hath suffered, and it is to be supposed that none hath escaped but at one time or another his part has been therein'.[1]

The collapse of the English cause in France and the civil strife of the 1450s and 1460s were experiences that left marked scars. Those which the civil wars left were visible in the sixteenth century, often literally, on the face of the land.

> The Lord Roos took King Henry VI's part against King Edward [John Leland wrote, as he listed the hands through which Belvoir castle in Leicestershire had passed], whereupon the Lord Roos's lands stood as confiscate . . . and Belvoir Castle was put in keeping to the Lord Hastings, the which coming thither upon a time to peruse the ground . . . was suddenly repelled by Mr Harington, a man of power thereabout and friend to the Lord Roos. Whereupon the Lord Hastings came thither upon another time with a strong power, and upon a raging will spoiled the castle, defacing the rooves and taking the lead off them. . . . Then fell all the castle to ruin, and the timber of the rooves uncovered rotted away, and the soil between the walls at last grew full of elders, and no habitation was there until of late days the Earl of Rutland hath made it fairer than ever it was.[2]

Wherever he went, the Tudor antiquary heard stories similar to this one, of the ways in which the wars had shaken the fortunes of families that had lived in this manor or that castle. Leland wrote in the 1530s; in some places memories of the troubled past were green for much longer, as at Nibley in Gloucestershire where, in the confusion of the year 1469, the last skirmish was fought in the feud between William Lord Berkeley and Thomas Lord Lisle. It must have been late in Elizabeth's reign that John Smyth here heard old country people

> relate the reports of their parents, kinsmen and neighbours present at this skirmish, some with the one lord and others with the other; and of such as carried victuals and weapons to some of those companies, as this lord's party lay hidden in the outskirts of Michaelwood Chase, out of which this Lord Berkeley broke when he first beheld Lord Lisle with his fellowship descending the hill from Nibley Church; and afterwards climbed up into the trees (being then boys of twelve and sixteen years) to see the battle.[3]

One important reason why the Tudor age was less disturbed than its predecessor by scenes such as this battle of Nibley Green was the accident of genetics which decided that the Tudors should never father any race of viceregal dukes of York or Gloucester, as the Plantagenets had done. But even more important was the fact that, by 1485, men were tired of the troubles and terrors of civil war, and disillusioned about the objectives which rebellious lords of the blood royal claimed to have in view in them. This is the extraordinary advice which, in the testament that he caused to be written within only a few weeks of the battle of Bosworth, John Lord Mountjoy gave to his sons: 'to live righteously, and never to take the state of baron upon them if they may lay it from them, nor to desire to be great about princes, for it is dangerous'.[4] John Blount had good reason to know how dangerous prominence could be. His father, the first baron, had risen with the rising fortunes of the house of York, but had been too close for comfort to Warwick in the 1460s. He himself had been allied by indenture with Lord Hastings, who lost his head at Richard III's command in 1483. His elder brother William had been killed at Barnet, fighting for the Yorkists. His stepmother, Anne, had lost her first husband, Humphrey Duke of Buckingham, at the battle of Northampton in 1460, and her eldest son at St Albans; both fell fighting for Lancaster. It is not much wonder, given experiences such as these, that the great families of the earlier Tudor period 'preferred almost anything to another civil war'.[5]

The loss of the English provinces in France left a mark that was at least as deep as that left by the civil wars. It is perhaps most clearly visible in the sense of England's isolation and her vulnerability to foreign invasion, which troubled Englishmen a good deal in the late fifteenth century, and after. 'Be it well considered', a speaker declared in parliament in 1473, 'how the next adversaries of this land, the Scots, be allied, and with whom, not only by an old league with the Frenchmen which be the greatest and ancient adversaries of this realm, but also now of late with the Danes; and what courage they have had to enter and trouble this land heretofore, the chronicles and histories be open.'[6] The day was drawing close, this speaker warned, when England, 'environed of mighty adversaries, destitute of old friends, should stand in greater doubt and peril than ever it did before'. Another fear expressed by this same speaker was that, if stern justice were meted out to all who disturbed the internal peace of the kingdom, there would be too few men left to defend it. A similar fear was among those uppermost in the minds of a growing host of critics of enclosure in the late fifteenth century. 'Where once the lord king had strong men for his warlike affairs, now instead of men nothing alive is found in some places but horses and mares and in other places sheep and oxen and cows.'[7] So wrote John Rous of Warwickshire. The sense of England's isolation, and of the necessity to provide for defence against outward enemies, was not just a feeling of Rous's generation, who lived through the times of trouble into the reign of Henry VII. It was a strong and lasting force in the sixteenth century.

The problem of the defence of the realm loomed large for another sector of opinion too at the end of the Middle Ages, for those who like Caxton and William of Worcester lamented the decline of chivalry among the well-born class. 'Now of late', Worcester complained, 'many who are descended of noble blood and are born to arms set themselves to singular practice . . . to learn the practise of law or custom of land . . . and waste greatly their time in such needless business as to hold courts and to keep and bear out a proud countenance at the holding of sessions and shires.'[8] How was it to be hoped that such men would uphold the martial reputation of England? Caxton was even more eloquently urgent.

> O ye knights of England [he cried in the epilogue to his *Book of the Order of Chivalry*], where is the custom and usage of chivalry that was used in those [past] days? What do ye now but go to the baths and play at dice? And some use not honest and good living against all order of knighthood. Leave this, leave it! And read the volumes of the Holy Grail, of Lancelot, of Galahad . . . of Gawain. . . . There shall you see manhood, courtesy and gentleness. And look in the latter days at the noble acts since the conquest; as in the days of King Richard Coeur de Lion; of Edward I and III, and of his noble sons; of Sir Robert Knowles, Sir John Hawkwood, Sir John Chandos. . . . Read Froissart! And also behold the victorious and noble King Henry V and the captains under him; his noble brethren, Montagu the Earl of Salisbury, and many others whose names shine gloriously by their virtuous and noble acts.[9]

Praise of a golden age in the past is a recurring theme in medieval literature, but there is more to this lament than romantic sentiment. Caxton made this clear when he rounded it off with an appeal to Richard III, king of England and France, to impose on the justices of the peace the duty of seeing that all knights in the kingdom had horse and harness in their possession 'so as to be always ready to serve their prince when he shall call them or have need'.

Caxton thought that something had been lost to English life that had been there in the days of the Black Prince and Chandos, and later too, in those of Henry V, and that the loss was real and dangerous. If we look back to what Philip de Mézières, the ex-councillor of Charles V of France, wrote, addressing the English just 100 years before Caxton's time, it begins to be plain that the latter was not in error.

> Listen, you who have sown such terrible shedding of man's blood [Philip wrote]. By your evil war, raised by pride and by lust for what is after all but a little land, the whole of Christendom has for fifty years been turned upside down . . . and, what is worse, what you have been empowered by God's permission to achieve for the chastisement of the sins of the Scots and French, you and your fathers have attributed solely to your own valour and chivalry, drunk as you are with pride and stirred up by stories of Lancelot and Gawain and their worldly valour.[10]

No French councillor would have dreamt of writing thus about the English in Caxton's time, and he and his like felt not only poorer in consequence, but less secure. Fear for the safety of the kingdom loomed uncomfortably behind the thought that, if a 'dire search' were now made as to how many knights there were in England that had the 'use and exercise of knighthood', there 'would be found many that lack'.[11]

Caxton's appeal for the revival of chivalry was one that went out too late. When he wrote the age of English territorial conquests in Europe was over, and so was the mood that had made them possible. A generation that had known only the humiliation of defeat in war overseas and the bitterness of internal strife was to be grateful to Henry Tudor for cultivating peace. There were deeper reasons, too, for lack of response to the chivalrous chauvinism that in Caxton and Worcester combined with fears for the safety of England. The 'bastard feudalism' of the late fifteenth century and of the Tudor age was fast losing touch with the martial ethos that had been its foundation in the days when indentures commonly recorded the retainer's duty to attend his lord, clothed in his livery, in the chivalrous mock-war of the tournament. Men were no longer looking to their aristocratic patrons for lordship in the old sense, for food in his hall, martial leadership, and justice in their quarrels with fellow retainers, but rather for patronage in a more modern sense, which would open avenues to advancement, and afford some kind of insurance amid the hazards of local and family feuding and litigation. That is why Worcester found himself complaining that men who knew the law were 'more esteemed among all estates than he who has spent thirty or forty years of his days in great jeopardy in your ancestor's conquests and wars'.[12] Though Worcester and his contemporaries could not see it, in a world in which esteem was thus bestowed, things could never be the same as they had once been. The future now lay not with noblemen for whom service in the king's wars was an ancestral duty, nor with the captains of men at arms, but more and more with the gentry. Worcester was paying a tribute to forces which already in his own day had gone far towards shifting the balance of political power in England and altering its nature out of recognition.

Notes

1 *Lit. Cant* (R.S.) vol. III, p. 275.
2 J. Leland, *Itinerary*, ed. L. Toulmin Smith, vol. I, pp. 97–8.
3 J. Smyth, *The Lives of the Berkeleys*, ed. Sir J. Maclean (Gloucester, 1883), vol. II, p. 114.
4 Quoted by K. B. McFarlane in 'The Wars of the Roses', *P.B.A.* 50 (1964), p. 119.
5 ibid.
6 *Lit. Cant.* (R.S.) vol. III, pp. 276–7.
7 J. Rous, *Historia Regum Anglie*, ed. T. Hearne, p. 121.
8 *The Boke of Noblesse*, ed. J. G. Nichols (Roxburghe Club, 1860), p. 77.
9 Caxton, *The Book of the Ordre of Chyvalry*, ed. A. T. P. Byles (E.E.T.S., 1926), pp. 122–3.
10 P. de Mézières, *Le Songe du Vieil Pélérin*, ed. G. W. Coopland (Cambridge, 1969), vol. I, pp. 396–7.
11 Caxton, *The Book of the Ordre of Chyvalry*, p. 124.
12 *The Boke of Noblesse*, pp. 77–8.

Bibliography

Since this book first appeared in 1973 there has been a spate of publications on later medieval England. The aim of the original bibliography was to provide, under subject headings, a series of lists of secondary works that might be useful as guides to the student looking for further reading. In revising it, I have kept to the original structure and aim, deleting some older titles, and adding in each section what seem to me the most important and formative of the works that have appeared since 1973. The original biography was eclectic, reflecting personal choice and the *lacunae* in my own reading: the same is true of the revised version, only more so. I hope that, its inevitable omissions notwithstanding, the revision will make the book more useful.

Two very substantial volumes of translated selections from original sources, *English Historical Documents*, vol. III, 1189–1327, ed. H. Rothwell (London, 1975), and vol. IV, ed. A.R. Myers (London, 1969), are invaluable companions to the student of the period covered in this book. The material is arranged in them thematically: the very ample selections from narrative sources are particularly helpful in following the political story. Other useful collections of primary materials that offer broad coverage include S. Chrimes and A.L. Brown (eds.), *Select Documents of English Constitutional History* (London, 1961); E.C. Lodge and G.A. Thornton, *English Constitutional Documents 1307–1485* (Cambridge, 1935): B. Wilkinson, *Constitutional History of England* (3 vols, London, 1948–58); and his *Constitutional History of England in the Fifteenth Century* (London, 1964). For all aspects of the fifteenth century, *The Paston Letters* are rewarding reading; there are two editions, from J. Gairdner (3 vols, London, 1872–5) and from N. Davis (2 vols, Oxford, 1971).

1. GENERAL SURVEYS

J.L. BOLTON, *The Medieval English Economy, 1100–1500* (London, 1980).

A.L. BROWN, *The Governance of late Medieval England, 1272–1461* (London, 1989).

F.R.H. DU BOULAY, *An Age of Ambition: English Society in the late Middle Ages* (London, 1970).

A. GRANSDEN, *Historical Writing in England*, vol. 2 [from 1307] (London, 1982).

G.A. HOLMES, *The Later Middle Ages 1272–1485* (Edinburgh, 1962).

E.F. JACOB, *The Fifteenth Century* (Oxford, 1961).

J.R. LANDER, *Government and Community: England 1450–1509* (London, 1980).

C.L. KINGSFORD, *Prejudice and Promise in Fifteenth Century England* (Oxford, 1925).

K.B. MCFARLANE, *The Nobility of later Medieval England* (Oxford, 1973). This volume publishes the Ford lectures of 1953, probably the most important lectures on late medieval England delivered in the twentieth century.

M. MCKISACK, *The Fourteenth Century* (Oxford, 1959).

A.R. MYERS, *A History of England in the Late Middle Ages* (Pelican History of England, 1952).

W.M. ORMROD, *Political Life in Medieval England, 1300–1450* (London, 1995).

A.L. POOLE (ed.), *Medieval England*, 2 vols (Oxford, 1958).

F.M. POWICKE, *The Thirteenth Century* (Oxford, 1953).

J.A.F. THOMSON, *The Transformation of Medieval England* (London, 1983).

Two older works deserve special mention because of their seminal nature:

W. STUBBS, *The Constitutional History of England*, vols II and III (Oxford, numerous editions).

T.F. TOUT, *Chapters in the Administrative History of Medieval England*, 6 vols (Manchester, 1920–33).

2. POLITICS AND POLITICAL BIOGRAPHY

The Hundred Years War and questions of Anglo-French relations are dealt with separately in section 3 below, and administrative and constitutional topics in section 4. Biographies of important ecclesiastical figures are mostly listed at the end of section 7.

(a) EDWARD I AND II (1290–1327)

G.W.S. BARROW, *Robert Bruce* (London, 1965).

P. CHAPLAIS, *Piers Gaveston, Edward II's Adoptive Brother* (Oxford, 1994).

J.C. DAVIES, *The Baronial Opposition to Edward II* (Cambridge, 1918).

N. FRYDE, *The Tyranny and fall of Edward II* (Cambridge, 1979).

J. HAMILTON, *Piers Gaveston, Earl of Cornwall, 1307–12* (Detroit, 1988).

J.R. MADDICOTT, *Thomas of Lancaster* (Oxford, 1970).

M. MCKISACK, *The Fourteenth Century* (Oxford, 1959).

C. MCNAMEE, *The Wars of the Bruces: Scotland, England and Ireland, 1306–28* (East Linton, 1997).

J.E. MORRIS, *The Welsh Wars of Edward I* (Oxford, 1901).

J.R.S. PHILLIPS, *Aymer de Valence, Earl of Pembroke 1307–1324* (Oxford, 1972).

M.C. PRESTWICH, *War, Politics and Finance under Edward I* (London, 1972).

—— *The Three Edwards* (London, 1980).

—— *Edward I* (London, 1988).

E.L.G. STONES and C. HAMPSON, *Edward I and the Throne of Scotland* (Oxford, 1978).

T.F. TOUT, *The Place of Edward II in English History* (Manchester, 1914).

M. VALE, *The Angevin Legacy* (Oxford, 1990).

F. WATSON, *Under the Hammer: Edward I and the throne of Scotland* (East Linton, 1998).

Articles

A.A.M. DUNCAN, *The Nation of the Scots and the Declaration of Arbroath* (Historical Association Pamphlet, 1970).

—— 'The war of the Scots', T.R.H.S. 6th series, vol. 2 (1992).

J.G. EDWARDS 'The baronial grievances of 1297', *E.H.R.* vol. 58 (1943).

E.B. FRYDE, 'The deposits of Hugh Despenser the Younger with Italian bankers', *Econ.H.R.* 2nd ser., vol. 3 (1951).

B.C. KEENEY, 'The medieval idea of the state: the great cause of 1291–2', *Univ. of Toronto Law Journal,* vol. 8 (1949).

W.M. ORMROD, 'State building and state finance in the reign of Edward I', W. Ormrod (ed.), *England in the Thirteenth Century* (Stamford, 1991).

M. PRESTWICH, 'The Ordinances of 1311 and the politics of the early four-teenth century', *Politics and Crisis in Fourteenth Century England,* ed. J. Taylor and W. Childs (Gloucester, 1990).

—— 'Royal patronage under Edward I', P.R. Coss and S.D. Lloyd (eds.), *England in the Thirteenth Century* (Stanford, 1986).

H. ROTHWELL, 'The confirmation of the charters and baronial grievances in 1297', *E.H.R.* vol. 60 (1945).

N. SAUL, 'The Despensers and the downfall of Edward II', *E.H.R.* vol. 99 (1984).

C. VALENTE, 'The deposition and abdication of Edward II', *E.H.R.* vol. 113 (1998).

S.L. WAUGH, 'For king, country and the patron: the Despensers and the local administration', *Journal of British Studies,* vol. 22 (1983).

B. WILKINSON, 'The ordinances of 1311', *Studies in the Constitutional History of the 13th and 14th Centuries* (Manchester, 1937).

B. WILKINSON, 'The negotiations preceding the Treaty of Leake', *Studies in Medieval History Presented to F.M. Powicke* (Oxford, 1948).
—— 'The Sherburn indenture and the attack on the Despensers', *E.H.R.* vol. 63 (1948).

(b) EDWARD III

R. BARBER, *Edward, Prince of Wales and Aquitaine* (London, 1978).
J. BOTHWELL (ed.), *The Age of Edward III* (York, 2001).
K. FOWLER, *The King's Lieutenant: Henry of Grosmont* (London, 1969).
G.A. HOLMES, *The Good Parliament* (Oxford, 1975).
W.M. ORMROD, *The Reign of Edward III* (London, 1990).
R. NICHOLSON, *Edward III and the Scots* (Oxford, 1965).
M.C. PRESTWICH, *The Three Edwards* (London, 1980).
J. VALE, *Edward III and Chivalry* (Woodbridge, 1982).
M. VALE, *The Angevin Legacy and the Hundred Years War, 1250–1340* (Oxford, 1990).
S.L. WAUGH, *England in the Reign of Edward III* (Cambridge, 1991).

Articles
A. AYTON, 'Edward III and the English aristocracy at the beginning of the Hundred Years War', M. Strickland (ed.), *Armies Chivalry and Warfare in Medieval Britain and France* (Stamford, 1998).
J. BOTHWELL, The English peerage and the 1337 Earls: estate redistribution in fourteenth century England', J. Bothwell (ed.), *The Age of Edward III* (York, 2001).
E.B. FRYDE, Edward III's wool monopoly: a fourteenth century trading venture, *History*, vol. 37 (1952).
—— 'Parliament and the French War, 1336–40', *Essays in Medieval History presented to B. Wilkinson* ed. T. Sandquist and M. Powicke (Toronto, 1969).
G.L. HARRISS, 'The Commons petitions of 1340', *E.H.R.* vol. 78 (1963).
G. LAPSLEY, 'Archbishop Stratford and the Parliamentary crisis of 1341', *E.H.R.* vol. 30 (1915).
W. ORMROD, 'Edward III and the recovery of royal authority in England, 1340–60', *History*, vol. 72 (1987).
—— 'Edward III and his family' *Journal of British Studies*, vol. 26 (1987).
—— 'Agenda for Legislation, 1322–40', *E.H.R.* vol. 105 (1990).
—— 'The domestic response to the Hundred Years War', A Curry and M. Hughes (eds.), *Arms, Armies and Fortifications in the Hundred Years War* (Woodbridge, 1994).
C. SHENTON, 'Edward III and the coup of 1330', J. Bothwell (ed.), *The Age of Edward III* (York, 2001).

C. TAYLOR, 'Edward III and the Plantagenet claim to the French throne', J. Bothwell (ed.), *The Age of Edward III* (York, 2001).

A. VERDUYN, 'The politics of law and order in the early years of Edward III', *E.H.R.* vol. 108 (1993).

(c) RICHARD II (1377–1399)

R. BIRD, *The Turbulent London of Richard II* (London, 1949).

E. CURTIS, *Richard II in Ireland* (Oxford, 1927).

F.R.H. DU BOULAY and C.M. BARRON (eds.), *The Reign of Richard II: Essays in Honour of May McKisack* (London, 1971).

J.L. GILLESPIE (ed.), *The Age of Richard II* (Stroud, 1998).

C. GIVEN-WILSON, *The Royal Household and the King's Affinity, 1360–1413* (London and New Haven, 1986).

A. GOODMAN, *The Loyal Conspiracy* (London, 1972).

D. GORDON, L. MONNA and C. ELAM (eds.), *The Royal Image of Richard II and the Wilton Diptych* (London, 1998).

J.S. ROSKELL, *The Impeachment of Michael de la Pole* (Manchester, 1984).

N. SAUL, *Richard II* (London and New Haven, 1997).

A. TUCK, *Richard II and the English Nobility* (London, 1973).

S.K. WALKER, *The Lancastrian Affinity, 1361–99* (Oxford, 1990).

Articles

M.E. ASTON, 'The impeachment of Bishop Despenser', *B.I.H.R.* vol. 38 (1965).

C. BARRON, 'The tyranny of Richard II', *B.I.H.R.* vol. 41 (1968).

—— 'The deposition of Richard II', *Politics and Crisis in Fourteenth Century England* ed. J. Taylor and W. Childs (Gloucester, 1990).

S.B. CHRIMES, 'Richard II's questions to the judges', *L.Q.R.* vol. 72 (1956).

J.G. EDWARDS, 'The parliamentary committee of 1398', *E.H.R.* vol. 40 (1925).

J.L. GILLESPIE, 'Richard II's knights: chivalry and patronage, *Journal of Medieval History* vol. 13 (1987).

—— 'Richard II's archers of the crown', *Journal of British Studies*, vol. 18 (1979).

C. GIVEN-WILSON, 'Richard II, Edward II, and the Lancastrian inheritance', *E.H.R.* vol. 109 (1994).

J. LYDON, 'Richard II's expeditions to Ireland', *Journal of the Royal Society of Antiquaries of Ireland*, vol. 93 (1963).

J.J.N. PALMER, 'The impeachment of Michael de le Pole in 1386', *B.I.H.R.* vol. 42 (1969).

C.J. PHILPOTTS, 'John of Gaunt and English policy towards France, 1389–95', *Journal of Medieval History*, vol. 16 (1990).

C.D. ROSS, 'Forfeiture for treason in the reign of Richard II', *E.H.R.* vol. 71 (1956).

N. SAUL, 'Richard II and the vocabulary of kingship', *E.H.R.* vol. 110 (1995).

G.O. SAYLES, 'Richard II in 1381 and 1399', *E.H.R.* vol. 94 (1979).

J.W. SHERBORNE, 'Perjury and the Lancastrian revolution of 1399', J. Sherborne, *War, Culture, and Politics in Fourteenth Century England*, ed. A. Tuck (London, 1994).

A. TUCK, 'The Cambridge parliament of 1388', *E.H.R.* vol. 84 (1969).

—— 'Anglo-Irish relations, 1382–93', *Proceedings of the Royal Irish Academy*, vol. 69 (1970).

S.K. WALKER, 'Richard II's views on kingship', R. Archer and S. Walker (eds.), *Rulers and Ruled in Medieval England* (London, 1995).

(d) THE LANCASTRIAN KINGS (1399–c.1450)

C.T. ALLMAND, *Henry V* (London, 1992).

A. CURRY, *The Battle of Agincourt: sources and interpretations* (Woodbridge, 2000).

R.R. DAVIES, *The Revolt of Owain Glyn Dwr* (Oxford, 1995).

R.A. GRIFFITHS, *The Reign of King Henry VI* (London, 1981).

G.L. HARRISS (ed.), *Henry V: the practice of Kingship* (Oxford, 1985).

—— *Cardinal Beaufort* (Oxford, 1988).

E.F. JACOB, *Henry V and the Invasion of France* (London, 1947).

C.L. KINGSFORD, *Henry V* (2nd ed. London, 1923).

J.L. KIRBY, *Henry IV of England* (London, 1970).

K.B. MCFARLANE, *Lancastrian Kings and Lollard Knights* (Oxford, 1972).

E. POWELL, *Kingship, Law and Society in the reign of Henry V* (Oxford, 1989).

T.B. PUGH, *Henry V and the Southampton Plot, 1415* (Gloucester, 1996).

S. SAYGIN, *Duke Humphrey of Gloucester and the Italian Humanists* (London, 1997).

P. STROHM, *England's Empty Throne: Usurpation and its Aftermath* (Yale, 1998).

K.H. VICKERS, *Humphrey of Gloucester* (London, 1907).

B.P. WOLFFE, *Henry VI* (London, 1981).

Articles

J.M.W. BEAN, 'Henry IV and the Percies', *History*, vol. 44 (1959).

A.L. BROWN, 'The commons and the council in the reign of Henry IV', *E.H.R.* vol. 79 (1964).

D. CROOK, 'Central England and the revolt of the Earls, 1400', *Historical Research*, vol. 64 (1991).

R.A. GRIFFITHS, 'The trial of Eleanor Cobham: an episode in the fall of Humphrey Duke of Gloucester', *B.J.R.L.* vol. 51 (1969).

G.L. HARRISS, 'Cardinal Beaufort: patriot or usurer?', *T.R.H.S.* 5th ser., vol. 20 (1970).

—— 'Marmaduke Lumley and the Exchequer crisis of 1446–9', J.G. Rowe (ed.), *Aspects of late Medieval Government and Society* (Toronto, 1986).

C.L. KINGSFORD, 'The policy and fall of Suffolk', *Prejudice and Promise in the Fifteenth Century England* (Oxford, 1925).

K.B. MCFARLANE, 'England: the Lancastrian Kings', *Cambridge Medieval History* vol. VIII, chap. XI.

—— 'Henry V, Bishop Beaufort and the Red Hat', *E.H.R.* vol. 60 (1945).

—— 'At the deathbed of Cardinal Beaufort', *Studies in Medieval History Presented to F.M. Powicke* (Oxford, 1948).

P. MCNIVEN, 'Prince Henry and the English political crisis of 1412', *History,* vol. 65 (1980).

—— 'The problem of Henry IV's health, 1405–13', *E.H.R.* vol. 100 (1985).

—— 'Rebellion, sedition, and the legend of Richard II's survival in the reigns of Henry IV and Henry V', *B.J.R.L.* vol. 76 (1994).

P. MORGAN, 'Henry IV and the shadow of Richard II', R. Archer (ed.), *Crown, Government and People* (Stroud, 1995).

A. POLLARD, 'The Lancastrian constitutional experiment revisited: Sir John Tiptoft and the parliament of 1406', *Parliamentary History,* vol. 14 (1995).

T.B. PUGH, 'Richard Plantagenet (1411–60), Duke of York, as the King's Lieutenant in France and Ireland', *Aspects of Late Medieval Government and Society* ed. J.G. Rowe (Toronto, 1986).

A. ROGERS, 'The political crisis of 1401', *Nottingham Medieval Studies,* vol. 12 (1968).

—— 'Henry IV, the commons and taxation', *Medieval Studies,* vol. 31 (1969).

J.S. ROSKELL, 'The office and dignity of Protector of England, with special reference to its origins', *E.H.R.* vol. 68 (1953).

P. and F. STRONG, 'The last will and codicils of Henry V', *E.H.R.* vol. 96 (1981).

A. TUCK, 'Henry IV and Europe: a dynasty's search for recognition', R. Britnell and A. Pollard (eds.), *The McFarlane Legacy* (Stroud, 1995).

R. VIRGOE, 'The death of William de la Pole', *B.J.R.L.* vol. 47 (1964–5).

—— 'The composition of the king's council 1437–61', *B.I.H.R.* vol. 43 (1970).

J. WATTS, 'The Counsels of King Henry VI, c. 1435–1445', *E.H.R.* vol. 106 (1991).

—— 'When did Henry VI's minority end?', D.J. Clayton, R.G. Davies and P. McNiven (eds.), *Trade, Devotion and Government: papers in Later Medieval History* (Stroud, 1994).

B.P. WOLFFE, 'The personal rule of Henry VI', S.B. Chrimes, C.D. Ross and R.A. Griffiths (eds.), *Fifteenth Century England, 1399–1509* (Manchester, 1972).

(e) THE WARS OF THE ROSES (c. 1450–c. 1461)

C. CARPENTER, *The Wars of the Roses: Politics and the Constitution, c. 1437–1509* (Cambridge, 1997).

J. GILLINGHAM, *The Wars of the Roses* (London, 1981).

A. GOODMAN, *The Wars of the Roses: military activity and English Society, 1452–97* (London, 1981).

A. GROSS, *The dissolution of the Lancastrian Kingship* (Stamford, 1996).

I.M.W. HARVEY, *Jack Cade's Rebellion of 1450* (Oxford, 1991).

P.A. JOHNSON, *Duke Richard of York* (Oxford, 1988).

A.J. POLLARD, *North Eastern England during the Wars of the Roses* (Oxford, 1990).

—— (ed.), *The Wars of the Roses* (London, 1995).

C.D. ROSS, *The Wars of the Roses* (London, 1976).

R.L. STOREY, *The End of the House of Lancaster* (London, 1966).

J. WATTS, *Henry VI and the Practice of Kingship* (Cambridge, 1996).

Articles

C.A.J. ARMSTRONG, 'Politics and the battle of St Albans', *B.I.H.R.* vol. 33 (1960).

J.M.W. BEAN, 'The financial position of Richard Duke of York', J.C. Holt and J. Gillingham (eds.), *War and Government in the Middle Ages* (Woodbridge, 1984).

N. CHERRY, 'The struggle for power in mid-fifteenth century Devonshire', *Patronage, the Crown and the Provinces*, ed. R.A. Griffiths (Gloucester, 1981).

D. DUNN, 'The Queen at war: the role of Margaret of Anjou in the Wars of the Roses', D. Dunn (ed.), *War and Society in Medieval and Early Modern Britain* (Liverpool, 2000).

J.P. GILSON, 'A defence of the proscription of the Yorkists in 1459', *E.H.R.* vol. 26 (1911).

R.A. GRIFFITHS, 'Local rivalries and national politics – the Percies, the Nevilles and the Duke of Exeter', *Speculum* vol. 43 (1968).

—— 'Duke Richard of York's intentions in 1450 and the origins of the Wars of the Roses', *Journal of Medieval History*, vol. 1 (1975).

—— 'The King's Council and the First Protectorate of the Duke of York', *E.H.R.* vol. 99 (1984).

G.L. HARRISS, 'The struggle for Calais: an aspect of the rivalry between Lancaster and York', *E.H.R.* vol. 75 (1960).

M.K. JONES, 'Somerset, York and the Wars of the Roses', *E.H.R.* vol. 104 (1989).

—— 'Edward IV, the Earl of Warwick and the Yorkist claim to the throne', *Historical Research*, vol. 70 (1997).

M. KEKEWICH, 'The attainder of the Yorkists in 1459: two contemporary accounts', *B.I.H.R.* vol. 55 (1982).

J.R. LANDER, 'Henry VI and the Duke of York's second protectorate, *B.J.R.L.* vol. 43 (1960–1).

K.B. MCFARLANE, 'The Wars of the Roses', *P.B.A.* vol. 50 (1964).

S. PAYLING, 'The Ampthill dispute: a study in aristocratic lawlessness and the breakdown of Lancastrian government', *E.H.R.* vol. 104 (1989).

T.B. PUGH, 'Richard Duke of York and the rebellion of Henry Holland Duke of Exeter in May 1454', *Historical Research*, vol. 63 (1990).

(f) THE YORKISTS (1461–1485)

C.A.J. ARMSTRONG, *The Usurpation of Richard III* (Oxford, 1969).

J. CALMETTE and G. PERINELLE, *Louis XI et l'Angleterre 1461–83* (Paris, 1930).

C. CARPENTER, *The Wars of the Roses: Politics and the Constitution in England* (Cambridge, 1997).

W.H. DUNHAM, *Lord Hastings's Indentured Retainers* (New Haven, Conn., 1955).

L. GILL, *Richard III and Buckingham's Rebellion* (Stroud, 1999).

A. GOODMAN, *The New Monarchy: England 1471–1534* (Oxford, 1988).

P.W. HAMMOND (ed.), *Richard III: Loyalty, Lordship and Law* (London, 1986).

M.A. HICKS, *False, Fleeting, Perjur'd Clarence: George, Duke of Clarence, 1449–78* (Gloucester, 1980).

—— *Warwick the Kingmaker* (Oxford, 1988).

R. HORROX, *Richard III: a study of service* (Cambridge, 1989).

J. HUGHES, *The Religious Life of Richard III: Piety and Prayer in the North of England* (Stroud, 1997).

J.R. LANDER, *Conflict and stability in Fifteenth Century England* (London, 1974).

—— *Crown and Nobility, 1450–1509* (London, 1976).

—— *English Justices of the Peace, 1461–1509* (Gloucester, 1989).

A.R. MYERS, *The Household of Edward IV* (Manchester, 1959).

A. POLLARD, *North Eastern England during the Wars of the Roses* (Oxford, 1990).

C. ROSS, *Edward IV* (London, 1974).

—— *Richard III* (London, 1981).

C.L. SCOFIELD, *The Life and Reign of Edward IV*, 2 vols (London, 1923).

B.P. WOLFFE, *The Crown Lands: an aspect of Yorkist and early Tudor Government* (London, 1970).

Articles

A. ALLAN, 'Royal propaganda and the proclamations of Edward IV', *B.I.H.R.* vol. 59 (1986).

C.A.J. ARMSTRONG, 'The inauguration ceremonies of the Yorkist kings and their title to the throne', *T.R.H.S.* 4th series, vol. 30 (1948).

J.G. BELLAMY, 'Justice under the Yorkist kings', *American Journal of Legal History,* vol. 9 (1965).

C. CARPENTER, 'The Duke of Clarence and the Midlands: a study in the interplay of local and national politics', *Midland History,* vol. 11 (1986).

M. HICKS, 'The changing role of the Wydevilles in Yorkist politics to 1483', *Patronage, Pedigree and Power in Later Medieval England,* ed. C. Ross (Gloucester, 1979).

—— 'The 1468 Statute of Livery', *Historical Research,* vol. 64 (1991).

J.R. LANDER, 'Edward IV: the modern legend: and a revision', *History,* vol. 41 (1956).

—— 'The Yorkist council and administration, *E.H.R.* vol. 73 (1958).

—— 'Council, administration and councillors 1461–85', *B.I.H.R.* vol. 32 (1959).

—— 'Attainder and forfeiture: 1453–1509', *Historical Journal,* vol. 4 (1961).

—— 'Marriage and politics in the fifteenth century: the Nevilles and the Wydevilles', *B.I.H.R.* vol. 36 (1963).

D.E. LOWE, 'Edward IV, the Wydevilles and the Council of the Prince of Wales', *Bulletin of the Board of Celtic Studies,* vol. 29 (1982).

D.A.L. MORGAN, 'The King's affinity in the polity of Yorkist England', *T.R.H.S.* 5th ser., vol. 23 (1973).

—— 'The House of Policy: the political role of the late Plantagenet Household', D.R. Starkey (ed.), *The English Court from the Wars of the Roses to the Civil War* (Harlow, 1987).

J.A.F. THOMSON, 'Richard III and Lord Hastings: a problematical case reviewed', *B.I.H.R.* vol. 48 (1975).

R. VIRGOE, 'The Benevolence of 1481', *E.H.R.* vol. 104 (1989).

B.P. WOLFFE, 'The management of English royal estates under the Yorkist kings', *E.H.R.* vol. 71 (1956).

C.T. WOOD, 'Richard III, Lord Hastings and Friday the 13th', R. Griffiths and J. Sherborne (eds.), *Kings and Nobles in the Later Middle Ages* (Gloucester, 1986).

3. ENGLAND, FRANCE AND THE HUNDRED YEARS WAR

(a) GENERAL SURVEYS

C.T. ALLMAND, *The Hundred Years War: England and France, c. 1300– c. 1450* (Cambridge, 1988).

P. CONTAMINE, *La Guerre de Cent Ans* (Paris, 1968).

A. CURRY, *The Hundred Years War* (London, 1993).

A. CURRY and M. HUGHES (eds.), *Arms, Armies and Fortification in the Hundred Years War* (Woodbridge, 1994).

K. FOWLER (ed.), *The Hundred Years War* (London, 1971).

R.W. KAEUPER, *War, Justice and Public Order: England and France in the Late Middle Ages* (Oxford, 1998).

M.C. PRESTWICH, *Armies and Warfare in the Middle Ages: the English Experience* (London and New Haven, 1996).

J. SHERBORNE, *War, Politics and Culture in Fourteenth Century England* (London, 1994).

J. SUMPTION, *The Hundred Years War: trial by battle* I (London, 1990).

—— *the Hundred Years War: trial by fire*, II (London, 1999).

M. VALE, *War and Chivalry* (London, 1981).

(b) THE WARS OF EDWARD I AND II, THE BEGINNING OF THE HUNDRED YEARS WAR

For literature on the Anglo-Scottish wars, see sections 2(a) and 8(a).

G.P. CUTTINO, *English Diplomatic Administration 1259–1339* (Oxford, 1940).

M. VALE, *The Angevin Legacy and the Hundred Years War* (Oxford, 1990).

Articles

J. CAMPBELL, 'England, Scotland and the Hundred Years War', *Europe in the Late Middle Ages*, ed. B. Smalley, J. Hale and J.R.L. Highfield (London, 1965).

P. CHAPLAIS, 'English arguments concerning the feudal status of Aquitaine', *B.I.H.R.* vol. 21 (1948).

—— 'Le Traité de Paris de 1259 et l'inféodation de la Gascogne allodiale', *Moyen Age*, vol. 61 (1955).

H.S. OFFLER, 'England and Germany at the beginning of the Hundred Years War', *E.H.R.* vol. 54 (1939).

W.M. ORMROD, 'England, Normandy and the beginnings of the Hundred Years War', *England and Normandy in the Middle Ages*, ed. D. Bates and A. Curry (London, 1994).

C. TAYLOR, 'Edward III and the Plantagenet claim to the French throne', J. Bothwell (ed.), *The Age of Edward III* (York, 2001).

M. VALE, 'The Anglo-French Wars, 1294–1340: allies and alliances', P. Contamine *et al* (eds.), *Guerre et Société en France, en Angleterre et en Bourgogne, xive-xve Siècle* (Lille, 1991).

(c) THE HUNDRED YEARS WAR, FOURTEENTH CENTURY

A. AYTON, *Knights and Warhorses: Military Service and the English Aristocracy under Edward III* (Woodbridge, 1994).

R. BARBER, *Edward, Prince of Wales and Aquitaine* (Woodbridge, 1978).

J. BRADBURY, *The Medieval Archer* (Woodbridge, 1985).

K.R. DE VRIES, *Infantry Warfare in the Early Fourteenth Century* (Woodbridge, 1996).

K. FOWLER, *The King's Lieutenant: Henry of Grosmont* (London, 1969).

—— *Medieval Mercenaries, I, The Great Companies* (Oxford, 2001).

H.J. HEWITT, *The Black Prince's Expedition of 1355–7* (Manchester, 1958).

—— *The Organisation of War under Edward III* (Manchester, 1966).

J.J.N. PALMER, *England, France and Christendom* (London, 1972).

C. ROGERS, *War Cruel and Sharp: English Strategy under Edward III* (Woodbridge, 2000).

P.E. RUSSELL, *The English Intervention in Spain and Portugal* (Oxford, 1955).

J. VALE, *Edward III and Chivalry* (Woodbridge, 1982).

Articles

A. AYTON, 'English armies in the fourteenth century', in *Arms, Armies and Fortifications in The Hundred Years War*, ed. A. Curry and M. Hughes (Gloucester, 1994).

C.C. BAYLEY, 'The campaign of 1375 and the Good Parliament', *E.H.R.* vol. 55 (1940).

E.B. FRYDE, 'Parliament and the French war 1336–40', *Essays in Medieval History Presented to B. Wilkinson* (Toronto, 1969).

J. LE PATOUREL, 'Edward III and the kingdom of France', *History* vol. 43 (1958).

—— 'The Treaty of Brétigny', *T.R.H.S.* 5th ser., vol. 10 (1960).

J.J.N. PALMER, 'The Anglo-French peace negotiations 1390–96', *T.R.H.S.* 5th ser., vol. 16 (1966).

—— 'The war aims of the protagonists and the negotiations for peace', K. Fowler (ed.), *The Hundred Years War* (London, 1971).

E. PERROY, 'The Anglo-French negotiations at Bruges', *Camden Miscellany*, vol. 19 (1952).

C.J. ROGERS, 'Edward III and the dialectics of strategy', *T.R.H.S.* 6th ser., vol. 4 (1994).

—— 'The efficacy of the English longbow: a reply to Kelly De Vries', *War in History*, vol. 5 (1998).

J.W. SHERBORNE, 'English expeditions to France 1369–80', *E.H.R.* vol. 79 (1964).

A. TUCK, 'Richard II and the Hundred Years War', *Politics and Crisis in Fourteenth Century England*, ed. J. Taylor and W. Childs (Gloucester, 1990).

(d) THE FIFTEENTH CENTURY

C.T. ALLMAND, *Lancastrian Normandy, 1415–1450* (Oxford, 1983).

P. BONENFANT, *Du Meutre de Montereau au Traité de Troyes* (Brussels, 1958).

A. BUCHAN, *Joan of Arc and the Recovery of France* (London, 1948).

A. CURRY, *The Battle of Agincourt: Sources and interpretations* (Woodbridge, 2000).

J.C. DICKINSON, *The Congress of Arras* (Oxford, 1955).

J.K. FERGUSON, *English Diplomacy, 1422–61* (Oxford, 1972).

E.F. JACOB, *Henry V and the Invasion of France* (London, 1947).

R.A. NEWHALL, *The Conquest of Normandy* (Yale, 1924).

R. PERNOUD, *Joan of Arc* (English trans., London, 1964).

A.J. POLLARD, *John Talbot and the War in France* (London, 1983).

M.G.A. VALE, *English Gascony 1399–1453* (Oxford, 1970).

R. VAUGHAN, *John the Fearless* (London, 1966).

—— *Philip the Good* (London, 1970).

Articles

C.T. ALLMAND, 'The Anglo-French negotiations 1439', *B.I.H.R.* vol. 40 (1967).

—— 'The Lancastrian land settlement in Normandy, 1417–1450' *Econ.H.R.* 2nd ser., vol. 21 (1968).

A. CURRY, 'The first English standing armies? Military organisation in Lancastrian Normandy, 1420–1450', *Patronage, Pedigree and Power in Later Medieval England*, ed. C. Ross (Gloucester, 1979).

M. DANIEL and M. KEEN, 'English diplomacy and the sack of Fougères in 1449', *History*, vol. 59 (1974).

M.K. JONES, 'John Beaufort Duke of Somerset and the French expedition of 1443', R. Griffiths (ed.), *Patronage, the Crown and the Provinces in Later Medieval England* (Gloucester, 1981).

—— 'Somerset, York and the Wars of the Roses', *E.H.R.* vol. 104 (1989).

—— 'Immunity from war and the lands of a captive knight: the siege of Orleans revisited', M.J. Arn (ed.), *Charles of Orleans in England* (Woodbridge, 2000).

—— 'The battle of Verneuil, 1424: towards a history of courage', *War in History*, vol. 9 (2002).

M.R. POWICKE, 'Lancastrian captains', *Essays in Medieval History Presented to B. Wilkinson*, ed. A. Sandquist and M. Powicke (Toronto, 1969).

C.F. RICHMOND, 'The keeping of the seas during the Hundred Years War 1422–40', *History*, vol. 49 (1964).

M. WARNER, 'The Anglo-French dual monarchy and the house of Burgundy, 1420–35', *French History*, vol. 11 (1997).

(e) THE ORGANIZATION OF WAR AND THE SOCIAL CONSEQUENCES

A. AYTON, *Knights and Warhorses: military service and the English aristocracy under Edward* III (Woodbridge, 1994).

J. BARNIE, *War in Medieval Society: social values and the Hundred Years War* (London, 1974).

H.J. HEWITT, *The Organisation of War under Edward III* (Manchester, 1966).

M.H. KEEN, *The Laws of War in the Late Middle Ages* (London, 1965).

P. MORGAN, *War and Society in Medieval Cheshire, 1277–1403* (Chetham Society, 1987).

M.R. POWICKE, *Military Obligation in Medieval England* (Oxford, 1962).

M.C. PRESTWICH, *Armies and Warfare in the Middle Ages: the English Experience* (London, 1996).

Articles

C.T. ALLMAND, see important articles listed in section (d) above.

E.B. FRYDE, 'Edward III's wool monopoly of 1337', *History,* vol. 37 (1952).

D. HAY, 'The division of the spoils of war in fourteenth century England', *T.R.H.S.* 5th ser., vol. 4 (1954).

G.A. HOLMES, 'The libel of English policy', *E.H.R.* vol. 76 (1961).

N.B. LEWIS, 'The recruitment and organisation of a contract army, 1337', *B.I.H.R.* vol. 37 (1964).

K.B. MCFARLANE, 'The investment of Sir John Fastolf's profits of war', *T.R.H.S.* 5th ser., vol. 7 (1957).

—— 'War, the economy and social change', *Past and Present,* No. 22 (1962).

—— 'A business partnership in war and administration, 1421–45', *E.H.R.* vol. 78 (1963).

J.W. MCKENNA, 'Henry VI of England and the dual monarchy: aspects of royal political propaganda 1422–1432', *Journal of the Courtauld and Warburg Institutes,* vol. 28 (1965).

M.M. POSTAN, 'Some social consequences of the Hundred Years War', *Econ.H.R.* 1st ser., vol. 12 (1942).

—— 'The costs of the Hundred Years War', *Past and Present,* No. 27 (1964).

A.E. PRINCE, 'The indenture system under Edward III', *Historical Essays in Honour of James Tait* (Manchester, 1933).

—— 'The payment of army wages in Edward III's reign', *Speculum,* vol. 19 (1944).

J.W. SHERBORNE, 'Indentured retinues and English expeditions to France 1369–80', *E.H.R.* vol. 79 (1964).

4. THE GOVERNMENT OF ENGLAND AND HER CONSTITUTION

Two important books offering general coverage under this heading are:

A.L. BROWN, *The Governance of Medieval England, 1272–1461* (London, 1989).

C. CARPENTER, *The Wars of the Roses: Politics and the Constitution in England c. 1437–1509* (Cambridge, 1997).

Works on military administration and organization are mostly listed in section 3(d) above. On topics where church and state interests overlap, see section 7 below.

(a) THE KING, CROWN AND THE CORONATION, ETC.

S.B. CHRIMES, *English Constitutional Ideas in the Fifteenth Century* (Cambridge, 1936).

C. GIVEN-WILSON, *The Royal Household and the King's Affinity, 1360–1413* (London, 1986).

A.R. MYERS, *The Household of Edward IV* (Manchester, 1959).

V.J. SCATTERGOOD and J. SHERBORNE (eds.), *English Court Culture in the late Middle Ages* (London, 1983).

P.E. SCHRAMM, *A History of the English Coronation* (Oxford, 1937).

Articles

C.A.J. ARMSTRONG, 'The inauguration ceremonies of the Yorkist kings and their title to the throne', *T.R.H.S.* 4th ser., vol. 30 (1948).

S.B. CHRIMES, 'Richard II's questions to the judges', *L.Q.R.* vol. 72 (1956).

R.S. HOYT, 'The coronation oath of 1308', *E.H.R.* vol. 71 (1956).

J.W. MCKENNA, 'The coronation oath of the Yorkist kings', *E.H.R.* vol. 82 (1967).

H.G. RICHARDSON, 'The English coronation oath', *T.R.H.S.* 4th ser., vol. 23 (1941).

—— 'The English coronation oath', *Speculum,* vol. 24 (1949).

N. SAUL, 'Richard II and the vocabulary of kingship', *E.H.R.* vol. 110 (1995).

C. VALENTE, 'The deposition and abdication of Edward II', *E.H.R.* vol. 113 (1998).

S.K. WALKER, 'Richard II's views on kingship', R. Archer and S. Walker (eds.), *Rulers and Ruled in Medieval England* (London, 1995).

B. WILKINSON, 'The coronation oath of Edward II', *Historical Essays in Honour of James Tait* (Manchester, 1933).

—— 'The coronation oath of Edward II and the Statute of York', *Speculum,* vol. 19 (1944).

—— 'Notes on the coronation records of the fourteenth century, *E.H.R.* vol. 19 (1955).

(b) ADMINISTRATION, LAW AND JUSTICE

Works on such topics as the Statute of York, impeachment and trials in parliament are listed in section (c) below.

J.M.W. BEAN, *The Decline of English Feudalism* (Manchester, 1968).

J.G. BELLAMY, *The Law of Treason in England in the Later Middle Ages* (Cambridge, 1970).

—— *Crime and Public Order in England in the Later Middle Ages* (London, 1973).

—— *Criminal Law and Society in late medieval and Tudor England* (Gloucester, 1984).

P. BRAND, *The Origins of the English Legal Profession* (Oxford, 1992).

—— *The Making of the Common Law* (London, 1992).

S.B. CHRIMES, *English Constitutional Ideas in the Fifteenth Century* (Cambridge, 1936).

A. HARDING, *The Law Courts of Medieval England* (London, 1973).

M. HASTINGS, *The Court of Common Pleas in Fifteenth Century England* (New York, 1947).

W.S. HOLDSWORTH, *History of English Law*, vols 1–3 (London, 1923).

H.M. JEWELL, *Local administration in the Middle Ages* (Newton Abbot, 1972).

J.R. LANDER, *English Justices of the Peace, 1461–1509* (Gloucester, 1989).

A. MUSSON and W. ORMROD, *The Evolution of English Justice: Law, Politics and Society in the Fourteenth Century* (London, 1998).

R.C. PALMER, *English Law in the Age of the Black Death: a transformation of Governance and Law* (Chapel Hill, 1993).

E. POWELL, *Kingship, Law and Society in the reign of Henry V* (Oxford, 1989).

B.H. PUTNAM, *The Enforcement of the Statute of Labourers* (Columbia, 1908).

T.F. TOUT, *Chapters in the Administrative History of Medieval England*, 6 vols (Manchester, 1920–33).

B. WILKINSON, *The Chancery under Edward III* (Manchester, 1929).

—— *The Constitutional History of Medieval England*, 3 vols (London, 1948–58).

Articles

J.G. BELLAMY, 'Justice under the Yorkist kings', *American Journal of Legal History,* vol. 9 (1965).

S.B. CHRIMES, 'Richard II's questions to the judges', *L.Q.R.* vol. 72 (1956).

W.E. IVES, 'The Common Lawyer', *Profession, Vocation and Culture in late Medieval England*, ed. C.H. Clough (Liverpool, 1982).

J.R. MADDICOTT, *Law and Lordship* (*Past and Present*, Supplement No. 4, 1978).

—— 'The County Community and the making of public opinion in fourteenth century England', *T.R.H.S.* 5th ser., vol. 28 (1978).

W. ORMROD, 'Agenda for legislation, 1322–40', *E.H.R.* vol. 105 (1990).

E. POWELL, 'Arbitration and the law in England in the late Middle Ages', *T.R.H.S.* 5th ser., vol. 33 (1983).

N. RAMSAY, 'Retained legal Counsel', *T.R.H.S.* 5th ser., vol. 35 (1985).

C. RAWCLIFFE, 'The great Lord as peacekeeper: arbitration by English noblemen and their councils', J.A. Guy and H.G. Beale (eds.), *Law and Social Change in British History* (Royal Historical Society, 1984).

I.D. ROWNEY, 'Arbitration in gentry disputes of the late middle ages', *History*, vol. 67 (1982).

R.L. STOREY, 'The wardens of the marches of England towards Scotland', *E.H.R.* vol. 72 (1957).

(c) PARLIAMENT AND THE COUNCIL

J.F. BALDWIN, *The King's Council* (Oxford, 1913).

M.V. CLARKE, *Medieval Representation and Consent* (London, 1936).

R.G. DAVIES and J.H. DENTON (eds.), *The English Parliament in the Middle Ages* (Manchester, 1981).

J.G. EDWARDS, *The Second Century of the English Parliament* (Oxford, 1979).

E.B. FRYDE and E. MILLER (eds.), *Historical Studies of the English Parliament*, 2 vols (Cambridge, 1970).

H.L. GRAY, *The Influence of the Commons on Early Legislation* (Cambridge, Mass., 1932).

G.L. HARRISS, *King, Parliament, and Public Finance in Medieval England* (Oxford, 1975).

G.A. HOLMES, *The Good Parliament* (Oxford, 1975).

F.W. MAITLAND, *Memoranda de Parliamento*, introduction (R.S., 1893).

M. MCKISACK, *The Parliamentary Representation of the English Boroughs during the Middle Ages* (Oxford, 1932).

J.E. POWELL and K. WALLIS, *The House of Lords in the Middle Ages* (London, 1968).

N. PRONAY and J. TAYLOR, *Parliamentary Texts of the late Middle Ages* (Oxford, 1980).

H.G. RICHARDSON and G.O. SAYLES, *The English Parliament in the Middle Ages* (London, 1981).

J.S. ROSKELL, *The Commons in the Parliament of 1422* (Manchester, 1954).

—— *The Commons and their Speakers in English Parliaments 1376–1523* (Manchester, 1965).

—— *Parliament and Politics in Late Medieval England* (3 vols, London 1981–3).

J.S. ROSKELL, L. CLARK and C. RAWCLIFFE, *The House of Commons 1386–1421*, 4 vols (Stroud, 1992).

G.O. SAYLES, *The King's Parliament of England* (New York, 1975).

Articles

(i) Parliament

C.C. BAYLEY, 'The campaign of 1375 and the Good Parliament', *E.H.R.* vol. 55 (1940).

L. CLARK, 'Magnates and their affinities in the parliaments of 1386–1421', R. Britnell and A. Pollard (eds.), *The McFarlane Legacy* (Stroud, 1995).

G.P. CUTTINO, 'A reconsideration of the *Modus Tenendi Parliamentum*', *The Forward Movement in the Fourteenth Century*, ed. F.L. Utley (Ohio, 1961).

J.G. EDWARDS, 'The *Plena Potestas* of English parliamentary representatives', *Oxford Essays in Medieval History Presented to H.E. Salter* (Oxford, 1934).

—— 'Justice in early English parliaments', *B.I.H.R.* vol. 27 (1954).

—— 'The commons in medieval English parliaments', *Creighton Lecture*, 1957.

E.B. FRYDE, 'Parliament and the French war, 1336–40', *Essays in Medieval History Presented to B. Wilkinson*, ed. A. Sandquist and M. Powicke (Toronto, 1969).

V.H. GALBRAITH, 'The *Modus Tenendi Parliamentum*', *Journal of the Courtauld and Warburg Institute*, vol. 16 (1953).

G.L. HARRISS, 'The commons' petitions of 1340', *E.H.R.* vol. 78 (1963).

—— 'War and the emergence of the English parliament', *Journal of Medieval History*, vol. 2 (1976).

—— 'The Medieval Parliament', *Parliamentary History*, vol. 13 (1994).

K.N. HOUGHTON, 'Borough elections to parliament during the later fifteenth century', *B.I.H.R.* vol. 39 (1966).

P. JALLAND, 'The influence of the aristocracy on shire elections in the north of England', *Speculum*, vol. 47 (1972).

G. LAPSLEY, 'Archbishop Stratford and the parliamentary crisis of 1341', *E.H.R.* vol. 30 (1915).

—— 'The interpretation of the Statute of York', *E.H.R.* vol. 56 (1941).

K.B. MCFARLANE, 'Parliament and bastard feudalism', *T.R.H.S.* 4th ser., vol. 26 (1944).

J.W. MCKENNA, 'The myth of parliamentary sovereignty in late medieval England', *E.H.R.* vol. 94 (1979).

E. MILLER, 'The origins of parliament' (Historical Association pamphlet, 1960).

A.R. MYERS, 'Parliamentary petitions in the fifteenth century', *E.H.R.* vol. 52 (1937).

S.J. PAYLING, 'The widening franchise – Parliamentary elections in Lancastrian Nottinghamshire', *England in the Fifteenth Century*, ed. D. Williams (Woodbridge, 1987).

D. RAYNER, 'The forms and machinery of the *Commune Petition* in the fourteenth century', *E.H.R.* vol. 56 (1941).

H.G. RICHARDSON and G.O. SAYLES, 'The king's ministers in parliament', *E.H.R.* vols 46 and 47 (1931–2).

A. ROGERS, 'Henry IV, the commons and taxation', *Medieval Studies*, vol. 31 (1969).

J.S. ROSKELL, 'The problem of the attendance of the lords in medieval parliaments', *B.I.H.R.* vol. 29 (1956).

—— 'Certain aspects and problems of the English *Modus Tenendi Parliamentum*, *B.J.R.L.* vol. 50 (1967–8).

J.R. STRAYER, 'The Statute of York and the community of the realm', *A.H.R.* vol. 47 (1941).

J.A. TUCK, 'The Cambridge parliament 1388', *E.H.R.* vol. 84 (1969).

(ii) The council

A.L. BROWN, 'The commons and the council in the reign of Henry IV', *E.H.R.* vol. 79 (1964).

—— 'The king's councillors in the fifteenth century', *T.R.H.S.* 5th ser., vol. 19 (1969).

J.L. KIRBY, 'Councils and councillors of Henry IV', *T.R.H.S.* 5th ser., vol. 14 (1964).

J.R. LANDER, 'The Yorkist council and administration, 1461–85', *E.H.R.* vol. 73 (1958).

—— 'Council, administration and councillors, 1461–85', *B.I.H.R.* vol. 32 (1959).

N.B. LEWIS, 'The continual council in the early years of Richard II', *E.H.R.* vol. 41 (1926).

R. VIRGOE, 'The composition of the king's council 1437–61', *B.I.H.R.* vol. 43 (1970).

J.L. WATTS, 'The Counsels of King Henry VI, c. 1435–1445', *E.H.R.* vol. 106 (1991).

(d) ROYAL FINANCE

Works on taxation in the context of parliamentary representation and consent are listed in the preceding section.

E.B. FRYDE, *William de la Pole: merchant and King's banker* (London, 1988).

G.L. HARRISS, *King, Parliament, and Public Finance in Medieval England* (Oxford, 1975).

W.E. LUNT, *Financial Relations of the Papacy with England*, 2 vols (Cambridge, Mass., 1939, 1962).

N.J. MAYHEW (ed.), *Edwardian Monetary Affairs, 1279–1344* (British Archaeological Reports 36, 1977).

J.H. RAMSAY, *A History of the Revenues of the Kings of England* (Oxford, 1925).

A. STEEL, *The Receipt of the Exchequer* (Cambridge, 1954).

B.P. WOLFFE, *The Crown Lands: an aspect of Yorkist and Early Tudor Government, 1461–1536* (London, 1970).

Articles

E.B. FRYDE, 'Edward III's wool monopoly of 1337', *History*, vol. 37 (1952).

G.L. HARRISS, 'Fictitious loans', *Econ.H.R.* 2nd ser., vol. 8 (1955).

G.L. HARRISS, 'Aids, loans and benevolences', *H.J.* vol. 6 (1963).

—— 'Cardinal Beaufort – patriot or usurer?', *T.R.H.S.* 5th ser., vol. 20 (1970).

—— 'Theory and practice in royal taxation: some observations', *E.H.R.* vol. 97 (1982).

—— 'Marmaduke Lumley and the Exchequer crisis of 1446–9', *Aspects of late Medieval Government and Society*, ed. J.G. Rowe (Toronto, 1986).

J.L. KIRBY, 'The issues of the Lancastrian exchequer and Lord Cromwell's estimates of 1433', *B.I.H.R.* vol. 24 (1951).

K.B. MCFARLANE, 'Loans to the Lancastrian kings: the problem of inducement', *C.H.J.* vol. 9 (1947).

R. VIRGOE, 'The Benevolence of 1481', *E.H.R.* vol. 104 (1989).

B.P. WOLFFE, 'The management of English royal estates under the Yorkist kings', *E.H.R.* vol. 71 (1956).

—— 'Acts of resumption in the Lancastrian parliaments, 1399–1456', *E.H.R.* vol. 73 (1958).

(e) CONSTITUTIONAL IDEAS AND POLITICAL WRITINGS

S.B. CHRIMES, *English Constitutional Ideas in the Fifteenth Century* (Cambridge, 1936).

R.F. GREEN, *Poets and Princepleasers: Literature and the English Court in the Late Middle Ages* (Toronto, 1980).

A. GROSS, *The Dissolution of Lancastrian Kingship* (Stamford, 1996).

R.H. JONES, *The Royal Policy of Richard II: Absolutism in the Later Middle Ages* (Oxford, 1968).

N. PRONAY and J. TAYLOR, *Parliamentary Texts of the Late Middle Ages* (Oxford, 1980).

V.J. SCATTERGOOD, *Politics and Poetry in the Fifteenth Century* (London, 1971).

Articles

J.H. BURNS, 'Fortescue and the political theory of *Dominium*', *Historical Journal*, vol. 28 (1985).

G.P. CUTTINO, 'A reconsideration of the *Modus Tenendi Parliamentum*', F.L. Utley (ed.), *The Forward Movement in the Fourteenth Century* (Ohio, 1961).

J.P. GENET, 'Political theory and local communities in later medieval France and England', J. Highfield and R. Jeffs (eds.), *The Crown and the Local Communities* (Gloucester, 1981).

P.E. GILL, 'Politics and propaganda in fifteenth century England: the polemical writings of Sir John Fortescue', *Speculum*, vol. 46 (1971).

J.L. GILLESPIE, 'Sir John Fortescue's conception of the royal will', *Nottingham Medieval Studies*, vol. 23 (1979).

J.B. GILSON, 'A defence of the proscription of the Yorkists in 1459', *E.H.R.* vol. 26 (1911).

M. KEKEWICH, 'The attainder of the Yorkists in 1459', *B.I.H.R.* vol. 55 (1987).

M.C. PRESTWICH, 'The *modus tenendi parliamentum*', *Parliamentary History*, vol. 1 (1982).

J.S. ROSKELL, 'Certain aspects and problems of the English *Modus Tenendi Parliamentum*', *B.J.R.L.* vol. 50 (1967–8).

5. SOCIAL AND ECONOMIC AFFAIRS

(a) GENERAL

J.L. BOLTON, *The Medieval English Economy, 1150–1500* (London, 1980).

A.R. BRIDBURY, *Economic Growth: England in the Later Middle Ages* (London, 1962).

R.H. BRITNELL, *The Commercialisation of English Society, 1000–1050* (London, 1993).

C.C. DYER, *Standards of Living in the later Middle Ages* (Cambridge, 1989).

P.J. GOLDBERG (ed.), *Woman is a Worthy Wight: Women in Medieval Society* (Stroud, 1992).

R. HORROX (ed.), *Fifteenth Century Attitudes: perceptions of Society in late Medieval England* (Cambridge, 1994).

M. KEEN, English Society in the Later Middle Ages (Penguin, 1990).

S.H. RIGBY, *English Society in the Later Middle Ages: Class, Status and Gender* (Basingstoke, 1995).

R.M. SMITH (ed.), *Land, Kinship and Life Cycle* (Cambridge, 1984).

(b) AGRICULTURE AND THE LIFE OF THE COUNTRYSIDE

M. BERESFORD, *The Lost Villages of Medieval England* (London, 1954).

B.M.S. CAMPBELL, *English Seignorial Agriculture 1250–1450* (Cambridge, 2000).

E. FRYDE, *Peasants and Landlords in later Medieval England* (Stroud, 1996).

B. HANAWALT, *The Ties that Bound; peasant families in medieval England* (New York, 1986).

B.F. HARVEY, *Westminster Abbey and its estates in the Middle Ages* (Oxford, 1977).

R.H. HILTON, *The Economic Development of some Leicestershire Estates* (Oxford, 1947).

—— *A Medieval Society: The West Midlands at the end of the Thirteenth Century* (London, 1966).

R.H. HILTON, *The Decline of Serfdom in Medieval England* (Economic History Society, 1969).

—— *The English Peasantry in the later Middle Ages* (Oxford, 1975).

W.G. HOSKINS, *The Making of the English Landscape* (London, 1955).

—— *The Midland Peasant* (London, 1957).

E.A. KOSMINSKY, *Studies in English Agrarian History in the Thirteenth Century* (Oxford, 1956).

J.R. MADDICOTT, *The English Peasantry and the Demands of the Crown, 1294–1341* (*Past and Present* Supplement, No. 1, 1975).

E. MILLER (ed.), *The Agrarian History of England and Wales*, vol. III (Cambridge, 1991).

E. MILLER and J. HATCHER, *Medieval England: rural society and economic change, 1086–1348* (London, 1978).

C.S. and C.S. ORWIN, *The Open Fields* (3rd ed., Oxford, 1967).

B.H. PUTNAM, *The Enforcement of the Statute of Labourers* (Columbia, 1908).

J.A. RAFTIS, *The Estates of Ramsey Abbey* (Toronto, 1957).

—— *Tenure and Mobility* (Toronto, 1964).

J.E. THOROLD ROGERS, *A History of Agriculture and Prices in England* (4 vols, Oxford, 1866–82).

—— *Six Centuries of Work and Wages* (Oxford, 1909).

J.Z. TITOW, *English Rural Society 1200–1350* (London, 1969).

Articles

J.S. DREW, 'Manorial accounts of St Swithun's Priory, Winchester', *E.H.R.* vol. 62 (1947).

F.R.H. DU BOULAY, 'A *rentier* economy in the later Middle Ages', *Econ.H.R.* 2nd ser., vol. 16 (1964).

—— 'Who were farming the English demesnes at the end of the Middle Ages?', *Econ.H.R.* 2nd ser., vol. 17 (1965).

C. DYER, 'A redistribution of incomes in fifteenth century England', *Past and Present*, No. 39 (1968).

B.F. HARVEY, 'The leasing of the Abbot of Westminster's demesnes in the later Middle Ages', *Econ.H.R.* 2nd ser., vol. 22 (1969).

J. HATCHER, 'English serfdom and villeinage: toward a reassessment', *Past and Present*, No. 90 (1981).

R.H. HILTON, 'A study in the prehistory of English enclosure', *Studi in onore di A. Sapori* (Milan, 1957).

E.A. KOSMINSKY, 'Feudal rent in England', *Past and Present*, No. 7 (1955).

S. PENN and C. DYER, 'Wages and earnings in late medieval England and the enforcement of the labour laws', *Economic History Review*, 2nd series, vol. 43 (1990).

L.R. POOS, 'The social context of the enforcement of the statute of labourers', *Law and History Review*, vol. 1 (1983).

M.M. POSTAN, 'The chronology of labour services', *T.R.H.S.* 4th ser., vol. 20 (1937).

(c) THE TOWNS

M. BERESFORD, *New Towns of the Middle Ages* (London, 1967).
R. BIRD, *The Turbulent London of Richard II* (London, 1949).
A.R. BRIDBURY, *Economic Growth: England in the Later Middle Ages* (London, 1962).
E. MILLER and J. HATCHER, *Medieval England: towns, commerce and crafts, 1086–1348* (London, 1995).
C. PHYTHIAN-ADAMS, *Desolation of a city: Coventry and the Urban Crisis of the late Middle Ages* (Cambridge, 1979).
C.P.S. PLATT, *The English Medieval Town* (London, 1976).
S.M.G. REYNOLDS, *An Introduction to the History of English Medieval Towns* (Oxford, 1977).
G. ROSSER, *Medieval Westminster, 1200–1540* (Oxford, 1989).
J. TAIT, *The Medieval English Borough* (Manchester, 1936).
J.A.F. THOMSON (ed.), *Towns and Townspeople in the Fifteenth Century* (Gloucester, 1988).
S.L. THRUPP, *The Merchant Class of Medieval London* (Chicago, 1948).

Articles
R.B. DOBSON, 'Urban decline in medieval England', *T.R.H.S.* 5th ser., vol. 27 (1977).
P.J.P. GOLDBERG, 'Women in fifteenth century town life', *Towns and Townspeople in the Fifteenth Century* ed. J.A.F. Thomson (Gloucester, 1984).
—— 'Female labour, service and marriage in the late medieval urban North', *Northern History*, vol. 22 (1988).
—— 'Women's work, women's role in the late medieval North', M. Hicks (ed.), *Profit, Piety and the Professions* (Gloucester, 1988).
D.M. PALLISER, 'Urban Decay revisited', J.A.F. Thomson (ed.), *Towns and Townspeople in the Fifteenth Century* (Gloucester, 1988).

(d) TRADE AND INDUSTRY

A.R. BRIDBURY, *England and the Salt Trade in the Later Middle Ages* (Oxford, 1955).
—— *Economic Growth: England in the Later Middle Ages* (London, 1962).
—— *Medieval English Clothmaking: an economic Survey* (London, 1982).
E.M. CARUS-WILSON, *Medieval Merchant Venturers* (London, 1954).

E.M. CARUS-WILSON and O. COLEMAN, *England's Export Trade 1275–1547* (Oxford, 1963).

W. CHILDS, *Anglo-Castilian Trade in the later Middle Ages* (Manchester, 1978).

E.B. FRYDE, *Studies in Medieval Trade and Finance* (London, 1983).

A. HANHAM, *The Celys and their world: an English merchant family of the fifteenth century* (Cambridge, 1985).

J. HATCHER, *English Tin Production and Trade before 1550* (Oxford, 1973).

M.K. JAMES, *Studies in the English Wine Trade* (Oxford, 1971).

T.H. LLOYD, *The English Wool Trade in the Middle Ages* (Cambridge, 1977).

E. POWER, *The Wool Trade in English Medieval History* (Oxford, 1941).

Articles

E.M. CARUS-WILSON, 'Evidences of industrial growth on some fifteenth century manors', *Econ.H.R.* 2nd ser., vol. 12 (1959–60).

G.A. HOLMES, 'The libel of English policy', *E.H.R.* vol. 76 (1961).

E. MILLER, 'The fortunes of the English textile industry in the thirteenth century', *Econ.H.R.* 2nd ser., vol. 18 (1965).

Y. RENOUARD, 'Le grand commerce des vins de Gascogne au moyen âge', *Revue Historique,* vol. 221 (1959).

(e) PLAGUE, POPULATION AND POPULAR UNREST

(N.B. Works on the labour laws and on serfdom are listed in Section (c) *ante*).

B.M.S. CAMPBELL (ed.), *Before the Black Death: Studies in the crisis of the early fourteenth century* (Manchester, 1991).

R.B. DOBSON, *The Peasants' Revolt of 1381* (London, 1970).

I.M.W. HARVEY, *Jack Cade's Revolt of 1450* (Oxford, 1991).

J. HATCHER, *Plague, Population and the English Economy* (London, 1977).

R.H. HILTON, *The Decline of Serfdom in England* (Economic History Society, 1969).

R.H. HILTON and T. ASTON (eds.), *The English Rising of 1381* (Past and Present Publications, Cambridge, 1984).

R. HORROX, *The Black Death* (Manchester, 1994).

C. OMAN, *The Great Revolt of 1381* (new ed. Oxford, 1969).

Z. RAZI, *Life, Marriage and Death in a Medieval Parish Economy: Demography in Halesowen 1270–1400* (Cambridge, 1986).

J.C. RUSSELL, *British Medieval Population* (Albuquerque, 1948).

J.F.D. SHREWSBURY, *A History of Bubonic Plague in the British Isles* (Cambridge, 1970).

G. TWIGG, *The Black Death: a biological reappraisal* (London, 1984).

Articles

J.M.W. BEAN, 'Plague, population and economic decline in England in the later Middle Ages', *Econ.H.R.* 2nd ser., vol. 15 (1962–3).

N. BROOKS, 'The organisation and achievements of the peasants of Kent and Essex in 1381', *Studies in Medieval History presented to R.H.C. Davis*, ed. H. Mayr-Harting and R.I. Moore (London, 1985).

R. FAITH, 'The "Great Rumour" of 1377 and peasant ideology', R. Hilton and T. Aston (eds.), *The English Rising Of 1381* (Cambridge, 1984).

C.M. FRASER, 'Some thirteenth century censuses', *Econ.H.R.* 2nd ser., vol. 10 (1957–8).

E.B. FRYDE, 'The English parliament and the Peasants' Revolt of 1381', *Studies in Medieval Trade and Finance* (London, 1983).

H.E. HALLAM, 'Population density in medieval fenland', *Econ.H.R.* 2nd ser., vol. 14 (1961).

B.F. HARVEY, 'The population trend in England between 1300 and 1348', *T.R.H.S.* 5th ser., vol. 16 (1966).

R.H. HILTON, 'Peasant movements in England before 1381', *Econ.H.R.* 2nd ser., vol. 2 (1949).

I. KERSHAW, 'The great famine and agrarian crisis in England, 1315–22', *Past and Present*, No. 59 (1973).

W. ORMROD, 'The Peasants' Revolt and the government of England', *Journal of British Studies*, vol. 29 (1990).

M.M. POSTAN, 'Some economic evidence of declining population in the later Middle Ages', *Econ.H.R.* 2nd ser., vol. 2 (1950).

6. BASTARD FEUDALISM, THE NOBILITY AND GENTRY

J.M.W. BEAN, *The decline of English Feudalism 1215–1540* (Manchester, 1968).
—— *From Lord to Patron: lordship in late medieval England* (Manchester, 1989).

M.J. BENNETT, *Community, Class, and Careerism* (Cambridge, 1983).

R.H. BRITNELL and A. POLLARD (eds.), *The McFarlane Legacy* (Stroud, 1995).

C. CARPENTER, *Locality and Polity: A study of Warwickshire landed society, 1401–1499* (Cambridge, 1992).

P.R. COSS, *The Origins of the English Gentry* (Past and Present publications, 2003).

W.H. DUNHAM, *Lord Hastings's Indentured Retainers* (New Haven, Conn., 1955).

A.B. FERGUSON, *The Indian Summer of English Chivalry* (Durham, N.C., 1960).

C. GIVEN-WILSON, *The English Nobility in the late Middle Ages* (London, 1987).

M. HICKS, *Bastard Feudalism* (London, 1995).

G.A. HOLMES, *The Estates of the Higher Nobility in Fourteenth Century England* (Cambridge, 1957).

M. KEEN, *Origins of the English Gentleman* (Stroud, 2003).

K.B. MCFARLANE, *The English Nobility 1290–1521* (Oxford, 1973).

—— *England in the Fifteenth century* (ed. with intro. by G.L. Harriss, London, 1981).

S.J. PAYLING, *Political Society in Lancastrian England* (Oxford, 1991).

C. RAWCLIFFE, *The Staffords: Earls of Stafford and Dukes of Buckingham, 1394–1521* (Cambridge, 1978).

C.F. RICHMOND, *The Paston family in the fifteenth century* (vols 1 and 2, Cambridge, 1990, 1996: vol. 3, Manchester 2000).

J.T. ROSENTHAL, *The Estates and Finances of Richard Duke of York (1411–1460)* (Nebraska, 1965).

N. SAUL, *Knights and Esquires: the Gloucestershire gentry in the Fourteenth Century* (Oxford, 1981).

—— *Scenes from Provincial Life: knightly families in Sussex 1280–1400* (Oxford, 1986).

S.K. WALKER, *The Lancastrian Affinity 1361–1399* (Oxford, 1990).

S.M. WRIGHT, *The Derbyshire Gentry in the Fifteenth Century* (Derbyshire Record Society, 1983).

Articles

C. CARPENTER, 'The Beauchamp affinity: a study of bastard feudalism at work', *E.H.R.* vol. 95 (1980).

—— 'The fifteenth century gentry and their estates', *Gentry and Lesser Nobility in Late Medieval Europe* ed. M. Jones (Gloucester, 1986).

P.R. COSS, 'Bastard feudalism revised', *Past and Present*, No. 125 (1989).

—— 'The formation of the English gentry', *Past and Present*, No. 147 (1995).

P. COSS, D. CROUCH, and D. CARPENTER, 'Debate: bastard feudalism revised', *Past and Present*, No. 131 (1991).

J. CORNWALL, 'The early Tudor gentry', *Econ.H.R.* 2nd ser., vol. 17 (1964–5).

C. GIVEN WILSON, 'The king and the gentry in fourteenth century England', *T.R.H.S.* 5th series, vol. 37 (1987).

H.L. GRAY, 'Incomes from land in England in 1436', *E.H.R.* vol. 49 (1934).

W.I. HAWARD, 'Economic aspects of the Wars of the Roses in East Anglia', *E.H.R.* vol. 41 (1926).

R. HORROX, 'Local and national politics in fifteenth century England', *Journal of Medieval History*, vol. 18 (1992).

N.B. LEWIS, 'The organisation of indentured retinues in fourteenth century England', *T.R.H.S.* 4th ser. vol. 27 (1945).

K.B. MCFARLANE, 'Bastard feudalism', *B.I.H.R.* vol. 20 (1945).

—— 'Parliament and bastard Feudalism', *T.R.H.S.* 4th series, vol. 26 (1944).

—— 'Had Edward I a policy toward the Earls?' *History*, vol. 50 (1965).

—— 'The English nobility in the later Middle Ages', *XIIme Congrès international des sciences historiques* (1965).

D.A.L. MORGAN, 'The individual style of the English Gentleman', *Gentry and Lesser Nobility in Medieval Europe,* ed. M. Jones (Gloucester, 1986).

T.B. PUGH, 'The magnates, knights and gentry', *Fifteenth Century England, 1399–1509,* ed. S. Chrimes, C.D. Ross and R.A. Griffiths (Manchester, 1972).

T.B. PUGH and C.D. ROSS, 'The English baronage and the income tax of 1436', *B.I.H.R.* vol. 26 (1953).

—— 'Some materials for the study of baronial incomes in the fifteenth century', *Econ.H.R.* 2nd ser., vol. 6 (1953).

C. RAWCLIFFE, 'Baronial Councils in the later middle ages', *Patronage Pedigree and Power in Later Medieval England,* ed. C.D. Ross (Gloucester, 1979).

7. THE CHURCH

(a) ECCLESIASTICAL ORGANIZATION AND RELATIONS WITH KING AND POPE

For works dealing with the church's estates and their exploitation, see section V(a).

G. BARRACLOUGH, *Papal Provisions* (Oxford, 1935).

A. HAMILTON THOMPSON, *The English Clergy and their Organization in the Later Middle Ages* (Oxford, 1947).

C. HARPER-BILL, *The Pre-Reformation Church in England, 1400–1530* (London, 1989).

B.F. HARVEY, *Living and Dying in England: the Monastic Experience* (Oxford, 1993).

M. HARVEY, *England, Rome and the Papacy, 1417–64* (Manchester, 1993).

P. HEATH, *The English Parish Clergy on the eve of the Reformation* (London, 1969).

—— *Church and Realm 1272–1461* (London, 1988).

J. HUGHES, *Pastors and Visionaries* (Woodbridge, 1988).

D. KNOWLES, *The Religious Orders in England* (3 vols Cambridge, 1947–59).

C.H. LAWRENCE (ed.), *The English Church and the Papacy in the Middle Ages* (London, 1965).

A.G. LITTLE, *Studies in English Franciscan History* (Manchester, 1917).

W.E. LUNT, *Financial Relations of the Papacy with England* (2 vols Cambridge, Mass., 1939–62).

W.A. PANTIN, *The English Church in the Fourteenth Century* (Cambridge, 1955).

S. RABAN, *Mortmain Legislation and the English Church, 1279–1500* (Cambridge, 1982).

R.N. SWANSON, *Church and Society in late Medieval England* (Oxford, 1989).

K.L. WOOD-LEGH, *Perpetual Chantries in Britain* (Cambridge, 1965).

Articles

L.R. BETCHERMAN, 'The making of bishops in the Lancastrian period', *Speculum,* vol. 41 (1966).

C. DAVIES, 'The Statute of Provisors of 1351', *History,* vol. 38 (1953).

R.G. DAVIES, 'The Episcopate', *Profession, Vocation and Culture in Later Medieval England,* ed. C.H. Clough (Liverpool, 1982).

—— 'Martin V and the English episcopate', *E.H.R.* vol. 92 (1977).

H.S. DEIGHTON, 'Clerical taxation by consent, 1279–1301', *E.H.R.* vol. 68 (1953).

C. ERIKSON, 'The fourteenth century Franciscans and their critics', *Franciscan Studies,* vols. 35–6 (1975–6).

E.B. GRAVES, 'The legal significance of the Statute of Praemunire of 1353', *Haskins Anniversary Essays* (New York, 1929).

J.R.L. HIGHFIELD, 'The English hierarchy in the reign of Edward III', *T.R.H.S.* 5th ser., vol. 6 (1956).

K.B. MCFARLANE, 'Henry V, Cardinal Beaufort and the Red Hat', *E.H.R.* vol. 60 (1945).

M.M. MORGAN, 'The Suppression of the alien priories', *History,* vol. 26 (1941).

R.N. SWANSON, 'Problems of the priesthood in pre-Reformation England', *E.H.R.* vol. 105 (1990).

(b) RELIGIOUS LIFE AND THOUGHT: LOLLARDY AND MYSTICISM

M.E. ASTON, *Lollards, and Reformers* (London, 1984).

M.E. ASTON and C. RICHMOND, *Lollardy and the Gentry in the Later Middle Ages* (Stroud, 1997).

S. BHATTACHARJI, *God is an Earthquake: the Spirituality of Margery Kempe* (London, 1997).

P. BOEHNER, *Ockham: Philosophical Writings* (London, 1957).

E. DUFFY, *The Stripping of the Altars: Traditional religion in England 1400– 1580* (New Haven, 1992).

M. GALLYON, *Margery Kempe of Lynn and Medieval Norwich* (Norwich, 1995).

M. GLASCOE, *The Medieval Mystical Tradition* (Exeter/Cambridge, 1980–).

A. GWYNN, *English Austin Friars in the Time of Wyclif* (Oxford, 1940).

A. HUDSON, *English Wycliffite Writings* (Cambridge, 1978).

—— *Lollards and their Books* (London, 1985).

—— *The Premature Reformation* (Oxford, 1988).

J. HUGHES, *Pastors and Visionaries* (Woodbridge, 1988).

A.J.P. KENNY, *Wyclif* (Oxford, 1985).

—— (ed.), *Wyclif in his Times* (Oxford, 1986).

D. KNOWLES, *The English Mystical Tradition* (London, 1961).

K.B. MCFARLANE, *John Wycliffe and the beginnings of English Non-conformity* (London, 1952).

—— *Lancastrian Kings and Lollard Knights* (Oxford, 1972).

P. MCNIVEN, *Heresy and Politics in the Reign of Henry IV* (Woodbridge, 1987).

G.R. OWST, *Preaching in Medieval England* (Cambridge, 1926).

—— *Literature and Pulpit in Medieval England* (Cambridge, 1933).

J.A. ROBSON, *Wyclif and the Oxford Schools* (Cambridge, 1961).

J.T. ROSENTHAL, *The Purchase of Paradise: Gift Giving and the Aristocracy* (London, 1972).

M. RUBIN, *Corpus Christi: the Eucharist in Late Medieval Culture* (Cambridge, 1990).

H.L. SPENCER, *English Preaching in the Late Middle Ages* (Oxford, 1993).

N.P. TANNER, *Heresy Trials in the Diocese of Norwich* (Royal Historical Society, 1977).

J.A.F. THOMSON, *The Later Lollards* (Oxford, 1965).

H.B. WORKMAN, *John Wyclif* (2 vols Oxford, 1926).

Articles

M.E. ASTON, 'Lollardy and sedition', *Past and Present,* No. 17 (1960).

—— 'Death', R. Horrox (ed.), *Fifteenth Century Attitudes* (Cambridge, 1994).

C. CARPENTER, 'The religion of the gentry of fifteenth century England', *England in the Fifteenth Century* ed. D. Williams (Woodbridge, 1987).

R. LOVATT, 'The *Imitation of Christ* in late medieval England', *T.R.H.S.* 5th ser. vol. 18 (1968).

W.A. PANTIN, 'The monk solitary of Farne, a fourteenth century English mystic', *E.H.R.* vol. 59 (1944).

H.G. RICHARDSON, 'Heresy and the lay power under Richard II', *E.H.R.* vol. 51 (1936).

C.F. RICHMOND, 'Religion and the fifteenth century English gentleman', *The Church, Politics and Patronage in the Fifteenth Century* ed. R.B. Dobson (Gloucester, 1984).

V.J. SCATTERGOOD, 'The two ways – an unpublished religious treatise by Sir John Clanvowe', *English Philological Studies,* vol. 10 (1967).

M.G.A. VALE, 'Piety, Charity and Literacy among the Yorkshire gentry' (*Borthwick Papers,* No. 50, York, 1976).

(c) EDUCATION

J.I. CATTO and T.A.R. EVANS (ed.), *The History of the University of Oxford, vol. II: late medieval Oxford* (Oxford, 1992).

A.B. COBBAN, *The Medieval English Universities: Oxford and Cambridge to c. 1500* (London, 1988).

N. ORME, *English Schools in the Middle Ages* (London, 1973).

—— *Education and Society in Medieval and Renaissance England* (London, 1989).

H. RASHDALL, *The Universities of Europe in the Middle Ages*, vol. III, ed. F.M. Powicke and A.B. Emden (Oxford, 1936).

R. WEISS, *Humanism in England during the Fifteenth Century* (Oxford, 1957).

(d) ECCLESIASTICAL BIOGRAPHIES

M.E. ASTON, *Thomas Arundel* (Oxford, 1967).

J.H. DAHMUS, *William Courtenay, Archbishop of Canterbury 1381–96* (Pennsylvania, 1966).

J.H. DENTON, *Robert Winchelsey and the Crown, 1294–1313* (Cambridge, 1980).

C.M. FRASER, *History of Anthony Bek, Bishop of Durham 1283–1311* (Oxford, 1957).

V.H.H. GREEN, *Bishop Reginald Pecock* (Cambridge, 1945).

G.L. HARRISS, *Cardinal Beaufort* (Oxford, 1988).

E.F. JACOB, *Archbishop Henry Chichele* (London, 1967).

R.J. MITCHELL, *John Free* (London, 1955).

G.H. MOBERLY, *William of Wykeham* (London, 1893).

R.L. STOREY, *Thomas Langley and the Bishopric of Durham* (London, 1961).

8. SCOTLAND, IRELAND AND WALES

(a) SCOTLAND

A.D.M. BARRELL, *Medieval Scotland* (Cambridge, 2000).

G.W.S. BARROW, *Robert Bruce* (London, 1965).

M. BROWN, *James I* (Edinburgh, 1994).

W.C. DICKINSON, *Scotland From the Earliest Times to 1603* (London, 1961).

A. GRANT, *Independence and Nationhood: Scotland 1306–1469* (London, 1984).

N. MCDOUGALL, *James III: a political study* (Edinburgh, 1982).

C. MCGLADDERY, *James II* (Edinburgh, 1990).

C. MCNAMEE, *The Wars of the Bruces: Scotland, England and Ireland, 1306–28* (East Linton, 1997).

R. NICHOLSON, *Edward III and the Scots* (Oxford, 1965).

—— *Scotland: the late Middle Ages* (Edinburgh, 1973).

E.L.G. STONES and C.G. SIMPSON, *Edward I and the throne of Scotland, 1290–96* (Oxford, 1978).

F. WATSON, *Under the Hammer: Edward I and the Throne of Scotland* (East Linton, 1998).

J. WORMALD, *Lords and Men in Scotland: Bonds of Manrent, 1442–1603* (Edinburgh, 1985).

(b) IRELAND

O. ARMSTRONG, *Edward Bruce's Invasion of Ireland* (London, 1923).
A. COSGROVE (ed.), *A New History of Ireland*, vol. II (Oxford, 1989).
—— *Late Medieval Ireland* (Dublin, 1981).
E. CURTIS, *Richard II in Ireland* (Oxford, 1927).
—— *History of Medieval Ireland 1086–1513* (London, 1938).
S. DUFFY, *Ireland in the Middle Ages* (Basingstoke, 1996).
R. FRAME, *Colonial Ireland, 1169–1369* (Dublin, 1981).
—— *The English Lordship in Ireland, 1318–61* (Oxford, 1982).
J.F. LYDON, *The Lordship of Ireland in the Middle Ages* (Dublin, 1972).
—— *Ireland in the Later Middle Ages* (Dublin, 1973).
—— (ed.), *The English in Medieval Ireland* (Dublin, 1984).
G. ORPEN, *Ireland under the Normans* 4 vols (Oxford, 1911–20).
A.J. OTWAY-RUTHVEN, *A History of Medieval Ireland* (London, 1968).
W.A. PHILLIPS (ed.), *History of the Church of Ireland*, vol. 2 (London, 1934).
H.G. RICHARDSON and G.O. SAYLES, *The Irish Parliament in the Middle Ages* (Philadelphia, 1952).

(c) WALES

R.R. DAVIES, *Lordship and Society in the Marches of Wales* (Oxford, 1978).
—— *Conquest, Coexistence and Change: Wales 1063–1415* (Oxford, 1987).
—— *The Revolt of Owain Glyn Dwr* (Oxford, 1995).
R.A. GRIFFITHS, *The Principality of Wales in the later Middle Ages* (Cardiff, 1972).
—— *Conquerors and Conquered in Medieval Wales* (Gloucester, 1994).
J.E. LLOYD, *Owen Glendower* (Oxford, 1931).
W. REES, *South Wales and the March, 1284–1415* (Oxford, 1924).
D. WALKER, *Medieval Wales* (Cambridge, 1990).

Genealogical tables

1 THE FRENCH SUCCESSION IN 1328 AND AFTER

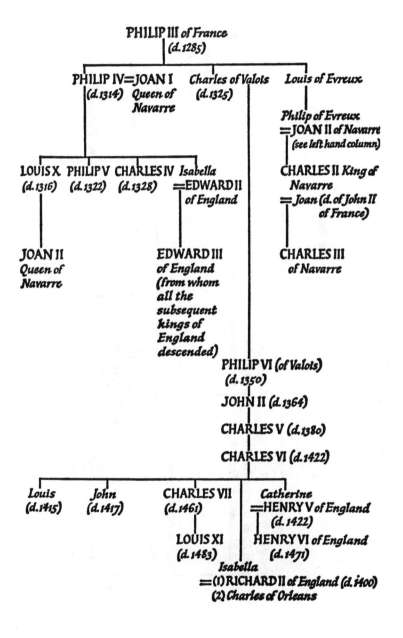

PHILIP III *of France*
(d. 1285)

PHILIP IV=**JOAN I**   *Charles of Valois*   *Louis of Evreux*
(d. 1314)   *Queen of*   *(d. 1325)*
     Navarre

Philip of Evreux
=**JOAN II** *of Navarre*
(see left hand column)

LOUIS X   **PHILIP V**   **CHARLES IV**   *Isabella*
(d. 1316)   *(d. 1322)*   *(d. 1328)*   =**EDWARD II**
    of England

CHARLES II *King of*
Navarre
= *Joan (d. of John II*
of France)

JOAN II
Queen of
Navarre

EDWARD III
of England
(from whom
all the
subsequent
kings of
England
descended)

CHARLES III
of Navarre

PHILIP VI *(of Valois)*
(d. 1350)

JOHN II *(d. 1364)*

CHARLES V *(d. 1380)*

CHARLES VI *(d. 1422)*

Louis   *John*   **CHARLES VII**   *Catherine*
(d. 1415)   *(d. 1417)*   *(d. 1461)*   =**HENRY V** *of England*
                       (d. 1422)

LOUIS XI   **HENRY VI** *of England*
(d. 1483)   *(d. 1471)*

Isabella
= (1) **RICHARD II** *of England (d. 1400)*
(2) *Charles of Orleans*

2 THE HOUSE OF PLANTAGENET AND ITS BRANCHES

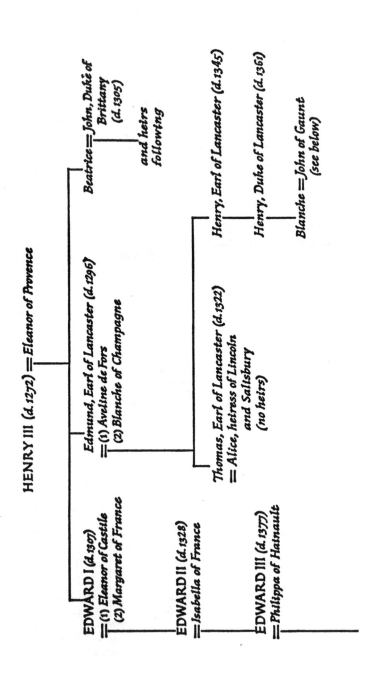

HENRY III (d. 1272) = Eleanor of Provence

EDWARD I (d. 1307)
= (1) Eleanor of Castile
(2) Margaret of France

Edmund, Earl of Lancaster (d. 1296)
= (1) Aveline de Fors
(2) Blanche of Champagne

Beatrice = John, Duke of Brittany (d. 1305)

and heirs following

EDWARD II (d. 1328)
= Isabella of France

Thomas, Earl of Lancaster (d. 1322)
= Alice, heiress of Lincoln and Salisbury
(no heirs)

Henry, Earl of Lancaster (d. 1345)

EDWARD III (d. 1377)
= Philippa of Hainault

Henry, Duke of Lancaster (d. 1361)

Blanche = John of Gaunt
(see below)

This is a genealogical tree of the English royal houses descending from Edward III.

Edward the Black Prince (d.1376) = Joan of Kent
- RICHARD II (d.1400) = (1) Anne of Bohemia (2) Isabella of France (no heirs)

Lionel, Duke of Clarence (d.1368) = (1) Elizabeth de Burgh (2) Violante Visconti
- Philippa = Edmund Mortimer, Earl of March (d.1381)
  - Roger Mortimer, Earl of March (d.1398)
    - Edmund Mortimer, Earl of March (d.1425) (no heirs)
    - Anne = Richard, Earl of Cambridge
      - Richard, Duke of York (d.1460) = Cicely Neville
        - EDWARD IV
        - George, Duke of Clarence
        - RICHARD III

John of Gaunt, Duke of Lancaster (d.1399) = (1) Blanche of Lancaster (2) Constanza of Castile (3) Katherine Swynford (from whom descend the Beauforts and, via them, the TUDORS)
- HENRY IV (d.1413) = (1) Mary Bohun (2) Joan, Dowager Duchess of Brittany
  - HENRY V (d.1422) = Catherine of France
    - HENRY VI (d.1471) = Margaret of Anjou
      - Edward, Prince of Wales (d.1471)
  - Thomas, Duke of Clarence (d.1421) (no heirs)
  - John, Duke of Bedford (d.1435) = (1) Anne of Burgundy (2) Jacquetta of Luxembourg (no heirs)
  - Humphrey, Duke of Gloucester (d.1447) = (1) Jacqueline of Hainault (2) Eleanor Cobham (no heirs)

Edmund of Langley, Duke of York (d.1402) = (1) Isabel of Castile (2) Joan Holland
- Edward, Duke of York (d.1415) (no heirs)
- Richard, Earl of Cambridge (d.1415) = Anne Mortimer (see left-hand column below)

Thomas of Woodstock, Duke of Gloucester (d.1397) = Eleanor Bohun
- Anne = (1) Thomas, Earl of Stafford (2) Edmund, Earl of Stafford (3) William Bourchier

3 THE HOUSES OF YORK AND MARCH

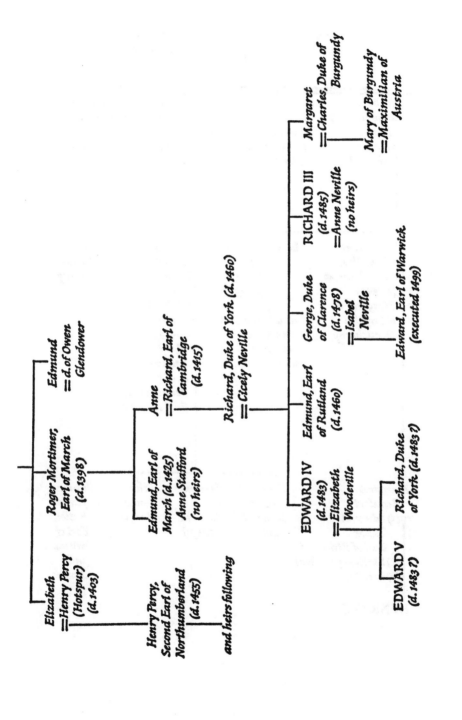

Elizabeth
=Henry Percy
(Hotspur)
(d.1403)

Roger Mortimer,
Earl of March
(d.1398)

Edmund
=d. of Owen
Glendower

Henry Percy,
Second Earl of
Northumberland
(d.1455)

and heirs following

Edmund, Earl of
March (d.1425)
=Anne Stafford
(no heirs)

Anne
=Richard, Earl of
Cambridge
(d.1415)

Richard, Duke of York (d.1460)
=Cicely Neville

EDWARD IV
(d.1483)
=Elizabeth
Wooderville

Edmund, Earl
of Rutland
(d.1460)

George, Duke
of Clarence
(d.1478)
=Isabel
Neville

RICHARD III
(d.1485)
=Anne Neville
(no heirs)

Margaret
=Charles, Duke of
Burgundy

Mary of Burgundy
=Maximillian of
Austria

Edward, Earl of Warwick
(executed 1499)

EDWARD V
(d.1483?)

Richard, Duke
of York (d.1483?)

John of Gaunt, Duke of Lancaster (d. 1399)
= (3) his mistress, Katherine Swynford

| John Beaufort, Earl of Somerset (d. 1410) = Margaret Holland | Henry Beaufort, Bishop of Winchester and Cardinal (d. 1447) | Thomas Beaufort, Earl of Dorset and Duke of Exeter (d. 1426) (no heirs) | Joan Beaufort = Ralph, Earl of Westmoreland (see Neville genealogy table 5) |

John Beaufort, Earl and then Duke of Somerset (d. 1444) = Margaret, d. of Sir John Beauchamp

Jane = James I, King of Scots (d. 1437)

and hence the Kings of Scots succeeding

Edmund Beaufort, Marquis of Dorset, Earl and then Duke of Somerset (d. 1455) = Margaret Beauchamp, d. of Richard Beauchamp, Earl of Warwick

Margaret = Thomas Courtenay

Margaret Beaufort = (1) Edmund Tudor, Earl of Richmond (2) Sir Henry Stafford (3) Lord Stanley

Henry, Duke of Somerset (d. 1464)

Edmund of Somerset (d. 1471)

John Beaufort (d. 1471)

Eleanor = James Butler, Earl of Wiltshire and Ormond

HENRY VII

5 THE HOUSE OF NEVILLE

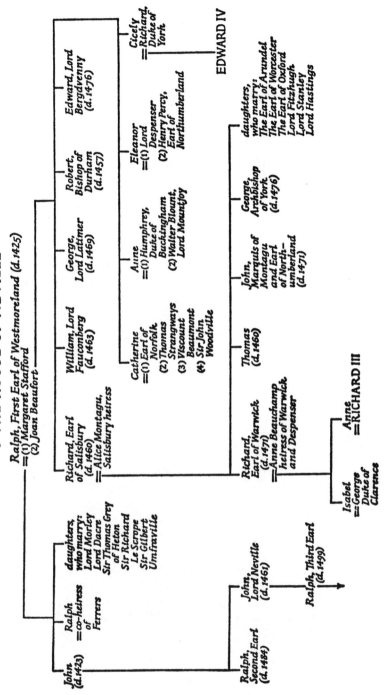

Ralph, First Earl of Westmoreland (d.1425)
= (1) Margaret Stafford
= (2) Joan Beaufort

John (d.1423)

Ralph = co-heiress of Ferrers

daughters, who marry:
Lord Morley
Lord Dacre
Sir Thomas Grey of Heton
Sir Richard Le Scrope
Sir Gilbert Umfraville

Ralph, Second Earl (d.1484)

John, Lord Neville (d.1461)

Ralph, Third Earl (d.1499)

Richard, Earl of Salisbury (d.1460)
= Alice Montagu, Salisbury heiress

William, Lord Fauconberg (d.1463)

George, Lord Latimer (d.1469)

Robert, Bishop of Durham (d.1457)

Edward, Lord Bergdvenny (d.1476)

Catherine
= (1) Earl of Norfolk
(2) Thomas Strangways
(3) Viscount Beaumont
(4) Sir John Woodville

Anne
= (1) Humphrey, Duke of Buckingham
(2) Walter Blount, Lord Mountjoy

Eleanor
= (1) Lord Despenser
(2) Henry Percy, Earl of Northumberland

Cicely
= Richard, Duke of York

Richard, Earl of Warwick (d.1471)
= Anne Beauchamp, heiress of Warwick and Despenser

Thomas (d.1460)

John, Marquis of Montagu and Earl of North-umberland (d.1471)

George, Archbishop of York (d.1476)

daughters, who marry:
The Earl of Arundel
The Earl of Worcester
The Earl of Oxford
Lord Fitzhugh
Lord Stanley
Lord Hastings

Isabel
= George, Duke of Clarence

Anne
= RICHARD III

EDWARD IV

6 THE WOODVILLE FAMILY

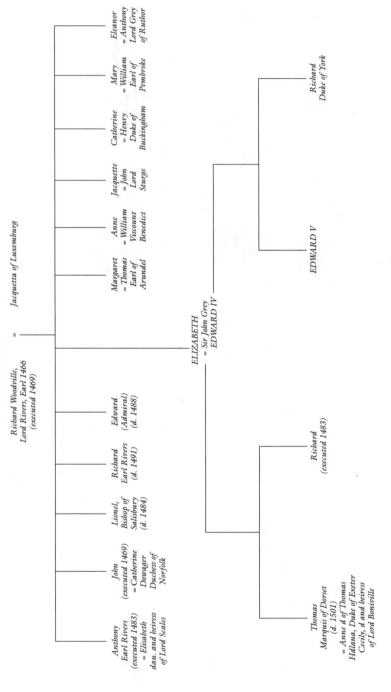

Richard Woodville,
Lord Rivers, Earl 1466
(executed 1469)

=

Jacquetta of Luxemburg

Anthony
Earl Rivers
(executed 1483)
= Elisabeth
dau. and heiress
of Lord Scales

John
(executed 1469)
= Catherine
Dowager
Duchess of
Norfolk

Lionel,
Bishop of
Salisbury
(d. 1484)

Richard
Earl Rivers
(d. 1491)

Edward
(Admiral)
(d. 1488)

ELIZABETH
= Sir John Grey
  EDWARD IV

Margaret
= Thomas
Earl of
Arundel

Anne
= William
Viscount
Benedict

Jacquette
= John
Lord
Sturge

Catherine
= Henry
Duke of
Buckingham

Mary
= William
Earl of
Pembroke

Eleanor
= Anthony
Lord Grey
of Ruthor

Thomas
Marquis of Dorset
(d. 1501)
= Anne d of Thomas
Hdana, Duke of Exeter
Cecily, d and heiress
of Lord Boniville

Richard
(executed 1483)

EDWARD V

Richard
Duke of York

Map 1 Southern Scotland and Northern England

Map 2 France after the Treaty of Brétigny, 1360

Calais
FLANDERS
PONTHIEU
Rouen
R. Seine
NORMANDY
Paris
BRITTANY
Brétigny
MAINE
ANJOU
Orléans
R. Loire
Poitiers
POITOU
Limoges
LIMOUSIN
R. Saône
Lyons
Bordeaux
R. Dordogne
GASCONY
Cahors
R. Rhône
R. Agenais
QUERCY
ROUERGUE
Rodez
R. Garonne
ARMAGNAC
Avignon
Toulouse
Narbonne

Land ceded to the
English in the treaty
Boundaries (approximate)
of the kingdom of France

Map 3 France at the time of the siege of Orleans, 1429

HOLLAND

Calais
FLANDERS Ghent
ARTOIS BRABANT
Agincourt HAINAULT
PICARDY

THE EMPIRE

Cherbourg
Harfleur
Rouen Compiègne
Formigny Caen Paris Rheims
NORMANDY
Verneuil R. Marne
DUCHY Fougères Troyes
OF
BRITTANY MAINE Orleans

R. Loire
DUCHY
OF
BURGUNDY
Chinon
Bourges
Poitiers

FRANCE

COUNTY OF BURGUNDY
R. Saône

Lyons
DAUPHINÉ
Bordeaux R. Dordogne

GUIENNE
R. Rhône
R. Garonne
Avignon
Bayonne Toulouse PROVENCE

Anglo-Burgundian
France
Lands of the house of Burgundy
Boundaries of the kingdom of France

Index